# LAKER

## The Glory Years of Sir Freddie Laker

Ania Grzesik
&
Gregory Dix

RECURSIVE PUBLISHING

First published in Great Britain and
in the United States of America in 2019
by Recursive Publishing Ltd

1 3 5 7 9 10 8 6 4 2



ISBN: 978-0-9956486-0-9
USA ISBN: 978-0-9992934-0-9

Typeset in Sabon by: Recursive Publishing, Ltd.
Cover repro by: Swan Press, Northampton

Printed and bound in England by
CPI Group (UK) Ltd, Croydon
CR0 4YY United Kingdom

Published by:
Recursive Publishing Ltd.
Distributed by:
The Myrtle Press
Billing Wharf, Station Road, Cogenhoe
Northamptonshire NN7 1NH, United Kingdom
Tel: 01604 890 208
www.themyrtlepress.com

www.Recursivepublishing.com

*"I want you to know,*
*there is nothing I haven't tried,*
*and one day it will all come out."*

*Sir Freddie Laker*

# Contents

# Contents

# Contents

# Contents

# Contents

# Introduction

## Why a book?

When the Internet really took off in the 1990's, the popular belief was that paper books and magazines would be superseded by electronic media and eventually cease to exist. This view was further endorsed as social media took a massive step forward, giving us the ability to instantly communicate with thousands (or millions) of people and also post images and video content.

Despite the doomsayers' predictions about the end of books, newspapers and magazines, in recent years there has been a revival. Bookstores, and supermarkets demonstrate the paper medium is far from obsolete. There are several reasons for this despite an increasingly media-savvy population who spend most of their waking hours attached to a tablet, smart phone or an electronic device of some sort. The first is that a paper product has a long shelf life. In fact, a book or magazine lasts as long as the paper it's printed on, which can be many hundreds of years. A book, especially a hard cover is great to have out on display or in a bookshelf alongside other great works of literature. We don't cut down nearly as many trees for paper as we once did, so the argument about saving the planet by not buying paper products has gone out the window. However, perhaps the main reason to buy a book, especially one that is non-fiction and in the case of Laker, biographical, is this. Because of the book's incredibly long life, authors of books as opposed to producers of electronic media, tend to fact check and do their research much more diligently. They have to, as their work, once printed cannot be retracted, edited, replaced or taken 'off-line'. If something in a book is found to be suspect, the publishers' only course of action is to try and withdraw existing unsold copies and then not print others until amendments are made. By then, it's too late as the first print run is already out in the world and its contents are being quoted and used by others, verbatim... no matter how inaccurate they may be.

The Publishers make this point because numerous film and video presentations about Sir Freddie Laker have been produced over the years, many of which were lacking. Almost without exception, they have contained inaccurate perspectives and statements, some relatively minor such as technical specifications or financial data and others that were considerably more erroneous (or even deliberately skewed) perhaps to cause sensationalism, sell more product or denigrate the subject.

As a result, Freddie is perhaps most remembered as the man who expanded too fast, bought too many aircraft and then went 'bust'. The success of Skytrain may well have been a myth, with the concept lasting just over four years and in its purest form a little over one year. But what Skytrain represented to the travelling public and the revolution that followed is considerably more important.

Because of Freddie's larger than life personality, media icon status and willingness to be publicly antagonistic to the establishment, he is not always remembered as the savvy, hard nosed businessman that he really was. He may not have been able to see through his ambitious plan for revolutionising civil aviation in the Far East,

Australia and Europe, but he should be forever remembered as the great visionary who foresaw the future as we experience it now. He was arguably the loudest of voices in the industry for the democratisation of air travel.

Freddie Laker was a true aviation pioneer just like others of the times such as Juan Trippe, Howard Hughes, Tom Braniff, Reginald Ansett, Ed Daly, Max Ward, and Herb Kelleher. They were all visionaries, they all changed the way we travel by air and they all perhaps had their own unique idiosyncracies - driven by ambition, single-mindedness and a self-belief mere mortals can seldom relate to. Freddie however, was the only British airline entrepreneur who became a household name and he remains so to this day.

Sir Freddie put Gatwick Airport on the map back in the 1970's when he bought his first wide-bodied DC-10s even though he had been involved in Gatwick's development in the BUA era. It's a travesty there is no memorial to him there and hopefully sometime in the near future this will be rectified, as it would be well-deserved and long overdue.

When you read this book, be assured that painstaking fact checking and research of the subject has been carried out. If at times the book occasionally reads like fiction, you can be certain it isn't. Apart from when personal experiences and recollections are being retold - typically accompanied by the individual's name and their role in the story - the facts stated can all be supported by documentation. The definitive story of the Glory Years of Sir Freddie Laker has been committed to print first and foremost. The objective being a literary product that can be passed on to future generations, so when electronic media devices and formats become obsolete, they may still derive something from reading a diligently written book.

*Recursive Publishing, Ltd.*

# Acknowledgements
## by
## Ania Grzesik

For as a long as I can remember, languishing at the back of the offices of the Myrtle Press, the Publisher where I had worked for over five years, were two large white folders. They contained a copy of Bob Beckman's 1988 unpublished book 'A Case of Corporate Murder'. The copy at Myrtle was given to Tom Rubython - the owner and Editor in Chief - in 1995 when he travelled to Florida and the Bahamas to interview Sir Freddie. Freddie was planning to launch his final transatlantic airline, Laker Airways, Inc.

I was given the task of researching and writing about the antitrust case following the collapse of Laker Airways. This became the starting point of a five-year project to document the extraordinary life of Sir Freddie Laker and the contribution he made to civil aviation. His legacy lives on today.

As any biographer knows it is impossible to do a book like this without the contributions of many others. Some, have never spoken at length about Sir Freddie or Laker Airways before. I owe them all a debt of gratitude for often patiently answering my questions and for my taking up a great deal of their time. Without exception, they are remarkable people with their own stories to tell.

In Washington DC, I would like to thank David Kirstein, Bill Barrett and Angela Beckman, all of whom showed extreme generosity in sharing their absolutely fascinating stories… not all of them printable.

I am sorry that one very special individual will never read this book - Christopher Morris, the Laker Airways' liquidator. Christopher sadly died quite suddenly in March 2015, just as he would have liked, following a day at the races and a good bottle of wine. It was a privilege to spend so many evenings and weekends in his company and to have had his friendship, for the last nine months of his life. His contribution and permission to use all the proprietary documents he had amassed has been an essential element of this book. I would also like to thank his legal team Christopher Grierson and Anthony Pugh Thomas, both of whom have been of enormous assistance and I thank them for their guidance. In Jersey, special thanks to Anthony Dessain for his research and specialised advice.

Of Sir Freddie's own legal team, heartfelt thanks go out to John Roney, Freddie's personal lawyer for many decades and also to His Honour, Harvey Crush.

Of the Laker Airways' management still with us, we have been most fortunate to have contributions by John Jones, Robbie Robinson and Christopher Brown, who gave us their superlative inside knowledge of the airline and the their reminiscences of Sir Freddie. Also Gerry Sharp (and Rufus) with whom we shared some excellent lunches. We appreciate the technical contributions of Capt. Harry Clark, Capt. Steve James, Capt. Geoff Brookes, Joy Poirrier, Jerry Penwarden, and Caz Caswell.

Thanks also to Professors Stephen Ison and Lucy Budd and we hope they will use this book for their own civil aviation tuition purposes.

A very special thank-you to Pierre Murphy - an unabashed propellor-head - who has given some terrific insights into life at the Beckman law firm. Also to Jacqui Watson for her photos and vivid recollections of the Hong Kong scene. 'Ta mate' to The Seekers' Athol Guy for his humorous anecdotes about Freddie. Ditto to Tramp's Johnny Gold who will likely remember the 1st of February 1982 like it was yesterday.

A person to whom we are most grateful for her contribution is Sir Freddie's only daughter, Elaine Seear. During our two exhaustive sessions, fueled by Earl Grey tea, Elaine gave extraordinary and candid personal insights of her father, her mother and of course her brother Kevin, who was tragically killed at age 17. That watershed moment in Sir Freddie's life, despite the immense sorrow it caused, created Laker Airways.

We would like to acknowledge Richard Moorhouse as well as the team at Myrtle Press for their assistance in distributing and marketing the book, David Peett, Mary Hynes, Will Adams and of course Tom Rubython who initiated the project originally.

Finally, thanks to my co-author, Gregory Dix. He opened up many new doors when he came on the scene in 2016 and brought unique perspectives of life with Sir Freddie and Laker Airways. He also contributed his personal archive of photographs, diaries and correspondence files, specialised industry knowledge, and his Laker Airways' contacts, all of which significantly changed the direction of the original story and has helped shape the final product.

*Ania Grzesik*
*Stratford upon Avon*

# Preface
## by
## Gregory Dix

I first met Freddie Laker in 1972 having just moved to Gatwick Airport from Luton where I'd worked for British Midland and Monarch Airlines. A colleague who had become the General Manager of Gatwick Handling, the airport's pre-eminent ground handling company had given me a job as a Ramp Coordinator. I'd already done this job as well as passenger service with Monarch and had been an Operations Controller with BMA, so I was fairly well-rounded. The job was a slight demotion but I wanted to get a foot in the door at Gatwick.

One day, I went to meet one of Laker Airways' recently acquired DC-10s arriving from Palma, Majorca. Laker's DC-10s were the first ones in Europe and they were a spectacular sight, resplendent in their distinctive white fuselage with red and black stripes. Supervising the turnaround of one of those magnificent planes was always thrilling. As I pulled my van up beside the towering aircraft, a Rolls Royce was sitting at the foot of the stairs. If I'd bothered to notice the number plate, I'd have seen 'FAL 1' and realised who it was, but thinking there must be a VIP aboard I called Movement Control to check. They radio'd back 'oh don't worry, it's just Mr. Laker and we've organised Customs clearance for him on the aircraft, he doesn't need anything'.

A few minutes after the Customs Officer had boarded, Freddie Laker – who I'd only seen in magazines and on television – suntanned with his hair blowing in the wind, appeared. He seemed larger than life in every respect as he bounded down the stairs yelling "hello Harry" to his uniformed chauffeur holding the front passenger door open for his boss. Then to my astonishment, he turned to me and said "hello Greg, how're you doing?" I wasn't wearing a name badge and he'd never set eyes on me before. He kept moving as I replied "great thanks Sir." He jumped into the Rolls and it glided off. That was the last I saw of him for several months. When I boarded the aircraft I said to the In-flight Director "Mr Laker just said 'hello Greg' to me which is really odd as he's never seen me before." She replied "while we were waiting for the Customs chap, he asked me if I knew who you were and it was good I did." She went on to explain that Mr. Laker made a point of knowing everyone's name he came across, and that he remembered them as well. It was a management style I hadn't experienced before and it made a lasting impression.

I made it a priority to seek a job with Laker Airways. After a brief and somewhat intimidating interview with ex Wing Commander 'Atty' Atkinson, Laker's Operations Manager, I landed one as an Ops Duty Officer. That relatively simple early career change, inspired by the first encounter with Freddie, changed my entire life. For the next two decades I had some of the greatest adventures any young man could dream of. I held huge positions of responsibility, traveled all over the world and was given the trust and latitude to pursue my professional and personal ambitions. In the many disparate roles I played during my association with Freddie, I always felt we were doing something incredibly worthwhile.

Fast forward to December, 2015, twenty-three years after Freddie and I went our separate ways. I received an email from John Jones, the former Commercial Manager for Laker Airways. He told me a new book was being written about Freddie based largely on an unpublished book of the Laker Airways' antitrust case. John suggested I get in touch with the author, Ania Grzesik, who at the time was working closely with Tom Rubython of the Myrtle Press, the Publishers of best selling biographies on world champions Ayrton Senna, James Hunt and others. Perhaps anticipating my reaction, he primed me further by saying they may send me a couple of their Formula One books if I helped. As a life-long motor racing fanatic, my interest in the project was naturally piqued.

A few back and forths on the telephone were followed by Ania making a couple of transatlantic trips in early 2016. First to Boston where I unloaded boxes of Laker files, photos and other material from my twenty years association with Sir Freddie. Then to Washington at which time we met with some of the key people involved with the Laker antitrust case and Freddie's last ventures. By that time, the book was heading in a slightly different direction.

In mid-2016, Ania and I acquired the rights and the original intellectual property from the Myrtle Press. When she suggested we co-author the book I admit to being somewhat skeptical as to the level of contribution I could make to the actual manuscript. However, it became clear fairly early in the process that perhaps I had more to offer than initially acknowledged. Biographies are invariably written by authors who never knew or met their subject. So having someone who had been involved in much of the main story and knew the principal character well was obviously helpful. Admittedly, it has been quite challenging and occasionally cathartic to delve into the past and recount what were unquestionably the very best of times, much of it spent in the company of such a unique individual.

I was keen from the outset that Sir Freddie's story should be much more than a straight-forward biography and that it should be written to benefit future generations of entrepreneurs, business and legal scholars, managers and executives. Freddie Laker's inspiring life story may be a case study for MBA students and for those operating their own business or in management.

Ania had already done incredibly thorough and detailed research prior to my involvement. The access she was given to key people involved in the Laker antitrust case is unprecedented and uncovered many previously unknown and unpublished facts about Sir Freddie and Laker Airways. The combination of her diligent fact-finding and face-to-face interviews together with my own recollections, diaries and materials has produced an accurate, no holds barred account of Sir Freddie's first sixty years and of Laker Airways up to its demise on the 5th of February, 1982.

Our working title for the project was 'Icarus'. But when it became apparent 'The Icarus Factor' mostly applied to just a few years of Sir Freddie's remarkable life, we changed it simply to 'Laker'. In the course of writing Laker, a massive historical data base and photographic library of Sir Freddie, his airlines, associates, and personal life has been amassed. Sincere thanks go to everyone who contributed materials, information and their personal experiences. We had to distill over 800 pages and a half million words of original manuscript down and in so doing we regrettably had to edit out many anecdotes and people who were part of the Laker story, for which we apologise. Similarly, we apologise in advance for any unintended errors or omissions. Over time, memories fade and documents disappear, however be assured we have done everything possible to ensure you read the most accurate and unbiased account of Sir Freddie and his ventures up to February 1982.

Although the years featured in this book, especially the '70s aren't all that long ago, the world was a very different place. There were no smart phones or personal computers, internet, satellite technology, or information devices we take for granted today. The workplace was quite different with a more formal dress code, secretaries adept in shorthand and typing, and communications by primitive telephones, telex, type-written letters and memos. Discrimination was acceptable, especially in high visibility service industries like airlines. You could be hired (or fired) for many reasons that would perhaps be illegal today.

They were still pioneering years in air transport; aircraft weren't as reliable as they are now, flying abroad was still considered special and passengers dressed up for the occasion. Every plane had a smoking section. Also in this era, governments and IATA strictly controlled civil aviation and every route, fare and service level was painstakingly evaluated (and fought over by lawyers) before being authorised. The breaking down and elimination of these regulatory measures was something Freddie Laker dedicated his life's work to.

The civil aviation industry and the travelling public owe a huge debt of gratitude to Sir Freddie. Thanks to his vision and perseverance, affordable air travel is now available to virtually everyone. This book is about the monumental achievements and experiences during the glory years of Sir Freddie Laker, one of Britain's greatest entrepreneurs.

We hope you enjoy it.

*Gregory Dix*
*Lenox, Massachusetts*

Above: Freddie Laker's official motif that he claimed was the mythical oozlum bird.

CHAPTER 1

# Action

## Ready or not...

Wednesday 3rd February, 1982

"Action."

"Are you Ready... for Freddie."

"Cut. Much better, Freddie, take five everyone."

Sir Freddie Laker was immaculately dressed in a dark double-breasted suit, a pale blue shirt and matching blue and white striped tie. He was standing in the hot passenger cabin of a Laker Airways DC-10 that had been transformed into a movie set. The lights were intense but Freddie was used to it, he was a born showman and enjoyed every minute of being in front of the camera. He had been doing the Laker Airways advertising, standing on the top of planes and poking fun at himself almost from day one ... and he loved it. The shoot was for a series of TV commercials for the upcoming 1982 spring / summer season of Freddie's world-famous Skytrain service between Britain and the USA. This ad campaign was crucial to generating more US-originating passengers and life-saving dollar revenue for his financially strapped airline.

The commercials were produced by Laker's relatively new Madison Avenue advertising agency, Lord, Geller, Federico & Einstein. Everyone was confident the ads were going to turn around Laker's fortunes after a disastrous previous year; ironically 1981 was the only time Laker Airways had not made a profit in its 16-year history. The LGFE creative team were seasoned professionals and directing the production crew was second nature. They had been planning this for some time, yet Freddie's endless meetings with bankers back in England had delayed their schedule several times.

The agency was understandably nervous about whether Freddie would cut the mustard as a front man. All they'd seen of him prior to the shoot showed him in a much darker frame of mind, dour and stressed due to all the problems he'd been dealing with during the latter part of 1981. Nevertheless, the spectacular

Laker DC-10 aircraft had been taken out of its normal transatlantic programme to allow the shoot to take place at JFK Airport. Earlier that morning, Freddie had been lifted on a cherry-picker to the top of the aircraft where he'd stood above the cockpit, more than 30 feet off the ground with no safety net, his arms outstretched in a posture that would proclaim in print ads 'Are you Ready for Freddie'. It was a deliberate reprise of an earlier campaign, when he had done a similarly dangerous act (but on a much smaller plane) with the punch line 'I've Got My Name on Every Plane', which had become one of Laker Airways' most enduring marketing themes.

The agency personnel were relieved as they finally got to see an upbeat and relaxed Freddie Laker doing what he did best. With Sir Freddie were a few of his Laker Airways' cohorts. Greg Dix, his New York-based general manager and executive producer of the ads, was as usual second-guessing anything that could potentially go awry. Two of Freddie's most glamorous In-Flight Directors, Meg Vesty and Amanda Cooper, together with popular steward Steve Wren, had been specially selected for the important shoot. They were having their make-up fine-tuned as they awaited a turn in front of the camera, while Freddie's long-serving publicity officer, the loquacious Robin Flood, fussed over him to his considerable bemusement.

"So what do you think?" he asked the gang about his first takes. Freddie was in a great mood, full of his old charm and playfulness the likes of which he hadn't been able to express for months. He barely heard their responses as his mind wandered back to the days before. After receiving confirmation that the re-financing of Laker Airways had been assured, Freddie had taken a few of his closest financial colleagues to one of the most exclusive nightclubs in London, impresario Johnny Gold's famous 'Tramp', to celebrate. There, he and his guests were treated to Tramp's renowned bangers and mash, washed down with half a dozen bottles of absurdly expensive Krug champagne. The celebration had given Freddie the boost of spirit he needed for the next morning's Concorde flight to JFK, allowing him to maintain his previously planned New York schedule.

Freddie had hit the ground running on arrival, enduring a challenging strategy meeting with his top managers. Then, with his back to the wall once again, he'd been coerced into giving up his dream of revolutionising air travel in Europe. It was a compromise that was nothing short of blackmail. Now, finally, he believed all his financial problems were behind him and he could get on with starring in the new television commercials, something he really loved to do.

Yet Freddie couldn't stop his mind drifting back to the months of aggravation and the seemingly endless meetings with bankers and lawyers that he'd endured. 'It shouldn't have to be this hard,' he almost said out loud. 'Why can't it be fun again?' he pondered, 'like it is now' as a familiar directorial voice interrupted his thoughts... "We'll do one more take Freddie and a safety, before we go to Scene 2" the director commanded. "Greg, silence Mrs Flood please or remove her from the set" he said, only half-jokingly. "Ladies and Steve, get ready for your scenes and are YOU ready Sir Freddie?" The director looked at his star, who seemed to be in his own world. Instantly coming out of his melancholic moment, Freddie

Laker, the master of composure, immediately retorted in his most authoritative tone, "Of course I'm bloody well ready … Mister Director."

Everyone laughed. They knew this was going to be a very good day indeed.

**Above:** Wednesday 3rd February, 1982. Sir Freddie in New York during the filming of the 'Are You Ready For Sir Freddie' TV commercials for the upcoming 1982 Summer season. Freddie was in high spirits believing his financial troubles were finally over and the airline's future was now assured.

# *Part 1*

## *First Fortunes*

CHAPTER 2

# Bruised Bananas
## Humble beginnings

1922-1946

"Just like New York!" A booming voice rang out around the offices of Laker Airways in a distinctive Kentish accent. Freddie Laker was referring both to himself and to the song lyric, 'New York, New York, so good they named it twice'. That wasn't a hit until 1978, so his mother Hannah must have had other reasons in naming him Frederick Alfred. In late adulthood Freddie loved to tell people that the reason he had 'Fred' in both his first and middle names was because his mother thought he was so good that she named him twice. Throughout his life, Freddie would seldom doubt that he really was twice as good.

Freddie was born on 6th August 1922 at his parents' home, an unremarkable terrace on New Ruttington Lane, Canterbury, Kent. The teenage Freddie nick-named the street 'Ruction Avenue' after the almost daily squabbles of the residents that spilled out onto the street. The country was still recovering from the First World War, with its tragic loss of life, emotional and financial damage. It was still the era of the biplane – the jet engine was a few years away, and commercial aviation was more fantasy that reality. Once the wartime ban on civilian flying ended in 1919, a few fledgling passenger services emerged, and the aircraft used were the now surplus military bombers modified to carry passengers across the English Channel between London and Paris.

By 15th June 1919 the first non-stop transatlantic crossing had been achieved by two Englishmen, Captain John Alcock and Lieutenant Arthur Brown. Their flight in a Vickers Vimy IV twin-engined bomber from Newfoundland to Ireland took 16 hours 27 minutes, and they landed heavily in a bog. It would be another 20 years before a scheduled crossing of the Atlantic became commercially available for those who were adventurous enough and could afford it, first by airship, then by seaplane.

The Laker family's modest circumstances were no clue as to what lay ahead for young Freddie, but a horoscope for his birth date is remarkably apt: "Being a Leo born, you are well known for your positive outlook and side-splitting humour. You gravitate to the spotlight, as you use being the centre of attention to entertain your friends and loved ones. Possibly even more important than your humour is your ability to deal with tough situations in an optimistic and hopeful way."

The family home has long since been demolished, replaced by 1960s social housing. With its two-up, two-down configuration, it had gas lamps and no indoor bathroom, instead a copper in the kitchen. It was typical of the accommodation afforded to the working classes of the day.

Freddie's 25-year-old father Frederick Henry was an able seaman in the Royal Navy, serving on HMS Repulse, a 'Renown' Class battle-cruiser built during the First World War. There were to be no siblings for Freddie, and within five years his father had abandoned his wife and infant son; Freddie's mother had gone down to the docks to welcome her husband back from one of his sailings only to find him in the arms of another woman. Frederick senior never returned to the family home, but he was perhaps not much of a loss, being a poor husband and father. The few memories Freddie had of a thoroughly unpleasant man were burned on his memory: "He was horrible to my mother and he was mean to me," he said. "When I was about five, and had done something, I don't know what, he locked me in the coal bunker. My mother was out and I stayed there for I don't know how long. I was afraid of the dark for years and years after that; I still am at times. He is dead and I am not sorry that he died."

Whatever his adventures at sea, Frederick senior died in Canterbury, the place of his birth, in 1970. Beyond the pain he left behind from those first years, he played no further part in the Freddie Laker story. Freddie met his father only one more time, during the war in 1942, when they met in a pub and his father bought him a beer. Freddie realised that as an adult he did not like his father any more than he had as a small boy. His father reappeared one more time to ask his son for money. He didn't get a penny. Frederick senior sold his very one-sided story to the papers. "It was the only time I have had nasty publicity," Freddie recalled. He did not attend his father's funeral and at the time referred to him publicly as a 'shit' and a 'nothing man'.

But Freddie had been blessed with a redoubtable mother, Hannah. Left to bring up her son single-handedly, she excelled. Undoubtedly Freddie's entrepreneurial skills and taste for hard work were inherited from his mother, who cleaned houses, picked fruit and bought and sold goods to survive. During the war she had worked in a salvage yard, then took it over and became a scrap dealer, a most unlikely profession for a young woman. In her own words, "I made a tidy sum." Later she had a grocery store in the town, another success: "We sold everything from toilet articles to stationery, cheese, fruit and clothes. That went well too."

Still, times were often hard for the two of them, and Hannah had to be careful with the little money they had. Bob Beckman, Freddie's American lawyer, recalls one story: "One evening, as dinner preparations neared completion, Freddie came into the kitchen and joined the conversation. He loved the bananas in the fruit bowl on the kitchen counter and started eating one that was clearly past it. I said, 'Freddie, you shouldn't eat those brown spots. My mother wouldn't let me eat bananas that looked like that.'" Freddie had grinned back at him and took another bite, brown spots and all. He said, "Those are the only kind my mother bought. She would stop at the market on the way home from her flower shop and buy the left-over vegetables and fruit."

Three years after the departure of his father, when Freddie was eight, Hannah Laker met William Allin. Unfortunately Hannah was still legally married to Frederick senior and with his whereabouts unknown was unable to file for divorce to marry again. So William changed his name from Allin to Laker in what Freddie said was an act of deference to Hannah and her young son, so that they would not have to change theirs. This implied that there had been a marriage, but there hadn't. In truth it was done to avoid the public scandal of an unmarried couple in the 1930s 'living in sin'. The lack of a marriage between the two was kept even from the closest of family. It was only due to an accidental slip of the tongue by Freddie to his grown-up daughter many years later that anyone ever found out.

William Allin could not have been more different from Freddie's biological father, and the boy adored him: "He was a wonderful man. I loved him. You know what he did to make things easier for me? He changed his name to Laker. I didn't know what to call him right off, but I loved him and wanted to call him something. So I called him 'Dear', and it stuck. He was an educated man. He came from quite a different world from my mother's – she had been really very poor – but he fell in love with her and he always loved her. He was a very loving man." That love lasted until William's death in 1966.

The new domestic arrangements in the Laker household were disciplined yet warm. At the Simon Langton Grammar School in Canterbury, Freddie was the undoubted dunce of the class and in his own words a complete "non-entity". School was a torment. "I hated school," he said. "And I was terrible, academically and otherwise. I still remember the roars of laughter from boys and master alike when, in answer to the question of what I wanted to be, I replied: 'A millionaire.' Ah well."

His school days came to an unfortunate end. "I hold a record there – on the day that I left I was caned on my backside seven times," recalled Freddie. As he was striking him, the headmaster, knowing that Freddie was leaving, told him: "This is the happiest day of my life." Many years later he was called back by the school to award prizes at graduation. Seeking information for his introduction, the school searched their records for his accomplishments. All they could find was that he had swum across a 25-yard pool as part of a physical education programme, but even this was a non-event. "What they did not know was that halfway across I put my feet down and walked part of it," laughed Freddie. His one notable achievement from his school days was running the school tuck-shop when he was 14. "Yes, I did well at that. I organised it properly, and it made money, and, of course, I got my sweets free."

Though poor academically, Freddie was good with his hands and enjoyed tinkering. Before the age of ten he had rebuilt an old three-valve Ekco radio, which was kept and treasured by his mother for her entire life. She also recalled that by the age of 12 he had rebuilt a car – an early obsession. With guidance from an uncle, who was a brilliant mechanic and bought and sold motorcars, when he was 14 Freddie took an automotive engineering course at night.

Freddie's mother instilled in her son her own values, and they would serve him well throughout his life. "I brought him up to be successful," she said, "and to know that if you tell me one lie, it will of necessity be followed by another."

Freddie's first paying job was helping his coal merchant uncle with his deliveries and, despite his mother's determination that her son should make something of himself, he had no idea what he wanted to do. The answer came from the heavens one day when a 15-year-old Freddie, on a day like any other, was standing outside the chip shop on the corner of his street with the other 'yobbos' and a scene unfolded in the sky above. As an adult he described what he saw with the same breathless excitement that had captivated him as a boy: "These two roads were like that, and straight down the military road was Canterbury Cathedral. And of course it really is a magnificent sight, with all the wall going round the cathedral, and I'm there with these mates of mine and having our fish and chips, two and one, you know, out of the old newspaper. Standing on the corner. And damn me if the Hindenburg was coming from Germany, going to America of course, and a Handley Page 42, a four-engine biplane, was coming from Croydon to go to Paris. I mean, you couldn't think of two dissimilar aerial objects than these two, and they crossed right over the top of Canterbury Cathedral. A magnificent sight. And I said to my mates, 'That's for me. I'm going into aeroplanes,' and that's what I did."

Fortunately for Freddie, a mere 30 miles away in Rochester was the Short Brothers factory. Short's specialised in flying boats, and Rochester was the ideal location due to its close proximity to the River Medway, where the planes could be tested.

The company had been founded in 1908 by Horace, Eustace and Oswald Short, and became the world's first aircraft factory; it had even built six aircraft under contract for the Wright Brothers themselves.

When Freddie left school in July 1938 he cycled over to Short's and managed to convince someone that he had some potential, despite the absence of any formal qualifications. On his first day – his 16th birthday – he was handed a broom and told to sweep the floor. Crucially Short's provided apprenticeships with basic instruction in aero-engineering and now, seeing a purpose in academic learning, he enrolled in maths and economics courses at night school. "It was very interesting. But of course I knew why – by then there was a purpose to it."

An apprentice's meagre wage of just over a pound a week was hardly sufficient to cover the rent on his lodgings and his other expenses. Freddie explained the situation regarding his landlady: "It was not going to work out very well for her. There I was, 16 years old, so I came to an 'arrangement' with her." The strapping, self-confident young man into which Freddie had grown embarked on another successful career that day, this time with the ladies.

Having sorted the rent and mastered the broom, the enterprising young apprentice's duties included getting the men's tea when they were working at the benches. All the men had billycans, which cost sixpence a can to fill. Freddie threaded the handles of the six cans onto a rod, and went off to the canteen to get them filled. He noticed that in the course of the journey back to the benches a lot of this tea was spilled, so next time, instead of buying six billycans of tea, he bought five and tipped some out of each one into the sixth, pocketing the extra sixpence. No one actually lost anything – they still got the same amount of tea. He then expanded operations to buying the tea in bulk after negotiating a better rate with the canteen staff, again pocketing the difference.

Freddie's apprenticeship as an engineer should have lasted four to five years, but was abruptly cut short not long after the outbreak of the Second World War. During the Battle of Britain, on Thursday 15th August 1940, Shorts was bombed heavily by the Luftwaffe. Much of the factory was destroyed, as were some of the Sunderland flying boats and Stirling bombers commissioned by the RAF. Freddie was offered a transfer to Swindon, a centre for wartime aircraft manufacturing. He declined. "I thought, well, I don't really want to go to Swindon, so I went with General Aircraft at Rochester."

In 1941 he enrolled in the Air Transport Auxiliary Corps (ATA) to spend his war time initially as a ground engineer at its home, White Waltham Airfield in Berkshire. Freddie's dream was to serve in the RAF as a pilot, but it was not to be; a perforated eardrum meant that he was unfit for active service. The ATA had an official motto, 'Eager for the Air', and two other unofficial nicknames, 'Anything to Anywhere' and 'Ancient and Tattered Aviators', referring to the pilots, most of whom were deemed unfit to fly by the RAF. Disabilities such as missing limbs and poor sight were often conveniently ignored in favour of ability. The ATA's ranks also included 166 women, among them Amy Johnson, who died while in its service, bailing out over the Thames estuary in 1941, never to be seen again. Johnson's ex-husband, Jim Mollison, from whom she was divorced just prior to the war, became one of Freddie's first mentors; he was a hard-drinking Glaswegian and thought by some to be a daredevil. He had qualified as a flying instructor aged only 22 and spent the years before the war breaking records alongside Johnson, sometimes in competition with her. Freddie became his flight engineer – it was quite a coup for a young lad to be paired with such a famous name in aviation.

Another man that Freddie teamed up with in the ATA, and who was a sort of father figure, was Arnold Watson. He was the ATA's chief test pilot, and the man who would teach Freddie to fly aircraft. Aware of his good fortune, Freddie recalled: "I was very lucky then, very, very lucky, in as much as I met a fellow – I wasn't much of an aviator, but I'd had a bit of engineering experience, but not very much – and his name was Arnold Watson. He was the joint publicity manager in fact for Castrol. And he wanted an assistant, and why he chose me I will never know, but I volunteered. He was absolutely wonderful to me. He taught me how to speak the Queen's – or King's – English of the day, more or less, and almost everything I know." It led to his greatest claim from the ATA years, which was that, "I was the only fella that he ever taught to fly on four-engine aeroplanes. Everyone started with one engine – I started with four and went downwards." During his years at British United Airways, Freddie repaid Watson by championing Castrol products above all else, and made sure that all BUA company cars and its aircraft exclusively used Castrol lubricants.

Being in the ATA was dangerous work and many people were killed. Freddie took on this perilous task of ferrying aircraft, "and then we were immediately seconded to, I think it was, 41 Group Air Transport Command, and that's where we did the ferrying." Mostly they were given aircraft to deliver, not always of a type that they had flown before – there were so many types of aircraft that needed to be moved around. Freddie tells of one near miss. Instrumentation was much more rudimentary in those days, and the artificial horizon in the aircraft he was flying, a twin-engined Avro Anson, was faulty, with the result that he actually fell sideways out of a cloud. He managed to recover the aircraft but it damaged one ear permanently and for the rest of his life he suffered partial loss of hearing. A close friend remembers the gloss that he put on the story, that he "came out the cloud, only aged about 20 or something," and he said, "There I was, I knew that I was still young and there were a lot of women that I hadn't met yet."

Amusingly for Freddie, he would explain that while working for the ATA he had actually been working for BOAC, the precursor of his arch-enemy British Airways. "I joined the ATA and we were ferrying aeroplanes in those days, of course, and I actually worked for BOAC, which is rather ironic in a way, and BOAC were in charge of the ATA." It wasn't quite like that, but Freddie liked a good story.

The administration of the ATA was initially under Gerard d'Erlanger, a director of British Airways Ltd, which became part of BOAC in 1939. Freddie joined in 1941 and it was controlled by the Ministry of Aircraft Production, although BOAC did provide the administration staff under d'Erlanger throughout its existence.

Remarkably for a man with such a keen interest in the opposite sex, Freddie settled down in a hurry. On 10th May 1942, still only 19 years old, he married Joan Stallwood. She was six years his senior, and he had been only 18 when they had first met at a wartime dance.

Had she known his real age, Joan said that she would never have married him, but clearly she'd eventually forgiven him for lying about his age. She describes their very first meeting: "He stood out from the crowd because he had a high starched collar and a suit and he looked very smart. He made a beeline for me and danced with me and said that he had bought a car for £2 and sold it for £4, but he had the use of it for the weekend. At the end of the evening, Freddie offered to drive me home. He dropped me well away from my house and after of course trying a bit of kissing and one thing or another, which we had a bit of a laugh about, he said, 'See you next weekend,' and that's how it started."

In January 1944, as the end of the war was approaching, their first child arrived, a daughter who they named Elaine. Freddie Laker was only 21.

CHAPTER 3

# Propellor Head

## Getting the aviation bug

1946-1948

In March 1946, at the age of 24, Freddie Laker was discharged from the Air Transport Auxiliary. After his demob, with a few pounds in his pocket, he moved with Joan and Elaine into a small flat in Streatham in the southern suburbs of London. He had £40 to show for his war service – three months' pay less deductions, after it had been worked out that he had lost two parachutes, two or three overcoats and a few hats. He needed to find work. It didn't take long. As chief engineer to Arnold Watson, he was in demand by post-war employers. Air travel was starting to boom and airlines were being set up everywhere, as Freddie remembered: "Towards the end of the war, the Brits, believe it or not, were actually thinking of airlines, and because I was in this exalted position, I suppose really, with Arnold, we were invited to sort of make ideas and plans and things for what's going to happen after the war."

As a consequence, on April Fools Day 1946 Freddie became one of the first eight employees of a new airline, British European Airways, formed as part of the British Overseas Airways Corporation. Freddie joined British European on the UNRRA (United Nations Relief & Rehabilitation Administration) flight. However, he found it boring and after three months he left.

He thought his time in aviation might be over and, still desperately short of cash, he tried his hand at door-to-door sales. He spent £25 on bedding plants from a nursery and started knocking on doors. He remembers his sales pitch: "Madam, would you like some bedding plants for your garden?" By his own admission he was not very good at the job, as he had no understanding of what he was trying to sell. To identify the plants he had a leaf from each one pinned on the back of an old Ford van; he couldn't spell 'antirrhinum', so wrote 'anti' under it. When he was asked for a dozen antirrhinums he would go back and look at the leaf, then compare it with the plants in the boxes.

This did not deter him from embarking on his second venture into horticulture very soon afterwards. Borrowing from friends and family in the spring of 1947, he bought a crop of cherries while the orchard was still in blossom. He and Joan picked the crop themselves and sold it for a small profit. He forced Joan to sleep in a tent in the orchard with their infant daughter. Joan was no pushover, being a strong and wilful woman unafraid to stand up to her husband during their marriage. According to her daughter, Joan could be totally impossible, but she had a strong sense of right and wrong and would correct Freddie whether he liked it or not. Few people had the confidence to do that.

Throughout their marriage, Joan was the steadying factor in Freddie's life. Freddie wasn't well educated when he met Joan. She had worked at the Amalgamated Press as a journalist and as such she was good with words, and played a big part in the running of the early business ventures.

Following these two enterprises he decided to get back into aviation, and found work with London Aero Motor Services (LAMS). This was a curious organisation founded by the most unlikely personality in post-war aviation. Dr Graham Humby was a plastic surgeon who interspersed his medical career with spells as a ship's steward, a dancer understudying Fred Astaire, a pioneer glider pilot, a garage-owner, and the operator of the most ambitious air charter company of its day.

LAMS had initially set up at Elstree airfield, which had a grass runway that proved impractical for the mix of Handley Page Halton aircraft and surplus Halifax bombers that were operating from it. The company soon moved to Stansted airport in Essex, which during the war had been a US bomber base and had fallen into disuse. A local journalist called Humby's operation at Stansted 'Squatters with 17 bombers'.

Humby was an enlightened man whose system of profit-sharing made every employee effectively a director. He also made the tea himself. This unconventionality was no doubt a better fit for Freddie. By now the company had grown to 250 staff, among them the newly employed, lowly flight engineer Freddie Laker, still proudly wearing the dark blue uniform of the ATA. But while LAMS was limping along, the ambitious and entrepreneurial Freddie, who was also dabbling in second-hand cars on the side, was soon branching out on his own. There were plenty of surplus wartime aircraft and spares knocking around, and for Freddie it was an opportunity that was too good to be missed.

In the autumn of 1947 Freddie left to set up on his own. He registered his first business, Aviation Traders, on 17th October. He bought surplus Army lorries, which were fixed up, repainted and sold. The following year's Bastille Day celebrations in Paris featured troop-carrying vehicles, at least half of which had been sold to the French army by Freddie. All forms of Army surplus followed, and he operated out of the boot of his car, with a typewriter for the invoices perched on the back seat. In essence, Freddie, just like his mother, was a dealer at heart and would trade in anything that would make a profit. Any man who admired his car would be asked to name a price for it. Years later, Freddie interrupted his return from a business meeting in East Africa to buy a pile of ships' chains rusting in Naples harbour, selling them later by telephone to a scrap dealer in Canada. As it grew, the parts business eventually moved to a lock-up garage near his home.

Despite his best efforts, Aviation Traders got off to a poor start. Freddie had spent all his £240 capital in less than three weeks and was borrowing money to survive. But he plugged away and as business picked up he started to make a small profit every week. Soon business was good, but this had not stopped the ambitious young Freddie from accepting a second job. By chance he had come across a Scottish entrepreneur named Bobby Sanderson who, with his brother, had set up an air charter company called Payloads in association with LAMS. Payloads operated out of London's Croydon and Hanworth aerodromes using three light aircraft to carry passengers. It had bought a batch of ex-RAF Halifax bombers with the idea of converting them into civilian freight aircraft, and the completed conversions were to go to LAMS to be flown from Stansted. In the end the plans did not work out and, after a series of accidents, Sanderson hired Freddie as his chief engineer to revive the business.

Freddie quickly realised that Payloads was a mess and he advised Sanderson to liquidate it and try and get his money out. "Get your money out as fast as you can," he said. Freddie sold off everything on his behalf and rescued some of Sanderson's cash, but in the process made himself jobless.

In May 1948 Freddie found himself sitting with Sanderson in the bar of the Silver Cross public house in Whitehall, London, drowning their sorrows. Sanderson, who was drawn to Freddie, bought him a drink, and the discussion turned to what Freddie was going to do next. Shrewdly, Sanderson saw past the brash ebullience to his friend's hidden qualities. "Freddie," he said, "you've done such a terrific job for me, what can I do to help you?"

"Well, nothing really," replied Freddie.

"Look, Freddie, if you had the money what would you do?" insisted Sanderson.

"If I had the money I would buy a fleet of surplus aeroplanes from BOAC," said Freddie with a laugh, but only half in fun.

"How much?"

"There are ten aeroplanes, Haltons, civilian versions of bombers, 600 tons of spare parts, and they are £42,000 the lot. For all ten aeroplanes and all of the spare parts, I'll need £42,000," he said, again only half seriously.

"How much have you got?

"Four," said Freddie. It was not nearly enough money.

Sanderson walked away for a few moments and sat at another table. When he returned he handed Freddie a cheque for the whole £42,000.

"Go and buy the aeroplanes," he told him.

Freddie was stunned. "When do you want the money back?"

"When you've sold the aircraft." It was Sanderson's way of saying thank you for rescuing him from Payloads. "I wouldn't have had any money if he hadn't got me out of trouble, and so I bought the aeroplanes," he explained. Once the Berlin Airlift started, Freddie was able to repay the money quickly. They'd agreed to split the profits 50:50 and share the losses equally too. Freddie recalled the act of generosity that proved the foundation of his business career: "He and his brother were great, great friends of mine until the day that both of them died. Of course the family and I are still great friends. He could have had anything but he didn't want anything. He was a real friend."

Freddie's intention for the Haltons was to move them on as quickly as possible, either whole or as scrap. He was now employing some former LAMS colleagues and was in need of a chief engineer of his own when another opportunity presented itself in the form of Jack Wiseman. Wiseman and his wife had been stranded in Sydney, Australia, on the demise of the LAMS world tramping organisation. On his return to England Wiseman contacted a former colleague, Ricky Brown, who told him that he was now working for Freddie and there was a job for him if he wanted it. When Wiseman visited Freddie at his office, he was invited to look after the engineering side of the company; he was one of the few engineers with an unrestricted A&C licence, and could certify any aircraft fit to fly on his own signature.

Freddie told him: "I've got all these Haltons from BOAC. I'm having to send them out for maintenance and I want someone to make sure I'm not being taken to the cleaners."

Wiseman was in his 30s, several years older than Freddie, and he was more experienced. Freddie couldn't promise a salary, only a share of the profits, but Wiseman was unfazed and had taken to Freddie immediately.

As 1948 closed, Freddie reflected on a great year. He now had a fleet of aircraft, a stable business, and his baby boy Kevin had been born in March. There had never been a prouder father. He felt his life was complete at last.

CHAPTER 4

# The First Big Break

## The Berlin airlift

1948-1949

All entrepreneurs need luck in their formative years, and Freddie Laker's early and extraordinary stroke of good fortune occurred in 1948, in the shape of the Berlin crisis.

But Freddie's first piece of luck came when he took delivery of the ten Haltons, which were quickly converted, the principal modification consisting of removing the gun turrets. They also came with hundreds of tons of spare parts. By August 1948 he and Jack Wiseman had fixed up half of the aircraft and sold the others; those retained were referred to, not entirely endearingly, as the 'Kennel Club', because the penultimate registration letter on all of them was 'D', as in dog (in the 1940s Dog rather than Delta was used in the phonetic alphabet). One went out on a long-term lease to Alpha Airways, an Anglo-South African charter operator.

The announcement of the Berlin Airlift sent freight rates – and the value of serviceable aircraft that could carry the freight – soaring. Freddie remembered: "Well, I thought, this is a bit of luck for three or four weeks." In the event his luck would last not for three or four weeks, but for 1 year and 14 days, to be exact. As Freddie later acknowledged: "From my point of view it was the best piece of luck I'd ever had. But of course, unfortunately for the wrong reason."

Freddie's good fortune would come on the back of misery inflicted on the inhabitants of Berlin, a city shattered by the events of the Second World War. When the conflict ended in 1945, the post-war fate of Germany was in the balance, and it was divided into four sectors, called 'temporary occupation zones', controlled by British, US, French and Soviet forces.

The city of Berlin posed a problem, as it was located 100 miles inside Soviet-controlled eastern Germany. It would have been unthinkable for the Allies to give the Soviets control of the capital, even though it was inside their designated zone, so it was decided to split control of the city between the Allies and the Soviets. It was generally believed that whoever controlled Berlin would eventually control the whole of Germany. The Western allies were frightened enough of Russia that any thought of a Soviet-controlled Germany was unthinkable. If Winston Churchill had had his way he would have driven the Soviets out of Germany altogether, but he didn't and the curious carve-up began.

Tensions slowly grew as Joseph Stalin tightened access to the city, using constant interruptions to road, rail and water supplies as a blatant attempt to undermine the fragile stability of West Germany. It was pure harassment designed to get the Allies to relinquish control of Berlin and vacate their half of the city. If that had happened nothing would have stood in the way of a Soviet communist-controlled Germany, with Europe possibly to follow. Stalin thought the West would roll over and would not deem Berlin worth the fight. But he was wrong. The Western leaders were determined that Berlin would not fall into Soviet hands.

The acute crisis began in June 1948 with the introduction of a new currency, the Deutschmark, to replace the highly devalued Reichsmark. The Russians objected and used the move as an excuse to begin the blockade of the city.

During talks between both sides on 22nd June, the Soviets made an explicit threat: "We are warning both you and the population of Berlin that we shall apply economic and administrative sanctions that will lead to the circulation in Berlin exclusively of the currency of the Soviet occupation zone." The same day they announced that they would introduce a new eastern currency, the Ostmark, in their zones.

Two days later, on 24th June, the Russians instigated a blockade around Berlin, preventing all access into the city in an attempt to drive out the American and British troops, who would cede it to Soviet control.

This was the first serious confrontation of the Cold War between the former allies. First the Russians turned off the electricity supply, which came almost exclusively from Russian-controlled power stations. On 25th June they cut off food supplies. The city was now under siege by the Red Army, which outnumbered the Allied forces by ten to one. Without supplies, the Western garrison inside Berlin, amounting to just under 25,000 people, would be forced to withdraw so the Russians could march in.

There was barely a month's worth of food inside Berlin, and just over 45 days' worth of coal. But the Russians had mistimed the blockade, as the summer just was starting. General Lucius Clay was the American Governor of Germany, and his gut response was to call the Russians' bluff and forcibly break through the blockade by sending a convoy, including a unit of combat engineers, up the autobahn to fix the bridge over the Elbe River that the Soviets were claiming was damaged. But while Clay believed that sending in an armed convoy was a risk worth taking, President Truman was against it, and the British military commander, General Sir Brian Robertson, was appalled by the plan, and told Clay that he was on his own if he went ahead.

In truth, the situation looked hopeless. Land-based access to Berlin had never been negotiated or formalised, which allowed the Russians to claim that the

Allies were in the city only with their special permission. Legally Clay could do nothing, and he was prevented by Truman from doing anything that could be deemed illegal.

But access by air was a completely different matter. On 30th November 1945 three 20-mile-wide air corridors into Berlin from Hamburg, Hanover and Frankfurt had been defined, and a written guarantee signed by all the participating nations. The presence of these three corridors, guaranteed in writing, was unarguable, and would eventually make the Berlin Airlift both possible and legal.

It was General Robertson who first suggested supplying Berlin by air. But Clay was dubious until Air Commodore Reginald Waite calculated that it would be possible with a big enough effort. Waite showed that Berlin's two million people required 5,000 tons of food, coal and diesel each day. The RAF reckoned that it could at a push fly in 750 tons a day, leaving the shortfall of 4,250 tons as the responsibility of the Americans.

General Clay decided to fly into Berlin to meet Ernst Reuter, the mayor-elect of the city.

"Look," he told him, "I am ready to try an airlift but I can't guarantee it will work."

On 25th June Clay gave the order to launch what was appropriately called 'Operation Vittles'. On the 26th the first aeroplane loaded with supplies left for Berlin. The RAF started two days later; its contribution was called 'Operation Plainfare'.

By the end of July it became apparent that the airlift would not be over quickly, and volumes would need to increase if Berlin was going to get through the winter. The RAF contribution could not be increased and the British Government discovered that BOAC and BEA owned the only aeroplanes that could carry cargo. Unable to take the aeroplanes off the existing commercial routes, the Government was forced to employ almost anything it could get its hands on.

Edwin Whitfield, manager of British European Airways, was given the job of coordinating the civilian end of the airlift. He had no idea what to do except commandeer every aircraft he could at any rate he was offered. This meant going to the 'sky tramps', the small commercial operators that had sprung up after the war, often operating war-surplus aircraft. The rates he offered were tempting, at £45 per flying hour, and £98 for carrying diesel fuel, which was deemed a dangerous cargo. The rates were a premium of 15 per cent over the going rate at the time.

Freddie Laker found himself in a very lucky position, owning six big planes when there weren't many people in England that had any aeroplanes at all, let alone a type that could meet the requirements of the airlift. But he was pessimistic about how long it would last, although potentially he could earn £1,000 from his fleet every day, which was a small fortune at the time. But he did not have the infrastructure or the personnel to mount such an operation. It was just him, Jack Wiseman, Ricky Brown and David Rosser, and all four were engineers by trade. It would be a struggle to get more than one aircraft in the air.

Freddie therefore sought the help of Bond Air Services, a company down on its luck that was already flying into Berlin from Wunstorf aerodrome, near Hanover. Bond owned two Halifaxes that it used to transport cargo, mostly cheese and fruit, into Britain from Europe. At the start of the airlift Bond was an aircraft down, one having crashed at Bovingdon airfield in Hertfordshire.

Freddie happened to be acquainted with Christopher Treen, Bond's chief pilot, whose brother Robert owned the company; they knew each other from Laker's ATA days. Freddie struck a canny deal with Robert Treen whereby Laker would supply the aircraft for Bond to operate, and they would share the freight fee. Freddie was further contracted to service the aeroplanes, from his enormous mountain of spares: "I had enough spare parts to maintain mine and everybody else's as well." Freddie described the deal as being "rather like Christmas."

With the deal with Bond in place, Freddie turned his attention to the huge servicing business that had resulted from the airlift. He expanded Aviation Traders to supply all the private operators with spares. A subsidiary company was eventually formed in March 1949, Aviation Traders Engineering Ltd (ATEL). He was also in need of an engineering base, and Jack Wiseman found just what they were looking for at Southend – a hangar filled with grain belonging to the Ministry of Supply. With a bit of coaxing from Freddie, the hangar was emptied and they moved in, with Wiseman setting up the engineering operation. Freddie later described the scene: "There was this sort of improvisation and of course we had to make all sorts of improvisations to change engines, get some form of cover. I mean, anything that looked like a tent was used."

As the airlift grew, so did Aviation Traders. Twenty-five companies were operating an assortment of 104 aircraft during the airlift, and most of them were using Aviation Traders for servicing and spares. Freddie was making two fortunes at once, sharing hourly revenues with Bond and servicing the entire civilian airlift at high prices for the spares he had obtained for nothing. At the peak of the airlift he had 400 men working away in Southend and 40 more in Hamburg. There was huge demand for Freddie's spares and engineering services, as the operators were only paid for the hours the aircraft were in the sky.

It was exhausting round-the-clock work, day after day, but for the participants it became a crusade. "I wasn't very much on the ground for the next year," commented Freddie.

It was almost as if the camaraderie of the bomber squadrons had been recreated, and they were out on a mission, but with a different enemy. Freddie ran his company autocratically, making instant decisions and backing them up unfailingly. He won a reputation for being as good as his word, and he expected anyone he dealt with to be the same.

Even though Freddie thought the Haltons "useless for civilian use", he hunted round and bought up as many as he could to profit from the freight rates. He found a couple being used by the RAF for target-towing and practice, and quickly commandeered them for the airlift. He was printing his own money – or so it seemed.

Freddie got the conversions down to a fine art. The plane, being a bomber, had a door that was only large enough for the crew to get into, so the bomb bay doors had to be taken off and the mechanism removed.

Berlin required a mass import of salt, and Freddie built panniers under the aircraft to carry the highly corrosive substance. Everything non-essential was stripped off the aeroplanes to save weight and increase the payload; on the Halton this was only 8 tons, which was totally uneconomic during normal times but, as Freddie said, "The aeroplanes came virtually free and we carried limited insurance on them."

The most difficult cargo to fly was coal. The bags would continually break open and spread dust throughout the aircraft, leading to a gradual build-up in weight. Crews would sometimes get out of the aircraft looking as if they'd just been down a coal mine, and would complain of headaches and breathing problems. The most popular cargo was potatoes.

Flying the cargo planes was almost as dangerous as a Second World War bombing mission. Friday 13th August 1948 was a black day at Tempelhof Airport when one aircraft crashed on landing, a second burst its tyres trying to avoid it, and a third landed on a partially constructed runway, all within minutes of each other.

The problem was that more than 500 aircraft were landing every 6 hours and being turned around again. Incoming aircraft were continually stacked in the sky, creating a risk of mid-air collision. Overloaded aircraft were aborting landings all the time. In the end new rules were instigated that allowed only one landing attempt, while loaded aircraft would fly at a different altitude from those returning unloaded. Under the new system aircraft flew three minutes apart and landed three minutes apart.

It was almost literally a flying circus, and the whole operation went round and round in a non-stop process. Freddie remembered: "Some pilots had as little as 800-900 flying hours, meaning we weren't talking about pilots that had got 15-20,000 hours, as they have today. So there is no doubt it was an incredible job that was done."

The airlift schedules became very precise. Each aircraft had a 40-minute window to take off, and if any pilots were not on time they did not go. "Work for Fred and burn your bed," was one slogan scrawled on the operations notice board at Hamburg, and that legend was to follow Freddie throughout his working life. Undoubtedly he was a hard taskmaster, and that often took its toll, as Greg Dix, Manager of the Laker Airways' US operation, explains: "A few of us had no life whatsoever outside of Laker for many years, which is probably why numerous relationships were forged within the company while others probably got dissolved because of it."

There was a tremendous pressure to keep flying, and the demands of the old aircraft were far in excess of normal. Frequent take-offs under maximum power strained engines and wore out parts, while repeated landings stressed the tyres and brakes. The airframes ate up spark plugs, brakes and tyres at an incredible rate, and the pounding caused by the frequent landings loosened bolts and rivets and fractured metal parts.

The weather was another problem. It was often appalling. Freddie said: "The aircraft, from an operational point of view, by today's standards, were really death-traps and junk. We had no de-icing equipment on these aeroplanes, no windscreen wipers. We used to put this paste on the wings to keep the ice off them. We were flying very low and the aeroplanes were buzzed almost daily by Russians fighters. Every kind of obstacle was put in the way to stop it. And the boys just kept going and going and going. And they never stopped. And I think it was that attitude, I suppose, that maybe the Russians saw, and there was no war, thank God."

Every pilot that operated on the airlift had come from the RAF. For them it felt like going back into service, back to war. Though no one expected it to last for more than three or four weeks, thinking that it would collapse, the only other possibility feared by everyone was the prospect of another conflict.

Freddie found that there was great enthusiasm to participate: "At first they had looked at it as, 'Oh well, let's go and do this and get on with the job and we'll earn a few pounds,' and something like that. But after a bit, two or three months down the road, and with nearly everyone involved having participated in some form or another in a war that had lasted for a very long time, Germany was not a popular place, but grudges were put aside. No one liked to think about their friends who in their hundreds had been killed. So we didn't think much of it when we first went into it. But then it became like a crusade. We thought, why did we do this war thing? It was all about freedom. And the freedom was for everybody, and here we were back in a worse situation than we started with. This was Hitlerism in a way, but under a different name. It was loss of freedom for people. Everyone volunteered, everybody wanted to do it. There was never a question of a crew member saying, 'I don't want to go today, I'm tired,' or 'I don't feel like it.' I don't think I can ever remember when every single member of the staff wasn't fit every day. Because there were no excuses to get out of it."

By December 1948 Joseph Stalin thought he had won. Freddie recalled, "Conditions that winter were terrible but I think the icing conditions were the worst." The steady drone of engines at three-minute intervals continued. A Russian front-line officer recalled years later: "One would appear overhead, another would disappear over the horizon, and a third emerge, one after another, without interruption, like a conveyor belt."

The Russians did interfere. They did their best to disrupt the airlift, but they could not be seen to be breaking their agreement, although there was plenty of provocation. The Soviets would carry out aerial manoeuvres in the corridor or right alongside it. Freddie said: "They would be off firing military equipment and the pilots could see them firing on the ground, and being buzzed and all that sort of thing by their aeroplanes. It wasn't nice. No one liked it. But of course it was all part of war games."

By the end the Berlin Airlift had delivered a total of 2.3 million tons of cargo to Berlin, of which the British delivered 541,936 tons. Freddie Laker was probably responsible for about 10 per cent.

The Russians finally admitted defeat after a counter-blockade of Russia's own western imports. Officially the Soviet Union lifted the blockade on 12th May 1949.

At the end of it, Freddie had repaid his debt to Bobby Sanderson. His planes had flown more than 2,577 trips. His half of the charter money came to £150,000, a lot of which was spent on wages; the pilots in particular were well paid at £65 per month, double the average monthly salary, and, with the added bonus of 3 shillings per round trip completed, many were earning £200 or more per month. Freddie's huge workforce of maintenance crews also needed to be paid, including overtime and bonuses, but Freddie had covered his overheads and there was enough left for a small profit. But the real money from the Berlin Airlift had been in the servicing and spares – the hangar full of ex-BOAC spares was an absolute goldmine for Freddie, their scarcity only increasing their worth. By the end Freddie was halfway to becoming a millionaire. It made him, by the standards of the day, a very wealthy man.

Freddie lost only one plane during the airlift when a Halton ran into a construction trench by the side of the runway at Tegel Airport close to the end of the operation. The plane was pushed out of the way by bulldozers so as not to delay those lining up to land and take off, and was immediately broken up for scrap by Freddie's men.

The aircraft, G-AHDO, had a chequered past. Six weeks earlier an engine had failed and it had been nursed home by its pilot, Joseph Viatkin. This was the aircraft that Freddie had leased to Alpha Airways, and it had only just come back into his possession, and then only by a whisker. In February 1949 it had been sitting in Johannesburg for nearly a month. The pilot, Dennis Parsons, and his flight engineer, Bob Batt, were tipped off that all was not well with Alpha Airways; someone from the company called at their hotel and asked for the plane's log book and registration papers. What might have been a perfectly innocent request was met with suspicion by Parsons and Batt, who refused to hand them over. Fearing that the company was in financial difficulties and the plane was about to be sold from under them, leaving them stranded in Africa, they decided to hold it to ransom, figuring that there would be someone who would pay to get it back.

Parsons pointed out that the plane was not Alpha's to sell, as it belonged to Freddie Laker. Both he and Batt knew Freddie from LAMS; only the year before Freddie had declined to give Batt a job at Payloads when he had asked for a very reasonable £9 a week salary. "That's more than I make!" exclaimed Freddie, and the two had left it at that. Batt sent a cable to Freddie: "Might be in danger of losing an aeroplane. Send carnet for fuel and will deliver Halifax to Southend." Freddie sent the carnet without further comment, and the crew began to make secret plans for a flight back to England.

Parsons still insisted that they find a payload to cover landing fees and overnight stops on the way home. Batt ran across nine African Merchant Navy seamen who had left their British ship in Cape Town, travelled as far as Johannesburg by rail, then been stranded by South Africa's colour bar. They were unable to buy tickets on scheduled airlines, which only allowed white passengers. They had plenty of money to pay their fare, having drawn all their pay in Cape

Town. In addition, Parsons picked up four white South African passengers, and another of the crew found a man wanting to re-export a paper pulping plant that he had bought from a London firm 25 years before.

In the early hours of 5th March the passengers waited as the plane was crammed with the freight. Parsons took the money when suddenly the situation turned ugly.

"But these men are coloured," complained one of the white passengers. "They can't possibly travel with us." Parsons explained that they would be travelling in a separate compartment, but that wasn't good enough for the white South Africans. The seamen, fed up with being treated like second-class citizens, were getting hostile. Parsons told them to go out to the plane and he invited the white South Africans to follow. When they refused, he climbed on board and ordered Batt to prepare for an immediate take-off.

The plane touched down at Bovingdon on 7th March. After handing over £100 profit to the managing director of Alpha, having deducted their own pay and expenses, Batt and Parsons flew the Halifax to Southend and handed it back to Freddie. Assuming that Freddie would show some gratitude for his part in the aircraft's rescue, Batt again asked for a job. He had been an airframe fitter in the RAF and had subsequently acquired a broad range of engineering qualifications and considerable flying experience, and already had an offer from the Lancashire Aircraft Corporation of £16 a week as a chief flight engineer. "All right," said Freddie, "you've got yourself a job. I want you to come as my Chief Inspector – and I will go as high as £8 a week." Batt accepted from sheer exasperation.

CHAPTER 5

# Scrap Merchant
## Wheeling, dealing and tinkering

1949-1951

By the time the Berlin Airlift finally ended in August 1949 Freddie Laker was a very wealthy man – by all accounts he was a multi-millionaire at today's values. It didn't seem to bother him a bit that the money had been made out of other people's misery and desperation, i.e. the unfortunate Berliners whom Stalin had sought to starve into submission.

He was enjoying it and didn't seek to hide his new-found wealth, as he remembered: "Let's put it that way – we had all made a lot of money." He was 26 years old and, as a close colleague recalled, "all made up." Others might have less charitably described him as an opportunist carpetbagger and they wouldn't have been far wrong.

He lost no time in enjoying the fruits of his success. He bought a five-bedroom house in the stockbroker belt in Carshalton, Surrey, and a brand-new Austin Princess for cash. He thought about a Rolls-Royce but decided that it would be too ostentatious for a man just turned 26 – not that he couldn't have easily afforded it. But the biggest satisfaction he got from having all that money in the bank was knowing that he had finally escaped the poverty of his childhood.

But there was a downside. During the airlift he had built up a formidable organisation and had a big company to support with high overheads and 400 people on the payroll. Suddenly there was very little for them to do and he started bleeding cash at the rate of £2,000 a week.

He became more and more worried as each week passed, and it got to the point where every day he added up how much time he had left before the money ran out, as he remembered: "I thought, what are we going to do now? What's going to happen?"

The short answer was nothing. Freddie was a one-hit wonder and any notions that he was a made-up businessman set for life soon vanished. He soon realised that he had just been lucky twice and that now his luck had run out. Surely lightning could not strike three times.

He knew what he should do and that was cease trading immediately and make everyone redundant. And that was the advice he kept getting almost every time he turned to his accountant and his bank manager. But he thought to himself that it was not them who had to look 400 men in the eye and tell them it was all over and they were on the scrap heap. Freddie Laker may have been many things, but he was not the cold-hearted ruthless bastard that some people thought he was.

But he was also nobody's fool. Freddie knew that it was time to stop flying. He knew everyone would try and keep flying their aeroplanes, which would mean cut-throat rates with too many aircraft chasing too little work. So he took the initiative and turned Aviation Traders into Britain's biggest scrap merchant almost overnight.

There was a desperate shortage of steel and aluminium in Britain and what existed was carefully rationed out. The shortages meant that the demand for metal scrap was still very high, especially the aluminium of which aircraft were chiefly made.

Freddie wondered aloud at the irony of it all. During the war housewives had been encouraged to give up their aluminium pots and pans for the war effort to be melted down into munitions. In a complete reversal, the planes were now being turned back into pots, pans and toothpaste tubes. The leader in this market was a Barnet-based company called John Dale Ltd, and it would buy as much scrap aluminium as it was offered at sky-high prices. It was also a huge gamble turning sophisticated aircraft that a year before had been worth tens of thousands of pounds into scrap.

But much as he disliked doing it, the transformation of Aviation Traders from a buyer and seller of aircraft and parts supplier into a scrap merchant was inescapable.

Freddie's acute knowledge of industrial processes once again came into play. On the back of a serviette in the café at Southend Airport he sketched out the design of a giant aluminium smelter and told his engineers to go and build it and have it ready by the end of the week five days hence.

The firebrick-lined tank he sketched was to be eight feet long by five feet wide, with a giant gas burner underneath. Freddie nicknamed it 'The Pot' and aluminium scrap would be piled in at one end and emerge from the other as pristine shiny aluminium ingots. It was a permanent fixture with the fires burning 24 hours a day, it was never allowed to cool down; it was designed to operate continuously. The smelter turned Freddie's fortunes around again, and he told anyone who cared to listen that he had finally found a machine that printed money, designed all by himself.

Freddie set to work buying as many aeroplanes as he could for prices as low as £50 each. He organised his men into teams and they cut the planes to pieces with oxyacetylene torches where they stood. From each plane Freddie's men produced ingots with a resale value of £500. It was a remarkably profitable business, as Freddie said, "We turned them into aluminium ingots and sold them to a saucepan maker called John Dale. It went very well."

The deep irony of selling the ingots to John Dale was not lost on Freddie. The aluminium had been smelted from old saucepans in the first place, originally manufactured by Dale, and Freddie neatly completed the circle by selling the metal melted within 'The Pot' back to the manufacturer of the saucepans. Freddie thought to himself that if this was the definition of raw capitalism, then it was clearly a world tailor-made for himself to prosper in. He thought to himself: "The others don't stand a chance." It was a thought that travelled with him for almost every day of the rest of his life.

But while he was full of bravado on the surface, marvelling openly and unashamedly at his own prowess as a businessman, deep down he hated turning perfectly good serviceable aircraft, some of which had flown only minimal hours, into scrap metal.

His chance had come purely because there were too many obsolete aircraft of the same type that no one wanted. There were literally tens of thousands of aircraft, many built in 1945 at a time when Lord Beaverbrook was doing too good a job and cranking up aircraft production to the same quantities that Heinz was turning out tins of baked beans. And no one at the Air Ministry seemed to notice that the war was coming to an end as Beaverbrook exhorted his workers to work harder and harder to produce aircraft that would never fly in anger. No one had expected the war to end as abruptly as it had after Germany collapsed under the twin assault of the Allied and Russian forces.

Just after the war Her Majesty's Government began selling off surplus aircraft engines. Often they were brand new and packed in wooden cases. Freddie would be regularly tipped off by someone in Government that they were coming up for auction. He knew that the numerous spark plugs in each engine were tipped with platinum. He managed to buy 6,000 aircraft engines for a ridiculously low sum, so low that he more than got his money back on the wood in the packing cases alone (sawn wood being scarce at the time). He then made a killing by extracting and selling off the metal from the points of the spark plugs, the value of which was as much as that of the engine itself.

A lot of it was made possible by inside information, which came to him because he charmed just about everybody with whom he came in contact. His job in the war allowed him to come into contact with many 'high-ups', as he called them, in HMG, the Civil Service and the Forces, and he made full use of the opportunities.

In the end Freddie even balked at paying £50 for each complete aircraft, and started hinting that he might have to charge as much to take the aircraft away and break them up at the sellers' expense.

Surprisingly, no one else caught on in quite the same way to the value of the scrap that could be extracted from dismantling an aeroplane. Aside from the aluminium, aircraft were made from very valuable and exotic materials, and Freddie's skill was unlocking the whole metal value.

The basic smelting operation only employed around 50 men, and the other 350 on the payroll needed more skilled work to keep them occupied. Freddie felt a sense of responsibility to the men to keep them employed, and he was glad he did as every part of value was carefully dismantled, catalogued and stored away to await a future buyer.

With the huge amounts of cash he was once again generating, he bought up every single piece of Government surplus equipment he could lay his hands on, which was being sold at numerous Government auctions up and down the country. At auction alone he bought more than 200 aeroplanes, including in excess of 100 Halifax bombers, and he also filled up the fields around Southend with ex-Army trucks and vehicles awaiting a market.

There were also plenty of munitions that no one wanted, which Freddie only had to stack on his lorries and take away. No one cared what he did with them. At one point Aviation Traders owned more guns and ammunition than the British Army itself. Machine guns and ammunition were stacked in the cavernous air-raid shelters that surrounded the edges of Southend Airport.

Freddie's activities at that time prompted some amusing moments. One evening he was with Batt, who was behind his desk in a wooden hut, when a police officer knocked on the door and said he was checking on the company's firearm licence to see if the licensed guns were in order. Batt took the policeman over to the shelters and showed him the piles of machine guns and cases of ammunition. The policeman was shocked and said: "I was talking about two Very Pistols." He realised his mission was somewhat fruitless, and simply told Batt to 'be careful', cursing the ineptitude of his superiors as he went.

It was a period of great opportunism as Freddie spent his cash pile wisely to snap up everything the old War Ministry had for sale. Since it was all priced well below scrap value, Freddie simply couldn't go wrong. As he put it, he was buying pound notes for ten shillings.

Not all the planes and war surplus materials were scrapped. Freddie managed to save three ex-BEA Vikings from 'The Pot'. He had picked them up very cheaply from the Ministry of Supply, intending to scrap them. But he changed his mind and the three Vikings were rebuilt as new and sold to BOAC at a sizeable profit. Rapidly Aviation Traders also became the largest supplier of Rolls-Royce Merlin power plants and parts, even supplying crankshafts to the engine manufacturer.

Freddie thought it highly amusing that he had bought the aircraft from the Government and had then sold them back to the Government, which owned BOAC. He marvelled at the never-ending ineptness of Britain's Civil Service, but thanked them for the thousands of pounds they were adding to his bank account every week.

With so many under his control, Freddie swapped parts around until he had assembled what were effectively a fleet of brand-new aircraft. And he managed to find buyers overseas who were swayed by the fact that Freddie was the only supplier who could offer brand-new aircraft. He contracted to supply the Egyptian Air Force with 12 new Halifaxes to carry paratroopers to their destinations.

Occasionally there came the opportunity for some profitable resales from the acres of military equipment stored in the fields. The Egyptian Generals looked at the shiny new aircraft their colleagues had bought and asked for Freddie's phone number. The resulting long-distance phone call saw them buy two dozen refurbished American-built Staghound T17 armoured cars, sight unseen. Freddie immediately went out into the wet fields of Southend in his wellington boots to see if he actually had any of that type of vehicle. He found well over 100, brought them inside one of the hangars, made up the required two dozen, and melted down what was left. The vehicles were better than brand new by the time they left the hangar and, painted in the proper Egyptian Army colours, were shipped to Egypt, where they gave many years of service, including seeing action in the Suez Crisis of 1956 and the attempted invasion of Israel in 1967.

The Egyptians also wanted the latest bombsights fitted to their aircraft. Freddie had agreed to supply them without any knowledge of what they were or how to get them. He contacted someone in the Ministry who told him that they were of American design and manufacture and that when the British had acquired them in the war it was on condition that they would eventually be destroyed. Freddie was then told that if he went to see the Governor of Brixton Prison, he might be able to help. Completely mystified, Freddie duly saw the Governor, who told him that HMG had handed the task of dismantling the sights to the prisoners. Did he have 12 (one for each aircraft)? Yes he did. Would he let Freddie have them? Yes he would. How much would they cost? At this point Freddie feared they would cost an arm and a leg. The Governor replied that every year there was a Christmas party for the prisoners, but this year it was in doubt as there were insufficient funds, but if Freddie cared to make a small donation... A donation of a few pounds was duly made and Freddie had his sights.

Freddie realised that what he needed was a war to truly cash in, so when the Korean War was conveniently started by General MacArthur the opportunities to make money were unbounded. Freddie had a huge stockpile of Mustang fighter engines and an almost unlimited supply of spare parts, which the US Army had left behind unwanted in England – the American Generals had deemed it uneconomic to ship the unwanted parts back to America. They had also closed down the factories and scrapped the tools and dies that had made the parts originally, thinking they had enough to last forever.

But the Korean War changed that and suddenly the Americans were buying everything Freddie had at the original new list prices. It was an unprecedented bonanza and pure luck. Another lucky purchase turned out to be hundreds of tons of snow chains, which he was able to sell at a handsome profit to the Canadian Army, which also wanted them for Korea.

But the overheads of paying 400 men meant that the whole operation had to run very fast to make money, and as others got in on the act the price of aircraft began to rise and Freddie started to face stiff competition at auctions. From margins of 500 per cent they dropped to 10 per cent, and Freddie with his 400 men was a high-cost operation. Soon he was only breaking even. The men who had proved such an asset when he needed to gear up quickly had become a liability again. But at least this time there were no losses.

When they had exhausted every avenue of profit and had nothing left to do, the remainder of Freddie's men broke up the surplus aero engines and salvaged the brass and copper scrap. Freddie paid them 5 shillings an hour and was most proud that he had not made a single one of his men redundant in the post-war period.

As time passed and the economy improved, many of the men, some highly skilled and in demand, began to drift away and the problem solved itself.

By then Aviation Traders was starting to prosper in the business it had been set up to do, under the control of Jack Wiseman. Freddie found a growing permanent market for refurbished planes for Wiseman to fix up and sell. Planes kept coming out of the Southend hangars like brand new.

Freddie thanked his lucky stars that he had been able to stay in business and keep hold of most of his cash. Most of the other Berlin operators had not been so fortunate. One casualty among many was his old partner, Bond Air Services, run by Robert Treen.

Freddie felt sorry for Treen and helped him out by partnering with him in a joint venture using four surplus aircraft running pleasure flights for Butlins holidaymakers in Skegness. They used the old airfield at nearby Ingoldmells, which had been built by Billy Butlin to fly holidaymakers directly into Skegness.

Suddenly the commercial aviation business began to boom as Britain recovered from the war, and any notion of scrapping the aircraft disappeared. In fact, Freddie realised that he had scrapped too many and the planes started to have a scarcity value as he marvelled at the turnaround and how quickly it had come. He sniffed the air and decided that it was time for another change of direction, and started to take his first small steps into the aircraft charter business.

CHAPTER 6

# Trooping Contracts

## Lucrative defence deals

1951

At the beginning of 1951, Freddie Laker was only 28 years old, yet he was on his way to becoming one of the richest men in post-war Britain. If he had thought he was rich in 1949, it was nothing to the noughts that would be added to his bank balance just two years later.

Seemingly Freddie had absolutely everything. He loved telling people he could do just about everybody's job as well as they could themselves. He had also become extremely confident in his own abilities and developed an extraordinary charisma that could seemingly make impossible things happen. It was clear that the confident man in his late 20s was nothing like the gawky 24-year-old he had been when he first got started in business.

In a magazine profile of the time he was described as: "Chirpily aggressive with the hint of a bright-eyed schoolboy and a drawer-full of bargaining treasures never properly hidden. He remains happiest with dirt on his hands whether it is helping to sweep snow from the runway outside his office or climbing a ladder to tinker with the engine."

The writer got it about right. The article noted the fact that Freddie was a very good engineer with an exceptional memory, and he could do just about everybody's job as well as they could themselves. He gave the impression that he knew every detail of what happened in his business. Freddie, together with his chief lieutenants Jack Wiseman, Bob Batt and Norman Jennings, was running a highly profitable business that was growing all the time. Below them was another cadre of managers and skilled engineers that he trusted. Most of the engineers were made in his own image. Throughout the aircraft industry, Freddie was known as a man who always fulfilled his side of any bargain. It was a fetish with him. In return, he demanded an equally high standard from anyone who dealt with him or worked with him. To his detractors – and there were many, usually jealous competitors – he was little more than a carpetbagger or some kind of East End wide boy.

But the success he had achieved was never enough, and one enduring characteristic was that Freddie Laker always wanted more. That raw ambition meant that what followed in the next 10 years was little short of phenomenal.

But first he had a personal problem he had to solve – because of his youthful looks he was not taken seriously by the much older businessmen (many twice his age) who dominated the aviation business. So as part of a serious mission to be taken more seriously he had a personal makeover. First he grew a moustache, which instantly made him look 10 years older. Then he threw out all his 'engineer's clothing' and bought a whole new wardrobe of smart suits and accompanying shoes, ties and shirts. It worked and he immediately found people took him more seriously as a man with a razor-sharp mind and an outstanding memory. He also found that some people he knew well didn't even recognise the old Freddie Laker any more. In 1951, encouraged by his new image and growing acceptance in the industry, and sensing a change in mood, Freddie decided to set up as a proper airline.

When he announced his plan to his managers and staff, however, everyone was stunned, and the news was certainly not favourably received. He had always told everyone that would listen that the airline business was a graveyard and a business to be avoided at all costs. He had told them to have him 'committed' if he ever attempted to enter that business.

In light of that, unsurprisingly his Aviation Traders managers were both angry and hostile. They immediately reminded Freddie that he had always insisted he was never going to operate planes, just service them and trade them. Almost everyone in the organisation considered running an airline a licence to lose money – no one, but no one, thought it was a good idea. Freddie's senior managers were already worried about their boss anyway. They believed he was on the way to becoming a megalomaniac, with delusions that he was master of the universe. They realised that they had been very lucky, and had it not been for the Berlin Airlift and the stupidly low prices at which the British Government had sold off Army surplus, Aviation Traders might well have gone bust.

In a tense meeting in Freddie's office, Jack Wiseman, Bob Batt and Norman Jennings argued desperately for their boss to drop the idea he had flamboyantly announced just a few hours before. Characteristically, Freddie brushed the protests aside and told them: "Things have changed, it's a new era." He had decided that there was going to be a growing market for air travel and there was room for another operator. The three men shook their heads and gave up the argument. It was just possible that there was a chance that Freddie was right – after all, he had been right so many times in the past. And for the next 31 years he was again.

An opportunity soon popped up to shortcut the start-up process. Freddie's top managers were using the fact of Surrey Flying Services having gone into receivership as an example of what could happen to Freddie if he went forward with his crazy plan. They told him again that he was making a big mistake. But Freddie waved them aside and instead went straight to the receivers of Surrey

Flying Services. On the spot in February 1951 he made a bid to buy up the assets and goodwill. To the chagrin of his managers the bid was accepted, and Surrey Flying Services became the platform for everything that followed.

Against all the odds the acquisitions proved to be a huge success – so successful that Freddie decided that buying up other failing operators was the way to go. He then went on a buying spree.

He bought a company called Air Charter for £20,000, which had belonged to his great rival, Harold Bamberg. It was in financial difficulties, but it also had huge tax losses that he could offset against the vast profits he had made as a scrap merchant.

In November 1951 he did his biggest deal and bought Fairflight Ltd from Air Vice Marshall Don Bennett, adding 300 employees to the payroll. Fairflight's main asset was a lucrative contract to carry cargo between Berlin and Hamburg. It also owned an Avro Tudor aircraft. The acquisition coincided with the second Berlin Airlift of 1951, which was about getting goods out of Berlin rather than in, as well as refugees fleeing the ravaged German city. The Russians had started impounding goods moving out of Berlin along the road and rail links, as well as blocking supplies of raw materials going in. This latest blockade threatened the newly won prosperity of West Berlin. Like the first, the second Berlin Airlift was highly lucrative and tailor-made for Freddie's skills at operating aircraft. Within a few months of taking over Fairflight, Freddie was running 75 flights a week between Berlin and Hamburg and Hanover. Once again, he systematically bought up every available aeroplane that was for sale and attempted to corner the market.

In July 1952 the companies he bought were reorganised under one banner, that of Air Charter Group (ACG). The new company quickly expanded to become the dominant operator on the Berlin route. As it had done the first time around, Aviation Traders was also supplying planes and servicing to all of Freddie's competitors. Freddie found himself in need of a traffic/commercial manager and could think of no one better than George Forster, an ex-ATA pilot he'd flown with. Freddie had bumped into Forster again since the war, when the latter leased a Halifax from LAMS for Lep Air Services, and they'd flown many times in each other's company on various 'commercial' missions. Something about these encounters stuck and Freddie telephoned him to offer him the job. Freddie not only hired Forster in August 1952 as his Commercial Manager, but also hired Forster's wife to run the office.

Freddie Laker always considered himself a sharp operator and quick to spot any opportunity in the then fledgling airline business. But one opportunity he did not spot and did not take advantage of was when the transportation of troops in the British Army made a switch from sea to air. As a result of his lack of foresight Freddie was a relative latecomer to a business that had grown into one of the most important markets for the independent operators.

The switch from sea to air transport for troops had happened in 1951 when Colonel Wilson, the owner of an operator called Airwork, had a brainwave, which was to turn the logistics operation of the British Army on its head. Previously soldiers had always travelled by ship. But Colonel Wilson, who was only known by his nickname 'Boy', convinced the War Office that flying soldiers around the world was much cheaper – £4 a head cheaper on a 12-hour flight to the Middle East. Even then there was scepticism, but Wilson finally won the War Office round by persuading them that using independent airlines helped maintain planes that at any time could be called on to augment the RAF's resources and get British troops quickly to trouble spots. The civil servants at the War Office were persuaded by such a strong argument and the trooping business for the independents exploded.

Wilson and Harold Bamberg's Eagle operation quickly cornered the market. Bamberg understood immediately what Freddie didn't, and rounded up all his old and unreliable aircraft to charter them to a gullible War Office, which was only interested in the lowest possible price. And for the lowest possible price it got the worst and most uncomfortable aircraft that a seat could be screwed into. As soon as it got traction Freddie realised his mistake, but could only look on as four operators cornered the market. The Air Ministry thought the four should only get stronger, awarding them the major contracts and preventing the likes of Freddie from making inroads.

Then he finally got a break. In a fit of pique Harold Bamberg had sold his fleet of ten York aircraft as a protest against the BEA and BOAC monopoly of carrying regular scheduled services passengers. Freddie took advantage of Bamberg's folly and bought four of his Yorks, and promptly had them flying troops to the Suez Canal Zone from RAF bases, albeit at a small loss. Freddie also landed trooping contracts from the British Government, deploying soldiers to the Middle East. Although the initial contracts were all loss-making, Freddie got a toehold in the market and it eventually proved to be the start of a hugely lucrative business. He won contracts because it was soon evident that he was the only reliable operator, thanks to his Aviation Traders division, while most of the other operators suffered chronic unreliability. Three- or four-day delays, with soldiers camping out on terminal floors, were common, and the aircraft the other operators used were uncomfortable as well as unreliable. Reports of flights were frequently scathing. One officer wrote sarcastically to his commander: "The flight was quite comfortable until we crashed at Malta."

It had not gone unnoticed that the flights operated by ACG had none of these problems, and Freddie's big opportunity came hand-in-hand with a terrible tragedy. A Skyways-operated York aircraft was lost over the Caribbean Sea with Army wives and children on board. It was a catastrophic and inexplicable loss, possibly caused by an engine fire or a major flight control failure. Freddie had already foreseen something like this and, when the inevitable happened, he was ready to capitalise on it.

The accident and the subsequent publicity caused a huge furore, especially when the *Daily Express* revealed that the War Office carried out no checks on the operators or their aeroplanes and simply awarded a contract based on the air carrier that submitted the lowest price. The Skyways crash completely changed the Government's attitude, and it appointed Major Douglas Whybrow to take over responsibilities for trooping contracts. His brief was to get improvements out of the unreliable private airlines. The York aircraft that were used for trooping varied greatly in standards and comfort, and Whybrow thought that there was an urgent need for a schedule of standards, embracing comfort and safety, including rearward-facing seats and penalties for delays. Unfortunately he wasn't given a larger budget to pay for the contracts and was told he would just have to use his powers of persuasion.

Whybrow found that the tenders were not honestly dealt with; decision-makers often had links with the airlines bidding for the contracts. He was aware of the name Freddie Laker and what his competitors were telling him – they were calling him a cowboy, East End opportunist and other unprintable terms. Whybrow deduced that the stories were so overdone as to be highly improbable. Air Charter was properly registered with the Ministry of Aviation, and Freddie had a very good reputation from the Berlin Airlift. Aviation Traders was well thought of for aircraft maintenance. The existing operators had very poor records, and the vilifying of the Laker-managed operations was nothing more than an attempt to smear Freddie's reputation because he was trying to muscle in on their patch. It was more likely that they feared Freddie Laker.

So it was rather unfortunate when an aircraft belonging to Air Charter – which had been chartered for some ad hoc trooping flights to Egypt – collapsed on take-off at Southend Airport. Fortunately there were no casualties. Freddie rang Whybrow and offered to collect him and take him to Stansted to see his operation, and he would explain about the mishap along the way. Freddie pulled up at the main entrance of the War Office in Whitehall in his sleek green Bentley, double-parking in spite of the horn tootings of displeasure from other drivers. He introduced himself with an outstretched hand. "I'm Laker," he boomed. Whybrow found Freddie's appearance rather unorthodox compared to the more formal and smooth front men employed by the operators to which had become accustomed: "A slightly brash manner and a cockney accent. He might have been mistaken for the chauffeur if not for the almost too smart suit and tie, confident twinkle in his eye and a well fed air."

During a long journey in heavy London traffic, Freddie explained what had happened to the York. It was an aircraft that had a reputation for being unreliable and notable for the length of runway it required for take-off at maximum weight. RAF pilots during the war had joked, 'If it were not for the curvature of the earth it would never get off the ground.' The flight engineer would monitor the engines while they were at 100 per cent thrust and therefore under maximum stress. He would then raise the undercarriage when the captain ordered him to do so. Raising the gear reduced drag, and speed would then build up so that the engines could be taken off maximum thrust as soon as possible, reducing the possibility of a failure.

The morning of the flight had been a miserable grey day. As Freddie told it, apparently the captain had looked towards the grim-faced flight engineer and told him to 'cheer up'. Unable to hear properly over the sound of the engines, the flight engineer misheard and thought it was the order for 'gear up'. The aircraft had not reached take-off speed and came to a grinding halt on the runway. Freddie's staff took the troops to a local hotel for a slap-up lunch. The

York was returned to the maintenance area and was ready to depart the next day. Whybrow thought the story implausible, but nonetheless amusing.

Freddie went to some lengths to impress upon Whybrow that he was honest and capable. He convinced Whybrow that he could give guarantees and keep promises in areas where he knew his competitors were likely to be cautious and non-committal. Only Harold Bamberg tried to strictly comply with the terms of his contract, but when efforts were made to convince him to go beyond the terms, even he was apt to hedge. Whybrow knew that things had to change, and Freddie seemed eager and claimed to be capable of delivering dramatic improvements. So Whybrow chose to overlook the embarrassing incident and felt that in Freddie he had found a man he could trust.

Freddie showed Whybrow around his operation and introduced his key people, including Jack Wiseman. Whybrow was impressed by Freddie's willingness to allow his workmen to talk openly. He and Freddie were now on first-name terms. On the return journey, Freddie wanted to know how he could get on the list for regular trooping contracts. Whybrow was surprised that Freddie had only been invited to tender for ad hoc flying contracts.

"What more can I do to impress the ministry?" asked Freddie.

"Reduce the dreadful delays, install rearward-facing seats and improve the furnishing of the aircraft," replied Whybrow.

"All that will cost more – are they willing to pay?" enquired Freddie, unwilling to fork out for it himself.

"No, but we are working on it," assured Whybrow.

A few weeks later Whybrow was invited back again with the contractual committee to inspect a York that Freddie had prepared. It had been completely stripped to save weight and the interior was now decorated in pink and maroon vinyl in an attempt to soundproof the cabin. The latest rearward-facing seats by the Rumbold company had been fitted, with no reduction in the number of passengers it could carry. It was the best trooping aircraft that Whybrow had ever seen, and it offered a measure of comfort that soldiers had never enjoyed before. In the days before the provision of headrests, which Wiseman had installed, soldiers had had to endure long-distance flights in uncomfortable seats that only came up to the middle of their backs. Freddie also promised to cut the delays. The Men from the Ministry were all impressed apart from the Treasury representative. He thought that the 'frills' were costly and unnecessary and he thought that the rearward-facing seats had stopped even more passengers being crammed in.

The committee was about to take tenders for a series of flights to Fiji via Singapore, the longest route undertaken by a private operator. There had been lots of lobbying. Air Charter had the lowest tender and committed itself to laying down spare parts and spare engines along the route. This was a practice that rapidly became standard procedure for all the other operators. As the flights were for servicemen and their families being relocated, Freddie had Aviation Traders move the toilets to the centre of the aircraft, find space for carrycots, and provide feminine items at no cost, together with newly available disposable nappies for the babies.

Whybrow advised the Under Secretary of State at the War Office, Sir James Hutchison, to award the new contract on merit and not price. He told Hutchison that ACG was the best operator and it duly won the contract regardless of price. The rate ACG quoted was £90 per flying hour, and it rapidly became an immensely profitable business for Freddie's company. In essence, all Freddie had to pay for was fuel and the salaries of the pilots, which was less than £60 per flying hour. It was a potential bonanza, and one might have thought the profit margin more than acceptable – but not Freddie Laker.

With the contract won, Freddie appointed George Forster as his General Manager to specifically run the troop charter business. Forster's first task was to organise the 25 round trips for the Singapore/Fiji contract. He soon found out why he had been hired, as Freddie wanted to use his expertise to extract every penny of profit from the contract. Together the two men examined every detail of the flights. They discovered that the flight to Singapore would be lighter than a conventional trooping flight of fully equipped soldiers because there would be a large number of women and children aboard. They also discovered that passengers on the Singapore to Fiji leg were all Fijian soldiers, who were being used to garrison Singapore. There were no women or children on that leg. But Freddie was misinformed that all the Fijian soldiers were small of stature, and told Foster to make his calculations accordingly.

When they had gathered the information and finished the research, Freddie told Forster to organise the flight planning to take advantage of any savings to be made. Freddie didn't want any extra fuel to be flown around or any planes that were not filled to the brim with passengers. Forster went out and bought the six-volume Tunes World Atlas and worked out the optimum routes to Singapore and Fiji with help from Norman Jennings. They measured the distance with a ruler and calculated the flight times with a slide rule. They discovered that the long leg to Fiji was crucial and calculated the weight of a small Fijian as instructed by their boss. It was obvious that the weight of the passengers was crucial.

With everything in place, Forster had found an extra profit of £10 per head. But he was in for a shock, for when he arrived at the end of the first proving flight he found that, far from being small, the Fijian soldiers were enormous, thus throwing out all his careful calculations. Forster was furious with Freddie; it would not be the last time this would happen.

Despite that first setback, Air Charter Group became by far the biggest operator in transporting British Army soldiers to their destinations worldwide. There were a few minor hold-ups, but there were no complaints. Freddie's staff had a good attitude towards their passengers, which was not something that could be said of the competition. The trooping business endured at profitable rates. George Forster also sought contracts with foreign armies and won most of them on the back of ACG's stellar reputation. Because of the company's reliability, high-quality service and impeccable safety record, in 1954 Air Charter was granted an unrestricted passenger licence, opening the door for it to grow and develop even further.

CHAPTER 7

# Cheating Death

## Quick thinking saves the day

11th March 1952

The aviation business in the early 1950s was an exciting place to be. It was the time of swashbucklers. Although every effort was given to making the planes safe, they were in reality creaking buckets held together by a few rivets, and a wing and a prayer were the most important ingredients in the success of any flight. Pilots thought nothing of taking off for long flights to Africa and beyond in these buckets.

Freddie Laker was at the centre of it and enjoying every moment. After all, he and his pilots had survived the Second World War, so what could happen to them now?

The mood was recreated many years later in the ITV drama series *Airline*, broadcast in 1982. The series starred Roy Marsden as Jack Ruskin, a pilot demobbed after the end of the war who starts his own air freight business called Ruskin Air, operating two DC-3 aircraft. *Airline*, created by Wilfred Greatorex, ran for one series of nine episodes and reflected the time.

Freddie was living his dream with his 400 employees. But one incident he may not have cared to remember came when he was aboard one of his four-engined York freighters in the second week of March 1952. They were returning the York to service in Germany after a routine overhaul. Captain Norman Jennings was the pilot and Captain Joe Viatkin was in the co-pilot's seat, with Freddie and Jack Wiseman on board. They were en route to Hamburg.

At 4.43 pm, on the final approach to Hamburg Airport, Wiseman, Jennings, Viatkin and Freddie were all in the cockpit for the landing. The numbers 4.43 became forever stamped on Joe Viatkin's brain. At 165mph and at 600 feet the landing gear had been routinely lowered and all four men were expecting nothing but a routine landing of the sort they had shared hundreds of times before. Jennings told Viatkin to take the plane down while he chatted to

Wiseman. But then suddenly both port-side engines cut out simultaneously. There was no precedent for this and no known emergency procedure – one engine maybe, but not two together. It caused a sudden unequal load on the plane, with the starboard engines still at full thrust. The complete lack of thrust from one side of the aircraft caused it to veer 70 degrees to the left. Viatkin tried frantically to correct with the remaining two starboard engines, but then they also cut out. Jennings as pilot in command shouted out, "I have control!" Losing all four engines is the one event that pilots hope will never happen to them. With plenty of height, a gentle glide-in landing may be possible, but a sudden total loss of power on the approach to land would typically not be survivable.

Added to that, the York was suddenly 90 degrees off course, losing height rapidly and, worst of all, headed straight for a cemetery and a brick-built crematorium building. Before 4.43pm there had been no sign of any problem with the engines, and the fuel gauges showed no indication of any shortfall. But the loss of all four strongly indicated a shortage of fuel. To Freddie Laker it was obvious that they had run out of fuel at a crucial moment. Freddie instantly assumed that the fuel must have leaked out unnoticed, near the end of the flight. He reached for the controls in the roof panel and retracted the undercarriage, which was standard procedure for the situation. Once the wheels were up, Freddie had a few seconds to think. Captain Jennings lifted the wing flaps, which raised the aircraft's stall speed. Then he kicked hard on the rudder. It was a desperate effort to flatten their angle of descent and get the plane over the crematorium. Freddie could see the irony of crashing into a crematorium and made a quip about saving funeral costs. Nobody laughed. At that moment everyone in the cockpit knew they were as good as gone and only a miracle could save their lives.

In those few seconds Freddie mentally checked through the fuel system of the Merlin engines fitted to the York. He suddenly remembered there was an accelerator pump between the throttles and the carburettors. He also reckoned that there would be a tiny amount of fuel left within the pump after the engines stopped. It was an engineer's reaction to a situation that was already hopeless from the pilot's point of view. Suddenly he grabbed the throttle levers and started to push them up and down rapidly. Jennings immediately knew what he was doing and focused on keeping the plane as level as he could. The accelerator pump responded by squirting fuel into the carburettors and the engines burst into life for a few seconds – enough to push the plane back up into the air. He kept pumping the throttles to squeeze the last bit of fuel available into the engines. It worked, and those ten seconds were just enough to lift the York over the crematorium. They had two feet to spare. Then the York hit some power cables, which slowed it down, but it cleared a school playground packed with children, gliding over the top of them with less than 3 feet to spare. The teachers, seeing something was amiss, screamed at the children, who ran for their lives. Then more luck as the plane's nose skimmed the roof of a small house, but the tail wheel took the roof off, exposing the bedrooms. Then Lady Luck really shone as the plane prepared to dive into a field of allotments, which were piled full of soft earth. It was extraordinary good luck and the soft ground absorbed the impact as the plane's nose buried itself in five feet of brown soil.

The impact was described later by Freddie Laker as being 'like in a car doing an emergency stop'. The four men in the cockpit ended in a heap on top of each other. Famously Freddie's first words to Jack Wiseman, when they realised they had survived, were: "Will you kindly take your bloody arm out of your Managing Director's face?" Wiseman was not amused as he got up with blood streaming from his face. It turned out to be the only injury – Wiseman had broken his nose. Meanwhile the mechanics travelling in the back were playing cards and completely unhurt – they barely knew what was going on as the cards and cash scattered around them. Joe Viatkin forced open a side window, pushed away the soil heaped against the side of the York, and pulled himself out into a pile of mud. He was immediately greeted by the owner of the house that had lost its roof and who seemed surprisingly cheerful considering what had just happened. He was a friendly man who seemed delighted that his otherwise mundane life had been brightened up that afternoon. He did not seem surprised to find someone crawling from a wrecked aircraft half buried in his allotment. He'd felt the building tremble, followed by a shaking of the ground outside. His delight at seeing the aircraft's crew and passengers survive was apparent. They were well aware they had only survived at all because Freddie's acute engineering mind had produced the two extra bursts of power that had avoided a head-on collision with the crematorium, which would have killed them all.

A few days after the crash, a German scrap dealer came along and made an offer for the wreck of the aircraft. Freddie sold it to him 'as is' in a hastily drawn-up agreement. The German was not at all pleased to discover later that his deal was only for the aircraft hull and not the four valuable Rolls-Royce Merlin engines, which had broken off in the crash-landing and landed a distance behind the fuselage and, conveniently, were nowhere to be seen.

# CHAPTER 8

# Creating an Empire
## Air Charter, Aviation Traders and beyond

1951-1958

Aviation Traders had grown into a huge organisation under Jack Wiseman's management. He had created a manufacturing division, and in 1951 had won a contract to make wing centre sections for Bristol Freighters. ATEL ended up building 50 wing sections for Bristol Siddeley, generating huge profits. However, much to the chagrin of Wiseman and his colleagues, Bob Batt and Norman Jennings, the profits were quickly reinvested.

With the facilities to fix anything, Freddie bought planes that others wouldn't touch. He bought nine damaged Yorks and Lancasters and cannibalised them to make three Yorks that were better than when they were new. He also rescued the ill-fated Tudor airliner. The Tudor was the first pressurised civilian airliner built by Avro and great things were expected of it, such as crossing the Atlantic. However, its early history was not a happy one and the aircraft had been rejected by BOAC. Two Tudors had mysteriously disappeared in the Bermuda Triangle, then another crashed in Wales killing 50 rugby supporters travelling from Dublin. Four of the aircraft had been destroyed since its certification in February 1945. After that, the Tudor was pretty much dead in the water and no one wanted it. Sensing an opportunity, Freddie studied the aircraft and learned all he could about the accidents. He talked to pilots who had flown Tudors, and learned that the aircraft weren't easy to get off the ground or to land. Though views were distinctly favourable once in the air, there were mixed feelings about the aircraft. He noted that there was no criticism of the Tudor from a technical or flying point of view in any of the accident reports; the type had successfully flown 9,500 hours during the Berlin Airlift. But there was a serious drawback in buying the aircraft. The Minister of Civil Aviation, Lord Pakenham, had issued an edict that no further passenger-carrying certificates would be issued for a Tudor.

Freddie was undaunted; he needed to replace Air Charter's Avro Yorks for his passenger and cargo charter work and began to investigate suitable alternatives. He needed an aircraft that could carry five-six tonnes of payload and fly stage lengths of 1,200 nautical miles. With the finances that he had available he had very few options; the Argonaut would have been the most suitable, but it would not be available to buy second-hand from BOAC for another five years. The DC-4, Freddie's preferred aircraft, cost £250,000 for a second-hand example – far too expensive even for Freddie's deep pockets.

In November 1952 he was left with a choice between two types of Tudor, the Mk1 and Mk4Bs looking like his best bet. Through Surrey Flying Services he already owned a Mk2 (G-AGRY), which was already certified to carry passengers, but it looked as though it would be uneconomic to operate in the way that he had intended, so he'd put it to good use on trooping contracts to Nairobi and RAF Fayid in Egypt. Freddie came to own three other Tudors, one out on lease to a Canadian carrier and two that were uncertified to carry passengers.

In addition to the Tudors, by the beginning of 1953 Air Charter's fleet had grown to seven Yorks, a Dakota, and a Mk31E Bristol Freighter. 1953 would prove to be the real breakthrough year, and ACG carried nearly 28 million pounds of cargo and 30,000 passengers.

Freddie's investigations led him to a fleet of ten nearly new Tudors, a mixture of Mk1s, 3s and 4Bs belonging to the Ministry of Civil Aviation. Without a passenger-carrying certificate, they were unsalable and each needed an extensive overhaul. Undaunted, Freddie began to negotiate for the aircraft. He examined them from end to end and flew as an observer on a series of test flights. After he had finished his evaluations he began negotiations for them, together with their spares and 88 Rolls-Royce Merlin engines. In September 1953 he got them for just 10 per cent of the £1 million they would have cost new. Freddie's confidence in the Tudor arose partly because he believed he had found the answer to the unexplained crashes.

In March 1953 there had been a very close call in one of the Air Charter Mk1 Tudors on a flight to Malta, when the aircraft had mysteriously gone out of control. It entered a spiral dive, from which thankfully the pilot managed to recover. Freddie's engineers found that there was nothing structurally or aerodynamically wrong, and there was nothing amiss with the engines. The cause turned out to be partial power failure. Freddie had Aviation Traders conduct a series of tests with the approval of Avro, the Air Registration Board and Rolls-Royce. The dive was recreated in the Tudor, then in a Dakota, a Bristol and a York. Freddie was confident enough to demonstrate the results to a number of observers, including a couple of brave journalists. They were shown the effect of using the carburettor heating system and cutting the power to the outer port engine. As the airspeed dropped the autopilot disengaged and the plane entered into a nose-down dive. The pilot showed how the ailerons and rudders were completely ineffective. Standard recovery action was taken and the aircraft returned to base and turned around for a trooping flight to Saigon. The conclusion was that the problem, once known and understood, was not dangerous or difficult to remedy.

In the hands of Aviation Traders, the aircraft underwent extensive modifications with an eye to improving safety. They removed the pressurisation system and replaced the light alloy hydraulic system with steel piping, carefully repositioning the pipes to avoid electrical cables. The electric cabling was rerouted clear of the floor of the aircraft together with all the electrical and radio components to reduce fire risk. The engines were modified to give increased take-off power and the main landing wheels were replaced with the latest available. There was a new ventilation system, a cabin heating system, and a fixed oxygen system for the crew.

ATEL added an emergency exit on the starboard side, together with numerous passenger amenities such as reclinable seats, extra windows, toilets, galleys and baggage compartments. Some aircraft remained as freighters exclusively to carry cargo, including G-AGRI, the first Tudor that had been delivered. A cargo door was cut into the side of the fuselage. Then, in a masterstroke, Freddie gave the aircraft a new name, the Avro Super Trader.

The modified Tudor easily passed its new airworthiness tests and went on its first proving flight between Stansted and Hamburg on 14th February 1954 in the hands of Jennings. Pakenham's successor reversed the stance on the Tudor and allowed it to certified for passengers, largely because of Freddie's efforts. The Tudors were soon in action carrying cargo and passengers at highly lucrative rates, which were high enough to pay for the whole project in six months. Air Charter would eventually own 17 Tudors between 1953 and 1959, six of which would be used for spare parts for the other 11.

However, one of the aircraft experienced a serious mishap, crashing on take-off in Egypt. The Egyptians phoned Freddie, who told them to leave the plane exactly as it was and to put a guard on it, and he would be down immediately. On arriving, he went straight to the plane and opened the access door at the rear of the fuselage. Inside were masses of carpets, which had caused the plane to be significantly overweight for take-off, but they had also shifted the aircraft's centre of gravity. There was simply no way it could have taken off. The aircraft had been due to be shown at the Paris Air Show, so the enterprising aircrew had intended to sell the carpets in France and make a profit on the side.

By the end of 1954 all of Freddie Laker's various enterprises were flourishing. Air Charter transported livestock to the continent and ATEL installed horseboxes and cattle stalls. They carried anything and everything including show jumping teams to Copenhagen and Hamburg and racehorses to Paris and Curragh.

Using his own cash, Freddie started up in the import/export business in Lagos, Nigeria. On a stopover in Lagos, he found that he could not buy ice cream or fresh meat in the capital. Sensing an opportunity, he purchased a cold store for a knock-down price and flew in vast supplies of both ice cream and fresh meat to satisfy the obvious demand. For a brief time he saw a new future for himself in West Africa, but found the business not really suited to his skills and quickly sold it for a profit.

Jack Wiseman remembered that Freddie had a mind like "a cash register".

He said: "He would do sums on the backs of envelopes, but he got the answers right. He saw planes in money terms. Pounds of pressure, revolutions per minute, all the details that other engineers saw as technicalities, Freddie appreciated, but he also looked at it as 'pounds, shillings and pence'."

In those days Freddie would have only one real rival, Harold Bamberg. Bamberg had the grandest vision of any of the independent operators in the early 1950s. Freddie was always very conscious of Bamberg and just a little jealous of his success. When Bamberg appeared at Freddie's Southend office to conclude a deal, he drove up in his new Bentley with stainless-steel bodywork. Freddie looked at it thoughtfully, then gazed over at his own Bentley and realised that it did not match up. There followed a visit to a Rolls-Royce showroom and an order for a new Silver Cloud.

Freddie was finally able to afford his first brand-new plane, a Bristol 170 Mk31F Freighter, which had arrived in February of that year. It was immediately nicknamed the 'Gold Brick', mainly because operating it was so profitable. Freddie then ordered another Bristol, which went straight onto the Berlin freight run. The Bristol Freighters were so profitable to operate because they had a large carrying capacity and shipped items that others couldn't manage. They were extraordinary aircraft and very versatile and led Freddie straight into competition with Silver City Airways, a company that had invented the cross-Channel air ferry service in 1948, and flew passengers and their cars directly into Europe from Lympne and Southend.

In 1952 Silver City terminated its Southend to Ostend operation as being uneconomical, and failed to take up another route from Southend to Calais. Freddie promptly applied for both in the face of protests from Silver City, which said that there was no room for another operator. But Freddie had strong support from Southend's airport commandant, who was keen to develop the airport, and he was granted the routes.

He entered the business in September 1954 with a new sub-division of Air Charter; he called it 'The Air Bridge', but later changed it to Channel Air Bridge because Silver City had used the term 'Air Bridge' in some of its marketing. He launched the new venture by flying his own Rolls-Royce and the Mayor of Southend to Calais and back.

Silver City operated mainly from Lydd and its catchment area was really South London. Before the motorway system in England was developed, if you lived in the Midlands or the North Lydd was hard to get to and Southend was a much better option.

Freddie hired another Mk31 from the Bristol Aircraft Company and placed an order with two more Mk32s for 1955. Silver City had bought up the rights to the whole production of the Mk32, but were unable to take up the option. Initially Freddie's Bristols shuttled several times a day between Southend and Calais until the grass runway at Calais became too badly churned up and flights had to stop for the winter. The flight cost £27 each way for a medium-sized car and four passengers. The Mk31 Bristol Freighter could carry three cars and 12 passengers.

The fare that Channel Air Bridge charged was actually a bargain for the convenience it offered. It was considered a better option than a long journey on an unreliable and uncomfortable Channel ferry, then hiring an unfamiliar rental car, even if it was slightly more expensive overall. About the only downside was having your right-hand-drive English car in Europe, where all the vehicles were left-hand drive.

The service earned Freddie plenty of kudos, but he felt that he had been spending far too much time on it himself. He seemed to be always on the scene greeting passengers and asking them what they thought and giving them that extra little bit of service. When one incoming flight was delayed, a disembarking passenger found the petrol pump at the airport shut. Freddie called for the keys and refuelled the car himself, returning with what was described as 'the cockiest grin, petrol cash in one hand, spinning a florin tip in the other'. After another flight that had landed in a storm, Freddie rushed up to a passenger carrying a sick bag. "You don't have to deal with that, give it to me," he offered. The man fixed Freddie with a jaundiced glare and in a booming voice with a northern accent said, "Nay, tha don't lad – ma teeth's in theer!"

Freddie wanted someone to run Channel Air Bridge for him, and he had just the person in mind, Douglas Whybrow. Whybrow had been posted to Hamburg, and Freddie called on him in February 1955 while visiting his base in that city from which he was operating on the second 'Little Berlin Airlift'. Freddie asked him to leave the Army and come and work for him as manager of Channel Air Bridge. He'd just announced that he would develop other routes and invest in a larger fleet of aircraft. Whybrow wasn't sure it was what he wanted, especially as the business was just a few months old. Freddie offered to keep the job open for as long as it took, and cajoled him, telling him about the 'marvellous results' – Channel Air Bridge had taken 10 per cent of the overall cross-Channel traffic in its first year. He had a new operation to Ostend and a licence for Rotterdam – it was going to be hugely successful, he eulogised. He had just taken delivery of a Mk32 Bristol Freighter – the 200th to be built – on 25th March and he was already operating three of the short-nosed Mk31s. He called the Mk32 'Valiant', and it was equipped with a movable bulkhead and a 23-seat rear passenger cabin. The plane joined the others on the Air Ferry routes, making it now 32 trips a day. The sister ship when it arrived was to be used on freight services in Germany.

After a visit to the Laker family home in Carshalton to discuss terms, Whybrow finally agreed. On the appointed day, Whybrow drove his family from Hamburg to Calais to meet the plane taking them back to Britain. He was a little underwhelmed when there was no one at the reception offices, just four uniformed men playing cards and smoking. It turned out that Freddie had sent the plane to Ostend by mistake.

On 24th January 1955, Air Charter bought its first American-built plane, the Douglas DC-4. G-ANYB was a C54 Skymaster, and Air Charter became the first British independent airline to buy an aircraft manufactured in the USA. It had originally belonged to a man even more colourful than Freddie Laker. Edward Daly owned an organisation called World Airways, and the DC-4 had been used as a troop carrier in the USA. Daly sold on the aircraft within a year to Air Carrier Service Corporation, part of California Eastern, which then sold it to Freddie. There was a prolonged negotiation before an import licence was granted; the DC-4 was an expensive plane and the Government of the time had problems with currency reserves. Freddie went to America to collect it in person, and flew back with his new prize to Air Charter's base at Stansted, where it was promptly put to work on trooping flights to Cyprus. Two more DC-4s were then purchased, the first delivered that same year.

By April 1956 Freddie's enterprises owned and operated 15 aircraft: two Yorks, six Tudors, three Bristol 170 Mk31s, two Mk32s and two DC-4s. He had another four Mk32s and a DC-4 on order. In the 12 months ending in September that year, Air Charter had carried 163,988 passengers and 29,808 tons of freight.

In 1956 Channel Air Bridge started services to Zeistenhoven in Rotterdam as soon as the new airport there had opened. The 75-minute flight was the longest air ferry route so far and enabled the aircraft to fly at a higher cruising altitude of 5,000 feet, with a resultant fuel saving. The high demand on the route made it an instant success. It had been the first British airline to advertise on Britain's first commercial television channel, ITV. By 1957 there were six daily services in the summer and four in the winter, often carrying freight as well. They transported a mixture of items including cheese, flowers, Dutch lettuce and ships' spares. On the Ostend route they moved large amounts of furnishing fabrics, chicory and exported British-made furniture. An early customer was John Bloom, the washing machine entrepreneur, who transported three planeloads of parts a week, but the contract ran into trouble when Channel Air Bridge made a mistake by not billing Bloom for the customs charges, which left a great deal of money owing. The Chief Accountant, Alan Nicholls, visited Bloom to collect the debt, but was physically threatened by Bloom's henchmen. Whybrow, who was less easily frightened, stepped in and did a deal for the debt, at the same time increasing the flights to four a week.

Air Charter was prevented from carrying some commodities by the terms of their licence, where the International Air Transport Association (IATA) set the rates. This business had to be left to the national carriers. However, after two years Channel Air Bridge had carried three times more freight than KLM and BEA. This in itself was a problem, and at the end of 1957 the company was forced into collaboration with Sabena. The Belgians had become increasingly concerned about the size of the Channel Air Bridge operation at Ostend and were considering withdrawing route authority. Freddie offered to operate in Sabena's livery by way of advertising to calm them down, and he and Whybrow went to Brussels to finalise the deal.

An old friend of Freddie's from the ATA days owned a nightclub in the city, and the three spent the night drinking and reminiscing about the war years until 5.00am. When they returned to the hotel there were urgent messages to call the company. Figuring that it was far too early and no one would be there, they left it and went to bed, but when they woke up to their horror in the morning papers was a photograph of one of their planes halfway across a railway track at the edge of Southend Airport. As they'd been drinking heavily all night, a driver had to be found to take them, together with Freddie's Rolls-Royce, to the airport. The hotel found someone while they both showered. Unfortunately the man was completely overawed by the Rolls-Royce and his driving was dreadful, even worse than Freddie's, which was notoriously bad.

Back at Southend Freddie conducted the investigation. There had been no injuries and the plane turned out to be undamaged. It had aquaplaned at the end of the runway in heavy rain. Somehow the adverse publicity did not affect bookings, and from 1st April 1958 two aircraft operated 24 flights a day to Ostend, one in each livery; Freddie liked the blue Sabena livery so much that he copied it in red for Channel Air Bridge.

Towards the end of the year he received a contract for transporting baggage for British troops and their families stationed in Germany – it was a useful fill-up. Profits had always been elusive, but by 1958 Channel Air Bridge had turned the corner and finally broken even. Operationally at Air Charter things could not have looked better. In the summer of 1958 Freddie bought two new Britannia 300s from Bristol Aircraft to replace the now aging Tudors on the long-haul charter work to Australia; the Government had already specified the Britannia to be used exclusively on trooping flights to the Far East. The first ten flights ran between Stansted and Christmas Island. Freddie knew that the Britannias would keep him ahead of the game and they were kept very busy from the moment he took delivery.

By December 1958 Freddie's fertile mind had thought up another brilliant idea. In conjunction with Horizon Holidays, Air Charter was to make Freddie's first attempt to fly a commercial service on the North Atlantic using his Britannias, which would be configured to carry 110 passengers. The plan was an all-inclusive two-week package holiday to New York for £165 (£3,750 at 2018 values). Freddie applied to the Air Transport Advisory Council to fly a once-weekly service from either London Airport or Gatwick from 1st March 1959, when the second Britannia was delivered, and this would rise to five a week if the packages were a success. The price of the whole two-week holiday was just £3 more than the IATA fare for the transatlantic flight alone. He would have to face down the state-owned airline BOAC and the IATA to do it.

Then Freddie won a Ministry of Defence contract to carry rockets and secret equipment to the Woomera rocket range in South Australia. This contract hastened the end of the Tudor; it was also the only time in Freddie's career in aviation that he was touched by a serious accident – one that involved multiple casualties. Freddie's safety record in every era of operating aircraft was exemplary. However, in April 1959 one of his three remaining Tudors, G-AGRH, crashed at 13,000 feet into the side of Mount Süphan near the North Turkish border. It took a special RAF mountain rescue team six days to locate the crash site, which was 50 miles from the Russian border. It was at the height of the Cold War and the heavily armed recovery party was sent with instructions to collect the paperwork and destroy the rockets that the plane had been carrying. Plastic explosives were dropped from an aircraft on the site, destroying all the evidence, which apparently included nuclear warheads. The location and the weather conditions, the most likely cause of the accident, had made it impossible to recover the dead crew members. Prayers were said for the 12 men who were buried at the site in a crevasse beneath rocks and ice. The nature of the cargo required the accident to be kept secret. Freddie was distraught – Air Charter and Aviation Traders were small enough for all the aircrew to be close personal friends of Freddie, some going way back to the Berlin Airlift days. The Tudors were retired but not before they had reputedly earned ACG £1 million of profit in just five years.

The Tudor operation had been created from absolutely nothing by the sheer ingenuity and inventiveness of Freddie and his men. Around that time Freddie had begun to believe his own publicity and believed he could walk on water. The signs of megalomania his managers had spotted a few years before, now manifested fully and Freddie's hubris was off the charts. It all spelled trouble. There was also no doubt that he was a radical thinker when it came to aircraft and their possible uses. No one doubted that Freddie had a brilliant mind as an engineer, but he lacked any formal academic training, which left him with a huge blind spot. One rival described his approach to aircraft design and performance as that of an 'inspired handyman'. And so it was ultimately to prove. Two concurrent projects were to cost Aviation Traders dear and ultimately lead to Freddie losing his independence.

The first was back in 1956 when the Royal Air Force decided to retire its fleet of Hunting Percival Prentice training aircraft. The Prentices were big, slow, safe single-engined trainers, with large glass canopies, fixed undercarriages and very large wings. They took off and climbed at a rate of 70 miles per hour with a top speed of only 150mph. The plane was big at more than 31 feet long, 10 feet high and a wing span of 46 feet. One of its disadvantages was high fuel consumption. Between 1945 and 1956 the RAF had bought more than 350 Prentices, and ten years later there were still 250 flying. They were excellent training aircraft and gave the trainee pilots a real sense of security, but were declared obsolete by the RAF in 1956. Freddie, sensing an opportunity that no one else saw, swooped in and bought them all.

On the face of it this was a good deal and Freddie paid scrap value for 252 aircraft in excellent condition fitted with very sophisticated radio equipment. He quickly stripped out the radios and made a killing selling them on. He had decided that the Prentices would make excellent private planes for wealthy businessmen, and there was no doubt that the market for private aircraft was growing fast. He thought the roomy and safe Prentice was perfect for the emerging market and he expected a queue for them at £1,500 each, 25 times what he had paid for them. He began to convert them all into civil light aircraft at a cost of around £500 each.

With so many aircraft, it took 18 months to gather them all up in one place, then another 18 months to complete the refurbishment. Bob Batt took charge and hired pilots who worked full time flying them into Southend, but he quickly ran out of space at Southend and was forced to use Stansted as well. There were just too many aircraft, and Batt and his small team were soon overwhelmed. But Freddie was undaunted and two years later the aircraft were repainted silver and upholstered in grey and red leather.

The converted Prentices could carry five people including two pilots, and at £1,500 each were a bargain for the time and an affordable private plane. But there were few buyers, and less than 20 were sold. The reason was simple. American manufacturers Cessna and Piper came in with a better aircraft aided by a very favourable dollar-to-pound exchange rate. Anyone who wanted a five-seater private plane bought a Cessna or a Piper. Freddie was left with more than 200 unsellable aircraft. Ever the pragmatist, he ordered them to be scrapped and took his losses. But it was not a total disaster, and the overall losses from the Prentice project were quite modest after having sold the radios.

But Freddie was not to be so lucky with his next project. At the beginning of the 1950s there were some, including Freddie Laker, who thought that a replacement for the venerable Douglas Dakota DC-3 was required. It was the most successful and numerically popular aircraft that small fleet operators ever had. For others, there was a strongly held belief that the only true replacement for a DC-3 was another DC-3. It was an outstanding aeroplane, versatile, with a low purchase price and efficient running costs. It was of a rugged construction and able to carry more that 2,300 cubic feet of cargo, loaded through its rear door. The DC-3 was also able to operate from short, poorly surfaced runways.

Freddie believed that the DC-3 was on borrowed time and not able to fulfil the needs of British civil aviation, and that something much better was needed – something that he could come up with. Freddie was about to go into the business of aircraft design and manufacturing. He anticipated the orders would come in thick and fast, as BEA had 40 DC-3s doing the jobs that the big jets and the Viscounts could not do.

The British Government looked it over and didn't argue that a British replacement should be manufactured; beyond that, it offered little by way of direct support. At the Ministry of Supply, one minister had suggested that Freddie's enterprises should receive Government help and cooperation. Aviation Traders had production and overhaul experience ranging from the Bristol Freighter to the North American Sabre, and as operators through Air Charter they had first-hand experience of the ruthless proving ground of day-to-day service. But as far as design and construction were concerned, there was an old engineer's saying: "I have a great advantage over everyone else, for I know nothing about the subject." As Freddie later himself admitted, it would prove to be the biggest mistake of his life.

Freddie had the misfortune to meet a man called Toby Heal, the assistant chief designer at Hunting Percival. Heal had become enamoured of a manufacturing process called tension-skin construction and had taken out a patent on it. It meant that thinner metal could be used to build aircraft fuselages, making them lighter and stronger. It was not a new idea, as Short's had used it on flying boats. Heal designed an aircraft in his head and pitched his idea to Freddie as a replacement for the Dakota. The lighter, stronger design meant that a larger payload could be carried with resultant increased profits. Because of this, the ATL.90 was nicknamed the 'Accountant'. The name stuck and was painted on the side, and the aircraft was advertised as the 'Accountant' from then on. Relatively quickly the name took on the opposite meaning, because of how much money the project had absorbed. As it swallowed more and more, Freddie ominously joked that the Mk2 would be 'The Auditor', and there would only ever be one more, the Mk3 version, which would be 'The Receiver'.

In the beginning Freddie was blown away by Heal and his ideas. Heal joined Aviation Traders at its second base at Stansted and formed a small design team to develop a plan for the aircraft before Freddie gave the official go-ahead. Freddie knew that if the project failed it could potentially break the company, and he naturally wanted to proceed cautiously. He initially put Heal to work on upgrading his Tudors, and the two of them thrashed out the ground rules for the ATL.90 Accountant project over a weekend. They would reproduce all the great features of the DC-3 with some advantages in performance and operating economics.

The brief called for a 28-seater (reduced to 25), twin-engined passenger/freighter capable of flying 1,500 miles, cruising at 275mph at a height of 25,000 feet. A higher cruising altitude would allow it to climb over bad weather, reducing noise and vibration and adding to passenger comfort. At this altitude the aircraft would need to be pressurised. The cost of fuelling the ATL.90 would be the same as a DC-3, but it would fly 50 per cent further.

The ATL.90 would have a higher rate of climb and cruising speed, while retaining the low landing speeds of a DC-3. It would have a level horizontal floor supported by a sturdy twin-wheeled steerable tricycle undercarriage. It would be designed for operation from short grass airstrips and airfields with indifferent surfaces. The twin undercarriage would give improved braking, and there would be additional braking effort from automatic pitch-controlled propellers. An innovative wing design using double slotted flaps would improve performance.

A MkII version would have a longer fuselage and carry 40 passengers. A third executive version for 12 passengers was mooted specifically for the US and Canadian market. Larger fuel reserves would give the MkIII an even longer range. Freddie even did a drawing for a nose-loading car-carrying air ferry version, which he designated the ATL.96. Heal decided it would be powered by a twin turbo-prop with the fuel tanks as an integral part of the wing, giving it a larger fuel capacity for long-range operation. The manufacture would be deliberately designed to be as simple as possible, with an estimated price tag of less than £150,000. It was undoubtedly a great concept. But it was an ambitious idea and far too big for what was still a relatively small private company. In fact, it was financial madness.

In 1953, the project got the green light from Freddie, and Heal and his team moved to Southend. When he announced the project publicly, most people in the airline industry shook their heads and thought that the project would only end in financial disaster. Many proclaimed that the aircraft would never appear, and even fewer thought that it would ever fly.

The first big decision was which engine to use. Freddie had built up a very good relationship with Rolls-Royce and became one of its biggest customers for spare parts. Aviation Traders still owned hundreds of Merlin engines, and Freddie had also been useful to Rolls as a supplier of spare parts. None of this was known to Lord Hives, the chairman of Rolls, who sternly rebuffed Freddie's request for an indefinite loan of its new state-of-the-art Dart engines. Roger Elgin and Berry Ritchie, Freddie's first biographers, best describe the haggling over the engines: "Hives let Freddie know that 'it would be easier to get the shirt off his back.'" Freddie owed him thousands of pounds going back years, and Hives was going to recover the debt. So Hives invited Laker, Wiseman and Batt to dinner to do just that. When the matter of the debt came up, Freddie nonchalantly told Hives that if he'd bothered to check he would know that Rolls-Royce owed him considerably more than he owed them.

Hives had the engines dispatched to Southend the next day, and they were perfect. Each engine had more power per pound of its weight than a piston engine. It was smaller and easier to clean and service, but the decision to use the Dart at the time that it was made was actually very brave, as little worldwide operating experience of the engine had been accumulated and its acceptance was not yet guaranteed. However, Rolls-Royce had high hopes for the Accountant project.

With such a crucial decision out of the way, Freddie realised that he could not contemplate manufacturing the plane himself; he simply did not have the resources to get an airworthiness certificate for the plane and set up a factory. Once the prototype was flying successfully, he hoped to sell the design to one of the major manufacturers and collect a royalty on sales.

Three years after the start of the project, and now dissatisfied with the slow progress of the ATL.90, in December 1956 Freddie appointed 'Johnny' Johnson as Manager, Aircraft Division. Ironically it was Johnson – another ex-Hunting Percival employee – who had turned down Heal's ideas. Johnson's brief was to coordinate the project, bring about the prototype in the shortest possible time, then plan for series production. During the development period Johnson recruited a workforce, which increased the number of men working at Southend to close to a thousand.

The prototype was finally completed early in 1957, but only after suffering an enormous setback. On 25th March three senior members of the design team, including Heal, apparently in collusion, resigned. Freddie lost his Chief Designer, Chief Aerodynamicist and Assistant Designer all on the same day. It left him with a difficult problem – obtaining approval to fly for the ATL.90 from the Air Registration Board, whose confidence was vested in the design team. Freddie immediately promoted the excellent assistant chief designer Arthur Leftley to head up the team, and hoped that this would satisfy the ARB.

By July the prototype was ready to fly. The plane had been built in a large old shed, which had to be knocked down to get it out when it was finished. The first test flight scheduled for the first week of July ended in calamity and public humiliation for Freddie. In front of the photographers and press that he had arranged, the mechanics accidentally set off the foam fire extinguishers in the engine while testing the aircraft's circuits. Freddie had a fit and immediately fired everyone. The following morning he rang Southend to check that they'd all come back to work. Fortunately they had.

The first flight finally got under way on the afternoon of 9th July 1957 with test pilot L. P. Stuart Smith at the controls. Freddie was watching from the airport control tower. It seemed like the whole of Southend Airport had come out to watch. His engineers had all left the hangar, many of them sitting on top of the Prentices for a better view. When the plane landed, Freddie ran across the airfield to greet his crew, who emerged from the now surrounded aeroplane to a round of applause. It had been a great day for Freddie Laker and Aviation Traders Engineering. His supporters called it 'one of the bravest and greatest achievements in the post-war era'.

However, during the test flight the aircraft experienced a major problem involving juddering from the elevator – not that anyone on the aircraft let on that there had been any difficulties, as it was huge moment for the small firm. After the flight the aircraft was grounded for five weeks while they identified the problem. They suspected it was either 'buffet' or 'flutter', two causes of potentially dangerous instability in an aircraft. It was decided to eliminate the possibility of flutter first, while the source of the buffet was finally traced to the extreme rear of the engine nacelles and the jet pipe fairings. After modifications were made, considerable improvements in performance were found, and the Accountant was back in the air, gaining 18 hours of flying time and exceeding its estimated cruising speed at 10,000 feet. Everyone was extremely pleased with the behaviour of the airframe, and it was in the nick of time as Freddie was desperate that the ATL.90 prototype should fly at the Farnborough Air Show between 2nd and 9th September. He badly needed orders and, more importantly, deposits to keep the project viable.

The plane was widely praised when it made its Farnborough debut. By then the controversial tension-skin concept had long been dropped, but it still performed well in the air. However, many individuals were highly critical of the engine installation mounted on top of the wing, and its cigar-shaped looks. By modern standards the Accountant was visually quite unappealing. Freddie didn't think this would ultimately be off-putting, citing the Bristol Freighter's inelegance as an example, and Bristol had built 210 of those.

There were a few tentative enquiries from the likes of Aden Airways, East African Airways and British West Indian Airways, but there were no firm offers and not a single order was taken. The prototype not being representative of the aircraft that would be available to buy didn't help. It was still missing some key features such as cabin air conditioning and pressurisation, de-icing, radio, and a full seating configuration. Freddie began a huge effort to persuade a major aircraft manufacturer to put the plane into production, telling them all that the Accountant "had the greatest potential of any aircraft in the world today." However, there were no takers.

A mini recession had begun and everyone was scaling back investment. Freddie was in touch with the big names of the day such as Gloster Aircraft, Saunders Roe and the Fairey Aviation Co, but despite his huge efforts he could not persuade a manufacturer to build the Accountant. The best offer he received was from Fairey for flight development and production capacity. The frankest and harshest assessment of the Accountant came from Hunting Percival, which had taken a very early look before the modifications to counter the buffeting.

The company's test pilot found that the control surfaces were too heavy and would require drastic changes, and that the thick wing sections created high drag. While it was thought that the design was sound, if conservative, there were areas where remedial work had been done but were still unsatisfactory. The oxygen, electrical and radio systems all needed to be redesigned.

It was felt that the amount of work done on the first prototype had been wasted in the special construction used on the fuselage. Even with all the resources of Aviation Traders poured into it, it was doubted that a second prototype with a new fuselage construction and a revised cockpit and windscreen would fly before the end of 1958, and not receive an airworthiness certificate before late 1959. It was also doubtful whether the Accountant would roll off the production line before 1960.

The slated MkII version with its 40 seats would have put it in direct competition with two other aircraft of that size, the Fokker Friendship and the Handley Page Dart Herald. Three to four hundred of these aircraft would be in existence before the Accountant made an appearance. The cost of completing the second prototype and preparing for its production was estimated to be another £1.9 million. Contrary to Freddie's expectation that the aircraft would sell for between £120,000 and £150,000, a more realistic price was put at £170,000, a long way off the expected low initial cost and therefore completely unmarketable.

In December 1957, Freddie called in a team of external accountants after it became clear that ACG was running out of money. The authorities at Southend Airport had granted him landing fees at 25 per cent of normal rates until the Accountant had flown commercially. The firm's accountants calculated that the plane had absorbed more than £750,000 of the company's cash, a colossal figure that Freddie had already guessed at. He realised that he had let the emotion of building his own aeroplane run away with him. It was not only his money that had been lost as he struggled to settle his accounts; the debts also included large amounts to companies like the Dunlop Rubber Company, to whom he owed £6,712. Freddie wrote to them all to ask that the debts be written off.

It was all Freddie needed to hear, and after reading the 100-page report by his accountants over Christmas he knew what he had to do. It was a miserable Christmas. Freddie went for long walks in the snow wondering whether he would still be in business by next Christmas. He tried one last time with the Under Secretary of State for Air, urging him to order 20 or 25 aircraft, or maybe just 10 to get things going.

On 10th January 1958, his first day back at work, Freddie watched the ATL.90 Accountant fly one last time, then he closed the project down. The aircraft had completed 50 hours of successful test flying. Without the backing of a larger manufacturer with the facilities to lay down a production line, it was pointless to continue. But Freddie still could not quite let go; he intended to initially mothball the Accountant and wait for a more favourable opportunity to proceed.

Many of the workforce were laid off and the project died instantly. Freddie hoped that there would be sufficient other work to build a new future for them.

He touted for any work he could, for his small design organisation, the several thousand square feet of workshop space and the several hundred men who were 'available for almost any kind of work'.

He was rightly proud of the effort put into what he knew was an impossible task for such a small company. He had already achieved more than any other British aircraft company had done or was prepared to do without the security of Government backing. He felt that he had been robbed of financial success. Freddie apportioned blame to the 1957 Government White Paper on Defence, authored by the new Minister of Defence Duncan Sandys, the son-in-law of Winston Churchill. The British aircraft industry was encouraged to consolidate into larger companies, and lucrative Government contracts would be selectively placed with those firms. By 1960 Hunting Aircraft, the Bristol Aeroplane Company, English Electric Aviation and Vickers Armstrong would be merged to create the British Aircraft Corporation (BAC). Hawker Siddeley swallowed up a number of others. All aircraft in development bar one during this period were cancelled.

It was the end of the Accountant. Freddie was so upset that he neglected to protect the intellectual property on which he had spent so much money. Soon aircraft were announced that strongly resembled the Accountant, while others used many of its design features. Freddie thought of taking legal action but was so worn down that he decided not to, even though many of the new planes were blatant copies. The final cost to Freddie's company of more than £750,000 had all come out of the cash flow of Air Charter and Aviation Traders. It had put a heavy strain on resources. Luckily he had been able to afford it, as the other side of the business was making substantial amounts of money. The Accountant had destroyed the group's overall profitability, and much of his own personal fortune in the process.

But it did have one positive outcome. Freddie realised that he was not quite the genius he thought he was and, as Jack Wiseman later told friends, "He was saved from himself." Something had to give. But the first humbling of Freddie Laker would prove to be short-lived.

At the unhappy moment when he returned the certificate of registration confirming that the Accountant had been completely destroyed, Freddie made a request that the rules be stretched allowing him to keep the registration number the Accountant had carried, G-ATEL. He wanted it for his planned DC-4 conversion, an aircraft that would become legendary in its own right, but at the time was still only known as the ATL.98.

Freddie was still waiting two years later for someone to rescue the Accountant, but help never came. So in February 1960 he ordered Jack Wiseman to scrap the prototype that was by now, like a rotting corpse, lingering on the fringe of Southend Airport, a sight that tormented Freddie every time he saw it. The break-up was brutal to watch for the 1,000 men who had worked on it, and not least for Freddie Laker, who realised almost too late that his dream of being an aircraft manufacturer was now over.

CHAPTER 9

# Selling Up

## If you can't beat 'em, join 'em

1958-1959

The failure of Freddie Laker's attempt to enter the market of aircraft design and manufacturing had been catastrophic for his two companies, Aviation Traders Engineering (ATEL) and Air Charter Ltd (ACG). The project had cost a total of £750,000, an amount equivalent to more than £20 million today. The money had seeped out of his companies' bank accounts gradually over a three-year period. The project had never been formally costed or budgeted, or had any cash allocated for it. It had just happened – almost by osmosis – and by the end the companies had no spare cash left. Luckily both firms had been exceedingly profitable throughout the period and generated enough on a monthly basis to cover the ever-increasing bills. In the previous two years, Freddie had taken no money out of his companies and he knew that the project had cost him personally in lost dividends. The economy was also slowing down and as he sat in his office once again contemplating signing redundancy cheques for the hundreds of engineers laid off from the project, he knew he had to sell his companies to survive.

ATEL and ACG had been fundamentally weakened. But at that moment it was known only to Freddie himself. Once competitors realised what had happened they could move in for the kill and there was a real danger the two companies would go bust. But he couldn't just go out and announce that his company was for sale so soon after the Accountant fiasco – it would have been commercial suicide. The balance sheets needed rebuilding, and to get the best price he knew he needed a good solid year of trading. So he embarked on a campaign of reverse psychology, telling the world how well he was doing and, if anyone asked, the companies were definitely not for sale.

As it turned out, 1958 was a very good year for both businesses. Freed from the Accountant losses, Freddie returned his focus to his core businesses, and by July it was clear that they were heading for a record year in revenues and profits. There was also an upside from the Accountant fiasco in that it had created a huge tax loss, and it was clear that the businesses would pay no tax for the next few years. That was soon reflected in cash flow and ACG received a large cheque from the Inland Revenue in the shape of a corporation tax refund, which helped to rebuild the cash reserves.

Freddie also got lucky when a gentleman named Gerald Freeman, a Director of Airwork Services, came calling at his office. Freeman, in his early 50s, was the founder of a very successful aircraft operator called Transair, a company that he had sold to Airwork in 1957 for a sum approaching £1 million. Freeman had begun as an air-taxi operator at Croydon Airport in 1947 and created a very profitable airline. The main business was transporting daily newspapers, running more than 3,000 newspaper flights a year for extremely time-sensitive products. Freeman expanded Transair into the air charter business and was hugely successful, earning a reputation for immaculately turned-out aircraft.

Transair's owner, Airwork, run by its Chairman Myles Wyatt, was a stock exchange-quoted company, majority-owned by some of Britain's richest men. It had been founded in 1928 by Sir Nigel Norman, who owned the original Heston aerodrome just north of Heathrow. The family also founded Britten-Norman, which built the Islander light aircraft. The shareholders of Airwork were substantial: Lord Cowdray was the richest man in Britain, while Lord Vestey and Lord Guinness were also substantial shareholders.

It was the second time that Freddie had been approached by Airwork Services with an offer to buy his companies. The first approach had happened during the summer of 1957 and had not been taken entirely seriously; talks had been protracted and were ongoing. But after the Accountant debacle, Freddie felt differently and was only too happy to accelerate the process. He had a desire to expand his increasingly successful air ferry operation, which had been engaged in a fare war with Silver City. To grow, he recognised that he needed to raise cash from outside sources.

Under Myles Wyatt, Airwork had been given the unofficial nod by the British Conservative Government that it could become the largest private airline and the third biggest behind BOAC and BEA. In those days the airline industry was highly regulated and everything of significance needed Government approval. Airwork expanded throughout the Second World War and beyond, using Douglas Dakotas and Vickers Viking aircraft. It operated worldwide and won many government contracts. In 1952 Airwork established a weekly scheduled service between London and Nairobi using 27-seat Viking aircraft, a journey that took three days to complete. The attraction was the £50 fare, half the price of the £100 charged by BOAC, but that journey only took 24 hours. But the company became too ambitious and started a transatlantic service, which was quickly smothered by BOAC. It lost Airwork a lot of money and thereafter the Government turned against the company; it took years for it to get back in favour. Myles Wyatt, the chairman, said at the time: "We discovered that playing in the first league was a very different affair to schoolboy football."

But the crisis established Wyatt as head of the company and he forged a reputation as a shrewd buyer and seller of aircraft, making handsome profits. Acquisitions were to be Airwork's future and its chairman wanted to build the biggest airline in Britain; its first big acquisition under its new strategy had been Gerald Freeman's Transair. After that, Freeman joined Airwork's board as head of acquisitions. Earlier in the year Airwork had held a board meeting at the Savoy Hotel in London's Strand. It was top secret and its agenda was to acquire companies. Present at that meeting were Freeman and Wyatt, Lord Poole, Lord Guinness and Geoffrey Murrant. They had a list of companies they might buy, and Freddie Laker's name was on it. However, the choice in front of them was somewhat limited. Besides Freddie Laker's companies, the others were British Eagle, Morton Air Services, Bristow Helicopters, Silver City Airways, and Hunting. Freeman approached them all.

Harold Bamberg's Eagle Aviation was the most likely acquisition, but when Freeman looked at the books he saw that all was not what it seemed, and Airwork quickly lost interest. Freddie's companies were the number one target, and after the Accountant fiasco Freeman smelled blood. So when he entered Freddie's office at Cumberland Place in London in 1958, he knew exactly what he was there for. Freeman was ex-RAF and looked the part, tall and slim with a permanent suntan. His good manners and dry sense of humour were legendary in the aviation industry. He and Freddie knew each other through their membership of the British Independent Air Transport Association (BIATA), and had worked together on the 'little Berlin Airlift'. Freeman had risen to be chairman of BIATA, although their operating styles were very different. When Freeman asked him if he would sell his company, Freddie naturally said "No," but he really meant "Yes".

After some verbal dancing around, Freddie agreed on the spot that he would sell his whole empire of nine companies and property to Airwork for a mixture of shares and cash provided the price was £1 million. With that the two men shook hands and put the takeover into motion. But what Freeman had actually agreed with Freddie was that Airwork would pay a million if the assets were worth a million. Freeman had no idea if the companies were worth that. ACG and ATEL were two totally different types of operation, and Freeman was really only interested in ACG. But Freddie said it was all or nothing. Freeman could put a number on ACG, but not ATEL. In fact, valuing ACG was very easy. It was a very good company run from the London office, and all its books were up to date. ATEL was a totally different animal and, as good as Air Charter was, Aviation Traders was the opposite.

In addition to the two Britannias, ACG owned 18 large transport aeroplanes outright and a host of long-term operating and charter contracts. Freeman valued the aircraft – including the three DC-4s, nine Bristol 170s, the six Avro Super Traders and still lingering Prentices that weren't even worthy of insuring – at £600,000. That was all agreed very quickly, but predictably there was a dispute over the value of ATEL. Freeman didn't want Aviation Traders at all, and was not sure it was worth anything. When Freeman visited ATEL's headquarters at Southend he didn't like what he saw. He thought the Southend operation looked messy. The lack of formal records meant that much of what Freddie had said his businesses were worth had to be taken on trust. But what also influenced the sale was that Freeman was keen to buy. He had a clear mandate from the board of Airwork to acquire Air Charter, and money was not the only criterion.

Freddie wouldn't budge on ATEL, and repeated 'all or nothing'. He proved the better negotiator, and Freeman didn't call his bluff. Freddie wanted £400,000 for ATEL and Freeman countered with £200,000 subject to an audit and normal due diligence. As expected, the audit proved somewhat difficult as Freddie had no stock lists of his spares and equipment and it had never been catalogued. Freeman was still unsure. When the accountants' report came back it showed that they were unable to value ATEL, as they had no idea what the spares were really worth in a sale.

The two men quickly reached a compromise. They arranged for Transair's chief engineer, Bill Richardson, to meet with Jack Wiseman and agree a joint valuation. The two settled on £300,000, which Freeman still thought was too high, but by then it was too late as the Airwork board had authorised him to buy the companies for up to £1 million, and word had got round the City that a big deal was pending. Airwork had to do the deal. Freddie got £900,000 for his companies. The deal was closed in January 1958, Freddie was paid £550,000, and the rest of the money was held back to cover any liabilities, being paid to him at £50,000 a month. A side deal was done for the Accountant; Freddie couldn't bear to part with it so Airwork was only too happy to sell it back to him.

Freddie, who owned 90 per cent, and his wife Joan, who owned 10 per cent, signed the deal in Airwork's boardroom. When Myles Wyatt leaned over with the blotter and pressed it down, Joan Laker threw her arms round her husband and cried tears of joy. She told Wyatt and Freeman: "I have got my husband back." Freddie, however, was in no mood to celebrate. He didn't really want to sell at all, but knew he had to. But his wife was delighted. Freeman invited both of them to dinner at his house in Surrey to celebrate. The Lakers took him a solid silver wine cooler, which sat on his sideboard until his death.

Once the companies were sold and the money was in Freddie's bank account, he had to tell his staff. He called his closest managers – Jack Wiseman, Bob Batt, Norman Jennings, Douglas Whybrow and Alan Nicholls, the Chief Accountant – to Cumberland Place and told them that he had done the deal. They had all been with him for a long time. By all published accounts Freddie apparently said: "I've just resigned for all of you. I'm selling out to Airwork. I've told them they can take my companies with no encumbrances at all. If they want you, they'll ask for you." He gave all his managers cash bonuses from his share, ranging from £250 to more than £10,000. It turned out that Gerald Freeman wanted all the managers to stay, and issued them with improved contracts. Freddie was staying on, too, sitting on the board of Airwork. So in many ways it was business as usual.

Freddie was 35 years old. He was a cash millionaire and splashed out £20,000 on the building a new house in a wealthy enclave on the outskirts of Epsom overlooking the Royal Automobile Club's golf course. He called the new house Charters, and it was on 'The Ridge'. The land came with lifetime membership of the golf club, so his children could use the fabulous indoor swimming pool. He also began indulging in a new hobby, racehorses. His daughter Elaine was friends with another little girl whose father was the racehorse trainer Ron Smythe, and Freddie caught the bug from her. He was so gripped that he bought a 75-acre stud farm, the Woodcote Stud, a stone's throw away from his new home. His life now consisted of nine holes of golf in the morning, lunch at the RAC clubhouse, and another 18 holes of golf, then an evening with friends playing poker until the early hours.

But it was not to last. By nature, Freddie was not a man of leisure and he was soon itching to get back into action. A return to Airwork alongside his old colleagues became inevitable.

# CHAPTER 10

# Tossing a Coin
## Buying Bristow Helicopters

### 1959-1960

Inevitably, as 1959 rolled into 1960 Freddie Laker was back at work, trundling into London to Airwork's HQ in Piccadilly, London, and putting his feet behind a new desk for the £3,500 a year they were paying him.

As part of the deal with Airwork he sat on the board and was still technically head of his old companies. But the board was very capable and had little interest in any of his ideas. His old companies were run far better by their managers than by him. He was an entrepreneur, and entrepreneurs started up companies. But Airwork only wanted to buy companies – it had no use for entrepreneurs like Freddie Laker.

Finally he presented himself at Myles Wyatt's office and asked if he could be assigned some tasks for the large salary they were paying him. Wyatt looked hard at Freddie; he wasn't that keen to have him around, and just as he was about to sidestep the request and fob him off, he said out of the blue: "Do you know Alan Bristow?"

Freddie replied: "Of course."

As it happened, Freddie and Bristow had met in Bermuda and they had spent a day together fishing. Bristow ran Bristow Helicopters, at that time probably the biggest helicopter operator in the world. It was highly profitable and Wyatt wanted to buy it. Wyatt had more than one reason for wanting to get Bristow's company in the group. Airwork had a loss-making helicopter operating business, which had been half owned by Fisons, the agrichemicals company. It had originally been set up to use helicopters for crop spraying and expanded quickly into all areas of helicopter operation. Wyatt had recently bought up the other half of the business from Fisons and had no idea what to do with it – or how to stem the losses.

Freddie was intrigued and volunteered to try to get Bristow to sell. Wyatt then told him that all Gerald Freeman's approaches to Bristow had been rebuffed. Freddie said, "I'll have a go," although he was not at all sure how he would be able to handle Bristow, a man whose tough reputation went before him, something that Freddie had seen at first hand.

Freddie wasn't at all surprised that the smooth Freeman had got nowhere with Bristow, who was a take-no-prisoners type of person and totally down to earth. He always said what he thought regardless of whether the other person wanted to hear it.

Freddie didn't tell Wyatt what had happened when they had met in Bermuda a few months previously. Bristow ran his company from Bermuda, where he lived in enforced tax exile with his wife and son and a secretary. He had finally been forced out of Britain because of his high personal earnings, which were taxed at a very high level due to something called the Surtax Direction Order (SDO); this had been introduced in 1922 by the then coalition Government, and had never been repealed. Bristow hated being away from Britain but he had no choice as the SDO was ruinous for really high earners like himself.

Freddie had gone out to Bermuda for a working holiday with his wife Joan and daughter Elaine after he had sold his companies. As well as sitting in the sun, he was doing some tax planning of his own with his accountant. It so happened that the Lakers were invited to a cocktail party at the home of Taffy Powell, who had founded Silver City Airways in 1948. In retirement, he represented Harold Bamberg's British Eagle in North America, and his son ran the radio station on Bermuda. Bristow was also invited, but arrived late at a party where he was sober and everyone else was nearly falling over. Bristow quickly found his wife Jean, and as he was chatting to her Freddie approached them. Bristow picks up the story himself: "A burly six-footer came over, swaying slightly. He was clearly tipsy. 'So, you are Alan Bristow,' he slurred. He poked a beefy index finger into my chest to accentuate every word. 'Yes ... who are you?' 'I'm Freddie Laker.' 'Pleased to meet you.'

"I carried on the conversation with Jean. The swaying Laker did not take the hint. Once again the index finger poked my chest. 'I'm going to buy your company,' he said. I looked at his finger still stuck in my sternum. 'You do that again, Mr Laker, and you'll be carried out of here.' That sobered him up a little and he let his finger drop. 'I want to buy your company,' he repeated. 'You couldn't afford my company,' I said. Just then his wife Joan appeared and sensed the tension. She pulled him by the arm. 'Come along, Freddie. You can talk business tomorrow.' 'Yes, let's talk tomorrow,' he said. 'I'm sorry,' I said. 'Tomorrow's my fishing Saturday.' 'I'd love to come fishing,' said Freddie. 'Can we all come?' 'Sure you can come. But you'll be seasick.' 'No, we're good sailors.' 'Okay, tomorrow morning at ten, down at the Flatts.'

"At the appointed hour Freddie, Joan and their daughter Elaine turned up dressed as though they were going to the Queen's garden party, and we went out to fish. Laker and I caught plenty of snapper, yellowtail and barracuda, and were satisfied fishermen when we anchored for a picnic lunch in Mangrove Bay on the North Shore of Somerset Village. No mention had been made of the previous evening's conversation, and I thought it must have been the booze talking. As we lay anchor, Freddie looked at his watch. 'I'm sorry, but we have to be at the airport this afternoon to fly to London.' 'Don't worry,' I said. 'We can put you ashore at the back entrance to the airport, so you can walk across to the terminal.' I headed for the airport at full speed, and the Lakers scrambled ashore on some rocks. I thought it odd, a family going to London with no baggage, but I found out later that Freddie was meeting with George Carroll at the airport, who had their bags."

The following day Bristow was talking to his chief executive, George Fry, on the transatlantic line and discussing the performance of the various Bristow subsidiaries around the world. At the end of the conversation he said to Fry, "By the way, I've met this man Laker. He says that he wants to buy the company." Bristow told Fry he had effectively told him where to go.

"Well, that was the right answer," replied Fry, and put the phone down, thinking nothing more of it. Fry knew of Freddie Laker and also knew that he did not have the wherewithal to buy Bristow Helicopters.

But within a few days Fry phoned Bristow and told him that he'd had an approach from Freddie Laker through a third party to buy the company. Fry had got it wrong and told Bristow that Freddie was not acting for himself, as he had thought, but for Airwork, Britain's biggest private airline. Suddenly Freddie's approach made sense to Bristow. The acquisition of Bristow Helicopters as part of Airwork would produce a substantial aviation operating company with fixed-wing, scheduled and charter services and helicopters. Bristow would also bring the profitable bottom line that Airwork mainly seemed to lack. Bristow told Fry: "You had better see what he wants." And he added to make sure that Freddie knew straight away how much Bristow Helicopters was making and how much it would cost to buy it.

A meeting was quickly set up between Myles Wyatt and George Fry in Airwork's head office in Piccadilly, London. Wyatt opened with a cheap offer and said that Alan Bristow would have to become an employee and report to him. Fry picked up his briefcase and made to leave barely 8 minutes after entering Wyatt's office. It had been the wrong approach, and Wyatt knew he had blown it almost immediately. He ran after Fry and called him back from the opening lift doors. He had miscalculated, not for the first time in his life, and thought that he could pick up Bristow Helicopters on the cheap. He had also misjudged the sort of man Alan Bristow was. Wyatt, now literally gasping for air, suggested that Freddie Laker and Alan Bristow should get together to negotiate. Fry agreed to pass on the message.

Alan Bristow was amenable to that and recalled in his memoirs: "Before getting any deeper into talks with Wyatt, I wanted to find out precisely how much Bristow Helicopters was worth, and what was the real motive behind Wyatt's offer in the first place. George and I took a good hard look at our cash flow and prospects for future contracts. The deeper we delved into the figures, the more thankful I was that George hadn't given the time of day to Wyatt's valuation. But I was not averse to selling – quite the opposite. The more I thought about it, the more the advantages impressed themselves upon me."

The advantage was that there was then no capital gains tax in Britain. If

Bristow sold out he could take all his money tax free and return to live in Britain, something he badly wanted to do. The helicopter operating business, despite being inherently profitable, also demanded the use of huge amounts of capital up front to buy helicopters for new contracts. Bristow often worried about the amount of debt he carried on his balance sheet. He recalled: "However good the living in Bermuda, I felt out of the mainstream. But more importantly, I thought it would ease the perennial problem of raising finance to enable us to win new contracts. To play ball in the international oil business one needed strong financial backing to provide muscle enough to persuade the manufacturers to take deposits and allow you to lease-purchase helicopters, an uncommon business practice at the time. BHL was operating in a highly competitive market, and finance costs were a heavy burden on the company. In the long term, the deep pockets of Airwork Holdings Ltd would surely give us the weight to win business on a global scale."

But Bristow didn't want to give up control of his company and he certainly didn't want to report to someone like Myles Wyatt, whom he regarded as little short of a buffoon. The impasse was broken by Freddie and Bristow handling the negotiations themselves, as Bristow recalled: "I rang Freddie Laker and made it clear that any attempt to subsume Bristow into Airwork would make discussions to acquire Bristow impossible. Freddie got the message loud and clear and relayed it to Wyatt. On that basis I agreed to meet Freddie for lunch to see if we could come together on price and terms of reference." Bristow flew in specially from Bermuda on a day trip. It was in and out for lunch.

Freddie and Bristow quickly agreed a deal. Bristow, who would return to Britain, would be left alone as chief executive to run the helicopter side of the business, and the Fisons subsidiary would also be turned over to him. He would be paid a low annual salary of £3,000 plus a Rolls-Royce and a chauffeur, but be entitled to 10 per cent of the operating profits of the helicopter business. On Tuesday 24th April 1960 Freddie Laker, Alan Bristow, George Fry and George Carroll, two entrepreneurs and their assistants, met for lunch at Simpsons in Piccadilly. By then Bristow and Freddie were getting on very well, as Bristow recalled: "This time he didn't poke me in the stomach." They had already agreed a price for the business, but found that they were £67,000 apart in valuation.

It was a long lunch and when they got to the brandy and cigars Bristow told Freddie he must have his price. Freddie retorted that Wyatt would fire him if he paid the additional £67,000. A desperate Freddie, knowing he couldn't leave Simpsons without a deal, offered to split the difference out of his own pocket, but Bristow wouldn't back down and said, "Freddie, I don't need to sell the business, and I don't think there is any purpose in pursuing the conversation. Let's forget about it." Suddenly Freddie reached inside his pocket and brought out a half-crown coin and shouted across the table, "Come on, Alan, I'll toss you for the difference."

After a moment's silence for Bristow to assess whether Freddie was serious, to his own astonishment he accepted the challenge, as he remembered later: "I'm not a gambling man. I take a calculated risk after weighing all the information, but I've never wagered money when I didn't think that I had a better chance of coming out ahead. Which makes it all the more inexplicable that I should end up tossing a coin for £67,000 with Freddie Laker – and this was in 1960, when £67,000 would buy a street of houses in Kensington."

George Fry was also astonished and kicked Bristow's leg so hard he drew blood. He told him not to do it. Bristow ignored him and the blood stained his suit trousers. Freddie tossed the half-crown in the air and said, "Call." Bristow called "Heads".

By then the whole restaurant had caught on to what was happening and had gathered around the table, together with an astonished head waiter who said he had never witnessed anything like this in his restaurant in the 30 years he had run the place. As Freddie raised his hand to reveal the coin it was turned up 'heads'. Relieved, but still in shock, Fry downed his brandy in one gulp and held his glass out for a refill.

Bristow breathed a very long sigh of relief. It had all happened in a moment. £67,000, more than £1 million at today's values, had been decided on the toss of a coin. Freddie was calm afterwards and said: "We'll have to sort that one out with Myles." Fry said: "Don't worry Freddie. I'll have a word with him on your behalf, and I won't mention anything about the tossing of a coin."

Bristow went straight to Heathrow to catch a flight back to Bermuda, barely aware of what he had just done. In the excitement, George Fry had actually strained his heart muscles and went straight to Harley Street to see his doctor, where he was prescribed a week's bed rest.

Myles Wyatt by now wanted Bristow Helicopters desperately and agreed to the extra money. He never found out about the coin toss. A few weeks later Freddie and Bristow met up again after the sale had gone through and Bristow had the extra £67,000 in the bank. He said to Bristow: "You're a lucky bugger, aren't you? Tell you what – there's a racehorse I fancy, a little filly. Why don't you share your good fortune and buy her for me?" And Bristow did so for £1,400.

The deal that Freddie negotiated was later to cost Myles Wyatt dear. Under Alan Bristow, the helicopter division of Airwork prospered mightily until annual positive cash flow reached a sum approaching £20 million, earning Bristow £2 million a year personally in bonuses, making him the highest-paid executive in Britain.

CHAPTER 11

# A Different Challenge
## The BUA years - Part 1

1959-1962

At the end of the 1950s, the then British Prime Minister, Harold Macmillan decided that airline travel should effectively be deregulated and no longer a monopoly between the state-owned British Overseas Airways Corporation (BOAC) and British European Airways (BEA). Macmillan appointed Duncan Sandys to head the Ministry of Supply in 1959 with the express intention of creating a separate Ministry of Aviation to rationalise the whole of the British aviation industry, both manufacturing and operations.

Sandys thought it was obvious that there were too many aircraft operators, most of whom were loss-making. After the lessons of the Berlin Airlift Macmillan had realised the strategic importance of Britain's independent aircraft operators and wanted Sandys to protect them from unfair and predatory competition from the state-owned companies.

Sandys found the independent aircraft operators very strong-minded and independent, so he shied away from dramatic change and set about rationalising Britain's aircraft manufacturing sector. After he was finished, eight manufacturing companies became effectively two and he made it clear that he intended to apply the same medicine to the independent airlines. The manufacturers had willingly gone to the slaughter, but the operators were resistant, as most of them were profitable and enjoyed their independence.

Harold Macmillan's Conservative Government therefore passed the Civil Aviation Licensing Act to enable Sandys to bend them to his will. When the bill passed into law, Sandys called the chairmen of the independent airlines in one by one to explain his new policy to them. The new Air Transport Licensing Board (ATLB) would have substantial powers to be able to order the operators around as it wished. It was a total abuse of executive power, but it worked and within a year, eight airlines were merged into two.

Much to the delight of Myles Wyatt, Duncan Sandys decided that Airwork should take the lead in nationalising the industry. He designated it to become the third biggest airline after BOAC and BEA. It was another gross abuse of Government power, but Wyatt didn't need any encouragement to make it happen.

The new regime also suited the powerful Cayzer family, which dominated the shipping industry by dint of its ownership of British & Commonwealth (B&C). If there was going to be a new third force in British aviation, the Cayzers decided they wanted to be it. Harold Macmillan's deregulation proposals were music to their ears as they sought a merger of their aircraft interests with Airwork.

The Cayzers were already in a strong position with their ownership of the Hunting Clan aircraft operating company. They were steeped in shipping and had bought Hunting as a way of hedging their bets on the future; many people at the time believed that air travel would totally eclipse travel by water for both people and cargo.

The original B&C Hunting Group had consisted of an aircraft manufacturer and an aircraft operator. To prepare for the new era the divisions were split and demerged. As part of a rather complicated arrangement, Hunting Air Transport, as it was called, became a subsidiary of Clan Line, the B&C-owned shipping company, and was hence renamed Hunting Clan, headed by Sir Nicholas Cayzer.

Although the Cayzers knew all about ships, they knew nothing about aircraft and soon ran into trouble with a series of loss-making contracts. The Government, the biggest customer of all the private aircraft operators, had squeezed prices until the profit margins had become almost extinct. The Macmillan/Sandys initiative was music to the Cayzers' ears. Airwork and Hunting Clan were already partners in Africa, so the two companies were every well known to each other. In March 1960 the merger between Airwork Holdings Ltd and Hunting Clan Ltd was announced. It was ostensibly a merger of equals where the big ship-owning families effectively took control of Airwork. Three major family-owned shipping companies, Blue Star, Furness Withy and British & Commonwealth, held 72 per cent of the shares. Hunting Aviation, the original manufacturing company, would own eight per cent, and Lords Guinness and Cowdray ten per cent each. Through all their cross holdings, the Cayzer family emerged the dominant shareholder. It was exactly what they had planned.

On 19th May 1960 Airwork grandly renamed itself British United Airways, pre-empting its official 1st July merger with Hunting Clan. The merger made it the largest independent airline in Britain.

BOAC and BEA were naturally furious at the creation of such a powerful and threatening competitor, but Duncan Sandys waved away their protests. The Government allowed the new company to be called British United Airways as long as it was never shortened to BUA, although inevitably it was and eventually caused much confusion among customers of BEA.

On the new BUA board sat Sir Nicholas Cayzer, Anthony Cayzer and Clive Hunting, with Myles Wyatt as chairman. It looked like a dream merger and the perfect solution to a tidying up of British privately owned airlines by Duncan Sandys. But there the good news ended. The newly formed British United

Airways was actually a ragbag of independent companies all managed separately with no common thread between them except that they all owned aircraft. Everyone thought Myles Wyatt was an ass and they ignored his frequent memos and even refused to return his telephone calls.

BUA was just a collection of independent fiefdoms and the individual subsidiary directors ran their own companies autonomously, all resentful of interference. Myles Wyatt may have run the head office and central finances, but he quickly found that he did not run the operating businesses. He therefore had no effective control of his own business.

Freddie Laker, elevated to the position of executive director, still ran ACG and ATEL, with Jack Wiseman, Norman Jennings, Bob Batt and Douglas Whybrow reporting to him as before. Even Gerald Freeman ran his own Transair business autonomously with his old managers Bill Richardson and Cliff Nunn reporting to him alone. The only company without a strong leader was Hunting Air Transport, and it had problems as a result of Wyatt's constant interference.

Freddie and Wyatt were keen to develop the opportunity offered by the Civil Aviation (Licensing) Act introduced in mid-1960. The Act bestowed automatic licences for the routes that airlines were already operating, and ended the BOAC and BEA monopoly of scheduled services. The independents could for the first time build businesses based on scheduled services. So BUA applied for a large number of domestic and international scheduled route licences to give its scheduled network the critical mass to become financially viable by 1965.

It applied for twice-weekly services to Istanbul, Tehran, Karachi, Delhi, Calcutta, Bangkok and Singapore, with a weekly extension to Hong Kong and Tokyo, utilising their existing fleet of Britannias and DC-6s. The company also planned a large expansion of its existing European network by filing applications for more than 20 cities, putting it in direct competition with BEA.

Freddie's strong challenge to BEA led him straight into conflict with the British Conservative Government. The Ministry of Aviation wanted a benign third airline, not a fierce competitor. But Freddie Laker never understood the meaning of the word 'benign'.

Although the monopoly may have ended, BEA and BOAC retained everything they had before the Act. The routes they owned were the best and the most profitable. The only real difference was that the newly formed Air Transport Licensing Board could now award routes to any air operator it liked. Freddie, in his usual style, put the cart before the horse and ordered new aircraft before he had the routes to fly them on. He planned orders for £20 million worth of new jets for the assortment of routes for which he wanted to apply.

He persuaded BUA to order the first ten BAC One-Elevens, a short-haul twin-engined jet, as a replacement for the turbo-prop-powered Viscounts. The British Aircraft Corporation One-Eleven had been conceived by Hunting Aircraft in the 1950s and was the great white hope of British Aviation; by 1961 Hunting had become part of the newly formed BAC, and decided to proceed with the One-Eleven project, even though lacking a launch customer.

Without Freddie Laker the One-Eleven may never have existed. Geoffrey Knight, BAC's sales director, with whom Freddie had forged a close personal friendship, called Freddie 'the father of the One-Eleven'. Knight had previously worked for Bristol, and had sold Freddie his Bristol Freighters and Britannias. To get things going Knight brokered a meeting between Freddie and Sir George Edwards, an aircraft engineer and the Executive Director of BAC who would later lead the British team on the Concorde project. Freddie pushed for a substantial improvement in performance over the Viscount and broadly outlined what he wanted. He insisted that the new aircraft be able to carry a full load of passengers non-stop to the far edges of the Mediterranean.

Freddie won himself an admirer that day. Edwards, who clearly enjoyed the sparring over the One-Eleven, is famously quoted as saying, "A few hundred years ago he would have had brass earrings, a beard, a bit longer hair and a cutlass," adding, "There are few people in this world who can give you a kick and you are happy as Larry when you have had it. Mr Laker is one of the few on my list." Freddie ordered ten BAC One-Eleven aircraft for BUA, subject to agreeing a price and specification.

The One-Eleven was planned as a smaller sister-ship to the Boeing 737, the dominant medium-range twin-engined jet. BAC gave the aircraft a similar spec; even the seat-track widths were the same, to broaden its appeal. The detailed negotiations were left to BAC's John Prothero Thomas, with BUA's Mick Sidebotham and Freddie Laker on the other side of the table. It was an uneven match; Prothero Thomas found himself facing tough, hard negotiators, and Freddie as ever would take every possible advantage, bullying him into submission. Sidebotham was worried about the aircraft's weight and payload, and told Freddie they would need to keep weight strictly under control. They spent a week trying to get the best possible deal for BUA. Freddie knew he had an edge.

In early 1961, Geoffrey Knight – tired of the apparent deadlock on price – wanted to pin down the deal ready for his spring quarterly board meeting. He had been talking the matter back and forth with Freddie Laker on the telephone and was getting nowhere. So he and Freddie went to the races at Sandown Park where the price was fixed in the paddock during the third and fourth races.

With that settled, on 9th May the public launch took place. It was announced that the BUA order for ten BAC One-Elevens was worth £8 million and there was a further option for five more. Soon after, the One-Eleven was ordered by Braniff as the American launch customer. It was highly unusual for a big American airline to place such a significant order for a European aircraft.

On top of this Freddie ordered four Vickers VC10s for an assault on long-haul services, at a cost of £2.8 million, but without having done any studies or in-depth investigations as to how they were going to be used. It was foolhardy to say the least. Freddie had gambled the whole organisation's future with this aircraft acquisition order.

To that end, preparation of the case for BUA's new routes was well under way. The selected destinations seemed to have been chosen randomly as being the most likely to have sufficient traffic.

Then in April 1961 BUA was hit with by a major setback. The executive responsible for preparing the company's case for the new routes suddenly died.

It was five weeks before the hearings at the ATLB. To Freddie and Wyatt's horror, when examining the contents of the man's desk it was apparent that work had hardly begun, and the little he had done was nonsense. They found all of his own arguments unsuitable and there was no case to present. Asking for a postponement would have been so embarrassing as to be utterly out of the question. So Freddie and Wyatt invited Douglas Whybrow for a drink at the National Sporting Club. Both parties were more than a little sheepish. Freddie had gambled the whole organisation's future on his aircraft order, and Wyatt feared that he would be the laughing stock of the whole industry. They asked Whybrow to take it on; he had little expertise but that didn't matter since the process was new for everyone. Freddie had shrewdly recruited Alastair Pugh, a former aeronautical engineer and aviation journalist, for Channel Air Bridge, and he too was redeployed to head up the application process. Freddie knew that Pugh could write and he understood aircraft. Pugh and Whybrow got down to work with a small team. Soon applications were made to present to the ATLB, accompanied by detailed economic and factual arguments in support of BUA's case to be awarded the routes.

They soon realised that the worst thing that could happen was for only some of the routes to be granted. A prime example was Rome, which already had a large frequency of flights and more than a dozen airlines serving it. The ATLB insisted that some of the applications be withdrawn. Naturally BEA opposed BUA's applications and at the official hearings argued strongly for BUA to get no routes awarded to it at all. The ATLB's verdict was now vitally important to Freddie as he already had delivery dates and had paid deposits on the 14 aircraft, which would start arriving soon.

BUA's entire business continued to be underpinned by the task of moving soldiers around the world; after all the mergers and takeovers, the company had a virtual monopoly on trooping contracts. With competitors gone, prices went up and Freddie know it would be good while it lasted. He knew it was only a matter of time before the RAF built up its own troop transport capability, which would kill the business for the independents. But for now BUA was making £4 million a year out of the business. In October 1961 BUA won its biggest ever contract to carry 11,000 troops a month between Britain and Germany.

Around this time Freddie commissioned BUA's new Air Terminal at London's Victoria railway station. BUA wanted its passengers to check in and drop off their baggage in a central London location before boarding a train to Gatwick. The convenience of relieving passengers of their bulky luggage would be a great selling point, as well as facilitating quicker handling for the airline. The man responsible for the development of Channel Air Bridge's rail/air traffic was George Parselle. He had been a railway apprentice before the war and his contemporaries now held high office at British Railways. BR was keen to develop the relationship, but explained that it was limited by space at Victoria. Parselle looked up above their heads at the arched roof of the steam-era train shed. Pointing upwards to the vast empty space, he said, "What about up there, over the lines?" BR agreed and expedited the building of the facility, spending £100,000 on it; it opened in late April 1962.

Meanwhile BUA was granted the first of the new licences by the Air Transport Licensing Board; it did rather well and won a series of 12 European scheduled route licences and the right to fly to Paris, Genoa, Amsterdam, Milan, Zurich, Madeira, Basel, Athens, Barcelona, Tarbes, Palma and Malaga. Although it seemed like a lot of routes, Freddie was disappointed, having expected to win a lot more.

BEA didn't agree and thought that the ATLB had been too generous, immediately appealing each route with detailed arguments to back up its appeals. Duncan Sandys had moved on and been replaced as aviation minister by Julian Amery. Amery refused every one of BEA's appeals and a year later BUA was cleared for take-off.

Rather late in the day BUA found that it also needed the approval of the governments to whose countries it was going to fly, and found it faced huge problems getting foreign governments to approve the new services. Myles Wyatt was very surprised at this turn of events, and said at the time: "A stranger to this industry might suppose that once a licence has been confirmed by the minister, the coast would be clear for the licensee to start operations without further ado." Nothing could have been further from the truth, and BUA began a long battle with foreign governments to get approval to fly to its new routes. Douglas Whybrow was not surprised by the outcome; he already knew about the intransigence of the French and Germans towards granting licences. and he knew that it would be a very long time before BUA aircraft would fly any of the routes.

Some of the new licences came with the proviso that they would not start for 15 months, in order to give BEA time to prepare for the new competition. In practical terms only four routes to European destinations were likely to be operated in the near future – Genoa, Tarbes, Palma and Barcelona – and these were marginal and seasonal routes at best. There were also internal routes to Glasgow and Edinburgh, which were reasonable. But it was too little work for the One-Elevens, and the airline was left with its basic existing business, charters, IT tours and trooping for its existing fleet of Viscount aircraft. The results were only satisfactory for BUA's African routes with the VC10 … and to the Canaries.

The summer of 1961 was a busy time at British United Airways. Wyatt and Freddie had become fascinated by the new hovercraft technology that was appearing. Hovercraft Developments Ltd (HDL) – an offshoot of the National Research Development Centre – had approached BUA as it wanted to showcase one of its machines in passenger service. Wyatt was especially keen. In May 1961 the search began for a suitable route. Alastair Pugh, in a borrowed light aircraft, flew the length and breadth of Britain surveying the various inlets for the perfect location. Route discussions ran late into the early hours, fuelled by coffee. Eventually it was Whybrow who came up with the Dee estuary in North West England, and a route between Rhyl and Wallasey. Whybrow knew it well, having grown up looking down on it; his childhood home was on Flint Mountain in Wales. The journey between the two points around the estuary and up the Wirral peninsula was long and tedious, and in the 1950s and '60s the drive could take many hours. The Dee estuary was also unusual as it would often contain very little water, and the hovercraft was the only vehicle that could operate in those conditions.

In October 1961, Freddie appointed a hovercraft committee to do a feasibility study. It was a committee of two, Alastair Pugh and BUA's planning manager, who reported to Douglas Whybrow. Whybrow and his colleagues at Channel Air Bridge were unimpressed by the results and thought that it would be uncommercial. However, since HDL and BP were going to fund it, there would be minimal cost to BUA and it would earn the company a great deal of publicity for pioneering a new form of transport. Freddie was all for it.

They had yet to decide on a vehicle, but it was thought that the Vickers Armstrong VA-3 was the best choice and BUA had a friendly history of dealing with Vickers. The VA-3 was 54 feet long, powered by two turbo-prop aero engines, and driven by propellers. It could carry a maximum of 24 passengers and had a top speed of 60 knots.

The project was flooded with enthusiasm and the start of the world's first scheduled hovercraft service took place on 20th July 1962. It attracted worldwide attention. The hovercraft bore the BUA livery across both sides and its particular shape soon earned it a nickname of the 'flying crab'. The 17 miles took 25 minutes, and the £2 fare was about the same as a 1st Class rail ticket. But the Vickers Armstrong VA-3 hovercraft was terribly unreliable and often broke down. The Dart engines struggled with the salt water. It only operated for a total of 19 days and managed only four consecutive days. For the first ten days of September there was no service at all, partly due to the terrible stormy summer. On what was to be its last trip, both engines failed and the hovercraft limped home.

The hovercraft project was a nice diversion for Freddie Laker and he said he was not surprised when it failed. However, it famously made him the man who put hovercraft services on the map.

# CHAPTER 12

# Car-via-Air

## The ATL.98 Carvair

1959-1961

1959 had marked the 50th anniversary of the first flight between the mainland of Europe and England by Louis Blériot, and the *Daily Mail* offered a £10,000 prize for the person who could make the fastest journey between London and Paris, by any method. It sparked huge interest between rival airlines desperate to win the race, and Freddie Laker was the most desperate of all. His competitor, Silver City Airways, hired legendary racing driver Stirling Moss to drive a Jaguar. Silver City would take Moss across the Channel on one of its planes and rely on him to do the rest. Not to be outdone, Freddie himself decided to enter, in his Rolls-Royce. At 18 feet long and weighing more than 4,600lb, it was hardly a racing car. Moreover, Freddie – used to being chauffeured – wasn't the optimal racing driver. He laid on a special flight from Southend Airport to Le Bourget with a Bristol Freighter aircraft belonging to Channel Air Bridge. Elaborate arrangements were made at each end to load and offload the Rolls as quickly as possible. Freddie then invited a select group of journalists to come along for the ride to witness the adventure.

During the Channel crossing the engines of the Bristol were on high boost for the whole journey, vibrating like crazy and deafening the passengers. Freddie started to panic, but the pilot told him not to worry; the engines might stop, but it was the airframe falling apart that he was really worried about – they didn't call it the 'Bristol Frightener' for no reason. As soon as the plane landed and the ramp was attached, Freddie jumped in the Rolls and sped towards the airport gates. But the gates were locked and the keys seemingly lost. Freddie suspected sabotage and backed up the car to ram the gates just as the key was found. One of the journalists vomited in the back of the Rolls. But despite the effort, it was all to no avail as Freddie lost the race, and it was little consolation that the illustrious Stirling Moss was beaten too. The eventual winner was Royal Navy Commander Ian Martin, who used a motorbike, a jet fighter and a helicopter.

For all the good times, there was a problem lurking for the highly profitable air ferry business. The converted Bristol Freighters would someday need replacing. After years of short hops and too many take-offs and landings they were suffering from metal fatigue, specifically in the wings. But it was not yet urgent, and it was estimated that there was still about eight to ten years of life left in them. Nevertheless, Freddie asked Bob Batt and Arthur Leftley to find a cost-effective replacement in January 1959. He asked them to carry out a feasibility study and gave them the freedom to evaluate a number of different aircraft.

It was easier said than done, as there was no other aircraft like it in the world. Freddie wanted an aircraft that was faster and could carry 25 passengers and five cars. It required a 70-foot cargo compartment, sufficient space for a toilet, and a galley. Ideally, the plane would be able to carry a 9-ton payload in all. Without something new, the long-term future looked bleak for the air ferries. Freddie wanted to expand Channel Air Bridge's services to further destinations in order to remain competitive; he wanted his air ferries to fly to Paris (Le Bourget), Dusseldorf, Bremen, Dijon, Lyon and Strasbourg, and most of these longer-range routes of 2-3 hours were unsuitable for the Bristol Freighters.

BUA owned three Douglas DC-4s, all inherited from Air Charter, which would soon be redundant. The fleet included Freddie's very first DC-4, G-ANYB 'Atalanta'. The aircraft had reached 37,000 flying hours and at the time it was mainly flying British tourists on day trips to Calais. The DC-4 had been superseded by the emergence of the jet age well before its natural life was over, and consequently there were plenty of second-hand models available, specifically the military C54 Skymaster variant, which could be bought for as little £40,000, with very few hours on the aircraft. A true civilian-configured DC-4 was nearly double the price.

Freddie's very own Archimedes moment struck him as he was bathing one Sunday morning. He shot out of the bath and, still dripping and naked, rang Jack Wiseman to explain his idea, but not before he'd asked Wiseman to get to the hangar at Southend and measure points in the fuselage of the DC-4. "What the hell for?" asked Wiseman. Freddie told him he thought that maybe they could move the cockpit up above the fuselage and put a big door in for cars. Meanwhile Freddie ran down to his garage and measured his car to see if it would fit. He even made a cardboard model, and decided that the Douglas DC-4 would make an excellent replacement for the ageing Bristols. It was ideal, and it was an aircraft with which he had plenty of operational experience. To this end, Freddie bought up enough parts and airframes to convert ten DC-4s into his new air ferry workhorse.

The DC-4 could carry a large payload of 20,000lb and it was wider than the Bristol Freighter – it could potentially hold five cars at once. Freddie's visionary design would see the front end and nose cut off and remodelled. The nose would comprise a massive one-piece door hinged on the port side, and the cockpit would be rehoused on top, above the main cargo deck. It would be the first commercial aircraft to have this unique double-decker configuration, many years before the Boeing 747. The DC-4 didn't have a pressurised cabin, but the low-altitude cross-Channel flights didn't need it. Batt and Leftley would have preferred to have waited for a DC-6 but, as Freddie explained to them, the DC-6 was too much aircraft for the job – it cruised nearly 100mph faster then the DC-4 and had a range of 4,000 nautical miles, far more than they would need for air ferry work within Europe. Not to mention the fact that the DC-6 was more than double the price. The new project was registered as ATL.98. Freddie was keen to promote Channel Air Bridge, so he held a naming competition for the plane in June 1959. The winners, two men from Southend, won a free trip to France for a car and two passengers. The name they came up with was the 'Carvair', an abbreviation of 'Car-via-Air'.

Freddie and Batt saw huge value to sell the Carvair project aircraft to other operators worldwide. They estimated the cost of an ATL.98 to be about £150,000-£160,000. Customers who wanted to save money could buy their own DC-4 and pay Aviation Traders for the conversion only. Before work could begin, however, permission was required from the Douglas Aircraft Company. Happily it was in favour of the project, recognising that it would extend the aircraft's lifespan, but it wanted to be absolved of any liability. Leftley needed the plans and data for the DC-4 from Douglas's archives, so he flew to the company's base in Santa Monica in March 1959 and obtained what he needed for $10,000. He left believing he had agreed to pay £10,000 – almost three times as much – as the exchange rate was $2.80 to the pound. Freddie was delighted when this was made clear.

By the time Bob Batt's men had finished with the plane it was barely recognisable, and Freddie was extremely proud of it. He said: "It was a complete rebuild. We kept the wings and the wheels and the tail section of the DC-4 and built a new nose on it and put the crew above the fuselage." The Carvair gave 72 feet of bookable space, carried 22 passengers and five vehicles – a payload of more than 8 tons. With a 200mph-plus cruising speed, it was considerably faster than the 165mph Bristol Freighter. The Carvair would never win prizes for its good looks, but it was functional in the extreme. It was ATEL's greatest engineering feat up to that time, more so perhaps than Freddie's ambitious and costly ATL.90 Accountant, as the Carvair had instant commercial success.

One of the biggest challenges had been in the rerouting of the mechanical controls from the cockpit to avoid obstructing the cargo hold. This needed nearly 600 additional pulleys and brackets that changed directions six times to make it all work.

The conversion was complex with many difficulties that had to be overcome, which was not something that Aviation Traders was keen to admit to. The number of variants of the DC-4 were all configured differently, some with four fuel tanks, others with six. Wing modifications and even the length of the aircraft could vary by a couple of inches, depending on whether the plane had been built in Santa Monica or Chicago.

There was one last problem to overcome: the nose was nine feet above the ground compared to the Bristol's five. Aviation Traders Engineering was busy building a scissor lift, called the 'Hylo', but in the meantime the Little Green Company had produced a simple mechanical chain-driven lift; this resembled a four-poster bed, was painted yellow and did the job until ATEL's Hylo was finished. Once in production, the Hylo loader was a huge success, generating contracts for other types of loaders from Aviation Traders Engineering.

The first Carvair, G-ANYB (ATL.98-1), made its initial test flight at 8.26am on 21st June 1961, piloted by Captain Don Cartlidge, Channel Air Bridge's chief test pilot. For the 2-hour flight Freddie, Batt and Leftley were passengers in a chase plane, a Cessna 310D belonging to BUA. The Carvair spent the next two months being tested and fitted out until on 28th August one of Aviation Traders' men ran a forklift into the back of the plane while it was parked by the hangar. The mishap almost ripped off the rear portion of the fuselage, which was split almost entirely around its circumference. Freddie, boiling with rage, fired the man responsible on the spot, as G-ANYB was undergoing certification by the Air Registration Board at the time. Fortunately, Aviation Traders had built a mock-up from the airframe of a retired KLM C54B-1-DC, which had been stripped for spares. The mock-up came in handy as ATEL's engineers attached it to Yankee Bravo, and the ARB airworthiness test flights resumed a month later on 29th September.

While the Carvairs were being constructed, Channel Air Bridge suffered an enormous setback when the French and Germans refused to grant licences. Eventually the Germans relented and allowed cars and passengers, but no freight. As an alternative the company sought licences to Basel and Geneva in Switzerland, but not without BEA putting up an almighty fight. They were the most popular routes and, even before the first flights were operated, the number of flights was doubled to four a day. Eventually the French relented and a flight to Strasbourg was allowed, but only because the city's councillor for tourism lobbied hard for the service.

G-ANYB received its Certificate of Airworthiness on 30th January 1962 and was delivered to BUA. Keen to promote Channel Air Bridge, the name had been changed from 'Atalanta' to 'Golden Gate Bridge'. Eight other Carvairs would be named in this way using a play on the word 'bridge'. On 16th February 1962 Yankee Bravo flew a demonstration flight to Ostend, and the next day flew its first revenue flight from Southend to Malaga.

The second Carvair, G-ARSD (ATL.98-2), wasn't far behind. Named 'Chelsea Bridge', it commenced commercial service in April with a flight to Geneva. G-ARSF (ATL.98-3) was named 'Pont de L'Europe' and received its C of A on 3rd August, operating its inaugural flight to Calais four days later. The next Carvairs converted at Southend by ATEL were for customers, the first of which was Interocean Airways of Luxembourg. The Channel Air Bridge Carvairs were deployed on routes to Calais, Basle, Geneva, Rotterdam and Strasbourg during 1962. Quieter, smoother, faster and with a significantly increased payload capacity than the Bristol Freighter, the ATL.98 Carvair was a huge success, and increased the popularity of all the routes it served. As soon as the new aircraft were in service and the single entity, Channel Air Bridge, was operating, it became very profitable. Freddie knew the bonanza would last as long as the aircraft lasted, then it would likely be all over. He was determined to milk it for as long as he could. Then, on Friday 28th December 1962 at 11.04am, tragedy struck.

Sierra Foxtrot (G-ARSF) was making a routine approach into Rotterdam. It was snowing and on short finals the landing gear struck a 6-foot-high dyke, 800 feet short of the runway threshold. The aircraft rolled and the right wing became detached. It slid inverted for 700 feet before coming to rest. Of the 14 passengers and four crew, one crew member perished. The cause was determined as pilot error; the final stage of the approach was below the normal glide path, with insufficient power. However, the accident didn't hinder production of more Carvairs, as it had nothing to do with the technical characteristics of the aircraft.

Nonetheless, after months of commercial service some faults began to appear. Channel Air Bridge's Carvairs were plagued with engine problems. Bob Batt analysed what was going on and concluded that the short sectors to Calais and Ostend were causing premature engine wear. The Carvair's four Pratt & Whitney R2000-7M2s engines were never designed for such short sectors. Aviation Traders' customer airlines for the aircraft, such as Aer Lingus and Ansett, flew longer routes and didn't have the same problems. So Channel Air Bridge, which had become British United Air Ferries (BUAF) from January 1963, rescheduled its Carvairs for longer sectors and resumed flying the short hops with Bristol Freighters.

In the end, a total of 21 of the aircraft were built and sold. Despite always saying that the Accountant was his greatest technical achievement, many would argue that Freddie Laker's most successful aircraft engineering project was the ATL.98 Carvair.

## POSTSCRIPT

*The British United Carvair is now probably best known for appearing in the 1964 James Bond movie, Goldfinger. The movie villain's black and gold Rolls-Royce Phantom III is shown being loaded onto the Carvair for a flight to Geneva. During the Carvair's lifespan it was used by Prince Philip, King Hussein of Jordan, King Faisal, and Crown Prince Gustav of Sweden. Rock bands such as the Who and the Small Faces, and legendary rally driver Paddy Hopkirk – who won the Monte Carlo Rally for Team Mini Cooper – were also Carvair customers. And a rugby team once chartered a Carvair as they wanted to use the cavernous cargo bay as an airborne playing field.*

CHAPTER 13

# Power Struggles

## Freddie's back-stabbing tactics

1962

There was another major leap forward in January 1962 when BUA merged with of one of the larger remaining independents, British Air Services (BAS). BAS had a fleet of 43 aircraft and was controlled by another prominent shipping company, Peninsular & Oriental (P&O). The President of P&O, Sir Donald Anderson, hatched a plan with Myles Wyatt to merge their businesses. Anderson was adamant that Freddie Laker was not informed of the plan, partly because BAS was bringing with it the larger but heavily loss-making Silver City, the main competitor to Freddie's jealously guarded Channel Air Bridge. The merger came as a very nasty surprise to Freddie, and had him seething for weeks. He had little respect for the management of Silver City and made sure that its former managers would have little or no influence on the combined business.

British United Airways did not have the cash to buy it, so Sir Myles Wyatt decided to create his own acquisition currency in a remarkable piece of financial engineering. He created a new holding company called Air Holdings Ltd out of thin air and issued millions of new shares. He then used his newly created shares to swap for the entire share capital of both BUA and BAS. It had Freddie Laker gasping in admiration. Wyatt made Freddie a Director of the company on 1st March 1962.

It proved to be a major coup and made BUA about half the size of BEA. The new Air Holdings Ltd had combined assets of £20 million and 4,000 staff. It was the world's largest privately owned airline outside North America. The takeover wiped out cross-Channel air ferry competition at a stroke. Freddie's own ferry airline, Channel Air Bridge, had boomed alongside Silver City and the cross-Channel businesses were carrying a quarter of a million passengers a year.

After the takeover British United Airways had 95 aircraft carrying 1.7 million passengers, 131,000 cars and nearly 87,000 tons of freight a year. It was an astonishing achievement thanks to both the operating nous of Freddie Laker and the financial nous of Myles Wyatt, whom Freddie started to treat with a new respect. But with the new giant company, it was not all plain sailing.

It soon became clear that the new incarnation of BUA needed a strong chief executive to knit the group together and restore corporate order. That man was clearly not Myles Wyatt, and only Gerald Freeman and Freddie Laker were contenders for the job. Forty-nine-year-old Freeman had the best claim. He was a serious businessman and a very talented manager. Transair was the most profitable part of Airwork and his business was run efficiently with good systems and excellent attention to detail. The latest annual profits were £400,000, and it was one of the most profitable companies in Britain. Freddie, at 37 years old, was 12 years younger than Freeman and with a totally different style of management. He was also the new boy in the company. His aircraft operating business, Air Charter, equalled Freeman's for efficiency, but Freddie's spares and servicing business was a nightmare.

Late into the process Myles Wyatt suddenly decided that he would also like the job and threw his hat into the ring. Certainly the 57-year-old looked the part; he was a large man, 6 foot 2 and heavily built at 18 stone (252lb). He patronised London's most expensive tailors, and was a member of the establishment and a Commodore of the Royal Ocean Racing Club, which organised the Admiral's Cup. His 19-metre racing yacht *Bloodhound* – a three-time Fastnet Race winner – was eventually sold to the Royal family for Prince Philip in 1962. Wyatt had joined Airwork in 1934 and climbed to the top in quick order. But he had never really managed an operational business, and his skill lay in trading aircraft options, which he did very successfully. Wyatt's management style was to divide and rule; it is said that he invented the process, and there was no one better at it than him, including Freddie Laker. Wyatt liked to have private and informal consultations with his directors. He enjoyed good food and wine, often ending the working day with a tongue-loosening dinner. As one biographer described him: 'Wyatt was older than Laker, bigger, tougher, better educated, better connected, better bred and something of a bully.'

But everyone assumed that Gerald Freeman would come out on top and get the job. He was best qualified to do it and on the surface seemed to work well with Wyatt. Certainly Wyatt and Laker had never really got on, which made Freddie an unlikely choice for the top job.

Amazingly the three men were deputised by the BUA board to appoint one of themselves to the post. It was the most extraordinary recruitment process for such an important job. So to decide who would run the group the three men met in Gerald Freeman's swank apartment in Eaton Square.

Unsurprisingly, Wyatt immediately applied his divide-and-rule technique, and what emerged from the meeting was a complete fiasco. Wyatt quickly realised he could not do the job himself and withdrew from the race. He settled for what was really a non-executive chairman position with the promise of a knighthood from Duncan Sandys. It was quickly decided that Freeman would run the short-haul business and Freddie Laker the long-haul routes. Effectively the company would split itself into two in the same manner of BOAC and BEA.

With that decided, Wyatt wasted no time in telling the two men how they should structure their businesses. But both Freeman and Freddie demurred; the latter told Wyatt: "I'm not going to be your bum boy, Myles." Wyatt looked at him quizzically, having no idea what a 'bum boy' was. Freeman just rolled his eyes and wondered what the future held with these two characters in such senior management positions. Freeman, somewhat naively, left the meeting contented; he was happy to run the short-haul business, which would all be merged into Transair. But when the dust settled, both Wyatt and Freddie realised that Freeman had come out on top. The short-haul business was 80 per cent of BUA, and they realised simultaneously that they had effectively given the top job to Freeman and demoted each other to subsidiary roles.

So the two men met again secretly and effectively cast Freeman out. They agreed a secret deal that saw them split power as group managing director and executive chairman. Then they called Freeman back in and told him that the original idea wouldn't work and in future he would report to them both. It was a fait accompli and Freeman was rightfully bitter about the outcome of the power struggle. He would never share a room with either man again. Freeman let his feelings be known and it divided loyalties at the airline. It was certainly a shocking betrayal to deny the best man the job. It was not Freddie's finest hour, as Gerald Freeman was a very decent man who had been ruthlessly stabbed in the back by Freddie Laker.

Although Freddie had won the power struggle, as a consequence he had put himself firmly in bed with Myles Wyatt, a bed he would find almost immediately extremely uncomfortable. His tenure as Managing Director began on 11th May 1962, at a salary £3,500 a year, a generous pension, company car, and two per cent of the net profits.

There was a period of wary fencing between Wyatt and Freddie, the latter hoping that he would eventually succeed Wyatt. He found Wyatt's ways irksome, but decided to make the best of it, and initially sucked up to him. The two agreed that they would not discuss contentious issues at board meetings. He found Wyatt a useful intermediary in dealing with the shareholders, and asked him to teach him everything he knew about high finance and the City. Wyatt relished wheeling and dealing and big business, while Freddie simply loved aeroplanes. Wyatt duly obliged, and in turn tied invisible 'puppet strings' to Freddie, monitoring his every move. Wyatt placed his own spies in every subsidiary, men who reported to him alone.

Freddie fought back and appointed George Carroll as his deputy Managing Director. When the two men had first met they had formed an immediate bond. Carroll was a grammar school boy, and admired Freddie for his drive and ideas. The two squared up to Myles Wyatt, but Wyatt had got exactly what he wanted. In truth it was Wyatt who had won the power struggle, using Freddie as his pawn to do so. Eventually he would emerge as the only man left standing.

With Gerald Freeman gone and ensconced at home in Surrey nursing his wounds, Freddie was feeling pretty pleased with himself, although he had no particular reason to do so. He had ruthlessly stabbed Freeman in the back, the same man who only three years earlier had made Freddie a millionaire. Now it was just him and Wyatt who stood at the helm of Britain's third biggest airline.

It really was a period in Freddie Laker's career to be forgotten. He did not at the time act in the manner of a gentleman, but instead as a ruthless pirate scything a swathe through BUA's operating companies. He rationalised and cut wherever he went until there was a unified airline whose planes all had the same colours and the same brand on the sides. This included the formation of British United Air Ferries, which took place on 16th July 1962, although the merger would not be complete until March 1963. Freddie installed his trusted friend Douglas Whybrow to run it.

While it definitely had to be done, Freddie could have done things in a much more sympathetic and caring way. His next victim was effectively Wyatt. Before long Freddie had sidelined him too, and soon Wyatt was taking little part in the day-to-day running of the business. Freddie was far more knowledgeable about aeroplanes than Wyatt and his relationship with BUA's pilots and engineers made him all-powerful. As expected, before too long Freddie had come out on top.

## CHAPTER 14

# Enter the One-Eleven, Exit Laker

## The BUA years - Part 2

### 1962-1965

Despite being given a small number of scheduled route licences to Europe by the ATLB, the failure to obtain any routes to Asia caused Freddie to have a rethink about the VC10s. In May 1962 the original order for four aircraft was halved to just two of the long-haul planes; Freddie did, however, keep his options open for the other two.

He was still fighting for reciprocal rights from many of the Europeans. The Greeks were the first to rule against BUA and its planned service to Athens in December 1962. Paris put up rock-solid resistance, as did Milan, Zurich and Basel, so much so that by the summer of 1963 BUA was only flying four routes of the 12 it had been awarded by the British licensing authority. Services commenced to Barcelona, Palma, Tarbes and Genoa, all of which faced strong competition from BEA, which was seemingly determined to put BUA out of business. As a consequence, none of the routes made much money and only covered costs at the height of the summer season when the flights were full. Then BEA made renewed strenuous efforts to get the Genoa licence revoked. It was so tough that Freddie considered handing the routes back to the Government, but he was persuaded to stay the course by Minister of Aviation Julian Amery.

The short-haul scheduled services soon fell into loss and Freddie was forced to issue a profits warning to the City. He became uncharacteristically despondent and said: "Commercially, we should not have operated these services with our bookings for the season, but politically we had to use them." Profits that a couple of years before had been £2 million had fallen away to just under £800,000. However, he was soon making plans to defeat BEA. His response for the following season was a proper marketing campaign for the routes, combined with some of the first package holidays – a flight and hotel for a single price. He authorised nearly £500,000 on an advertising campaign with the theme 'Fly British' to cock a snook at BEA. He appeared in some of his own adverts and was becoming increasingly well known. *The Daily Express* newspaper took a shine to him and promoted his airline relentlessly. To get past the French veto on flying directly between London and Paris, Freddie came up with a typically novel solution. A year after it opened, he made good use of BUA's Victoria air terminal when BUA inaugurated its 'Silver Arrow' service on 26th May 1963. This was a collaboration between British Railways, the French national railway SNCF and BUA; passengers would travel first by rail to Gatwick, from Gatwick by plane to Le Touquet, and from Le Touquet into Paris by train. Freddie even persuaded the French to build a spur line from Le Touquet to Paris to make the 5-hour journey less arduous. At an unbeatable return fare of £10.9s, it was substantially less than any other alternative.

It was not long afterwards that the first flight of Freddie's eagerly awaited One-Eleven aircraft took place. He had been keeping a close watch on progress with his engineer's eye and had spent ample amounts of time at the BAC factory in Hurn. The future of BUA and his own reputation hung on the One-Eleven's success. The short-haul jet was to be the great white hope of the British Aviation industry and after BUA's launch order, Sir George Edwards had managed to secure orders for 60 more. Gabe 'Jock' Bryce, the One-Eleven's former chief test pilot, described the scene as he and co-pilot Mike Lithgow flew the aircraft for the very first time, late in the afternoon of 20th August 1963: "As we accelerated down the runway, there was a huge rainbow at the end of the runway, and we took off straight into it. So the omens looked good. Flew for about 20 minutes, then came in and landed safely just before the light began to fail."

Bryce could not have been more wrong. At 10.40am on 22nd October the prototype aircraft G-ASHG, already painted in its BUA livery, crashed after entering a deep irrecoverable stall during flight-testing. It had completed 52 successful flights and nothing seemed amiss. On the fateful 53rd flight it had already completed four successful stalls without any problems – the stalls were an important requirement for the One-Eleven's airworthiness certificate.

The pilot was the brilliant and celebrated Mike Lithgow, one of the most experienced test pilots in Britain. In 1953, he'd set a world air speed record in a Vickers Supermarine Swift F.4 of 737.7mph.

The early test flights had given the pilots immense confidence in the One-Eleven. On its 47th flight, a stall testing programme began. Stalling an aircraft is allowing the plane to decelerate while pulling the nose up until it falls to a speed at which the lift generated by the wing suddenly drops and becomes much less than the weight of the plane ... and the plane then stalls. Normally the nose of the plane will drop, building up speed again until it recovers from the stall of its own accord.

The programme of testing had reached the point of identifying the handling characteristics at the point of stall and establishing the precise stalling speeds at various centres of gravity. By flight 53, the test programme had been very successful. The One-Eleven had already completed four successful stalls and recoveries and they now progressed into the territory of extreme characteristics. As part of this testing, the centre of gravity was moved back to its furthest point.

That morning Lithgow was the pilot in command, as Bryce was busy with VC10 work. He put the One-Eleven, G-ASHG, into a fifth stable stall from 16,000 feet, just like the 40 or more stalls that he and Jock Bryce had carried out before. The aircraft began to drop from the sky, almost level, at a rate of 10,000 feet per minute. Lithgow did everything he could to save the out-of-control aircraft, but in little more than 90 seconds it crashed into open farmland near Chicklade in Wiltshire and was almost totally destroyed by fire. Captain Lithgow and the other six members of the flight test crew all lost their lives. The news reached Hurn at around 12.15pm. Brian Trubshaw – who later found fame as Concorde's test pilot – called from Wisley.

"You'd better get across here quickly – I think we've lost the One-Eleven," he told his colleagues.

The One-Eleven project was in crisis and the aircraft's future was now in jeopardy. That evening the analysis began. Lord Portal, Chairman of BAC, took personal charge, but the immediate concern was for the families of the men who had died.

The following day the data recorder was analysed and a picture of what had gone wrong emerged. In paying tribute to Mike Lithgow, senior BAC test pilot Gabe 'Jock' Bryce described what happened.

Lithgow had begun the manoeuvre at a speed one-and-one-third times the stalling speed and then decelerated at 1 knot per second until the 'G' meter – the instrument that records the amount of lift being generated by the airflow over the wings – read '1'. The lift was then equal to the weight. At this point, the One-Eleven was docile. As he eased the stick back, pulling the nose up, the moment came when the aircraft entered the stall and the lift available would no longer support its weight. Gravity then took over. The One-Eleven was now flying below its stalling speed, tilted nose up at 25 degrees above the horizontal. Lithgow reduced the speed even further and the One-Eleven began to sink rapidly.

It did not pitch forward on its nose, as had been expected, but continued to fall out of the sky with its nose tilted slightly upwards. When Lithgow pushed the stick forward there was no response. He pulled up the flaps and banked the aeroplane steeply, first to starboard, then to port, then to starboard again, pushing all the time on the elevators. The nose tilted forward, but only very slightly, and the elevators had very little effect. The angle of descent meant that the wing was shielding the tail plane and starving it of airflow, so the elevators had nothing to act on but disturbed, turbulent air. There was enough airflow coming up under the tail plane from the downward velocity to blow the elevators fully up and keep them there. The aircraft was locked in a 'deep stall'.

There was one more chance – the application of full power. For the next 15 seconds Mike held the throttles wide open. The only result was a rapid pitch up of the nose, causing him eventually to pull off the power. All the engine power available could do no more than reduce the rate of descent. It could never effect recovery – the drag remained greater than the thrust.

The deep stall phenomenon was something that Lithgow had never experienced before; in fact, it had only ever previously been encountered once, the year earlier. No one could have foreseen it and the stall was totally unexpected. This was the first accident to be attributed to this phenomenon, peculiar to T-tailed aircraft. The cause of the accident was officially stated as: 'The One-Eleven entered into a deep stall condition, recovery from which was impossible due to the wings blocking the airflow over the elevators on the T-tail.'

After the thorough investigation, everyone returned to work on redesigning the One-Eleven to correct its flaws. The wind tunnel work on the aircraft was reviewed and further tests carried out; models were built and launched from helicopters at various flying altitudes. The leading edge of the wing was modified, causing the wing root to stall more fully, ensuring that when the pilots carried out further stall tests on the One-Eleven it would develop a pronounced nose-drop. The original elevators were discarded and a new powered system designed. As the T-tail design of the One-Eleven had helped to create this aerodynamic phenomenon, to his credit Sir George Rogers, in a bid to avoid further loss of life, shared what they had learned from the One-Eleven's accident recorders and wind tunnel information with Lockheed, Boeing and Douglas. The Americans were all working on aircraft designs with a similar T-shaped tailplane design. After approximately two months, flight-testing quietly resumed. The test pilots were initially expressly forbidden to repeat the stall manoeuvres, as at that stage the fault was yet to be corrected. 'We're back in business' BAC reported to the press. But it wasn't quite so simple.

Some months later, on 18th March 1964, another One-Eleven bound for BUA, G-ASJB, made a heavy landing at its base at Wisley, sliding more than 1,000 feet along the runway. The aircraft was badly damaged but fortunately no one was hurt this time. The cause was found to be pilot error. Fearing press and public reaction to the second accident, BAC issued a statement that the accident had been caused by a crosswind. Freddie backed them up, even though he knew it wasn't true.

Eventually stall testing had to resume, but a third flight-testing crash, of another One-Eleven, G-ASJD, was to test Freddie's resolve. After the earlier fatal accident, the One-Elevens were specially modified with a new powered elevator and modified wing leading edge, and in order for the aircraft to recover in the event of a deep stall it was also fitted with a large tail parachute. The reverse thrust actuators were also altered so that they could provide upward thrust in the air and pull the One-Eleven into a nose-down pitch.

On 20th August 1964, the anniversary of the first flight, G-ASJD was engaged in stalling trials when the pilot mistakenly concluded that the plane was in a deep stall and deployed the parachute, while also using the specially adapted reverse thrust. But the aircraft had not stalled and was dragged down by the parachute. Unable to jettison the parachute, the aircraft landed with its wheels up on Salisbury Plain, lying on its belly in the middle of a field. Its BUA livery was crudely covered up with brown paper and sticky tape as it was recovered.

Initially, the plane appeared to have suffered remarkably little damage, but upon inspection the flaps and the bottom of the fuselage were severely damaged. So the wings, tail and engines were removed and the aircraft was transported back to Hurn by road.

By now the One-Eleven was being referred to by some as the new 'Comet', the world's first jet airliner, which had its reputation irreparably tarnished by a serious of accidents.

The news of the latest One-Eleven accident reached Freddie as he was holidaying on his yacht, coincidentally with Geoffrey Knight. It was Knight's birthday and during that evening, while consuming copious amounts of champagne, Knight took the call. He told Freddie about the accident – the One-Eleven project seemed doomed. Freddie's apparent response was, "You cannot have two crashes." With the cause found to be pilot error, Freddie continued to keep the faith, when others may have faltered.

But while BUA's European short-haul routes were facing all kinds of problems, the long-haul routes to Africa were starting to prosper, thanks to the arrival of the new Vickers VC10 four-engined jet aircraft. At a combined cost of more than £10 million, the two planes were to be put to work on BUA's African routes. To boost profitability, Freddie concentrated on developing these company operations, focusing on under-served countries like Sierra Leone, Uganda and Gambia.

The first new VC10, G-ASIW, arrived on 11th September 1964, and was proudly shown off at the Farnborough Air Show. Under the terms of its licence, and to protect BOAC from competition, BUA could not offer a 1st Class service, so Freddie had a large cargo door installed near the front of the plane on the port (left) side, and where wealthy passengers would have sat in deluxe accommodation, there would be crates full of freight. Flying cargo wouldn't be as lucrative as flying 1st Class passengers, but it filled a gap. India Whisky completed an eight-day series of proving and demonstration flights in Africa, carrying both Freddie and his Rolls-Royce Silver Cloud, the massive vehicle only just fitting through the cargo door. Commercial flights began on 1st October with a bread-and-butter trooping flight to the port city of Aden. The second VC10, G-ASIX, arrived a month later.

The two VC10 jets replaced the old piston and turbo-prop aircraft such as the Britannias and DC-6s. They were smooth and comfortable over a long flight and flew twice as fast as their predecessors. But they were 30 times more expensive. For a long time BUA was the only airline running scheduled jet services to Africa, and scooped up much of the high-margin business as a result. As soon as the African VC10 service was established, BUA also won the rights to fly to South America. BOAC was losing money on its South American routes and had applied for a £1.25 million-a-year Government subsidy for four years to cover its losses and keep the route open, BOAC's chairman, Sir Giles Guthrie, having declared the VC10 to be uneconomic. Minister of Aviation Julian Amery turned BOAC down flat, but when the company called his bluff and ceased the service, Amery asked BUA to take it up with the Government's backing. He said: "It deserves and will receive the Government's full support."

Freddie quickly realised that BOAC's decision to withdraw from South America was an opportunity not to be missed. Although the routes had been loss-makers for BOAC, so overwhelming were their attraction that Freddie immediately made plans to start flying as soon as BOAC stopped. It was the first time an independent airline was offered the chance to operate a major scheduled international route to Brazil, Argentina, Uruguay and Chile. *The Daily Express* ran the news on its front page with the headline 'Rolling down to Rio'. Buckingham Palace also announced that Prince Philip, Duke of Edinburgh, would fly BUA on his upcoming tour of South America.

A new licence was quickly granted and it gave BUA the right to operate as many flights a week as it liked, with 1st Class included, thus negating the need to carry freight. Amery helped where he could and allowed BUA to retire its VC10s from trooping contracts to place them on the South American routes, using the slower and less comfortable Britannias for the troops.

But then came a shock: the Conservatives lost the General Election to Labour and Julian Amery left his post. When he had originally announced that BUA had been awarded the South American routes, he had been roundly criticised by the opposition party. Labour accused Amery of sharp practice and undermining the operations of BOAC, stating that a Labour Government would be in no way bound by this 'hurried and highly questionable deal'. A senior Labour figure also said that the deal was corrupt and had been cooked up by BUA's shareholders and the Tory Government. Freddie feared that the South American licences would be taken away and dreaded receiving the morning post. His riposte was to inaugurate the routes before Labour could stop them; he figured that, once started, it would be harder to close them down, and the first passenger-carrying proving flight took off on 12th October. BUA's VC10s would be flying in competition with the Boeing 707s of the rival American airlines, with a start date for the first scheduled service proper pencilled in for 5th November. No letter arrived in the post, and with that the Labour opposition faded away. After the trial flights, the new Government even confirmed the licence with no objections. BOAC's managers were astounded.

The Brazilian and Argentinian governments saw the withdrawal of BOAC as an opportunity to reduce the frequency of flights to their territories. A reciprocal designation from the South Americans for BUA was going to be tricky. It had been clear from the outset that BUA was not going to be welcomed by the South Americans and there would be plenty of bureaucratic corruption to overcome.

However, the British Government refused to stand for this and sent a delegation to Sao Paulo – led by Neil Marten, a junior Aviation Minister, and including Freddie Laker – to negotiate terms. What the route really needed, and what Freddie wanted, was three flights a week. When he realised that he was going to be turned down, Freddie lay down on a sofa at the side of the room. When the leader of the Brazilian delegation asked if he was unwell, Freddie replied, "When you are about to be raped you might as well lie down and enjoy it." The Brazilians were deeply insulted by Freddie's comment. They were already upset that BUA had conducted a promotional tour of South America using a VC10, carrying both a sales team and Freddie's Rolls-Royce. Nevertheless, Freddie got his way. It wouldn't be the last time that he would use that negotiating ploy. Only a matter of weeks after BOAC's service to Rio de Janeiro ended, the route was operational again and flown by BUA.

The new Minister of Aviation was Roy Jenkins. He was not a fan of Freddie Laker and the two often clashed. Freddie went on the attack against the minister on a number of subjects, taking great offence when Jenkins wrongly maligned Freddie's approach to safety. But Jenkins was a fair-minded man and, once he saw that it was a success, he gave BUA a 15-year licence for the London-Rio route.

Jenkins had good reason to be fond of BUA. It was the lead airline for the new British-built VC10 aircraft, on which thousands of jobs depended. Meanwhile BOAC was conspicuously buying Boeing 707s, ignoring the British-built plane.

BUA had a stroke of luck in 1965 when Brazilian airline Panair do Brasil went under, reducing competition. When the Brazilian Government threatened to revoke BUA's licence, Jenkins said he would ban Varig, Brazil's premier international carrier, from flying to London. The dispute was quickly resolved.

By the third year of operation the route started to make money and proved that a private airline could take over a loss-making route and turn it into a success, even against great odds. BUA's South American performance had a big impact on future Government aviation policy for years to come; the private airlines had come of age and were a force to be reckoned with. BOAC realised that it had made a huge mistake in giving up the routes, and had been made a fool of by Freddie Laker. This triggered a vendetta against Freddie that became integrated into BOAC's culture, irrespective of who its top management was.

Following its South American success, BUA applied for routes within the British Isles, the playground of BEA and Harold Bamberg's British Eagle airline. But Bamberg was so fed up with being squeezed continually by BEA and the British Government that he gave up Eagle's routes altogether in February 1965. BUA promptly applied for Eagle's domestic routes, but this prompted Bamberg to resume the flights. The Air Transport Licensing Board resolved the dispute by allowing BUA to fly to Scotland from Gatwick, and BEA and Eagle to fly to Scotland from Heathrow. BUA would use the first of its new BAC One-Elevens on the routes.

The first One-Eleven had been delivered on 22nd January 1965, and on 9th April, after a series of proving flights, it entered service for BUA. The inaugural commercial flight of a BAC One-Eleven was from Gatwick to Genoa. Lord Douglas of Kirtleside, former Marshall of the Royal Air Force, cut the ribbon, with BAC's Geoffrey Knight and BUA's Managing Director Freddie Laker in attendance. The One-Eleven went on to become the most successful British airliner ever, with 235 examples built. The aircraft's very existence would be forever entwined with Freddie Laker.

After three years as Managing Director and trying to turn BUA into a fully integrated and well-managed airline operating modern planes, Freddie began to feel frustrated. It was a thankless task, and there were 35 separate companies under his umbrella for which he was responsible. He was becoming increasingly personally disenchanted. He was not happy as a paid employee as he had no personal financial stake in the venture. He regarded himself as the creator of what was probably the biggest success story in aviation since the war, but although he was getting the recognition he was not getting the reward. He was bored and tired of the constant bickering of Sir Myles Wyatt. More than once he had threatened to resign, but could never quite bring himself to do it.

It just wasn't the same any more. He'd effectively fallen out with Douglas Whybrow over how British United Air Ferries fitted within BUA back in the summer of 1963. Freddie was heavily engaged with BUA's main scheduled service operations, and Whybrow, among others, felt that Freddie, in his lofty status as Managing Director, was becoming more remote from his old pals. The bickering increased and their exchanges became more and more acrimonious. They therefore met to thrash out their differences. In a meeting that took nearly a whole night, neither saw to eye to eye over the future of Whybrow's division, BUAF. Freddie didn't think the air ferries would ever make money. He had a £20 million fleet of new aircraft to think about, whereas Whybrow had a fleet of Carvairs and old Bristols worth less than £1 million.

Another source of friction with Whybrow came in the form of BUA's new headquarters, Portland House, an ultra-modern skyscraper in London's Victoria. Whybrow was dead against it, especially the expense of the costly futuristic sales offices provided for BUAF. The design featured decorative lighting strips, clocks and world maps. He had been highly critical of the move, which he felt went against the trend – airlines were moving out of central London rather than into it. An extra floor for BUAF's expansion was taken, but it would never be occupied. Ultimately Freddie offered Whybrow the job of Chief Commercial Executive of BUA and Commercial Director of BUAF. Reluctantly Whybrow took the job, but his relationship with Freddie was never the same again.

In October 1965 Freddie gave a lecture to the Royal Aeronautical Society, where he unleashed his venom at the Government and its policies. He called its approach to licensing and International negotiations as a 'fine specimen of Victoriana'. He bemoaned the lack of public investment in British aviation, blaming the politicians who were in his mind 'restrictionist and anti-liberal', and had hamstrung the private sector. "It is a young industry, it should be free," Freddie told the audience.

He was also frustrated with Chairman Myles Wyatt's rejection of his idea to start a transatlantic service. In a forerunner of what would eventually be called 'Skytrain', Freddie tried to interest the BUA board in a 'cheap and cheerful' North Atlantic service. He was strongly supported on the BUA board by Alan Bristow, who remembered: "I was in favour of it, but it was always a marginal thing and the shareholders didn't care for it. Even if it worked flawlessly you would have made three per cent gross."

When the idea was finally rejected, Freddie made his plans to leave.

# CHAPTER 15

# The Unthinkable

## Freddie's darkest hour

1965

By the end of 1965, Freddie Laker was getting tired of playing second fiddle at British United Airways (BUA) to its overbearing chairman, the now knighted Sir Myles Wyatt. Wyatt had been knighted in July 1963 in the Queen's Birthday Honours list. Freddie had never worked for anyone and he reported to Wyatt mainly by accident when his company had been taken over by BUA.

Sir Myles Wyatt and Freddie had come to terms on the running of BUA between them in February 1962. They agreed that Wyatt as chairman would look after the shareholders and Freddie as managing director would run the company. The two men could not have been more opposite – they were like chalk and cheese. Wyatt was as smoothly urbane as Freddie was brutally blunt. That the two men had worked together for so long was a miracle, but now that time was nearing its end. The only thing that had kept them together for so long was some sort of latent mutual respect. Freddie had to admit that he had learned some valuable lessons at the feet of Wyatt; he appreciated that Wyatt had deep City connections and knew how to cosy up to merchant bankers. Likewise Wyatt respected Freddie's ability to get things done operationally. But ultimately, Wyatt's micromanagement style rankled Freddie – he was unused to such close scrutiny of his actions. Similarly Freddie's coarse brashness ate away at Wyatt's notions of how business in the civilised world should be done.

Freddie had almost walked out of BUA midway through 1964 but thought better of it. However, by mid-1965 he had had his fill of Wyatt, and their relationship was increasingly peppered with disagreements. Alan Bristow, who was close to both men, observed the gradual disintegration of what had started off as a promising partnership. Bristow said it was Freddie's talent for self-publicity that really grated with Wyatt. Wyatt once told Bristow: "You get the impression from reading the newspapers that Freddie Laker owns this company."

However, the part of the group that Freddie was personally responsible for was beginning to lose money after a net profit of £792,936 in 1963 and £523,130 a year later. In 1965, BUA posted a loss of £211,130. Freddie was not unsurprisingly fed up with pushing mud uphill with a spoon. He'd seen the first One-Elevens and VC10s into service and he was now ready to leave. The Wyatt/Laker arrangement had run perfectly well and to the satisfaction of the latter for a number of years, but in the spring of 1965 he decided that he was going to quit BUA. In early July, with the problems mounting at BUA, Freddie resigned, his departure timed to come into effect at the end of the year. It was agreed that he would leave on 31st December, but the timing and method of making his departure known to the outside world were yet to be decided. Even so, Wyatt had requested that Freddie stay on the board of Air Holdings Ltd as an expert on aeronautical and technical matters. For his services he would receive a substantial salary of £5,000 plus expenses, and a pension that would cost Air Holdings another £800 a year.

From that point, Freddie had one foot out of the door of BUA and half an eye on the future. He continued to work full on and people doubted whether he would in fact leave when the time came. Wyatt's greatest fear was which of them the board of directors would pick for the top job if given a straight choice. But Wyatt had nothing to fear – Freddie had other plans for the future.

At the time, the 43-year-old Freddie and his wife Joan lived together with their two teenage children, Elaine and Kevin, in a spacious house called Charters on The Ridge, near Epsom in Surrey. Charters, which the Lakers had built themselves, was idyllic and adjoined the RAC's Woodcote Park country club and golf course. They holidayed on Freddie's first yacht, aptly named King. Seventeen-year-old Kevin Laker was the apple of his father's eye and his Dad had big plans for his future; he intended to set up a business with both of them in partnership. Freddie remembered: "I resigned from BUA to go into the airline business with my boy Kevin; we were also going into the holiday tour business and buy a couple of hotels and all that."

But that was for the future and young Kevin, when not at school, whiled the time away with his friends, many of whom came from the other side of the tracks. Over the road from The Ridge were the less salubrious homes of families with somewhat lower incomes. Kevin became friendly with a young lad named John Jones, and the two became inseparable. John Jones remembers those days well: "Kevin was about a year and a half younger than me. But we'd been mates since we were about 14 years old. He was as wild as I was wild, but he was settling down and becoming more mature as he got older." Nobody knew then that Kevin was probably dyslexic. Despite being coached at school after numerous stand-up fights with his parents, he was eventually sent away to a boarding school. This didn't help and, at his wit's end, Freddie, who had grown fearful of his son's wild and rebellious streak, sent Kevin to London to work for John Plumer & Partners, his insurance company. It had the desired effect, and after less than a year Kevin's behaviour dramatically improved.

Elaine Laker also remembers those days vividly: "My father saw so much of himself in Kevin. Kevin was so like him both physically and in character. When Kevin was very young they would sit and build model aeroplanes together and then they were in the garage building go-karts. Both were very mechanically minded and loved machines. Kevin was an absolute speed merchant – he had so many accidents I can tell you, but they were minor."

John Jones worked in a bank in Battersea and almost became a member of the Laker family – he would often go to their house and sit down for supper cooked by Joan. He and Kevin Laker both shared a love of cars, as Jones recalled: "We would be in the garage mucking around building go-karts or whatever. Then I got my driving licence and Kevin would come around with me after I had passed my test. When Kevin got his provisional licence, I would be his qualified driver accompanying him on the L-plates." Then Freddie bought his son a Morgan three-wheeler, which he could drive on his provisional licence, followed by a Reliant Robin three-wheeler. The bizarre three-wheelers fell into the category of a motorcycle and sidecar, so someone with a provisional licence could drive them unaccompanied. Jones remembers that the cars were kept on the road by the mechanics at British United Airways. Both vehicles were unreliable and the Morgan used to strip the cogs in its gearbox every other week as it was raced up and down the Dorking bypass. Eventually, the absurdly dangerous Reliant Robin was rolled over on the bypass, with seemingly no ill effects for the occupants.

As soon as he turned 17, Kevin took to the road. He passed his driving test first time and became a true speed demon. His wealthy father indulged him with a red Austin Healey Sprite. In those days it was perhaps the ultimate four-wheeled transport for a young tearaway, the car of every 17-year-old's dreams. Freddie had been careful in his choice of the Sprite. It was a soft-top sports car that had its two headlights sticking up out of the bonnet, hence its nickname of 'frogeye' Sprite. But while the car may have looked the part, it only had a 948cc engine of a little over 40 horsepower, its 0-60mph time was more than 20 seconds, and it struggled to reach a top speed of 80mph. It was a marvellous springtime for the two teenagers, as Jones remembered: "Once he'd passed his test, we would drive all over the place in this thing to parties."

And then it all ended suddenly in the most tragic of circumstances, as John Jones recalled many years later: "We went to a party in Dorking on a Saturday night in July 1965. The party was at Anne Dunlop's house. My parents were away, so afterwards Kevin was planning to bring Angela, his girlfriend, back to my place. When it got late I went home first, with Kevin following in the Sprite. He left with a guy called Adrian Birdseed, who we called 'Chick'." But Kevin never arrived at Jones's house, as he recalls: "I don't know what happened, we never really found out." He continues: "It appears that Kevin went round the first corner of the Mickelham bends, a tricky section of the A24 south of Leatherhead, and something caused him to lose control of the car. It spun round and crossed over to the opposite carriageway so that Kevin was facing the oncoming traffic. A van drove straight into his side of the car, right where Kevin was sitting." Kevin Laker was taken to Redhill Hospital in a bad way with a punctured lung. Adrian Birdseed was miraculously unharmed. Fifty years ago a punctured lung was a serious injury and not easily treated. Kevin was put into intensive care, barely alive.

The police tracked down Freddie and Joan Laker who were in Genoa, Italy, for a few days holiday. Freddie kept his new yacht, the 'Kevela', there under the eye of the BUA station engineer. He used his connections to charter a plane to get them home that night. It was almost dawn by the time the Lakers arrived at John Jones's house.

Jones said: "They came and knocked on my door and Freddie just said, 'What the hell has happened?'" Freddie, Joan and Elaine went up to Redhill Hospital to see Kevin, but he died very shortly afterwards. Elaine remembered: "You could see it was very, very serious; he was yellow and there were tubes everywhere. Thirty-six hours later he was dead."

It was truly the most terrible blow for Freddie Laker. He described himself as 'raging at the world', trying to make some sense of his loss. He recalled many years later: "I kept trying to find an explanation. I sat for hours in churches, just thinking, waiting. But nothing ever happened, no explanation ever came, I never understood." Some say the hammer blow of losing his son and all his dreams caused Freddie to become permanently unbalanced and they believe he was never the same person again. After the post-mortem the undertakers delivered Kevin's coffin to the Laker's house before the funeral, where it lay in the dark dining room with the curtains closed. Between Kevin's death and the funeral, Freddie took to the bottle to ease the raw pain. After getting through a bottle of wine by lunchtime, he polished off another in the afternoon, then went to the local pub until midnight. Freddie was utterly inconsolable with grief, and it was the only way he could cope. Joan was not far behind, but with her strength of character she wore it somewhat better.

Freddie and John Jones conducted an aviation-style investigation into the circumstances of the accident. But they never discovered what had happened that night on the Dorking bypass, as Jones says: "Freddie and I took paint samples off the cars that we thought had been involved and there was a guy who was a real bad piece of work and he was involved somehow, but we never pinned it down." The best theory is that Kevin was racing his friends back home and was nudged in the back, causing him to lose control of his car.

On the evening before Kevin's funeral, Freddie finally cracked. Alan Bristow came over to comfort Joan in her husband's absence; he had heard of Freddie's absences and thought it was best that someone was with Joan, so he came over from his home at nearby Ashtead. Bristow often flew his Widgeon helicopter to the Laker's home, deliberately landing it on the back lawn with the rotor blade inches away from the Laker's bedroom window. Freddie was the only one who didn't see the funny side of it. That evening Bristow thought it prudent to leave the helicopter at home.

When Freddie arrived home that night shortly before 1.00am, Bristow put him to bed after a large tumbler of brandy and a long chat. On the morning of the funeral the undertaker's hearse arrived early in the morning and Kevin's coffin was loaded up for its last journey. Freddie, Joan and Elaine, together with Alan Bristow, saw the coffin off, then ate breakfast silently around the kitchen table. There was really nothing left to be said. What had happened was unimaginable, inexplicable and inescapable.

On a wider front, Kevin Laker's death had far-reaching consequences. His death was a tragedy that could not be reconciled, that time didn't heal. All the Laker family could do was cope from day to day, which Freddie did to the end of his life. He would often go to where Kevin was buried, in secluded parkland. He'd sit on a seat there and talk to him.

Neither Freddie nor Joan ever got over Kevin's untimely death; it was a void in their lives from then on. In fact, never a day went by for the rest of his life that Freddie did not remember his son. "You have to live with it, it is your problem and you have to stay with it," he would say. John Jones coped by telling himself that it had never happened. He carried on his relationship with the Laker family as if Kevin was still there, as he remembered: "I was a young man of 18 years old and I had lost my best mate and I did not feel like going down the pub or going out at all in the evening, so I would do what I had always done, which is walk across the field from my house to the Lakers' house and sit down and have supper with them. I must have reminded them of Kevin, so they were happy to have me around."

Freddie Laker was 43 when Kevin died. He was an extremely wealthy man by the standards of the day. He had long ago left behind his impoverished background. He had all the things that money could buy, a beautiful home, a stud farm, a string of racehorses and a yacht, but it all meant nothing. The shattering loss of Kevin had flung Freddie into a pit of despair and all the ideas for the new business that he and Kevin were to run were scrapped – it was just too raw. After a few weeks of idleness and grief, Freddie pulled himself back together and went back to work at BUA.

The following account of what took place when Freddie returned to work is taken from Freddie's own report, written for Sir Nicholas Cayzer. However, it may well have been sanitised to make Freddie look better and to damage Wyatt.

At the beginning of August, rumours were flying around BUA that Myles Wyatt was taking advantage of Freddie's absence. He was short-circuiting Freddie, making executive decisions without consultation and generally being disloyal to his managing director. It was not the first time that Wyatt had gone behind Freddie's back; he had done exactly the same thing when he bought the shares of British Aviation Services – owners of Silver City – three years earlier. The seeds of war had already been sown back then. The most serious rumour was that Wyatt was secretly negotiating with Jack Jones – the owner of Channel Airways Ltd – to buy his company or a majority shareholding. Channel was a small independent airline based at Southend Airport and in trouble, and Freddie had already rejected a rescue; he didn't care for Jack Jones and declared that BUA was not interested. He declined to make any sort of offer, calling it a 'complete bust'. He had kept the board of BUA and Myles Wyatt fully informed, giving them his reasons for rejecting a deal. Freddie knew the operation well and had no interest, not even its nuisance value to Air Holdings or BUA.

While Freddie was away Wyatt had spoken to Jack Wiseman about Jones and the deal, sufficiently to give Wiseman the idea that BUA was interested. Wiseman asked Freddie if this was so, and Freddie replied, "No, I haven't heard of it." Freddie dismissed the rumour as malicious, until the evening of Monday 15th November.

At 5.30pm Freddie was in Wyatt's office talking generally when Wyatt handed him a grey folder, saying, "I'd like you to read this overnight – it will surprise you."

Freddie didn't look at the folder and its contents until early the following morning while eating his breakfast. He quickly noted the words 'several weeks ago' before reading on that Jones had approached Wyatt, who had agreed that under the greatest of secrecy he would investigate the possibility of buying his companies. In that moment Freddie realised that all the rumours had in fact been true.

To Freddie this demonstrated the lack of confidence that Wyatt had in him. It was a great personal blow that, at such a late stage of their association, Wyatt had thought it necessary to keep secrets from him, especially when members of his own staff at Southend knew as well. He came to a split-second conclusion that he and Wyatt had lived through a life of lies. Freddie scrawled a hasty resignation letter that was typed by his secretary, Mrs Jarvis. At around 11.00am that morning the letter, together with the folder, was sent to Myles Wyatt in the internal mail. And with that, Freddie cleared his desk and left. His letter informed Wyatt that he could no longer continue with his duties at Air Holdings Group because he could not tolerate the 'hole in the corner' way of life between them. He had no wish to fight or argue about the rights or wrongs. Freddie's mental make-up made him unable to compromise on many things, and a betrayal like the one he had just endured was not negotiable. He let Wyatt know that he had left his company car at Gatwick, from where they could collect it.

In less than an hour the news had reached Sir Nicholas Cayzer, and he immediately sought to track down Freddie, who was in the Eccentric Club in Ryder Street drowning his sorrows. Sir Nicholas begged Freddie not to take precipitous action until they had talked. They arranged to meet at 5.30pm in privacy, away from Portland House. They talked for more than two hours and Cayzer somehow convinced Freddie that he should endeavour to meet with Wyatt and at least resolve their problems.

After a brief phone call the next morning a summit was arranged for 3.00pm at Portland House. Wyatt couldn't see why Freddie had taken offence. Freddie conceded that in normal circumstances the chairman could negotiate in secret, but he and Wyatt had made a pact not to. As far as Freddie was aware it had never happened before. He couldn't understand why he was suddenly not good enough to negotiate for what he thought was a two-bit operation. He had after all been good enough to act for the company and take the lead in negotiations with other companies like HCA, Bristow, SCAL, Jersey, Leroy and Whitehall, and buy new aircraft on behalf of BUA. Wyatt apologised. "I made an error of judgement," he told Freddie. "There is and never has been a lack of confidence, and if it has hurt you I'm sorry because that was not the intention." To Freddie this was a very handsome apology. In reply he said that it had never been his intention to get Wyatt or Sir Nicholas Cayzer to apologise or lick his boots – it was all a matter of principle and integrity that could not be compromised.

But Wyatt was economical with the truth when he explained to Freddie what he had been up to. Jones had said that any deal would have to be conducted in complete secrecy. Under no circumstances was Freddie Laker to enter the negotiations, and he did not want anyone nosing around Southend. Wyatt told Freddie that he was the first person that had been told, and as soon as Wyatt had been released from his promise he had handed the folder to Freddie. Freddie asked Wyatt if anyone else had known. Wyatt said no, not even Richard Cayzer. It was a barefaced lie. Wyatt and Freddie discussed how they could move forward, by delaying the purchase of Channel Airways until after December when Freddie would no longer be managing director. Freddie wouldn't agree to this – he would still be the expert on the AHL board, and would still need to look the deal over, and that might result in fouling it up. Between them they agreed a plan that Wyatt would phone Jack Jones and tell him that Freddie Laker, as the AHL expert, would be in charge. Freddie assured him that he would not deliberately sabotage the deal. The following day Freddie rang Wyatt and said he could not agree with the proposal because it was only a method for him to compromise on his principles, something he could not do. Freddie's letter of resignation stood.

Freddie had a number of appointments that he was still required to honour and that he agreed to fulfil. Wyatt and Freddie met one last time on 19th November. Wyatt wanted Freddie to stay until the end of the year, but Freddie wouldn't agree to this. Finally it was arranged between them that Freddie would go to Las Palmas and stay out of the country for a week while Wyatt dealt with the shareholders.

That evening Freddie was at the flat of Eric Rylands of Skyways – he and Rylands went all the way back to the Berlin Airlift. They were about to leave for the Guild of Air Pilots & Air Navigators (GAPAN) annual general meeting when Freddie's secretary rang – the cat was out of the bag. Joan, keen to protect her husband's position and angry at how he had been treated, had telephoned Arthur Brennard, the news editor of the *Sunday Express*, and told him that Freddie Laker had walked out of BUA. The newsman smelled a very juicy exclusive. Freddie immediately telephoned Wyatt at home and apologised, assuring him that he would try and play it down. However, the story would not go away; Freddie begged Brennard not to publish what he knew, but Brennard refused. Eventually they agreed he could write a story, but it would be vetted and Wyatt would be asked for his comments. Privately, Freddie told the author that if he came out of it grey he would spit back at Wyatt because he was right and had behaved impeccably at all times. Later, Freddie called Sir Nicholas Cayzer and thanked him for his help and counsel, and told him he could not carry on. Freddie asked Cayzer to make sure that Wyatt did not start a smear campaign against him or he would 'slay Wyatt'.

Freddie left for Las Palmas, but by complete coincidence the VC10 carrying him to the Canary Islands turned out to be flying Richard Cayzer back to the UK. So as they crossed paths in Las Palmas, Freddie felt duty bound to inform him of the position. Richard Cayzer's version of what he had known about the events turned out to be remarkable. Cayzer had been aware of the deal despite Wyatt having told Freddie that no one knew; in fact, he had said to Wyatt, "Will you tell Freddie?" Wyatt had replied, "Yes, I will tell Freddie." Furthermore it turned out that Richard Cayzer had been to Southend to see Jack Jones and his organisation, assuming that Freddie knew. Freddie was shown a file with private correspondence that proved his suspicions about Wyatt. The secret wasn't a secret at all, and at least three people had known about the negotiation. Freddie never spoke to Wyatt again and never returned to the BUA offices at Portland House. From then on he and Wyatt aired their differences through the newspapers.

In 1965, and throughout the life of Freddie Laker, there are a number of conflicting stories that this book and its writers have endeavoured to resolve. These stories more often than not were concocted by Freddie himself.

There is another version, a more sensationalised account of the events surrounding Freddie's falling out with Sir Myles Wyatt. Freddie himself repeated this version when he was in his late 70s. It was also recounted by Alan Bristow, and is told below. Some of the confusion lies with Freddie's own personal correspondence with Myles Wyatt, which right up until November 1965 was both friendly and cordial. The alternative, more dramatic version is as follows, and picks up with Wyatt's negotiations with Jack Jones of Channel Airways. Elements of both versions may well be true.

Jack Jones had sensed the management divisions at BUA, and went behind Freddie's back to contact Wyatt separately. Wyatt paid a secret visit to Jones at Southend to view his operation. But he had the bad luck to be spotted in his Rolls-Royce by one of Freddie's former managers at Aviation Traders, which was also based at Southend. It was a dead give-away, as Wyatt had a very distinctive Rolls-Royce. When Freddie next went down to Southend, the manager told his boss about Wyatt's visit.

Freddie knew instinctively what Wyatt was up to and could barely contain his rage as he drove back to Portland House in London that afternoon. He left his car by the pavement outside and stormed up the stairs of the building to confront Wyatt in his seventh floor office. He brushed Wyatt's secretary aside and went straight through to find Wyatt on the telephone behind his large desk. Freddie stood in front of the desk for a few seconds with his arms folded, staring straight at Wyatt. Wyatt declined to look up and carried on with his call. A fuming Freddie put his finger on the telephone button and cut off the call. Wyatt looked up and said: "What the blazes...?" but before he could get any more words out Freddie barked, "Put that telephone down!" Stunned by the sudden interruption, Wyatt could only confirm what Freddie Laker already knew. When he had recovered his composure he told Freddie that BUA was buying Channel Airways. Freddie exploded. As one eye witness described it, 'Freddie took off and went into orbit.' He said: "Over my dead body!" A fierce row erupted between the two en and the loud exchange of words could be heard right across the seventh floor. Freddie was by this time virtually frothing at the mouth. He called the 62-year-old Wyatt a buffoon and a dinosaur and told him his unwelcome meddling was destroying BUA. Wyatt told Freddie that it was no longer any of his business. "None of my business?" Freddie shouted back. "I'm the Managing Director of the company. You're going to saddle me with a lame duck airline, and it's none of my business? If you go ahead and buy Jones out, I'm resigning now."

The whole incident was witnessed by Alan Bristow and his colleague Reg Cantello, who was sitting in a nearby office, and he rushed in when the commotion started. The two men were afraid that Freddie was going to punch Wyatt, who wasn't in particularly good health. Eventually they got Freddie out of Wyatt's office, sat him down and attempted to pacify him. Over a cup of tea Freddie told Bristow exactly what had happened. Bristow later recalled that he thought Freddie was wholly in the right and concurred with his view that Channel Airways was a basket case and that BUA shouldn't touch it. The next day there was a real atmosphere on the seventh floor and Freddie asked Bristow to accompany him for a meeting with Wyatt.

Bristow spoke first: "Look, you can't expect Freddie to take this lying down. He's the managing director and he thinks that you are negotiating behind his back." Then Freddie and Wyatt started going at it again, as Bristow recalled: "They were like a pair of bull elephants charging at each other about – what the rest of us thought was – the stupidest thing."

Realising that he was getting nowhere, Freddie cooled down and eventually backed off. Wyatt continued with the Channel Airways negotiations and Freddie kept his distance. The row caused the news of Freddie's resignation to become public knowledge, but he continued to come to work every morning as usual for days afterwards as though nothing had happened. Wyatt saw the incident as his opportunity to rid himself of Freddie once and for all at the earliest opportunity, and put pressure on him to leave immediately. But Freddie wouldn't go. It was a bizarre stand-off.

The story extends to the day of Kevin Laker's funeral, as the family were about to leave for the service. The silence was broken by the telephone ringing. Joan Laker rushed to answer it, as she had every telephone call since her son's death, momentarily thinking that it was Kevin and that he was all right after all. Her face quickly dropped and she shouted: "It's for you, Freddie – will you take it? It's Myles." Freddie walked to the phone, thinking that his adversary had rung to offer his condolences. It turned out to be far from that, and Wyatt had rung neither to offer his support nor his sympathy. When Freddie came on the line he simply said: "You've got to make up your mind, Freddie – are you resigning or aren't you?"

Freddie was in too much of a state to respond or be angry, and said quietly: "Well, right now I'm taking my son to be buried. The hearse is outside and we're going off now. It'll have to wait. I'll let you know."

But seemingly lacking any humanity or compassion, Wyatt pressed on. "I need to know now, Freddie – are you resigning or aren't you?"

With that Freddie lost it and shouted down the phone, "Oh, fuck you – I've resigned."

Alan Bristow, listening, was appalled at Wyatt's behaviour, and later John Jones said: "Wyatt was a fool and had no emotional intelligence at all."

Freddie put the phone down. Without saying a further word to anyone he left the house, motioning everyone to join him in the funeral cars taking them to the cemetery ... with Kevin.

Irrespective of how or why he left BUA, once he had gone Freddie started planning a new airline, just as he was going to do with Kevin. He and Joan worked tirelessly on the details around the kitchen table, planning their new venture in the aviation business. There was a constant stream of business people coming in and out. The phones went non-stop and people stayed over. John Jones remembers: "Because I worked in the bank, I was the figures man ... it was exciting." Eventually it morphed into a plan that involved flying passengers for package tour operators. Before he'd even left BUA, Freddie had already hatched a scheme to buy three BAC One-Elevens. Jones recalls: "We started adding up the costs and I can remember it to this day. We came out with a figure of £232 per hour for overheads before the direct operating costs. The aircraft needed to be flown for 2,600 hours before it would turn a profit." They didn't believe that would be a problem. For want of a better name, Freddie decided to call his new venture 'Laker Airways'.

# Part 2

## His name on every plane

CHAPTER 16

# Get Back on Your Feet Again

## Laker Airways is conceived

1966-1969

In the spirit of the hit song 'Pick Yourself Up', Freddie Laker announced that he had 'dusted himself off and was back on his feet again'. It was 4:00pm on Tuesday 8th February 1966 at the St Ermin's Hotel near Victoria in London. Freddie held a press conference to announce the launch of his new airline. He'd called it 'Laker Airways'.

The announcement was a hugely confident display of bravado, as Freddie told the small group of assembled press all about his new venture. He told them Laker Airways was going to be a low-cost operation dealing not with the public directly, but exclusively with package holiday tour operators as a 'contract carrier to the trade', and that it would be 'a personalised airline'. Freddie intoned that his company would not be the 'biggest' or the 'cheapest' – it would simply be 'the best'. This applied mainly to the way that he operated his fleet of aircraft, which would be done both economically and impeccably.

None of the people assembled that day thought it was a bad idea. The package holiday market to European sunspots was booming in the mid-1960s and British families were travelling abroad in greater numbers. Destinations in the Mediterranean, Canary Islands and even North Africa were rapidly becoming in vogue. Most of the holidaymakers were going overseas for the first time and for many it was their very first time flying on an aeroplane, something they perhaps never thought they would do in their lifetimes.

Freddie revealed that he had already signed an order with the British Aircraft Corporation to buy three 89-seat BAC One-Eleven 320L series aircraft, which would be delivered the following December. His would be one of the first airlines in Britain using brand-new jet aircraft for holiday flights. Freddie held back from bragging that, unlike BUA and Dan Air, the only other independent jet aircraft operators in Britain at the time, he was the one person who already had a history of making the concept work.

Freddie had ordered the One-Elevens for Laker Airways before he left BUA, conspiring with BAC sales director Geoffrey Knight over prices and delivery dates well before he resigned. Laker Airways had been planned to be a 'proper' family business between father and son until Kevin's death. The £4 million cost of the aircraft was all borrowed from Clydesdale Bank, to be paid back over eight years. Freddie didn't name the Clydesdale at the press conference, but described his lenders jokingly as 'a big banker – come to think of it, he is a very big bloke indeed'.

Freddie had learned how to borrow large sums of money from the master of the game, BUA's chairman, Myles Wyatt. Much as he disliked Wyatt personally, he admired his fund-raising skills immensely. He'd built up a relationship with BAC when he was managing director of BUA, and the aircraft manufacturer had every confidence in Freddie's operating skills; indeed, it guaranteed part of the loan for the aircraft. Freddie had been instrumental in the success of the BAC One-Eleven, which may never have gone into production without his support. When British European Airways (BEA), the national carrier, had opted for the Hawker Siddeley Trident jet, it put BAC's entire One-Eleven project in jeopardy, but Freddie rescued it by ordering the first ten One-Elevens for BUA's fleet.

At the press conference, Freddie publicly lavished BAC with high praise: "The service I have had from that company could not be better. It is impossible to beat it. I have been in trouble in the middle of the night and rung them up and they have never let me down, never." Despite the favourable reception at the press conference, over the next week, as is somewhat typical with the fickle British media, especially the specialist aviation writers, Freddie's plans were debunked. Financial journalists wrote that his projections were way off. Others called the venture potentially suicidal. It's fair to say that in 1966 they probably didn't get the concept. Freddie said his planes would fly 4,100 flying hours in the first full season, 2,600 summer hours and 1,500 winter hours. With each aircraft carrying approximately 73,000 round-trip passengers, at an average round trip flight time of 5 hours, it equated to 820 flights. He said his flying costs would be £300 per hour. No one thought he could make any money. Sceptics believed that revenues would be nowhere near enough for him to cover his overheads and pay back the loans on three brand-new, state-of-the-art jets, together with depreciation and interest payments. But Freddie had done all the planning down to the minutest detail, and he knew the aviation business perhaps better than anyone else. He was confident of his business model and was determined to prove the naysayers wrong.

The planning had taken a few months between himself and his wife Joan, with John Jones occasionally participating whenever he came over to the Laker's house, following the tragic death of his best friend, Freddie's son Kevin. Before the company was christened, while still in its embryonic stages, Freddie would refer to it as 'Fred Air' for his own amusement. A constant stream of people were coming in and out of the house and the telephone rang non-stop, just as Freddie liked it.

The first official recruit to the new airline was Leonard 'Atty' Atkinson. The tough, former RAF Wing Commander was BUA's flight planning manager and he'd been its station manager in Las Palmas. Atty, who only had one lung, was given the job of Operations Manager. For a brief spell he moved in with the Lakers, working round the clock on getting the new airline up and running. John Jones was working for nothing, late into the evening, as the plans took shape around the Laker's dining room table. Finally Freddie casually looked up from the table and said, "I suppose you want a job?" Jones replied, "You bet your boots I do," having already anticipated the question for weeks.

Otherwise, recruiting for the new venture was not going that well. When he was still at BUA, Freddie had discreetly sounded out two of his oldest and most loyal lieutenants, Jack Wiseman and Bob Batt. Wiseman was particularly crucial and was still in charge of Aviation Traders Engineering, which performed all of BUA's manufacturing and engineering operations. But neither he nor Batt wanted to take the risk. They were both well settled in the organisation and preferred a more comfortable existence. It had been fun in the 1950s when they had both been young men with no commitments and had agreed to split the kitty four ways. Starting from scratch again was not an option they would consider. Knowing Freddie as they did, they knew there would be too much toil for uncertain rewards, and no firm promises of salary, security or pension. They weren't willing to 'burn their beds' again. Luckily there were other good people who were more than willing to leave BUA for such an exciting adventure. In the place of Batt and Wiseman, Freddie managed to poach two key managers from his old company. Peter Yeoman, who had been chief engineer at Southend Airport and the works manager at Aviation Traders for 16 years, joined Laker Airways as Chief Engineer. Together with the talented Yeoman came the equally competent Brian Wheelhouse as Purchasing Manager; he had done five years in the RAF and six years at BUA. Then came George Forster, Freddie's former commercial manager at Air Charter, then at BUA. He was not getting along well at BUA and figured he would be far happier dealing with the devil he knew and became Laker's Commercial Manager. Perhaps it was because he hadn't quite given up some of the habits he'd formed in the fledgling era of post-war aviation and the ex-Second World War Halifaxes. John Jones recalls his old mentor's flight costing technique: "George had a map of the world on the wall behind his desk, and he had the end of a bit of string pinned on London with a series of knots in the string, each knot representing £1,000. If someone rang up and said, 'I want to go to Tripoli,' he would swing the other end of the string around to Tripoli, count the number of knots and say, 'That will be £4,500 please.' That was his method of flight costing and if they said that was too much he would retort, 'Make the buggers walk!' I learned a lot from George."

Atkinson recommended Captain Alan Hellary to be the new company's Chief Pilot. Hellary was a great admirer of Freddie and had already written to him when he had heard about his resignation from BUA to say how sorry he was. When he read later in a newspaper that his former boss was starting up his own airline, he telephoned Freddie from his home at Bournemouth. He was about to fly to Aden on the BUA VC10, and Freddie asked him to come to his house at Epsom directly after his flight arrived back. Hellary said that would be at 4:00am. "That's OK," said Freddie. "See you around 6:00am and we'll talk."

During the war Hellary had served in RAF Bomber and Transport commands. He and Freddie had a history going all the way back to November 1951, Hellary having flown with Freddie on the 'Little Berlin Airlift' between Berlin, Hamburg and Hanover. He had then spent three years flying Tudors on the Australian run from Stansted to Adelaide. In those days it was a gruelling 11-day round trip, logging 110 flying hours. Captain Hellary saw no future or further promotion at BUA and was delighted that there might be a job for him even though, as a senior VC10 pilot, it was initially a big step down. Forced to work out his notice, Hellary couldn't join Laker Airways until 1st June.

Like so many others, Hellary thought that Freddie Laker's departure would be a disaster for BUA, and that's exactly what it was. Joining Hellary were a number of BUA's VC10 pilots, all willing to trade flying prime long-haul routes on perhaps the best aircraft of its time for an initial 'demotion' and an unknown future. Their departure left BUA with a shortage of senior pilots, and clearly demonstrated the influence and charisma Freddie wielded.

After Freddie's resignation, Myles Wyatt employed Max Stuart-Shaw as BUA's Managing Director. He had limited experience in the industry, most recently as East African Airways' Managing Director. As a result, although a perfectly affable man, he was never on top of the job. He was not cut from the same cloth as his predecessor. When Freddie left BUA, it was still marginally profitable, but under Shaw seemingly overnight it went £16 million into the red. Shaw couldn't cope. He just couldn't understand how Freddie had managed to 'see everyone in the large queue of people outside his door'. Alan Bristow recalled the situation years later: "It was quite simple. Freddie would have had them all in at once. He'd give them their orders in rapid fire while simultaneously arranging lunch and instructing his bookie, and all the while he'd have his trousers round his ankles while his tailor measured him for a suit." Bristow continued: "Freddie was a natural entrepreneur, and he knew every inch of the business. He was the making of BUA as an airline operating successfully in the scheduled and charter markets."

Not only had Freddie lucked out by hiring Hellary, he also recruited 50-year-old former Wing Commander Dennis Hayley Bell; his sister Mary married the actor John Mills (later Sir John) and their two daughters, Juliet and Hayley, were also famous actresses. Hayley Bell was a decorated war hero who had flown Avro Ansons, Handley-Page Harrows, Bristol Beaufighters, de Havilland Mosquitoes and several American-made planes. He was one of the first pilots to fly Viscounts on behalf of BOAC, and in 1956 he became a test pilot for Vickers on the VC10. Freddie hired him as his Chief Training Captain for Laker's BAC One-Eleven fleet, in another enormous coup.

By 13th March 1966 the key management positions of Laker Airways had been filled. The final three were Bill Townsend, who was ex-RAF and came on board as Technical Director, Ian Allan, another ex-RAF pilot, and Cliff Nunn. Nunn had served in the Fleet Air Arm before joining Transair, which became part of BUA. At the outset, Freddie also recruited his first cabin crew from BUA.

Nina Griffin, whom Freddie made no secret that he was sweet on, resisted his charms and would become Laker Airways' Chief Stewardess. Joining her was Joy Harvey, who had been with BUA since 1956. The executive line-up was a close group made up of mostly trusted old confidants upon whom Freddie could rely to perform to the very best of their abilities. Freddie told them that it would be a small tight operation growing in size to no more than six planes. He told his new management team, "If it grows any larger you can kick my arse." And he told the press, "I don't intend to get big and I reckon with all the tricks of the trade that I've learned in the past 27 years I can keep this a personal airline for the next 22 years until I retire." It was a good plan, but everyone acquainted with him knew that Freddie would never stop at just six planes.

Freddie rented part of the old Air Couriers' hangar at Gatwick as an engineering base, where the airline would take care of its own maintenance, with major overhauls contracted out to Air Couriers just next door. When Atkinson turned up at the new Laker Airways HQ for the first time, he found the hangar on the perimeter of the airfield and three offices of barely a thousand square feet lit by unshaded light bulbs. Inside was Freddie's old oak desk from BUA with a couple of telephones perched on it and empty crates to use as chairs. "This," said Freddie Laker, "is Fredair." Atkinson immediately shopped for stationery and furniture at a bankruptcy sale in Reigate, and Freddie enlisted friends and family in the redecoration of his new premises. It was all dirt-cheap, just as Freddie liked it.

Now that Freddie had acquired the offices for the new Laker Airways it spoiled everything for Joan. Kevin had died and their daughter Elaine had married John Trayton Seear just eight weeks later. Elaine recounts: "My mother was now home alone. She was in her fifties, which back then seemed old, and she felt she no longer had a purpose. It was awful for her."

With the first of Laker Airways' new BAC One-Elevens not due for delivery until December, Freddie arranged to borrow BAC's demonstrator aircraft for training his crews. In April, keen to get flying again, two Bristol Britannia 100s were bought from BOAC for a respectably low amount. Freddie had borrowed £190,000 from Clydesdale Bank, which gladly sanctioned an overdraft for him. He liquidated some assets, including his interest in J. K. Seear & Co, which was an agent for Lloyd's of London, for £50,000, and his share in the Casanova Club, a gentlemen's gambling club in the West End of London, for £80,000.

The two Bristol Britannia turbo-prop aircraft were perfectly good workhorses, but had become passé with the arrival on the market of the jet-engined competition in the form of the Boeing 707. Freddie's two examples, Bravo November (G-ANBN) and Bravo Mike (G-ANBM), were quite famous. Among other trips, one had flown the young Princess Elizabeth, now the Queen, back from Africa after she had learned that her father, King George VI had died.

Freddie's flight crews and engineers were already type-rated for the Bristol Britannia and didn't require much re-certification training. The aeroplanes were pressed into work on ad hoc charters once they had come back from their overhauls at Scottish Aviation in Prestwick. The first Britannia was delivered at the end of April and the second in August, coinciding with Freddie joining the board of Castrol. Both had been given a coat of paint at Prestwick in the simple new Laker Airways livery, white with a black and red stripe down the fuselage – an adaptation of his horse racing colours. The name Laker appeared only on the tail, with a simple logo – a stylised bird flanked by a small Union Jack – on the fuselage. He boasted that the logo was based on the imprint of a wet martini glass on a serviette. From then on he said it was the 'Oozlum bird', a mythological creature that flies round in circles until it disappears up its own backside. At the time there were no marketing or PR experts on his team, as they might have steered him away from his choice of logo. Freddie thought his own name – both short and written small – would be good because "You could quickly whip someone else's name on it for charter work. There was nothing egotistical in the choice of name, just that I couldn't think of anything better."

The new Laker Airways was up for anything and everything, often at short notice. The first customer was Cunard, when the entire crew of the QE2 was stranded in Le Havre after a dock strike at Southampton. The crew wanted to come home for their long weekend, and the only way back was by air. The man from Cunard asked John Jones, "Would you send one of your aeroplanes to bring our crew home for the weekend?" He said, "Yeah that'll be £95 each," having quickly done the sums in his head. Jones heard the Cunard man on the other end of the telephone shout across to a shed full of seamen, "It's 95 quid a seat!" They shouted back, "No, it's too much." Jones replied as quick as a flash, "All right, it's 75 quid a seat, OK?" It was OK and Jones and the empty Britannia immediately set off for Le Havre.

As the passengers embarked, Jones collected £75 off each as they went up the steps, putting the cash in a big brown envelope. Some of them didn't have English pounds, so he accepted American dollars and French francs; Jones had no idea whether they had paid enough or not. When he got back to Gatwick he stuck his head round Freddie's office door to tell him, "That worked OK, the Cunard charter." Freddie asked slightly dubiously, "Did you get paid?" The delighted Jones emptied the contents of the envelope onto Freddie's desk in front of Geoffrey Knight. The latter, who was visiting his old friend, looked bemused at the turn of events. Freddie smiled at him and said: "This is the airline business, you know."

Freddie had hired two accountants to take care of the airline's finances, a senior man who had worked for Tate & Lyle and a younger assistant accountant named Robbie Robinson, aged just 21½. He was Britain's youngest chartered accountant when he qualified in November 1965. He found working for Freddie, which often included working weekends, 'bloody tough but fun'. Then one August morning the finance director of the airline never returned from his holiday. While he had been away Robinson had been putting papers on his desk ready for his return, but he never came back, so by default Robinson became the airline's Chief Accountant. He was just 22.

Last to join the Laker Airways management group was John Trayton Seear, a chartered surveyor by profession with no prior experience in the airline business. Seear had married Freddie's daughter Elaine and still grieving, Freddie insisted that his new son-in-law come to work with him, begging and begging until Seear was reluctantly convinced to join Laker Airways in 1967 as a full Director of the company. The addition of the suave and handsome Seear to the Laker management team immediately raised the issue of 'succession'. Everyone was aware how hard the loss of Kevin had been, and that Freddie would probably never get over it. John Jones was still young and impetuous and, while clearly extremely bright and driven, still had lots to learn, not least in terms of interpersonal skills. But in John Seear, Freddie had potentially an heir apparent, someone who'd already cut his teeth in another profession and had the maturity the company needed. Freddie figured that it wouldn't take him long to learn the aviation industry and he put him in charge of a mixed bag of departments and activities. John Seear's arrival at the airline rankled John Jones, who had naturally seen himself as the heir apparent. Their relationship was strained from the outset, something Freddie never took the time or effort to rectify. It was almost as if Freddie encouraged internal conflicts as part of his 'divide and conquer' management style, despite it often being counter-productive.

In April 1967, Freddie set up the formal company structure, creating new companies. Laker Airways Leasing Ltd was formed in the UK, which in turn bought an off-the-shelf company registered in Jersey, in the Channel Islands. Laker Leasing was set up purely for the purposes of obtaining the UK air operator's licence needed to run a British-based airline, and was subsequently renamed Laker Air Services Ltd. It owned the aircraft and employed the staff. Having a Jersey company meant that Britain's restrictive labour laws, which were limiting for independent aviation operators, could be circumvented, because they did not apply in the Channel Islands. Under the UK's labour laws, wages and benefits had to be identical to those paid by the heavily subsidised state-owned carriers, BOAC and BEA, and they were a real burden on the independents. The fledgling Laker Airways needed better efficiencies and a lower wage bill to make their numbers add up.

Freddie had already had his fill of the behaviour of the 13 trade unions at BUA and told close associates that the unions were the real reason he left. He found working with the unions impossible and was not going to be held to ransom again by the bitter strikes against which he had fought. He said he had spent more time bickering with the trade unions over their seemingly endless demands than running the airline. At BUA, management staff routinely took over striking workers' jobs; during a porters' strike in December 1964 Freddie could be found loading the passengers' luggage onto an aircraft. Shedding the unions didn't stop plenty of candidates for the 120 jobs on offer.

Initially, Laker Airways had jobs for 18 pilots, 28 stewardesses, 48 engineers and 26 administrative and clerical staff. When Freddie advertised these positions, there were applications from more than 2,000 people. Freddie recalled: "Letters have been coming through my letterbox at the rate of 100 a day. I had a telephone call from Zurich from a captain who had asked for a job for himself and his entire crew. Apparently they wanted to 'work for an airline with personality'. That's us, all right."

Freddie focused his mind on finding customers for the One-Elevens. There was plenty of growth in charter travel from Britain during this period; the total inclusive tour market serviced around 1.5 million passengers in 1967. And Freddie had an ingenious scheme to win the work, which he called 'Time Charter'.

Under the scheme, holiday operators would commit to wholly charter an aircraft for a year and guarantee to use it for a minimum of 2,600 flying hours; they were charged £300 per hour. However, Freddie anticipated that all 2,600 hours would be flown in the six months of summer, after which he would offer an hourly rebate of £100 per hour for every extra hour until the maximum practical number of hours per year was reached.

After adding up the costs, the standing overheads that Freddie incurred, including the repayments on the aircraft, and paying pilots, office staff and insurance premiums, whether the aircraft flew or not, were £232.50 per hour for 2,600 hours. So, with the fixed overheads already covered out of the revenue, any other flying would be for the burning costs only. As he gleefully put it, there was always 'a bit for mum'.

It was a way of smoothing out the year-round costs in what was a risky business for the charter airlines, while remaining attractive to tour operators. Flights might be chartered to deliver holidaymakers in only one direction, and the aircraft would fly back empty without a paying customer. In summer, prices were high and in the winter any work they got was often operated at a loss.

The tour operators had the surety of an available aircraft at a fixed price without having to charter extra aircraft during the high season or pay the exorbitant prices that charter operators would charge during that period. Their own flying costs were covered in the summer and they could increase their profits by offering extra tours in the winter at 'bargain basement' prices. They could therefore fly holidaymakers to faraway locations like the Canary Islands for fantastic fares.

There was an added attraction in Freddie's calculation of the time flown. Unlike in Europe, where this was rounded up to 15 minutes, Freddie was going to copy the Americans and charge for exact minutes. In his sales pitch he told prospective clients: "A BAC One-Eleven costs £8 a minute to fly," exaggerating the real cost to make his point. "If you add up all those odd minutes over a year, you are paying for a lot of extra flying." A contract with Laker defined the flying hours as the time elapsed between the moment the aircraft departed from the terminal at one airport – the 'off-blocks' time – to the minute it came to a standstill at the terminal of another or 'on-blocks'.

At the time, Britain's inclusive tour holiday trade was led by Thomas Cook, which was owned by the British Transport Commission, the owner of British Rail. Freddie had been trying to sell the company his new 'Time Charter' innovation, but the decision-makers at Thomas Cook didn't have the vision to embrace the concept and turned him down. Single-handedly, Freddie Laker had invented the concept of tour operators blocking seats (at full financial risk) on his aircraft.

It was trend-setting and it became de rigueur for just about every tour operator/airline partnership operating in Europe in the late 1960s through the 1980s. But it didn't catch the imagination of the bureaucratic Thomas Cook organisation; for that company the concept was far too risky. There would not be many occasions when Freddie's salesmanship failed him, but this was one of them. Thomas Cook's rebuff was a big disappointment to Freddie and he could barely conceal his despondency. With no alternative he grudgingly had to talk to smaller operators. As a result of the Thomas Cook turndown, Freddie focused on Wings, the up-market travel offshoot of the Ramblers Association, which had been operating air tours since 1956 and offered holidays to more exotic destinations outside Europe. But Wings was no easy pushover. Its Managing Director, Ernest Welsman, was a savvy businessman and knew what he was about when it came to tours and travel. In 1966, Wings was running quality, high-value tours to Majorca and the Riviera; the company specialised in opening up more exotic destinations for the times, such as Tunisia, Cyprus, Rhodes and the Middle East. It had grown exponentially and Welsman was initially attracted by the opportunity of having exclusive use of a brand new BAC One-Eleven.

Unbelievably, Freddie had dropped the ball when Welsman first got in touch. His initial enquiry was treated with curt rudeness as Freddie was not up to speed with how big Wings had become. Welsman was not taken seriously for a month, until the mistake was realised then Freddie went all out to get the business, putting on a bravura performance in front of Wings's executives. Freddie knew every tiny detail by heart, never referring once to the contents of his briefcase, which in reality only contained his sandwiches in case he wasn't offered lunch.

Welsman was asking himself whether Wings could fill a plane of its own, but soon came to the conclusion that it could. He had a greater concern about the imposition of tough conditions, including heavy financial penalties, and an airport turn-around time of no more than 50 minutes. Freddie was taken aback when Wings said that it was ready to sign, and Welsman presented Freddie with a contract. He was a good match for Freddie in negotiations, and had accepted most of Freddie's terms, including a few safety clauses of his own. One of them was if the value of the pound fell by 15 per cent or more he could re-negotiate his charter rate. In the event, the Wings devaluation clause was never invoked, but they came close; on 18th November 1967 the pound was devalued by 14.3 per cent courtesy of Prime Minister Harold Wilson after Arab countries switched their sterling balances to dollars in Zurich. The value of the pound against the dollar went from $2.80 to $2.40, and led to Wilson's famous 'pound in your pocket' speech, telling Britons that the pound at least in Britain was worth the same. The first commercial flight of a Laker Airways' BAC One-Eleven flew to Djerba, off the coast of Tunisia, on 27th February and the lucrative Wings contract began on 24th March. Lady Luck was still smiling upon Freddie.

Freddie had opened up talks with Lord Brothers in mid-1966 to take the second One-Eleven. Lord Brothers was run by three siblings, Christopher, Basil and Stephen Lord, from a tiny office in Wimbledon. The company had been formed in 1957, a year after Wings. In 1958 it had booked its first clients, 200 of them, on flights to Yugoslavia using a Douglas DC-3 aircraft. The Lords were bright, well-educated young men and were big enough to be taken seriously by BUA, from which they chartered 75 per cent of their aircraft. Myles Wyatt's arrogance had turned them off, and they were only too happy to talk to Freddie Laker. Like Welsman, they were attracted to the new BAC One-Eleven jets on offer.

Freddie, knowing that he had to, turned on the charm, wining and dining the Lord brothers and telling them that the reason he was offering them the opportunity was because he thought 'they were among the best'. In an avalanche of bluff and flattery, Freddie told them they could take it or leave it. Their business, like everyone else's, was booming, and without hesitation or careful analysis as to whether or not they could fill the plane, they gladly signed a contract in June 1966 almost identical to the one Wings had signed, to take one plane exclusively. The contracts with Wings and Lord Brothers together were worth well over £1 million a year to Laker Airways (£18.5 million at 2018 values).

Before the One-Elevens arrived and his newly signed contracts could take effect, Freddie found his Britannias and their newly appointed crews a more consistent operation. He picked up a six-week contract with Air France from 27th July flying holidaymakers all over Europe from Paris Orly to Cologne, Rimini, Venice, Dubrovnik, Rome, Dublin, Cherbourg, Athens, Amsterdam, Valencia, and Las Palmas. It all went smoothly and without incident, bar one occasion when a technical fault on one of the Britannias seriously delayed a departure. The Air France operations manager naturally figured that Laker would fly in a substitute aircraft, but there was only that one plane available. Captain Alan Hellary couldn't find it within himself to tell the Air France man this was it ... that there was no other plane. The two Britannias carried 9,798 passengers for Air France in the 1966 summer season; the contract made a significant contribution and neither crews nor planes ever stood idle. Laker Airways' revenue for 1966 was £98,000 (£1.8 million at 2018 values). The net result was that the fledgling carrier managed to turn an unexpected profit of £3,079, an unprecedented achievement for the airline's first year of operation.

It had been a late start for the new airline and, as the holiday season came to a close, Freddie Laker went searching further afield for another source of work for the off-season. Sometimes it came from the most unexpected places.

Rhodesia (now Zimbabwe) had unilaterally declared independence from Britain on 11th November 1965. Instead of responding to the UDI with force, Britain (and the United States) had imposed tough economic sanctions. Unintentionally, severe effects from this action were suffered by Rhodesia's next-door neighbour, Zambia, a landlocked country reliant on an oil pipeline that ran between Beira in Mozambique and Umtali in Rhodesia.

To mitigate the damage, the RAF had been airlifting supplies of oil since December of that year from Dar es Salaam in Tanzania (the largest city in East Africa) into Lusaka, the capital of Zambia. It was a costly exercise and the British Government had already spent almost £6 million on the operation. The airlifts into Zambia were grossly inadequate to sustain the nation; the country was still on its knees and a second airlift needed to be organised, but this time with civilian aircraft, as the Zambians objected to the use of military aircraft.

Civilian aircraft were therefore chartered, mainly from Caledonian, Lloyd International and Transglobe.

Sensing an opportunity, Freddie Laker flew to Lusaka with Joan, without bothering to tie up contracts before leaving Britain. He simply touched down in a glistening Britannia and quickly got word around that his plane was for hire. Somehow he gained an audience with the Zambian leader, President Kenneth Kaunda, who was the nation's first President after it had declared its independence from Britain in 1964. Freddie told Kaunda that he should take over the airlift. It took him a matter of days to convince the President, but he eventually managed to pull off the deal.

For that winter, Freddie had the interiors of both the Britannias stripped out for the oil lift. However, the operation got off to a disastrous start only hours after Freddie had signed the contract. On 30th December 1966, the first Britannia en route to Zambia from Tanzania captained by Lyndon Griffith (whom everyone called 'Griff') was forced to land in Entebbe, Uganda with engine trouble. The aircraft was carrying a cargo of rifles and 243 cases of .303 ammunition for a sporting club in Ndola. It was cleared into Uganda at 6:00pm and the crew went off to stay in a local hotel. At 10:00pm, Entebbe's Chief of Police came by and took the captain's passport. At midnight, three CID officers arrived and interviewed the crew. The next morning they were rounded up, taken to the airfield police station and questioned about 'alleged illegal importation of ammunition'. The crew were detained in a police mess in Kampala awaiting release when a similar fate befell the second Britannia, which landed at 10.00pm on 4th January in Dar Es Salaam, Tanzania. It had arrived early to pick up its cargo of oil for delivery to Lusaka, but the authorities promptly seized it and put it under armed guard for landing without permission. Freddie was holidaying with Joan at the time and took the blame for the incident. "I should have been more careful about checking things out with the Tanzanian authorities before my plane flew there for the airlift." Two days later the Britannia was on its way.

John Jones, who was sent down with the crews, engineers and loaders to run the operation, recalled: "We loaded the oil drums one at a time through the passenger door of this Britannia, humped them down onto palettes, then lashed them down eight at a time. We'd then have six palettes down the floor of the aircraft and flew these to Lusaka. We then flew back to Dar empty and did it all over again."

It was a great operation and there was a real esprit de corps amongst the staff; it was fun and everyone mucked in. Robbie Robinson recalls manually sawing a shed in half with Peter Yeoman to get it into the hold of a Britannia to take down to Africa. It was nailed back together at the other end. "It's like being in the old Air Charter days, back to when staff wanted to work," declared Freddie, clearly relishing being his own boss again. When the contract ended in March 1967, it reaped Freddie a cool £250,000 (£4.6 million in 2018), paid for by the British Government out of public funds.

But as the winter of 1967 drew closer, there was still no customer for the third BAC One-Eleven that Freddie had ordered. Delivery was imminent and, despite strenuous efforts and a series of heroic sales pitches, there was no interest from tour operators.

Then, as he had often done before, Freddie Laker pulled yet another rabbit out of the hat. Spending so much time in Africa had yielded some unexpected rewards and high-level connections, one of which was in Kinshasa (formerly Leopoldville) in the Congo, previously known as the Belgian Congo.

After five years of war and political instability, termed the 'Congo Crisis', power had been seized in a coup d'état in 1965 by Colonel Joseph-Désiré Mobutu. He was now President Mobutu and, as dictator and ruler of the nation, had the full responsibility for the national airline. Air Congo had two new Sud Aviation Caravelles on order, but they would not be delivered until late 1967, and the carrier was an aircraft short after one of its fleet had been damaged in a thunderstorm. Freddie, using his African connections and now with a solid reputation from operating the Zambian operation successfully, managed to lease his third BAC One-Eleven to Air Congo. The deal was concluded in London on 20th April 1967 with Everest Katanga, Air Congo's director of foreign operations. The value of the contract was rumoured to be almost twice what Freddie had derived from the other One-Eleven charter deals.

It was Zaire's turn to host the African Unity Conference in September 1967, and President Mobutu was keen to impress, regardless of cost. He had already built a delegates' village with a colour television in every one of the huts, and had to set up a colour TV station specially to service the fewer than 100 colour sets in the country.

The Zaire BAC One-Eleven was delivered on 13th May, already painted in Air Congo livery. It was the most visible sign of Zaire's new prosperity and went into service two days later. John Jones stayed for the whole year together with the six crew members and the eight engineers required to carry out the maintenance. The crews flew on rotation three weeks at a time, with Air Congo supplying the cabin crews. Alan Hellary captained the plane on its first flight out of Kinshasa. When he taxied out for take-off he found himself refused flight clearance because he carried no radio officer. He advised the control tower that he was flying a British jet equipped to British international standards and that under British regulations he did not need a radio operator. He got nowhere. He taxied back off the runway and called up Freddie to sort it out. Fortunately, Freddie was in Africa and staying in Kinshasa, as he was pursuing a new love interest, named Rosemary Black. He rushed to the airport and demanded clearance for his plane to take off. He was told that the only man who could give it was the aviation minister, and it was a Congolese national holiday. Freddie bullied the minister's address out of the airport officials and shot off into the countryside in a rental car. Three hours later he zoomed back waving a piece of paper signed by the minister giving permission. The contract ran for a year, although the original aircraft had to be switched out because it developed corrosion in its wings from water in the fuel. Initially Freddie had been hopeful that the contract might continue, but it was not to be. The plane was recalled.

Laker Airways experienced a few body blows in its formative years that might have put any other emergent airline out of business, but not Laker. It survived the early difficult years because its operating costs were so low. The cost-saving innovations were mostly devised by Freddie's chief navigator, Dick Bradley, who had joined Laker Airways from BOAC, where he had been an instructor at its central training unit and chief examiner on Comets. Bradley was a man who could 'sharpen pencils better than anybody', according to John Jones. Bradley worked through the payloads, the weather conditions, and length of runway at any airport they were flying to or from. From these calculations, he introduced the reduced-thrust take-off technique, making Laker Airways the first airline ever to implement it. Each pilot was given a graph containing the One-Eleven's take-off weight, the ambient temperature and headwind conditions on any given day. Bradley calculated the take-off thrust settings for the conditions, as Jones explains: "So you were coming out at the absolute minimum power required for take-off, whatever the temperature or wind strength at Gatwick. He had the aircraft operating like sewing machines and we were incredibly efficient." There were significant maintenance advantages with the reduced-thrust take-off procedures, which increased overall engine life; fewer overhauls were needed and it gave better fuel consumption. When Laker's Rolls-Royce Spey engines were sent back to the factory for rebuilds, the manufacturer acknowledged that they were the best maintained of any BAC One-Eleven operator.

Bradley's other genius was for weight saving. He changed the passengers' baggage allowance, limiting it to 15kg, 5kg less than the usual 20kg. What would have been nearly half a ton of baggage was put on as fuel instead, significantly extending the range of the aircraft. Wings and Lord Brothers were encouraged to restrict the load to 70 passengers on certain flights. If they wanted to fill the plane to the maximum 89, it would be them, not Laker Airways, that would pay the extra landing charges and time on the ground if the plane needed to refuel en route. That way, Freddie's pilots could get the BAC One-Elevens all the way down to Tenerife in the Canary Islands non-stop, despite it being considerably beyond the BAC manufacturer's maximum range specifications.

Naturally, extending an aircraft's operating range like this still depended on good weather, the strength and direction of the wind and other factors, not least of which was great airmanship by Freddie's crack pilots. By making the aircraft lighter, even on shorter routes, it created better fuel consumption. Laker Airways was competitive with charter operators who used longer-range aircraft that could carry more passengers, but could rarely fill them during the slower winter months. Extending the maximum range also meant fewer cycles (take-offs and landings), which resulted in less stress for the engines, airframes, wheels, tyres and brake units. Freddie's early flight crews were mostly former Royal Air Force pilots, so their airmanship and flying abilities were of the highest standard. For many of them, the BAC One-Eleven was their first experience of a jet-powered aircraft. Freddie's good fortune in securing the services of Capt Dennis Hayley Bell paid off as he had done much of the test and development work for the One-Eleven. He trained Laker's pilots to derive the absolute aximum performance from the aircraft. Optimum speeds and flight levels, asking ATC for direct (off-airways) routings, minimising approach patterns whenever possible, climbing using reduced power settings, and a host of other operational techniques became part of a Laker pilot's MO. The efficiencies reduced fuel consumption and minimised wear and tear on the engines. The smallest things made all the difference, and Laker Airways easily outperformed BAC's calculations for the One-Eleven by a healthy margin.

Upon its return from Zambia in May 1967, Freddie had the Britannia reconfigured from a freighter to a passenger aircraft. He then leased it to Treffield International Airways in a contract that was supposed to last until the end of 1968. Treffield took the plane on one of Laker's standard 'Time Charter' contracts. The company was a newcomer to the inclusive tour business, having been set up in 1965, and its entry into the holiday charter market wasn't established until the beginning of 1967, with a single four-engined turbo-prop Vickers Viscount leased from Channel Airways. Treffield primarily targeted the North of England for its customers. However, it was struggling financially, and it lacked the financial means to pay for the chartered Laker Britannia; when it failed to pay up, Freddie was forced to cancel the contract. Treffield went into bankruptcy on 23rd June and brought Laker Airways its first bad debt of £16,000. It could have been much worse.

Treffield's downfall put Freddie in contact with Arrowsmith Holidays of Liverpool, which now needed a new aircraft supplier. Its owner, Harry Bowden-Smith was a sometime band leader who had pioneered very low-cost package holidays for Britain's working man and his family in the North West of England. It had all begun from an office in Oldham, Lancashire, offering bus tours to First World War battlefields in France. Within a couple of years, Arrowsmith was offering holidays to farther-flung destinations that required the use of aircraft. Bowden-Smith became one of the founding members of the Association of British Travel Agents (ABTA). From a humble start in Liverpool in 1967, the business grew over the next 20 years purely based on the lowest-cost holiday possible with no frills, apart from the sun. Bowden-Smith would often refer to his greatest triumph as being 'introducing fish and chips to the Spanish coast'.

The success of Arrowsmith had made Bowden-Smith a wealthy man. He had just turned 50 and was already thinking of selling his company, his decision influenced by the death of his wife Edna in 1966 from cancer. But the real incentive to sell came after an air disaster on 4th June 1967. A British Midland operated C4 Argonaut, chartered by Arrowsmith Holidays flying from Palma to Manchester, went down on the outskirts of Stockport while making a second approach to Manchester Airport. Seventy-two people on board were killed, but amazingly 12 got out and survived. Bowden-Smith was devastated. He developed a heart condition and urgently needed surgery. After that ordeal he wanted out of the business.

Freddie negotiated a first option to buy Arrowsmith, which had always been highly profitable but was then suddenly in trouble following the crash. The immediate effects of the accident had meant customer confidence had been lost and Arrowsmith was on the edge of collapse.

Freddie closed the deal in November 1967 and announced that he had acquired the business for between £300,000 and £500,000, a fraction of its real value. He immediately installed Cliff Nunn to manage it. After the deal went through, Freddie said, "After acquiring Arrowsmith, we controlled both the flight and the package holiday components, so we were vertically integrated." He was using the latest industry buzzword; it was the theory that as many aspects as possible of the holidaymakers' entire experience should be controlled by one entity – the flight, ground transfers, hotel, food and beverages, even recreational activities. The customer paid one price and wasn't aware of (or even interested to know) the breakdown for each component of the vacation experience. Naturally, the revenue from these integrated elements of the package holiday all fell to the company, which then paid the respective costs, which were greatly stabilised and negotiated to the lowest possible level. Freddie also ordered a fourth BAC One-Eleven and a launch order for three BAC Two-Elevens, a longer and wider version of the earlier plane. He also bought the prototype VC10, G-ARTA, but decided not to operate it and leased it out to Beirut's Middle East Airlines (MEA) instead.

Laker Airways' first full summer season in 1967 saw the company carry 101,793 passengers. That year Freddie even won an industry award from the Daily Telegraph newspaper for 'the greatest contribution to the travel industry'.

Not so great, however, was the outcome for Freddie and Joan Laker's marriage. While he was in Lusaka, Freddie had met the attractive 32-year-old South African divorcee, Rosemary Black. Freddie thought he had fallen in love, but it probably could have been anyone, as he was actually on the rebound from another extramarital affair. Freddie often asked his wife, "Why can't I just have two?" Rosemary had two young boys and a daughter, and it was hard to swallow for Joan and Elaine that Freddie had found a replacement 'off-the-shelf' family. It was the final straw for Joan, who had often overlooked the fact that Freddie had never been a particularly faithful husband, with a weakness for stewardesses in the BUA days. He often used to disappear, but typically he and Joan would make it up. This time, however, Freddie had set his heart on divorce, but was too frightened to put it to Joan himself. So one day he asked his daughter Elaine to collect him from the station and on the drive home urged her to do his dirty work for him. Elaine was close to her father and had been put on a pedestal by him, but was most definitely her mother's daughter. She replied firmly, "Sorry, Daddy, you do that yourself." Freddie grinned boyishly and replied, "I thought you'd say that."

After 25 years of marriage, the Lakers divorced, with Joan maintaining her 10 per cent shareholding in Laker Airways. Freddie was now free to remarry, which he did just as soon as his divorce came through. Freddie and Rosemary were married on 10th July 1968. Needless to say, this created significant disruption within Freddie's original family; he lived in the next village to his pregnant daughter and her husband, John Seear. He would often visit for breakfast and was in and out of their house on a regular basis. Joan could not bear the thought of Rosemary being so close to her daughter, even though they rarely met. It also placed John Seear in an awkward position, as he witnessed the hurt that Freddie was causing his wife and mother-in-law. When Seear took

Joan's side, Freddie went mad, threatening him to make a decision: "It's either me or you're out." Freddie felt betrayed. He was the type of man who took anything less than 100 per cent loyalty and total agreement with anything he did to mean you were 'against' him ... and therefore an enemy. After much consideration, Seear somewhat reluctantly remained in his director role with Laker Airways, as he had a wife and a future family of his own to support. However, the relationship with his father-in-law would never be the same again.

Both of Laker Airways' prime customers, Wings and Lord Brothers, were thriving, with the latter chartering a second BAC One-Eleven for the 1968 season. But then Lords reneged on the additional aircraft, and Freddie was furious. It emerged that Lords was using a brand-new computer supplied by a company named ICL to forecast its likely customer demand, and due to a glitch things were not as good as they seemed. ICL used Lords as a guinea pig, and the overestimates almost destroyed the business, as hotel rooms had to be cancelled and staff laid off.

Lord Brothers began to experience cash flow problems, and owed Laker £50,000. After the takeover of Arrowsmith, Freddie was waiting to pounce as he badly wanted a London-based tour operator. Stephen Lord had bought back the 49 per cent that had been sold to a private shareholder, Gellatly Hankey, only two years before. The company tried to negotiate with Forte and BUA to take it over, but to no avail, so Stephen Lord sold 50 per cent of his stake to Freddie. Not long afterwards Christopher Lord, wanting to sever ties with the company, sold his 25.5 per cent stake at the end of January, giving Freddie the majority shareholding. Neither brother had been given much entirely free choice by Freddie. Stephen, who was already managing director and deemed the most responsible even after the computer debacle, kept his position.

In the winter of 1968, Lord Brothers offered a weekend in Palma for £9.99, with flights departing at lunchtime on a Friday. The package included the flight to Palma, three nights' accommodation including breakfast, and the ride home on Monday morning – £6 of the total was the airfare and the rest was paid to the hoteliers. The latter were absolutely delighted because they could keep their staff on over the winter and knew they were going to make money in the hotel bar. John Jones remembered: "They were absolutely up for it."

Freddie revelled in the tour business and dreamt up a catchphrase for the advertising, which read 'Live like a lord, on a Lord Brothers holiday'. When delays occurred, Freddie had an almost miraculous ability for soothing passengers. They invariably emerged smiling, forgiving and relaxed even after long delays following an explanation and an apology from the boss himself. He used to tell them, "I have my name on the side of the plane, it has got to do well," and they loved it. Freddie was determined that Laker Airways would earn itself an unmatched reputation. In the first season he flew on many of the flights himself, mingling with the passengers, flattering them and impressing them with his attention to detail. There wasn't an airline boss like Freddie, anywhere.

By the time the fourth One-Eleven was delivered, Laker Airways no longer needed the two Britannias and they were sold to Indonesia in January 1969. One of their final missions showed just how unconcerned Freddie was in taking on controversial contracts; in August 1968 he chartered one of his two Britannias (G-ANBM) to the Nigerian Government to carry a consignment of rifles for the Nigerian Army. Nigeria was in the midst of a civil war and Britain was accused of taking sides. The Britannia left for Lagos having spent the previous 24 hours under armed guard on a remote corner of Elmdon Airfield near Birmingham.

There was no doubt that business was thriving despite the shock of the six-day Arab-Israeli war, which increased oil prices sharply, albeit temporarily. Harold Wilson's Labour Government was suffering a currency crisis and imposed a £50 limit on the amount of currency a Briton could take out of the country. Margins were slashed to a profit of just £1 per head per tour, and load factors dropped below 90 per cent, signalling hefty losses for other operators and forcing some out of business. But the downturn proved to be a blip and the appeal of the cheap foreign holiday had become so great that the industry quickly recovered. UK airlines carried 27 per cent more passengers than they had the previous year.

Flug Union, a new tour company from Germany, entered into a 12-month deal for a Laker Airways' BAC One-Eleven. Rolf Teichmann, its founder, was attracted by the brand-new aircraft on offer, but feared he could not fill it outside of the peak summer months, just by offering inclusive tours. But he found that there was a secondary market, flying Turkish 'guest workers' in and out of West Berlin; they were in the country due to an acute shortage of labour there in the 1960s. German airlines were still excluded from flying to Berlin, still isolated in East Germany. Access was strictly controlled via the three air corridors.

Freddie also found a steady income in the off-season from flying the many thousands of pilgrims to Jeddah for Mecca on the Hajj, initially from Turkey. He also picked up work with the British India Steam Navigation Company, a division of P&O, flying passengers to meet cruise ships in the Mediterranean.

On 6th November 1968, Harold Bamberg's British Eagle, which operated 24 aircraft and had annual revenues of £16 million, closed down. It was brought down by a crash and the withdrawal of its licence to fly to Bermuda and the Bahamas after a complaint by BOAC. The latter accused Eagle of trying to turn a charter operation into a scheduled service. After that, Hambros Bank withdrew its support and the airline collapsed overnight owing £5.5 million to its creditors.

Laker Airways gained from the collapse of British Eagle by taking over the leases of its two Boeing 707-138Bs, which had originally done service with Qantas. Kleinwort Benson, Eagle's receivers, were only too happy to have Laker take over the 707s with an unprecedented 'pay as you fly' deal of £69 per block hour. These two aircraft were unusual as they were the short-fuselage versions built especially for the Australian national carrier. They had 158 seats in an all-economy configuration and a full tank range of approx 4,100 miles (3,565 nautical miles). Freddie immediately painted them in the Laker livery and planned to use them for the growing affinity group charter market on the North Atlantic.

In February 1969, Freddie signed an order for four BAC Three-Elevens, a twin-engined, 270-seater, wide-bodied aircraft. They were scheduled for delivery in 1974 and would cost £5 million each. Freddie had a unique rapport with BAC who was looking for someone to place an order and back the project. Geoffrey Knight once again turned to Freddie Laker ... the man he called 'the father of the One-Eleven'. And Freddie, whose mantra was 'Fly British, Buy British', was pleased to help. Sadly, just like the BAC Two-Eleven project before it, the BAC Three-Eleven never got off the drawing board. Britain's Government of the day failed to support the British aircraft industry, handing over what could have been a triumphant and innovative concept to the new European Airbus Industrie consortium and the Americans. At the time, no-one knew that the twin-engine wide-body would become the industry standard, as it would be a few more years before the Airbus A300, then the Boeing 767 would be launched. The McDonnell Douglas Corporation had a twin version of its wide-body DC-10 on the drawing board but, as with the BAC Three-Eleven, it was never built. Both companies rued the day they decided to terminate their respective twin-engined, wide-body projects and hand the concept to Airbus.

During the 1969 summer season the competition between the inclusive tour operators became increasingly fierce. Margins at Lord Brothers and Arrowsmith were cut to the bone. Clarkson's Holidays, under the management of Tom Gullick, blazed a trail of low-priced holidays to the sun; the company was a subsidiary of the Shipping & Industrial Holdings conglomerate, and had capital to develop the market and fund losses. It quickly became the market leader, undercutting everyone's prices, including Freddie's.

With all the expansion, Freddie proclaimed that his airline was valued at £6 million and that a Stock Exchange flotation was likely, as soon as he had the minimum three-year profit record. Freddie had hit the ground running and was delighted to be in profit right away. He had no difficulty in raising money for all his expansion and was seeking to get permission from the Bank of England to buy a stake in three hotels in Majorca. In the first three years of Laker Airways' existence, the passenger numbers had increased dramatically for such a small airline. By 1968 the company's passenger numbers had more than doubled to 233,739, and it was generating more than £8 million in revenue; Arrowsmith was contributing £1.7 million and Lord Brothers £3.7 million. Profits for the financial year-end in March 1969 were a handsome £482,687. By then Laker's passenger numbers had grown to 334,514, and the company employed more than 200 staff.

In anticipation of this rapid expansion, Freddie had leased 11 acres of land at Gatwick from the British Airports Authority. He assigned his son in law, John Seear, to project manage the construction of what he called the '£1 million Laker Airways' International Jet Centre'. Whether it cost as much as £1 million was anyone's guess, but construction began on a complex to house several aircraft undergoing maintenance, together with a five-storey suite of offices.

It took only 15 weeks to construct, and was 204 feet long by 180 feet wide. The hangar could theoretically house anything currently flying except a Boeing 747. Laker Airways settled into its new home in November 1969. Freddie's office was on the third floor and overlooked the old Air Couriers' hangar and offices where he had started. His other directors were a shout away down the corridor, the first floor was for Purchasing and Engineering, while Operations and Navigation were assigned the second floor. Accounting and the Commercial department were on the top floor. Laker Airways was growing fast, and so were Freddie's boundless ambitions. To no-one's surprise, following his devastating loss just a few years earlier, it hadn't taken Freddie Laker long to get back on his feet again.

CHAPTER 17

# Second Force Ambitions

## Round One to Thomson

1969-1970

After two years of waiting, the parliamentary committee investigating the future of British air transport finally published its long-awaited report on 2nd May 1969. The committee, headed by Sir Ronald Edwards, came to the somewhat obvious conclusion that Britain's airline industry was still grossly out of balance – namely that 90 per cent of scheduled routes were in the hands of the two state-owned corporations, British Overseas Aircraft Corporation (BOAC) and British European Airways (BEA). BOAC had all the long-haul international routes and BEA the European short-haul routes. The other 10 per cent was operated by independent airlines, struggling to find a few profitable destinations. Basically, the independents got the 'leftovers' – the routes BOAC and BEA didn't want. And they couldn't make them profitable.

Edwards, a member of the 'great and good' and chairman of the Electricity Council, was a recognised economist and recommended that the United Kingdom should have a licensed and designated 'second force' airline from the private sector, which should be 'financially sound and managerially strong' and 'embrace more than one of the existing airlines'. According to Edwards, the new second force airline should offer competition on some domestic and international routes and it would be licensed to operate a viable network, which would mean BEA and BOAC surrendering some its own routes. Freddie Laker had nothing but contempt for the report; he said it had recommended special privileges for Caledonian while "finding room for independents like me in the attic."

The Edwards report singled out two air operators that might be afforded 'second force' status. The first was British United Airways (BUA), which already had all the expertise of running scheduled services, although it fell far short of the requirement of being 'financially strong'. BUA had previously been managed by Freddie and during his tenure he had built it up into the UK's largest independent airline. But after he left, its finances had deteriorated and the only part of BUA that was financially successful was Bristow Helicopters, run by Alan Bristow. Bristow had wanted to leave, but was given a 20 per cent shareholding to stay and run the whole airline, replacing Freddie's successor, Max Stuart Shaw, who had presided over the financial disaster. Inevitably Bristow had found sorting out BUA a tough job. Everything was wrong. The only saving grace was that the company had many good people, particularly those who had been recruited by Freddie. Bristow, like Freddie before him, found dealing with the unions at BUA the main problem. Clive Jenkins, leader of the Association of Scientific, Technical & Managerial Staffs, was a particular nuisance. Seemingly he had 'declared war' on BUA and Bristow. For his part, Jenkins detested Bristow almost as much as he disliked Freddie Laker.

Realising that the situation at BUA was probably hopeless, three of the largest shareholders, Guinness Mahon, Blue Star and Hunting Aviation, sold their stock, leaving British & Commonwealth Shipping controlled by the Cayzer family as the principal shareholder. B&C also wanted to get out and put its shares up for sale. Bristow tried everything he could to get B&C to stay, but to no avail. The shareholders had all been terribly shaken by Freddie's departure, coupled with the fact that he had set up his own airline and was now a competitor.

Sir Nicholas Cayzer offered to sell BUA to BEA for £9 million, but BEA politely turned him down; the ongoing financial commitments involved in buying BUA and its order book would have been huge. The buyer needed to have £5.3 million for three new BAC One-Elevens, repay a loan of £5.7 million, and make good on lease payments for four One-Elevens and their spares amounting to a further £9 million. There were also two loan guarantees of £1.5 million for a Vickers VC10 and £2.5 million for another One-Eleven. All in all the debt was in excess of £24 million, and the buyer would need to have the money to pay for the share capital.

Cayzer lowered the price and offered BUA to BOAC for £8.7 million. BOAC was interested and the two parties entered into serious negotiations. The latter's managing director, Sir Keith Granville, whittled the price down to £7.9 million. The British Government gave preliminary approval to a proposed takeover after Cayzer warned Roy Mason, President of the Board of Trade, that there was no realistic prospect of a merger with another independent airline to create an independent 'second force'.

But there was another contender to buy BUA and take on the title of 'second force'. It was Caledonian Airways, run by the feisty and fiercely nationalistic Adam Thomson. Based in Scotland, the company flew charters across the Atlantic and wanted BUA's scheduled routes. Edwards believed that Caledonian should merge with BUA to become the much-vaunted 'second force' and that it should put in a bid. There followed long discussions about how the deal could be structured, but Thomson and his bankers, the Royal Bank of Scotland, couldn't see how they could possibly raise the capital to complete a deal and beat out BOAC. However, Adam Thomson was an ex-Navy pilot with ambitions that knew no bounds.

Harvey Crush, a well-known QC and at the time heavily involved in aviation, remembered: "Adam Thomson's ego was vast – it was as big as Scotland." Interestingly Crush also said of Freddie Laker: "Freddie's ego was as big as Kent." Crush believed that the independent sector was a contest of egos between Freddie and Thomson. He was right, and it lasted until the day Thomson retired. Crush preferred Freddie and believed that Thomson thought that he should be allowed to be the unopposed second force.

Eventually details of the agreement between BOAC and BUA were leaked to the press, by BOAC itself. Thomson was furious and unleashed all his forces, which was mainly unrestrained bluster. Caledonian applied to the Air Transport Licensing Board to revoke BUA's scheduled route licences and immediately applied for them itself, setting the scene for an ugly and protracted legal battle. Caledonian leaked its own ambitions to the press and said that it was Caledonian, not BOAC, that was closing in on a deal for BUA.

The Board of Trade's Roy Mason was seriously embarrassed and on 18th March came before the House of Commons and explained that Sir Nicholas Cayzer and British & Commonwealth had misled him. His approval for the BOAC-BUA merger was withdrawn until the situation was clarified and other bids considered.

In April 1970, British & Commonwealth had no choice but to act, and through its brokers, Baring Bros, it put its BUA stake up for auction. The asking price was trimmed a little more to £7.5 million and at that price Freddie smelled a bargain, throwing his hat into the ring even if he did see the pitfalls: "From a personal point of view, it will be a tremendous amount of hard work and I don't doubt that I will wind up being the richest man in the cemetery, not in the too distant future." By acquiring BUA he saw that he could combine it with Laker Airways into one big profitable airline. And who better to run it than the man who'd made good profits while running BUA? He reasoned that merging the two air-operating companies was in line with the Government White Paper on Air Transport, while at the same time it would produce the backbone of the second force.

Freddie moralised that it would be quite wrong to take away the competitive stimulus that the country needed so badly. If BUA was allowed to go to BOAC, it would probably mean the end of private scheduled airlines operating in the United Kingdom. However, despite his blather about the good of the country and the good of all, Freddie's interest was purely financial. He forecast that the combined airlines would make a pre-tax profit of £1.5 million a year for the next few years – not that he would be paying any tax. BUA had some very attractive capital allowances to offset against corporation tax for the foreseeable future, which could be worth as much as £2.5 million.

This was Freddie's two-year plan. By the summer of 1972 he saw himself taking the company public, valuing it at £22.5 million with revenues of £30 million. That was "the real motivation," he repeated to his executives. The attraction was obvious; Laker Airways combined with BUA would be the largest independent airline in Europe with the most up-to-date fleet of 26 jets.

Between them, Laker and BUA occupied an enormous 37 acres at Gatwick. The two companies would make a vast airline employing more than 4,000 people. But there was one problem: Freddie was still spooked by the unions, which were demanding parity with the employees of the national corporations, who enjoyed substantial advantages over their independent colleagues. They demanded equal pay and conditions; even a small increase in wages was calculated to be considerable. They were unreasonable and unacceptable terms.

It didn't matter that Freddie didn't have the money to buy BUA. Laker Airways made only £330,000 in 1969 and its net asset value was £1.2 million. He knew that he needed £7.5 million in cash and he expected to pay a further £1.082 million back to British & Commonwealth in repayment of more debt that had been borrowed to get BUA through the tricky winter months. Freddie's solution was to borrow from a consortium of banks, securing the loan on the assets of the combined group and an option to buy equity in the future. But this time even Freddie couldn't pull it off and he quietly backed out. His bid for BUA generated a few column inches and attracted some barbed comments from the likes of Clive Jenkins, who said that Freddie was nothing more than 'an old film star trying to make a comeback'. However, it was unlikely that Freddie gave a damn what Jenkins thought.

The 23rd May deadline expired and, with BOAC out of the picture, Caledonian was left as the only bidder when Alan Bristow's management consortium couldn't find any financial backing for its own plan. BUA was forced into negotiating with Caledonian again, and Thomson, now in the driving seat, stipulated publicly that this time it had to be Caledonian buying BUA – it was no longer a merger, it was a takeover. At Bristow's suggestion they came up with a form of hire-purchase deal with a payment plan of £100,000 a month, spread over 60 months. But the drama was not over. Caledonian couldn't even raise the small deposit required, so the sale talks were temporarily broken off. Eventually Thomson managed to find the money and the deal, however precarious, was done. The Government set about facilitating the merger of BUA and Caledonian on 3rd August in line with the recommendation for the second force. The BOAC and BEA objections were over, and both were brought to heel, but not before BEA had called in the lawyers again to try and block the sale.

Caledonian got BUA for a knockdown price of £6.9 million, and the deal was finally concluded on 30th November. The newly combined Anglo-Scottish company renamed itself British Caledonian (BCal) and looked to transform itself into a full scheduled airline. It installed itself in BUA's complex at Gatwick, barely a couple of hangars away from Laker Airways. The two were now near neighbours and set to become each other's greatest rivals.

Freddie slipped away quietly, but for the benefit of the press he gave his own version of a famous saying in corporate defeat: "They won, we lost – next?" And there were to be plenty of 'nexts'.

The first occurred in October 1970. Freddie involved himself with a new (non-IATA) airline called International Caribbean Airways, licensed by the Barbados Aviation Authority for an unrestricted worldwide service. The airline had the support of the Government of Barbados and its Prime Minister, Errol Barrow. Freddie held a 49 per cent stake and, partnered with a number of others including Major Norman Ricketts, who co-founded International Air Bahama in 1968, was the first Managing Director and chief executive.

The new airline ran scheduled weekly flights between Gatwick and Barbados via Luxembourg from 14th December 1970, using one of Laker's Boeing 707s, G-AVZZ. The arrangement called for the aircraft, flight deck crew and one or two Laker cabin staff to be supplemented by Barbadian stewardesses. Luxembourg was a low-fare friendly point that allowed the airline to bypass bilateral agreements. Fares in low season were £56 for a single and £106 for a round trip, while in the high season a single was £69 and the round trip £132. The livery of the aircraft was only altered with 'International Caribbean' in bold gold lettering and the national flag of Barbados.

Before the year was out Freddie bought his fifth and final BAC One-Eleven, G-ATPK, from Bahamas Airways; it was a 301 series aircraft, originally owned by British Eagle. Papa Kilo, as it was known, was every bit as good a One-Eleven as its four newer stablemates, yet it was perceived almost like the runt of the litter, likely on account of it being 'pre-owned'. For some reason, unbeknownst to everyone including those who flew the aircraft, Papa Kilo seemed to be able to perform slightly better than its stablemates. Perhaps it was slightly lighter – no one really knew. It again went to prove that aircraft in that era had individual personalities and perhaps even unique performance capabilities too.

Like all good entrepreneurs, Freddie was never satisfied. He personified the mantra that 'standing still is tantamount to going backwards'. His fleet of five BAC One-Elevens and two Boeing 707s was never going to be sufficient to do what Freddie had in mind. He was even overheard to say, "They're not really proper 707s," meaning that they were the short-fuselage version with a smaller capacity of 158 seats rather than the full-sized model, the 320 series, which could carry 189 passengers 1,250 nautical miles further, making them perfect to fly to Los Angeles, San Francisco and Vancouver. Similarly, while the One-Elevens were reliable workhorses for flights down to the Mediterranean sun spots, Laker Airways was already feeling capacity limitations on its most popular routes such as Gatwick and Manchester to Palma, Ibiza and Alicante.

With this in mind, Freddie asked his Purchasing Manager, the astute Brian Wheelhouse, to start looking at options for the future, while his Chief Navigator, Dick Bradley, was tasked with evaluating the routes, payloads and aircraft performance data of every aircraft currently flying, as well as any others that were still in development.

The BAC Three-Eleven cancellation still haunted him. He couldn't get over the short-sightedness of the British Government, which with the stroke of a pen had essentially cratered the future of the British aircraft industry.

CHAPTER 18

# The Skytrain Dream
## A solution to a problem?

1970-1971

"Bob, it should be like going to a station, buying a ticket and getting on a train. And that, Bob, is it."

"What is?" asked an exhausted Bob Beckman, looking back at Freddie Laker quizzically.

"It's the solution," asserted Freddie.

Beckman was the specialist Washington-based aviation lawyer that Freddie had hired in 1969 after he'd bought the two Boeing 707-138Bs from the receivers of British Eagle. It was already the early hours of the morning and the pair were still working, long into the night. They were holed up in Freddie's hotel suite in Washington DC in late 1970.

The mysterious problem, and the solution to it, was a subject that had been occupying Freddie's mind almost exclusively. It revolved around the problems of operating 'affinity group' charters, the only way anyone in Britain could access cheap non-stop transatlantic flights at the time.

In the modern world, and to those outside the aviation industry, it was a system that was completely baffling. The affinity group charters were a small niche in international air transport where governments allowed the smaller, mostly independent airlines to operate ad hoc charter flights. Carriers like Laker Airways would operate on a selection of routes, mostly transatlantic, and charter the entire aircraft to a single entity for a fixed amount on behalf of a group that was organised for purposes other than air travel. A qualifying group was allowed a maximum of 20,000 members, thereby excluding the most common clubs the public might be enrolled in, such as trade unions or motoring organisations. The rules stated that to qualify for a cut-price air ticket, members of the travelling group were required to have 'sufficient affinity', which was defined as at least six months membership before the date of departure. The group had to be clearly distinguishable from the 'general public'. As a further disincentive, travel agents were limited to charging a maximum of five per cent commission. The airline took no part in selling individual tickets.

The International Air Transport Association (IATA) had allowed the affinity group operations for the benefit of its own members, mainly because Pan American and BOAC had formed non-IATA subsidiaries to operate charter flights with their older aircraft. The complexity of the rules was designed to shut out any cut-price competition.

It had all started near the end of the Second World War at a meeting of governments in Chicago to discuss the ground rules for international civilian air transport, which was expected to become a major industry after the war. The governments considered applying the same freedoms to air transport that were historically available to ships engaged in international commerce by sea. Wars had been fought for the principle of 'Freedom of the Seas', and in the 1970s ships could go pretty much anywhere they liked. 'Should the air be treated like the oceans?' was the question. The governments decided it should not. International scheduled air transport would be permitted only between those countries that agreed to allow it. For example, unless both Britain and America agreed, no airline could fly between Britain and America, no matter how big they were or how much they lobbied their respective governments for approval.

The agreements between the governments controlled the number of airlines that would be permitted to operate, the number of flights that could be flown between the desired points in the different countries, the number of seats on each flight, the price that could be charged, the number of inches of legroom a passenger could be provided with, and even the size of the sandwich the passenger could be served.

The power of governments to decide, implement and control the details of international air transportation was, for practical purposes, exercised by the airlines. Back in April 1945 the airlines had formed the International Air Transport Association (IATA), to meet and decide by unanimous vote the prices they charged customers on all the world's air routes. That way, the larger airlines could not outvote the smaller ones. IATA would protect its own, regardless of their size and efficiency, which of course did not always go together. However, it did succeed in keeping airfares unreasonably high.

The United States Government agonised over whether it should allow its biggest international air carriers of the day, Pan American and TWA, to join IATA, and therefore engage in international price-fixing, which was a crime under US law. After an intense debate, the United States joined the price fixers. Air travellers flying the Atlantic therefore became the prisoners of IATA.

Freddie Laker despised IATA. He believed that air travellers, no less than purchasers of shoes or cars or radios, should have the freedom to buy the product of their choice, and airlines, no less than manufacturers of shoes, cars or radios, should be able to sell their services at home and abroad in free and open competition. Freddie, a self-acknowledged 'de-regulator', had always been a champion of free enterprise and IATA's iron hand on air travel was anathema to him. Transatlantic routes had been Freddie's dream for years. He'd tried to interest Myles Wyatt in a cut-price transatlantic operation when he worked at British United Airways (BUA), but Wyatt had always resisted.

Laker Airways was a latecomer to the market, mainly because it didn't have any jet aircraft that could fly across the Atlantic until 1969. The trailblazer of affinity groups was Adam Thomson's Caledonian Airways, the forerunner of BCal. Caledonian received the first permit in1963 by applying to the Civil Aeronautics Board in the United States. There were powerful objections by the major scheduled airlines but the permit was signed by President John F. Kennedy and forced the hand of the British Air Transport Licensing Board (ATLB). When Bob Beckman applied on behalf of Laker Airways for the same licence six years later, obtaining a permit had become almost a formality and only required the services of an experienced aviation lawyer.

Caledonian exploited the loophole with a strategy that traded on the ethnic links between Scottish expatriate communities in the US and Canada. It was big business for Caledonian and by 1970 it had flown more than 800,000 charter passengers, with a large percentage of these being affinity groups crossing the Atlantic. With very high standards of service and operation, Caledonian had the edge over most of the legacy airlines.

Freddie Laker embraced the system and worked it for all it was worth. In 1970 alone his hardworking little fleet of six planes flew 369,461 passengers, and affinity groups made up about 15 per cent. But affinity group charters were a strange business. People were put into fake organisations, and given an imitation back-dated membership card. Fictitious club names were used, like the Left-Handed Canary Club. These clubs would then advertise charter flights, and people from all over the place would book up on the Left-Handed Canary Club's flight to New York. Of course they had nothing to do with any such organisation and had never even heard of the Left-Handed Canary Club. The names of the clubs became absurd; however, what was going on grew to be an open secret and virtually impossible to police.

Tickets were readily available from bucket shops, primarily in the Earls Court area of London, the shop fronts openly advertising these charters. Carefully worded small ads appeared in the back of newspapers. There were just as many opportunities in New York, where some of the businesses were run by semi-criminal elements. It wasn't the airlines' fault; technically they had done nothing wrong, as they hadn't sold the tickets. But the responsibility was put upon the airlines to regulate the charters by removing suspect passengers or face punitive fines imposed in British Courts, or by the American Civil Aeronautics Board.

It was Ray Colegate, a senior official at the Board of Trade, where he had worked in the aviation department since 1967, who had the thankless task of enforcing the rules on affinity group charters. Colegate, noted for his fashionable cigarette holder that hardly ever left his lips, was a practical man. His roles at the Board of Trade and later the CAA made him all-powerful. Nevertheless, those upon whom he delivered judgement all agreed on one thing – he was a very fair man. As a trained government economist, Colegate had held various civil service posts in the Treasury and Central Statistical Office, so he understood the problems better than almost anyone. The previous November he had called the affinity group charters 'the biggest can of worms on the travel scene' when he spoke at the annual ABTA conference.

Unfortunately, Laker Airways had devoted its two Boeing 707s to the transatlantic charter market just as the affinity group debacle imploded. At the urging of their national airlines, the governments of Britain, Canada and the USA hounded Laker's flights. Government inspectors swooped in unannounced to grill each passenger on whether he or she was a member of the club that had chartered Laker's aircraft. The governments didn't go after the clubs that had improperly sold the tickets to non-members – they went after the airlines. Laker Airways, the upstart newcomer, became a particular target for the authorities.

Laker Airways' planes were raided twice in early 1971. On 26th March 112 American and Canadian tourists were stopped from flying home to New York. Investigators had been given a tip-off and arrived at Gatwick to interrogate the passengers about their right to be on the charter flight. It was being operated on behalf of the seemingly innocently named European Immigrant Families of New York and the Inter-University Student Programme. The impromptu 'sting' left many of the passengers stranded without the means to pay for an alternative flight home. Laker Airways was not guilty of selling the dodgy tickets and refused to refund the passengers. From then on, Laker tickets were boldly overprinted with charter regulations so that there would be no further doubt that the risk was with the purchaser. Not that anyone took the slightest bit of notice, and in mid-May of the same year the inspectors from the Department of Trade struck again. This time lying in wait were film crews from Britain's BBC and ITV television networks and a handful of journalists. Freddie accused the DoT of tipping off the media for maximum publicity, although the department denied it.

Freddie railed at their 'disgusting behaviour and Gestapo-like tactics' and said that they had 'trampled human dignity into the ground'. He called the inspectors 'second-class policemen'. Women were reduced to tears, and after the five inspectors had done their work 46 Americans were refused permission to board the flight home. Three hours later, the flight, which had been booked by a New York ticket broker called 'Aeromatic', departed from Gatwick with 30 per cent of its capacity empty. Those who were left behind complained that they had 'been treated like animals'. The interrogations of the passengers were tantamount to public trials. "It was disgusting and I was hopping mad at the way it was all handled," Freddie said angrily in a public statement, vowing to do whatever he could to change things.

What really upset Freddie was the public exposure and how Laker Airways had been unfairly targeted; he blamed the Department of Trade, claiming that it had organised the set-up with the TV crews and newspaper journalists, when in fact it hadn't. The affair hadn't made the Government entity look good either and, following the incident, the DoT sensibly stuck to quietly tipping off the airlines instead. Following the debacle, Freddie thought up his own typically novel solution, making much of his own statements that 'an ordinary man does not lie'. Freddie liked to think of the ordinary man as being very much in his own image, 'a glowing example of honesty'.

So at the check-in counters at both ends of the operation Freddie positioned a notary public with a Bible in hand for passengers to swear an oath and sign an affidavit that they had been a member of the group for a year, double the requirement in the rules. If nothing else, it demonstrated that the system was a complete nonsense. Little old ladies were swearing on a Bible because if they didn't they were not getting on the flight. The passengers signed the affidavits, they went into the pile and, if they were ever looked at, everyone had attested to being a bona fide club member. There was no one who wasn't prepared to knowingly perjure themselves for a cheap flight, including lawyers, doctors and even Catholic priests. It was ridiculous and against public policy to have people lying to get on an aircraft, even with charter fares costing anything between £25 and £50 compared to a one-way fare with BOAC of £140.20. Even BOAC's cheapest round trip excursion ticket on offer cost £144.20. So it was no surprise that people were prepared to 'lie to fly'. Seeing just how many people disavowed themselves just for a cheap airfare solidified Freddie's belief that the rules had to change and cheap air travel should be available to everyone without deceit.

Freddie and his deputy, Cliff Nunn, debated what to do. As was his way, Nunn hummed and hawed; he was somewhat ambivalent about how to deal with the pressing affinity group issue that had now reached crisis point. "Cliff, we need to shut the bloody affinity groups down once and for all," Freddie ranted. "We've just had another fine for carrying illegal pax and I'll have Geoff's head for it." Geoffrey Street was a former Royal Air Force Wing Commander that Freddie had somehow picked up during the formative years of the airline. He had been awarded an OBE for war services, and was in the company of numerous others from Freddie's past, some of whom had been given jobs and responsibilities they were not qualified to do or suited for. "He's a pleasant enough fellow," John Jones said of his slightly built and nervous Commercial department colleague, "but completely ineffectual."

Nunn agreed that the North Atlantic charters were most assuredly out of control and that Street had failed to maintain control over the affinity group programme. He didn't want to appear to be taking sides by pointing out to Freddie that most of the problems were outside Street's and Laker Airways' control. Instead he took a safer route: "What if you put John Jones in charge of the charters," Nunn suggested, but that was met with a firm shake of the head by his superior. Both Nunn and Freddie knew that there was a fair bit of tension between the younger and more dynamic John Jones and Street, which Commercial Manager George Forster often had difficulty in mediating.

With the future of the North Atlantic charter business appearing uncertain, Freddie wanted to unlock Australia as an alternative, knowing that it could be very lucrative. Fares to and from Australia were literally sky high. Under existing rules from Australia to Europe, Qantas had a virtual monopoly on discount flights, which could be priced at no less than 55 per cent of the IATA fare. Freddie had already been turned down once in the summer of 1970 when he had asked for permission for 60 round-trip charters. That had come about because of a chance meeting with Athol Guy; he was quite a celebrity as his band, the Seekers, had enjoyed a number of hits in every part of the globe, the biggest being Georgy Girl from the 1966 movie of the same name, which starred Lynn Redgrave in the title role.

The two men had been first introduced when Guy was in England on tour with the Seekers in 1969. Freddie's son-in- law, John Trayton Seear, had invited an old school friend, Bill Astling, to the airline's Gatwick headquarters to present a project he was involved with at Gaffneys Creek to the east of Melbourne; it was an old mine that needed investment and it was just the kind of thing that Freddie loved to put his money in. Astling brought Guy along with him and during a break he and Freddie got chatting. Freddie asked Guy what he knew about the Australian mining scene. "Not a thing," ventured Guy.

"Well, you're not much use to me then, are you?" exclaimed Freddie with a grin.

"Guess not, Fred," Guy grinned back, just as Freddie got called away to take a phone call.

Guy wandered down the stairs, into the hangar, past the two Laker 707s and out onto the tarmac to experience the roar of the jet engines on the runway. Within 15 minutes Freddie was sitting beside him on the grass offering an apology for his rudeness.

"Didn't take it that way."

"Typical Aussie!" boomed Freddie. "So, what do you know about the tourism industry in Australia?"

"We haven't got one!"

"Now you're talking! Come back upstairs. I want your help."

The two men just clicked. Guy loved what he called Freddie's 'cheeky integrity', and what followed was years of what Guy calls 'a boys own manual of how to be bloody serious whilst having the time of your life fighting governments, international airlines, bureaucrats and their barristers.' Guy appreciated Freddie's spirit: "One hour of rest, and you could not stop him from being a party animal. Many times I would put him in the lift to his hotel room after a long day and long haul travel, only to catch him an hour later emerging from the same lift to rejoin the team." Athol's wife Toni considered Freddie a loveable rascal, but liked the open character that he continually displayed.

Rather handily, Guy had become a Member of Parliament in his state of Victoria in 1971, and in April Freddie decided to try again, pitching his case to become an approved charter carrier on the route. Australian travel agents were already getting around the high scheduled fares between Australia's main cities and the UK by selling scheduled seats to Singapore, where passengers could book a cut-price charter ticket to Europe and enjoy a substantial saving. The planned operation would initially utilise Laker's two Boeing 707-138Bs, and offer an all-inclusive holiday to Europe for the attractive price of AUS$925.

Freddie registered a company, Laker Airways (Australia) Pty, in Melbourne, which was housed within Guy's own company, Athol Guy International, to ensure that it was Australian-managed. Guy had cleared his unpaid position with Laker Airways with the state's Premier, Rupert 'Dick' Hamer, and was engaged in longer-term discussions about the benefits to the whole country of Laker-style long-haul travel. One of Guy's roles as co-chair of the parliamentary parties' tourism and state development committee was as liaison with federal ministers and the select committee on tourism. There was no question that Athol Guy was a very useful man to know.

Freddie went to Australia with John Seear. Guy set up discussions with the governing Liberal Country Party coalition's Minister for Civil Aviation, Senator Bob Cotton, and the director of the Department of Civil Aviation, Sir Donald Anderson. The meetings were very cordial, but no more. Freddie argued that cheap charters were good for the Australian national economy, and Australia needed to do something about its tourist deficit, adding that it was all down to expensive airfares. He expected to gain rights to fly into Australia within a year, but not this time. As well as being the minister in charge of fares, Anderson was on the board of Qantas, and Sir Reginald Ansett, owner of Australia's biggest domestic airline, told Anderson to reject the proposal. Freddie returned home empty-handed to more uncertainty.

"I've tackled a lot of governments and won nearly every time. The only exceptions so far are South Africa and Australia," he said on his return.

By the early summer of 1971, the North Atlantic charters were completely unravelling. The ATLB started prosecuting air charter firms through magistrates' courts in England for breaking air transport regulations. The rules got tougher, plans for charters had to be filed with the ATLB long before departure, and any that were suspicious went to a hearing. The effect on Laker's business was devastating.

In the US the Civil Aeronautics Board was mounting its own crackdown. Its enforcement chief, Richard O'Melia, was of a mindset that just about all affinity groups were fraudulent and existed only for the purposes of cheap travel. The CAB sent its staff under cover to buy tickets and travel on suspect flights, and Laker continued to be caught out by spot checks. The CAB's approach was highly aggressive, asking details of the charters, and any airline failing to cooperate would receive a substantial fine. It compiled lists of all suspect charters, and the Laker list was said to run to more than 200 flights. But Laker Airways wasn't alone, as every charter airline was affected in some way.

Freddie sought legal advice from Bob Beckman. "What should I do?" he asked. "Stop operating," Beckman told him, which wasn't the answer he had been looking for. Freddie told his expensive American lawyer that telling him he couldn't do something just because it was unlawful was unacceptable to him. What he had really asked for was a way around it, and Beckman had failed to supply one.

Freddie came up with all sorts of ideas of his own, including 'blacklisting the bandits', but Beckman explained that this would violate US anti-trust laws. Freddie contacted Raymond Colegate at the Department of Trade to check, and he agreed with Beckman. Undeterred, Freddie sent Colegate a long letter containing his ideas on how to clean up the illegal charters. He suggested requiring clubs to submit passenger lists six months in advance, the period of membership required to qualify. The existing rules and the highly regulated regime that existed didn't make much sense to Colegate either, but he didn't make the rules, he just enforced them. Notwithstanding, Colegate came up with his own innovative idea. He called them 'Advanced Booking Charters', which was quickly shortened to 'ABCs'. Colegate's ABC fares required a lengthy advance purchase period of 90 days and the customer had to spend a minimum of 14 nights away. The airline operating the ABC flight had to submit to the CAB a certified passenger list in advance of the flight.

Freddie told Colegate that he didn't entirely disagree with his approach, but he maintained that the neglected 'short-term booker', like the 'long-term booker', was in need of cheap air travel without the frills and expense associated with travelling on the IATA carriers.

Freddie took the problem apart and examined each piece to find a solution. There were millions of people on both sides of the Atlantic who wanted to fly but could not afford it. He guessed that many people would be willing to accept uncertainty and even some discomfort in exchange for cheap flights. He decided to go back to basics. Freddie thought and thought, until finally he believed he had the answer.

The germ of the idea had taken shape in Freddie's mind some years before, after he had watched rail passengers arriving at Victoria station from Gatwick. When he had pitched a similar idea at BUA, no one had listened, but why would they? It was crazy.

But now he had combined those thoughts with another experience while on a trip to the United States. He'd flown the 'on-demand' shuttle service operated by Eastern Airlines between New York's La Guardia Airport and Washington National. Eastern also flew a shuttle service between La Guardia and Boston's Logan Airport. Freddie had been impressed by the simplicity of the operation. Long before today's intense airport security, shuttle passengers could turn up, board the plane and pay on board by either cash or credit card. The flights went every hour and the one-way fares were between $10 and $15. Empty or full, the shuttle would fly continuously. Freddie thought that a no-booking (just turn up), no-frills, single-fare 'shuttle'-type operation across the Atlantic could work in much the same way. When he had finished deliberating all this with himself he had devised a service that nobody working in air transportation would have thought could ever work. Freddie's passengers would not be able to make reservations. Food was not included in the price. People who wanted to fly could come to the airport, buy a ticket and, if there was space on the flight, they could go. If there were no seats left for that day they would go away or wait until the next day to try again. They could bring their own food or buy it on the plane. Freddie realised that he was proposing to offer in the sky essentially the transportation service that trains offered on the ground. And then in another burst of inspiration (according to Freddie), he shouted out loud while in his bath: "I know … I'll call it Skytrain!"

Freddie thought his idea was a stroke of genius, but would anyone else? After bouncing the idea off Beckman, he shared his vision with his own board of directors. "What we want is something simple like a train," he told the

**Above:** "My Greatest Technical Achievement and my Greatest Commercial Failure" was Freddie Laker's often used statement about the ATL.90 'Accountant.' Designed and built by Freddie's Aviation Traders (Engineering) Ltd. in the mid-50s as a successor to the Douglas DC-3. Competition from the more established manufacturers was intense, the 'Accountant' failed to attract any customers and the single prototype was eventually scrapped. Despite Freddie's considerable worldwide fame and success as an airline owner, he is less known for his achievements as an aircraft designer, engineer and innovator.

## From Canterbury to Berlin (1922-48)

Frederick Alfred Laker was born on 6th August 1922 in Canterbury, England. After troubled school years, he joined Short Brothers as an apprentice at age sixteen. Freddie's well-documented inspirational sighting of a biplane crossing the Hindenberg airship started a successful and tumultuous aviation career.

**Left:** Freddie Laker aged three.

**Right:** An early school photo of the young Freddie (centre) with class-mates and masters of the Simon Langton Grammar School in Canterbury.

© Mirrorpix

**Above:** Freddie (second from left) with a Lancaster Bomber whilst in the Air Transport Auxiliary.

© Elaine Seear

**Above:** Freddie(top) with a Hawker Typhoon.

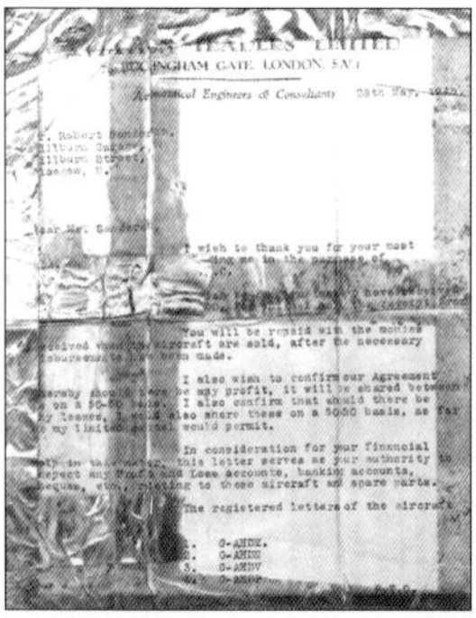

BUCKINGHAM GATE, LONDON, S.W.1

Aeronautical Engineers & Consultants

28th May, 1948.

Robert Sanderson,
Kilburn Garage,
Kilburn Street,
Glasgow, N.

Dear Mr. Sanderson,

I wish to thank you for your most

You will be repaid with the monies received when the aircraft are sold, after the necessary disbursements have been made.

I also wish to confirm our Agreement whereby should there be any profit, it will be shared between us on a 50-50 basis. I also confirm that should there be any losses, I would also share these on a 50-50 basis, as far as my limited capital would permit.

In consideration for your financial help in this matter, this letter serves as your authority to inspect any Profit and Loss accounts, banking accounts, cheques, etc., relating to these aircraft and spare parts.

The registered letters of the aircraft

1. G-AHDX.
2. G-AHDU
3. G-AHDV

**Left:** Freddie's letter of 28th May 1948 to Bobby Sanderson. He was confirming the terms of a loan of £42,000. It was his first big break and enabled Freddie to buy ten ex-BOAC Handley Page Haltons. Freddie treasured the torn & tattered copy for the rest of his life.

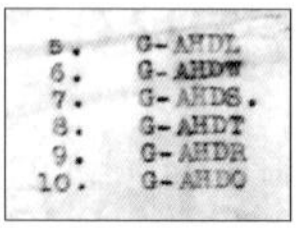

5. G-AHDL
6. G-AHDW
7. G-AHDS.
8. G-AHDT
9. G-AHDR
10. G-AHDO

**Above:** One of the ten Halifax (Halton) aircraft Freddie bought from BOAC in May 1948. Aviation Traders made further modifications to the Haltons for service on the Berlin Airlift with Bond Air Services during the blockade by the Soviet Union of 1948. The airlift made Freddie's first fortune.

© Elaine Seear

**Above:** Freddie and Joan. After his stint in the ATA, in 1942 Freddie married Joan Stallwood. He was just 19 and Joan was 25, but she was smitten by the young man's drive as well as his charm. Joan helped Freddie with his early businesses, wheeling and dealing WW2 surplus materials.

## Scrap Merchant (1949-1952)

After a couple of years buying and selling surplus WW2 engines and parts with Aviation Traders, Freddie acquired Air Charter in 1951 from Harold Bamberg. He then had an integrated airline with a maintenance, spare parts and engineering division, all under one umbrella.

© Elaine Seear

**Left:** Freddie's key executive, Bob Batt (R) with the 'melting pot' (of WW2 surplus aircraft and spares) at Southend Airport. Aviation Traders did anything and everything to turn the mass of scrap metal and parts into products that would yield a profit. The timing was right and the project made Freddie his second fortune.

© Elaine Seear

**Right:** The Dragon Rapide of Surrey Flying Services, the first airline Freddie purchased in 1951.

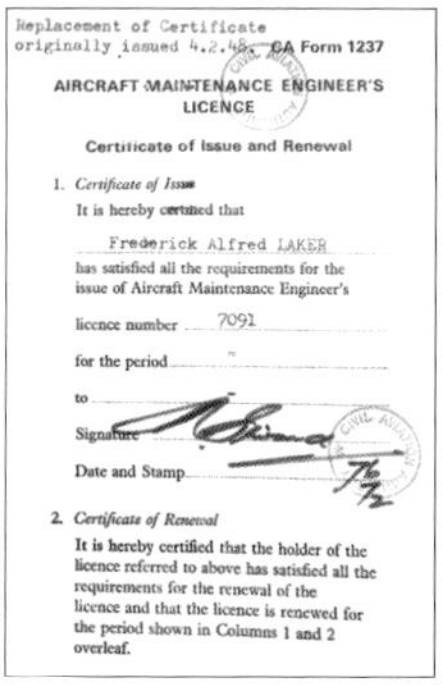

Replacement of Certificate
originally issued 4.2.48. CA Form 1237

AIRCRAFT MAINTENANCE ENGINEER'S LICENCE

Certificate of Issue and Renewal

1. *Certificate of Issue*
It is hereby certified that
Frederick Alfred LAKER
has satisfied all the requirements for the issue of Aircraft Maintenance Engineer's
licence number 7091
for the period
to
Signature
Date and Stamp

2. *Certificate of Renewal*
It is hereby certified that the holder of the licence referred to above has satisfied all the requirements for the renewal of the licence and that the licence is renewed for the period shown in Columns 1 and 2 overleaf.

© Elaine Seear

**Above:** Freddie's Aircraft Maintenance Engineer's Licence he'd held since 1948 and kept current thereafter.

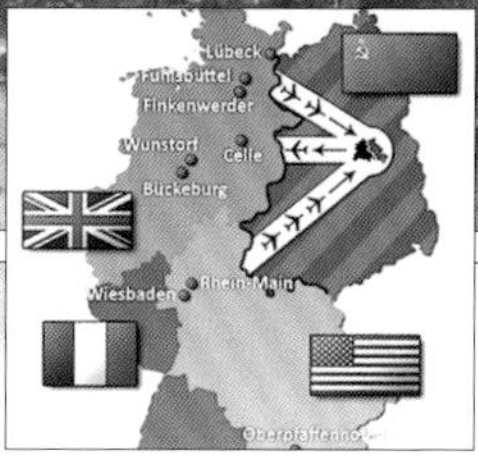

© Elaine Seear

**Above:** An Air Charter Avro York 685 aircraft carried refugees from Berlin in 1952. Derived from the famed Avro Lancaster bomber, the Yorks had done extensive work during the Berlin blockade of 1948-49 and were still capable and reliable. **Inset:** A map of the area around Berlin showing the British, French and American sectors of Russian-controlled East Germany and the three air corridors.

Air Charter was Freddie's first real airline venture. The carrier had a mixed fleet of Avro Yorks, Avro Tudors, Bristol Britannia 300s, and Bristol Freighters. It was a highly profitable airline.

**Above:** Bristol Britannia G-ANCE. Along with its sister-ship G-ANCD, the 'Whispering Giants' - as Britannias were known - were deployed on trooping flights and used as freighters.

**Above:** Joan (L) and Freddie leaving the Aviation Traders' building. Joan played a pivotal role in Freddie's early business successes and was a 10 per cent shareholder of the companies.

**Below:** An Air Charter Britannia after a trooping flight.

**Left:** The Avro Tudor 689 'Super Trader' was operated by Air Charter until the mid-fifties after Aviation Traders had modified it. Freddie was later called the 'Tudor King' by his adversaries.

**Right:** An Air Charter Bristol Britannia 307F in the Aviation Traders Engineering hangar at Southend. When Freddie sold out to Airwork in 1958, the Britannias were repainted in the livery of British United Airways (BUA).

## His 'Greatest Technical Achievement' (1957)

'and his greatest commercial failure.' The cost of the ATL.90 'Accountant' nearly put Freddie under.

Freddie (in hat) being interviewed after the successful proving flight of the Aviation Traders' ATL.90 'Accountant'. The aircraft was later re-registered as G-ATEL.

**Above:** Freddie emerging from the Accountant to be interviewed by dozens of reporters.

**Left:** The high setting of the Rolls Royce Dart engines was the Accountant's most unorthodox design feature.

**Right:** The sectional drawing of the 'Accountant' as seen in '*Flight*' magazine's review of the aircraft on 12th July, 1957.

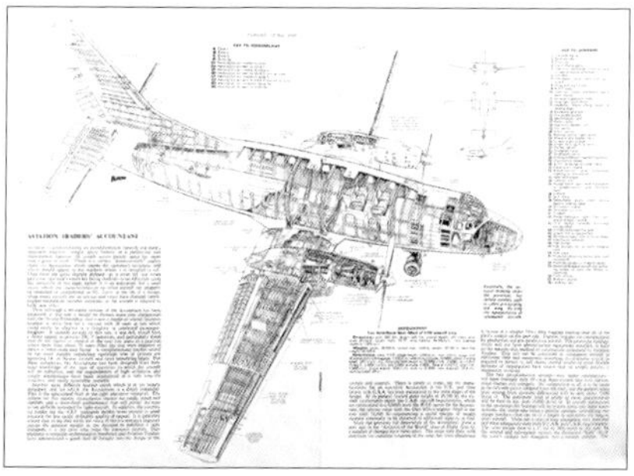

The ATL.90 'Accountant'

**Below:** Freddie (L) with Mr. L.P. Stuart Smith - Chief Test Pilot for ATL, Mr A. I 'Johnny' Johnson and Mr. D. Turner - Chief of Flight Test after the successful proving flight of the ATL.90 Accountant.

**Above:** The 'Accountant' had blind flying instrument panels for both pilots and a central panel for the engine instruments. The centre console housed engine, propellor, undercarriage, flap, and trim controls.

© Elaine Seear

## An Early Passion for Horses & Farming

Freddie sold Aviation Traders to Airwork which became British United Airways. The sale netted him nearly a million pounds (£21M in 2018), some of which bought him a stud and a nearby working farm.

**Above:** Freddie riding 'Pip' near his home on the Epsom Downs.

**Above:** Freddie with his farm manager George Plowes and 'Jasper' at the Woodcote Stud. George was much more than an employee - he was Freddie's best friend in the world.

**Left:** Freddie with one of his thoroughbreds at the Woodcote Stud. Racing and breeding horses were his main passions. Motor yachts were another.

**Below:** Freddie and his farm manager, Tim Haines (L) and George Plowes (R) with a prize Hereford bull at Woolgars Farm, in Surrey, England.

## Air Ferry (1954-58)

Freddie Laker was one of the innovators of the air ferry concept in 1954, where cars, passengers and cargo were transported across the English Channel to points in northern Europe. The air ferries were faster and arguably safer than the ships that ferried vehicles across the channel to France and Holland.

Freddie's Rolls Royce about to be loaded on to the Channel Air Bridge Bristol Freighter. He was racing against Stirling Moss and others in the Bleriot London to Paris air race.

**Right:** The Bristol Type 170 Freighter (often referred to as the 'Bristol Frightener') was the only mid-sized aircraft that could operate the air ferry at the time. Bristol 170 Mk31 and Mk32 were used by Freddie's Air Charter and its Channel Air Bridge division. The aircraft held three medium-sized cars, twenty passengers and flew at 165mph for 800 miles.

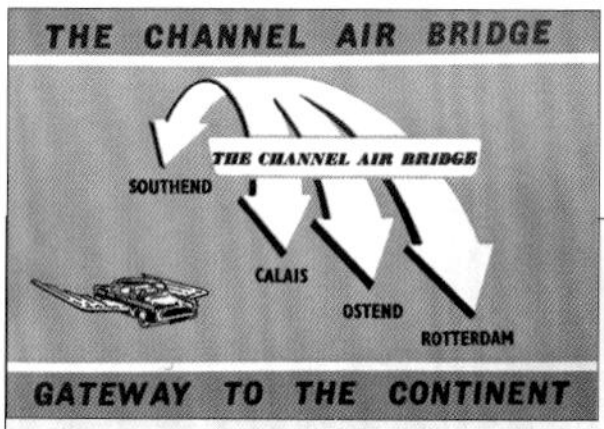


**Left:** The key routes in northern Europe flown by Air Charter's Channel Air Bridge division.

**Above:** Competition was fierce between Channel Air Bridge and Silver City Airways. The air ferries weren't just for the wealthy and on any given day, an assortment of vehicles were driven onto the Bristol Freighters.

**Right:** An Air Charter Douglas C-54 (DC-4). Freddie obtained a licence from Douglas Aircraft Corp. to modify the C-54 to carry cars, as the Bristol Freighters had limitations for the job.

## Family

Freddie had been married for 18 years in 1960. He had sold his companies and was a multi-millionaire, but he soon tired of playing golf and raising horses at his stud farm. It wasn't long before the domestic bliss Joan craved throughout the turbulent Air Charter and Aviation Traders era would end.

© Elaine Seear

**Above:** Freddie with his family, 12 year-old Kevin, wife Joan, 16 year-old Elaine and Jasper in 1960. Two years earlier, the Lakers had moved into their new home, 'Charters' in Epsom, Surrey where they overlooked the Royal Automobile Club's golf course. Woodcote Stud was just down the road. Freddie wasn't suited for a life of leisure with his family and soon landed a new role... at BUA.

**Above:** Kevin Laker and Freddie enjoying a serenade.

**Right:** Freddie's mother, Hannah. Freddie never forgot the sacrifices his mother and step-father, William Allin made for him when he was growing up. Once successful, Freddie always provided them with a lovely home and anything else they needed. His close relationship with his mother more than likely influenced the Lakerism 'there are three genders... men, women and mothers'.

## Enter the One-Eleven (1960-65)

Freddie's 'Aviation Traders' was bought out by Airwork in 1960 and it became part of the BUA group. He continued to oversee his division until he became British United Airways' first Managing Director soon after. His first initiatives at BUA were to commission the central London Air Terminal, place orders for new aircraft, combine the air ferry operations, and launch a successor to the Bristol Freighter.

**Above:** Freddie (R) with Station Master W. Fearne as work begins on BUA's passenger terminal at London's Victoria Station in 1961. BUA's passengers could check in at the city terminal and then board a train, direct to Gatwick Airport.

**Above:** The recently appointed British United Airways' Managing Director in his office celebrating ordering ten new BAC One-Elevens for BUA. It was farsighted on Freddie's part as the aircraft had yet to be built and tested and BUA wouldn't take delivery for several more years.

**Above:** BUA's Victoria Station Air Terminal. Freddie used his contacts at British Rail and committed substantial funds for the off-airport facility. The city terminal concept was then adopted by airlines in the USA and elsewhere.

**Above:** Freddie and Douglas Whybrow (R), the Director and General Manager of Channel Air Bridge at a press conference to announce their plans for the consolidated British United Air Ferries.

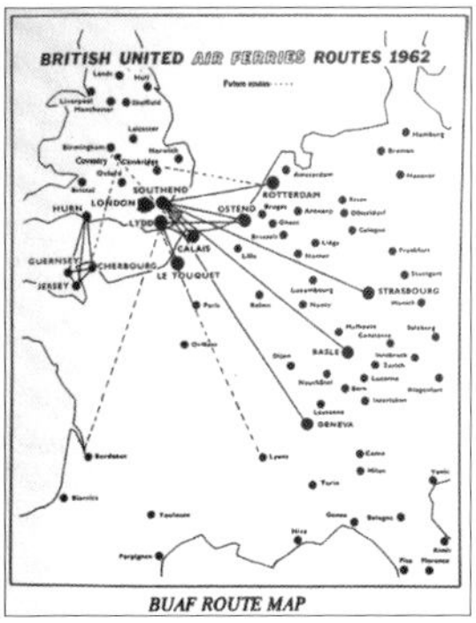


**Right:** The British United Air Ferries' route map. Bristol Freighters did the short hops while the longer flights deeper into continental Europe would be flown by the soon to be delivered ATL.98 Carvairs.

## The Aviation Traders ATL.98 Carvair (1961)

Freddie saw an opportunity to replace the Bristol Freighter with a larger aircraft for long haul car ferry operations from England to continental Europe. The first Carvair took flight on 22nd June, 1961.

**Above:** The ATL.98 Carvair, built by Aviation Traders (Engineering) Ltd. at Southend was a radical modification of the Douglas C-54 Skymaster (DC-4). Seeing a need for people to have their vehicles transported more expeditiously across the English Channel and beyond, Freddie had twenty-one C-54s modified to carry up to five cars and twenty two passengers. The aircraft was a very successful venture and fourteen international airlines followed BUA and bought Carvairs. The four Pratt & Whitney Wasp engines gave the Carvair a cruising speed of over 200mph and a range of over 2,000 nautical miles.

**Above:** An ATL.98 Carvair under construction at the Aviation Traders (Engineering) Ltd. facility, Southend.
**Below:** A BUA/Channel Air Bridge ATL.98 Carvair.

**Below:** Bob Batt (L), Managing Director of Aviation Traders (Engineering) Ltd. presents Douglas Whybrow, General Manager of British United Air Ferries with the Aircraft Manual for the ATL.98 Carvair.

## Car-via-Air (1961-62)

Freddie got off to an auspicious start in his first years at BUA. Following an enviable run of initial achievements, expectations were high as to what he would do next.

**Above:** Freddie with one of BUA's attractive hostesses.

**Above:** A custom lift, built by 'Little Green Engineering' that resembled a four-poster bed was positioned at each airport to transfer vehicles (& occasionally boats) to the Carvair's main deck. Later, Aviation Traders built their own lift which was faster, lighter and more reliable.

**Right:** Freddie proudly views a large model of the Carvair at a trade show where he took orders for the aircraft from a number of international airlines.

**Below:** An ATL.98 Carvair operated by British United Air Ferries was used in the blockbuster James Bond movie 'Goldfinger'. The movie villain's Rolls Royce is being loaded into a Carvair at Southend using the Aviation Traders' designed scissor lift.

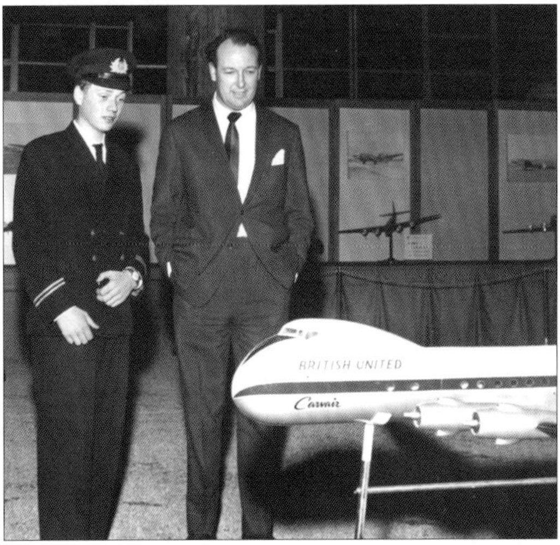

## Innovation (1962)

Freddie was an innovator and always keen to try something new and unproven. There was never a more pioneering approach to fast surface transportation across water than the hovercraft. Freddie seized the opportunity to promote British United Airways with the hovercraft, even if it was short-lived. His job at BUA also offered a Rolls-Royce, his own plane and some of the best-looking air hostesses in Britain.

**Above:** The British United Airways' liveried Vickers Armstrong VA-3 hovercraft on its inaugural service between Rhyl in North Wales and Wallasey (just across the River Mersey from Liverpool) on the 20th July 1962. BUA's Managing Director, Freddie Laker pioneered the world's first commercial hovercraft service.

**Above:** The VA-3 hovercraft arrives at Wallasey and is greeted by hundreds of astonished onlookers, civic leaders and most of Britain's press.

**Below:** Freddie liked having his own personal aircraft that came with the job at BUA. The Cessna 320 Skyknight had a range of over 1200 miles and could cruise at 250mph, giving Freddie lots of opportunities to visit BUA's out stations in Britain and Europe.

**Above:** Freddie with BUA air hostesses in 1962. He always enjoyed being in the company of attractive women and resisted hiring male cabin crew as long as possible. Freddie was now forty and in his prime, savouring the job he held and the privileged lifestyle he enjoyed.

© Alamy

## Image Building (1963)

Freddie disagreed with the extravagant remodeling of Portland House in London after the consolidation of BUA's various airlines and companies. Chairman Myles Wyatt and the Cayser family, the majority owners of BUA, wanted a classier image in the heart of London.

**Left:** British United Air Ferry's sales office at Portland House. Freddie and the new head of BUAF, Douglas Whybrow fell out over the extravagance.

**Right:** Freddie continued his 'hands-on' management style into BUA. He is painting the propellor tip of a Britannia to the amusement of his engineers.

**Above:** Freddie at BUA's new Portland House headquarters in 1963. Models of the two VC10s and ten BAC One-Elevens he had ordered dominate the boardoom's conference table. Freddie perpetuated his visionary forward thinking by buying aircraft years ahead of having the routes to fly them on.

## Ups and Downs (1964)

Freddie was thrilled to take delivery of BUA's new VC10s and immediately deployed them on routes to East Africa. He then took over BOAC's loss-making flights to Rio de Janeiro, Santiago, Montevideo, and Buenos Aires. Freddie's vision using the VC10s was about to make the routes profitable. BUA was having increasing trades union disputes which were abhorrent to the airline's staunch anti-union Managing Director... but first he had to celebrate his 42nd birthday.

**Left:** Freddie is presented with a golf club birthday gift by Geoffrey Knight, Managing Director of BAC. The two men had considerable mutual respect after cementing the deal for the One-Elevens.

**Below:** Freddie waves the flag to start a BUA VC10 sponsored vintage car race.

**Left:** Freddie cuts the birthday cake iced with his widely-used motto 'Fly British.'

**Left:** Freddie and BUA's Capt. Jennings about to board a VC10 bound for Rio de Janeiro that BUA served in late 1964.

© Getty Images

**Above:** Freddie satisfyingly holds a model VC10. Despite now being disillusioned by his role at BUA, he wanted to stay long enough to realise his vision of flying the VC10s profitably on prestigious routes to Africa and South America, and get one over BOAC.

© Mirrorpix

**Left:** Freddie helps his managers load luggage onto a BUA plane during a strike by BUA's Gatwick Airport baggage loaders in late 1964. The unreasonable and disruptive union action was a turning point for him.

## Exit Laker (1965)

Freddie felt he had accomplished everything he could at BUA. The new VC10s were operating reliably and profitably. He was now looking forward to BUA's first One-Eleven arriving. After a troubled period of flight testing that included one fatal crash, the aircraft was now certified and would be in service later in the year. BUA was destined to become Britain's first all-jet airline, but for Freddie, it was time to go.

**Above:** Freddie's Rolls Royce Silver Cloud 3 being off-loaded from a BUA VC10. Freddie had a cargo door installed on the VC10s as the bilateral agreements restricted BUA from having a first class section on their routes to east and southern Africa. It was an inspired move, as it reduced the break-even passenger load factor and there was always a heavy demand for air freight capacity.

**Right:** Freddie's Rolls was used in BUA's print advertising to promote their freight services on the VC10.

**Above:** Freddie (C) stands on the steps of a BUA One-Eleven before the inaugural flight from Gatwick to Genoa with former Marshal of the Royal Air Force, Lord Douglas of Kirtleside (L) and Geoffrey Knight.

**Above:** Freddie being interviewed by journalist Phil Holt. Shortly after, Freddie resigned as British United's Managing Director. Many of his key BUA management resigned soon after to follow him in his next venture. Freddie took his old oak desk when he quit, for good luck.

**Below:** Britain's first BAC One-Eleven went into service for BUA in April 1965, flying scheduled services and I.T. holiday flights throughout Europe.

## The Unthinkable (1965)

Freddie's days at BUA were coming to a close. He and BUA Chairman Myles Wyatt weren't seeing eye to eye and the union disputes were becoming unbearable. He had amassed a great deal of experience and achieved a lot, but Freddie wanted to realise his vision... with his son. Then the unthinkable happened.

© Mirrorpix

**Above:** Freddie pondering his future at BUA with a Vickers Viscount in the background. Despite being Managing Director of Britain's third largest airline, playing second-fiddle to Chairman Myles Wyatt proved all too challenging for someone with Freddie's personality and ego.

**Right:** The rift with Sir Myles Wyatt gave Freddie no alternative but to resign as BUA's Managing Director and then resign his Directorship of the Air Holdings Group a few months later.

© Elaine Seear

**Above:** Kevin, Freddie and Elaine Laker at Elaine's 21st. birthday celebration in January 1965. Elaine's future husband, John Trayton Seear was also at the party. A few months later, Freddie's beloved son Kevin was killed in a mysterious car crash while driving home in his Austin Healey Sprite. He was only seventeen. Freddie and Joan were devastated and Freddie spent weeks in solitary introspection. His friends and family weren't sure whether he would ever recover from the loss.

assembled executives. They had total faith in their boss's vision and readily bought into the idea; it was a fairly easy sell after the debacle of the affinity group charters. Now all he had to do was persuade the British and American Governments to give his idea a chance. Freddie asked Bob Beckman to help prepare and present the application to the British Government.

And so began a gruelling effort to get a presentation ready. Every morning while the process went on, Freddie would call Bob Beckman at his home from his office at Gatwick just as soon as the lawyer rose from his bed. Then, just as Freddie was getting into bed around midnight, he would call Washington again for news of the day's progress, usually just as Beckman was sitting down to dinner. Beckman would never dream of not answering or asking Freddie if he could call him back.

Freddie kept the pressure on and thought about little else, as was his way. In only a matter of weeks Laker Airways' first application to operate the new 'Skytrain' service from London to New York was made to the Air Transport Licensing Board (ATLB) in London. On 15th June 1971 the ATLB received a dossier outlining a simple no-booking, walk-on scheduled service with a fare of £32.50 each way in the winter and £37.50 in the summer. There would be one daily flight throughout the summer and four a week during the winter. Tickets could only be purchased six hours before departure. Freddie was determined to break the stranglehold on fares and liberate air travel, for the people. In doing so he was taking on the might of the British and American Governments as well as the major transatlantic airlines, BOAC, Pan Am and TWA.

Two weeks after filing the application, on Wednesday 30th June, he invited the press to the Savoy Hotel to reveal his plans. As always, journalists focused on how Freddie Laker was going to fund such an ambitious undertaking. And as he had always done, he assured them that his airline had the financial wherewithal to support the revolutionary Skytrain service. Laker Airways' application to operate Skytrain was scheduled to be heard on 19th September, giving him four months to prepare for the hearing.

After he had filed his application, he approached the young lawyer Harvey Crush to represent him. Crush, already a QC, was 30 years old and was well known to Freddie as he had prepared many air transport licensing cases before the ATLB, acting for numerous independent airlines. Crush also attended all the board meetings of the Tour Operators Study Group, and it was at one of these meetings that Freddie approached him.

"Harvey, I've got a new type of long-haul service I want to do."

"Is it a charter service?" Crush asked logically.

"No, it's a scheduled service and it's called Skytrain – you just turn up and board," Freddie responded enthusiastically.

"I'll do it," Crush said immediately, sensing that Freddie was clearly onto something. He was entranced by the idea and went off to Gatwick to meet with Bob Beckman, who had flown over from Washington. Already Beckman had been sounding out officials at the Civil Aeronautics Board in Washington with Freddie's grand plan, as the application process would have to be repeated in the United States. But Beckman's initial enquiries had been met with complete scepticism at the CAB.

Crush realised quickly that he had a lot to learn from Beckman. Presenting the case for Skytrain would be unlike anything he had ever done before. So he flew back to Washington with Beckman to consult with Tom Riley, an aviation economics analyst from Systems Analysis Research Corporation. Riley would present the economic case with all the costings and traffic forecasts. When Beckman and Crush returned from DC, the Laker Airways executive team were all sitting around the boardroom table waiting for them: Freddie, Cliff Nunn, John Seear, and most of the other senior managers. The meeting was a big let-down, as Beckman said he that didn't have answers, just more questions. He said that as it stood the idea could not be floated. It needed to be developed further and in more detail to have a chance of winning over the US authorities and defeating the opposition of the scheduled airlines. So Freddie told Beckman to retrieve his bags from his hotel and move in with him for a few days so they could brainstorm together. Late into the evening they debated ideas back and forth to meet any roadblocks that the British and Americans may throw up.

However, before any hearings were convened the Conservative Government led by Edward Heath passed a new Civil Aviation Act, which would come into effect in August 1971. The Act established a new public body that was called the Civil Aviation Authority (CAA), which would regulate civil aviation in Britain, as recommended by the Edwards report. Previously, the Director of Aviation Safety issued Air Operators Certificates on the advice of the Air Worthiness Registration Board, while the ATLB issued the licences. The new CAA would bring the responsible bodies together to oversee the airworthiness and financial health of the airlines, then issue licences. The mantra was that the well-financed airline would always be the safest. A secondary function would be to oversee the state-owned airlines, BOAC and BEA, which Professor Edwards had proposed remain as two separate entities.

The advent of the CAA meant that it wasn't the most auspicious time to be making the Skytrain application in the United Kingdom – the ATLB, already a toothless tiger, was in limbo. The ATLB had been created after the passing of the Civil Aviation Licensing Act of 1960, but all too often the board's decisions had been reversed by government ministers or civil servants at the Department of Trade who selected 'tame commissioners' to hear appeals, usually brought by BOAC or BEA. The commissioner did not make the decision, only a recommendation. When a recommendation did not suit, all the minister had to do was ignore it. The new, completely independent CAA with decision-making powers would solve this problem.

However, for the time being the ATLB would be deciding whether Laker Airways would get a licence. A man called Jimmy Lawrie chaired the board, and he didn't like Freddie Laker one bit – but loved Freddie's arch-rival Adam Thomson. This was crucial, as there was aggressive objection throughout the public hearings from British Caledonian and its lawyer, Leonard Bebchick. The Skytrain hearings, taken in the round, became a battle of two egos. British Caledonian's stated intentions were to become a full scheduled carrier, as Thomson put it 'to become the British TWA', and to do that it needed access to 'all available sources of traffic'. But, as Harvey Crush recalls: "Undoubtedly Adam ran a very good airline. It did do very, very well. But it was never actually big enough or powerful enough to stand on its own two feet through thick and thin."

Thomson didn't think that Skytrain could succeed, but even a 'living failure' was a source of concern because of a diversion of traffic. This would adversely affect the viability of the 'second force', as the London-New York market was the cornerstone of any viable system of a second force status to the United States. By concentrating only on one section of the market, Laker Airways would defeat the effort of the second force carrier to fight foreign airlines.

Freddie's counter argument was that he sought only to bring a little order to the chaotic situation in which the law served some people badly and made others resort to breaking it because simple, low-cost transport was not available to them legally. Affinity groups would continue, or Colegate's 'ABCs' would be introduced. With cheaper fares than Skytrain, and with reserved seating and free meals, they would not attract the same passengers who wanted to use the Skytrain service. Freddie wanted a niche for himself and for those passengers who wanted simple, regular, reliable, safe and comfortable transport between two points. "No frills," he said. "They don't have to pay for anything they don't want." Little did he know what he was about to start.

Beckman forewarned his client that undoubtedly Skytrain, even without a conventional booking system, would be perceived as a scheduled service and therefore it would be diverting traffic away from the scheduled IATA airlines. Freddie had to concede that passengers who had reservations on the lunchtime flight from Heathrow might call in at Gatwick first in the hopes of taking a cheap flight. If successful they could claim a refund from BOAC as a way of saving money. Beckman and Freddie prepared for these questions as well as numerous others. How could they stop touts selling tickets on at a profit? Was there a danger of a destructive price war? If it looked like being a success, surely the competition would want a piece of the action.

The ATLB's negative response to Skytrain came as a surprise; it said that it was concerned about crowd control in the queue for tickets. Freddie was taken aback by this concern – it was a question that neither he nor Beckman had anticipated.

"I have never known a reason for turning down something because it may be too successful," he started off. "Twenty years ago the London Palladium had the opportunity to book Frank Sinatra. Do you think they said, 'Oh, we probably shouldn't book him as we may have a queue around the block outside'? It's a ridiculous argument. What we are going to do is what the manager of the Palladium did ... he opened his doors and filled the theatre to capacity and when he had a full house, he put a sign up that said, 'Sorry, house full,' and the perhaps disappointed Sinatra fans disappeared off to the pub or did something else. We'll do exactly the same, except in our case the passengers who don't get on that day's flight will simply wait until the following day and travel then."

Bob Beckman and Freddie spent that evening devising more answers to unanticipated and off-the-wall arguments against Skytrain.

Over the course of the public Skytrain hearings, much was made of whether or not Freddie Laker's latest brainchild was adequately financed. The success of Skytrain had been predicated upon selling 100 seats per flight on a Boeing 707 with 158 seats, i.e. a 63 per cent load factor, but Freddie expected he could achieve at least 70 per cent. He had John Jones methodically plot the load factors, average revenue per flight, and the respective profit and loss sensitivities.

"We can afford to invest and lose £400,000 on this service without it having any impact on the actual fabric of the company," Freddie countered to BCal's lawyer, Leonard Bebchick's assertion that with a load factor of 48 per cent Skytrain would lose £400,000 in its first year. In effect, Freddie was only gambling a year's profit on the service, and he was certainly not going to allow Skytrain to bankrupt Laker Airways. The costs he considered would be lower since they wouldn't be providing free meals, and there would be extra income by charging for them instead – 25p for a cup of tea, 50p for breakfast and £1 for a main meal was the tariff his catering and cabin services departments had come up with. Freddie told the ATLB that he had set aside £30,000 as launch costs and for promotions. His gut feeling was that this was perhaps on the high side as he was banking on deriving considerable free publicity for the service. Freddie was masterful at promotion and with a phone call could have the British press corps with notebooks and cameras descending on the Laker offices.

In the latter stages of the hearings, BCal's Bebchick highlighted the potential problem of passengers who flew one way and then couldn't get a ticket to fly back. He told the hearing: "A family who at the end of their two-week holiday found that Skytrain was full by the time they reached the booking desk might have problems such as no cash to pay for overnight accommodation and local transportation, or for a more expensive flight. Our embassy and your embassy there are going to get a lot of phone calls from people who can't get on the Skytrain and don't have funds to get a scheduled flight back." Bebchick urged, as one of his final actions at the ATLB, that "Skytrain was not the sort of albatross you should willingly put around your necks."

Freddie was livid about British Caledonian's intrusion into the Skytrain hearings. BCal's application for North Atlantic scheduled licenses to New York and Los Angeles were shortly to be heard. And he was thoroughly annoyed with Adam Thomson. When the time came, Freddie played tit-for-tat and voiced all the objections he could think of at BCal's hearings for its routes. These were made in the genuine belief that BCal's case was very weak and about to inflict grievous self-injury. This he felt would rebound on the rest of the independent airline industry. Harvey Crush shared Freddie's opinion that BCal's case was weak: "They had equipment which was out of date. And the size of the market was not there. Nevertheless, Thomson and Bebchick put up a pretty good case and the ATLB awarded BCal a licence for a service they called 'NYANDLA' (New York and Los Angeles) and it was set to begin the following year."

In November 1971, the ATLB turned down Laker's application for a Skytrain licence. The prevailing feeling was that it should not be licensing something as innovative when the whole new structure of the Civil Aviation Authority, with a clear policy and guidance, was coming in the following year. The virulent internal arguments of IATA over North Atlantic fares, it said, were 'all too delicately balanced'.

However, the Board acknowledged that it seemed to be 'a very good idea' and said that it was possibly even worthy of a trial, especially if it drew off 'some of the present illegal traffic'. The ATLB did question the existence of Laker's 'forgotten man', and thought Skytrain would divert passengers from existing carriers.

Freddie could have waited for the CAA to be put in place, but instead appealed against the refusal. However, he would have to wait until March of the following year to have his appeal heard.

While pursuing his new idea, Freddie continued to take a stand against the American Civil Aeronautics Board. Laker Airways was one of the foreign airlines operating charters that refused to pass on information about its flights, its passengers and the respective charterers, despite repeated requests. Finally, Laker was given 20 days to respond and produce the information the CAB said it needed. Freddie didn't want to give it over and cited civil liberties and privacy as the reason: "It's simply a matter of what we feel they have a right to know." Freddie's stance just upset the Americans even further. Together with another British charter carrier, Donaldson Airways, he had further sanctions imposed after not providing the requested information. The CAB told both airlines that if they wanted to continue flying to the US they were required to submit detailed supporting information 28 days prior to each flight.

The tightening of the rules and the stringent policing by the authorities meant that the British, American and Canadian authorities turned down 90 per cent of Laker's proposed charters for 1972 – only 12 round-trip flights were approved. The affinity group charter flight bonanza was effectively over, and Laker Airways virtually closed down its transatlantic charter business, despite the enormous demand from passengers. The risks were simply way out of proportion to the benefits.

However, Freddie's vision was rapidly taking on a life of its own. It was now much more than the Skytrain dream, it was a quest akin to the search for the Holy Grail, and it would test Freddie's resolve like nothing he had ever attempted before.

CHAPTER 19

# Laker Goes WideBody

## Can the DC-10 cross the pond?

November 1971

"Oh bugger." The phone was ringing and it woke Freddie out of a deep sleep; his utterance was typical when being disturbed in the small hours of a cold November night in England. He turned on the bedside light and looked bleary-eyed at the clock sitting on the ornate marble-top bedside table. New Manor Farm, set in the Surrey countryside, was a family-size house which was unfortunate, as Freddie was now effectively a single man again. After less than a couple of years it was clear that he had perhaps made a mistake in divorcing his first wife Joan, who had been at his side since his late teens, and taking up with Rosemary. It was the latest of just a handful of errors Freddie had made so far in his life, his other faux pas having been mainly to do with aircraft. He was now living apart from his second wife, whom he had met in Africa a few years earlier, when he had been totally smitten by the beautiful woman. The pairing was ill suited; the bombastic, often crude, habitual philanderer was not a good match for the slightly nervous yet elegant Rosemary, who had exquisite tastes and style. Now Freddie entertained an assortment of female 'house guests', usually one-nighters, some of whom worked for him and probably thought it would advance their careers. But most nights he spent alone.

Freddie wondered who could be calling him in the middle of the night. Then his mind kicked into gear – several of his planes were operating through the night hours. A One-Eleven was heading back from Tenerife, an 1,800-mile flight and one of the longest the company did with the aircraft. Freddie marvelled at the skill of his pilots in extending the usable range and regularly undertaking 4-hour flights without a fuel stop. One of the aging 707-138Bs was returning to Gatwick from Toronto. He knew these old workhorses were getting towards their sell-by date and needed to be replaced before the next major check. He thought about what the weather was like across Europe. There was a time when Freddie knew the whereabouts of his aircraft at all times, but as the company grew he relied on the Operations department to keep him informed about how everything was running. And Ops always called him if there was an issue with something.

The phone kept on ringing. He jumped out of bed, grabbing his dressing gown, his mind going over all the potential scenarios. In the still of the night the phone's shrill double-ring seemed louder as he turned on lights and started down the stairs. Calls in the middle of the night were an airline owner's biggest fear and in his mind there could only be one reason why the phone was ringing at 3 o'clock in the morning. It had to be Ops calling with a problem, or worse.

Freddie picked up the receiver. "Hallo – Freddie Laker," he said breathlessly.

"Good evening, Mr Laker. Please hold for Mr McDonnell" said a crisp-voiced, middle-aged American woman.

"McDonnell?" Freddie said to himself. "Surely not James McDonnell. Must be someone else."

"Go ahead sir," said the female voice.

"Hi Freddie! So glad I could get hold of you. I hope it's not an inconvenient time." The caller was an obviously well-educated American man.

"Well, it's two in the morning here – who is this?" Freddie said abruptly.

"It's Sandy, Freddie – Sandy McDonnell. I know we haven't seen each other in a few years. How are you?"

"Er, very well, Sandy, thank you," Freddie responded, immediately sounding more civil. It wasn't often the owner of a small private airline received a personal call from the recently appointed President of the illustrious McDonnell Douglas Corporation.

Freddie had met Sanford's uncle, James McDonnell, a few years earlier when the recently merged McDonnell and Douglas entities were trying to sell their DC-9 and DC-8 aircraft to British airlines, with no success. Freddie was a red, white and blue flag-waving Englishman, and decided to buy BAC One-Elevens, the DC-9's biggest competitor, instead. Then, when British Eagle went into receivership in 1968 he was able to do a sweetheart deal for its two 158-seat Boeing 707-138B aircraft on the cheap. The 707 was the DC-8's main competitor at the time. Truth be told, Freddie didn't much care for the nose of the DC8 and thought the 707 was a much 'prettier' aircraft.

His brain now in overdrive, Freddie was thinking fast. "Why would Sandy McDonnell be calling me at this hour? They know I'm committed to the One-Eleven. Surely they aren't trying to get me to buy their DC-8s."

"How is Mac?" Freddie asked the junior McDonnell about his uncle James. Freddie was in awe of the elder McDonnell's vision and his achievements; the esteemed Princeton and MIT-educated aeronautical engineer had received numerous awards for his contributions to aviation and had founded the McDonnell Aircraft Company in St Louis, Missouri. Freddie had only briefly dabbled in military operations with Department of Defense work, but he knew McDonnell Douglas was a preferred US Government contractor and its military work was the company's primary focus. The California plants manufacturing the DC-8 and the DC-9 had now shifted much of their operations to the DC-10 as the DC-8 programme was winding down. Freddie knew that the anticipated regulations concerning engine noise would likely put an end to the DC-8 and they'd all end up in Africa and South America, or the desert airparks and graveyards in the USA. DC-9 sales had literally gone through the roof over the previous few years since they had started the line in 1965. Long before CAD and robotics were in everyday use, McDonnell Douglas was turning out as many as four DC-9s a week. Moreover, Freddie knew that the three American carriers, United, American and National, had pretty much grabbed all of the first batch of DC-10s and had firm orders and options on many more.

"My uncle's fine, thanks – in his seventies now but as active as ever. He asked me to send his best regards to you. Freddie, the reason I'm calling at this late hour is because we have a bit of a problem." McDonnell continued with a heavier tone in his voice, "I obviously can't get into too much detail but there's been some dirty dealing on the other side of the world."

Freddie was intrigued and suddenly didn't feel the least bit tired. "Go on, Sandy."

"Well, All Nippon Airways signed a deal with us for six DC-10s and for reasons best known to them and perhaps the Japanese Government, they've suddenly cancelled. Apparently All Nippon came under pressure to not introduce wide-body jets for the time being."

"Can't you just pocket their deposits and sell the options on?" Freddie responded with typical logic.

"It's not quite that simple, Freddie, because all the financing is coming from Mitsui." Freddie knew of Mitsui. It was one of Japan's largest conglomerates that owned companies in banking, shipping, insurance, steel, chemicals, and many other industries. McDonnell continued: "All $150 million, to be exact. So Mitsui are the de facto owners of these DC-10s." Freddie let out a sigh as he acknowledged the magnitude of what McDonnell was telling him, especially as dirty deals were not part of MDC's culture. Sanford Noyes McDonnell was well known and respected for his work ethics. He wasn't called a 'boy scout' just because of his high morals and adherence to strict rules. He had actually been a top level 'Star Scout' as a young man growing up in Little Rock, Arkansas, and had introduced the legendary 'Scout's Promise' as the foundation of MDC's code of ethics.

As soon as McDonnell mentioned the DC-10 Freddie was on familiar ground, as he had studied that MDC project. Originally conceived to fly between the east and west coasts of the USA for United and American Airlines, MDC's DC-10 was a wide-body tri-jet similar to Lockheed's L-1011 TriStar. The two aircraft were alike in size and design, the main difference visually being that the DC-10's centre engine was an integral part of the vertical stabiliser, whereas the TriStar's S-ducted centre engine was housed in the fuselage. Opinions were divided on which tri-jet was superior, and Freddie, as would any respecting airline executive, had compared the specifications of both aircraft, as well as Boeing's 747. He knew that wide-body was the future, but also appreciated the enormous risks involved with operating a large-capacity aircraft with the high price tag that came with it. Freddie always preferred to buy British if he could, and the L-1011 did at least offer British-made Rolls-Royce RB211 engines. He also favoured the DC-10 more than Lockheed's tri-jet for numerous reasons, not least of which was the DC-10's better range, but the cost of both aircraft was prohibitive. When he had enquired about the TriStar he had been informed that the earliest delivery dates were not until 1974 or 1975. Freddie had tried to obtain two of the aircraft from Pacific Southwest, but it came down to one thing – no one would give him the financing terms he needed.

Freddie knew that McDonnell Douglas and Lockheed were in competition for military and civil aircraft sales and there was no love lost between the two companies. Airline contracts for the two aircraft were being sought in an aggressive manner, with MDC winning American and United for the first DC-10s and Lockheed securing deals with Eastern and TWA for its TriStars. He was aware that sales teams from both manufacturers were banging on the doors of every major carrier across the globe and were sparing nothing on lavish entertainment and other 'incentives' in an effort to woo the airlines' key decision-makers. Freddie held back a laugh. "And I suppose you think I should buy six DC-10s from you, Sandy, even though I haven't any work for them and they won't fly to anywhere I want to go, such as across the Atlantic."

"Actually, Freddie, the DC-10, even though it was originally designed for coast-to-coast operations, may well be OK for transatlantic if you reduce the all-economy capacity down from the maximum 380 seats and do a few other relatively minor things." McDonnell had now said something that really grabbed Freddie's attention; he thought about this for a second or two, but before he could respond McDonnell said the magic words, "and between MDC and Mitsui we'd give you a drop dead purchase price and some great financing. We've managed to get the Turks to take three of them, so what if you made a commitment for two, Freddie, with an option on a third? They aren't quite finished yet but the first ones will be coming out of the shed at Long Beach fairly soon. You should pop over and take a look at them."

McDonnell was gently persuasive and he knew which of Freddie's buttons to push. He had intuitively figured that Freddie Laker would be interested in the DC-10s. Freddie's reputation as a wheeler-dealer was unsurpassed and McDonnell knew that he wanted to expand his operations on the North Atlantic. MDC had already hit on Freddie's arch-nemesis, British Caledonian's Adam Thomson, to take the three aircraft, but Thomson, a typically tight-fisted and oftentimes belligerent Scot, baulked at the price. Truth be told, Thomson was nowhere near the visionary that Freddie Laker was and it's likely the thought of expanding BCal into wide-body jets brought him out in a sweat. McDonnell strategically kept his conversation with Thomson from Freddie for fear of having the phone slammed down on him; the long-standing acrimony between Laker and Thomson was well known throughout the entire civil aviation industry.

"Let me give you a ring back tomorrow, Sandy," Freddie responded, trying to sound as if he couldn't really care less. "I need to speak with some of my chaps about it, especially the bloke who does all the aircraft performance analysis.

He'll be able to say based on your data whether he thinks we can get across the pond and still have enough reserves for New York. If they can't make JFK and Toronto, then the Tens aren't for us, I'm afraid," he concluded.

"OK, that sounds good, Freddie. I'll look forward to hearing back from you and meantime I'll telex over some financials for you so you can see the plane's operating cost data and work out the approximate repayment schedules. I know Mitsui are really keen to do a deal with someone – heads will roll there if they don't offload. They may even be getting the swords polished up." Freddie laughed at the thought of how embarrassing this must be, and in Japan of all places. "The timing is really good for this to happen, Freddie, and I know I speak for my uncle and everyone at MDC when I say we'd love to see some of our planes with 'Laker' painted on the side. Speak soon. Bye."

"Cheers, Sandy," Freddie said almost reluctantly, as in a way he wanted the MDC top man to keep going with his sales pitch. Like many brilliant men, Freddie's ego needed continual massaging and having someone of McDonnell's stature sucking up to him like this was the fuel that kept him going. Freddie was astute enough to realise that a deal with a small British independent airline like his would open the doors for DC-10 sales to many airlines other than the major flag carriers. This he figured would give him a bit of leverage for negotiating a better deal.

As McDonnell rang off, Freddie started to get that feeling he always got when he could smell an incredible deal in the making. It was like a gambler's 'high' when he wins at the tables or, in Freddie's case, when one of his thoroughbreds won a big race. "It's better than sex," he was famous for saying after a victorious moment, whether in business or at the race track. Freddie had a history of gambling on buying aircraft before he had any work for them, or had even figured out how to pay for them. It had always worked before, so why not now? He knew his old Boeing 707s had to achieve high load factors to break even. Their early-generation turbofan engines consumed more than 1,800 US gallons of fuel an hour, and the next major check would cost more than the planes were worth. Quiet, wide-bodied jets with modern high-bypass turbofan engines were the future – the Boeing 747 had proved that already. But the purchase of a 747 was out of his league and the demand for the aircraft ensured that there were no deals to be done. A tri-jet made much more sense for Laker Airways: cheaper to buy, less costly to operate with only three engines rather than four, and a smaller seating capacity than a 747 meant fewer empty seats in the low seasons and a better break-even load factor. The DC-10 could be perfect for Skytrain, he thought.

The medium-range DC-10 would be quite at home operating flights down to the Mediterranean too. "If we can get it across the Atlantic with enough reserves..." His thoughts trailed off, even though the impromptu call from McDonnell dominated his entire being. Freddie envisaged a couple of DC-10s freshly painted in his traditional white with the red and black stripes and a big 'LAKER' on the tail sitting on the MDC flight line at Long Beach. They'd be next to other brand-new DC-10s destined for every major American carrier and a host of other internationally known airlines. He imagined the press reaction as the first of his new wide-body jets landed at Gatwick. Laker would be the first DC-10 operator in the whole of Europe. “All the free publicity I’ll get will help fill the planes,” he thought.

Now wide awake, Freddie went to his study and started making notes and ‘to do’ lists for all his key executives. He resisted the temptation to immediately call Dick Bradley, his chief navigator. Instead, Freddie pulled out books and magazines and anything he could find on the DC-10. Realising that sleep was now impossible, he made a strong pot of tea, had a hot bath and picked a dark grey ensemble from the row of two and three-piece suits in his wardrobe. As he got dressed for work his mind was focused only on McDonnell Douglas DC-10s and what he would do with them.

When Freddie got to his office the first person he spoke to about the conversation with Sandy McDonnell was John Jones. Freddie had a strong affinity with his young and assertive protégé, whom he was unofficially grooming for a promotion in the Laker organisation. Freddie knew that the venerable George Forster, Jones’s immediate superior, was going to retire soon for health reasons and he was mentoring Jones to take over from him in what was perhaps the most crucial job in the company, after his own. But Jones still had a few rough edges, and quite a few of Laker Airways’ management team had on occasion marched into Freddie’s office complaining about the young man’s abrupt manner and that he was ‘impossible to work with’. Freddie took it all in his stride and usually told the complainer that he’d deal with it, but hardly ever did. He gave Jones a lot of latitude as he knew he had one of those rare analytical minds and work ethics that could steer the company’s future, and he wanted to develop that potential to the full. Freddie told Jones what McDonnell had offered a few hours earlier. He also confirmed that the deal couldn’t happen until Dick Bradley had worked some magic with his slide rule, because it wasn’t known yet if the DC-10 could get to New York with enough reserves.

Jones left Freddie’s office knowing that for the next few weeks the old man would be thinking about nothing else but DC-10s. He’d be living and breathing the aircraft, running around the office holding a DC-10 model, hanging photos of them in the hallways and talking about them ad nauseam. In no time at all Freddie would become the world’s most knowledgeable individual on the DC-10. His excitement and boyish enthusiasm would, as always, be completely infectious and, no matter how busy they all were with their main jobs, Freddie would relentlessly enrol, coerce and browbeat everyone in the Laker organisation and beyond into having a DC-10 mindset, just like his. Nothing would be allowed to dilute his latest vision. Jones had been down this road before and knew the form, but if this deal with MDC came off it would seriously raise the bar for the company. Jones likely had on his mind how on earth he would fill these massive planes with passengers, but there were other considerations for Laker operating DC-10s, perhaps even bigger challenges than those that Jones would have on his plate.

To start with, finance director Robbie Robinson would have to juggle the books, as Laker’s cash resources were virtually non-existent and its current cash flow from operations couldn't handle the anticipated debt repayment and interest. McDonnell Douglas surely knew that Laker didn't have the money or any immediate work for DC-10s. The hangar would need to be modified to accommodate the aircraft. Freddie's son-in-law, John Seear, had helped design the hangar that currently made no height allowance for anything taller than a Boeing 707 tail. This point may have given Jones cause for a wry smile, as there was no love lost between himself and Seear. All the engineering equipment would need to be upgraded. How would Laker's brilliant engineering team managed by Peter Yeoman change the DC-10's centre engine sitting more than 30 feet off the ground? Where would the huge wheels and tyres be stored and the brake units serviced? An expansion of the engine shop would be needed to accommodate the massive new and relatively untested GE CF-6 engines. Purchasing manager Brian Wheelhouse would have to procure all the spare parts, seats, catering equipment and other capital items they would need; at the time Laker didn't even possess a set of steps long enough to get onto the aircraft. Operations manager Atty Atkinson and Captain Alan Hellary would have to decide who would be the first pilots and flight engineers to be trained in California, then in turn become the DC-10 fleet's training personnel. Head of cabin services Joy Harvey would have to create new positions and promote the most senior and competent cabin crew to operate the DC-10. It would require at least ten hostesses. Catering manager Nina Griffin would have to ramp up the flight kitchens and bonded store operations to provide an excellent food and beverage service for more than 300 passengers and 13 crew. Cliff Nunn would have to find a new source of bonded fuel as the DC-10 would consume more than 2,400 US gallons of fuel every hour. Airport logistics at each point the DC-10 would operate would have to be planned and suitably equipped. Gatwick Handling didn't even have a tug that could push back a fully loaded DC-10 from the gate, as no airline operated wide-bodied aircraft there. The list went on and on. It would all be moot, of course, if the aircraft couldn't make it across the Atlantic from Gatwick to New York and Toronto. So the future of Laker's DC-10 acquisition was arguably in the hands of Dick Bradley.

This was another example of Freddie Laker's genius, and why he had been so successful. Just as things had stabilised and were running reasonably smoothly at Laker Airways, he would have another whim and throw everything and everyone into virtual chaos. The airline's dedicated senior executives and their respective departments would be expected to work 15-hour days to achieve Freddie's latest vision, with the obvious compromises to family life and their health. And Freddie would resist hiring any more staff than absolutely necessary. He was also a master at keeping things close to his chest and he had effectively used this management style since he was a young man. He typically told each of his key executives what they needed to know to do their job and not much more. He was the only one that would have the entire picture. It was an old-fashioned technique and an extension of his insecurity complex, but it had always worked for Freddie ... and he wasn't about to change.

George Forster had been with Freddie for close to two decades since the Air Charter days. Nothing much fazed him. Forster would map out a strategic plan for Jones, Gerry Sharp, Geoff Street and the rest of the Commercial department for the DC-10 operations. They had Lord Brothers and Arrowsmith to sell seats to their UK client base. The Laker companies all had an enviable reputation with the travel trade so there would be terrific support from travel agents. On the other side of the Atlantic, they had well-respected tour operators in the USA and Canada who would be excited about the opportunity to sell packages to the UK on a brand-new wide-body jet.

Freddie needed Dick Bradley to do a quick performance assessment and give him assurance that the DC-10 Series 10 aircraft could fly across the Atlantic. Above every other consideration, this was pivotal before going to the next step. It would be key to Freddie calling back Sandy McDonnell and potentially agreeing in principle to the purchase of the first DC-10s in Europe.

Sandy McDonnell had been vague as to why All Nippon had suddenly cancelled the purchase of six wide-body DC-10 jets. Freddie wanted to know why. He knew that if he had all the information, he'd have better negotiating leverage with MDC and with Mitsui. So he called Bob Beckman in Washington and asked him to do some digging and try and find out the real reason behind the sudden ANA cancellation.

"Mr Laker, I have Mr Beckman holding for you," Lesley Chilton said not half an hour later as she handed Freddie a fresh cup of tea.

"What've you got, Beckers? What have you found out about the ANA stuff."

"Freddie, I'm sorry but I've never experienced such silence on something this big. No one, I mean no one, is talking. I spoke to a lawyer friend in Tokyo who works with Mitsui."

"And?" asked Freddie anxiously.

"Well, I'm sorry Freddie but there's no 'and'. There's nothing. Zero. A dead end. This probably goes higher than you can imagine." That wasn't what Freddie wanted to hear, as he knew that not having good intelligence on what had gone down in Japan could weaken his negotiating position with Mitsui and MDC. But he was still in control.

"OK, Bob, well thanks for trying and if you hear anything at all, no matter how insignificant, call me any time."

Dick Bradley confirmed that he had MDC's data but that it was all based on what American and United were doing with the planes, and didn't really show their maximum potential. It all came down to payload, headwinds on the Atlantic, and some take-off considerations. With a reduced seating configuration instead of the maximum 380, and with Gatwick's current runway length, the DC-10-10 could possibly make New York with enough reserves. But the notoriously long ATC delays at JFK had to be considered. The last thing anyone needed was for a captain to declare an emergency landing because the aircraft was out of fuel from circling for an hour or more. Freddie only really heard the first part of Bradley's analysis. Like all good entrepreneurs he only focused on the positives. He just wanted confirmation that on most days – average days – the DC-10 could get to New York from Gatwick.

Freddie was confident that the 47-year-old, 6-foot former Royal Air Force officer could make the aircraft do what he needed it to do. After all, Bradley was a guy who was not only a world-class navigator and aircraft performance specialist, he'd also spent a year doing computer programming in 1965, years before the word 'computer' was part of the lexicon. When he'd decided to take a year's sabbatical, he'd built a house and learned Mandarin on the side. Dick Bradley wasn't just your average guy. Alan Hellary used the term 'genius' to describe him, so if Bradley was confident the DC-10 could fly the Atlantic, then it could. And it would. Freddie also knew that his pilots were masters at stretching the operating range of every aircraft they flew; whether it was the One Elevens or the Boeings, they'd squeeze every ounce of performance from the plane. Fuel conservation was in every Laker pilot's DNA. He instructed Bradley to go and do some magic with his slide rule and give him a 100 per cent assurance that the DC-10s could cross the Atlantic and not risk anything. "Right boss, back to you in a bit," replied Bradley.

As Freddie sat pondering what he was about to commit to with McDonnell Douglas, he started doodling on his pad, thinking about the press release he'd need to draft for the announcement. It was going to be a very big deal. Every newspaper would have it on its front page, he thought as he scribbled down the headline 'Laker Goes Widebody'.

CHAPTER 20

# The Battle for Skytrain

## A watershed year for Freddie

1972

In March 1972 the Commissioner who heard Freddie's Skytrain appeal was Sir Dennis Proctor, a former managing director of the Maersk shipping line and a retired career civil servant. Harvey Crush represented Laker Airways again and the second time around it went a lot better. Crush told the panel that if Freddie wanted to lose money that was up to him, as it was his money to lose. Proctor was impressed and Freddie told Proctor that Skytrain could be flying by August if his licence was granted expeditiously.

Freddie successfully convinced the panel that the need for Skytrain existed and, on appeal, won permission for Skytrain to fly. Proctor said that he "had no hesitation in recommending this appeal." The board accepted that there was a demand for a standby service of this kind from passengers who were not prepared to travel at the IATA fares – to such an extent that it feared that a 'near chaotic' situation might arise at the airport from an uncontrollable demand.

Incredibly, John Davies, the new Minister for Aviation, disagreed. He vetoed Proctor's decision pending the arrival of the CAA. Freddie was going to have to go through the whole process all over again if he was to ever realise his Skytrain dream. Freddie hoped that the Prime Minister, the Rt. Hon. Edward Heath, would force Davies to uphold the original appeal decision, thus avoiding another round of hearings before the new CAA.

On 30th March 1972 Freddie was received at 10 Downing Street. But Heath followed the advice of the civil servants that the new CAA could not be excluded and must hear the case. The fear was that the new body would be 'irreparably weakened before it had convened' if it was excluded. The very next day, the 31st, the reign of the ATLB ended and that of the CAA was due to start. Davies's decision was upheld and Laker Airways' Skytrain approval lapsed.

There were a number of problems facing the CAA when it came into being on 1st April 1972 under the chairmanship of 63-year-old Lord John Boyd-Carpenter. He had been the Conservative MP for Kingston-upon-Thames for 26 years, held the position of Minister of Transport & Civil Aviation briefly between 1954 and 1955, and latterly had been Chief Secretary to the Treasury.

In the short space of time since Laker Airways had operated its first 'affinity group' charters, three or so years earlier, the aviation industry had changed forever. Pan Am had landed its first Boeing 747 at London's Heathrow Airport in January 1970. Boeing hadn't just replaced its 707, it had triggered a revolution with its wide-body, twin-aisle aircraft. Over-capacity had arrived. Very quickly, the established airlines were losing millions of dollars and it would be even harder to argue for an entirely new service bringing increased competition, such as Laker's envisaged Skytrain service. The IATA carriers couldn't agree among themselves on how to deal with all the empty seats, let alone see off the charter flights that had garnered more than 30 per cent of the transatlantic market share by 1971. Everyone, not just Freddie, was looking for alternatives.

This was also the beginning of an era where airlines could make properly considered forecasts using the latest computer technology. The first introduction of a computerised reservation system by American Airlines in 1964 had been another huge shift in the industry. The SABRE system (Semi-Automated Business Research Environment) was developed by IBM for American Airlines, which participated in its development and was the first to use it. By 1968 BOAC had developed its own version, called 'Boadicea'. BOAC came up with the idea of a cheaper 'advance purchase fare'; it was called APEX that gave the company the ability to mitigate against unfilled seats. But it wasn't received very well by IATA, whose members preferred things just the way they were despite the glut of empty seats caused by the wide-body revolution. BOAC also received a poor response from IATA for another version of APEX known as 'Earlybird'. There was complacency among the IATA carriers, who were mainly funded by their nation's taxpayers. In 1971 as much as 50 per cent of the capacity on the North Atlantic went unsold.

Boyd-Carpenter was a strong, outspoken leader, contemptuous of IATA and primed for action to reduce fares – a popular move with the British public. He recruited like-minded independent thinkers such as Ray Colegate and later Hugh Welburn for key positions. Welburn left BOAC, where he'd worked in market research, to take up his post; APEX had been his original idea and actually predated Freddie Laker's Skytrain concept by a year. He'd also worked at BEA, the other British state-owned carrier, where institutional complacency caused his resignation. Both carriers were content to plod along with low load factors subsidised by the state, while overcharging passengers by edict of IATA.

Ray Colegate, as the head of the new CAA's economic policy and licensing division, was less radical than Welburn but shared similar views. He gave more importance to the consumer than his colleagues at the Department, who were preoccupied with the health of the industry, and most particularly of the state airlines, BEA and BOAC. Prime Minister Heath's Government was wedded to the idea that competition, the free play of market forces and less regulation, would bring about the dynamic lift the British economy so badly needed. This set the tone for Lord Boyd-Carpenter's tenure as head of the CAA and gave Freddie Laker a modicum of hope that soon he would receive a more favourable ruling on Skytrain.

Freddie seemed undaunted about all the waste of time and resources of the earlier Skytrain hearings and presented another application. A hearing was scheduled before the newly formed CAA for 6th April 1972. The new application was unchanged except for one important point. The 158-seat Boeing 707 in the original Skytrain application had now been replaced by the new 345-seat DC-10-10s due to arrive in six months. The prospect of the McDonnell Douglas DC-10s transformed the economics of Skytrain. With the new plane at a 75 per cent load factor, Freddie predicted the service would carry 200,000 one-way passengers a year based on a once-daily round-trip flight, a tripling of his earlier forecast, and raising the potential profitability exponentially. The forecast passenger numbers with the new aircraft were a terrifying prospect for Laker's competitors, especially BCal, but Freddie played it down: "Obviously it would be ridiculous for me to make a statement that there will be no diversion. I am saying that it is my considered opinion that there will be no measurable diversion with Skytrain."

The arguments for and against Laker's Skytrain service that opened on a dull and rainy April morning in London were all thrashed out over three days, presided over by Lord Boyd-Carpenter himself; his and Freddie Laker's paths had never crossed before. The CAA procedures were much the same as those of the ATLB, but they were now acting under proper policy guidance, issued by the Secretary of State, which gave broad directions regarding what the CAA ought to be doing. Boyd-Carpenter was supported by his deputy, Robin Goodison, and John Bowley, another former civil servant and an economics and licensing expert. In the rerun, Freddie appeared with his two lawyers, Harvey Crush and Bob Beckman, and Tom Riley appeared again on their behalf to present the economics of the case. The atmosphere was relaxed and informal.

Boyd-Carpenter set the scene with a few but important opening remarks. There were two questions uppermost in his mind. What sort of traffic would Skytrain attract? How could services at such low fares be economically viable? The CAA's terms of reference enjoined it to look at the health of the industry and the well-being of the traveller. Boyd-Carpenter's two questions were the core of the case, and Freddie would have to produce satisfactory answers to them in order to win.

Harvey Crush, for Laker, opened with some strong popular rhetoric, which had a distinct echo of his client about it. "The British working man requires to be able to travel without paying for an entrepreneur to take his cut in the charter, without paying for the reservation item, without paying for the middleman's advertising. He wants transportation pure and simple without having to wait two or three months before he can go." Then he cited Freddie's immense industry experience – his work with the Tudor, Accountant and Carvair, and the development of BUA, which had made a profit in every year under Freddie as managing director. After Crush's introduction, there was no apparent reaction when Freddie testified to the immense profit potential he envisaged with Skytrain. It was as if they expected nothing less from him.

Each side presented its case and was cross-examined by the opposition lawyers and the panel. Sometimes the questioning was fierce, but exchanges were occasionally humorous. The arguments were also now becoming familiar. Would Skytrain have a monopoly? How likely was it to succeed? Was 'the forgotten man' – Freddie's preferred term – a figment of the imagination? Boyd-Carpenter was keenly interested in Freddie's claim that in 'the forgotten man' there was a neglected market. When his opportunity to test the strength of Laker's case arose, this was the topic he turned to first.

"Mr Laker, you said several times you were going for a wholly new market?"

"Yes." The 'forgotten man', who was regarded as the prime customer for Skytrain, was defined as a typical semi-skilled or skilled manual worker, earning around £1,500 a year in Britain and $7,000 in America. Freddie estimated that there were millions of them, and that the market was a bottomless barrel. In 1971, three million travellers had used charter flights on the North Atlantic. Freddie said there were eight million 'forgotten people' in the United Kingdom and 120 million in the United States. He reckoned that there had to be at least 200,000 who needed to use his instant-booking, no-frills Skytrain service, and that was all he needed to make the service profitable.

Lord Boyd-Carpenter had a strong interest in encouraging competition among the established airlines and wanted to get at IATA. He quickly asked Freddie and his lawyers to define the traffic being aimed at, the profitability of such low fares, and how much diversion there would be from the scheduled carriers. At that time Freddie had proposed a fare of £32.50 one way in winter and £37.50 one way in summer, which amounted to a saving of 37 per cent on IATA's cheapest fares. Freddie may have been contemptuous of IATA, but he had no interest in declaring war on it just yet.

Objecting vehemently once again was British Caledonian. BCal tried to demonstrate that the venture was a risky one, while simultaneously arguing that large numbers of passengers would be poached from existing services. British Caledonian fought even harder before the CAA than it had in the earlier hearings. Its top management, Adam Thomson and Alastair Pugh, attended the hearings to give evidence.

Freddie knew that if he made Skytrain too simple, he would stand no chance of getting official approval for it. There were limits to how much competition for the established airlines even the likes of Boyd-Carpenter would tolerate. So Freddie explained his solution: "When Skytrain was conceived, we had to propose a service that would cater to the genuine spontaneous purchase passenger and yet put a sufficient artificial barrier in their way that it would not divert traffic from the traditional scheduled services. And this is where the no-reservations idea came from. This is the artificial barrier that we dreamed up."

Boyd-Carpenter couldn't help but notice Harvey Crush wriggling at the question of diversion. Crush quoted the words of civil aviation pioneer, Harold Bamberg: "The airlines of the world have developed, and by now fully exploited the market represented by the wealthy and the business traveller.

It must find new markets among more modest travellers. The answer is to reduce the cost of air transport. If fares were reduced, many more people would travel." Boyd-Carpenter took this to mean that Freddie was arguing that there would be no diversion at all from the existing carriers. Harvey Crush was not keen to state that this would be the case exactly: "It is obviously impossible to say there would be no diversion at all, because one passenger is technically diversion. We are saying that it is our considered opinion that there will be no measurable diversion with Skytrain."

Freddie admitted that there were no statistics to prove that the potential Skytrain market actually existed and that it would take two months of experience of flying Skytrain to tell. He told the hearings that he thought Skytrain would be very profitable and that it was "the best idea I have ever dreamed up". He pointed out that the Icelandic airline, Loftleidir, had built up a three per cent share of the North Atlantic market on the basis of cheap fares, although there was some inconvenience as passengers had to put up with a stopover at Reykjavik. Nevertheless, not one scheduled carrier claimed that the quarter of a million or so Loftleidir passengers had been diverted from them. At the April 1972 hearings, Freddie went out of his way to demonstrate that Skytrain would not cause a price war. Previous experience had taught everyone that a price war was no good to anyone. Low prices yes, but not a price war.

Boyd-Carpenter summed it up, posing the central question: "The more important reason for these people not travelling on the North Atlantic – is it the rigidity [of the affinity group rules] or the fares?" It was obviously the fares, although no one was keen to say so outright. Boyd-Carpenter also asked Freddie whether Skytrain's eventual success depended on the airline having a monopoly. Freddie replied: "We cannot plan the future on the basis that we would ever have a monopoly."

BCal said that Laker Airways' loss in the first year would be £1.3 million on revenue of £8 million. Adam Thomson said that Skytrain could place the whole 'second force' experiment on the North Atlantic in grave jeopardy. Freddie tried to reassure them that he would try to schedule Skytrain so that passengers would find it impossible to cancel BCal reservations and switch to Skytrain if a seat was available. BCal's Alastair Pugh pointed out that one Skytrain departure with Laker's DC-10 aircraft could carry 50 per cent of all the daily average scheduled traffic between New York and London in the months of January and February, which was a stretch even by BCal's standards of extreme hyperbole.

BOAC, the only licensed British carrier on the Atlantic, behaved throughout as though it was a neutral observer and only questioned Skytrain's profitability – it had very much backed off with its objections. BOAC's solicitor and legal director, Bob Forrest, told Laker's Harvey Crush what it was up to, which was to nobble British Caledonian's second force Gatwick ambitions: "We would quite like you to be alongside Caledonian at Gatwick. It would spoil the economics of Caledonian's case," he said. Freddie's and Crush's determined advocacy of the Skytrain case and their claim that the airlines were neglecting a substantial portion of the travelling public had hit their mark. The Laker team had put up a good showing. All they could do now was await the CAA's decision. Freddie was confident that it would grant him a licence for Skytrain. He informed his directors and the Engineering, Flight Operations and Commercial departments to press ahead with the preparations as they awaited the decision.

Freddie had committed to buying the two McDonnell Douglas DC-10s with an option on a third, although his Chief Accountant, Robbie Robinson, hadn't yet worked out the intricate details of the repayment schedules. The finer points of the financial aspect of the contract were still to be finalised. Regardless, in the early summer of 1972 Freddie, Harvey Crush and Bob Beckman flew to Los Angeles to meet with McDonnell Douglas President John Brizendine and VP of Sales Charlie ('Widebody') Forsythe. They were shown the aircraft, still under construction in the main production hangar, the hull painted with anti-corrosive green paint. Clearly awed by what they saw, they posed for photographs holding hands to show how wide the plane was. Freddie cannily won over the McDonnell Douglas executives, who weren't used to someone with his magnetic personality, in-depth knowledge of engineering and aircraft manufacturing, and shrewd negotiating skills ... all complemented by an indefatigable sense of humour.

Freddie and his two lawyers then flew straight to Tokyo to see Mitsui and spent a week negotiating the financing for the aircraft. Crush remembered the meetings: "Everyone that I have ever met who has negotiated with the Japanese tells the same story – they just sit there and say nothing, and it's completely disconcerting." The three men left unconvinced that they had a satisfactory deal. The only purpose seemed to be to arrange a second round of negotiations in Bob Beckman's Washington office the following week.

The Japanese liked business trips to the USA and they loosened up once the business was all done, as the Laker team had experienced after the meetings had ended in Japan. So Beckman pulled out all the stops for the visitors. He booked the Mitsui delegation into the best hotel in DC, then arranged for some appropriate female 'entertainment' for their guests afterwards. Freddie knew this would all be on his tab, but he didn't say anything, as he assumed Bob was well versed in the Japanese business culture. After the usual pleasantries and preliminary discussion, which meant that Freddie spoke a hundred words to every one uttered by the Japanese, he got serious. With a deadpan face, he told the Mitsui executives that he wanted to pay for the aircraft out of flying revenues only. He told them that if he couldn't fill the aircraft he didn't want to have to pay and would pass the risk back to Mitsui. He convincingly told them it was called 'Freddie Laker's just in case clause', at which Beckman, stifling a snort, had to turn away. The Mitsui executives didn't understand what Freddie meant by 'just in case' or how it had any relevance to the negotiation.

Anticipating this, Freddie decided to tell them a well-honed tale of a wealthy ranch-owning cowboy wearing a ten-gallon hat, visiting a Rolls-Royce dealership in Texas. Perplexed by a hole in the radiator grille of the luxury automobile, apparently for a starting handle, the cowboy asked why on earth would a Rolls-Royce need to carry a starting handle to crank the engine? The salesman replied, 'Just in case,' then said to the still perplexed cowboy, 'Well, look what you've got under your shirt? You've got a pair of nipples underneath your shirt haven't you? What is the purpose of nipples? They're to feed babies. Are you ever going to have a baby? Of course not. So why have you got fucking nipples then? Just in case.' Beckman, who had not heard this one before, nearly fell off his chair as Freddie grinned enthusiastically from ear to ear. This well-recited anecdote was one that had sealed many previous deals. To their credit, the stone-faced Mitsui delegation eventually forced a laugh, probably more out of politeness than out of comprehension. Notwithstanding, the deal for the DC-10s was concluded on terms acceptable to Freddie, even if his 'just in case' clause wasn't written into the contract quite as he would have liked. The Japanese were for once out-manoeuvred by a man from Kent. Without knowing all the details of what had gone down with the ANA cancellation, Freddie had the upper hand to negotiate a once-in-a-lifetime aircraft purchase. Dinner that night and what followed was a raucous affair and, as Beckman had anticipated, their Japanese guests, after quite a few whiskeys, delved right in. And of course, so did Freddie and Bob.

On 26th September 1972, as many expected, Lord Boyd-Carpenter announced that Laker Airways was to be awarded a 10-year licence and could begin its service on 1st January 1973, with at least one daily flight. The CAA had accepted that a demand existed for Skytrain, and Boyd-Carpenter said: "We welcome Freddie Laker's enterprise in seeking to meet this demand and we view with favour the innovation involved with this application." But there was a sting in the tail. The licence was granted for departures from Stansted Airport, not Laker's home base of Gatwick. Stansted was an old Second World War airfield in Essex, where a passenger terminal had only just been built. There were no regular airline services from it, and it was the one airport on which the British Airports Authority regularly lost money. There was no direct rail link to London and the proposed M11 motorway was still not confirmed, as all the environmental impact considerations were being debated. The Americans referred to the airport as 'Stansted Field'. So any joy Freddie had derived from the announcement was immediately dashed.

His first reaction was to reject it, but Bob Beckman correctly predicted, "Accept it Freddie – we can negotiate this later."

Another sting was that Freddie could only sell 189 seats on each aircraft, the typical maximum capacity of a Boeing 707-320. The remaining seats would have to be roped off. Despite these onerous and absurd restrictions, British Caledonian was still unhappy and appealed against the CAA's decision, clearly more out of spite than logic. Ironically, the awarding of a scheduled service licence now qualified Laker Airways for IATA membership, whose annual general meeting opened in London the very day the licence was granted. No doubt Freddie balked at the price of the membership fees, which ran into hundreds of thousands of dollars. For state-subsidised airlines this money came from the taxpayers' pocket, but for a small independent airline like Laker it would come straight off the bottom line. He dismissed IATA as 'an airline trade union that spends half its time circumventing its own rules'.

Britain's Prime Minister, Ted Heath, spoke on the opening day of the IATA AGM, emphasising the desirability of providing individual excursion fares for air travellers. It left no doubt that it was for IATA to make sure the benefits of travel were made available to as many people as possible and as cheaply as possible. Ray Colegate had in fact written large parts of Heath's speech, and the awarding of the Skytrain licence could be seen as the first manifestation of that warning to IATA. Colegate was in alignment with Freddie when it came to IATA.

Needless to say, Laker Airways never became a member of IATA and Freddie remained its sworn enemy that intensified as his battle for the Skytrain licence gathered momentum.

# CHAPTER 21

# The DC-10 Changes Everything

## Scaling up in every sense

### 1972-74

Freddie Laker's genius was that he immediately saw how he could use the cancelled ANA DC-10 Series 10 order with McDonnell Douglas to his advantage. Despite the planes being the medium-range version of the DC-10, designed for US transcontinental use and not initially built for crossing the Atlantic, Freddie couldn't resist a terrific deal and the terms being offered. He was gambling that he could make the DC-10s work for him. On paper, according to MDC, a fully loaded DC-10-10 with maximum fuel would be right on the limits for the flight of 3,016 nautical miles (3,470 statute miles) between London and JFK, New York. However, Dick Bradley worked out how the DC-10-10 could get to New York or Toronto, firstly by some finessing of the payload. The planes would be fitted with 345 seats (rather than the maximum of 380) in a 10-abreast configuration, and passengers' checked baggage would be restricted to 15kg instead of the usual 20kg. That would permit the maximum fuel of 21,670 US gallons to be uplifted at Gatwick for the 7½-hour journey westbound across the Atlantic. Bradley then reworked the DC-10 performance data, mostly with nothing more than a slide rule and a pencil, and concluded that Gatwick to JFK would be achievable on most days. Laker's DC-10 pilots, masters of extending the range of everything they flew, would get the plane to optimum flight levels en route, which would minimise fuel flow, typically averaging around 2,400 US gallons per hour. Occasionally, extreme weather conditions such as a hot day with still air at Gatwick and strong North Atlantic headwinds en route may require a fuel stop in Bangor - Maine, or Gander in Newfoundland but this would be the exception rather than the rule. Stansted had a longer runway, so Gatwick was used as the benchmark. Eastbound due to the prevailing tail winds; the flight time was 45 minutes shorter than in the other direction and JFK had longer runways.

In establishing that the DC-10-10 could operate westbound across the Atlantic, Freddie looked at the seat-mile costs. They were unsurpassable. After taking into account the repayment and interest on the aircraft loans, John Jones worked out that the break-even load factor on the London to New York route would be 63 per cent, or 217 passengers. The DC-10-10's seat-mile costs were vastly superior to the 158-seater Boeing 707. Freddie had always liked Boeing aircraft, but the 747 was too big for what he had in mind and, while the Lockheed L-1011 TriStar was perhaps more technologically advanced than the DC-10, it didn't have the range, cost considerably more, and Freddie couldn't possibly finance it. He was thrilled to have been given the opportunity to buy the DC-10s, so he ran some basic numbers by Chief Accountant Robbie Robinson. Robinson's job would be to ensure that the company had enough cash flow from its flying operations to pay for the aircraft. The terms MDC and Mitsui had offered were unbeatable, even by Freddie's standards. He would finalise the details of the financing with Mitsui later, but he now had enough to be able to commit in principle to MDC for the aircraft.

As a result, on 24th February 1972, Freddie Laker finally announced to the world that he had signed an order to buy two McDonnell Douglas DC-10 Series 10 aircraft with an option on a third. One of BCal's objections to Skytrain was that Laker Airways didn't have a wide-body aircraft. "I have now dealt with that objection," Freddie gloated. This was big news by anyone's standards, as small privately owned airlines like Laker didn't buy new wide-bodied jets every day. It was a punt such as Freddie had never made before. Laker Airways' profits for 1972 were forecast at a quarter of a million pounds, and on paper the company was hardly able to fund the purchase of new aircraft to the tune of nearly $65 million ($350 million in 2018) – unless Freddie was able to get Skytrain off the ground as soon as the planes arrived. First, though, he had a few internal issues to deal with.

Throughout the Laker organisation there was a growing and increasingly challenging juxtaposition of young, keen go-getters and a decidedly less adaptable old guard that Freddie had brought along, almost like a security blanket, from the early days of Air Charter and BUA. Despite the considerable progress and Freddie's innovative ideas, the early years of Laker Airways were in reality only a step away from the post-war era of propeller-driven Halifaxes and Yorks; more often than not it felt that way, especially to the aforementioned younger team members. They impatiently had to endure their more senior colleagues' endless reminiscing about the 'good old days' and the war, not to mention a long-established practice of liquid lunch breaks, a throwback to their RAF Officers' Mess ritual, which invariably rendered them ineffective for most of the afternoon. The company was at a critical juncture in its life cycle. If Laker Airways was ever to become a significant fixture in civil aviation, Freddie would have to address some of the huge disparities that existed within his organisation, and he needed to address them immediately, or risk getting left behind. The arrival of the DC-10s in late 1972 would spark a necessary and overdue growing-up process, where Laker Airways would have to elevate itself to another level.

That next level was the North American Advanced Booking Charter (ABC) market, a concept that had been devised by Ray Colegate, the Economics Director of the soon-to-be-initiated CAA. The ABCs would supersede the old 'affinity group' charters, which had proven to be a travesty. Freddie told Cliff Nunn that Geoffrey Street wouldn't be managing the ABCs. "I have something else in mind for him," Freddie said emphatically. "John Jones will take charge of the ABC programme," and that was that. It was typical of Freddie's dictatorial management style. Then, surprisingly to many in the company, he gave the plum job of Skytrain Service Manager to Street. Freddie rightfully had a soft spot for anyone who'd been in the military, and he was giving the decorated former RAF Wing Commander another chance to shine after he, at least in Freddie's eyes, had bodged the affinity group charter operation.

With those two key positions filled and with the new aircraft on the not too distant horizon, Freddie decided that he wanted a better image and more autonomy at his home base, so he applied for Laker Airways to perform its own ground handling. But the British Airports Authority didn't want that ... and neither did Dan Air, which was a growing independent airline owned by the Davies & Newman shipping company. Dan Air had a large mixed fleet of aircraft and did its own ground handling at Gatwick. So the BAA brought Laker and Dan Air together in something akin to a forced marriage. Freddie and Dan Air's Managing Director, Alan Snudden, struck a deal and Gatwick Handling Ltd (GHL) was formed, each airline taking a 50 per cent equity position in the new entity. Untypically, Freddie didn't play hardball over this initiative, as he quickly saw the joint venture as an opportunity to reduce his airline's ground handling costs. He committed capital to purchase new equipment necessary for the wide-bodied aircraft, while Dan Air contributed all its existing ground services equipment and its passenger services personnel. Gatwick Handling's staff would have their own uniform to distinguish them from the parent airlines.

Dan Air was already performing ground handling and passenger services for a number of foreign airlines transiting Gatwick, but the new GHL entity would now aggressively solicit more third party carriers to offset Dan Air's and Laker's costs. It would be pitting GHL against BCal and British Airtours, the other Gatwick-based airlines able to offer third party handling at the time. A separate board of directors for Gatwick Handling was formed, with both parent companies equally represented. Cliff Nunn and John Seear were the Laker directors on the board, while Dan Air's Snudden and Frank Horridge, the engineering director, made up the other side. Harold Whincup, also a Dan Air director, became the first managing director of GHL, while Sir Robert Hardingham, former Chairman of the CAA, was appointed chairman. In February 1972 the formal agreement for Gatwick Handling to undertake ground handling and passenger services at Gatwick Airport under a 10-year licence was signed by Freddie Laker and Alan Snudden of Dan Air in the presence of David Livingston, the general manager of Gatwick, for the British Airports Authority.

With the organisation in place, someone was needed with the experience and capabilities to run the day-to-day operation, but there was no one at Gatwick up to the task. Snudden suggested they bring Jerry Penwarden down from Luton, where he had been Dan Air's base manager for a couple of years following a tour in the Middle East. So without too much discussion, Penwarden became GHL's general manager. It was a good decision as he was one of the most knowledgeable and skilled experts in all aspects of aircraft ground handling and passenger services; there wasn't a piece of ground handling equipment he didn't know how to operate and he could quote the zero fuel weight of pretty much any aircraft off the top of his head. Penwarden always modestly claims that he was merely in the right place at the right time. He had six months to get Gatwick Handling up to speed for the arrival of Laker's DC-10s. Fortunately there was already a fairly well-honed operation in place, so Penwarden's main focus was on the acquisition of new equipment and training the staff to handle a considerably larger aircraft.

For the anticipated expansion into wide-body operations, new and more powerful push-back tractors were needed, so he ordered a new Dennis/Mercury four-wheel-drive MD400 tug with a 40,000lb capacity; the tug was capable of pushing or towing any wide-body aircraft including a fully loaded Boeing 747. Compared to its predecessor, the ubiquitous MD300, the massively long and low MD400, painted in bright red Laker livery, looked almost space age at the time. It was the first MD400 tug at Gatwick, something the GHL ramp guys loved to rub in over a pint if their BCal counterparts were within earshot. New Houchin 140kVa ground power units, pallet dollies for cargo containers, and large adjustable passenger stairs were also purchased, as there were no air bridges/jetways at Gatwick's North Pier from which Dan Air and Laker operated. Gatwick Handling was now ready to handle any of the new generation of aircraft that came through the airport, long before it was a regular occurrence. Freddie, never shy at cocking a snook at BCal's Adam Thomson, derived particular pleasure from GHL being the first at Gatwick able to handle wide-body aircraft. Everything was ready for the arrival of the first Laker Airways DC-10 later that year and for the much-vaunted Skytrain service.

One of the components that would make Freddie's DC-10 acquisition commercially viable was Lord Brothers, the London-based tour operation he had acquired in 1968. Bob Lewis, Lord Brothers' managing director, having replaced Stephen Lord, was now stricken with cancer and didn't have long to live. Freddie needed a well-qualified replacement as he was relying on Lord Brothers for a large percentage of the group's profits to help fund the DC-10 purchase. Ernest Welsman, who had owned and operated Wings, had retired in 1970 and had no desire to return to top management of a tour operation, so Freddie contacted George Carroll, his former assistant at BUA.

George Carroll had risen through BUA to look after its IT business, Castle Holidays. He had grown it into a major operator, with more than £7.5 million in annual revenue, and was perfect for the job of running Lords, as he was chairman of both the TOSG Trust Fund and the Tour Operators Council. He had become one of most important and influential men in the industry, but had been effectively demoted from his position of general commercial manager when BUA was sold. The Cayzers had retained Castle, and Carroll found himself no longer making the decisions, answering to Hon Nicholas Cayzer. Understandably he felt insulted. Freddie swooped in and snatched him away, and successfully negotiated a £5,000 pay-off from BUA for a loss of position. Carroll needed no persuading to return to the Laker fold, and joined his old boss in May 1972, although officially he was on 'gardening leave' until June. To Freddie's considerable joy and relief, George Carroll took over managing Lord Brothers Holidays just in time to commence planning for the increase in potential capacity with the new Laker DC-10s.

Every Laker department was already well into the preparations for the DC-10s, but once the deal with Mitsui was finally consummated Freddie gave the green light and all his key department heads went into overdrive. During the summer of 1972, Laker Airways' Technical Director, Bill Townsend, practically lived in Long Beach; preparing the engineering side for a new aircraft type, especially one that was a considerable step up in technology as well as size, was an enormous undertaking. Led by Manager of Flight Operations, Captain Alan Hellary and newly appointed DC-10 Fleet Captain Steve James, the Laker pilots and flight engineers who had been selected for the initial training on the DC-10 were also living in Long Beach for the summer. They undertook the type conversion on the McDonnell Douglas simulator, followed by flying the DC-10 demonstration aircraft over the nearby Pacific Ocean. MDC had assigned Captain Jack Allavie and Captain 'Red' Kaffenberger, two of their most experienced training pilots, to the Laker Airways' flight crew team. The MDC demonstration pilots could do things with a DC-10 (albeit empty and therefore very light) that few would believe possible... Fortunately most of the extreme manoeuvres and aerobatics took place over the Pacific and well out of sight.

The MDC training captains were impressed at how fast the Laker pilots and flight engineers converted to the DC-10. A high point was when Captain Basil Bradshaw, who had previously been on Laker's One-Eleven fleet, managed to just keep the DC-10 in the air even after the MDC Flight Trainer had cut two engines at take-off to replicate a bird strike ... on the simulator, of course. Many of the flight crew had graduated from Laker's Boeing 707s, arguably a more difficult aircraft to fly than the DC-10, so they were already experienced on large, multi-engined aircraft with at least three guys sitting up front. One of the biggest variations over what they were used to was the absence of a fourth cockpit crew member for long-haul flights ... a navigator.

Laker's DC-10s were to be fitted with state-of-the-art Litton Inertial Navigation System (INS) technology, which would allow the pilots to conduct all the over-water navigation themselves without a navigator. Freddie himself had specified that he wanted three separate INS systems installed in his planes and not the more typical two. When asked why he wanted the considerable additional expense of three, he responded pragmatically, "Well, if you have only two and they both say something different, which one do you believe?" This was typical of Freddie, who would never compromise when it came to anything related to the engineering, the technology, or the operational safety of his aircraft.

Laker's DC-10s were effectively on a hire-purchase-type agreement, with interest pegged at the current Eurodollar base rate plus two per cent. To pay the deposit, $7.35 million was borrowed from the Export Import Bank of America (EXIM) at six per cent interest over ten years. Thus Freddie managed to buy the aircraft without using any of his own money – Mitusi and EXIM provided it all. The British Government also did its bit and waived any import duty on the two planes and there were no 'progress payments' either. It made Laker Airways Britain's biggest investor in new aircraft after BOAC.

Laker's aircraft, powered by the new General Electric CF-6 engines, were an absolute steal at around $21 million apiece. Freddie signed the final contract in Tokyo on 6th October 1972, after eight months of negotiating over the details. It was mostly gamesmanship, and he had been deliberately stalling until the CAA had made its decision concerning his Skytrain licence. As he and Beckman walked into Mitsui's tastefully grand board room to conclude the deal, Freddie whispered into the other's ear, "Is this where I ask them for my commission?"

Everything went to plan in California, and in mid-October Freddie flew to Long Beach where he would officially accept delivery of the first DC-10. He and his technical director, Bill Townsend, stood with John Brizendine and the McDonnell Douglas top brass for publicity photographs alongside the Laker DC-10. They were presented with plaques, medals and aircraft models. It was a milestone for the McDonnell Douglas Corporation, as Laker Airways was the first non-scheduled (charter) airline to purchase the DC-10, and the MDC management knew that the Laker deal would prompt other independent airlines to follow suit. And they soon did.

'Zulu Charlie' – the first Laker Airways DC-10, registration G-AZZC – flew from Long Beach across the Atlantic, non-stop as it was empty, arriving at London Gatwick on 26th October 1972. The historic delivery flight was piloted by Captain Alan Hellary, and almost the entire workforce at Gatwick stopped what they were doing to welcome the plane. Its landing gear came down, the nose tipped upwards and the distinctive sound of the GE engines permeated the Surrey landscape. A huge cheer went up as the aircraft touched down.

The DC-10 looked stunning painted in Laker's distinctive gleaming white fuselage with its red and black striping. The name of the aircraft, 'Eastern Belle', was painted in white on the black stripe immediately under the cockpit. The British flag was at the front, and right behind it was Freddie's familiar 'Oozlum bird' motif; on the port (left) side it looked like a stylised letter 'L'. Hoards of eager plane spotters and enthusiasts descended on Gatwick Airport to get a glimpse of the first DC-10 to land there; the airport had to provide special viewing areas to accommodate them all. The second DC-10, G-AZZD, named 'Western Belle', arrived three weeks later on 16th November to a similar welcome ceremony. For many days following the arrivals of each of the Laker planes, newspaper articles and television news clips invariably showed a euphoric and emotional Freddie Laker with the headline 'Freddie Laker's DC-10 Lands at Gatwick', or simply 'Laker Goes Widebody'.

Late 1972 represented a watershed moment in the Laker company's life cycle. Freddie was like an excited schoolboy who'd just been given his first bicycle.

His DC-10s were the first in Europe, beating KLM and SwissAir by a few weeks but, more importantly for Freddie, he had beaten British Caledonian in getting the DC-10 into service. Freddie's decision to buy the aircraft had undoubtedly been more spontaneous than planned, but the timing of the purchase was inspired. Boeing's mighty 747, which had been launched a couple of years earlier, was proving to be uneconomical unless it flew with a very high passenger load – its fuel costs were exorbitant. The recession of 1969-70 had affected Boeing considerably and sales of its flagship jumbo jet had plummeted. The (mostly state-owned) carriers who had initially bought the 747, perhaps more for status than commercial viability, were now second-guessing themselves and looking hard at the considerably more economical trijets offered by McDonnell Douglas and Lockheed. Almost by default, Freddie Laker found himself in a commercially advantageous position thanks to the DC-10s.

As expected, once the aircraft arrived at Gatwick and were finally a reality after months of anticipation, the daily lives of everyone at the airline changed exponentially. During the weeks that followed, it was typical for staff members to take a short diversion into the hangar to gawk at the massive aircraft before heading to their respective offices. No one had seen anything like them and the DC-10s lifted everyone's spirits. They were the instigator of increased productivity, longer working hours, more congeniality, and a host of other positives. Freddie couldn't have found a better staff motivator than these new aircraft, and he enrolled everyone in DC-10 euphoria.

Dozens of Laker's skilled engineering staff pored over the new planes, fitting seats and galley equipment and preparing them for the upcoming demonstration flights Freddie had planned. The advanced avionics and the revolutionary GE CF-6 high-bypass engines were like nothing they had ever experienced. The innumerable tasks faced by Laker's world-class Engineering division were at another level. Changing out the Number Two (centre) engine of the DC-10 was going to be one of their most challenging engineering feats and special equipment had to be custom-built for the job. Laker's engine bay, which until then had housed a few Rolls-Royce Spey engines for the One-Eleven fleet and a couple of Pratt & Whitney JT3s for the 707s, now had to be enlarged to house at least one massive spare DC-10 CF6. Ground equipment such as longer sets of stairs, upgraded ground power units and a larger, more powerful tug to move the DC-10s around at the Laker International Jet Centre had all been acquired.

No other department in the Laker organisation faced the challenges experienced by the Engineering division. Fortunately, it was managed and staffed to an extraordinary high standard. As Freddie was a licensed engineer himself, he was as uncompromising when it came to Laker Airways' Engineering department as he was with the Flight Operations division.

Meanwhile, Laker's then all-female cabin staff were being introduced to the plane for the first time by chief stewardess Joy Harvey and her deputy, Bernadette Higgs. Laker's One-Elevens had three cabin crew and the 707s six, but the DC-10s required ten. Irrespective of the stipulation requiring one crew member per 50 passengers, or the number of emergency doors to be manned,

Laker Airways typically overstaffed its aircraft. It prided itself on exemplary cabin service as well as a 100 per cent safety record. Before the DC-10 came into the Laker fleet, the most senior cabin attendant or stewardess flying the line was called a 'Number One'. With the arrival of the DC-10, a new and more senior role was initiated, the 'In-Flight Director'. It was shortened to 'IFD', and the first group of IFDs was hand-picked from the most senior and competent Number Ones. Coordinating the in-flight service of a 345-passenger wide-body aircraft was completely different from anything they had done before. It required a higher level of management skills than had been necessary on the smaller aircraft types.

Yet the in-flight service challenges were nothing compared to proving that the cabin crew could safely evacuate 345 passengers within the legally required 90 seconds. The 'mini-evacs' were held outside the hangar and Laker staff were enrolled to participate as simulated passengers. It was terrifying and quite dangerous as the eight evacuation slides deployed from the doors were ignited by an explosive charge, inflated and unfolded down to the ground. The Number three left and right doors had a slide that went over the wing and a second section that went from the wing to the ground at an angle. The passenger deck of the DC-10 was 15 feet above the ground. The cabin staff yelled directions and pushed the simulated passengers towards the exit doors, where they had to quickly remove their shoes and one by one slide down to safety, fast. Fortunately, the evacuations only produced a few minor bumps and bruises, which was unusual. The CAA inspectors signed off Laker's cabin crew in record time, much to the relief and delight of Freddie and Joy Harvey.

Unlike the first group of pilots and flight engineers who had been trained at McDonnell Douglas in California, the cabin staff did all their training on the aircraft once they arrived at Gatwick. They had only a couple of weeks before the demonstration flights to learn how to provide a top-class service in a twin-aisle aircraft. Laker's DC-10s came with the innovative lower galley configuration, whereby the downstairs galley was located adjacent to the forward cargo hold and was accessed from the main deck via lifts located between the forward passenger cabin and the centre cabin; one lift was for crew members while the other was for the galley carts containing the food and beverages. It was an extremely efficient way of preparing food for a large number of passengers. The lower galley had direct access to the forward baggage hold, which was useful for storing supplies that would otherwise have to be stored somewhere on the main deck. Keeping the food preparation out of sight of the passengers had many advantages and crew members assigned to lower galley duties invariably enjoyed it, despite the immense workload of heating the food and preparing the lay-ups for 345 passengers, twice each flight. Meanwhile, over in Laker's flight kitchens located in the ageing low-rise buildings next to the hangar, the flight catering and bonded store team had to ramp up equipment and manpower. Their challenge of preparing meals for more than twice as many passengers per flight than they had done before for the 158-seat 707s, together with meals for the 13 DC-10 crew members, was considerable.

In the 1970s, airlines typically gave their passengers a full meal on almost all flights. Even short IT flights on the One-Elevens to the Mediterranean invariably included a full meal, two rounds of drinks and a duty-free service. The cabin crew were challenged to get all this done in a flight time perhaps as short as the 1hr 45min flight to Palma. They typically started the in-flight service almost immediately the landing gear had been retracted after take-off and the no smoking sign had been extinguished, and they would still be wrapping up the service as the gear came down on the final approach to the destination. Long-haul flights gave a bit more latitude, but the cabin crew still did much more than on a typical flight today. With the new DC-10s, Laker's cabin staff became trendsetters for exemplary, high-volume in-flight service.

The first group of pilots who had been trained at Long Beach became the training staff for the next batch, many of whom were converting from the Boeing 707s. Laker Airways only had two 707s, so to crew the first DC-10s some pilots came straight from Laker's 89-seat BAC One-Elevens. This was unusual at the time, as airlines invariably used aircraft size as the criterion for promotion. Laker Airways had no choice; it was either that or go outside the company for pilots, and that wasn't the Laker way. Fortunately, some of Laker's most experienced pilots were flying the BAC One-Elevens and were more than competent to transfer to the DC-10. A few less senior One-Eleven captains opted to be DC-10 first officers (co-pilots), with the knowledge that they would likely be promoted to the left-hand seat in short order when more DC10s were purchased. Other One-Eleven pilots moved over to fill the vacancies on the Boeing 707s, and would then be mostly operating transatlantic flights to North America, charters to the Middle East, Asia and Australia, and the hugely popular Barbados trips, as opposed to pounding around Europe every day from Gatwick, Manchester or Berlin.

Throughout civil aviation, there wasn't a great deal of logic in the way pilots were promoted to different aircraft types. It was pretty much industry standard to start less experienced flight crew members on smaller aircraft, but in practice the two-man One-Eleven flight crew needed significant skills and experience to fly four or even six sectors within Europe during a duty day. The short flights, often in atrocious weather, with congested airways and approach patterns to airports such as the challenging Category 'D' Funchal on the island of Madeira or the Category 'C' Innsbruck in the Austrian Alps, took top-level skills. A pilot rostered to fly to those airports had to have done simulator training or a flight in the jump seat behind another captain to familiarise himself with the approach. An argument could be made that it often took greater skills to fly multiple sectors in Europe on a One-Eleven, especially in winter, than to fly across the Atlantic on a much larger aircraft, although airports such as New York's JFK were often challenging. As a result of Laker's 'promote from within' philosophy, some of the company's pilots were promoted to the left-hand seat of a DC-10 long before they ever thought possible.

The new McDonnell Douglas DC-10, call sign Zulu Charlie (G-AZZC), sat proudly at Gatwick Airport in November 1972. It had been fitted with its seats and galley equipment, the cabin crew had been trained, evacuations completed to the satisfaction of the CAA inspectors, and a thousand other tasks completed. The first mission was to show off the plane. Freddie had personally selected the flight deck crew and hand-picked his most experienced, friendly and attractive cabin staff to take care of his guests.

For an entire week 'ZC' took off from Gatwick for a quick local demonstration flight or flew to an airport in Laker Airways' key markets such as Liverpool, Manchester, Prestwick, Stansted, and other strategic UK population bases. Freddie even had the DC-10 land at the Royal Air Force base at Manston in Kent so he could pick up his mother, Hannah, and take her for a ride. She lived in nearby Ramsgate and he didn't want her to have to travel far, so he took the plane to her. Needless to say, when the massive plane touched down at Manston it brought the RAF's day-to-day activities to a grinding halt.

As Laker Airways had an important base at Berlin's Tegel Airport, Freddie had his Operations department obtain a slot for the Berlin air corridor. The Commercial department set everything up with Laker's tour operator Flug Union; they were thrilled to be able to invite travel agents and VIPs for the eagerly anticipated demonstration flight. It was the first time a wide-body aircraft had visited Berlin, and Freddie was keen to show it off at the scene of his first aviation venture, where he'd made his first fortune. About 20 minutes out from Tegel, the captain radioed Laker's office to give the plane's ETA. Laker's base manager, Arno Angermeir, panicked when he realised that there were no stairs at Tegel large enough to reach the DC-10's passenger doors. He rushed into Dan Air's office next door to confront Jack White, who was in charge of logistics at Gatwick but was in Berlin doing staff training.

White remembers the moment: "Arno came rushing in and asked if we had any steps big enough for a DC-10. Obviously we didn't as no wide-body aircraft had ever been to Tegel before. So I took him outside and showed him our biggest set." Laker had never needed steps at Tegel, as its One-Elevens all had integrated stairs. White continued, "Our steps were big enough for a 707 or DC-8 but a couple of feet shy for the DC-10. So we grabbed some milk crates and when the DC-10 got to the gate we stacked them at the top of the stairs so the guests could climb aboard. Freddie wasn't too pleased and did a bit of yelling. We took bets in the Dan Air office that Arno would probably be looking for a job with us the following day."

At all the principal Laker airports, the on-board team would pick up a large group of travel agents, travel wholesalers, civic dignitaries and regular consumers including lots of schoolchildren. Freddie was keen to explain his logic of having the kids experience a flight on the DC-10: "They're the future and who do you think they'll book with for their first holiday or trip to the States?" It was a good argument, as first impressions and experiences when you're young stay with you as you grow up. The guests were taken up for a quick excursion, served drinks and experienced the in-flight entertainment systems. Freddie would make speeches and extol the DC-10's size, and comfort, and the fantastic Laker in-flight service. Many of the guests were invited to the cockpit to see the flight deck crew at work. Freddie did the rounds and shook hands with everyone on board. His enthusiasm for the plane was so infectious that by the time the guests deplaned back at their home airport they were sold on it.

They'd been given 'I'm a Laker Liker' and 'Fly a Laker DC-10' stickers, which were now stuck on their bags, jackets and sweaters, together with a package of information on Laker Airways. The DC-10 cost over £2,000 an hour to do these publicity flights, and in a week Freddie spent more than $100,000, but the PR value was arguably worth five times as much. There wasn't a newspaper or TV channel that hadn't covered the DC-10 demonstration flights. The name 'Laker' had now been planted firmly in the minds of the public all over the UK, and this would definitely pay off later – annoyingly for Freddie, much later than he would have liked.

While Freddie and his hand-picked crew, together with PR and sales personnel, were busy demonstrating the new aircraft, John Jones and Robbie Robinson pored over the financial spreadsheets. 'How do we make these DC-10s work?' they asked themselves. Jones doesn't recall much in the way of advance costings, budgets or revenue forecasting having been done for the aircraft before they arrived; all he remembers is that 'the DC-10s arrived as more blank lines on my sheet of paper'.

Nevertheless, the first revenue-earning flight for Laker's new DC-10 aircraft was a charter on 21st November 1972 with a day trip to Palma, Majorca, on behalf of Britain's leading aviation magazine. The 331 press corps, travel agents and subscribers had each paid £22.90 for the *Flight International* 'Seminair', as they called it. A detailed inspection of the aircraft, a talk on 'the DC-10 and its operation' by John Morris from the MDC design team, and a visit to Palma's new and controversial airport were followed by lunch at the Christina Palma Hotel. The cabin staff showed off their glamorous new red Laker uniforms. Freddie was typically bullish to the press at the lunch: "I'll fly them wherever people want to go, at prices they can afford. And if need be, I'll have a different price for every day of the year, and I'll fly my planes full and make money as always. This is a business, not a charity."

Late in 1972 George Carroll was joined at Lord Brothers by Gordon Nichols, another former Air Holdings man, as Commercial Director. Nichols had entered the travel business in 1960 after leaving the Royal Air Force, where he had been a Squadron Leader. He had joined Whitehall Holidays and become executive director when the company was taken over. The addition of Nichols strengthened Lord Brothers' management team significantly. With the reversals taking place in the British tour operating industry, there was a need for depth of management like never before.

The major operators – big names like Horizon, Thomson and Clarkson – were posting losses in the millions. The Top 20 tour operators lost £7.2 million between them. However, Laker's travel companies enjoyed profits of £40,000 (£538,500 at 2018 values) at Lord Brothers and £100,000 (£1.5 million) at Arrowsmith.

Freddie made a considered decision to expand the Laker group of companies against the background of the new shape of the air travel industry in what he called 'a government and IATA controlled monopolistic industry based on higher and higher fares'. He didn't really have a choice, as the first two DC-10s had increased Laker Airways' overall seat capacity by 90 per cent.

In many respects the Laker group was lucky that it was the end of the boom in the IT industry that had started in 1968. In 1971 eight million holidaymakers had been carried by UK airlines, albeit at wafer-thin margins. Ruthless price cutting, in search of higher and higher volumes and elusive profits, was to be the undoing of some of the biggest package tour operators in the business. The CAA had abandoned price controls on charter flights to Europe, citing them as ineffective, so there was no limit to capacity on the IT charter flights. Lords stepped back from outlandish pricing such as the £9.99 weekend in Palma just as the UK's IT industry was finally bitten by the global and political problems of 1973. Since it had begun trading in 1966, the Laker group's accumulated balance at the end of the 1972 financial year stood at £1.9 million (£28 million in 2018), of which £1.38 million was credited to Laker Airways International and £517,000 to subsidiary and associated companies.

George Carroll and John Jones got together on the monumental task of filling the DC-10s they now had at their disposal. Carroll naturally wanted as much wide-body capacity as possible for the European inclusive tour holidays, as the large-capacity aircraft dramatically reduced the seat cost component of the package. Given that the other ingredients of the package holiday such as hotels and ground transfers were similar, any savings in flight costs would be passed on to the consumer. Lords didn't need to slash its prices to the bone – the DC-10 gave it an edge over every other tour operator in Britain. Meanwhile Jones wanted to maximise the DC-10s for flights to New York, Toronto, Halifax and Montreal, at the extreme limit of their operating range. For 1973 Lord Brothers and Arrowsmith advertised a round-trip air-only product to North America as well as fully inclusive tour packages and fly-drive holidays. The planned, comprehensive programme of Advanced Booking Charters between Britain and North America interspersed with short hops down to Palma, Ibiza and other Mediterranean sun spots in between the transatlantic flights was an efficient way to maximise utilisation of the DC-10s. One of Canada's leading tour operators, Suntours, based in Toronto, inked a deal with Laker Airways worth more than $15 million whereby it would share capacity on Laker's DC-10s with the UK tour operators. This created a space management situation the likes of which Laker Airways had never experienced before.

On 1st April 1973, instead of the anticipated Skytrain service inauguration, a Laker DC-10 operated the first transatlantic Advance Booking Charter flight between Manchester and Toronto on behalf of Arrowsmith Holidays. The passengers on the flight paid only £45 for the round trip and it paved the way for a more regular service to Canada's premier eastern city, three times a week out of Gatwick. And that was just the tip of the iceberg.

Freddie had decided to unleash John Jones's energy and enthusiasm exclusively on the ABCs, appointing him manager of this new division of Laker Airways. Jones was sent up to the Lords' offices at Grosvenor Street in London to take up his new post. The compact offices began to bulge with boxes of booking forms that had once been filled with sworn affidavits for the affinity group charters. But instead of booking through a bogus club, prospective passengers now booked 90 days in advance directly with the tour operator or the airline. Passengers' names, together with their passport numbers, were added to a manifest that was then filed with the CAA. The compilation and submission of the manifests created an enormous administrative task for the airline, and Jones often found himself on the telephone to the CAA requesting that it bend the rules and allow him to add new names to the passenger list at the last minute.

During 1973, Laker Airways operated five 89-seat BAC One-Elevens, two 158-seat Boeing 707-138Bs and two 345-seat DC-10-10s. The small fleets meant considerably reduced flexibility if any aircraft experienced a technical problem. And when a DC-10 experienced a problem, it was particularly challenging, especially if the station engineer called Ops and advised that an aircraft was 'AOG', or 'Aircraft on Ground'. When AOG was written on the movement board it didn't mean that the aircraft was on the ground and sitting at the gate as part of its operating schedule. It meant that it was on the ground and unable to fly due to a major technical problem, often for an unspecified period. An AOG was an air carrier's second worst possible scenario (it is obvious what the first was), as it invariably meant delays for passengers, intense additional work for the Engineering department and the rescheduling of other equipment in the fleet, or possibly a sub-charter from another airline. Whatever the remedial action, it was sure to be a costly exercise. How the airline handled the problem and dealt with the passengers could affect the carrier's reputation with its customers as well as with travel agents and tour operators.

The purchase of the McDonnell Douglas DC-10 aircraft had propelled Laker Airways into the big time. It was now a wide-body operator when very few independent airlines could boast that. But in the 1970s, passenger aircraft were not as reliable as they are today and equipment failures were frequent. Whenever a breakthrough technology was introduced there were the inevitable downsides. The newly developed high-bypass turbofan engines such as GE's CF-6s that were fitted to Laker's DC-10s were initially prone to problems. In the early days of operating the DC-10, Laker Airways experienced several, unanticipated disintegrations of their GE engines, mostly at some point during the take-off when the engine was at its maximum power setting. If the engine failed before the aircraft had reached its critical V1 speed, the pilot in control could bring it to a safe – albeit very rapid – stop within the runway's length. However, an engine failure after V1 invariably meant that the pilot had to continue the take-off on two engines. The crew then had to get the plane back on the ground as soon as possible.

Ideally it would return to its origination point if safe to do so, but before it could land, the crew would have to reduce the overall weight of the aircraft to its maximum landing weight – and the only way to get the aircraft to its MLW quickly was to 'dump' fuel. However, the crew couldn't just open up the fuel purge valves and dump jet fuel (which is similar to kerosene) all over the countryside. The only alternative was to fly out over the sea and dump fuel there. Everyone on board would be aware that the aircraft was now operating in a compromised situation and had perhaps suffered serious damage, as hydraulics and electrical systems might also have been affected by the failed engine. The captain would have made a reassuring announcement over the PA and would have advised the nervous passengers that they were returning to the departure airport. The cabin staff would also be feeling the pressure trying to maintain a calm atmosphere. Once fuel had been jettisoned, the aircraft's weight was recalculated to be at or below its MLW when it landed back at the origin airport. From London's Gatwick Airport, the sequence of events, depending on the quantity of fuel to be dumped, could take an hour or more. All this time the aircraft would be flying with one engine out, something that was not lost for a second on the flight crew, or the now seriously inconvenienced and skittish passengers.

The Laker Airways fleet was scheduled tightly and when one of its DC-10s suffered an engine failure the next similarly sized replacement aircraft to operate the flight might not have been available for many hours. Meanwhile the Operations team would evaluate all the options. They would assess if a couple of smaller aircraft could perhaps do the service and, if not, would advise the passenger services department and down-line airports of the delays. A last resort would be to sub-charter from another carrier such as Dan Air. In any event, the immediate travel plans of up to 345 people would now be in tatters, through no fault of their own, while another 345 returning passengers – who may have already checked in at the destination airport for the flight home – would be informed that they had an indefinite delay. The knock-on effect, depending on the day and time of year, was significant. In the early years of the DC-10, delays sometimes went into an overnight situation. The passenger capacity of a DC-10 presented logistical challenges the airline had never faced before. If the delayed passengers had to be put up in a hotel, as the airline would have to do for a long delay, whereas the passengers aboard a One-Eleven would need two buses and perhaps 50 hotel rooms, a DC-10's complement needed seven buses and more than 200 rooms.

For Laker Airways, a failure of one of the DC-10's CF-6 engines was always a massive problem. The downside of having such a small fleet of aircraft meant that Laker would typically only have one spare CF-6 engine to fall back on. As the only DC-10 operator in Europe using that particular engine type, the availability of spare engines was almost non-existent, not to mention that they were incredibly expensive. The sheer size of the engine meant that transporting one from the USA could only be done by sea or by specialised cargo transport planes. Unlike Laker's One-Elevens, which had readily available Rolls-Royce Spey engines, or the ubiquitous Pratt & Whitney JT3 engines of the 707s, the DC-10's GE CF6-6 engine was a rare commodity in the early 1970s. They weren't sitting around in a neighbour's hangar, because the closest airline operating with this engine type was based in Istanbul, more than 1,500 miles away. It meant that a failure was exponentially more serious and potentially more costly than with any other engine type.

After experiencing several catastrophic failures of the DC-10's CF6 engine, Laker's engineering team, after consultation with General Electric, conceived an ingenious system of borescoping the engines. By inserting a probe fitted with a light and a camera lens into the CF6's combustion chamber, the engineers could check for hairline cracks. These cracks were the result of the considerable temperature variances experienced by the engine during its everyday operation. The combustion chamber, located between the high-pressure compressor and the high-pressure turbine, reached temperatures of more than 600 degrees Celsius. The constant heating and cooling cycles created some hairline cracking of the combustion chamber walls. Eventually this led to the combustion chamber letting go and the subsequent disintegration of the entire engine behind the fan assembly. When one of the DC-10's engines blew up it was terrifying for passengers, especially if they were sitting by a window and could see it shooting flames and metal parts out of the back.

Apart from the obvious disruption and costs incurred with respect to the engine, the delayed passengers, aircraft rescheduling and so on, the effects of these early technical incidents were felt throughout the company and beyond. The sheer size of the DC-10 meant that everything was amplified. In the 1970s every airline suffered from technical delays; in fact, it was an almost everyday occurrence. But when a Laker DC-10 had a technical issue, especially something as serious as an engine failure, it literally reverberated throughout the entire airport and was regularly reported in the newspapers. Fortunately, these early teething problems with the DC-10 and the new GE CF6 engines were fairly short-lived and 'AOG' became less and less of a routine notation on the Ops department's movement board, much to Freddie's relief.

Early technical issues aside, Laker's DC-10s were unquestionably the best advertisement that Gatwick Airport had ever had. They put Britain's number two airport on the map, and finally Gatwick began to be taken seriously, especially in the United States. At the time, Laker's DC-10s were the largest aircraft carrying the largest ever passenger load on a single aircraft that Gatwick Airport had ever experienced. They were the most modern plane based there by almost a decade. The other Gatwick airlines were still using much older jets such as BAC One-Elevens, Boeing 707s and 727s, Vickers VC10s, and Hawker Siddeley Tridents. British Airtours and Dan Air were still operating sizeable fleets of the De Havilland Comet, the world's first commercial jet airliner that dated back to the early 1950s. Single-handedly, Freddie's DC-10s had enhanced the status of Gatwick Airport. Together with Laker's affiliated ground handling company, capable of handling wide-body jets, Gatwick became a viable alternative to numerous foreign airlines unable to get traffic rights at London's Heathrow. Gatwick Airport owed Freddie Laker a considerable debt of gratitude for his inspired decision to buy the DC-10s and for everything he did on the airport's behalf to make it what it eventually became.

The arrival of the DC-10s meant that everyone had to up their game. It was exhilarating, and working for Laker Airways increased everyone's status in the industry considerably. Naturally, there was the inevitable jealousy from colleagues in other airlines, and nowhere was this more noticeable than with British Caledonian. The respective employees of the other Gatwick-based airlines at the time, Dan-Air and British Airtours (BA's charter division, which was located next door to Laker) all cooperated and got on well with their opposite numbers at Laker Airways, be it the Operations, Commercial or Engineering departments. BCal, however, seemed to withdraw and become more and more isolated, and unhelpful. This attitude was clearly driven from the top and was likely an extension of the animosity between its managing director, Adam Thomson, and Freddie Laker. Cooperation and support within the airline community was essential, whether it was for an occasional sub-charter, spare parts or even a replacement engine or simply some peer to peer insight about the weather.

Laker Airways was suddenly in the power position at Gatwick and they assumed the role of lead carrier there, for the last few years a status held by BCal after it had bought out British United. Unwittingly, Laker was now perceived as Britain's de facto number two airline after BOAC, this despite BCal, Britannia and Dan Air being larger carriers in terms of fleet size and numbers of passengers carried. It was exciting for the Laker staff to be a part of this new era of civil aviation, and the enthusiasm permeated throughout the entire company. As Bob Dylan once sang, 'The times they are a-changin', and nowhere was that more evident than at Laker Airways. The DC-10s had literally changed everything.

CHAPTER 22

# Obstructive Bureaucracy

## Not as easy as ABC

1972-74

British Caledonian Airways' objection to the Laker Airways Skytrain licence was summarily dismissed on 28th December 1972, and on 26th February 1973 the airline was designated as a national flag carrier under the Bermuda II Agreement. This bilateral agreement between the United Kingdom and the United States paved the way for Laker Airways to apply to the United States Government for an Air Operators Permit. It would be a formality for Laker Airways to be declared the second British scheduled airline on the prestigious London to New York route.

Certainly Freddie Laker believed that under the 1946 Bermuda Agreement, the granting of a reciprocal operating permit from the United States would be little more than a formality. The agreement called for 'comity and reciprocity', and the Civil Aeronautics Board (CAB) should have recognised Laker Airways as the second officially nominated airline on the New York route. Crucially, the treaty did not specify a timescale and only stated that it 'should be done within a reasonable time'. Neither Freddie nor his lawyer, Bob Beckman, anticipated any problems or any delays; it simply did not occur to them.

Freddie prepared to commence his new Skytrain operation from Stansted on 1st April 1973. Geoffrey Street, the new Skytrain Service Manager, had ensured that everything at Stansted was arranged and the New York end was all ready to go at JFK. Laker would still have to operate through the north charter terminal at JFK rather than the International terminal, where most of the other international scheduled airlines were based.

Laker Airways' official submission was made formally through diplomatic channels by Rowland Baring, the British Ambassador. He wrote formally to US Secretary of State, William Rogers seeking ratification.

Under normal circumstances the forwarding of a licence application from the

State Department to the CAB and ultimately for a presidential signature should have happened within days. Mysteriously, Laker's application was lost, then lost and lost again. It eventually arrived after the intervention of the British Foreign office on 18th April, and in response the Americans played dumb and replied that they 'did not understand what exactly Skytrain was'.

The delays that followed were unprecedented. As Freddie Laker later recalled, they were, "pure undiluted delaying tactics ... played out by middle distance nobodies." British diplomats in Washington warned their American counterparts that, unless the application was processed, the United States would be in breach of the Bermuda II Agreement.

The CAB's hostility towards Laker Airways' Skytrain gradually became all-embracing. It was led by the CAB's chairman, Secor D. Browne, a 56-year-old Bostonian who was about to retire. Browne did not want Skytrain approved on his watch and found every possible reason to deflect it. Freddie, who had once said, "I have the utmost confidence in Mr Secor D. Browne – in my opinion Skytrain falls bang within his thinking," was now eating his words.

At the heart of Browne's resistance was the introduction of ABC fares, which had ended the affinity group charter fiasco. Browne had recognised the insanity of the letter rules, and one of the most important actions of his incumbency was the CAB's adoption of the ABCs (Travel Charter Groups, or TGCs in the United States) to make bargain charter flights available to all travellers, regardless of whether they belonged to an affinity group. Browne believed that Skytrain would upend his greatest achievement. When the idea of ABCs was first introduced, he said: "This will bring low-cost air travel to a bigger part of the population who are not necessarily three-legged Armenians or librarians from Ashtabula belonging to a librarians' society."

Aside from ABC, Browne was an unflagging critic of deregulation of the airline industry as a whole, fearful of how it would affect the fortunes of the scheduled carriers, especially the American ones. He did not like Skytrain and could not see how it would fit among the existing services offered by the legacy/IATA airlines.

When Browne finally retired, President Nixon appointed Robert Timm, a former US Marine, as the new chairman. Timm had been a board member of the CAB since 1971 and was the former boss of the Washington State Utilities & Transport Commission. Like Browne, he was an arch-protectionist whose stance was to support US airlines, effectively taking a stand against the American consumers who were denied lower ticket prices. Timm was entirely against competition and believed that the solution to the problems was discounted seats, perfectly served by the ABC system.

Richard O'Melia, the head of the CAB's Bureau of Enforcements (BoE), went even further, and inferred that he thought Skytrain was a con to get around the charter rules. He believed that Freddie Laker had previously engaged in 'massive violations of American law' in his various schemes to exploit the charter market. In January 1973 O'Melia reacted and asked the BoE to temporarily suspend Laker's United States air carriers permit, a move designed to knock out Skytrain and bring Freddie to heel. Laker's fractious history with the CAB and the alleged breaches of affinity group charter rules were then cited as the reason for rejecting Skytrain, even though Laker Airways had not even flown a charter to the US without the CAB's express permission since March 1972. Ironically, Laker was one of the few airlines obeying the rules, and as a result its North Atlantic charter passenger business had declined to 31,621 passengers in 1972 from more than 50,000 the year before.

Freddie felt he had done more than any other operator to prevent illegal charters. At his Gatwick offices and those of Beckman in Washington there were literally thousands of sworn affidavits from passengers. It was Freddie who had most recognised that the charter market had been sullied, and drafted a code of practice. The code was never adopted, but many of the proposals it contained were embodied in the rules that accompanied the introduction of the ABCs that replaced the affinity group charters.

O'Melia was unmoved by Laker's record and imposed a $90,000 fine. Worse, he demanded an admission of guilt. The fine was easy to pay, but admitting guilt publicly was something else altogether. Freddie realised that he was being held to ransom and was told that the situation could delay indefinitely his case going before the CAB; he was told that the proceedings concerning the charter violations could easily take another two years to process. Bob Beckman immediately called O'Melia and asked him what it would take to make the matter 'go away'. But Beckman had miscalculated, and O'Melia smelled blood. He immediately upped the fine demand to $101,000 ($570k-2018), which would be the highest ever paid by an airline for a commercial infraction. It was a huge sum in comparison to the $40,000 that British Caledonian had paid, or the $8,000 that Dan Air was fined for similar violations.

Freddie reluctantly authorised Beckman to pay the fine. In hindsight it was a colossal misjudgement, but Freddie felt he had little choice, as he said: "I was faced with the question of do I sell my pride for that figure or do I fight and put my whole business in jeopardy? I said I would capitulate. We agreed a confession but it was watered down because I have never been accused of cheating, lying or falsifying documents. Being in front of the game, and trying to outsmart my competitors, yes – but cheating, no. I said I would never give in, but in the end, like everyone else, I had my price."

Payment of the fine and the muted admission certainly cleared the air, and O'Melia and Freddie developed a cautious friendship. When O'Melia was later proposed as a board member of the CAB, Laker wrote to the Senate committee describing his former adversary as a 'man of great fairness and professionalism'.

The payment of $101,000 in July 1973 cleared the way for the first pre-hearing conferences on Skytrain, set for 11th September, a full five months after the application had first been submitted. The British embassy in Washington threw its weight behind Laker Airways, making it plain how seriously it was taking America's failure to honour the Bermuda II Agreement.

The case came before Judge Greer N. Murphy, an experienced CAB judge, who made it clear he wanted to fully understand what Skytrain was before he approved it. The threats were numerous. Murphy was concerned that Skytrain threatened Pan Am's survival. By 1973, Pan Am, one of the world's premier airlines, was well past its heyday, making huge financial losses and relying on government subsidies to survive. US charter operators were also reeling; they relied on lucrative contracts carrying soldiers to and from Vietnam, and the war there was now coming to an end. Pan Am, TWA and the other US airlines all joined together to lobby against Laker's Skytrain, which they deemed unfair competition. They tried to persuade Judge Murphy to strangle it.

Then came the Yom Kippur War, fought out over 19 days in the Sinai and Golan Heights between Israel and Egypt in October 1973. The Arab members of the Organisation of Petroleum Exporting Countries (OPEC) imposed an oil embargo against the United States and other countries that supported Israel. The price of oil doubled, then quadrupled. Not only that, but there was also a shortage caused by the short-term disruption in supply, which sustained the dramatic price hike. The drastic reduction in the availability of jet fuel caused by the OPEC boycott had a dire effect on civil aviation and the associated inclusive tour industry.

The 1973 Hajj pilgrimage to Mecca was somewhat muted because of the Arab-Israeli war. This annual event fell during the autumn when the supplemental airlines had capacity to spare, as it was typically their off-season. Laker Airways assisted Saudi Arabian Airlines (Saudia) and sent a Boeing 707 down to Jeddah, and a DC-10 was dispatched for the second phase of the Hajj. A high-capacity aircraft was a massively attractive feature for the host airlines and charterers and meant that more pilgrims could be transported in a shorter time. From that point on, Laker Airways would become one of the preferred international airlines for every subsequent Hajj pilgrimage. The revenue derived from chartering aircraft for these flights was significant, it was worth the effort, despite the potential risks in order to maintain cash flow out of season.

On Monday 10th December 1973, Laker Airways presented its case before the CAB. The hearings started with the Americans deciding whether or not Laker had been properly designated as a carrier. It was another delaying tactic.

Freddie grew more and more frustrated, and after day three of the hearings he went on the attack, telling journalists: "When you talk with the lawyers privately, they admit it's just a big game. They say, 'Of course we know you are designated. Of course we know you are in the bilateral agreement.' It is just a big charade. They are having a very expensive day out on the airlines. This is why my airline makes a profit consistently and theirs do not. At least half of the bloody stupid questions would never have been asked by an airline man; only a lot of lawyers who don't really know what they are talking about."

Freddie also had many harsh words for the USA itself: "I don't mind saying that the United States of America does not have many friends in the world of aviation. They are just about to lose the best one they had. This isn't for the CAB to decide, it has been decided by Uncle Sam himself."

When it was Freddie Laker's turn to testify, Bob Beckman feared that his client would launch into a diatribe, so he coached him to answer either 'Yes', 'No' or 'I don't know'. Beckman told him that unless it was absolutely necessary to elaborate, he should not.

The main thrust of Laker Airways' case was that there would be no diversion of passengers from other carriers and any airline trying to match Laker's fares would lose hundreds of thousands of dollars doing so. Freddie said: "There is a strong incentive for them not doing so."

For once, Freddie followed his lawyer's advice and Beckman breathed a sigh of relief when his client stepped down from the witness box. When Freddie cheekily asked, "How did I do Bob?" Beckman confirmed that it had gone as well as it could have done. The alleged affinity group rule breaches had not even been mentioned, but Laker Airways had faced some unexpected opposition from the Port Authority of New York, who was concerned about Skytrain passengers camping out overnight at Kennedy Airport to get tickets.

The verdict was published the following March and recommended that a permit for Laker's Skytrain should be issued for a temporary two-year period, and it was now in the public interest to do so. The CAB said that it had only one concern – it believed Laker's fares of £37.50 in the summer and £32.50 in the winter were set far too low; having been set before the fuel crisis, they were now three years out of date.

Freddie sang Judge Murphy's praises and complimented him for ignoring the opposing American airlines: "This is what we have been working on and waiting for over the past three years." He was certain that President Nixon would now sign off on the Skytrain permit and he hoped to start the service within weeks.

However, the CAB had a different agenda and would ignore Judge Murphy's recommendations. Freddie had underestimated the determination of the board, which was acting apparently on the orders of the White House. The CAB had been secretly running a campaign to protect the existing carriers and it never had any intention of reciprocating the British CAA licence and its Bermuda treaty obligations.

Robert Timm had the power to review his CAB's decision, which he exercised. Another hearing was scheduled, which replayed all the previous arguments. The only change was that Laker Airways revised its Skytrain fare to £52 westbound and $125 eastbound. The new fares had been approved by the CAA in London, but US approval was still not forthcoming.

Amidst all his tribulations, Freddie looked to his own Government for their support. But he would be disappointed. Winds of change had blown through Britain in February 1974 when the Conservative Prime Minister, Edward Heath, had unexpectedly lost the General Election after a bitter battle with the British trade unions and the coal miners. Harold Wilson's new Labour Government had very different ideas about aviation policy, and the new Secretary of State for Trade, Peter Shore, was no friend of Freddie Laker. It did not bode well for the future.

Luckily, Laker Airways' charter business, under ABC rules, was booming. Even without Skytrain, the company was carrying more charter passengers across the Atlantic on its ABC flights than all the British and American charter carriers put together. Gradually, as the 90-day ABC advanced purchase stipulation was reduced to 60 days, Laker Airways became the leading operator of ABCs on the Atlantic, with more than a third of the overall charter market.

Laker Airways was still the smallest of the British charter operators overall. British Caledonian, Britannia Airways, Dan Air and Court Line were carrying more than a million passengers a year against Laker's 668,777 in 1973. Yet Laker was the most profitable, and its revenue per passenger mile was second only to that of BOAC.

Despite Laker's success, trading conditions were challenging because of the mid-1970's recession and the oil crisis. A number of airlines would go under during 1974. Horizon Holidays, run by Vladimir Raitz, went into receivership in January and was then bought by Court Line. Soon afterwards, Donaldson International Airways collapsed. Donaldson had been in trouble with both the CAB and CAA over affinity group charters, and as a result it hadn't been able to find work for its sharp-looking 707-321s, with their large red thistle painted on the tail, three of which had been converted to carry freight as well as passengers. The increased cost of the venerable 707s finally brought the airline down, and Freddie bought the old two-storey wooden Donaldson maintenance shed. He had his men move it out and erect it alongside the Laker hangar, then once electricity and phone lines were installed, Freddie gave it to John Jones as the headquarters for Laker's rapidly expanding ABC operation. He even sanctioned another telex machine and coffee-maker, thus ensuring Jones wouldn't have to leave too often. More than a few of Laker's staff members breathed a sigh of relief when the 'take no prisoners' Jones moved out of the main building and into his new quarters.

Laker Airways came through the crisis better than most, and in the first four months of 1974 carried five times more passengers on scheduled ABC flights than all the other British carriers put together.

With all this going on, in April 1974 Freddie made a bid to win the contract to operate Concorde, the Anglo-French supersonic airliner. No airline had wanted to buy Concordes, so the French and British Governments were forced to lease them out to their flag airlines, Air France and the newly named British Airways. After merging with British European Airways (BEA), British Overseas Airways Corporation (BOAC) had changed its name to British Airways. They told the Government that it couldn't operate Concorde without an annual subsidy of £25 million.

Freddie sensed an opportunity and held an impromptu press conference to announce that he could operate Concorde better than the national flag carrier: "If I can have the same terms and conditions as British Airways, I will make a profit with the SST." Laker wrote to Tony Benn, Secretary of State for Industry, and Peter Shore, Secretary of State for Trade, suggesting that they hand Concorde to him rather than pay British Airways a subsidy.

Freddie proposed a 'souped-up package holiday service' for Concorde. He likened it to his experience as managing director of British United Airways with the VC10 as his example. When BUA took over the South American routes that BOAC did not want to run without a subsidy, Freddie had demonstrated that it could be done. He had also supported the BAC One-Eleven, another British aircraft, without the need for subsidies. Freddie considered Concorde to be just another aeroplane, and that it should assume no premium beyond the price of a 1st Class fare between London and New York. He predicted that in his hands, the five British Concordes would fly 3,000 hours per year on prime routes to New York, Toronto, Miami, Caracas, Rio and possibly Tokyo, carrying 500,000 passengers annually. He chose the routes for environmental acceptability and flights over water to maximise supersonic speeds, government relations, and ease of licensing. Freddie figured that after 15 months of operation, he would make £585,000, a 3.76 per cent return on his investment.

But that was as far as the proposal got. Freddie later told friends had he never really expected to be allowed to operate Concorde but he hoped that his suggestions would get the Government to end 'once and for all the insane idea of scrapping Concorde'.

Another diversion was Laker's appearance in the new British hit movie 'Stardust', which starred David Essex, Adam Faith, Dave Edmunds and The Who's drummer Keith Moon. Laker had loaned a Boeing 707 to the film's producers, and the action depicted band members disembarking from the plane with Laker hostesses standing by the door and the Laker 'Oozlum bird' logo prominent. The scene was set in Los Angeles, but was actually shot outside the Laker hangar at Gatwick. Fortunately it was a sunny day in Sussex despite the absence of palm trees. Gerry Sharp, who had organised the event recalled that Keith Moon, true to form, demolished two bottles of brandy during the shoot. Plane spotters and aviation enthusiasts who saw the movie were quick to point out that the band members started on a BOAC VC10 but then disembarked from a Laker 707; clearly the producers had little regard for continuity.

On 20th May 1974, Laker Airways' third DC-10, registration G-BBSZ, arrived at Gatwick Airport, and Freddie named it 'Canterbury Belle'. The DC-10 purchases had turned out to be an inspired decision; Laker's first two had generated more than £11 million in revenue since their arrival.

Any excitement over Concorde, the new DC-10 or Keith Moon quickly evaporated when Bob Beckman telephoned Freddie from Washington. He had been privately warned by US Government officials that there was little chance the White House would ratify Skytrain. He said the excuse given was Freddie's admission of guilt and payment of the £101,000 fine the previous year. It made Laker 'unacceptable' as the second British designated airline. Freddie naturally reacted angrily: "The actions of the United States have cost us $20 million in lost revenues, while they've gladly accepted $65 million from me for the McDonnell Douglas DC-10 purchases."

On 6th June, the final decision was passed to President Nixon for an early August announcement. By then, Richard Nixon had other, more pressing matters on his mind. In a matter of a few weeks, Gerald Ford took over the presidency following the Watergate scandal and Nixon's resignation.

There was more disruption on 15th August when Clarksons, one of the UK's biggest tour operators, ceased trading after its owner, Court Line, collapsed. Court Line had fallen victim to a perfect storm of events and circumstances, some of which were perhaps outside its direct control. The package holiday boom of the early 1970s led to unsustainable pricing and the company expanded too fast, taking on $55 million of debt to finance the purchase of Lockheed L-1011 TriStar wide-body aircraft. It had also purchased the Caribbean airline LIAT and a couple of resort hotels on the island of Antigua, as well as Horizon and Clarksons. In the early 1970s, Court Line was like the Braniff of England. They echoed the American carrier's Alexander Calder-painted aircraft and Pucci-attired stewardesses with their multi-coloured BAC One-Eleven 500s and TriStars, with glamorous stewardesses dressed in style-setting Mary Quant uniforms. At the time, Court Line was the only British airline with any real pizzazz. Had they stayed in business it is likely their innovative branding and vertically integrated operations would have given the Laker group some serious competition, perhaps more than any other British independent airline.

More than 40,000 holidaymakers were stranded abroad and Laker Airways scrambled its DC-10s to repatriate Court Line's passengers. Meanwhile 100,000 people who hadn't yet travelled anticipated losing their money. But Tony Benn stepped in and assured the Clarkson ticket holders they would get their money back. With Clarksons gone, and a major competitor off the scene, Laker Airways prospered.

Freddie would have done well to look closely at the reasons behind Court Line's collapse, but he was too absorbed with Skytrain and the expansion of Laker Airways, the tour companies, and his new DC-10s for any introspection. The collapse prompted him to write to Peter Shore, extolling the solid financial base of Laker Airways. He told him that, with the Skytrain licence, Laker Airways would 'be without doubt the most successful and most financially sound company in the UK'. He added that if he got the go ahead, he suggested it would create jobs, He ended his letter by saying, "I'm still convinced that in the final event one of our ministers will have to contact Dr Henry Kissinger, the US Secretary of State himself, to win Skytrain approval."

Shore deputised a junior minister, Stanley Clinton Davis, to reply and make reassuring noises to Laker that the problem would be solved. Freddie also appealed to the International Civil Aviation Organisation (ICAO), which governed the Bermuda II Agreement. He did not receive a reply.

In reality, Peter Shore was just paying lip service to Freddie. He had bigger things to worry about. The Labour Party's coalition pact with the Liberals fell apart and there was another General Election in October, which Labour won comfortably.

Meanwhile the airline industry was suffering as the oil crisis intensified. After BOAC and BEA merged on 31st March 1974 and their operations were combined, the newly named British Airways became the largest carrier on the North Atlantic with 35 per cent of all traffic. It had made a £16.6 million profit in 1973, then was blighted by the fuel crisis and ran up a £14 million loss the following year. There was now enormous overcapacity with 20 major airlines flying the prime routes between the UK and the USA. Almost every airline was in trouble. By August 1974, Pan Am had debts of $400 million and was as good as bankrupt. TWA was seeking hundreds of millions from the American Congress, and Pan Am asked for $50 million and a further $10 million a month to ensure its survival. The two airlines were forced into merger talks, discussed the sharing of routes and dividing up capacity within the United States, and were given temporary immunity from US anti-trust laws.

To alleviate the crisis on the North Atlantic, discussions between British Airways, British Caledonian, TWA and Pan Am began with the blessing of both governments. They were ordered to come up with an Anglo-American agreement to reduce capacity so that Pan Am and TWA could raise fares. Laker Airways was not invited to the forum, but insisted that as a designated transatlantic carrier it had the right to participate in the discussions. Freddie started a verbal battle about the matter with George Rogers, the Under Secretary at the Board of Trade and the most senior civil servant in charge of aviation.

Freddie wrote to Rogers on 12th September 1974 and reminded him that while scheduled traffic had gone down, Laker's transatlantic charter traffic was growing. He told Rogers it was the high fares of the scheduled airlines that had pushed the passengers onto his aircraft. Freddie said Britain needed to stop being negative, encourage lower fares, authorise more flights and grow the market. Anything else would be economic suicide. He accused the scheduled carriers of tacitly using widespread practices of discounting their own fares, often illicitly. He also charged them with offering overinflated commissions for the business and muscling into once spurned charter markets to preserve their ailing schedules. The scheduled carriers and other less efficient operators were demanding the introduction of minimum fares, combined with the introduction of the scheduled airline APEX fares, all of which Freddie viewed as harming the industry rather than expanding it.

Rogers was responsible for negotiating the international traffic rights for British airlines, but had never cared much for Freddie Laker or his ideas. Likewise Freddie loathed Rogers, whose only previous experience had been as a negotiator of agricultural prices in the European Common Market; it was said that he specialised in the price of pig meat yet somehow had inveigled himself into a position of power where he could exert influence on the aviation policies of the day. Freddie described him as 'arrogant, manipulative and untrustworthy'. This time, Freddie was not on his own, as this was a view shared by the CEOs of almost every other independent British airline.

Rogers feigned surprise at Freddie's criticisms that he had been excluded from the forum and referred him to correspondence between Freddie and Stanley Clinton Davis, the Parliamentary Under Secretary of Trade for Companies, Aviation & Shipping.

On 23rd September 1974 Peter Shore announced that the UK/US delegations had come to an agreement for the coming winter months of a 20 per cent reduction in capacity compared with the previous year. Shore also revealed that the American airlines were worried about the effect the Skytrain would have between November 1974 and April 1975.

The release provoked anger and suspicion in equal measure; Freddie wrote a furious letter scolding Rogers, demanding that he explain what right he, as a mere civil servant, had to decide as to whether or not Skytrain operated that winter. When Rogers showed his hand against Skytrain, Freddie accused him of a gross betrayal of his office. He reminded him of his duties to obtain traffic rights for Skytrain as speedily as possible. He said Rogers's action up to then had been 'plain dishonesty'. Freddie also said that he would be taking the matter up at the highest level.

This time the reply came from Shore, who told Freddie that he would not get his US permit in time for the winter of 1974/75 and therefore there had been no provision for Skytrain in the agreement. As far as Shore was concerned, the national interest in reducing excess capacity was a matter of urgency and took precedence. But Shore reiterated that they were doing everything they could to help Laker Airways by reminding the US Government of its obligations, in the strongest terms. Freddie believed that the words were not Shore's but those of Rogers.

Freddie couldn't understand how Shore seemed to be supporting an agreement that sidelined Skytrain. His response was to order Bob Beckman to find out exactly what had happened during the talks in Washington. Beckman secured a transcript through a freedom of information request and Freddie learned the truth. When the transcript landed on his desk, Beckman phoned Freddie and dictated the key passages of what had happened in Room 726 of the CAB's offices in Washington on the morning of 18th September 1974.

The meeting to secure cuts in capacity had taken place between William Waltrip of Pan Am, William Slattery and K. L. Briggs of TWA, Ossie Cochrane of British Airways, and Charles Powell and Peter Jack from British Caledonian. The CAB also had an observer present called Richard Derisden. The British Embassy sent Alexander Gordon-Cumming, a former civil servant, to watch over the proceedings. During the talks, the possibility of a fifth carrier on the route was brought up by Slattery and the transcript read: "One point I'm not clear on in terms of drafting the agreement is: What do we want to say regarding the possibility of a fifth carrier on the New York line. How do you want to phrase how that will affect what we've accomplished today?"

Pan Am's Waltrip said: "My recommendation would be that it automatically would terminate the New York-London agreement."

Charles Powell asked for them to clarify what they meant: "In other words, if Laker receives approval for its Skytrain tomorrow, the agreement would be null and void immediately, even if they don't pick it up until next June or something."

Slattery replied: "The advent of another carrier on the route just doesn't make any efforts that we've gone through in the past five days worthwhile. We've been discussing a rational situation here and trying to rationalise capacity. The advent of a fifth carrier makes this a kind of nonsense."

The British delegation wasn't pleased about the inclusion of the clause excluding Skytrain, but the agreement had taken a long time. Ossie Cochrane queried whether the Americans were talking about the entire agreement or just New York to London. Slattery said: "New York-London terminated immediately."

Waltrip made clear that the cancellation clause excluding Laker would carry on through 1975, while adding they would like the right to review the rest of the agreements for cuts in capacity they had between them. Powell was perturbed, and warned that BCal would not sign the agreement without specialist legal advice.

Freddie Laker could hardly believe it. Behind the scenes, he suspected that elements within the British administration, notably Rogers, were working hand-in-glove with the IATA airlines to thwart the granting of the American licence that Freddie needed to operate Skytrain to New York. However, he tried to put it to the back of his mind as he was due to go to Palma for the day with John Jones and a group of travel agents to promote Laker Holidays at a travel industry conference. Freddie had often hurled insults across the trenches, at officialdom, IATA and the executives of other airlines, deriding them as morons, stupid in the extreme or worse. On arrival in Palma he could no longer contain himself. He decided to throw caution to the wind and let rip. Speaking at a travel industry conference in Majorca, Freddie called British civil servants 'bums and gangsters'. He roared: "If any of them want to victimise me I will die for England with the Union Jack in my hand. I don't want any hammer and sickle in my back."

His audience was startled and the civil servants furious. They resented being labelled 'bums and gangsters'.

Rogers took the comments personally and telephoned Ray Colegate of the CAA to ask him what he was going to do about it. Colegate replied: "He could not have been talking about you, or it would have been bums, gangsters and bastards." The CAA's response was no surprise, as Rogers did not have very many friends within it, and he was particularly despised by Colegate. Eventually everyone saw the funny side, even the so-called 'bums and gangsters' themselves. At Christmas that year and for years to come Freddie and Jones received a card from the Department of Trade with the message 'Merry Christmas from the bums and gangsters'. Not, however, from George Rogers, Freddie's main target, who had taken the comments personally.

Freddie found he had many friends at the CAA. Aside from Colegate, he was supported by the chairman, Lord Boyd-Carpenter. Laker said publicly, "Lord Boyd-Carpenter's support was unprecedented." Boyd-Carpenter himself was boiling over with rage that such a thing had happened on his watch. Ray Colegate, who had flown to Washington to negotiate new charter rules, found that the whole business had gone on right under his nose, without him knowing. He was both embarrassed and annoyed by what had taken place.

Freddie's response was to order Bob Beckman to sue the airlines that had taken part in the lock-out of Laker Airways from the London-New York route. In October 1974, Beckman duly issued a lawsuit in the US District Court in Washington against Pan Am, TWA, British Airways and British Caledonian under American anti-trust laws. The suit claimed \$19 million in damages, the amount that Laker Airways calculated it would lose between 1st November 1974 and 31st March 1975 as a result of not being able to operate the Skytrain service due to the void clause in the restrictive capacity agreement. The CAB had given the participants immunity from anti-trust laws, but only for the purpose of coming to an agreement on reducing capacity, not for the exclusion of a competitor. The suit contended that 'the defendants have conspired and combined ... to influence the agencies of the United States Government to delay Laker's authorisation ... by coercion, threats, intimidation, and other unlawful and improper means.'

Beckman wanted to turn the screw even further and issue writs against the individuals personally and government bodies in the UK and US, but the airlines hastily decided to settle. By November, the writs were settled and the four defendant airlines amended the agreement to remove the offensive voiding of the clause.

Nevertheless, even without Skytrain Laker Airways was thriving on the North Atlantic thanks to the ABCs. Laker carried 179,690 passengers across the Atlantic during 1974, up by 77,588, an astonishing 76 per cent increase. For the end of the summer season John Jones had worked a substantial deal through the shipping brokers Furness Withy, with whom Laker had performed a number of charter flights. Two of the DC-10s were contracted to operate from Casablanca, Rabat and Fez in Morocco on behalf of the Moroccan national airline Royal Air Maroc during October and November. Jones sent his colleague Gerry Sharp to Morocco to oversee the operation and apart from a few minor hiccups it was a very successful Hajj.

Peace had temporarily been made between Freddie and his enemies after Beckman's threats of a suit. But it was not to last. On 23rd December, British Airways filed an application with the CAA calling for Laker Airways' Skytrain licence to be rescinded, citing the enormous losses experienced by existing North Atlantic operators. BA was backed up by British Caledonian, which said that Skytrain would disrupt its transatlantic business and harm all the IATA airlines. BA's lawyers claimed that ABCs catered perfectly well for travellers seeking low fares, and were available to everyone. The Advanced Booking Charter rules were considered a high enough wall to stop the charter airlines diverting full-fare-paying passengers, never mind that their fares were up to ten times what the supplemental airlines were charging.

Five years after the Edwards Report had advocated there should be a 'second force' airline designated to serve routes and compete, British Airways was seeking to reverse the principle. It had a monopoly as the only UK airline offering scheduled services on the Atlantic and it desperately wanted to keep it that way. Skytrain, it said, was no longer a necessity and British Airways was no longer neutral on its existence. It suggested that if it were to suffer any competition at all, it would rather it be from British Caledonian, who had supported BA's application to crush Skytrain.

Arguing to remove Laker's transatlantic permit on the basis of overcapacity was a little tricky for British Caledonian, since it had pulled out of both its US routes in October the previous year after citing 'catastrophic losses'. Starting the US routes so soon after the merger with BUA had been misguided and a commercial disaster. BCal was still running old and thirsty 707s on its routes, at a time when aviation fuel was both scarce and expensive.

The protracted legal wrangling about Skytrain had already cost Laker Airways dear, and Freddie's faith in the rules of international aviation had been severely shaken. He called the opposition a "delinquent example to set before the world out of pure selfishness and vested interests" and "the failure of the British government to enforce the Bermuda Agreement is an irredeemable act of weakness."

Meanwhile, in December 1974, Robert Timm was forced to resign from his exalted position of chairman of the CAB. He was exposed by *The Washington Post* newspaper for accepting hospitality from United Airlines by way of an all-expenses-paid golfing trip to Bermuda with other airline cronies. There were also other accusations of misconduct. President Ford replaced him with John Robson, general counsel to the Department of Transportation. Under Robson, the CAB set about reversing some of its anti-competitive policies. Despite the unprecedented obstructive bureaucracy he'd had to endure, there was still hope for Freddie and his Skytrain quest.

CHAPTER 23

# See You in Court Minister

## ... as Cupid's arrow strikes again

1975

As 1975 dawned, Freddie Laker was back where he had started in pursuit of his Skytrain dream. Moreover, he was now a quarter of a million pounds (£2.5 million at 2018 values) lighter, due to the legal fees. Freddie was furious about BA's application to revoke his Skytrain licence on the grounds of economic recession; he said their heavy-handed move was akin to 'using a sledgehammer to crack a nut'. He would regularly use this metaphor thereafter.

Prior to the obligatory two-day hearing on the matter, scheduled to take place on 22nd January, Laker Airways called for public support, issuing a rallying postcard to 5,000 of the 20,000-plus members of the public who had taken the trouble to write to the airline in support of Skytrain, which was by then already a household name. The call to arms asked for their help in seeking to prove there was a demand for the Skytrain service by returning the postcard. Eighty per cent of the cards were returned within the first week, and even after the hearing, the cards continued to flow in. On the morning of the hearing, standing on the steps of the CAA building in London, Freddie unfurled a scroll with the collated names of all the Skytrain supporters.

He'd brought a phalanx of his senior management, including Deputy Managing Director Cliff Nunn, Financial Director Robbie Robinson, Managing Director of Laker Air Travel George Carroll, Skytrain Service Manager Geoffrey Street, Group Solicitor Christopher Brown, and his Personal Assistant Lesley Chilton. They all raised the petition up across the doorway to make Freddie's point and it was duly photographed and reported on by the press.

Later that month the CAA threw out BA's application to revoke the Skytrain licence, but, while not taking Laker Airways' licence away, the CAA suggested that Freddie might wait a year until conditions were better. And there remained the question of American approval, which after a year was still unforthcoming.

Freddie's feelings of frustration were mingled with applause when National Airlines in the USA proposed a 'no frills' transatlantic service, reducing fares by 35 per cent. It was termed by the US Government's Department of Transportation a 'first breath of fresh air' in airline pricing in the last decade; Freddie thought perhaps they were beginning to realise the truth of his crusade. However, on 5th February 1975, Laker's Skytrain application in the United States was rejected again. Any conventional businessman would probably have given up at that stage and moved on, but not Freddie Laker. To all intents and purposes, Skytrain was dead. Although he held a licence in Britain, it appeared that there was no chance of it ever being upheld in the USA.

But Freddie was not made like conventional businessmen, which was just as well. He'd already expended millions on DC-10 loan repayments, infrastructure and the aforementioned legal costs for the new 'stillborn' service. Practicalities aside, the Skytrain licence was now a matter of principle. His tunnel vision was in high gear and Freddie wasn't about to give up his quest now, or ever.

Laker's three DC-10-10s were a long-term commitment of more than £26 million. Meanwhile, thanks to the ABCs and tour operations the Laker group of companies made £185,000 profit for the year 1974/75. Freddie's battles with authority had taken their toll, and the airline division of the group posted a loss of £300,000. So far, it had taken seven full hearings and he still couldn't operate his Skytrain service. Freddie forecast that the Government's reticence in enforcing the bilateral agreement between the USA and UK was going to cost him another three-quarters of a million pounds in lost revenue for the year.

In early 1975, Laker's Skytrain was facing yet another threat of extinction because of the arbitrary power wielded by Peter Shore, the Minister for Trade, and his Government White Paper on Civil Aviation Policy. The policy review had been initiated when Harold Wilson's Labour Party had won the election in February 1974. It was to consider what changes might need to be made to the policy in light of the oil crisis and the general economic recession. The Skytrain service was subsequently included in Shore's review on 21st March 1975. Whatever this meant for Laker Airways, Freddie was sure of one thing – it wasn't going to be good.

For airlines like Laker and BCal, it actually meant a tightening of regulations and less competition that had been encouraged by the previous administration under Conservative Prime Minister Edward Heath. On 17th April 1975, Freddie submitted a Skytrain Supplement to the Department of Trade policy review board. He could only sit and wait until Shore's review was complete, so he took some time to finally address his increasingly messy personal life.

For some time, Freddie had been living apart from his second wife Rosemary, although the couple were not yet divorced. Rosemary had moved to a house in Fulham without any animosity and she was being maintained by Freddie. He had pretty much sworn off marriage, claiming that he was married to his business and that life with him was impossible for any woman. He would say, "I am never there. I am off in the morning and in the course of the day may fly to America and back without her knowing. It's too much to ask of a woman."

Freddie was in no hurry to divorce Rosemary and he didn't want to make the big payout he knew would come with it. He had no intention of remarrying as he was having a great time as a single man. When Freddie wasn't working, he kicked back and spent as much time as he could with his Spanish friends on his yacht in Palma, Majorca. He'd named the latest vessel 'Tutinela'. It was a combination of 'Tutin', his nickname for Rosemary, as she reminded him of actress Dorothy Tutin and his only daughter, Elaine.

Aboard 'Tutinela', Freddie would be the ultimate playboy, chasing women around the deck of the yacht and being physically amorous. He would party ashore until 3.00am most nights in the bars and nightclubs of Palma, where he was naturally the centre of attention. The on-shore parties would invariably transfer to the yacht when the bars closed and carry on there until the dawn hours. 'Tutinela' was a magnet. The bikini-clad or topless women, seductively cycling their two-seater Mediterranean 'pedalos', would circle around the yacht in the hope of being invited up for a glass of champagne, a photo with the famous celebrity... or more. Freddie was wary and understood these women were there for the yacht and the spoils, and not necessarily for him. But Freddie being Freddie, it was a rare occasion when he resisted the temptation of inviting the women aboard, although very few made the cut for a second night.

Then, out of the blue one day, he met a stunning blonde from Oklahoma. She was a widowed mother of two who was enjoying a winter holiday in Majorca. Her name was Patricia Gates and Freddie fell head over heels for her. Following the first soirée in Palma with his new love interest, Freddie flew back to Gatwick on one of the Laker One-Elevens and stopped by the Operations office as he always did. Greg Dix, who was the day shift Ops duty officer, vividly remembers the moment when Freddie came bounding in, shouting, "I've met this American, Dix – she's an Okie."

Dix laughed and, as no one else was in the room, sarcastically responded, "Well, remember that you always tell us to steer clear of American women as they're all crazy."

Freddie laughed too, as he'd often warned his young men to avoid Americans, but he continued, "Well, this one's a stunner and she has two kids. You won't believe the name of her son."

"Go on," Dix replied.

"It's Biff!" Freddie shouted. Then, seeing his man's quizzical facial expression, he went on, "Honestly Dix, that's his real name and... he's a dead ringer for Hoss Cartwright from Bonanza."

And with that he ran out of the Operations office, still laughing and clearly on a high about his latest conquest. Dix shook his head as Freddie left. In the couple of years that he'd worked in Laker Ops he'd witnessed Freddie's moods vacillate depending on how life at home was going. It was apparent that if his domestic scene was going well, he would be in good spirits, and that became infectious throughout the airline. It was more than a coincidence that every area of the business seemed to follow him, so if Freddie was focused and upbeat, the airline prospered. Conversely, when Freddie's domestic life was in chaos, it took his usually buoyant personality with it and the efficiency, employee morale, motivation and even the commercial results of the airline tended to follow. One of the senior engineering managers swore that 'if Mr Laker's mood is down, the planes go tech more often'. Freddie's power and influence were immeasurable and the dynamics of Laker Airways were totally interdependent with his own. It was unquestionably a rare phenomenon.

As Freddie's relationship with Patricia, his latest fixation, progressed in early 1975, a divorce from Rosemary became a priority. In the 1970s, it would be considered scandalous for a married man of Freddie Laker's stature to have an affair with another woman and it would have been splashed across the tabloids. During their courtship, Patricia reassured the naturally concerned Freddie that she loved him and did not want any money from him.

Freddie was a high-profile figure and needed to steer clear of any public scrutiny; he was already making enough headlines with the well-publicised 'Battle for Skytrain'. Then Patricia announced to him that she was pregnant. Panicked, Freddie expedited his divorce from Rosemary and arranged to marry Patricia. He fortunately avoided being publicly humiliated on the front page of the ruthless News of the World, Britain's most hard-line Sunday gossip and scandal tabloid. In May 1975, Freddie broke the news to his first wife, Joan that he was marrying for a third time. Joan was the only other shareholder and a non-executive director of the Laker group of companies and had remained Freddie's trusted confidante, long after their divorce in 1968.

Freddie's solicitor, Kenneth Titmuss, referred to Joan as Freddie's 'Catherine of Aragon' (the first wife of Henry VIII), because of her belief that she was his 'true and only wife'. On hearing about Freddie's latest plan to marry for a third time, Joan was horrified. She had her suspicions about Patricia, founded on not much more than a woman's intuition. She distrusted Freddie's fiancée and suspected that her motives were perhaps less than honourable. Joan still had tremendous love and respect for Freddie as well as concern for their daughter, Elaine, whom she sought to protect from her gullible ex-husband's decision-making. It turned out that Patricia had possibly used the oldest ruse in the book to compel Freddie to marry her, by becoming pregnant. As they both desperately wanted to make their first child 'legitimate', on 9th July, Freddie and Patricia married in haste at the local registry office.

Incensed by Freddie's perceived lack of good judgment in his personal affairs, Joan, who did not know Patricia was pregnant, unexpectedly turned up at their wedding reception. Upon seeing the size of Patricia and realising that she was obviously well into her pregnancy, Joan caused a scene. She was intent on disrupting the union and letting everyone within earshot know her thoughts about the marriage. To Freddie's obvious embarrassment, Joan had to be physically removed from the premises by Elaine and her husband John Seear.

At the end of July, as Freddie and Patricia were enjoying their honeymoon, cruising peacefully around the Mediterranean on 'Tutinela', the tranquillity was suddenly interrupted by a radio-telephone call from the Secretary of State for Trade, Peter Shore. Shore said he urgently wanted to see Freddie in London, as the final draft of the Labour Party's Civil Aviation Policy review was sitting on his desk. Freddie was reluctant to break his holiday and upset his new bride, but deep down he was bored with the sea, the endless sun and not working. So he made his excuses, left Patricia on the boat and hopped on a plane to London.

On 29th July, upon landing at Gatwick Freddie collected his deputy, Cliff Nunn, and they drove straight to the Ministry. There they found the 50-year-old Minister for Trade, Cambridge graduate Peter Shore, in his grand office with his top civil servant, George Rogers. While Freddie did not fear Shore, he was apprehensive about Rogers, who fancied himself as a tough guy and saw Freddie Laker as a prime adversary. Rogers had wormed his way into a position of power and had been advising Shore, who knew little about aviation and relied on his ambitious and arrogant assistant, who was only too happy to share his own prejudicial opinions. When he saw Rogers, Freddie knew it would be bad news, and it was. Shore told him that the report recommended carving up British aviation between British Airways and British Caledonian and that there would be no room for Laker's Skytrain. He went on to say that Freddie's licence to operate Skytrain was being revoked, adding that he regretted being the deliverer of such bad news. He felt an affinity with Freddie, as he had served in the RAF during the Second World War. But there was little he could do, having commissioned the review, and he was forced to accept the report's recommendations.

Freddie tried arguing but quickly realised that Shore and Rogers weren't listening. He suggested an experimental trial period, but that was refused. When he realised that dissent was fruitless, he yelled at the two men, asking why they hadn't told him this in a letter or over the phone, instead of interrupting his honeymoon. He glared at Rogers, blaming him, and said that he would get even. Rogers, as cool as a cucumber, told him that the decision had been made in the best interest of the taxpayers. As Freddie stormed out, deliberately leaving the door open, he asked Shore's secretary how she could work for such a devious man. Peter Shore, the son of a Merchant Navy captain, was not used to such incivility and expected better of Freddie, even when he was delivering bad news.

After the meeting, Shore went straight to the House of Commons so that he could announce his decision before the MPs broke for their summer recess. He declared the new policy for long-haul routes, which were to be single designation – there would be no more than one UK airline in scheduled service on any route. The clock was being turned back 30 years on British civil aviation by this threatened return to a state monopoly, and the proposed liquidation of civil aviation's private sector would ensure that international airfares would be governed by IATA. Shore's stance lacked any social or economic justice or moral values. He told the House of Commons, "I am satisfied that if it [Skytrain] is allowed to go ahead in the conditions likely to prevail in the North Atlantic market for a considerable time ahead, it would divert traffic away from existing services and in particular damage British Airways. I have accordingly told Laker Airways that in these circumstances, the Skytrain service cannot be allowed to start." Freddie had followed the minister to the Commons and was observing from the public gallery. As Shore delivered his report to the House, Freddie sat watching and listening. He was seething with anger.

Shore told the house that he must do everything he could to protect the 4,000 jobs at British Caledonian that, he had been advised, would be seriously threatened by Laker's Skytrain. He went on to say that Skytrain would never fly. The report spelt out what the future was for Laker Airways and Skytrain. It said: 'The Secretary of State for Trade has decided that Laker Airways' designation as a scheduled service operator under the United Kingdom/United States Air Services (Bermuda) Agreement should be cancelled.'

However, this backfired on Peter Shore and he got a roasting from MPs as well as from journalists in the following day's newspapers. Freddie said in a prepared statement: "We still hold a licence. Any changes in the policy guidelines have to be approved by Parliament. Before they become law there has to be a debate. I will continue to be a buccaneer. I can assure Mr Shore and all who think like him that Skytrain will remain on the books until the day I die." Freddie stated firmly that he would 'see the Minister in court' in order to uphold his licence. It was by no means an idle threat.

In the parliamentary debate that followed, Shore, together with his Under Secretary Stanley Clinton Davis, who was regarded by Freddie Laker and his managers as a complete and utter bastard, tried to defend their absurd position. It contradicted the words of Sir Dennis Proctor of the ATLB, who had on appeal granted Freddie a Skytrain licence back in 1972, stating that there was a demand for the service. They argued that allowing Skytrain would undoubtedly cause damage to British Airways, despite the approved Skytrain capacity being only 1.3 per cent of the whole market. Even if 50 per cent of passengers on Skytrain were diverted from other carriers, the incursion would have been only 0.76 per cent. "A Pandora's box of problems could be opened... We would be inviting a shambles on the North Atlantic route when we require order," Clinton-Davis told his fellow MPs.

The prospect of 'diversion' had always been a bone of contention throughout the Skytrain hearings; Freddie maintained that Skytrain was not in competition, but was actually a stimulus. When the news reached Washington, American Government officials were ecstatic and relieved, as Peter Shore had just done their dirty work for them. Freddie called it 'both immoral and illegal as well'.

Freddie gathered his solicitors to see what could be done. His external counsel was John Roney, a fourth-generation lawyer who had inherited Freddie and Laker Airways from Kenneth Titmuss when their respective law firms merged. Titmuss, whom Freddie affectionately called his grandfather, was very blunt, which Freddie liked. Despite his diminutive stature, he refused to be told by Freddie what to do. The more genial Roney was a commercial litigator at the time and told Freddie that he would take a look at it. He engaged Andrew Bateson, a QC with a brilliant reputation, and at their initial conference on the Shore issue, Bateson claimed that the Minister had acted 'ultra vires' or beyond his powers and outside what he could do within the Act. Upon hearing this, Freddie ordered them to take action against Shore by way of a judicial review. He alleged that the Secretary of State for Trade had overreached his powers by ordering the cancellation of the licence for Laker Airways' Skytrain.

The Labour Government had turned its back on Freddie Laker, who had now told Minister Shore that he would see him in court. It was game on.

CHAPTER 24

# I'm Freddie...

## Keeping the show on the road

1975-76

"Mr Laker, I have the Palace on the line for you."

"Which palace, Lesley?" came the reply, which opened the door for Freddie's secretary to offer an untypically sarcastic response, "You know more than one?"

Lesley Chilton pressed her hold button as Freddie picked up the phone. "Yes, yes of course we can, we'll arrange everything," she heard her boss saying at the conclusion of the call. When he'd put the phone down, Freddie told his private secretary what he'd just committed to.

On a cold, rainy morning a week later, a large black Daimler limousine drove through the security gate at Gatwick and straight up to the stairs of Laker's Boeing 707 'Zulu Zulu', as it was known. The plane had 'International Caribbean' painted in gold letters on the tail and fuselage, and instead of Britain's Union Jack it carried the flag of Barbados, which was where it was headed that day. Barbados was served on a scheduled service basis via the Laker affiliate, International Caribbean Airways. The Gatwick to Barbados via Luxembourg flights remained a popular – albeit unprofitable – fixture.

A diminutive woman in a raincoat and headscarf quickly scurried up the stairs, brushing aside the umbrella being offered by a Gatwick Handling traffic officer. She was followed by a slightly built man and another woman. The regular passengers bound for Barbados via Luxembourg that day had already boarded and were likely wondering what the delay was for. At the top of the stairs the specially selected crew comprising Laker 707 senior training captain John Page and number one stewardess Sandy Doherty met the royal party, HRH Princess Margaret and her companion, the handsome and considerably younger Roddy Llewellyn. HRH also had her prerequisite lady-in-waiting along for the trip. The front few rows of the aircraft had been curtained off for their privacy and passengers had been advised not to enter the forward cabin area and to only use the rear toilets. Buckingham Palace had specifically asked that nothing special be done with the exception of providing proper glasses instead of the usual plastic ones and full bottles of liquor instead of miniatures. The economy seats for the party hadn't been replaced with larger ones but Freddie had insisted that his flight kitchen organise special food.

The quasi-royal flight was going smoothly until about five hours after leaving Luxembourg, when Doherty's presence was summoned. In her distinctly royal voice, HRH exclaimed, "Excuse me, my dear, but the sun was shining through the left-side window not long ago and now it's shining through the right side." After consultation with Captain Page, Doherty returned to advise the Princess that they had originally thought they could make the nearly 4,500 miles from Luxembourg non-stop to Barbados, but then realised that they couldn't and had turned back to Santa Maria in the Azores for fuel. After the somewhat embarrassing extended flight, the plane finally landed at Barbados more than two hours later than planned. Despite the considerable amount of drinks and fatigue from the long flight in an economy class seat, HRH immediately regained her royal composure. Clearly thrilled to be in the sunshine again, the Princess stepped through the front passenger door, smiled and waved to the group of Barbadian dignitaries who were all waiting anxiously below – so much for 'secrecy'. The royal party was quickly transferred to a light aircraft that would whisk them off to the exclusive enclave of Mustique, a private island in the northern Grenadines just 115 miles away. There they would be guests of the renowned Colin Tennant, who had introduced HRH and Mr Llewellyn a few years earlier and regularly hosted their trysts on his island. Freddie was only mildly annoyed that the crew had miscalculated getting to Barbados non-stop from Luxembourg with royalty aboard; it wasn't the first time it had happened, as the route was right at the limit of the 707-138B's operating range.

In the days before computer technology was present on every commercial aircraft, trans-oceanic navigation was not always an exact science. Freddie would be the first to say, "Better to always play it safe going down there 'cos if you get it wrong, your feet get wet," as there is simply nowhere to land for fuel between the Azores and Barbados. As the transportation of a senior member of the Royal Family in this case was to all intents 'secret', Freddie was unable to put the coveted 'By Appointment' seal on his notepaper, denoting that he had been of service of some sort to a member of royalty. That was fortunate, as the bloodthirsty British press would have called him a hypocrite, after he'd declared himself the 'champion of the forgotten man'.

While he continued his battle for the elusive Skytrain licence, Freddie's empire was growing fast. The organisation that Freddie built was already one with a colourful past and an equally exciting future. Going into 1975, the Laker group now comprised 16 companies, ten of which were 100 per cent owned, with the two most dominant being Lord Brothers and Arrowsmith Holidays. Gatwick Handling, owned equally with Dan Air, provided aircraft and passenger handling services for more than 70 airlines. In Scotland, Thistle Air Brokers, in which Laker had a 26 per cent share, had been running its own

ABC programme out of Prestwick under the Lord Brothers banner. In Spain, Laker's interests included two companies: hotel operator Trans Espana SA and travel agency Viajes Trans-Espana. Palma, Majorca, was unquestionably Laker's principal Spanish destination. Nothing happened at Palma without Tony Estella's involvement and approval. He was one of Freddie's closest friends as well as Laker Airways' agent for all the Balearics. In the Canary Islands, Mike Sy played a similar role as expeditor and agent for Laker while Costas Nicolopoulos kept everything running smoothly in Greece. Laker was fortunate to have such dedicated professionals as their agents in their strategic package holiday destinations.

Lord Brothers, the main Laker group holiday company, was poised to become one of Britain's most respected tour operators. Under the management of George Carroll it continued to thrive with Freddie's patriotic motto of 'strong, independent and British'. Carroll was responsible for the huge success aided by a highly competent and experienced management team. The revenue of the Laker group in 1974 had grown by 60 per cent and in 1975, Freddie decided the time was right for a rebranding of his principal tour company, so Lords became known as 'Laker Air Travel'. This simple name change unified the Laker group's travel and tourism interests under one banner; Freddie was staking a claim to an even greater position in the travel industry. Behind the move he spoke of the desire to present a more understandable brand identity to his customers when the same name followed through from booking to flight to hotel. "Now people will book a Laker holiday and fly on a Laker aircraft. And they will book a Laker rather than a Lords ABC to North America." Freddie's reasoning for grouping everything under the 'Laker' name was sound. He was incensed by the advertising of IATA carriers and their ABC fares that contained only the scantiest of references that they were ABC rates and therefore could not be sold by airlines. When the airline and the operator name is common to both, "quite legitimately we can urge book a Laker ABC on a Laker flight," Freddie explained.

This wasn't the case up north, however. Arrowsmith, managed by Harry Bowden-Smith, continued to promote its own holidays and ABC programmes separately in the North of England via Laker's Manchester operational base. The company had a great reputation and Freddie was in no hurry to rock the boat with the no-nonsense Bowden-Smith; there was never a discussion about changing the Arrowsmith name to Laker.

The new 'Laker Air Travel' name was launched in time for the group's expanded 1975 summer holiday programme. There had been another worryingly slow start of early bookings for the year due to the industry's problems, but soon they were coming in at a great rate, 30 per cent more than at the same time the year before.

No time was lost in promoting the new identity. 'Take a Laker' was the new catchphrase promoted by Freddie himself in flamboyant style. To promote the newly badged operation he rented a vintage Vauxhall car and travelled the countryside handing out leaflets at pubs along the way. Publicity consultant Robin Flood organised travel agent seminars around the country, and George

Carroll, Gordon Nichols and Don Evans of Laker Air Travel would attend and give speeches. Carroll wouldn't miss any of these events if his favourite Laker airhostesses like Bev Blum or Julie Poole were on the roster. Taking a tip from his master, Carroll fancied his chances with some of the company's cabin crew members. The star of the show, Freddie himself, would be brought out to rapturous applause and cheers. He loved going on the road with his ladies in red and garnered a good deal of publicity by donning a stewardess's hat and wearing a sandwich board that read 'I'm Freddie Fly Me', usually with a big clown-like grin on his face. It was the sort of thing that he excelled at; he would do whatever it took to ensure the Laker name became a household word. No other airline chief executive had ever been so publicly acclaimed or been so at ease at making fun of himself while promoting his brand. He didn't know it at the time, but Freddie's unique style of 'self-promotional' marketing was being watched by others with great interest.

Freddie predicted tremendous growth for 1975. "Our new Laker Holidays, Laker Night Riders, and Laker ABC programmes allow for an expected 20 per cent increase in capacity over 1974," he boldly proclaimed. The unsurpassed seat cost of the DC-10 made a short-stay package holiday to the most popular Mediterranean destinations a cheaper option than staying at home.

For its long-haul transatlantic programme in 1975, Laker Airways extended its offering to 167,000 round-trip ABC seats. The Arrowsmith programme from the North of England was raised to 20,000 seats, and Laker provided a 30,000-seat programme for Suntours out of Canada. During the summer of that year Laker's aircraft were scheduled to cross the Atlantic up to 22 times a week. Prices between March and October started from only £71 for a round trip. In 1974, Lord Brothers had offered 51,550 round-trip ABC seats, but in 1975 as Laker Air Travel its transatlantic ABC capacity increased to 117,000. The more than doubling of available capacity came about mainly because seat allocations previously offered to other tour operators on Laker's ABC flights were now exclusively sold by the Laker group. New York and Toronto, the routes with the highest demand in both directions remained the major North American ABC destinations for 1975. Flights to these destinations were planned months in advance; they went on the same days each week with the same flight numbers, ans were more reliable in terms of being able to plan a trip than any typical scheduled service. In fact, Laker published its ABC flight programme further in advance than the transatlantic airlines' scheduled flights.

Los Angeles had started off as primarily a destination originating in the UK, but a deal with LA-based tour operator Jetsave meant that a sizeable seat allocation on the LA flights would now be for Americans coming to Britain. Freddie sent a team of stewardesses out to Los Angeles where they travelled around the western states in their distinctive red Laker uniforms with personnel from the tour operator to promote the new service from LAX. Freddie flew out to LA to host a function for Jetsave where he worked the show with two of his original USA-based staff, Linda Earls, who usually worked at JFK, and Ricki Walsh who was Laker's representative at LAX.

In addition, ABCs were offered to Oakland, Windsor Ontario (for Detroit),

Montreal, Halifax, Winnipeg and Vancouver. In the USA Freddie became well known for his TV commercials produced by the renowned advertising agency, D'Arcy MacManus & Masius. The TV spots had Freddie on camera saying, "My name's Freddie Laker. I own Laker Airways and I think it's outrageous what you have to pay to fly." The commercial ended with him saying, "Look, I've got to give you a better deal. I've got my name on every plane."

Freddie believed it was absolutely vital that ABCs were adopted in Europe as soon as possible. The increasing popularity of self-catering apartments and the need for the cheapest holiday available, which needed flights only, was on the rise. Freddie had been in the forefront of protests against the usurping of charter airlines' European holiday traffic by IATA airlines using the part charter concept, where they were permitted to sell charter seats alongside scheduled seats to fill their aircraft. He felt that it should have been negotiated with a potential introduction of European ABCs. Freddie thought it was ridiculous that scheduled carriers were permitted to 'cross-subsidise' their passenger seats while he still had constraints like having to package a hotel room with air to make a package holiday.

He complained that the CAA was laying plans for minimum pricing on ABCs, a move that Freddie totally disagreed with. He did not want minimum prices imposed on him; that, he said, should be "left to our commercial judgment and what the market would stand, compatible with economically viable operations." He had a particular problem with having to charge a price based on an old aircraft, the 707. "Why should airlines buy quieter, more efficient airplanes when those with older noisy airplanes are being protected and we are being forced to put prices up to high levels?" he asked. Freddie lodged the strongest possible objection to the CAA's imposition of minimum ABC selling prices, accusing the CAA of blatant contravention of government-decreed policy guidelines.

Freddie believed he still had the edge, even if a free market ceased to exist. He made a strong case for booking with Laker Airways; he had the best aircraft, the DC-10, and with a more efficient aircraft he could offer considerably better value and service. Complimentary drinks, in-flight stereo and cinema were all included on Laker's ABCs, and his year-round operation offered more frequency and more capacity, giving the ABC passenger a much wider choice of travelling dates. Freddie thought that the scheduled airlines' new APEX fares would have no effect on his ABCs; they were restricted to only those airlines with IATA licences and there remained a 25 per cent price difference in favour of ABCs. The rules were more stringent than those for ABCs, although the 60-day advance booking rule was the same. The minimum stay requirement for an ABC was 14 days in the summer and 10 days in the winter. The minimum stay for an APEX was 22 days, one day more than a three-week holiday, putting it out of reach of the average working family. Further restrictions on APEX passengers meant that they had to return within 45 days, whereas ABC passengers could stay away for up to a year.

Freddie didn't think that Skytrain, if and when it was given the go ahead, would harm his ABC business – he believed that there was a need for both.

"There are two distinctly different types of Laker Airways' transatlantic passenger," he said. "The Skytrain passenger wants instant booking and will probably pay in cash for immediate travel at the lowest fare. Many will want only a one-way ticket and they don't want a restriction on how long they can stay. The Skytrain passenger won't mind some inconvenience or even waiting for the next flight, so long as the price is the lowest." Freddie was adamant that Skytrain was geared towards the 'forgotten man' who, in his opinion, comprised almost half of the adult population of Britain and about the same percentage in the USA. "Our typical ABC passenger on the other hand wants the security of an advanced round-trip purchase with set dates of travel in each direction. They accept a few restrictions such as the 60-day advance purchase, which we are trying to reduce down to 45 soon, the minimum stay of two weeks and, of course, the deposit they pay when booking." Freddie felt that neither Skytrain, when approved, nor the ABCs would affect the IATA airlines' scheduled services, which offered everything from 1st Class to promotional fares from the more favoured London Heathrow Airport. "And one more thing which is of even greater importance to my Finance Director," he quipped. "The ABCs give us perhaps the best positive cash flow I've ever experienced in all the years I've been in this business. We get paid, in full before we have to deliver the service, and there are hardly any cancellations. There aren't many businesses that can say that."

With three DC-10s available since the arrival of G-BBSZ ('Canterbury Belle') the previous year, and being fully utilised for the ABCs as they awaited their true purpose, the Skytrain service, Laker's Boeing 707s had more availability for special ad hoc charters. One of these was a two-month tour of North America in the summer of 1975 for the Rolling Stones and their party. The tour was originally slated to include concerts in Central and South America, but ended up being just Canada and the USA. It was guitarist Ronnie Wood's first tour with the Stones since the departure of Mick Taylor. Laker's 707 G-AWDG was assigned to the tour with the appropriately long-haired and irreverent Captain Jack Allum in the driver's seat and senior In-Flight Directors Irene McAdam and Meg Vesty taking care of Mick, Keith, Charlie et al.

By the late summer of 1975, Freddie was winning his battle for approval of Skytrain, but only in the USA. The Americans had run out of ways to scupper it and had softened their stance. On 27th August, the Department of Transportation assured Laker Airways by letter that the US Government – if at some time in the future the UK's Secretary of State decided that a Skytrain service would be appropriate – would give prompt attention to the issue of a reciprocal permit for Laker Airways. Unfortunately Freddie needed Peter Shore, the Minister for Trade, to support the application. Shore's department, which was nothing more than a bunch of BA protectionists had no intention of asking for a US permit on Laker Airways' behalf. It wrote a report and a directive explaining why British Airways would be severely harmed by Skytrain, effectively leaving Freddie Laker rejected in his own country.

Freddie was so convinced of public support, and so sceptical of those who sat in judgement above him, that he was determined to prove it. He commissioned a third independent public opinion survey from MORI (Market & Opinion Research International), the largest independent research organisation in the United Kingdom.

One of the few political voices that was vociferous in support was Stansted Airport's local MP. Laker's Skytrain, if designated, was due to operate from Stansted, which was 30 miles north-east of London in rural Essex. While it wasn't many miles further from central London than Gatwick, it was nowhere near as convenient. Unlike Gatwick, it had no direct rail service and the M11 motorway had not yet been constructed, so fast access by road was limited. But Laker Airways had no choice if it wanted to operate Skytrain. Upon hearing the report on the Minister for Trade's directive, the Stansted Airport Action Support Group sent a telegram to each member of the Cabinet and the Trades Union Congress (TUC) General Manager at the September 1975 Labour Party Conference in Blackpool. The group warned that the lack of employment prospects would be aggravated by the loss of potential generated by Skytrain.

When Commercial Manager George Forster retired, John Jones took his place after having successfully guided Laker's lucrative ABC programme between the UK and numerous North American cities. As the 1975 summer season concluded, Laker Airways was the undisputed leader of North American Advanced Booking Charters, and set a new record of 228,726 passengers flown – 55 per cent of the total flown by the five British carriers on the North Atlantic, BCal, Dan Air, British Airways (and its charter division, British Airtours), and Laker. The ultra-efficient DC-10s coupled with a vertically integrated product marketed via in-house tour operations created unprecedented pricing and service quality that gave the Laker group a distinct advantage. Jones was rightfully proud of how they had turned around a challenging situation of potential overcapacity with the DC-10s into a record-breaking triumph. If nothing else, the success of Laker's ABC programme demonstrated that there was a sizeable untapped market for all segments of travel across the Atlantic, whether for business, vacation or visiting friends and relatives, providing the fares were competitive. Freddie was smug about his decision to allow Jones the freedom to exploit the ABC programme's potential. Not only had it generated significant revenue, but it had also showcased the true potential of the DC-10-10 as a bona fide transatlantic aircraft. This, Freddie felt, would give him leverage with McDonnell Douglas when it came to ordering more aircraft, the first of which was imminent.

Things had gone so well that Freddie was negotiating for a fourth DC-10. He loved his DC-10s and, after the demise of Court Line with its Lockheed TriStars, Freddie was happy that he had hedged his bets with MDC and not with Lockheed. He had always wondered about what had led to the All Nippon cancellation that had led to such a fantastic windfall. The official line was that ANA had come under pressure not to go into wide-body jets, but had subsequently gone ahead and ordered the L-1011 from Lockheed. Something clearly was not above board, and in 1975 the cover-up was finally exposed.

In the early 1970s there were only three wide-body commercial aircraft models to choose from, all American, from three manufacturers, McDonnell

Douglas, Boeing and Lockheed. Only the world's biggest airlines could afford to buy and operate these aircraft.

The Lockheed Aircraft Corporation was one of the USA's largest defence contractors. During the Cold War its 'Skunk Works', or Advanced Technology Division as it was later called, had carved its name in the history books with the development of the U2 spy plane, then the revolutionary SR71 'Blackbird'. The latter set speed and altitude records that have never been broken – it could outrun missiles. Even more remarkable was that its only weapon was a camera. The 'Skunk Works' was home to some of the most brilliant engineering minds in the world. The Pentagon had permanent staff there and the facility was held in awe by the entire aerospace community. In addition to the aforementioned cutting-edge aircraft, Lockheed's portfolio also included history-making planes like the C-130 Hercules and the gargantuan C5 Galaxy. Lockheed also devised and built the Polaris submarine-launched ballistic missile. Despite Lockheed's unparalleled technological achievements, the four-engined turbo-prop Constellation and Electra were the manufacturer's last venture in civil air transport until the L-1011 programme. In the 1960s Lockheed had essentially owned the corporate jet market with the ubiquitous Lockheed Jetstar. With its four jet engines, ten-passenger capacity and a 2,500-mile range, the Jetstar was a popular choice of the rich and famous. Elvis had a red one. But Lockheed wanted to try its hand in the commercial aviation arena again, and in 1967 American Airlines presented it with a challenge to build a tri-jet that could fly coast to coast. Lockheed knew it was up against McDonnell Douglas, which had also been requested to submit a proposal to build a transcontinental, high-capacity tri-jet. Lockheed's aircraft was named the L-1011 TriStar. McDonnell Douglas Corporation meanwhile named its competitor tri-jet the DC-10.

In committing itself to the challenge, Lockheed put itself in serious competition with not just McDonnell Douglas's DC-10 but also with Boeing's 747, the original 'jumbo jet' and the undisputed industry leader of wide-body, high-capacity, long-haul air transportation. Lockheed spent $650 million on R&D for its L-1011 project, all borrowed from US banks. Unlike Douglas and Boeing, which had never stopped building and developing civil aircraft, Lockheed had to play catch-up. They spent many millions on developmental technology for the TriStar.

Almost immediately after committing to the project, it proved a mistake. Lockheed lost numerous defence contracts amidst a severe recession that put 60,000 highly skilled jobs at risk, and only survived because of a government-guaranteed loan. Lockheed desperately searched the world for customers for the TriStar – it needed to sign orders for 300 L-1011s to break even on the ambitious venture.

Lockheed's initial sales targets hinged on an order from either (or preferably both) of the major Japanese airlines whose markets were rapidly expanding. A prestigious sale to All Nippon Airways (ANA), the domestic carrier, and Japan Airlines (JAL), the state-owned flag carrier, would unlock doors to other Far Eastern carriers such as Hong Kong's Cathay Pacific and Korean Air. However,

JAL was not interested in Lockheed's L-1011 due in part to the carrier's long-standing affiliation with Boeing. ANA meanwhile had already agreed terms to buy six DC-10-10s from McDonnell Douglas, with $150 million of financial backing from the giant Mitsui Corporation.

Upon hearing about the ANA deal, Lockheed sought to scupper the contract with MDC. They hired an agent called Yoshio Kodama, who had close ties with the Japanese ruling party as well as less savoury links in the Japanese underworld. His reputation had survived after being imprisoned for three years at the end of the Second World War as a suspected war criminal. Under direction from Lockheed, he managed to persuade ANA to seriously consider switching its order to the Lockheed TriStar. At $30 million per aircraft, the L-1011 was considerably more expensive than the DC-10s to which ANA had already committed. In order to accomplish the objective, Carl Kotchian, the President of Lockheed, via Kodama, undertook a penetration of the very top level of Japanese political decision-making. It could have gone either way due to the strict Japanese culture and ethics, but for once the 'bad guys' prevailed. For his services in promoting the TriStar, as well as for other services rendered, Kodama was paid $7 million by Lockheed. A further $2 million was paid out through other channels to Japanese government officials, in order to grease the wheels. The Lockheed bribes went as high as the Japanese Prime Minister, Kakuei Tanaka.

Kodama also sought to frustrate the ambitions of ANA's rival, Japan Airlines. The minute the deal with ANA was signed, Kodama conspired to stop JAL buying any wide-body jets. ANA officials, through Kodama, bribed the Japanese transport minister to prevent JAL buying either 747s or DC-10s ... and it worked. In November 1971, in a dramatic volte-face, ANA switched its order to the Lockheed L-1011 TriStar and cancelled the six DC-10s.

The ANA scandal finally emerged in 1975. A bribery ring was revealed and a slew of prosecutions followed, including that of Prime Minister Tanaka. Meanwhile, the instigator, Yoshio Kodama, was side-lined by a stroke the same year. But that did not stop Mitsuyasu Maeno – a right-wing activist and 'pink film' actor, who felt personally betrayed by the scandal – taking matters into his own hands. On the morning of 23rd March he and two friends dressed up as Kamikaze pilots had rented two light aircraft, ostensibly to film a sequence for one of Maeno's films. Maeno piloted one of the Piper Cherokees himself and flew to Kodama's residence. He was heard on the plane's radio calling out in Japanese 'Long live the emperor' before crashing his aircraft into the house. Maeno died instantly, two servants in the house were injured and a fire started. Kodama, however, was unscathed, and shortly afterwards stood trial for the bribery scandal.

This was all unknown to Freddie when he bought the DC-10s. Corruption and collusion had put him in the pound seats for buying the DC-10s at just the right time and at the right price. It was profound, and the irony of it was certainly not lost on him.

At the end of the 1975 summer season it was time for Laker's flagship aircraft to earn their keep on another Hajj operation. The year before, two DC-10s had been used for the Mecca pilgrimage flights to Jeddah in Saudi Arabia from points in Morocco. However, for the 1975 Hajj, Jones had contracted two Laker Airways' DC-10s to Nigeria Airways. They would operate from Kano in Northern Nigeria to Jeddah, on a tight schedule of daily flights. Operating from a somewhat remote point in Nigeria presented Laker Airways with operational challenges they had not experienced since the 1960s, when Freddie had sent the Britannias down to sub-Saharan Africa for an extended period.

John Jones had cut his teeth in Africa and he of all people should have been aware that the considerable revenue he could extract from Nigeria Airways may not offset the risks of operating Laker's brand-new wide-body aircraft in what was unquestionably a 'hostile environment'. Nigeria, a country ruled by a military junta, had just gone through another coup d'état.

At the first Hajj planning meeting Jones told the assembled departmental managers that he was in no rush to go down to Africa again. He was also far too busy with Laker's burgeoning ABC programme and his new job overseeing the entire commercial department. Gerry Sharp had indicated no interest in going to Nigeria either, likely on account of the food there not being to his liking, or some such excuse; he felt he would be more useful at the Jeddah end. Operations Manager 'Atty' Atkinson suggested they send Greg Dix down to manage things in Kano. "He's been in sub-Saharan Africa before when he was with Monarch. He'll kick things into shape down there," Atkinson said confidently.

The aircraft had to be modified and the engineering department fitted plastic covers to all 345 passenger seats. The carpets were removed and the toilets replaced with a shallow bowl set into the floors of all but two of the toilet compartments; the latter would be blocked for crew use only. Catering would be simple and to a large extent would depend on what the Nigeria Airways' flight kitchens in Kano could provide. Jones said the host airline had been helpful and accommodations for the crew had been arranged, the runway had been widened and everything was arranged at Kano for the first ever wide-body aircraft to land in that part of Africa. Little did he know.

For three weeks, the aircraft were scheduled to fly each day to Jeddah from Kano filled to capacity with pilgrims, then fly back empty to immediately turn around and do it all again. There was a pause in the flight operations of approximately two weeks while the Hajj took place before the return flights commenced from Jeddah. With well in excess of half a million pilgrims flying out of Jeddah Airport in the 1970s, it was chaotic. Checking the passengers in and making sure they were going on the right flight to their destination was challenging, then on their return they would be carrying everything imaginable purchased in Saudi Arabia and hard to find in their home country.

The advantage at the Jeddah end was that there were so many airlines there, and a much better support system existed if anything was needed. This was particularly important for the engineering team, who got to know their counterparts working for other DC-10 operators such as the American supplementals, Trans International, Capitol and Overseas National. It was a completely different story, however, in Kano, Nigeria.

After getting all his vaccinations updated at the BCal medical centre and drawing a large float of US dollars from the Accounts department, Dix flew to Kano a few days ahead of the arrival of the first of Laker's two DC-10s. Upon arrival in Nigeria it was obvious that far from everything being arranged, in fact, nothing whatsoever had been arranged. It was total chaos. For the next few days, Dix rushed around trying to get everything organised, including crew accommodation; eventually, with a fair bit of bribing, this was established in what looked like old military barracks at the only hotel of merit in Kano.

The first DC-10 duly arrived and as there was no taxiway, it had to do a 180-degree turn at the end of the runway. In turning, the nose gear went on to the fresh tarmac that had been hastily installed at the side of the existing runway and promptly sank into it. The tarmac had been laid straight onto dirt, with no foundation. The DC-10 was stuck. The only tug available was inadequate to pull a DC-10, especially from a small crater, so Laker's engineering team, who were aboard the aircraft, quickly disembarked and organised the Nigerians. With considerable effort and power being applied on the DC-10's engines, the aircraft was finally extricated from the crater and taxied into the terminal area.

In 1975, Kano International Airport had no air bridges and no tugs capable of pushing back a fully loaded DC-10, so the planes had to park nose out on their stand for departure. A Nigerian marshal flagged the DC-10 into the ramp area and signalled that he wanted the captain to do a 180-degree turn so that the plane faced out for its first departure. What he had not considered was that to turn the huge aircraft in its own radius, almost maximum thrust had to be applied not only on the outboard wing engine but also on the three-storey-high Number 2 (centre) engine. As the aircraft commenced its turn in the confined space, the jet wash from the centre engine tore through the windows of the terminal building and those of the Kano control tower that sat above it. Nigerian air traffic control was fairly basic back then, and the controllers were still using paper strips to monitor flights in their airspace. These all scattered when the windows blew in, so no one had any idea of the whereabouts of any of the aircraft in the area. Fortunately, no-one was injured inside the terminal from the flying glass caused by the lethal jet wash. Needless to say, the Nigerians initially blamed Laker for the damage and confusion and it seemed possible they may arrest the captain of the DC-10. After Dix had tactfully explained what had happened, the authorities eventually realised that it had been the fault of one of their own staff, who was immediately taken away in handcuffs.

The next day, the first bus loads of pilgrims arrived from the holding camp. Some of them had lived in squalid conditions with almost no sanitation or food for many weeks, and it showed. They had all been given an orange, so the entire cabin of the plane had a peculiar aroma of orange mixed with extreme body odour. Some of the pilgrims had also thoughtfully brought along their pet parrots; typically these would be the exotic African grey, and they were confiscated before the pilgrim set foot on the steps, which naturally created hysteria. The cabin crew were challenged like never before, especially when pilgrims tried to light fires in the cabin to boil water for tea. Many of the pilgrims had come from remote villages and had never seen an aircraft before. Moreover, some had never even experienced climbing up steps before and created confusion as they tried to crawl up the steep stairs or slide up them on their backs. Then came the first casualty – a pilgrim collapsed on the steps, likely from heat exhaustion. The Nigerian doctor who had been summoned pronounced him dead, so Dix, as the Laker man there, had to pick up the body and place it in the back of his small pick-up. He then drove the body over to a spot at the corner of the airport that had been designated as the area for dumping corpses. Over the course of the three-week outbound Hajj, more than a dozen dead bodies ended up in a heap after dying, just before taking the Laker flight to Mecca. Fortunately, none of the pilgrims died while flying, as that could have seriously jeopardised Laker's 1975 Hajj programme.

The first phase of the Nigerian Hajj went as well as it could and fortunately neither DC-10 suffered any major mechanical issues, as that would have been very serious. Dix had been warned that if Laker failed to meet its part of the contract, including technical delays that compromised the pilgrims' Hajj experience in any way, the aircraft would be seized and used as collateral. He was left in no doubt that he and others of the Laker team would also be arrested. Dix informed all the captains and the engineering staff of this threat, inferring that they were to get the aircraft out of Nigeria at all costs.

Dix was assigned to the Jeddah end for the outbound Nigerian Hajj while a Laker colleague, John Greenhead, went down to Kano for the less intense incoming phase. Unfortunately, Greenhead got into a car accident almost immediately and ended up in a Nigerian prison. It could have ended badly had it not been for Laker's new Lebanese contacts in Kano, who Dix had befriended a few weeks earlier. They ensured that Greenhead was sent food and water and then negotiated his eventual release.

At the Jeddah end of the Hajj in Saudi Arabia, Commercial Executive Gerry Sharp had organised the Al Attas Hotel in downtown Jeddah for Laker's crews and ground personnel. The hotel was close to the souk, or marketplace, which became a favourite haunt for Laker's cabin staff. Sharp had made several good contacts in Jeddah, one of whom was a low-ranking member of the Royal Family who opened up his beach-front villa at the Jeddah 'creek' for Laker's crew members. Despite alcohol being forbidden in Saudi Arabia, there was clearly no shortage and the Laker crews on layover in Jeddah enjoyed the hospitality. For Laker's flight crews, being assigned to a Hajj was either a high point of their calendar or one of the most challenging experiences of their life, depending on where the Hajj was operating from and who was on their crew. One thing was certain, without a significant amount of flexibility, resourcefulness and an above average sense of humour, no one would have lasted long on a Hajj assignment.

After the Hajj had finished, Dix debriefed John Jones and the Laker management. He recommended that they never contract for a Nigerian Hajj again, as the risks obviously outweighed the rewards. It also took several days of intense cleaning to get the DC-10s back to where they could be used for normal services again.

At the close of 1975, Freddie Laker's most successful year to date, his personal life took another turn. In expectation of the arrival of their new baby, whom Freddie naturally hoped was going to be a boy, he moved his wife and her daughter Bettina to Furzegrove Farm. The main house was a six-bedroom Tudor-period mansion, with stable blocks, servants' house and 100 acres of prime land in North Chailey, Sussex. Freddie bought the estate for £83,500, and Patricia immediately started to furnish the house with expensive antiques. Freddie's mother was a frequent visitor and she had her own room at Furzegrove decorated in yellow and white chintz.

It had all the makings of a blissfully perfect lifestyle. Freddie was playing the dutiful stepfather to the hilt. He enrolled his 13-year-old stepdaughter Bettina in the exclusive Rodean private girls' school, located just outside Brighton. He was clearly enchanted by her, partly through their shared love of horses. Patricia tightened her grip on Freddie, and his daughter, Elaine, now 31 with a daughter of her own, saw less and less of her father. Patricia was typically present whenever Elaine visited. Freddie's constant referring to Bettina as his daughter upset Elaine's mother Joan, who wrote to him expressing her concern and asking him to stop. Once again, he had selfishly replaced his original family with another family to whom he now devoted most of his domestic energy, as well as his resources.

On 10th November, much to Freddie's initial delight, Patricia gave birth to a son. They named him Freddie Robert. However, the joy was short-lived as sadly the baby died just three hours later. Freddie was devastated. He was the kind of man who held dynastic ambitions, and a male heir meant absolutely everything to him. A son to whom he could teach the business and pass the baton to, as well as bequeath his empire, was his ultimate goal. With the memory of losing his first boy Kevin still raw, Freddie had now lost another. It was an immense second tragedy.

He could never be described as being the most considerate husband, so Freddie being Freddie left his distraught wife in hospital and took his daughter Elaine and stepdaughter Bettina horse racing ... to cheer himself up.

CHAPTER 25

# ...Fly Me

## Staying busy while the battle intensifies

1976 - 1977

It was no secret at Laker Airways that ever since 17-year-old Kevin Laker had been killed in his Austin Healey Sprite, Freddie had an open disdain for fast cars, spirited driving and motor racing; motorbikes were not up for discussion under any circumstances. However, Freddie's position on this did not stop John Jones, Kevin's best friend from the days when they were teenage tearaways, continuing to drive like a hooligan. On any given day Jones could be seen ripping down the Gatwick perimeter road past all the hangars at 70 miles per hour with the rev-counter red-lining and the underpowered four-cylinder engine screaming in agony. Jones's face would be contorted in a stern grimace, his reddish long hair and dark glasses giving him a menacing presence. He'd have the seat reclined at a rakish angle, arms fully outstretched with his hands firmly gripping the wheel, 'boy-racer' style. As the abused vehicle limped into the executive parking area, the acrid smell of overheated brakes would permeate the morning air. Jones's driving was a direct extension of his personality – no holds barred and full-on all the way, with little consideration for the vehicle or for Laker's dedicated MT division, whose job it was to keep the growing fleet of vehicles and ground equipment operating ... including Jones's company car. Fortunately, Jones had a few redeeming qualities that offset the daily mistreatment of his vehicle.

John Jones wasn't alone when it came to spirited driving. His colleague in the Commercial department, Gerry Sharp and Greg Dix, both drove excessively fast, albeit less aggressively than Jones, as did Freddie's son-in-law, John Seear, many of the engineers and even some of Laker's pilots. Freddie would witness the perimeter road being used as a race track from his office window and he'd asked Cliff Nunn to 'have a word with the hooligans'. However, Nunn fancied himself as a bit of a 'motorhead'; he always drove a sporty company car, and for once he ignored the old man. So when Jones told Freddie that Sharp had made a deal with Bernie Ecclestone, then head of the Formula One Constructors Association (FOCA) and owner of the world-championship-winning Brabham F1 team, for Laker Airways to transport the F1 teams' personnel on special charter flights, it wasn't met with the usual enthusiastic response to new business.

Notwithstanding, for several years Sharp scheduled Laker's BAC One-Elevens for F1 charters within Europe, then blocked capacity for the Grand Prix teams' personnel on Laker's DC-10s operating the Los Angeles ABC flights. Apart from the revenue and perhaps some prestige provided by the contract with FOCA, there were a few perks. Dix recalls Sharp coming into Ops one day in early May when he was on duty saying, "Fancy going down to Monaco for the race?" and, upon seeing his colleague's reaction, followed up with, "I can get us FOCA passes."

As a life-long F1 fanatic, Dix didn't need much persuading, so "I swapped one of my 12-hour shifts giving me four clear days, and tightly grasping our FOCA credentials Gerry and I headed to Monaco on the chartered Laker One-Eleven for the entire Grand Prix weekend." Some of Laker's cabin crew who were chatted up by the F1 teams' mechanics during the DC-10 flights to LA landed invitations to visit the F1 paddock at Long Beach, where the annual US Grand Prix was held during the 1970s. Dix continues: "Being on the inside of a scene like F1 was a massive privilege as well as an eye-opener. We worked hard and intensely at Laker Airways, but F1 teams operated at another level altogether. It was a shame Freddie didn't come and see what went on, as there was a lot to learn from them." A high point for Sharp and Dix was being on the pit wall for the start of the controversial 1976 British Grand Prix at Brands Hatch when James Hunt and Niki Lauda were vying for the World Championship. Hunt won the race on track but was disqualified following an appeal from Ferrari.

"My shot of the Ferrari and the McLaren on the front row of the grid at Brands is probably one of my most treasured photographs," Dix says. "I showed it to Freddie when he came into Ops one evening while we were all viewing the slides, but he wasn't particularly moved by it. Hmm, perhaps if they'd been horses..."

The Laker contract with Bernie Ecclestone and FOCA was kept going for several years by Sharp, who became quite a fixture in the pits and paddock, but no one really knew why he was there or what he did. Purposefully striding down the pit lane with his Samsonite briefcase, Sharp just looked important. He was on first-name terms with Bernie and in F1, that's all that mattered.

Freddie was approached by numerous racing teams for sponsorship during the 1970s. The era of the major cigarette brands dominating motor sports was doomed following the USA banning of tobacco advertising on television in 1971. A prominent British airline would have been a coup for a Formula 1 team. However, Freddie's negative position on motor racing was reasonable; he said the fear of flying was already a challenge that airlines faced and it would only be intensified if a racing car carrying the Laker name ended up in a crash, especially one that involved injury or a fatality. But everyone knew he also had personal reasons for not wanting any involvement in motor sports.

While he might have said no to sponsoring a racing car, true to form, in 1976 Freddie couldn't say 'no' when McDonnell Douglas offered to sell him its demonstration DC-10-10 aircraft, the second of its type to be built and at a considerable discount. It was an act of supreme self-confidence by Freddie, as Laker Airways didn't need another wide-body aircraft on its books and there really wasn't any work for it at that time. This particular DC-10 had been used for pilot training and demonstrations since its first flight on 29th January 1971.

The Laker pilots who had trained at Long Beach had already flown the plane, which was to be registered as G-BELO and named 'Southern Belle'. It was scheduled for delivery in June the following year. It had low hours but quite high cycles (take-offs and landings) due to the nature of the flights for which MDC had used it. This DC-10 differed from Laker's first three aircraft in that it was to be fitted with an auxiliary fuel tank where the rear cargo hold was located. Its maximum take-off weight was also increased by 15,000lb. The additional fuel would give 'Bellow', as it became known, an increased range, allowing for non-stop ABC flights to North American destinations such as Chicago and Winnipeg.

Throughout 1976, Freddie was as immersed as ever with the protracted Skytrain applications and encouraged his ever-loyal staff to lobby hard for the service. So early that year a staff action group was formed and they marched on London demanding that Skytrain be given the go ahead. Christopher Brown, Laker Airways' company solicitor, was its leader. The coach-loads of uniformed Laker staff, all carrying placards that read 'Ever heard of the consumer, Mr Shore?' marched along the south bank of the Thames and across Westminster Bridge to the House of Commons. They then filed into the old chamber, the great hall of the House, to the astonishment of the other visitors.

Freddie posted Brown in the lobby of the House of Commons to seek political support for his cause. They published a pamphlet 'Skytrain – A National Scandal?', distributing it to all MPs. The document was a full-scale attack on Peter Shore and strongly debunked the statistics supplied by the CAA to the Department of Trade in his White Paper on Aviation. It challenged every word spoken by Shore and Clinton Davis on the matter. The pamphlet called the reasons for killing off Skytrain as miscalculated, distorted and misdirected. It was an emphatic refutation of the arguments and reasoning given by Shore in defence of his decision, and an attempt to place on record the facts.

It turned out that Laker's lawyers had been correct about Peter Shore overstepping his authority as a minister in instructing the CAA to revoke the Skytrain licence. Parliamentary approval was required for Shore's implementation of radical policy changes. Publication of the White Paper was delayed until February 1976 when Shore, somewhat belatedly, realised he could not just change civil aviation policy. Turning it into law required a vote in the House of Commons and the House of Lords. The letter came to Laker's rescue and the Lords voted 83 to 68 in Laker's favour. But Shore had no intention of acting on a motion by the Lords. So on 6th March 1976, in an unprecedented move, having reached the end of the line, Laker Airways sued Minister Peter Shore for acting beyond his powers.

Just a month later, Shore was replaced by Edmund Dell as Secretary of State for Trade. Freddie initially thought that this was a stroke of luck, as Shore was a hard-line left-winger and Dell's politics were more moderate. The 55 year-old Dell, a former merchant banker, was a capitalist, just like Freddie.

Dell's support for Skytrain caused problems at the very top of the Labour Government and put Dell and Prime Minster James Callaghan at loggerheads. Dell told Callaghan that ordinary people deserved the right to travel at reasonable prices and that it was a betrayal of the working classes by the Labour Party. Dell said he could not see why Laker Airways should be prevented from running its Skytrain service, and told Callaghan that the concept of Skytrain was hugely popular with the British public. Callaghan told Dell he lacked political judgement, and reminded him how powerful an influence the unions were in Labour Party politics. Despite Edmund Dell's support, Laker's Skytrain remained becalmed and its future would be decided in court. Freddie had long ago realised that a Labour Government would never allow Skytrain to fly.

However, Dell's stance on Skytrain became an irrelevancy when the Department of Trade's senior civil servant, George Rogers, somehow convinced him that the 1946 Bermuda Agreement with the United States was outdated. On 23rd June 1976, Dell gave notice that Britain was exiting the treaty when it ended on 22nd June 1977.

Dell was keen to strike a much better deal for British airlines. He was brainwashed by Rogers that the objective should be something called 'single designation', which meant that only two airlines, British Airways and Pan Am, could operate the London-New York and London-Los Angeles routes. If Rogers' dastardly and absurd plan succeeded, Skytrain would still never fly even if Freddie beat the Government in the upcoming court case.

The presiding judge for the Laker Airways Ltd vs Peter Shore hearing, Justice Sir Alan Mocatta, knew which way the wind was blowing. On 30th July 1976 he wholeheartedly ruled for Laker Airways that Minister Dell's predecessor, Peter Shore, overstepped his powers in revoking Skytrain's licence. Mocatta's view was that the minister was wrong to restrict competition so severely and he overturned Shore's decision. However, he forewarned the Laker side that it would not be the end. "I strongly suspect this will be a pyrrhic victory. The end result will not reflect the ruling that I have just given. Hard luck."

Justice Mocatta was right. The Government immediately said it would appeal Mocatta's decision. Sam Silkin, the Government's solicitor, was particularly unhappy about losing on a matter that he saw as a principle called 'the Crown's prerogative'. A date was set for an appeal, to be heard in late November. The Government was now preoccupied with the need to reaffirm the 'Crown's prerogative' as a matter of absolute predominance, and Silkin's team of government lawyers assured him they would win easily. Meanwhile Freddie went back to making money.

By the end of 1976 Laker Airways and its integrated tour operations had become a force to be reckoned with. By now, the airline had a mixed fleet comprising three 345-seat DC-10-10s, two 158-seat Boeing 707-138Bs and five 89-seat BAC One-Elevens. This gave the airline considerable flexibility for both long- and short-haul operations. In the four years since the first DC-10s had arrived, Manchester had grown exponentially. Servisair did all the ground handling and passenger service, while Laker's own engineers and uniformed ground staff supervised the One-Eleven flights to the Mediterranean and Canary Islands and the DC-10s operating the ABCs to North America. Pilots and Flight Engineers rotated through Manchester while Chief Stewardess Beryl Booth managed a permanent group of cabin attendants who were qualified on both aircraft types. On any given day they might be heading down to Tenerife on a One-Eleven and the next day to Toronto on a DC-10. The package holidays and ABCs were mainly sold through Arrowsmith Holidays, headed by the incomparable Harry Bowden-Smith and his General Manager, Sid Owens.

Freddie's history with Berlin went back to 1948, when he had first participated in the Berlin Airlift. By 1976, Laker's presence in West Berlin was significant; his full-time base there was overseen by Station Manager Arno Angermeir, with permanent uniformed ground staff, engineers and a dozen attractive young German stewardesses – who were instantly recognisable by the higher hemlines of their Laker uniforms. A small, select group of One-Eleven Captains and First Officers relocated on a temporary basis; it was a popular assignment as Berlin was a vibrant city with an active night life and numerous cultural attractions.

However, West Berlin in the 1970s was a veritable island, separated from Russian-controlled East Germany by a wall. Checkpoint C or 'Charlie' was the only crossing point by road into East Berlin and it was a stark reminder of the Cold War that was still very much in existence. From the visitor area you could see over the wall into the grey and depressing East Germany. The Checkpoint Charlie museum was also an eye-opener as it included exhibits of some of the extreme measures East Germans had taken to escape, such as being welded into the petrol tank of a car and other ingenious methods to evade border security.

Laker's One-Elevens flew West German tourists to the Mediterranean sun-spots for tour operator Flug Union. Laker also established its own company, Laker Air Travel Gmbh, which coordinated a lucrative operation transporting Turkish 'guest workers' between West Berlin and Istanbul, Ankara and Izmir. The Turks were brought into Berlin to do all the jobs the West Germans didn't want to do; it was almost like slave labour, as the Turkish workers weren't paid well. Notwthstanding, when it was time for them to return to Turkey after their stint in West Berlin, the check-in for the flights resembled Jeddah after a Hajj. The Turkish workers turned up with everything they couldn't buy at home, from household appliances to windscreens for their cars. Needless to say, the check-ins took a while and as possessions were confiscated or disallowed for travel, hysteria and mayhem occasionally ensued at Berlin's Tegel Airport.

Several times a week charter flights operated between Laker's Gatwick base and Berlin Tegel. Operationally, they were perhaps the most challenging flights the company undertook at the time. The strictly controlled air corridors in and out of West Berlin were patrolled by the Russians, and adherence to slot times for the corridor and maintenance of airspeed and flight levels was paramount. There was literally no margin for error; slot times were inviolate and if a plane strayed from the corridor, a Russian MiG would be on its wingtip, pronto.

North America was also caught up in the Cold War, but it wasn't as obvious. The signs to the nearest fall-out shelters had almost disappeared in the USA's major cities, tourism was booming and Laker Airways was a major player. The Advanced Booking Charter programme had paved the way for the airline to be a dominant force in North Atlantic travel. By the end of 1976, Laker had three North American bases – New York (JFK), Los Angeles (LAX) and Toronto (YYZ). The DC-10s and 707s both operated ABCs to numerous points in North America, but the three main destinations were served on a scheduled basis. At JFK, the Laker planes operated through the North Terminal, which was for charter flights only. Lee Stevens and Butler Aviation handled the flights while Laker's three uniformed staff, Linda Earls, Cathy Green and Mickey Meunier, supervised the check-ins. They also did double duty as sales reps whenever there was a travel trade function. The operation at JFK had been on standby for Skytrain to start at any moment, and in anticipation Freddie had Charles Maxwell relocate from Barbados, where he had worked for one of Freddie's stalwarts, Ian Allan, at International Caribbean.

LAX could just be flown non-stop by the Boeing 707s, but the DC-10s always had to make a stop westbound at Bangor in Maine for fuel and a crew change. Laker's flights to LAX operated in and out of the West Imperial Terminal (WIT), which was only for charter flights and was located a couple of miles from the central terminal area. The WIT was quite efficient if somewhat primitive; for example, passengers baggage was picked up outside by the road. Ricki Walsh supervised the ground handling, which was facilitated on behalf of Laker by her father's company, Mercury Services, who also did the refuelling at LAX. Like her New York counterparts, Walsh similarly undertook sales functions as needed. The tour operator Jetsave took capacity on the flights for LA-originating passengers heading to the UK on vacation, or to visit friends and relatives there.

Toronto was Laker's only other manned outstation in North America. Jean Docherty was Laker's representative there and General Aviation did the ground handling. What made Toronto so viable was sharing capacity for passengers originating in Canada. There was an especially large English and Scottish expatriate community in Eastern Canada and the VFR (Visiting Friends and Relations) market segment was vital to the Canadian ABC programme. Cliff Wenzel was a go-getter in the early ABC days and almost single-handedly put Laker on the map in Canada, while the lucrative Suntours contract that came later was essential to the success of Laker's Toronto operation.

With Greg Dix's post-Nigerian Hajj report from 1975 still ringing in their ears, compounded by the Engineering division's complaint about having to spend a week deep-cleaning both aircraft when they came back from Kano, the commercial executives decided not to re-sign with Nigeria Airways for the 1976 Hajj. Instead, John Jones and Gerry Sharp did a deal with Iran Air for two DC-10-10s to operate the Hajj from Tehran's Mehrabad Airport to Jeddah from October onwards.

Iran in 1976 was governed by Shah Mohammed Reza Pahlavi, whose family dynasty had ruled Persia for more than 2,000 years. The Shah had befriended the USA and westernised the ancient Persian culture. He and his family had accumulated massive wealth and power and ran the country with an iron fist. Anyone overheard talking about the Shah in a public place could face execution. Notwithstanding, Tehran had a healthy and vibrant middle class, and women were not only allowed to work but, incredibly, also be seen in public with their faces uncovered. However, it was clear that bubbling under the surface was considerable political unrest and public resentment, especially from the poor, uneducated and more gullible citizens. Having been in Nigeria the year before, where the country was ruled by a military government, Dix and the Laker Hajj team who were sent to Iran were aware of the risks they faced for the 1976 operation and thought they had planned for every eventuality.

The first phase of the Iran Air Hajj went quite smoothly. The only hiccup was a last minute pallet of cargo the Iranians insisted on loading after Dix had already finished calculating the weight and balance of the aircraft and given the load sheet to Captain Mike Kennett.

"What's on the pallet?" Dix asked the Iran Air ramp supervisor.

"Wheat," he replied.

"OK, bulk load it into Hold 3," said Dix, as the two main cargo holds were already full and had been closed up.

The ramp was a mass of humanity all trying to dispatch the aircraft on time, as the Shah was due to fly in at any moment, which would shut the airport down for at least three hours. The pressure was on to get Laker's aircraft off the blocks as soon as possible. So Dix quickly calculated the weight of the pallet of wheat being loaded into the most rearward baggage hold, adjusted the load sheet and gave the new take-off trim to the captain. The doors closed and the DC-10 taxied out to the runway. It was always exciting to watch one of the DC-10s take off; the unique sound of their engines made everyone stop what they were doing and turn their attention to the runway, which at Mehrabad was one of the longest of any international airport at almost 13,000 feet. In October the temperatures were mild and generally below 20 degrees Celsius, but Tehran sits nearly 4,000 feet above sea level and in midsummer the temperatures reach more than 30 degrees. Iran Air operated its Boeing 747SPs non-stop from Tehran to New York, a 13-hour flight of more than 5,300 nautical miles. Mehrabad was also a joint military airfield, where the gargantuan US Air Force Lockheed C5A Galaxy was a regular visitor, transporting American-made helicopters, tanks and munitions for the Iranian military – hence the extraordinarily long runway.

Laker's DC-10 was halfway down the runway, building speed for lift-off for the flight to Jeddah, 7½ hours away, when the unthinkable happened. The nose of the DC-10 suddenly snapped upwards, putting the aircraft at an extraordinarily steep angle with the tail of its fuselage inches from scraping the tarmac. Almost instantaneously the captain pushed the nose back down and continued at take-off speed for another 1,000 feet while they retrimmed the horizontal stabiliser before executing a perfect take-off.

"What the hell?" everyone exclaimed, but Dix knew immediately what had happened, so he rushed into Iran Air Operations to communicate with the aircraft before it got out of VHF range. As he suspected, the take-off stabiliser trim setting he'd given to the captain after adjusting it for the last-minute 'pallet of wheat' had been incorrect. Dix spoke on the radio to the captain and, after apologising, called the Iran Air staff in for an enquiry. If the take-off had been on a 9,000-foot runway there was a possibility that the aircraft may not have made it. After a lot of finger-pointing and hedging, Iran Air ground personnel finally admitted that the pallet hadn't contained wheat but molasses, perhaps four to six times the weight. Loading it in the very rear of the aircraft had created an unacceptable mis-trim. They knew that the additional true weight would have put the aircraft over its maximum take-off weight so they lied about it, risking the aircraft and crew as well as all the Iranian pilgrims aboard. In different circumstances or with a less experienced pilot it could have been a disaster. Senior management were called in and, after hearing what had happened, the guilty Iran Air ground staff were taken away by armed soldiers.

Iran Air was a superbly professional airline that prided itself with a 100 per cent safety record, so what had happened went against everything the company stood for. Just as Dix was accepting the apology of Iran Air's management, they were informed of the Shah's imminent arrival. The airport was on lock-down – no one could leave, and all aircraft movements were frozen. The Shah's private 707 was on approach with fighters on each wing. As it touched down, two Iranian military helicopters took up station alongside until it was at its special terminal, where a small army was waiting together with limousines and heavily armed military vehicles.

"So, how did it go in Tehran?" asked Freddie one evening when Dix was back at his desk in Operations. Dix told his boss about Iran and how impressed he had been with the people he'd got to know there. Freddie was intrigued as he hadn't spent much time in the Middle Eastern countries. Dix told him that the Iranian women were unquestionably the most beautiful he had ever seen, "and the blokes weren't too shabby either," he concluded, which brought a chuckle from Freddie. Dix then got serious and in no uncertain terms urged Freddie to tell John Jones that no matter what the potential revenue, operating the Hajj from countries with so much political upheaval like Nigeria and Iran was massively risky. "We could have lost a plane in Tehran, and it would have been my bloody fault." Freddie said he would have a word with Jones, thanked Dix for the Caspian caviar he'd brought back, and rushed off to continue his quest for the Skytrain licence.

Laker Airways defied all odds in 1976 and once again grabbed the lion's share of the UK's ABC market with 280,409 passengers carried on its North Atlantic routes. This represented 53.5 per cent of the overall UK ABC market and, while it was a point and a half down on the previous year, it still meant that Laker was top dog for UK to North America affordable advance booking travel. Laker's ABC programme and the European tour operations, since the rebranding of Lord Brothers the year before, were performing at the highest level, both operationally and commercially. The two main parts of the business were aptly supplemented by ad hoc charters and the annual Hajj. The International

Caribbean route from London to Barbados via Luxembourg was the only marginal division of the Laker group's diversified business.

More than one senior manager of the airline wondered why so much energy, time and resources were being expended pursuing the elusive Skytrain, when the company was doing so well in almost every area of its operations.

But Freddie's Skytrain dream had become an obsession, in a similar way to the Accountant project, 20 years earlier – a venture that almost bankrupted him.

CHAPTER 26

# Victory at Last

## Bermuda breakthrough

1976 - 1977

On any UK constitutional matter, it was Lord Justice Denning who was most favoured to hear the appeal. Lord Denning was pro-democracy and, as it turned out, also very pro-Laker. In November 1976 the Court of Appeals ruled on Freddie Laker vs Peter Shore.

George Rogers, who was behind it all, was adamant that the Government would win the appeal, but Sam Silkin's appeal was thrown out. As the judgement was read out, the Laker team knew that they had won. Lord Denning put on his very best Hampshire burr so that everyone listening knew that he too was a man of the people.

His Lordship proceeded to firmly put the Government in its place. He argued that the Civil Aviation Act took precedence over the wishes of the Secretary of State for Trade, whose prerogative was only to persuade Parliament to change the law, a strategy that had already been previously rejected by government lawyers as unnecessary.

Lord Denning, Lord Justice Roskill and Lord Justice Lawton ruled that the British Government had gone beyond its power in cancelling Laker Airways' licence. George Rogers was said to be white with shock and very shaken, and asked the Americans for a postponement of the next session of the Bermuda treaty negotiations until January, after the dust had settled. It seemed impossible that Rogers could continue in his role after such a devastating blow.

The ruling came as somewhat of a surprise, as Lord Denning had stated earlier that it was a 'serious matter' for the courts to declare that a minister of the crown had exceeded his powers. He said, "It is so serious that we think very hard before doing it. But there comes a point when it has to be done." The Judges came out strongly in favour of Laker Airways and their ruling essentially killed the Government's attempt to destroy Skytrain. Skytrain was once again alive and kicking.

Sam Silkin, the Attorney General, was present in court when Lord Denning read out his judgement. He immediately stood up to ask for permission to appeal to the House of Lords; he was refusing to give up and wanted another opinion. Lord Denning told him, "Certainly you may appeal to the Lords, Mr Attorney General. But I would fail in my duty if I did not point out to you that the score at present stands three-love in favour of Mr Laker."

But Lord Denning did give the Government a possible way out. He said that Edmund Dell could have used a section of the 1971 Civil Aviation Act to stop Skytrain, as a section of law allowed the Secretary of State to give orders to the CAA in times of war and national emergency. He could have ordered the CAA to revoke its permission for Skytrain. But Dell had no intention of doing that and made it clear that he totally rejected Denning's advice to use the foreign policy exemption, saying, "It would have been politically impossible, having lost, to pull a new rabbit from the hat." As a result, Skytrain still had a British operating licence for the London-New York route.

Much still depended on the negotiations with the Americans over a new Bermuda treaty, and they were not going well for the British. The lack of a detailed, well-prepared case saw the Bermuda II negotiations stall. The Americans had been surprised to see the extent of the British negotiators' unpreparedness when the talks opened. George Rogers and his team had arrived with no economic analysis underpinning their arguments. The UK Government's plan for 'single designation', come what may, was clearly untenable, although Rogers refused to see it that way. He would not listen to any word against his spoken position in either the Bermuda II negotiations or the Laker case. But he was on his own, as it had been the CAA's view from the start that 'single designation' was ridiculous and unobtainable. A CAA official whispered in journalists' ears that it was 'wishful thinking' to believe that the American Government would take either Pan Am or TWA off the London-New York route just to 'humour the British'. The Americans were hugely irritated by Rogers's abrasive style; he prided himself on being, as he put it, 'the hard man negotiator'. Minister Dell had been initially pleased to have such a tough operator in the senior bureaucratic role at his disposal, but Rogers's macho approach was rapidly becoming a liability for the Department of Trade.

The Americans reached the point where they were unwilling to continue to negotiate with Rogers. They let it be known at very high levels that he was a serious impediment to the outcome and it was better if he were replaced. They argued that the British view of designating just two airlines, Pan Am and British Airways, to fly two of the most profitable airline routes in the world (London-New York and London-Los Angeles) was nonsense. The Americans wanted dual designation on the two prime US-UK routes, with TWA and one other British airline, preferably British Caledonian, flying them.

Laker's Skytrain would become a key component in the Bermuda II negotiations with the Americans. As far as Britain and America were concerned, Skytrain was a scheduled service and not a charter. The issue was whether Laker Airways should be the second designated carrier on the London-New

York route alongside British Airways, and whether the British would accept both TWA and Pan Am on the route. British Airways naturally wanted just itself and Pan Am, and said any other result would cost it £6 million a year in lost profits. The Americans refused to budge on the position of dual designation and were scathing about the amateur approach of the British delegation.

The lack of agreement in the Bermuda II negotiations continued to put Laker's Skytrain service at serious risk. To try and speed up negotiations the Americans appointed a special ambassador, Alan Boyd, a former US Secretary of Transportation. Edmund Dell finally realised that George Rogers was not up to the job and reluctantly put Patrick Shovelton, a formidable international negotiator, in charge. Shovelton was a highly genial man with a ready smile and, more importantly, was an under-secretary who outranked Rogers in the Civil Service; he was elevated to ambassadorial status for the talks. There was also air carrier representation at the hearings, and Laker Airways, which now held an official scheduled carrier's licence, was invited to join in. Commercial Manager John Jones was the Laker Airways representative, and he and his counterparts from BA and BCal sat alongside Shovelton.

Patrick Shovelton was the man for the moment, having been heavily involved in the EEC negotiations. He was regarded as a troubleshooter and a problem-solver in his department. He thoroughly enjoyed his new role and if he felt the Americans were getting too inflexible and over-demanding he told them, "Be careful or I will get George back." They weren't sure whether he was joking or not, and usually backed off, just in case he wasn't. The 57-year-old proved to be a breath of fresh air for the negotiations, even though the two sides were miles apart on the dual designation and capacity issues.

However, the breakthrough came on 18th February 1977 when Shovelton agreed with the Americans for dual designation on the routes to New York and Los Angeles. British Caledonian had virtually dropped out of the North Atlantic market because of financial problems, leaving the second carrier status wide open for Laker Airways. With Freddie having won approval to operate on the most important long-haul route in the world, he was now in a position to threaten the concept of the 'second force' that was so precious to BCal.

The British Embassy in Washington immediately restarted the process to get Laker Airways an American licence to operate, and officially asked the State Department to resume processing the company's application for a foreign air carrier permit. It was good timing as the American public were also demanding lower air fares. Senator Edward Kennedy, Chairman of the Senate committee dealing with administrative practices and procedures, took up the cause. He began asking why it cost so much to fly from Boston to Washington when it was so much cheaper to fly from Los Angeles to San Francisco, a route where competition had dramatically forced down fares. Freddie Laker appeared before Kennedy's committee in person and told it: "People seem to have lost their senses out of concern over what will happen to Pan American, TWA and British Airways. I submit that it is reasonable to believe that these carriers are taking advantage of the problems which in large measure they have brought upon themselves."

Much of the previous deadlock and anti-Laker feeling had been broken due to the efforts of Professor Alfred Kahn, who had become Chairman of the US Civil Aeronautics Board (CAB) in June 1977. Kahn was a new broom and decided that the time had come to give Laker Airways a licence. He admired Freddie Laker, related to his ideas and pushed the virtues of deregulation. Kahn believed in encouraging as many airlines to fly on as many routes as possible, with fares as low as possible.

Alongside that new thinking at the CAB was the rise of the consumer movement in the United States, led by consumer rights campaigner Ralph Nader. Jimmy Carter had taken notice and had campaigned on a platform of less government and lower prices. When Carter was elected, all the past obstructions to Laker Airways in America seemed to melt away.

On 6th June 1977, Laker Airways was given approval for a foreign air carrier permit by the Civil Aeronautics Board, subject to the conclusion of the Bermuda II negotiations. A few days later, on the 14th, President Carter signed it off with the words, "I strongly endorse and have approved the decision of the CAB permitting Laker Airways to provide a low fare 'Skytrain Service' for one year between New York and London." It was the fastest-ever presidential signature on record for the issuance of a foreign air carrier's permit. The catch was that Laker Airways would have to wait for 60 days to give US airlines time to put their cases forward to the CAB for operating similar services.

At Laker Airways' Gatwick offices, Freddie Laker raised the Union Jack and popped plenty of champagne corks. Characteristically he celebrated the decision by leaping into the air for the assembled staff and press photographers outside his headquarters with a bottle of champagne in hand. He confidently named the day when Skytrain would commence services as Monday 26th September, which marked the end of the holiday season when the Laker Airways' DC-10s would be released from their summer charter contracts.

After six years of trying, Laker Airways finally had an American licence for its Skytrain service. When Freddie received the formal document he found it was 40 pages long and full of petty restrictions to keep him in check. After the initial jubilation he was fuming again because of the conditions that had been attached to it. He said, "It is the most disgraceful document ever produced by any country as a form of reciprocity." Amidst all this change, Bermuda II had hit another snag.

President Carter wanted to do away with much of the fare control mechanism that existed. That was a step too far even for the genial Patrick Shovelton. But Carter was insistent. The President phoned James Callaghan threatening that direct air links between the United States and Great Britain would be cut off if a deal was not reached. Callaghan, however, made a speech and declared that air links would not actually be severed.

Nevertheless, Brock Adams, the US Secretary of Transportation, said that it would be effective from midnight on the equinox, 21st June 1977. The airlines began to instigate emergency procedures. British Airways said it would fly passengers to Canada and arrange connections, while Pan Am and TWA would do the same through Brussels and Amsterdam. Freddie was aghast and realised that he might have nowhere to fly to in September.

The pressure from the USA forced the negotiator's hand, and Alan Boyd steered through a settlement with Patrick Shovelton that was acceptable to both sides, after Britain's Ambassador, Sir Peter Ramsbotham, warned that UK-US relations were in danger.

The final outcome was a good one for Great Britain, thanks to Shovelton, who outwitted Boyd. The deal was agreed at 5 o'clock on the morning of 22nd June. It was just in time, as the CAB was on the point of issuing the paperwork to cancel the British permits as flights were actually circling New York waiting to land. Freddie could breathe again.

The new Bermuda II agreement added Atlanta, San Francisco, Seattle and Dallas to the schedule, together with the existing New York, Los Angeles, Boston, Chicago, Detroit, Miami, Philadelphia and Washington. Thirteen gateways into the United States. At British insistence, Bermuda II furthermore contained clauses that made it illegal for any airline operating scheduled flights between the UK and the US to resort to predatory pricing or capacity dumping. Air fares would have to reflect the real cost of operating the routes. This was welcome news for Freddie Laker.

The Americans got their way on capacity and dual designation but, as John Jones recalls, "The British eventually got the upper hand and the agreement they wanted. We certainly beat the Americans hands down on Bermuda 2A, we just ran rings around them, and we came out with such a favourable agreement to us, the British, that they didn't know what had been done to them." It was the most liberal air service agreement the US had signed so far and would be the source of friction for years to come.

Despite the licence restrictions, Freddie was delighted and placed a call to the White House to thank President Carter personally. He wasn't sure whether Carter would take the call. Freddie told him, "You are my kind of man. A man dedicated to competition. Now we'll get the show on the road."

CHAPTER 27

# Bully Boy Tactics Backfire

## A homecoming for Skytrain

July and August 1977

Freddie Laker felt confident as the launch date for his well-publicised Skytrain service approached. "I hope to make a 10 per cent return on my investment with Skytrain ... and I will," he vowed to the press.

The major airlines had scoffed at Skytrain before it was initially approved, but now they were taking it very seriously. Freddie's reputation in the industry as a maverick airline operator who never lost was about to be severely tested.

Freddie's problems, however, were far from over. The initial go-ahead for his Skytrain service had ignited a bitter price war by the major carriers serving the North Atlantic. Some industry pundits predicted that Skytrain was doomed before it even started because of the fierce competitive response coming its way.

British Airways, Pan Am and TWA struck immediately. Air India, Iran Air and El Al, who had also flown the London to New York route for years under the 'fifth freedom' regulations, responded later. 'Fifth freedom' rights were granted for a carrier to operate between two foreign countries, providing the flight originated or ended in its own country. While such airlines were rarely viewed with as much significance as the main 'point-to-point' carriers, they nevertheless quietly diverted a fairly high percentage of the market. They also used the ethnic 'bucket shops' to their considerable advantage, as these consolidators bought large blocks of seats at a heavy discount. The bucket shops typically used classified advertising at the back of the Sunday newspapers, and savvy customers could shop around for a low transatlantic fare, as long as they didn't mind flying on an Asian carrier.

The major airlines anticipated being granted massively reduced fares so they could compete with the renegade Laker Airways. Without waiting for the authorities on both sides of the Atlantic to approve the new fares, they slashed their advertised ticket prices dramatically and launched aggressive multi-million-dollar promotional campaigns to let potential passengers know about the savings they could experience with their airlines. They made sure the perceived shortcomings of Laker were publicised loudly by their expensive advertising agencies. 'Don't Fly the Budget Airline' screamed the newspaper ads. They told the public on radio, TV and in print that they offered better service than the forthcoming Laker Skytrain ... and they did.

They pumped up their Boeing 747 aircraft, the flagship wide-body aircraft with large spacious cabins and complimentary meal service. Some offered complimentary alcoholic beverages in economy class. Their service allowed a passenger to book in advance, order a special meal and check in a bag that weighed 20kg. The list of all the things they did better was long ... and now they were going to offer their superior product at the same low price as Laker. The majors were so anxious to hit Laker hard and fast and so bullish their fares would be approved that they didn't even add a disclaimer in their ads that stated 'subject to governmental approval'. British Airways came up with a Super Apex (Advance Purchase Excursion), Pan Am called its low fare 'Budget', and TWA offered a 'Standby' that was similar to Laker's Skytrain product but with a few of the usual TWA frills.

The aforementioned major airlines, many of whom were already losing money on the transatlantic routes, filed their fare revisions to commence on the 15th, 23rd and 26th September 1977, to compete head-on with the proposed launch of Laker's Skytrain service, slated for the latter date.

Buoyantly, Freddie claimed that he was so certain of success that he didn't plan on responding with any advertising to contradict them. "I'm not going to compare my product with anyone else's," he said confidently. "Pan Am and TWA are doing the work for me." For years, Freddie had been disparaging of the two American carriers; he regularly described Pan Am's business practices, which he regarded as stupid, as 'Panamania'. At a lunch held in his honour at the International Civil Aviation Club in Washington DC he joked that TWA stood for 'Teeny Weeny Airlines' – later it was 'Try Walking Across'. They had played right into his hands and Freddie couldn't believe their stupidity. They were spending a fortune to create a market for low-fare air transport, a market that might not have existed before September 1977. Freddie spent nothing, yet his picture was on the cover of international news magazines, in the daily newspapers, TV news, everywhere. During the spring and summer of 1977 there was perhaps no one in the civilised world who had not heard of Freddie Laker. He was a household name in the UK, the USA, Europe, and way beyond. He was celebrated as the pioneer of a new era in air transportation. He didn't have to spend a penny on advertising. His 'advertising' was front-page news, and it was free. His often self-mythologising and hyperbolic sound bites were a dream for the media. Over the decades that he'd been in the airline business, he'd built a symbiotic relationship with the press that worked well for both sides. Much of the airline's publicity was Freddie Laker himself, almost irrespective of what the story was about – and it helped that Freddie and the company were both called Laker.

This in itself helped blur any delineation between Freddie the man and Laker

Airways. Never before had a privately owned airline owner been given the sort of publicity usually reserved for politicians and entertainment industry celebrities. The public in turn lapped up everything 'Freddie Laker'.

Meanwhile, Freddie countered the hostile advertising of the majors by highlighting in the press that the price-cutting schemes would cut their revenues without inhibiting his own operation. However, the 'Big 3' airlines, BA, Pan Am and TWA, protected their existing traffic and any potential revenue loss from the proposed low fares. They limited the availability of their Super Apex, Budget and Standby fares to 700 one-way seats per week, per airline. This quota basically filled their existing empty seats or excess load factor in the off-season. In BA's case, its Super Apex availability would be a maximum of 25 per cent of the total seats available, amounting to about 80 seats a day on its 747s.

The 'fifth freedom' carriers meanwhile had their respective availability limited to 545 one-way seats each per week. The combined low-fare capacity they offered dwarfed Laker's offering, especially with Laker's reduced capacity restriction of 189 seats per flight instead of the 345 physically available seats in a DC-10, so their interests were more than protected.

As expected, Laker's competitors defended their efforts as simply a competitive measure. Pugnacious in his response, Freddie said the effort was "nothing more than an effort to kill Skytrain before it has even commenced operations."

Freddie set out to prove his assertions and, with the willing assistance of his Washington lawyer, Bob Beckman, who liked to practise 'preventive medicine' on behalf of his client, sought the initiative to expose IATA as the evil fare-fixing cartel both Beckman and Freddie had always decried. Beckman fired off a Freedom of Information Act request to the CAB for Pan Am's submissions in support of its proposed 'Budget' fares. It had worked in 1974, so why not now? He received minutes of three IATA meetings in Geneva and it immediately confirmed their suspicions.

In the summer of 1977, Freddie's enemies had gathered at IATA's Geneva headquarters to decide what to do about the Laker curse and what would be an appropriate response to Skytrain. Their proposed low fares would not only put a stop to Skytrain but would counter the threat of the equally pressing problem of competition from the supplemental charter operators. Twenty-eight per cent of all North Atlantic passengers flew on charter flights, with only about a third carried by the IATA member carriers. The cost of competing with the supplemental airlines ate into the major carriers' profits. Freddie forecast that this conference would scuttle the ABCs and increase fares.

At the time, apart from Laker, the UK supplemental airlines weren't big players in the North Atlantic charter market. In the USA, several that had been in business since the 1940s had created niches in the market. Overseas National, Trans International (TIA), Capitol and World Airways were the main protagonists, all of whom were major players in the respective charter markets. TIA boasted that it had operated to every airport in the world that had a runway on which a DC-8 could land. There was a natural camaraderie when the privateeers found themselves operating away from base, as on the Hajj, and a considerable level of cooperation existed between them, especially if one was in trouble and needed a sub-charter, spares or even an engine. Despite there being some competitor dynamics for ad hoc charters and the Atlantic ABCs, there was nothing like the acrimony they all felt towards the IATA carriers, with the exception of BCal, which never really fitted in with either group. BCal hated Laker Airways because it was stealing all its thunder, and it couldn't stand the thought of Laker's further expansion making it bigger than it already was.

Thus civil aviation in the mid-to-late-1970s on both sides of the Atlantic was clearly delineated between the majors on one side and the supplementals on the other. Another difference between the two airline factions was that almost all the supplemental carriers were owned and managed by dedicated air transport fanatics like Freddie Laker.

On 5th July 1977, 23 airlines had sent representatives to participate in a traffic conference; all flew the North Atlantic and all had an interest in the decision. There was only a partial agreement on North Atlantic fares in place and IATA rules called for a unanimous decision. The President of the European Civil Aviation Conference (ECAC), an IATA offshoot warned of the 'possibility of an open fares situation on the North Atlantic beginning in September and called on IATA to take the necessary steps to restore order as soon as possible.' Open fares were the most dreaded two words in air transport.

The meeting was, as always, cloaked in secrecy and the minutes never identified the speaker by name, only as 'the member' or 'members'. However, the routes, fares and self-interest being discussed revealed their identities and the airlines they represented.

Some airlines argued that IATA should not try to respond to Skytrain. IATA airlines had high cost structures. They could not afford to sell seats at Laker's low prices. The CAB had already reviewed the costs of a Boeing 747 as flown by TWA and Pan Am on the London-New York route in 1976 and found their advertised low fares were only slightly in excess of their cost per available seat mile (CASM).

A degree in mathematics wasn't necesary to work out that if they needed a fare of $376.26 at a 58 per cent average load factor (i.e. the average load factor the major carriers were experiencing) to break even, their lowest proposed average fare of $276.44 would necessitate a 95 per cent load factor. This was, of course, completely unrealistic, yet was still in excess of the fares they had proposed to offer in order to compete with Laker. The caveat however was that they weren't offering the entire aircraft at these low prices and they could almost always make a case that their first class and full fare economy passengers more than compensated for what was nothing more than a loss-leader. It would be a debate that would continue for many years.

IATA airlines carried 30,000 passengers a day between the US and Europe, while Laker's no-frills, no-reservation Skytrain service would carry just a few hundred a day. 'Let it go,' said some of the delegates. 'It will be too disruptive to mount a low-fare response '

But they wouldn't let it go. They wanted Skytrain destroyed in its infancy, or before. The spectre of Laker's Skytrain now gave them an opportunity to drive all the charter operators off the Atlantic by introducing predatory fares, after years of trying.

In the guise of competing with Skytrain, IATA could sanction them offering high-value product with advanced reservations and other frills at such low prices that not only Skytrain but also every charter carrier would be driven out of business. Sure, there would be some initial losses, but they would be short-term losses and, once the dastardly charter operators were gone, the fares could be hiked back up to 'normal levels' again.

BA, Pan Am and TWA were each proponents of a different option as the best competitive response to Skytrain. TWA opted for a 'like for like' with Skytrain, a 'Standby' fare of $256, just $20 higher than the proposed round-trip Skytrain fare of $236. TWA calculated that Laker's Skytrain could dilute $8 million of its revenues if it didn't respond with a similar product.

Pan Am, wanting 'the US flag to stay competitive on the Atlantic', came up with a 'Budget' fare, also at $256, with a three-week advance booking and the passenger could have their seat confirmed ten days before the flight. The downside was that there was no guarantee of a seat and the date of travel was uncertain. It was nicknamed the 'we'll tell you when' budget fare. Pan Am was later forced to admit that the fare was 'unjustifiable on economic grounds, except purely as a competitive response to Laker'.

BA's filings with the CAB had followed a different course, concentrating on a reduced 'Apex', termed the 'Super-Apex'. The $290 proposed fare was to compete primarily with the charters and not with Skytrain. However, the two US airlines rejected British Airways' Super-Apex as being 'not cheap enough to properly take on Laker'.

Determining round-trip fares in 1977 was made doubly harder due to the fluctuating dollar-to-pound exchange rate. Earlier, in October 1976, the pound had plunged to an all-time low of $1.63. It was recovering from mid-1977 and the economists were hopeful it would get back to being above $2 during 1978.

Apex fares had not been acceptable to many of IATA's members, driven by a fear of contagion and that they would distort fares on their own routes. Many of the IATA carriers wanted a 'get-out clause' included, so they could cancel their cheap fare offerings if Skytrain failed.

At a second IATA meeting on 22nd July 1977, the North Atlantic carriers attempted to establish a compromise on Apex fares in a concerted move against the charter operators. BA was still pushing for the reductions and did manage to thrash out a quota of cheap seats that it could offer.

The Joint Meetings of Traffic Conference reconvened for a third and final time at 2.30pm on 10th August, and deliberated over three days. The conference amounted to less about Laker than horse-trading over Apex fares.

Lufthansa felt the 'Big 3' had gone too far; the German national carrier thought that Skytrain would 'tap a completely different market' from its own services, and the Big 3's proposed Apex fares, should they spread into Europe, would threaten Lufthansa's profits. Another opponent of the fares considered the proposition that 25 per cent of available seats being sold at the Apex level was far too high compared with Skytrain's reduced-capacity 190 seats per day restriction.

Together with Super-Apex, BA had filed a 'part-charter' proposal where blocks of seats could be sold to middlemen, 40 seats at a time. These middlemen would set the price and fill the seats, the only condition being an unprecedented 50-day advance booking. To get the others to agree, BA used this as the bargaining chip, taking it to the table and obtaining more than a few nods of concurrence.

The last voice of dissension against the Apex onslaught was Olympic, the Greek national carrier. Its representative expressed his annoyance that "this reconvened meeting has basically dealt with the requirements of a few members regardless of majority opinion in order to rush a new level of service between New York and London."

All the proposed new fares were incorporated into an IATA agreement, then presented to the CAB for approval.

Freddie Laker denounced the IATA agreement made in Geneva as pure, unadulterated, predatory price fixing. It was a conspiracy. It was illegal. It was immoral. "Their idea of 'predatory' is praying over my dead body," he said. Freddie maintained that government-owned airlines should not use taxpayers' money to deny the public the choice of a new way to travel without frills and at a low cost.

Freddie and Beckman handed out copies of the IATA meeting minutes and publicly exposed IATA as anti-competitive and acting against the interests of the travelling public. "It's like climbing into the ring at a boxing match and finding you have to take on the audience as well," complained Freddie.

IATA was afraid, and with good reason. Governments of the time had never been closer to taking the process of setting fares away from them. They had usually focused on the approval and rejection stages of route licensing and in formulating guidelines for their national carriers, and tended to turn a blind eye if they perceived minor illegalities, typically giving IATA a free rein. Now government observers were predicted to attend future traffic conferences in a matter of months. IATA feared that their iron grip on services and fares was going to be eroded by regulation, not just competition.

The mood in the White House and the CAB under its new Chairman, Alfred Kahn, had turned firmly against the IATA cartel. Professor Kahn was a champion of deregulation and had worked with other progressives such as consumer advocate Ralph Nader and Democratic Senator Edward Kennedy in trying to dismantle anti-consumer cartels and monopolies. In his role at the CAB, Kahn issued an order that effectively removed anti-trust immunity for US airlines. The order also included any foreign carrier that flew into the United States. As a result of this action, Pan Am and TWA were forced to resign their membership of IATA as they could no longer safely take part in fare conferences for fear of contravening American anti-trust laws.

The American Society of Travel Agents (ASTA) supported the approval of Pan Am's 'Budget' and BA's 'Super-Apex' fares, as these were distinguishable from conventional fare tariffs. In contrast, however, ASTA urged the disapproval of the TWA's 'Standby' fare, considering it 'an improper way to market scheduled air transportation'. What ASTA meant was that, because TWA's

Standby would be sold direct to the customer at the airport on the day of departure, travel agents would be unable to earn commission on the fare. It was the travel agents both in Britain and the US who felt most bitter about Skytrain for the same reason; the service was a direct sell to the customer at the airport on the day of departure and therefore precluded them from earning a commission. Any travel suppliers who chose a direct sell business model risked the ire of the travel agent community, often to their downfall. Travel agents were a powerful group and their respective trade associations, ABTA in the UK and ASTA in the USA, vehemently protected their members' interests.

The CAB heard oral arguments on the fare filings on 30th August 1977, and had to answer the critical question, 'Were the proposed Apex fares an appropriate response to Skytrain and were they a proper, healthy competitive product?' The board argued that since there was no way of precisely predicting what would happen in the marketplace, the market itself would unfailingly determine the outcome.

The complainants expressed a view that the proposed Apex fares of the 'Big 3' were inappropriate. Their fares included meals and a reservation service and the overall product was superior in price and quality than either Skytrain or the charters.

Freddie Laker suggested that "The airlines applying for similar permits to mine should reflect on their words of 1971 when they said that Skytrain would destroy air transport as we know it. They have not acquired any new expertise, but some of them – who declared Skytrain as uneconomic but are now promising to match Laker's new service – are subsidised by the taxpayer." He continued: "There's a conspiracy by the other carriers to gang up on me and kill me off before I've even started. I think their plan is that they want Freddie Laker's head neatly chopped off and on a platter."

Freddie said that the application amounted to unethical predatory pricing. And he was not alone in his opinion. Charter airline officials were also up in arms over the major airlines' new pricing schemes. Tour operators – upon whom the charter carriers depended for their business – had been heavily solicited by the majors to sell their new low-fare offerings. Unable to resist, despite their allegiance to the supplemental carriers with whom they had done business for years, the tour operators reluctantly cancelled existing contracts with the independents and switched their business to the major carriers.

In Washington, the US Justice Department (DOJ) took heed of the charter airlines' complaints. Stating that he was appearing on behalf of the transatlantic passenger, the acting Assistant Attorney General, John H. Shenfield, urged the CAB to investigate whether the bargain offers were designed to force charter airlines out of business. The DOJ concluded that the fares were so disproportionate with the existing fares that it was difficult to imagine how they were lawful. The CAB's Office of the Consumer Advocate agreed with the DOJ, stating that the 'Big 3's' respective Apex, Budget and Standby fares should be higher to reflect the higher level of product they all offered.

Officials at TWA and Pan Am rejected Shenfield's testimony and claimed that their fares were justified: "We've watched the charter carriers gain an enormous increase in business," said one Pan Am official. "But now we feel the pendulum has swung the other way and it's time for us to be restored to where we once were." Laker's Skytrain had kick-started an unprecedented level of paranoia.

Freddie contended that the fares they proposed were essentially conventional services at Laker prices. There was no difference between BA's Super-Apex product and its regular Apex product, apart from the price. He called Pan Am's Budget fare, with its booking service, gimmicky and expensive. TWA's Standby product was really just a late-booking, full-amenity economy service. All the majors used the preferable London Heathrow Airport, had sales agents, airline sales offices, offered sales on credit, provided full meals, and had no weight limitation on baggage.

The American CAB was not prepared to risk unravelling the thread of competition, saying that "The theatre of competition on the North Atlantic has thus far been limited to a cast of two classes of carrier; it would be a genuine tragedy if the newest player was knocked out in the first act of the drama about to be performed." It ruled accordingly, automatically allowing TWA's Standby fare as the most appropriate response to Skytrain. TWA's free meals and all the other frills offered were more than enough value-added components to justify Laker's $20 lower fare differential. The CAB found that the remainder of the IATA agreement was contrary to the public interest.

Notwithstanding, the CAB could not ignore BA's Super-Apex. The Board regarded the supplementals as the low-price innovators and the primary source of competition on the Atlantic, as well as many other international markets. It felt that the Super-Apex fare offered by Britain's flag-carrier could put many of the American independents out of business. The CAB therefore decided it was not a reasonable response to Skytrain.

The CAB recommended the liberalisation of Skytrain so that it stood a better chance of success against the major airlines' low fares and superior product. The unnecessarily burdensome restrictions imposed on Laker Airways by its UK licence might threaten the ultimate viability of the service to the public. The rigid predetermination of the capacity offered was flatly contrary to US policy.

Freddie now had justification to take matters back to the CAA. It was the second week of September 1977 and there were just ten days to go before the Skytrain service was due to start.

What had helpfully come out of the earlier Bermuda II affair as far as Laker Airways was concerned was that in order to boost Gatwick Airport and to relieve some of the congestion at Heathrow, the British Government was trying to persuade airlines to switch from one to the other. The incumbent airlines naturally refused, so the Government announced that the two new American carriers flying between the USA and the UK, i.e. Delta and Braniff, would have to use Gatwick. This was the judgement that Freddie needed to obtain the rights to use his home base of Gatwick for Skytrain.

Freddie told the CAA that it was 'unfair, unreasonable and unrealistic' to force Skytrain to use Stansted. All the scheduled North Atlantic IATA carriers, including the 'fifth freedom' airlines, were using Heathrow. In the face of predatory fare-pricing as described by the US Department of Justice, Freddie said he felt nervous. "I am terrified – they have got me by the throat," he told the CAA tribunal, adding, "but I'm not counted out yet and I'm relying on fair play from the British."

Freddie asked for four other major changes to his Skytrain licence. He asked for an increase in baggage allowance from 33lb to 44lb, in line with the IATA carriers' 20kg allowance. He also sought a removal of restrictions on the number of flights per week and, most importantly, on the number of seats offered. Laker Airways wanted to be able to sell every one of the 345 seats on its DC-10s. Furthermore, he requested CAA approval to sell seats on the Skytrain service from 4:00am on the day of departure and the freedom to sell open date tickets in advance through travel agents. "The issue on the table," said Freddie, "is about whether Skytrain is going to be destroyed. Gentlemen, our future and the future of British civil aviation, is in your hands."

Predictably BA and BCal protested – Freddie hadn't realistically expected them to remain silent in response. BA said the changes Freddie proposed would mean that Skytrain was not Skytrain any more and would take on the characteristics of a typical scheduled operation. It was a feeble and inane argument and observers caught panel members' eyes rolling at BA's decidedly lame presentation.

The British Airports Authority (BAA) also made representations. It was worried that passengers would be queuing in the airport for many hours for the proposed 4:00am ticket sales start time. It also made a point about passengers' baggage tying up the bag rooms at the airport for equally as long. The BAA also put the case that it had spent (a meagre) £15,000 on preparing Stansted Airport to handle Laker's DC-10s. While it thought that Skytrain deserved support,it felt that it 'had to look after its parochial interests'.

Freddie put forward a strong rebuttal to counter the BAA's argument on behalf of Stansted. Gatwick, by contrast, had spent £100 million to bring its capacity up to 16 million passengers a year, yet currently only six million passengers were using it. Freddie calculated the additional costs of flying from Stansted would be in the region of half a million pounds a year, including £358,000 in fuel and £105,000 in additional crew costs, as he would have to either house crews at Stansted or position them daily from their base at Gatwick.

BCal predictably objected to having Skytrain operate from Gatwick, as it would undermine its own services that it was about to restart to the USA in October. Its argument was seriously flawed and potentially insulting to the CAA board's knowledge of American geography; BCal was to start operations to Houston, 1,400 miles from New York. Freddie countered that the question of diversion did not apply since BCal no longer operated a service to New York and that the Texas market was entirely different from that of the greater New York market. "It's a bit like saying if you fly to Athens, you'll be in competition with Barcelona," Freddie said convincingly.

BCal, straight out of Chairman Adam Thomson's playbook, pathologically objected to everything. The company was paranoid about any threats to its perceived position as Britain's 'second force' airline. "It's the 'Little Man' syndrome masquerading as an international airline," said Freddie, without trying to hide the disdain he felt for his tartan-clad neighbours at Gatwick.

The CAA gave Freddie a sympathetic hearing, but to his dismay allowed the predatory fares of the majors. Denying them, it stated, would be seen as an attack on the US carriers. It said it was '100% happy with the fares'. It had in fact been powerless to prevent them, as any other decision would have caused Freddie to have his US permit revoked by the CAB in retaliation.

However, the CAA did come to Freddie's aid, dismissing the opposition to his requests and making an immediate decision to drop all the measures that stopped him being competitive. A liberated Skytrain, the CAA proclaimed, would now fly from Gatwick.

Freddie was delighted. The airlines had overplayed their hand, thereby strengthening the chances of Laker's untested Skytrain service succeeding. Freddie would have to come back to the CAA the following week for a hearing on the question of additional flights during May and September, but for now he could proceed with his Skytrain launch plans for 26th September 1977.

To appease the British Airports Authority, the CAA attached some new conditions, ones that Laker Airways could live with. Ticket sales and baggage check-in had to take place outside the boundaries of the airport. The company had three weeks grace during which passengers could initially book and check-in at Laker's desks at Gatwick.

Laker's Skytrain Service Manager, Geoffrey Street, after spending months setting up for a Stansted operation, had to hastily switch to a check-in system at Gatwick, one that would cause the least amount of disruption to the other airlines and to the airport.

Over in New York, the local manager there, Charles Maxwell, had been tasked with finding an off-airport terminal facility as he had been unsuccessful in obtaining on-airport check in facilities for Skytrain. United agreed to handle Laker's aircraft but refused permission for passenger check-in at the United terminal, fearing long lines of prospective Skytrain passengers disrupting its own operations. So Maxwell had settled for a 15,000sq ft ground-floor space in Rego Park, Queens. It was a reasonable commute to JFK, less than 10 miles away, although traffic congestion would need to be considered for the 7:30pm daily departure from JFK. Passengers would check in at Rego Park and be transferred by bus to JFK Airport while their checked baggage would be transported by truck directly to the aircraft. United had no Federal Inspection capability at its terminal, so the Skytrain flight from Gatwick would have to arrive at JFK's International Building, then be towed round to United's terminal for departure. In anticipation of air traffic delays compounding its turnaround time at New York, Laker Airways played it safe and allowed an extended ground time at JFK of 3hrs 45min. It was far from an ideal situation at either end, but compared to what Laker was going to have to do before the CAA's last-minute decision, just a few days earlier, this felt like a major triumph.

Freddie hadn't dared to increase his Skytrain fares, even though by now they were three years out of date, for fear of further objections from the competition and the inevitable delays it would create. He would have to live with them for the time being. "Whatever people say about me," the 55-year-old Freddie gleefully declared, "they've got to recognise that air travel will never be the same again." For now, Freddie had survived his adversaries' 'Bully-Boy Tactics'

POSTSCRIPT

*On 26th September 1977 – the day of the first Skytrain flight from Gatwick to JFK – US President Jimmy Carter, the man who had authorised Skytrain, made a devastating decision. He overruled the CAB's recommendation for suspending the Apex and Standby fares filed by the six major airlines as being inconsistent with his administration's foreign economic policy. He therefore would not interfere with the IATA airlines' vicious plan, citing 'a commitment to low-fare, competitive international air service for the benefit of American consumers'. Only if the CAB obtained new evidence that the fares were indeed predatory would he consider an extension of their suspension.*

*The UK Government had also supported the IATA conspiracy. Using its formidable diplomatic powers, with the support of the European Governments, it was the British Government that had persuaded Carter to overturn the CAB's judgment. The two nations had come to some kind of an ad hoc agreement on 9th September.*

*The shortsighted decision by Carter ignored the warnings of his Department of Justice that the new low fares appeared 'predatory'. Privately, one airline executive who was linked to the 'unholy six' disclosed their evil intentions: "We can undercut Freddie Laker in one season. When he's out of business, we'll get back to the job."*

*Freddie stated that Laker Airways' once-a-day service with around 250,000 available seats per year was only about 1 per cent of the existing capacity between Europe and the USA, yet even this was more than the major airlines could stomach. The predatory fare filings were nothing more than an overreaction to Laker. What they did was an unnecessary knee-jerk response to something they hadn't properly thought through. But that was not the point; it was what Laker represented that was the problem. Freddie Laker, like no other airline figurehead before him, represented something that touched a nerve.*

*From this point on, without any of them saying it aloud, or even perhaps to each other, the major airlines were dedicated to seeing the demise of Laker Airways. If not now, then at some time in the future.*

# Part 3

## The Icarus Factor

CHAPTER 28

# GK10 Clear for Take Off

## Air travel is changed forever

26th September 1977

The Rolls-Royce glided to a halt and parked in its usual spot right outside the glass-panelled door marked 'Reception' at the International Jet Centre, Laker Airways' HQ at Gatwick Airport. It was a chilly morning and still dark. The traditional Kienzle analogue clock embedded in the walnut dash read 5:35am, but it meant little as this was a very special day.

The driver's door opened and a 6-foot-tall, broadly built man dressed in a black tracksuit stepped out; his hair was uncombed, he hadn't shaved and looked as if he hadn't slept either. He threw the keys on the seat and didn't bother locking the door of the Rolls as he strode quickly towards the small metal door that led from the car park into the hangar. He paused briefly to savour the next moment.

As he opened the door and stepped inside, the bright lights made him shield his eyes and he stopped in his tracks. As his eyes became accustomed to the glare and he witnessed the spectacle inside, he had to hold back tears. This was a defining moment in his life and he knew it. He was transfixed, standing there for what seemed like an eternity just taking it all in. His thoughts went back to the endless battles he'd had at the British CAA, the American CAB, the Department of Trade and Industry, the armies of lawyers, the ups and downs of being told 'OK' one minute and 'get lost' or worse, just a few minutes later. He thought about the hostility and opposition he'd endured from total strangers who were mere representatives, often in low-level jobs at other airlines and governmental departments. He wondered why on earth he was so vilified and why they hated him so much. What were they all scared of?

"Good morning, Mr Laker, you're up early" It was the upbeat Tim Cremin, Freddie's on-duty Station Engineer dressed in his black uniform with three gold rings on the sleeve to denote his rank. The diminutive, energetic and popular senior engineer had walked quickly over to his boss when he saw him standing at the hangar entrance door.

"Morning, Tim," Freddie responded, immediately coming out of his wistful moment and suddenly not looking or feeling tired at all. "The plane looks fantastic, Tim – the lads have done a super job, thank you." Both men looked up at the gleaming black, red and white nose of Laker's first McDonnell Douglas DC-10, G-AZZC, or 'Zulu Charlie' as everyone called it. The name of the plane, 'Eastern Belle', was clearly visible in white block letters on the black stripe under the cockpit, but it was never referred to by its name, instead always by the phonetic alphabet version of ZC. This was an era when large commercial aircraft had almost lifelike personalities. Crew members knew intuitively which plane they were on and they had their favourites. This was occasionally subjective, especially in the 707 fleet, where 'Zulu Zulu' was typically favoured over 'Delta Golf', likely because ZZ's main job was flying to Barbados, with three-day layovers. While 'Zulu Charlie' had 'seniority', being the first in the fleet, the third DC-10, 'Sierra Zulu' (G-BBSZ, 'Canterbury Belle') or 'S Zed' was everyone's clear favourite, whereas the latest acquisition, which everyone called 'Bellow' (G-BELO, 'Southern Belle') had already earned a reputation for being a bit of a 'dog' and somewhat unreliable.

One of Laker Airways' tugs was already attached by a tow bar to the front wheels of 'Zulu Charlie'. The night shift had washed and waxed the tug, getting it ready to push the DC-10 out of the hangar and down to the ramp for its historic flight to New York that afternoon. The aircraft had been given a 'deep clean', which meant every square inch of the interior had been meticulously gone over and was now sparkling. The plane looked even better than when it had been delivered five years earlier on 26th October 1972, as the first DC-10 to land in Europe.

Cremin beamed at his boss's compliment, which he knew was well-earned. He and his regular team of line engineers, together with more than a dozen others who had volunteered for that important night shift in order to prepare the DC-10 for the next day's flight, had all worked especially hard. They knew what lay ahead that day. 'Zulu Charlie' would be photographed by the world's press and appear on the front page of every newspaper, as well as on the evening news of television channels in the UK and the USA. Laker's flagship DC-10 was soon going to be as famous as the first Concorde, and Freddie Laker would be acknowledged in a similar way to Lindbergh. Ironically, 1977 was the 50th anniversary of Lindbergh's historic flight from New York to Paris, and that fact wasn't lost on anyone in the Laker organisation.

Cremin's night shift team of engine, airframe and avionics specialists had put in an extra effort to ensure that absolutely nothing could possibly go wrong and the plane was 'tip-top'. In a couple of hours he'd be handing over to his counterpart Station Engineer, the equally affable Bob Townsend, whose brother Ron was Deputy Chief Engineer and older brother Bill was Laker's Technical Director. Bill had been instrumental in the acquisition of Laker's DC-10s and had lived out in Long Beach for months, working with the McDonnell Douglas technical staff. He had a terrifying crash on the San Diego freeway while out in California and for a few days Freddie feared he may lose his chief technical guru. Freddie knew his engineering team were amongst the best in the business. He'd always considered Laker Airways to be an engineering-driven company first and foremost, and he never compromised when it came to his aircraft and their safety, technical reliability and appearance. As Freddie walked around the magnificent DC-10, looking up in wonder at the centre engine, more than 30 feet above him, and taking in the bustling activity in his hangar, the stress of the past few weeks fell away. He had been embroiled in the final hearings for the Skytrain licence and the battle to improve the operating terms, such as the last-minute change from a Stansted operation to Gatwick. It had taken a toll, but standing in his hangar Freddie felt exhilarated. An aeronautical engineer at heart, as well as by qualification, he was never happier than when he was in the company of his engineers and his aircraft. It was here that Freddie felt most at home, and his incredibly dedicated team of aeronautical engineers all knew it.

"Have the galleys been checked, Tim?" Freddie asked. "You know Joy's running the show today, so it better be tickety-boo." He was referring to his head of Cabin Services, who as Joy Harvey had been with him since the BUA days. She'd since married one of his pilots, Tony Poirrier, in 1975. Joy had taken over managing the cabin crew when Nina Griffin retired from flying duties and had been assigned Laker's burgeoning in-flight catering and bonded store operation. Following the arrival of the first DC-10s in 1972, the Cabin Services department had grown exponentially and was the largest department in the company. Despite spending more and more time in the office administrating the intricacies of the department, Ms Poirrier, who was known as a perfectionist, still regularly did 'surprise' check flights. Any of her ladies who turned up with hair or make-up less than perfect, their name badge crooked or perhaps becoming slightly overweight, would be hauled in for a 'chat' with Joy. She was known to be a stickler but always very fair; her cabin staff both feared and revered her. Nonetheless, after the inaugural flight was over it was likely that she would eagerly join in the much-anticipated revelry in New York and let her hair down.

Laker's DC-10s had lower galleys where all the food preparation was done. McDonnell Douglas had recommended this 'unique at the time to the DC-10' galley configuration and, after some initial scepticism, Freddie soon realised it was an innovative and practical way to prepare an efficient in-flight food and beverage service, well out of sight of the passengers.

"The galleys, loos, seats, everything has been gone over several times. Don't worry, Sir, we're good to go," the Station Engineer reassured his boss.

"OK, thanks, Tim, I'm just going to run up to Operations and see who's on the crew. I hope it's a few of my favourites," Freddie said, grinning.

"Well, Greg's on in Ops tonight and he's been down a few times bugging the hell out of us and checking everything," Cremin said humorously, referring to his Operations department colleague who was a personal friend. "I bet he's made sure all the lookers are rostered for the flight." Freddie laughed, as he hurried off to the side door that led to the office block and the Ops department.

"You're up early. I hope you got some kip as you've got a bloody long day ahead of you." Laker's Ops Duty Officer, Greg Dix, who was busy writing up the day's movement board, looked up and greeted his boss with a smile as

Freddie strode into Operations. It was Dix's fifth year in Ops and they had a familiar rapport, despite the younger man not yet being part of the airline's senior management.

Unlike many of his Laker colleagues of that generation, Dix wasn't a home-grown Laker man. He'd started as a junior manager at Britain's famed retailer, Marks and Spencer, owned his own business in California, sailed large yachts in the Pacific and Caribbean for a couple of years, and then cut his teeth with other British airlines. While never discourteous, Dix nevertheless was quite irreverent when interacting with his boss and wasn't afraid to tell him what he thought. Cliff Nunn had at one time said that Dix was a bit like Freddie's son Kevin, which in spite of Dix's passion for motorbikes perhaps explained the affinity the older man had with his young protégé. Freddie knew Dix was itching for a bigger challenge and that he may lose him if he didn't give him a promotion, or send him off abroad to manage something. It was a problem he had throughout the company as it grew. Freddie knew the younger, keener guys would have to take over from some of his senior loyalists if the airline was to stay ahead of the competition. One Saturday, when they were alone in Ops sorting out a massive problem with the fleet, Dix had mentioned to Freddie that he'd been offered a management position with Saudi Arabian Airlines. It wasn't blackmail or leverage, but the 29-year-old wanted Freddie to know that he had ambitions and if they couldn't be fulfilled at Laker Airways there were other opportunities out there. It had been duly noted, unbeknown to Dix at the time.

"Who's down the back today, Greg?" Freddie asked.

"Hmm, it looks like you have all the players," Dix said as he reviewed the crew list for GK10. "Joy, of course, is heading things up, but all your usual favourites of the old guard, Bev, Sandy, Meg, Fiona…"

"Oh God, Scott-Dickson," Freddie interrupted. "Last time I flew with her she got into it with a passenger and I had to intervene as she was giving the bloke an earful. Mind, she was right, we should have flung the obnoxious drunk out the door at thirty-five thousand feet."

"Siobhan too."

"Which one?" Freddie asked quickly.

"Hunter, the tall one. You know – the one Gerry fancies," replied Dix, referring to his Commercial department colleague Gerry Sharp, who made no secret of his soft spot for Ms Hunter. Dix continued: "Faith, Pam Birtles, and of course the lovely Sue Barnes. Oh, and the one you were asking about who flew you back from Palma – Kym."

Freddie laughed, as he'd mentioned earlier that he'd spotted one he quite fancied on a recent flight. "She seems a bit reserved, Greg, definitely not like the others."

"Well, actually she's the flavour of the month with the flight deck from what we've heard in here, but the crewing guys say she's keeping a modest profile and we don't have anything scandalous on her yet."

Freddie laughed heartily. He loved all the gossip about his aircrew and liked to keep in touch with what was going on, and, more to the point, who was doing who. Laker was famous in the industry for its flight crews' merrymaking, frequently encouraged by Freddie himself who was no stranger to hard partying or fraternising with his cabin staff. Recently, though, Freddie had been a bit out of touch as he dealt with all the licensing aggravation and because the company had grown so fast since the arrival of the DC-10s. He used to know everyone by name and even knew the names of their husbands, wives and kids too. Regrettably, he didn't now have the time he once had for partying with his flight crews, but he was looking forward to putting that right in New York that very evening.

"You know Baz is driving, right?" Dix asked Freddie. "Mike Willett and Spud are up front too, so you can probably count on a few shenanigans."

'Baz' was Captain Basil Bradshaw, one of Laker Airways' most popular captains. Aside from being an ace pilot, Bradshaw was a relentless practical joker. He often dressed up in drag, did impersonations on the PA system or wore Dracula teeth when a passenger visited the cockpit, which in the 1970s was not just permitted, but encouraged. One of Bradshaw's favourite japes was to arrange for a new stewardess, perhaps only 19 years old, fresh from training and on her first flight, to sit in the jump seat right behind him for take-off. The three seasoned flight deck crew would make the blushing 'newbie' feel at home as they strapped her in, paid her compliments and generally made her feel like a VIP. As the plane accelerated down the runway, the girl's nerves would be peaking. Just as Captain Bradshaw was about to lift the DC-10 into the air, the flight engineer would flip a single switch that would activate the test for the ground proximity warning system (GPWS), which had an obnoxiously loud digitised voice that yelled out 'Pull up, pull up, pull up'.

The unwitting girl would be terrified, while the crew would remain totally calm and execute a perfectly normal take-off. All her colleagues down the back would have been in on the prank. She was now properly initiated into Laker Airways' renowned 'sisterhood', which at the time was an all-female cabin staff department. A trip with Captain Bradshaw was invariably memorable and it was his unique type of humour, fully in step with disciplined professionalism, that set Laker Airways apart. Almost everyone in Britain's airline industry at the time wanted to work for Freddie Laker, except perhaps for a few down the road at BCal who were loyal to Freddie's nemesis, Adam Thomson.

"Right, well I'm heading upstairs to clean up a bit. It's going to be a long, crazy day, I expect" Freddie announced as he reviewed the movement board.

"OK, I'll see you at the plane as I'm hopping on board later. I want to see what's going on in New York as I hear there's a bit of aggro at JFK. John said there'll be a few spare seats, but for the life of me I don't know why."

Freddie's face winced at Dix's observation – more than anything he wanted the first flight to be full.

"I'm off for a couple of days now and Sandy's on the flight so you know it'll be a good evening," Dix continued, referring to the 'renowned for après-flight, hard-partying' Sandy Doherty, one of Laker's senior In Flight Directors with whom Dix lived and was one of Freddie's favourites.

"Oh, that's great! We'll have a bloody good thrash in New York then ... that's if we can send Robin off with Maxwell. Maybe he'll take her down to one of his haunts on the lower west side." Freddie laughed as he left Ops, knowing that it would be a good night in New York if he could for once get clear of his local manager, Charles Maxwell and publicity officer Robin Flood. He knew that would be a challenge, though, as Mrs Flood had a tendency to smother Freddie like a possessive mistress, to the chagrin of the rest of his staff.

At 8:30am Lesley Chilton arrived to find her boss already in his office, freshly shaved but still in his black tracksuit. As it was a big day for everyone, Lesley was wearing the special gold and diamond pendant depicting London and New York landmarks that Freddie had commissioned and given to a select few. "We were all so nervous if it would go OK," Lesley said later. Of all the people close to Freddie in those last few weeks before Skytrain finally became a reality, Chilton had probably borne the brunt. She was undeniably his rock at Laker Airways, doggedly loyal and discreet; she literally had no life at all outside the airline and her boss.

"I'm heading over to the terminal, Lesley, to see how the check-in's going and greet all the passengers."

"Aren't you going to change first?" she replied, looking up and down at his tracksuit. Freddie ignored the admonishment and rushed out, grabbing Cliff Nunn on the way, who'd just arrived. The two of them jumped into the Rolls with Freddie driving and sped off to Gatwick's terminal building.

Geoffrey Street was standing behind the check-in counters anxiously tapping his foot. Dressed in a natty cream suit and colour-coordinated tie, he looked quite out of place amongst the immaculately uniformed Laker and Gatwick Handling personnel. Street was observing the well-trained staff checking passports and taking money, mostly cash, for the flight to New York. The passengers could purchase meal tickets if they hadn't brought their own food. Checked bags were weighed carefully and any that were over 15kg were rejected and the passenger had to lighten them. There were no exceptions, even though Laker had recently been given permission by the CAA for 20kg of checked baggage per person, the same as all the major airlines. It wasn't because the company wanted to penalise the passengers, but if the individual baggage allowance wasn't restricted, 345 passengers multiplied by 5kg each could have meant the difference between making it non-stop or having to refuel en route.

The first DC-10-10s had already been flying full to New York and back on the Advanced Booking Charter flights and had experienced no difficulty making it non-stop westbound, including the occasionally long air traffic holds at JFK. But no one knew what the average Skytrain passenger would try and bring, despite their being advised of the 15kg checked bag restriction. Many passengers would be students with time on their hands to trek around for weeks or months and have enormous backpacks. Because Skytrain was a walk-on, same-day service with no fixed return date, it was likely that numerous passengers would bring extra luggage for an extended stay in the USA. At the New York end the checked baggage allowance wasn't so critical, as the flight time eastbound to London was 45 minutes or more shorter than westbound due to the prevailing North Atlantic tail winds. JFK also had longer runways than Gatwick, so even in the height of a New York summer, when temperatures were regularly over

30 degrees Celsius, the Laker DC-10s would be able to carry maximum fuel as well as a full payload from New York. Another consideration in 1977 was the additional weight of duty free goods that passengers purchased at the airport. The airline had no control over how much duty free the passengers bought before getting on the plane, but if 70 per cent of the passengers on a Laker DC-10 bought duty free liquor, the additional weight could have been more than 1,500lb. Everything really was that tight.

"How's it going Geoff?" Freddie said abruptly without a 'good morning' or any pleasantries, as he and Nunn walked up to the check-in desks. They viewed the uniformed passenger service agents smiling and chatting to the passengers as they processed them. Freddie spotted Gatwick Handling's General Manager, Angus Kinnear, standing in the gallery observing the check-in procedures. He smiled and waved, giving Kinnear a thumbs-up as he knew he'd pulled out all the stops to make Skytrain a success. Freddie liked Kinnear as he was a mad-keen aviation enthusiast like himself. He had been appointed GHL's General Manager a few years earlier after Donaldson collapsed, replacing Jerry Penwarden, who had taken a top job with Cathay Pacific in Hong Kong, managing all Cathay's stations worldwide. Kinnear was a tall, well-dressed workaholic who knew everything there was to know about pretty much any aircraft, as well as all the disparate pieces of ground handling equipment, from ground power units to de-icing rigs. His reputation for perhaps being even more fastidious than his predecessor was well-earned.

Freddie worked the crowd and shook hands with the passengers standing in line, most of whom showed surprise and genuine delight to meet him in person. No other airline before Laker had been represented by the owner in quite this way. Freddie thanked them for flying on the Skytrain service and many asked for his autograph; a heavily made-up peroxide blonde asked Freddie to sign her leg, lifting her skirt well above her knee. He duly obliged, getting down on the floor for the task while flirting outrageously with the astonished woman. The other passengers clapped and cheered as Freddie instructed, "You're not to wash that leg ever again!" This was Freddie Laker at his best, and he never disappointed; he was an absolute natural at public relations and always had a kind word to say, never forgetting his own humble beginnings. Nunn and Street looked on, incredulous at how Freddie mingled with the crowd of passengers at the check-in counters. They marvelled at how he could have them eating out of his hand with such ease, and also what he was able to get away with. They'd seen him do it many times before, but on this important day he'd stepped up his PR game to another level altogether.

"Nice suit, Geoff!" Freddie, tongue firmly in cheek, complimented his nervous Skytrain Service Manager while noting that Street was dressed more for the tropics than a 63-degree day in England. He wasn't sporting the Skytrain tie he'd been issued, or even a company name badge. "How many have checked in so far? We'll have a full flight, won't we?" Nunn noted the sarcasm in Freddie's tone, as he knew he had already checked on the expected passenger count with Commercial Manager John Jones. Jones, who had monitored the inaugural flight's passenger count, had told Freddie that the flight wouldn't be quite full based on the numbers he had. Freddie's reaction to this news was predictably visceral. Jones explained, "We blocked a good portion of the plane for Robin Flood's press corps, but many of the reporters won't show now since you told Robin that everyone had to pay full fare, including the press."

There weren't enough standby passengers to make up for the shortfall of reporters, but this wasn't all Street's fault, much as Freddie wanted to point a finger. There had been so much publicity about the first Skytrain flight that many expected there would be no seats available on such a historic occasion, and therefore stayed away. Freddie had been quite angry upon hearing Jones's forecast, as he desperately wanted a full inaugural flight. That was the whole point of Skytrain. "There should always be more people waiting than we have available seats," he'd emphatically told his staff. It was an entirely different pitch from the one he'd given the licensing authorities when they had expressed concern about queues and possible airport disruption.

As if the thought of the first Skytrain flight having some empty seats wasn't enough to potentially spoil this landmark day, Freddie then heard the unpalatable voice he'd been hoping to avoid for a little while longer. Robin Flood, his publicity representative, appeared through the crowd, fussing that he was needed elsewhere. She promptly whisked the compliant Freddie off for a press and photography session, without offering an acknowledgement or any courtesy to the bemused Cliff Nunn, whose presence she appeared oblivious to, or more likely had deliberately ignored.

Cliff Nunn was a quiet and patient man who often had difficulty saying what he wanted to in a clear and concise way. He typically used 'er' or multiple 'ers' and 'hmms' to commence a sentence, and invariably gave the impression that he was dithery and indecisive. While this was arguably true, he nevertheless on occasion came up with something brilliant. In collaboration with fellow director John Seear, who was a chartered surveyor and handled all the complex architectural and building work for the company together with numerous other tasks, they had designed Freddie a beautiful new office suite with an en suite bathroom. Nunn felt that this would be the only way he could relocate Mrs Flood from the executive floor and have a quiet life.

Freddie's new office utilised the third floor space that had been occupied by Laker's company solicitor Christopher Brown, insurance manager Tony McCarthy and their secretaries, as well as Robin Flood and her two assistants. They were all relocated down to the first floor, much to Brown and McCarthy's eternal appreciation. It was ingenious. Freddie had moved into his new spacious suite with lots of room for all his aeroplane models, pictures and memorabilia, together with a connecting office for Lesley and a separate secure area for files. Meanwhile his old office at the far end of the corridor became the conference room. They even furnished his new office with an expensive rosewood desk to replace Freddie's old oak desk that he'd brought from BUA; the bar located in the old desk had to be housed elsewhere to facilitate their late evening cocktail hours.

However, the obsessed Mrs Flood had put up a huge fight with Nunn to stay on the third floor. She had desperately wanted to remain in close proximity to Freddie, and had given all manner of bizarre reasons why she should, such as "He needs me by him at all times" and "Nobody knows him like I do," the latter being a clear insult to Lesley Chilton, who was Freddie's undisputed confidante. Freddie sensibly stayed out of the infighting, while the resolute Nunn, like a pitbull, prevailed in achieving his objective.

At 10:30am, after dealing with his last-minute office work, Freddie, now smartly dressed in a dark suit with a Skytrain tie, was driven down to the Gatwick terminal building by his chauffeur Harry Freeman. Harry hadn't had the best morning – when he had woken up at 7:00am and gone to get the Rolls to drive his boss to the office, it was gone. He panicked, thinking it had been stolen, but then common sense prevailed and he called the Laker Operations department. Once assured that Freddie had in fact arrived at the hangar already and the Rolls was safe, he had driven Freddie's wife Patricia, who was five months pregnant, to Gatwick to join the celebration. Her condition meant that she wouldn't be on the first Skytrain flight. Freddie's daughter Elaine Seear was not going to New York either, as she had an acute fear of flying; this allegedly stemmed from what she had to endure as a young girl during Freddie's early adventures in Africa, flying in barely airworthy planes and having to fend off the unwanted advances of numerous rough characters.

Freddie was ushered into the terminal area, already filled with press and dignitaries. He was interviewed and photographed by reporters from virtually every media outlet in Britain and beyond. When asked how he was feeling, he told them, "I'm as tense as an electric wire." Discussing the fares that Laker's competitors had introduced in order to defeat Skytrain, he told them, "It didn't occur to me that Pan American would be so foolish as to divert thousands of passengers from themselves just to defeat me. But people have been trying to gobble me up for years and found me indigestible. I expect I will remain so."

Then he and the press corps were ushered into a conference room where champagne was opened and hors d'oeuvres offered. There, Freddie cut a large celebratory cake with an appropriate 'Skytrain' message written on it. After the celebrations, it was time to move the 'dog and pony show' down to the ramp. The aircraft had been towed from the hangar to its designated hard stand at the end of Gatwick's north pier for passenger boarding. Special enclosed stairs had been acquired with the 'Skytrain' logo on the side, and Gatwick Handling's Herculean MD400 was already positioned to push 'Zulu Charlie' back from the stand. Freddie dutifully posed for photographs by the plane. He adopted several unforgettable postures including his signature arms outstretched flying pose. When he was handed the national flag of England to wave, it was met with loud applause. Freddie was making another intentional taunt at his Scottish arch-nemesis, BCal's Adam Thomson. He could of course have waved the Union flag, which incorporated the flags of England, Northern Ireland and Scotland and is what most people associate with Britain. The Union flag was also half of the Skytrain logo painted on the side of the aircraft. But Freddie's deliberate waving of the English flag with its red cross on a stark white background was a typically antagonistic gesture, in addition to being a well-intentioned act of pure patriotism.

At around midday the Gatwick Handling staff told him they were soon to be releasing passengers for the 1:00pm departure. This was deliberately early, but Freddie wanted to be photographed with as many of the inaugural passengers as possible. With several glasses of champagne giving him the additional lift he needed, he was on top form. The passengers were eating out of his hand, laughing at all his quips, the women responding positively to his flirtatiousness and more than happy to be hugged and kissed by one of Britain's most famous celebrities. His signature line of "Should I kiss you on all four cheeks?" was met with an agreeable laugh of encouragement, which at any other time he would have followed up on. The only downer for him was that the inaugural Skytrain service, perhaps the most important moment of his life since the first flight of the Accountant 20 years earlier, wasn't going to have a full load of passengers. He really had no one to blame for this but himself, and he knew it.

Sitting next to 'Zulu Charlie' was Freddie's latest acquisition, being readied for an ABC flight to Toronto. Laker Airways had taken delivery of its fourth DC-10-10 (G-BELO) in June 1977 at a price of $21 million, $8 million less than the cost of a brand-new aircraft, and Freddie hadn't been able to resist the 'deal' when the plane had been offered by McDonnell Douglas. It was delivered 'as new' with a few modifications, one of which was designed to preclude the catastrophic depressurisation similar to the one that occurred in Paris to a Turkish Airlines DC-10. The additional 4,775 US gallons of fuel BELO could carry put a host of new North American destinations within range as well as Gatwick or Luxembourg to Barbados. Laker Airways had funded it with a loan organised by the Clydesdale Bank; Freddie had good credit and was receiving assistance from both British and overseas banks.

At 12:45pm, it was nearly time for GK10 to depart. After thanking all his ground engineers and the Gatwick Handling staff, Freddie climbed aboard. Robin Flood had blocked the entire front row on the left side of the forward cabin for herself and Freddie, but he ignored her and went straight into the safe haven of Zulu Charlie's cockpit.

"Hello, Baz," he said cheerily to Captain Bradshaw, who was already strapped into his seat and about to do the pre-flight checks with Mike Willett, his First Officer. Flight Engineer Spud Murphy was busy with his own check list and was about to shoot off down to the ramp for one quick last-minute walk around before they closed the doors. The atmosphere in the cockpit was calm; these were all seasoned aircrew and for them it was just another flight from Gatwick to New York. They'd done it dozens of times already since 1972, when Laker's DC-10s first arrived.

"OK if I sit up front for take-off?" Freddie politely asked the captain, as he always did, no matter that he owned the airline and the planes. "And please, no practical jokes on this one Baz, we've got the world's press watching us."

Seizing the opportunity he had been given, Bradshaw quickly reached down in his flight bag, installed his Dracula teeth, turned around and grinningly acknowledged the directive, to Freddie's astonishment.

Back in the cabin, Joy Poirrier and her team of very senior and experienced cabin crew had all the passengers strapped in, checked that the overhead bins were secure and in position to start the emergency demonstration as soon as they felt the aircraft moving. The atmosphere in the DC-10 was electric; the passengers were excited, as they all knew this was a very special event. They'd been given complimentary champagne before departure and most of them had been thanked by Freddie himself for waiting in line for hours.

It had been a long hard battle to get Skytrain off the ground, and this wasn't lost on anyone that day. The press were in the forward cabin, but there were some noticeably empty seats due to the no-shows. In retrospect, insisting that the press had to pay their way was perhaps not one of Freddie's better decisions, as he needed good press coverage; however, it was too late to do anything about it now.

Captain Bradshaw commanded "Start Three" to commence the engine start procedure as the DC-10 was pushed back 'off blocks' right on time. The six years of effort had paid off at last. Flight GK10, Freddie Laker's history-making inaugural Skytrain service, was on its way to New York.

As Zulu Charlie taxied towards the runway, Freddie could see the throngs of spectators at the terminal building viewing area who had turned out to watch the historic event. He listened on his headset to the flight crew communicating with the Control Tower while they ran through their pre take-off check list. The cabin crew meanwhile had finished the emergency demo and were strapped in at their assigned stations by the doors. The mighty DC-10 lined up on the displaced threshold of Gatwick's runway 26. It sat stationary for a few moments as Freddie nervously waited for those half-dozen words from ATC.

Fighting to keep his emotions in check he muttered 'here we go' then he heard... "Laker One-Zero, Clear for Take-Off." Air travel had been changed forever.

CHAPTER 29

# What's Next?

## Developmental Initiatives

1977-78

After all his years in the civil aviation business with its rough and tumbles and everything that went with it, Freddie was euphoric as the inaugural flight landed at New York's John F. Kennedy Airport on 26th September 1977, with the passengers all cheering and clapping. The first Skytrain flight had gone well, no one had misbehaved and Freddie had done the rounds as he always did, chatting to the passengers as well as doing interviews with the journalists. Hundreds of onlookers crammed the viewing gallery to witness Laker's DC-10 pulling up to the gate at JFK's International Arrivals Building.

The passengers were all buzzing as they disembarked, with Freddie standing at the door thanking each one of them for flying with Laker Airways on the historic flight. New York's press corps was waiting to interview Freddie, but first he had to thank his crew for a job well done. After he had toasted a successful inaugural flight and been photographed with some of his cabin crew, he told Captain Bradshaw and Chief Stewardess Joy Poirrier that he'd join them all at the hotel later. First, he had to see the inaugural JFK to Gatwick flight off in a few hours. Freddie's stamina was superhuman. It was already past 9:00pm on his English-time body clock, he'd been up since before 4:00am and had probably consumed more than a dozen glasses of champagne. He'd been interviewed and photographed and spent almost the entire flight chatting to passengers and crew members. But he showed absolutely no signs of fatigue, as this was what he thrived on. At one point he'd considered returning immediately on the inaugural eastbound flight, until common sense prevailed.

The American press was often kinder to Freddie than their counterparts across the Atlantic. During the six-year battle for Skytrain, the notoriously fickle British press alternated between lauding Freddie and attacking him. In the USA, while the general travelling public may have applauded what Freddie was trying to do, the travel industry and airlines in particular had been quite vocal about their opposition to the almost unheard of British airline.

One of New York's TV presenters asked Freddie how he was feeling on this memorable day. "Well, first off thank you New York for having us in the Big Apple," he responded. "We've been flying here for years, of course, with our charter flights, but now affordable travel to Britain is available every single day of the week."

A reporter asked about his choice of aircraft for the Skytrain service. "Well, I just love our DC-10s. Look at it," Freddie said, pointing to the magnificent aircraft sitting at the gate. "I can tell you that if I see one of my planes out on the tarmac I can't take my eyes off it and if I see one rolling down the runway I stop whatever I'm doing to watch it take off and if I see one on approach I watch it land. And every time I think to myself, 'My God, how lucky you have been, Freddie Laker!' It is an absolute thrill I assure you. I feel like I am coming home at last. It has taken six years and millions of pounds of my money to get to this moment, as well as many millions of dollars in lost revenue for Britain and the USA. But now all that's forgotten and we can look ahead and embrace the future of affordable transatlantic air travel for everyone."

From then on it was a downhill run. Day after day, many of the Skytrain flights were full and queues immediately began to form for the next flight. The first month brought revenues of more than £1 million and a profit of £127,439. The number of passengers on every flight averaged 269 against a break-even load factor of 228. Freddie was ecstatic and everyone at Laker Airways breathed a sigh of relief as Skytrain was finally up and running. And it was a success, at least for now. Freddie said, "The only thing that will get me off the North Atlantic is a hole, six feet under."

The euphoria over the first Skytrain service from London Gatwick to New York gave Freddie and his Washington lawyer, Bob Beckman, unbridled motivation to expand Laker's routes further. The success of Skytrain did not satisfy a man like Freddie Laker or stop him poking more sticks at windmills. This was just the beginning according to Freddie and Beckman. They were now planning to enlarge the Laker operation from a low-frequency, no-reservation service from London to New York into a worldwide threat to the international airlines' cartel. Freddie wanted to challenge countries with fare protectionist policies and compete directly with major legacy airlines – many of which were government-owned – on some of the world's most sought-after air routes. It was a typically ambitious, albeit perhaps premature, objective.

London to Los Angeles (LAX) was always considered the next logical US Skytrain destination, and Beckman had started planning it before the New York inaugural. So Laker Airways formally applied to operate a daily Skytrain service from London (LGW) to LAX, one of the world's most coveted routes. Freddie described this application as 'a natural progression of the Skytrain concept', announcing one-way fares of £113, or the US equivalent of $250. Alfred Kahn, the new Civil Aeronautics Board (CAB) Chairman, who was putting a wrecking ball through the red tape of airline regulation in the US and doing everything possible to encourage a low-fare trend, said he was delighted that Laker wanted to fly to Los Angeles.

Then, less than a month after the launch of Skytrain, in October 1977, Freddie and Beckman threw in an application to the British CAA for Laker to operate an extensive Advanced Booking Charter series to three key Australian cities, Sydney, Melbourne and Perth. Ideally Freddie wanted to operate at least twice weekly to Australia via Singapore from London, and possibly from Luxembourg if it helped keep fares low. He called Australia 'virgin territory' and felt that there was a fortune to be made from flying 'down under'.

Freddie had already alerted his man in Australia, Athol Guy, to get started. Athol was Laker Airways' director and go-to guy in Australia. It was now more than six years since their first unsuccessful attempt to fly charters to Australia. What Freddie needed to know from Guy was what new licensing challenges he may face from the Australians. In the intervening years Athol Guy had become a Member of Parliament in his state of Victoria in 1971. He was well-versed in Australia's complex political structure and the red tape Freddie would face in his second attempt to fly on the 'Kangaroo Route', as the London to Australia route was known.

Freddie readily extolled the continent's virtues: "Australia is situated between the two most competitive countries in the world, Japan and America. It is ideally placed to develop a booming tourist industry and it has so much to offer. Great beauty, glorious weather, superb sports facilities and all sorts of leisure activities. And the people are very nice." Despite Freddie's confusion regarding Australia's geographic location in relation to Japan and the USA, its government was wholly opposed to any kind of charter flights. British Airways and Australia's national flag carrier, Qantas, maintained a lucrative high-priced monopoly. Both airlines were part of the protective IATA cartel, maintaining privilege and profit margins. But ordinary Australians did not agree and would have happily hung out the welcome banners for Laker.

Throughout the early 1970s, Athol Guy, on Freddie's behalf had tried to convince the Australian Government of the benefits of a Laker-style operation to and from Australia. The Government's prime interest was in protecting Qantas, nevertheless Guy continually argued that the new operation would not draw a single passenger away from the national carrier.

Athol Guy's 'non-diversionary' angle would be used continually and repeated non-stop by his parliamentary friends and supporters. Freddie Laker was such a popular figure that during a visit he was described in the Australian Parliament as attracting the most favourable public reaction since the Beatles had visited in the mid-1960s. Freddie told the Australians that he would bring in 25,000 British tourists a year. The Australian public and press were won over – they lapped up Freddie's (typically Aussie) humour and directness.

Freddie's plans had struck a chord with the Select Committee on Tourism, headed by Duke Bonnet, and later by David Jull from Queensland, who was popular with both ends of Australia's political spectrum. Freddie made a formal submission to the select committee that recommended Laker Airways be granted a licence. The committee duly agreed that the company should be given charter rights to bring British tourists to Australia on package tours.

Freddie and Bob Beckman knew that their new application was still a long shot because, even if the British gave the go-ahead, the ultra-protectionist Australians were likely to baulk at someone they considered an upstart British carrier arrogantly snatching traffic from Qantas and British Airways on the prized 'Kangaroo Route'. Laker's proposed fares ranged from £345 to £550 per round trip. Freddie told the CAA the very opposite to what he had said in Australia – that most of his passengers would be Australian originators. Later he would double-back on his own comments as being 'for British Ears'. The anticipated traffic mix was an important point to both governments anxious to bring more tourism money in than taking it out. Changing the originating traffic numbers to suit Freddie's purpose did not go unnoticed.

The board of Qantas, Australia's flag carrier, attacked; it had a new chairman, Sir Lenox Hewitt, who had referred to Freddie Laker as a 'great huckster'. Hewitt did as much as anyone to spoil Laker's chances of getting an Australian licence. Among other criticisms, he said: "They are flying DC-10s – there won't be enough toilets." Freddie claimed that all the critics were "speaking pure unadulterated rubbish and that Qantas has failed to do one thing, and one thing only ... and that is to produce a tourism industry for Australia." Freddie was correct and the situation had hardly improved since Athol Guy's response of 'there isn't one' years earlier. He now sought a way to change matters.

Officially, Qantas did its best to respond graciously to the new application, telling the Australian Government that it favoured charter flights, but any changes should await a renegotiation of the bilateral agreement and the number of points served.

British Airways also got in on the act and objected, claiming that the new application would 'damage the route'. While Freddie was still talking enthusiastically about a Christmas or New Year start date, any licence decision on the 'Kangaroo Route' was kicked into the long grass for some time and would likely not happen before a total review of Australia's air transport policies. Freddie's dream to fly to Australia was once again in an indefinite holding pattern, although he still proclaimed that Laker would fly 'down under' soon.

With just one daily Skytrain flight in operation at the end of the 1977 European summer holiday season, two of Laker's DC-10s were contracted out to Air Algerie for the 1977 Hajj pilgrimage flights to Jeddah in Saudi Arabia, in deference to Freddie's insistence that future Hajj operations should be as risk-free as possible. Laker had been flying to Algiers with its One-Elevens for years and Air Algerie was its handling agent there, so Algiers was familiar ground, unlike the previous Hajj operations in Nigeria and Iran. Commercial executive Gerry Sharp opted for the Algiers end, as the French-inspired cuisine was to his liking, while Greg Dix was assigned to Jeddah for both phases. Little did he know that this would be his last Hajj assignment.

To everyone's relief, everything went well and there were no major delays or technical issues with the aircraft, although during Phase 1 Dix was summoned before an irate Jeddah Airport management to explain why Laker's empty DC-10 returning to Algiers had executed an abnormally sharp-angled take-off manoeuvre followed immediately by a steep turn with the wingtip just feet from the ground. The take-off had concluded with an extremely low and very fast fly-over above the main runway. Thinking quickly, Dix told the angry airport officials that the captain had radioed in that they weren't sure if the gear had retracted and had to do a fly past for a visual check. It wasn't all that convincing but it was a spectacular bit of flying, by one of Laker's top jocks.

One day towards the end of the first phase of the Algerian Hajj, just as Dix had dispatched an empty DC-10 from Jeddah, a limousine with a Saudi flag waving from the front fender appeared on the ramp and drove up to where he was standing with a group of Laker's engineers. An important-looking young Saudi dressed in his ankle-length white 'thobe' introduced himself as the cultural attaché to the Saudi Royal Family. He enquired if they could charter an empty DC-10 to Algiers and return three weeks later on one of the empty legs from Algiers, after Phase 2 commenced. Dix enquired as to the nature of the charter. It was for a party of some 16 members of the Royal Family together with a cast of falcons and their handlers, and how much would it cost? After the initial surprise at this request, and wondering why they wouldn't be attending the Hajj instead of going off on a three-week falcon hunting trip in Algeria, Dix told the attaché that they could have the flights for $10,000. The royal representative didn't bat an eyelid and shook hands to confirm the arrangement, saying that the royal party needed nothing special for the flights. He confirmed the dates, hopped back in the limo and sped off. A few days later a convoy of exotic vehicles all sporting Saudi flags drove up to Laker's DC-10 as it was being prepped for one of the last Phase 1 empty flights back to Algiers. The same attaché who had met with Dix earlier handed him a briefcase that he said contained $10,000 in cash. Dix knew better than to open the briefcase and check its contents. The royal party, more than a dozen hooded falcons and their raptor handlers emerged from the cars. When asked if he'd like to hold a falcon, after donning a special glove, Dix somewhat reluctantly did so for fear of insulting the clients. "It was bloody terrifying," he told Freddie after returning home for the two-week break between Hajj operations and relaying the story of how it felt to be a few inches from the beak of a 200mph peregrine falcon.

"Didn't they give you a commission for organising the trip, Dix?" Freddie asked, knowing that it was a Middle Eastern custom to take care of the agent or middleman of a business deal.

"Well, they offered, of course, but I couldn't accept anything. Heck, it's my job after all." Noticing his boss's quizzical look, he continued: "But guessing that I liked cars more than gold watches they asked if I'd take a 911 as my 'commission' and what colour did I want?" Freddie shook his head in complete disbelief at his man's stupidity.

On the return phase of the Algerian Hajj, while taking the pilgrims back to Algiers, in almost a reprise of the previous year's near catastrophe in Tehran, a Laker DC-10 again narrowly averted a serious incident. The Saudi ground handlers had overloaded the aircraft and given false weights to the Laker staff. This wasn't unusual and contingency allowances were always made for the extra weight; however, on this occasion they went too far. The DC-10 commenced its take-off run towards where the Laker team were all standing to watch. But to their horror, instead of lifting off about where it normally would, it just kept going, further and further towards the very end of the runway, more than 2¼ miles of concrete with an ambient temperature well in excess of 30 degrees. The DC-10 used up every inch of the available runway and when the nose finally lifted off the ground the main wheels were literally kicking up sand. The plane staggered into the air and a disaster was narrowly avoided by superb airmanship.

Another 'disaster', although not nearly as potentially calamitous, was when a Laker DC-10 was chartered by the production company of the movie adaptation of Ira Levin's novel *The Boys from Brazil*. On the day of departure from Gatwick, the DC-10 assigned to fly to Lisbon that day carrying many of the cast, the production crew and all the equipment, sat at Gatwick's north pier alongside another Laker DC-10 that was destined for Toronto. Three hours after both planes had taken off for their respective destinations, instead of the standard arrival message from Lisbon, Laker Operations received a frantic call from the ground handlers. Apparently, upon opening the aircraft hold doors, instead of crates of studio equipment to offload there were more than 300 suitcases tagged with a 'YYZ' label, the three-letter airport code for Toronto. Needless to say, the other plane, now halfway across the North Atlantic en route to YYZ, had its holds filled with crates, bags and studio gear all labelled 'LIS'. When Operations informed Freddie, he got onto Angus Kinnear of Gatwick Handling and unleashed a John Jones-style 110-decibel tongue-lashing. But this wasn't a simple problem to fix, and in fact it took three days for the film's gear to finally arrive in Lisbon. Meanwhile the 'A list' stars, Laurence Olivier, Gregory Peck and James Mason, together with the entire crew were sitting around in Portugal sipping wine and playing backgammon. It was quite ironic that Freddie's airline was responsible for delaying the production of such a controversial film, in which Peck played the infamous Nazi experimental doctor at Auschwitz, Josef Mengele. The demurrage costs for the production delay were off the charts; at that time Olivier and Peck were two of the highest paid actors in the world, and Commercial Manager Jones naturally hoped that Laker's underwriters would pick up some of the compensation. Through no fault of his Commercial department, it was a black mark on what was otherwise a very successful year.

By the end of 1977, Laker Airways' overall business had increased by 25 per cent and for the first time the airline had carried more than 1 million passengers in a single year. The Skytrain service between London and New York had carried 54,489 passengers at a load factor of 80.8 per cent. Gross revenue was in excess of £2.5 million (£17 million at 2018 values) and Skytrain had made a profit of £450,000 in just one calendar quarter.

Skytrain was an instant success, and not just in terms of load factor and revenue. It stood for free enterprise and value for money. Laker Airways had considerably lower overheads than its North Atlantic competitors, and the administrative costs of Skytrain were minimal, passengers paid up front mostly in cash and, as all ticket sales were now direct with the customer, Laker did not have to pay any travel agent commissions.

The big question that went unanswered was how sustainable the Skytrain business model was in its present format. However, that wasn't a question the supremely confident Freddie Laker was asking himself in December 1977 as he planned more and more Skytrain-type operations.

To cope with all the proposed expansion and meet the existing demand, Laker Airways had the need to replace its two former Qantas and British Eagle Boeing 707-138Bs that were fast reaching the end of their commercial lives; replacing these older aircraft was a considerably better option than continuing to maintain them. Two much newer Boeing 707-351Bs together with spare engines and rotatable spares were purchased for £7.1 million from Cathay Pacific, who at the time was replacing its 707 fleet with Rolls-Royce-powered Lockheed L-1011s. The 707-351B, a Cathay variant of the venerable 707-320 series, was a proven long-haul workhorse. Cathay had purchased them from Northwest Orient Airlines, which had operated them successfully for years on its trans-Pacific routes. NWA was perhaps even more experienced in trans-Pacific operations than Pan Am, something Dick Bradley pointed out to Freddie.

Captain Geoff Brookes, Laker's Boeing 707 Fleet Captain, was sent out to Hong Kong to oversee the pre-delivery modifications, then fly the first 351B to Gatwick. Brookes and his flight crew spent four weeks in Hong Kong while the Hong Kong Aeronautical Engineering Co (HAECO) prepared the aircraft. The modifications and pre-delivery work included fitting the planes with Litton Inertial Navigation Systems (INS) similar to those on Laker's DC-10s, Ground Proximity Warning System (GPWS), new HF radio sets, the mandatory pre-delivery 'C' Check, and finally repainting the aircraft in the Laker livery.

Captain Brookes flew the first 707 back to the UK via Bangkok, Bahrain and Istanbul on the 3rd and 4th December 1977. A spare engine was bolted on as a fifth pod and they picked up a CAA inspector in Bahrain so the crew could demonstrate the new INS operation on the final legs to Gatwick.

Laker's first 707-351B went into service in the third week of December, while the second was planned for May the following year. The acquisition was timely as the 189-seater 351B had a range of 5,000 nautical miles, considerably more than the 138B's 3,600. It could fly non-stop to Barbados from Luxembourg for Laker's subsidiary, International Caribbean Airways, without a stop in the Azores for an uplift of (expensive) jet fuel. The 351Bs could also make it to the west coast of North America non-stop to facilitate Laker's ABCs to Los Angeles and Oakland as well as to Vancouver, Calgary and Edmonton.

The 707-351Bs could also operate Laker's London to Los Angeles Skytrain service non-stop. In fact, given the nature of the route, the 707 was a better plane for the task than Laker's DC-10-10s; if the latter were used on the LA Skytrain flights, the necessary stop for fuel and Federal Inspection (US Customs and Immigration) in Bangor, Maine, added significantly to the operating costs, increased the flight time by three hours and necessitated a crew change in Bangor with the added costs of hotels, per diems and other expenses.

Never one to miss a chance of buying aircraft, Freddie, ever the opportunist, took advantage of a scheme that had been nicknamed 'Samurai money'. He ordered two more new DC-10-10s from McDonnell Douglas before the year's end. Japanese cash was made readily available to solve the considerable trade imbalance between the United States and Japan. Needless to say, the scheme was creating considerable political controversy in the USA. Japanese banks provided the money and McDonnell Douglas technically 'exported' the planes first to Japan, then on to Britain and elsewhere. The two new DC-10-10s were scheduled to arrive at Gatwick in the first few months of 1979. When Freddie was asked what the intended use was for the additional medium-range wide-bodies he was typically arrogant: "By the time they arrive we'll have four or five Skytrain flights a day to New York as the demand will be so great and daily flights to Toronto as well." Based upon what he'd achieved so far only a fool would bet against him. Nevertheless, Laker Airways' 1977 financial commitment for aircraft had now topped $80 million dollars ($330 million in 2018) and it wouldn't end there. The early edict to his staff that 'if we get bigger than six planes you can kick my arse' had by now gone out of the window.

New aircraft, new routes and developmental initiatives notwithstanding, there was no question that the event Freddie was looking forward to the most was due to occur in early January 1978. His wife Patricia was pregnant again and Freddie once more had high hopes that it would be the son he wanted more than anything else in the world.

CHAPTER 30

# Lakerville

## Arise Sir Freddie

1978

Just after the 1978 New Year, amid considerable joy, Freddie's wife Patricia gave birth to his third son on 4th January. It was the male heir he desperately craved and had been so cruelly denied. The now 55-year-old Freddie was a father once again. In deference to his beloved stepfather, William Allin, they named the boy Freddie Allen, although he affectionately became known by his parents as 'Charlie'. Freddie said that the victory over his Skytrain service paled in significance compared to the birth of his son. He saw his future clearly: "I have a new ambition, I have one job in life, and that is to see him on his 21st birthday, and this makes me look after my health and things. I have something to do ... stay alive." This time Freddie vowed to keep his son safe and give him all he wanted. Insiders knew that this boy would likely be spoiled rotten, but he would never be given a sports car when he passed his driving test. Freddie meanwhile had a new Rolls-Royce, and he'd authorised £663,787 (£3.9 million at 2018 values) of Laker funds to purchase a 27-metre Benetti yacht that he had named 'Patrina' – a combination of the first names of his wife Patricia and stepdaughter Bettina. 1978 was starting to shape up well.

Laker's JFK Airport operation was being managed by John Greenhead, but long-time Laker employee Linda Earls and her colleagues were becoming exasperated by his performance, or rather the lack thereof. Earls had made noises to Gatwick, specifically to Cliff Nunn, that JFK needed better management. Maxwell was way too busy at the Laker Travel Centre and overseeing the remote ticket offices around New York City to give JFK Airport any attention, and airport operations weren't anything he knew about anyway. So Nunn spoke with Freddie about the situation at JFK and they made a decision about what to do. One evening, after he'd finished his shift in the Operations department where he was the daytime Duty Officer, Freddie asked

Greg Dix to come and speak with him in his office. It was mid-March 1978 and the Skytrain service had been operating for six months. It hadn't exactly been trouble-free at either end of the operation, but while they had plenty of competent people at Gatwick to make things happen, it was a different matter in New York.

"How would you like to go to New York, Greg?"

Thinking that Freddie meant for him to go and fix a problem or coordinate something there for a day or so, Dix responded, "Sure – when and what do you want me to do there?"

"I want you to take over the JFK station from Greenhead and run it properly," Freddie replied. "Cliff will sort out your money and give you a brief about Maxwell as you'll have to report to him for now." What Freddie didn't mention was that when Cliff Nunn had told Maxwell they were replacing John Greenhead, and with whom, it hadn't been met with much enthusiasm. Apparently, Nunn had said to Maxwell, "Be careful or Dix will have your job too." So, after thanking Freddie for the opportunity, Dix got his personal affairs in order and a week later his life dramatically changed as he took over perhaps one of the most challenging jobs in aviation at the time. Living in an airport hotel, Dix's feet didn't touch the ground once he arrived in New York; the problems he inherited in his new role at JFK were at another level.

A few days after he'd started his new job at JFK, Dix was summoned to a meeting with the head of the Port Authority of New York and New Jersey's Aviation Division. Dix's secretary Diane told him that the Port Authority was sending its helicopter to pick him up at 10:30am from the United Airlines ramp for the meeting, but they hadn't said what they wanted to see Dix about. The yellow and white Sikorsky helicopter arrived on time and scooped Dix up for his meeting.

Caesar B. Pattarini ran all of the Port Authority's airports, which included JFK, La Guardia, Newark, Stewart Newburgh, Teterboro and Atlantic City, as well as New York City's two heliports. He was one of the most important men in American aviation, respected and feared in equal part by everyone who came in contact with him. But Dix was unaware of that. Waiting at New York's downtown heliport was a black stretched Cadillac limousine and standing beside it was a short man dressed in black who looked like a wrestler. He announced that he would drive Dix to the Port Authority offices in the north tower of the World Trade Center, despite it being a two minute walk away.

The high-speed elevator stopped at the 66th floor and Dix was shown into Caesar Pattarini's dark wood panelled office. The immaculately dressed Pattarini had an intimidating presence: "Mr Dix, I'll get straight to the point. When I first met Mr Laker before you started flying your Skytrain, I told him there was no room at JFK."

Dix responded quickly: "I didn't know that, Mr Pattarini but Laker had been operating into JFK's charter terminal for years before we started Skytrain."

Pattarini continued: "Surely you can't be happy with the present arrangement. Your planes arrive at the International Arrivals Building for customs clearance, then they have to be towed around to United's terminal for departure. United won't let you check in there for fear your passengers will dirty up the terminal – their station manager Jack Genader has been very firm on that. Checking them in at your Rego Park building, bussing the passengers and trucking the baggage out to JFK can't possibly be satisfactory long term."

Dix said: "Well, no, it isn't optimum of course, which is why we want counter space at the IAB just like all the other international carriers. It's one of the main reasons why Mr Laker has sent me here."

Pattarini glared at the cocky, youthful individual sitting in front of him: "That's not likely to happen any time soon, Mr Dix. But we have a good option for you, where you can check in your passengers right at the airport." Dix didn't respond, wondering what was coming next. "We want you to operate out of Newark instead. In fact, we insist you move your operation to Newark as soon as possible."

Dix wasn't exactly sure how to respond to that. One wrong word may have threatened the future of Laker Airways in New York, perhaps even the entire USA. After a pause to collect his thoughts, he replied: "Mr Pattarini, having the ability to check our passengers in at the airport would be a big plus, I admit. However, we have a licence from both governments to operate Skytrain between London Gatwick and New York's Kennedy. It's taken us six years and cost millions in lost revenue. There's no way – and I speak for Mr Laker and our Washington counsel – now we are flying the route that we will agree to switch airports."

It was as well Dix had only been in New York in his present role for a few days, or he would have perhaps thought twice before standing up to Pattarini. He hesitated before saying anything derogatory about Newark, and that New Yorkers at that time had a mental block about crossing the river into New Jersey. Not to mention that Newark fell under a separate bilateral agreement that would have meant Laker applying for a new licence from both governments, something Pattarini surprisingly hadn't eluded to.

Realising his demands were going nowhere, Pattarini quickly dismissed Dix and had him escorted down to the Cadillac where the driver held open the back door. As he settled into the plush leather rear seat, Dix wondered if he was about to take an unwilling part in a reenactment of a scene in *The Godfather*, where a disloyal family associate was taken for his last ride in an identical vehicle. But he was safely helicoptered back to JFK and immediately called Freddie, who was still in his office at Gatwick.

"How did you get on with Pattarini?" asked Freddie.

"He wanted us to move to Newark," Dix replied.

"Oh God, not that again? What did you say to him?" Freddie asked.

"Oh, I basically told him to fuck off," Dix responded as he heard Freddie suppress a laugh at the other end.

"OK, good lad. By the way, Dix, I need you to go to Los Angeles soon and start setting it up for Skytrain. Cheers!"

Laker Airways remained at JFK thereafter and Dix wondered how on earth he was supposed to get JFK into shape and set up LAX at the same time. A call to Bob Beckman in Washington may offer some insights.

When the Los Angeles application was heard in mid-March 1978, the only opposition it faced was from British Caledonian. Laker Airways' bid to serve the number one California destination had stirred BCal into action; the company was now preparing to reapply for the prestigious route itself. BCal had very different ideas from Laker about the market profile on the route and proposed a radically new fare structure, a three-class aircraft. The addition of an Executive class was a completely new concept to airlines at the time and shifted the nature of the battleground. In its submission, BCal's mixed-class DC-10-30 it had on order but didn't yet operate, was planned to have 80 seats in its basic economy class at fares lower than Laker's Skytrain. However, BCal's rigorous attempt to regain the Los Angeles licence came to nought. The CAA was clearly annoyed with BCal for having done a lack-lustre job on the route when it had earlier held the rights, so in April it handed the LA route to Laker Airways, much to the chagrin of Adam Thomson, BCal's Chairman, who called it 'a serious and inexplicable error of judgment'. The wording of BCal's subsequent appeal was derogatory to the CAA, calling its ruling 'shabby and unconvincing', even suggesting foul play. It inferred that the CAA could not have reasonably reached its decision based on the evidence.

With the approval of the Los Angeles Skytrain pending, Freddie called John Brizendine, the President of McDonnell Douglas. 'Briz' and Charles 'Wide-Body' Forsythe, MDC's Vice President of Sales, had been instrumental in Laker's acquisition of the four DC-10-10s already in service and the two new DC-10-10s scheduled for delivery in February and March 1979. After the usual cordial greetings, Brizendine asked Freddie why he had called.

"We're going to need a couple of 30s for our LA Skytrain and perhaps some other long routes we're applying for in Asia and Australia. What do you have available, mate?" he asked, hoping that 'Briz' had some long-range DC-10-30s available soon. But MDC's senior executive confirmed that the earliest delivery of a new DC-10-30 was many months down the road. "You can have one in time for Christmas '79 Freddie – I'll put a bow around it for you and have Santa deliver it," he said with a chuckle. Freddie explained that he needed the aircraft pronto for the LA service, but MDC had a lot of DC-10-30 orders for major carriers, many of them European state-owned airlines, and 'Briz' couldn't justify Laker jumping the queue.

"Just between us, Freddie, ONA are in a bit of trouble and may not make it. They have two low-hours 30CFs they're looking to offload if you need something fast."

The 'CF' (Convertible Freighter) version of the DC-10-30 appealed to Freddie, so he immediately placed a call to Bob Wagenfeld, the Overseas National Airways President, whom he vaguely knew, as in many respects ONA was somewhat like the Laker Airways of the USA. It was a substantial independent carrier that was continually embattled by the major US airlines with whom it competed. Together with its counterpart, Trans International Airways, ONA was the first US independent airline to operate the DC-10-30 for its extensive charter flight programme. Freddie learned from Wagenfeld that ONA would prefer a quick sale with both aircraft going to a single customer, but they clearly wanted a lot more than Freddie was prepared to pay for them, so nothing came of it.

Apparently BCal had already approached ONA about buying its DC-10-30s and couldn't come to an arrangement either. After a moment or two of glee at perhaps getting another one over on his arch-nemesis, Adam Thomson, by having a DC-10-30 ahead of BCal, common sense thankfully prevailed. So more communications to Brizendine, Forsythe and VP of Commercial Contracts, Pete Burns, followed, with Freddie eventually giving MDC a verbal commitment for two DC-10-30s, albeit with an earliest delivery of late 1979. Freddie wasn't happy about having to wait so long for the aircraft, but he had no choice if he wanted a place in the queue for MDC's long-range tri-jet.

With the commencement of the 1978 early spring travel season, the crowds of would-be Skytrain passengers clogged up Gatwick Airport's departure lounges. New York had become the new Mecca as thousands were prepared to endure considerable discomfort and lack of sleep to reach their goal. The British Airports Authority (BAA), Gatwick's owner, was left with no alternative but to relocate them in a large temporary tent to alleviate the chaos. Then the British CAA intervened and directed that in future Laker's Skytrain service tickets would have to be sold away from the airport. London's Victoria station was felt to be the most appropriate location to house the new sales office, as fast Gatwick-bound train services departed from there. Freddie found an empty kiosk in a small arcade next to a platform and had it moved into the old Victoria station medical centre due to construction work taking place at the station. It was far from ideal, but Laker Airways could at least function.

In New York, despite some early resistance, United Airlines had agreed to do the aircraft ground handling, and Laker's Skytrain flights departed from the United terminal at JFK Airport every evening, seven days a week, with few problems. The passengers were checked in at the Laker Travel Centre in Queens, then transferred to the United terminal by bus and went straight to the gate for departure. Meanwhile their baggage, which had been checked in and tagged at the Rego Park terminal, went by truck straight to the aircraft. It was an efficient system in spite of the highly restrictive circumstances Laker faced.

Laker Airways' Skytrain service licence for the London-Los Angeles route was officially granted on 5th May 1978. Despite Bob Beckman's urging to start earlier, Freddie decided that the service would commence on 26th September, the first anniversary of the first flight of the London-New York Skytrain. Prices ranged between £84 and £96, less than had first been intended in order to meet the competition of the new Apex and Standby fares from the competing airlines, which were now quite deliberately attacking Laker's ticket prices. Once licensed, Beckman pressured Laker Airways to commence operations as soon as possible or risk losing it, with little or no consideration for airport logistics, marketing, staffing or anything, giving noone time to catch their breath. No new route was so vigorously and perhaps prematurely inaugurated as Laker's London to Los Angeles Skytrain service.

British Caledonian made one last attempt to derail the Los Angeles Skytrain service with an appeal to Edmund Dell, the Secretary of State for Trade, to overturn the decision. Thomson threatened to take the matter to 'the highest courts in the land'. It was a long shot – since the formation of the CAA six years earlier, not one single appeal to the Secretary of State had been successful. The LA route was forever a 'bit of sand in the oyster' between the two airlines. Once again, the feud between Adam Thomson and Freddie was being perpetuated.

During a planning meeting for the LA route, Freddie asked two of Laker's key managers for their opinion.

"We operate the 707 non-stop now on the ABCs – why don't we start with them on Skytrain?" John Jones suggested. "We may not fill the DC-10s to start with at such short notice. We can always paint 'Skytrain' on the side if you're worried about branding."

But Freddie was reluctant to use the Boeing 707-351Bs on the Los Angeles Skytrain service, even though they could fly there non-stop and would carry 189 passengers, which, as Jones had said, would probably be more than enough available seats to kick things off to LA. Newly appointed Operations Manager USA, Greg Dix, who after less than three months stateside now managed all Laker's North American airport activities, chimed in.

"Freddie, I agree with John about starting off with the 707, but no one will have us in their terminal at LAX – it's like JFK all over again. We are probably going to have to operate out of the West Imperial Terminal like we do with the ABCs as they're all scared to death of having queues of backpackers lined up down Century Boulevard."

Freddie heard what his key managers were saying, and knew that what they recommended was logical, but as usual he dug in. He felt he had a track record of being right and he would be this time too. So despite all the obstacles at LAX, and not having the right equipment to fly the route non-stop, Freddie insisted that the new West Coast Skytrain service would be flown by Laker's DC-10 aircraft. And they would stop at Bangor in Maine for fuel and a crew change in both directions. And that was that.

Laker's DC-10-10s could never make it to Los Angeles non-stop unless they were empty and there were minimal headwinds; London to Los Angeles was an 11½-hour flight non-stop and more than 4,750 nautical miles. Freddie recognised that having to stop in Bangor en route to LAX wasn't optimum in the long term. The first of the long-range DC-10-30s he had made a commitment for wouldn't arrive until late 1979 to facilitate a reliable non-stop West Coast service. However, there was one advantage to stopping in Bangor. As a US Port of Entry, passengers could clear customs and immigration while the plane was being serviced and a new flight crew took over. They would arrive in Los Angeles as domestic passengers and avoid the typical long queues at the LAX immigration and customs checkpoints. "See!" Freddie said smugly. "Stopping at Bangor is a selling point – let's be sure to make the Bangor stopover sound like a benefit, not a disadvantage. They'll love it, an empty terminal, polite customs officers and fresh Maine lobster to take to LA." But despite the 'perceived' advantages of stopping at Maine's premier international airport en route to LAX, Freddie knew that flying to the West Coast of the USA non-stop was ultimately the only way it could ever be commercially successful.

Throughout the first half of 1978, the rival airlines had competed hard with 12 daily flights between New York and London between them, and they bracketed Laker's flight times. They offered a small percentage of their capacity each day to match Laker's fare, gave a full reservation service, complimentary meals and a 20kg baggage allowance. Their low-fare seats were full but so were Laker's. The other airlines couldn't quite match Laker's fares and they lost money on every low-fare passenger; Laker was winning the battle ... at least for now.

From 10th May 1978, another daily round trip using a Boeing 707 was added to the New York Skytrain schedule for the build-up of student vacation travel when the demand would clearly outstrip supply. The DC-10s were flying full of passengers; they couldn't fill the aircraft fast enough and at any given time there were enough prospective passengers waiting in line to fill several days' worth of flights. The high load factors Laker was achieving to offset the low fares increased the likelihood of returning passengers having to wait in line again, sometimes for days. The additional capacity didn't alleviate the queues snaking around Victoria or at the Rego Park terminal in New York, as travellers flocked to use the Skytrain service in ever greater numbers.

And it wasn't just Laker Airways. Even before Skytrain started, it caused the competition to behave like headless chickens, their executives making knee-jerk and irrational decisions based purely on Laker's presence in their coveted transatlantic market. It mattered little that Laker's initial one flight a day with 345 seats was hardly a threat to the unrestricted scheduled service capacity offered by the legacy airlines. Between them, British Airways, Pan Am and Trans World Airlines, together with the 'fifth freedom' carriers that operated from New York over London, El Al, Air India and Iran Air, had a combined daily capacity exceeding 4,000 seats. Nevertheless, panicked by the spectre of Freddie Laker, they launched rival Standby and Budget fares to compete with Laker Airways, all with strictly controlled capacity at these low prices. They would never have dreamed of bringing in these loss-leader type standby fares – which had only been previously tried in the American domestic market – if Laker Airways hadn't existed. Laker's competitors flew people to London and New York, then found they couldn't (or wouldn't) fly them back, thus leaving them stranded. The scheduled airlines were completely unable to cope with the demand. The massive newspaper coverage devoted to the Skytrain service together with the competitor airlines' own advertising had built up public expectations that unlimited cheap travel was simply there for the asking.

Because of the legacy carriers' irrational move to compete with Laker, Heathrow Airport also became choked. The BAA, in desperation, stopped standby tickets being sold there as well. This pushed the problem into central London and into the airlines' city ticketing offices, where large queues of passengers formed, desperate to get a seat home. There were instances when the harassed airlines – anxious to move the queues of standby hopefuls – placed some of the angry, tired and dishevelled travellers into their empty 1st Class seats. This was to the obvious distaste of the well-to-do and the premium business travellers who were paying full fare in the neighbouring seats at the front of the aircraft.

As the attacks on Laker Airways by the legacy carriers continued through the summer, it was fortuitous for Laker Airways that Alfred Kahn had taken the helm at the USA's Civil Aeronautics Board (CAB). Under Kahn, the spirit of deregulation was being taken into the international sphere. With a new sheriff in town, IATA traffic conferences were severely curtailed by the actions of his CAB – the CAB began to wage its own war on IATA. Any fares and rates agreed under its auspices at its regular traffic conferences would no longer be accepted, effectively pulling the US airlines out from IATA fare controls and reducing the influence of IATA in other markets where US airlines benefitted from 'fifth freedom' rights. It brought the airlines into the sights of the US anti-trust laws that had never before been rigidly enforced for IATA member airlines. It should have offered some hope of protection for Laker. The CAB before Kahn had always preferred bilateral agreements that it called 'friendly, mutual and beneficial' – in other words, a protectionist system for the legacy airlines of which Freddie was highly critical.

As an emergency response, IATA called a special annual meeting in Montreal in late June 1978. The queues of people both in London and New York clamouring to get on a Laker aircraft only hardened the negative opinions of Freddie Laker held by his competitors. Speech after speech heavily criticised Laker's Skytrain service, scapegoating Freddie for the Carter administration's envisioned policy of 'open skies'. The American President's planned US domestic deregulation was determined to bring the benefits of lower fares and more competition to the American public. Needless to say, many airline executives questioned the logic behind deregulation, while industry analysts forecast that it would be the death knell for many airlines, some of which were household names. But Freddie's popularity with the public stood at an all-time high.

Nothing reflected this more than when it was announced that Freddie Laker was to be given a knighthood in Her Majesty the Queen's Birthday Honours List for services to the airline industry. The recognition of his achievements was the crowning glory of his career, yet the knighthood was a surprise as it had come from the Labour Goverment's Prime Minister, James Callaghan.

Freddie took full advantage when notified of the honour by saying, "I think the Government must have now accepted that competition is the name of the game." Freddie received hundreds of congratulatory notes, even from some of his competitors, all acknowledging that the honour was well deserved. Prior to his investiture, Freddie was invited to Buckingham Palace on 1st June 1978 for a special luncheon with the Queen and the Duke of Edinburgh. As guest of honour he was seated next to Her Majesty on her left-hand side, while the rest of the luncheon guests were a disparate group that included film director Fred Zimmermann, architect and town planner Elizabeth Chesterton, Treasury civil servant Sir Leo Pliatzky, Roman Catholic Bishop Alan Clark. and others who were to be honoured at the investiture in July. At the lunch Freddie kept the conversation light by asking Her Majesty how she put up with her sons flying helicopters, parachuting and doing all manner of dangerous activities. Without hesitation the Queen pointed across the table at her husband Prince Philip and in a raised voice said, "It's him." As they sat in the surreal Buckingham Palace dining room enjoying the privileges of aristocracy, Freddie quietly hoped that Her Majesty or any of the other guests at the royal luncheon wouldn't bring up the fact that hundreds of prospective Skytrain passengers were at that very moment standing in long lines around Victoria station, just a half mile away.

For once, Freddie exercised constraint and didn't mention to HM that her sister, HRH Princess Margaret, had secretly flown to Barbados on the Laker-operated International Caribbean Airways 707 a few years earlier. She had been en route to the Caribbean island of Mustique for a tryst with her lover, Roddy Llewellyn. It was a national scandal and an embarrassment for the Royal Family, and the relationship triggered Princess Margaret's highly publicised divorce from Lord Snowdon.

On 19th July, Freddie, immaculately attired in his dark grey morning suit, went back to Buckingham Palace with his mother Hannah and wife Patricia to receive his knighthood. Afterwards, he and the stylishly dressed and very glamorous Oklahomian, now 'Lady' Patricia Laker, went to a local pub for a game of darts and a pint. Freddie received a gift of a ceremonial Wilkinson sword from his American lawyer Bob Beckman, which he promptly used to prop open one of the creeky old doors at his Furzegrove estate. Most visitors were never told that the sword was from Beckman, and Freddie was happy to let them assume that the Queen herself had given it to him. These were proud moments for a man of his modest background, as he said: "I always thank fate for what I was. It taught me the biggest lesson – that nobody should ever have to live like we did – two up, two down, outside lavatory and no bathroom. I never cared about social differences, and I have no time for people who do."

That was just as well, for while Freddie now mixed with royalty, his Skytrain passengers camped out for days, sleeping rough around Victoria station and the Thames embankment in makeshift shelters of cardboard, discarded plastic, old banners and anything they could find in the trash, or steal. Mostly they were students with limited funds who had no money for accommodation. The streets of Westminster were turned into shanty towns. Laker's Skytrain had quickly earned itself the reputation of being the airline service of 'grubby backpackers sleeping outdoors in unsanitary conditions'. 'Lakerville' was born.

The summer of 1978 was particularly wet and the conditions for Laker's prospective passengers were dire, with Freddie lamenting that there had 'only been two days of sunshine since 1976'. However, his personal presence, visiting the encampments around Victoria station and mingling with the potential passengers, quelled much of the frustration. Many of the would-be Skytrain passengers had camped out in extreme conditions and Freddie wanted to make sure they knew he appreciated their efforts. The 'anti-establishment' revered him; Freddie was already the hero of the 'common man' and now, as he sat among them on dirty pavements in the rain, it only brought him greater adulation, which of course he lapped up.

The scenes around Victoria station and the banks of the Thames were the stuff of legend. The illusion only grew as thousands of people decided that this was what they had been waiting for. A kind of grass roots movement evolved, its mission being to secure a cheap seat to America or Britain no matter the hardships and inconvenience. Unlike earlier 'movements' that supported political or sociopolitical causes such as the Vietnam War, gay rights or environmental issues, the Skytrain 'grass roots' movement was an unofficial and transient campaign on behalf of a commercial product. It was totally unprecedented. Prospective Skytrain passengers thought they would never get a seat and would have to spend the night on the pavement by Victoria or at posh Eccleston Square, a small park-like residential area nearby. The affluent residents of this exclusive enclave continued to be subjected to the Laker passengers camping out for days just outside their multi-million-pound, five-storey, terraced mansions. There, the Laker devotees lit fires for cooking, had late-night sing-alongs and, as there were no sanitation facilities, urinated and even defecated on the marble steps of the mansions.

The passengers organised themselves into their own queuing systems, grouped by the dozen with two of the group staying in the queue on behalf of the rest. If they ignored the hand-written warning signs, queue-jumpers were quickly identified and punished, sometimes physically. As most of the passengers of the summer of '78 had camped out, often for days without any sanitation facilities, Skytrain unintentionally took on the persona of a Hajj operation, where the pilgrims had endured similar hardships. Needless to say, this backfired on all the positive publicity Laker Airways had enjoyed for initiating the Skytrain service less than a year earlier. As a result, Freddie was called by Edmund Dell, the British Minister for Aviation. Dell was desperate to find an answer to the chaos in London that was being caused. Freddie explained to the minister that it wasn't only his fault and that the other carriers wouldn't take their own passengers back. Dell responded, "Yes, I know, but I still want you to solve the problem."

Freddie's idea was a 'rollover system' to store the names of the people in a computer, whereby no one would have to wait more than a day to fly. It was merely a more formal version of what Laker was already doing in New York. The best idea that one of Laker's competitor carriers could come up with was to house the passengers in temporary holding camps on Hackney Marshes to the north-east of London. 'Lakerville' ironically set Laker Airways on a path towards its Skytrain service becoming a full scheduled service akin to its competitors. It was fairly obvious that the original Skytrain model championed by Freddie was unsustainable and the turmoil of 'Lakerville' drove the point home loud and clear. Freddie's 'forgotten man' – whose demographic he had clearly described in order to get his licence – simply wasn't flying on Skytrain. Because of the restrictions imposed upon it, Skytrain had inadvertently become a niche for the lowest demographic of traveller, who was prepared to endure inhuman levels of discomfort to obtain a cheap ticket.

On the other side of the Atlantic a similar scene had emerged. The expansive Laker Travel Centre (LTC) terminal building located on Queens Boulevard, in Rego Park, was the epicentre of Skytrain in the USA. Laker Airways wasn't allowed to sell tickets or check in its passengers at JFK Airport, so all Skytrain customers either purchased their tickets to London at the LTC, at the 59th Street Airline Ticketing Office or downtown in the lobby of One World Trade

Centre. Regardless of where they bought their ticket, it didn't guarantee them a seat on a flight until they had checked in at the cavernous Rego Park facility. Unlike Laker's Victoria station location, which had no undercover facilities for prospective Skytrain passengers, the Laker Travel Centre was large enough to accommodate more than 500 people.

A Laker flight check-in at the LTC comprised a system where a passenger service 'lobby agent' would make sure the passenger's passport was valid while they waited in line. When passengers arrived at the counter and presented the tickets they had purchased at one of Laker's remote ticket locations, they were asked if they wanted a smoking or non-smoking, window or aisle seat. Laker's check-in staff in New York had discretion on where to seat each passenger. The back of the aircraft was the smoking section, and was where anyone was given a seat who, after spending a few days outside in the queue, appeared a bit worse for wear. The non-smoking forward cabin and the flexible centre cabin were held for passengers who appeared to be in fairly 'good shape' and unlikely to create discomfort for those around them. A seat was then selected by the Laker agent from a seating chart, and the seat number peeled off and stuck on the passenger's boarding card.

The system was quite primitive, but it was also fast. Once the 345 passengers for that day's flight had been checked in, they were transferred 10 miles by bus to the United Airlines terminal at JFK for departure. Their bags were taken by truck directly to the aircraft and bulk loaded; at that time Laker was unable to use a containerised baggage system. Almost by default, the Skytrain check-in was extremely efficient and caused minimal inconvenience to the passengers once they'd been processed. The next day's passengers could be accommodated inside the Laker Travel Centre, where they were given a number from 1 to 345; they could then sleep in the building or go out for a meal without fear of losing their places. The LTC had turned out to be a life-saver for Skytrain.

However, as the summer progressed and more and more passengers joined the queue, the line stretched outside Laker's terminal and down the sidewalk of Queens Boulevard for more than 100 metres. One enterprising Skytrain passenger, who turned out to be a gay hooker, pitched a tent on the pavement at the corner of Queens and Junction Boulevards. There he proceeded to do 'favours' for prospective passengers willing to pay for his services, and that was how he bought his passage to London and back. Another, a competent singer and guitar player, strode the pavement entertaining the hundreds of people in the line and collected enough tips to buy his ticket. One day a black stretched Cadillac limousine was cruising down Queens Boulevard. Just as it went by the line of prospective Skytrain passengers, the back door opened and a body was tossed into the street, rolling into the gutter right in front of the startled, mostly British passengers. This was all fed back to Freddie at Gatwick, who laughed his socks off at the chaos, completely oblivious to the backlash that 'Lakerville' had created or how it may affect his future ambitions.

While Manager USA Charles Maxwell and his sales team were busy setting up ticket offices in the greater LA area, Operations Manager Greg Dix had contracted with Braniff to co-host that company's state-of-the-art 'Cowboy' system for airport check-in both at LAX and JFK. At that time Laker was unable to take forward reservations and prospective passengers had to turn up on their day of departure to buy a ticket. However, Dix felt this would change, especially with 'Lakerville' and the unacceptable queues in London and New York. In anticipation of being able to make advance reservations, he determined that Braniff's 'Cowboy' computer system would do the job.

Two weeks before the London to Los Angeles Skytrain was due to start, Dix took a few of his key staff to Dallas to train on Braniff's reservations system at the company's Love Field headquarters in Texas. Upon returning, and before the first Los Angeles flight, Dix called Gatwick and spoke to Director John Seear. He enthused about 'Cowboy' and urged Seear to do whatever it took to get London to also adopt the superb Braniff system. Seear reported back that they had already contracted with software developers in the UK to write a custom programme for Laker to use on a worldwide basis. Clearly this wasn't the most expeditious way forward to meet Laker's immediate needs; Braniff and other American carriers were using far superior systems to anything a UK software company with no prior airline experience could devise.

Braniff was a joy to work with; it was a much bigger airline than Laker Airways, but shared many of the same characteristics, with a loyal and upbeat employee group, innovative brand management and cutting edge marketing. Their CEO, Harding Lawrence, was primarily responsible for Braniff's development and he was ably assisted by advertising legend Mary Wells, of the famous Wells, Rich & Greene agency in New York, whom Lawrence had married in 1967. Braniff was the first airline to have leather seats, the first to paint its aircraft in wild colour schemes, courtesy of the renowned American sculptor Alexander Calder, and the first to dress cabin crew in brightly coloured ensembles created by the renowned Florentine fashion designer Emilio Pucci. In 1977, famed American designer Halston was commissioned by Braniff to design new uniforms; the tasteful, muted beige dresses made Braniff's attractive stewardesses look as though they were headed to a Beverly Hills cocktail party rather than to Bogota on a DC-8.

With their founder's name, Tom Braniff, on the side of the planes, Braniff shared its British counterpart's personalised brand identity. The similarities between Braniff and Laker didn't end there. Braniff had successfully competed with the biggest and the best American carriers of the times. It essentially 'owned' South America and its international network was growing rapidly. Domestically, the company competed head-on with American and United, and in the early 1970s it had tried to buy Pan Am.

Just as Laker had irked its British foes, BA and BCal, Braniff had done the same with its US rivals, United and especially American. However, Harding Lawrence, Braniff's CEO, who was unquestionably a tough executive, didn't rankle his competitors in quite the same way as Freddie Laker did. Nevertheless, the Braniff-Laker relationship came about because of Laker's LAX Skytrain needs, and both parties were keen to develop things further. Co-hosting Braniff's 'Cowboy' computer system also gave Dix a bit of leverage he desperately needed at LAX. He was keen to avoid the LA Skytrain flights having to operate out of the West Imperial Terminal (WIT), which was located on Imperial Highway on the south side of LAX and more than two miles from the central terminal area. The WIT was satisfactory for Laker's advanced booking charter (ABC) flights, which were planned to continue with the Boeing 707s even after Skytrain had commenced. But for the first year of Skytrain – with the passengers already pre-cleared into the USA at Bangor and arriving as domestic passengers – Laker needed to be located in the central terminal area.

Just as Laker had experienced in New York, no one at LAX wanted the carrier in their terminal building, fearing a similar fate awaited them with thousands of grubby backpackers queuing for days to fly to London. After convincing Braniff that there would be no long lines of would-be passengers, as they would arrive at the airport already ticketed, Dix secured two check-in counter spaces at Braniff's Terminal Two facility. Terminal Two also had customs and immigration, so once the LA Skytrain service went non-stop with the DC-10-30 aircraft there would be no need to tow the aircraft from the international arrivals terminal to the departure terminal, as they had to do at JFK. Upon hearing of this development, Freddie was naturally relieved.

Laker Airways' potential DC-10-30 order kept escalating from the original two aircraft the company needed for the London-LA route, as Freddie and McDonnell Douglas tried to reach a satisfactory deal. A sticking point was a payload/range performance issue with the DC-10-30. Laker had already proved that it could surpass MDC's original performance specifications of the DC-10-10 by flying it to New York from Gatwick, even on hot still-air days with a full payload. By proving that the DC-10-10 could be operated on longer sectors, it opened up new customer markets for McDonnell Douglas and General Electric. This wasn't lost on MDC, which had been mightily impressed by Laker's Chief Navigator Dick Bradley's DC-10-10 evaluations. So when Freddie debated aircraft performance issues, MDC listened. The company had even made a tentative offer for Bradley to come and work at MDC, but he wasn't interested.

To satisfy Freddie's concerns about the potential performance shortfall of the DC-10-30, MDC suggested that the Laker aircraft be fitted with the higher-rated GE engines, the CF6-50C2B. This upgraded engine was typically reserved for the ER (Extended Range) variant of the DC-10-30, and would, according to MDC solve the performance deficit issue and also give Laker an increased Maximum Take-Off Weight (MTOW) from the standard 565,000lb to the maximum available for the type of 580,000lb. This, MDC said, would 'guarantee' a full payload from Gatwick to the West Coast of the USA in any headwind and ambient temperature conditions.

Freddie wasn't entirely convinced, but he had to accept MDC's estimates until Laker started to fly the aircraft and had accumulated performance data of its own. After considerable wrangling to get the price closer to what Freddie wanted to pay for each aircraft, on 14th September 1978 he signed an agreement to buy five brand new long-range DC-10-30s at a total cost of $228 million ($884m in 2018). The planes were to be delivered from Long Beach between December 1979 and the summer of 1980.

The DC-10-30 order was perhaps a ludicrous over-expansion of capacity, considering that the only long-haul route for which the aircraft were for at the time was London to Los Angeles. Yet no one at Laker Airways batted an eyelid at the almost doubling of Laker's DC-10 fleet. Freddie had been right so many times before, so he must be confident about this latest acquisition, everyone reasoned. Clearly, the airline now needed to completely re-evaluate its entire future route network for deployment of these massively expensive planes.

The financing for the five DC-10-30s proved easy to arrange, and $161 million was provided by the Export Import Bank of the United States (EXIM). The remainder of the money came from McDonnell Douglas and General Electric. Freddie personally persuaded EXIM's chairman, William Draper, to do the deal despite the amount of leverage it entailed. It was perhaps the greatest sales pitch of his life. In Draper's plush Pennsylvania Avenue office in Washington, overlooking the White House, Freddie gave a tour-de-force, unscripted pitch. Draper and his colleagues had never heard anything like it. Freddie charmed them with his overpowering eloquence.

Although the deal was perhaps unwise financially, everyone had an incentive to make it happen. And they did. So after considerable laughter, back-slapping and handshakes all round, Freddie suggested they all go to one of his favourite haunts in DC to toast the occasion. The young Laker executives accompanying Freddie at the meeting, Christopher Brown and Robbie Robinson, were coerced into joining their boss and the EXIM team at Archibald's, Washington's oldest strip club, to celebrate. While in DC, Freddie couldn't wait to see Bob Beckman over at his office and tell him about this latest development. After complaining about why he hadn't been there for the EXIM negotiations and the Archibald's soirée, Beckman's unadulterated joy at hearing that Freddie had just ordered five long-range DC-10-30 aircraft was entirely predictable. His mental wheels were already turning as he mumbled potential Laker destinations such as Hong Kong, Australia, Japan and South America, to Freddie's amusement. "Don't start anything until I give you the go ahead, Bob!" he commanded. As Freddie left his lawyer's office he was thinking, 'this is going to cost me a fortune, the planes are going to seem like a bargain compared to Beckman's fees'.

As a result of, or perhaps despite of 'Lakerville', Freddie's airline had in his own words 'a marvellous summer'. However, the figures from the UK actually went down slightly due to the negative publicity the huge queues had created. Prospective Skytrain passengers thought they would never get a seat and would have to spend the night on the pavement by Victoria station or squatting on doorsteps in Eccleston Square.

At the same time, Skytrain had deterred tens of thousands of conventional travellers... vacationers, those visiting friends and relatives or flying for business; in fact anyone who wanted to book in advance and know what their dates of travel would be. The same people who had booked a flight on Laker's Advanced Booking Charters.

The hugely successful ABC programme between London and New York, which had carried more than a million travellers since 1970, had now been replaced by the Skytrain service. Another downside of Skytrain was the loss of the regular, repeat customer generated by the ABC programme, especially those visiting friends and relatives, arguably one of the most valuable customers for an airline. Until some major changes were in place, it was unlikely that any sane traveller would want to repeat the Skytrain experience. When Skytrain was conceived, no one imagined it would create such hysteria. Within just one year of the service commencing, its innumerable flaws were obvious to all and 'Skytrain' was fast becoming a dirty word, a hindrance to progress and anathema to airport authorities, handling agents and other airlines.

The 'Skytrain' moniker had become double-edged. Yet a year into the experiment and fuelled by what he perceived as a tremendous success, Freddie's plans called for a massive global expansion of Laker Airways' Skytrain services. What he conceived was nothing short of breathtaking.

When the inaugural Skytrain service to New York took off on 26th September 1977, the Laker Airways' fleet had grown to four DC-10-10s with 345 seats, two 707-138Bs with 158 seats, and five BAC One-Elevens with 89 seats. The total seat availability had increased by 1,380 or over 180 per cent from 1972. By the time the LA inaugural flight took off just a year later, the 707-138Bs were up for sale, although still in the fleet, and two 189-seater Boeing 707-351Bs from Cathay Pacific had been delivered earlier in the year. Then, Freddie ordered another two new DC-10-10s scheduled to arrive in February and March 1979, plus no fewer than five new DC-10-30 aircraft, all scheduled to be at Laker's Gatwick base between December 1979 and mid-1980. The arrival of these new aircraft would take the available seat capacity of the fleet (even with the old 707s gone) to 4,618, a whopping 116 per cent increase from 1977. And no one believed that Freddie would stop there.

At the time, Laker Airways didn't have any new route licences on which to deploy all these new planes, except for a few advanced booking charter destinations in North America and two new marginal 707 routes from Boston and Baltimore to Barbados, which no one considered would work in the long term. Moreover, the company was stretched thin organisationally. And soon, despite a promising year, its finances would be stretched thin as well.

Why so many aircraft? Lots of people asked this, including senior executives within the organisation; competent managers with responsibilities for filling the planes with passengers, making sure there was enough revenue flowing in to pay the massive loans, handling the enormous engineering and maintenance burden, training all the new pilots and cabin staff, and all the other monumental challenges of operating a rapidly expanding international airline. Laker's infrastructure had grown considerably when the first DC-10s had arrived. Now it was going to have to ramp up every area at an unprecedented rate to effectively operate all these aircraft … and 'where the hell are we going to fly all the planes to?' was a question asked by many in the company, not unreasonably. Airlines typically had routes in mind before buying the planes to fly them. Freddie's business model from his earliest years with Aviation Traders had always been to buy aircraft as cheaply as possible when they were available… then find something to do with them. But these weren't second hand Yorks; Freddie was committing the company to an unprecedented debt burden.

Freddie was on one of his highs at this point in his life. His recent knighthood and all the accolades and awards that followed, a stable domestic situation topped off by the birth of his long-awaited son, had given him a 'superman' persona. Not only did he now consider himself unassailable, virtually all those around him were caught up in the euphoria and thought so too. 'SuperFred' had got one or two things right in the past so 'he must know something we don't' everyone concluded, including his directors, senior department managers and those closest to him. Freddie was always a 'fearless leader' type of boss, but now he assumed a veritable 'godlike' status within his organisation and beyond. Everyone diligently did his bidding and went along with his schemes, no matter how off-the-wall some of them may have initially appeared. His tunnel vision was in overdrive and he typically had an answer for every objection or different perspective to his own. In no time at all, Freddie had any naysayers turned around; he was no stranger to psychological bullying if anyone ever challenged his decisions. He was almost never questioned, and to do so would be tantamount to heresy.

Freddie deliberately had no 'non-executive directors' on the Laker Airways board. His first wife Joan was a 10 per cent shareholder in the company, although she played no day-to-day role. In many respects this was a seriously missed opportunity, as Joan was strong-minded, competent and extremely well thought of by all those who knew her. Unfortunately, since Freddie's third marriage to Patricia – that Joan considered abhorrent – she had distanced herself from him. Unquestionably, Patricia offered some pizzazz, especially at cocktail parties and promotional events, but she knew nothing of the business. Joan's once much-needed and valuable counsel that she'd given Freddie in the past was now, for the first time in his adult life, missing. So Freddie didn't have anyone who might question his 'over the top' vision and occasionally inject some reality into his thought processes. Instead, he had strategically formed a board comprising a small group of only four 'executive directors' who were basically nothing more than senior managers (in America they would be 'Vice-Presidents'), each with a specific portfolio of responsibilities. The only time they were all in the same room together was for the mandatory annual general meeting stipulated by the UK's corporate laws and Freddie's traditional (men only) Christmas luncheon.

The Laker Airways' executive directors essentially did Freddie's bidding. His management style in the 1970s, the same as it had always been, was dictatorial rather than inclusive. He used a 'divide and conquer' philosophy that – perhaps deliberately – pitted some key executives against each other to the point that they simply didn't communicate. It was a bizarre and somewhat dysfunctional way to run a business in the 20th century and, as the company grew, Freddie became less and less effective as the overall chief executive. There wasn't a General Manager or Chief Operating Officer at Laker Airways – it was just Freddie. Fortunately, the airline had extremely competent and self-motivated individuals heading up each major department, most of whom had been with Freddie since the BUA days, or earlier. Even without day-to-day top management direction that might be typical in most organisations, Laker

Airways worked. For the most part, especially operationally and technically, it worked very well indeed. However, Freddie's outdated, autocratic style of management wasn't conducive to the monumental growth the company was about to experience.

Consequently, when Freddie ordered another seven massively expensive wide-body DC-10 aircraft no one seriously challenged the decision. Finance Director Robbie Robinson may have wondered how they were going to pay for the planes and Commercial Manager John Jones might have scratched his head as to how they'd use them all, let alone fill them with passengers. The genius Chief Navigator, Dick Bradley – with the help of his slide rule – would have assessed whether the new DC-10-30s, even with the upgraded engines, would make it to Los Angeles on a hot, still-air day out of Gatwick with 100mph North Atlantic headwinds. Freddie had proven his ability over several decades of buying aircraft at just the right time and for the right price, so everyone naturally assumed he must have it 'spot on' this time too.

Thus, when they learned about the new aircraft acquisition plan, Freddie's key managers at Laker Airways dutifully put their heads down, and worked at a fever pitch for unimaginably long hours. Most jobs at the firm in those days paid considerably less than contemporary positions in the industry, yet no one complained and no one would have wanted to work anywhere else. They intuitively knew that they were caught up in something special – perhaps one of those rare opportunities in life when you look back many years later and say, 'I was there; I was part of that.' It's debatable whether any individual leader in the airline industry – or perhaps any industry for that matter – had created a culture such as existed at Laker Airways at that time. The 'esprit de corps' was unique. Without such a talented and dedicated team of people around him, Freddie could never have embarked on all the massively ambitious initiatives that he had started almost immediately after the Skytrain service had launched in September 1977.

Behind Freddie's bold aircraft acquisition plan, his vision of colossal global expansion was frantically urged on by Bob Beckman, arguably one of Washington's top specialist aviation lawyers. Beckman had played a key role for Laker Airways by obtaining the Skytrain licences, dealing mostly with the obstructive USA side. Freddie listened to Beckman, even though Beckman would never tell Freddie that he was wrong about any developmental initiatives or route procurements. Beckman saw an opportunity for himself to be the catalyst for Laker Airways becoming an international phenomenon. He'd be able to charge the top rate for his services and he and his wife would enjoy lots of all-expenses-paid, 1st Class trips out of it too.

Freddie and Beckman's new international routes for which they were applying were in three categories: Pacific Rim, North America & Caribbean, and Europe.

1. Pacific Rim: London to Hong Kong (via Sharjah), operated as Skytrain; Hong Kong, Tokyo (via Guam and/or Honolulu) to Los Angeles, San Francisco or Seattle and on to Vancouver (US-UK Bilateral Route 6), operated as Skytrain; London to Sydney, Melbourne, Adelaide and Perth in Australia (via Sharjah

and Singapore), operated as Skytrain; and Advanced Booking Charters between Hong Kong and Colombo, Kuala Lumpur, Manila, Taipei, Seoul, Chiang Mai, Bangkok, Tokyo, Fukuoka and Osaka.

2. North America & Caribbean: London to Detroit, Chicago, Boston and San Francisco/Oakland (US-UK Bilateral Route 1), to be operated as Skytrain; Baltimore to Barbados and Boston to Barbados (for International Caribbean Airways), operated as a scheduled service; and Advance Booking Charters to several new cities in Canada.

3. Europe: London to 36 European cities, operated as Skytrain; and 630 European city permutations not routeing via London, operated as Skytrain.

4. Former BUA routes to South America (evaluated but not applied for).

The seeds for many of these routes had been planted earlier; now Laker's licence applications became an urgent priority as all the new aircraft Freddie had ordered needed to be deployed somehow. Despite 'Lakerville' and the chaos Skytrain had created in the summer of 1978, the company's mission was clear. Now, Freddie and Bob Beckman's quest for 'global domination' really began.

CHAPTER 31

# Quid pro Quo

## Coerced to buy the Airbus

1978 - 1979

During the first week of September 1978, the annual Farnborough International Air Show took place in England. Second only to Paris among the world's air shows, Farnborough showcased the latest and the best aircraft and equipment from the world's top manufacturers. That year Farnborough was to be the scene of a big Laker announcement. Riding the first year's phenomenal success of his breakthrough Skytrain transatlantic service, the recently knighted and ebullient Sir Freddie Laker had revealed that he would be more than doubling his DC-10 fleet. He had already committed to the purchase of five new long-range DC-10-30 aircraft, in addition to the two DC-10-10s under construction at McDonnell Douglas's Long Beach factory.

However, there was a rumour blowing around that there was a bigger deal in the offing and that Freddie was about to also purchase six Airbus A300-B4 aircraft. In the days long before airlines routinely announced orders for 50 aircraft or more, the news, scooped by the BBC, was very big news indeed. Freddie wasn't pleased; he had wanted to save making the headlines for his next Skytrain inauguration. Notwithstanding, within a week of the Farnborough show, a letter of intent for ten A300 aircraft had been signed in a deal worth nearly £250 million.

The total value of the aircraft orders placed by Freddie that September was $725 million ($4.3 billion at 2018 values). It would raise the airline's debt-to-equity ratio from 9:1 the year before to a staggering 11:1. Laker Airways didn't have much working capital, but the lenders were not worried about participating – their only concern was protecting their own positions.

At the age of 56 Freddie had fallen victim to a salesman's patter. The first overtures by Arthur Howes, Airbus Industrie's European sales manager, had been met with stiff resistance. Freddie should have seen Howes coming – after all, he had given him the nickname 'Maisonette', a maisonette being half a house. Freddie had taken the Cockney pronunciation of Arthur Howes and got 'Arfur 'ows', which became 'half a house'. At least that was the explanation he gave. Perhaps only a true Cockney would have understood the logic.

During one of Howes's regular but fruitless 'courtesy visits' to the Laker Airways HQ, Freddie indicated that he might be interested after all in something that Airbus Industrie had to offer ... its A310. But that model was still on the drawing board and couldn't be delivered until 1983. When Howes gave Freddie the quotation, Freddie shouted, "It resembles a bloody tallyphone number," and he was again put off doing a deal.

Showing any interest at all was a spectacular change of heart by Freddie, who'd always dismissed the Airbus project with scorn and bought only American or British-built aircraft. He'd famously said, "Airbus is useless – since it would be like a horse designed by committee, it would fly like a camel." Freddie had no intention of ever buying any aircraft from Airbus.

"He came over to New York shortly after I had relocated there and I met him as I always did," Laker's US Operations Manager, Greg Dix, said of Freddie as he ranted on about Airbus Industrie during the drive from JFK to the city. "You can't believe what they're like," he growled. "Imagine it – cocky German Doctors of Engineering in their crisp white coats and Brylcreemed hair, the French having two-hour 'Parisian' liquid lunches and a bunch of complaining Brits shuffling around in their grubby brown overalls and chuffing on Woodbines, all trying to build a plane together!" Fortunately there were no members of the press nearby as he continued: "It won't happen, I'm telling you, Greg. They won't do it – it'll be a bloody great disaster and take us down with it if we go with them. Let's stick to who we know." By that remark he meant let's stick to buying aircraft from McDonnell Douglas, which at the time actually had a twin-engined version of the DC-10 already conceptualised to compete with the Airbus wide-bodied twin.

Dollar by dollar, the price of the A300s came down until Howes eventually wore Freddie down to the point where he somewhat reluctantly said 'yes', incredibly, to no fewer than ten Airbus A300s. The first aircraft was pencilled in for delivery in December 1980, with two more in February 1981, two in June 1981, three more in 1982 and the final two destined to arrive in the spring of 1984. Freddie wanted the planes for his planned European scheduled services to take on British Airways. He believed that Europe was ripe for the introduction of his brand of competition. Someday soon, he speculated, three of the aircraft would be put into service on his proposed schedules serving multiple European markets, foretelling the future of European civil aviation. What he planned to do with the rest of the aircraft was anyone's guess. However, it would fulfill another of Freddie's objectives, which was for Laker Airways to be the UK's first all-wide-bodied airline. This was clearly ego-driven and not based in practicality, as Freddie hadn't considered that many, if not most, of the European routes he envisaged flying couldn't support a high-capacity wide-body aircraft. The traffic simply didn't warrant it, not unless the routes were flown just a few times a week; European routes needed frequency more than capacity.

Freddie stands with the President of McDonnell Douglas Corp. John Brizendine as they survey the DC-10, the aircraft that would become the defining factor of Laker Airways. Freddie started the airline that bore his name humbly, with just two old BOAC Britannias, but the new company expanded fast with more planes and routes. Freddie had a dream of affordable air travel for everyone that he called 'Skytrain'. He spent six years chasing his goal, fighting government obstructions on both sides of the Atlantc. But it was the DC-10 that ultimately made Freddie's dream a reality.

## 'Get Back on Your Feet Again' (1966)

Freddie Laker epitomised the song 'Pick Yourself Up' written for the popular musical 'Swing Time.' Following the tragic loss of only son Kevin and his sudden resignation as Managing Director of British United, after a brief period of introspection, Freddie got back in the saddle and with his wife Joan and help from Kevin's best friend John Jones, Laker Airways was born.

**Above:** A Laker Airways' Bristol Britannia 100. Initially, the fledgling airline only had two Britannias sourced inexpensively from BOAC in April 1966. The aircraft were painted in the distinctive white fuselage with red and black stripes, emulating Freddie's racing colours.

**Above:** Laker Airways' Britannia (G-ANBM) in Treffield International livery at Gatwick before Treffield collapsed. Treffield was one of Laker Airways' first charter customers.

**Left:** John Jones was Laker Airways' first employee. After a formative period in the Ops department, the twenty year old Jones was sent to Lusaka with the Britannias and he managed a programme of cargo flights, transporting oil to Zambia from Tanzania.

Laker Airways' first group of executives and managers. some of whom had immediately left BUA to join Freddie's new venture. **Clockwise:** Cliff Nunn - Director, Bill Townsend - Technical Director, George Forster - Commercial Manager, Leonard 'Atty' Atkinson - Operations Manager, and Nina Griffin - Chief Stewardess.

**Inset:** Captain Alan Hellary left BUA to join Freddie at Laker Airways as his chief pilot.

**Above:** A Laker Airways' Bristol Britannia in the stylish Laker livery.

## The Father of the One-Eleven (1966)

Drawing from his prior experience with the One-Eleven at BUA and his close association with Geoffrey Knight, the Managing Director of the British Aircraft Corporation (BAC), Freddie placed an order for three brand new 89-seat BAC One-Eleven 300 aircraft for Laker Airways.

**Above:** Geoffrey Knight Managing Director of BAC and Freddie upon signing the contract for the One-Elevens. Knight hailed Freddie as the 'Father of the One-Eleven'.

**Above:** The first One-Eleven 320L (G-AVBW) being checked out by Laker hostesses at BAC's production hangar at Hurn Airport. Bravo Whiskey was delivered to Laker Airways in December 1966.

**Right:** Freddie in the cockpit of a BAC One-Eleven. When it came to flying the aircraft his credo was always 'Leave it to the Professionals' but he enjoyed having a go on empty legs occasionally.

**Below:** Freddie and his wife Joan, who was a shareholder in the company, with a model of a BAC One-Eleven they planned to operate with their newly formed Laker Airways.

## Early Work (1966-68)

One of Freddie's initial successes was the introduction of the 'time-charter' concept, where tour operators - such as Wings and Lord Brothers - bought blocks of time on Laker's aircraft. With a long term African contract for one aircraft, the first One-Eleven year exceeeded all expectations.

**Above:** Ernest Welsman of 'Wings' was the first tour operator customer to time charter a Laker BAC One-Eleven aircraft.

**Right:** The original 'Laker Lovelies' on the front stairs of Laker's first BAC One-Eleven. Nina Griffin (front) was the first 'Chief Stewardess' and she went on to manage Laker Airways' in-flight catering unit. Joy Harvey (next up) became head of Cabin Services shortly after and managed Laker's in-flight service for the package holiday operations.

**Below:** Joy Harvey welcomes a holiday-bound family aboard a Laker BAC One-Eleven.

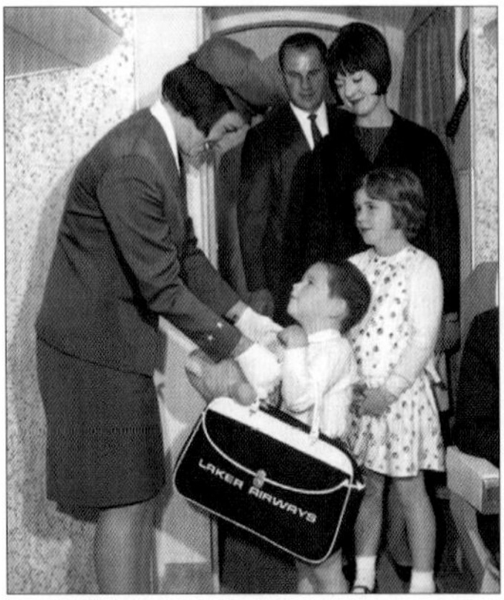

**Above:** Laker's engineers checking a One-Eleven's Rolls Royce Spey engine.

**Above:** Christopher (L) and Stephen Lord, owners of 'Lord Brothers Holidays' time chartered the second Laker One-Eleven. Freddie bought them out in 1968.

**Right:** Laker's third BAC One-Eleven (G-AVBY) was leased to Air Congo for a year. John Jones was sent down to manage the operation. It was risky work as the country had recently been taken over by a military coup and the aircraft flew to African destinations such as Entebbe, Lagos and Lusaka.

## Moving Fast (1969)

1969 was a developmental year with the building of a new hangar and offices and several key people who would be pivotal to the future of Laker Airways.

**Right:** A Laker Airways' BAC One-Eleven outside the Air Couriers' hangar at Gatwick where Laker was first based. By 1969, the company had outgrown the facilities so Freddie leased the empty land next door for a new hangar & office complex.

**Left:** Freddie's son-in-law, John Seear (a chartered Surveyor by profession) and a Director of Laker Airways was tasked by Freddie to oversee the building of the new Laker hangar facility.

**Below:** Freddie by the rear stairs of G-AVBY, one of his new BAC One-Eleven 300s. As most airports didn't have air bridges (jetways), the innovative integral front and rear stairs enabled fast embarkation and deplaning.

© Mirrorpix

**Above:** The 'Laker Airways International Jet Centre' was opened in 1969. The ultra-modern building could accommodate a Boeing 707 and two One-Elevens with office space for several hundred employees.

**Right:** Athol Guy of the world famous 'Seekers' was introduced by John Seear. "There isn't one" Athol famously replied when Freddie asked him about Australia's tourism industry. Realising the opportunity for charter flights to Australia, Freddie asked Athol to be Laker's main 'guy' down under.

**Below:** Harry Bowden-Smith of Arrowsmith Holidays in Liverpool was an early customer. After he was bought out by Freddie, Harry continued to run Arrowsmith in his own unique style.

**Above:** Manchester based air hostesses Carolyn Waldron (L) and Beryl Booth flew Arrowsmith customers from Manchester to the Mediterranean. Laker based a One-Eleven and support staff at Manchester exclusively for Arrowsmith.

**Above:** Freddie helped with the concept of the BAC Three-Eleven in the late 60s. He placed an order for the wide-body aircraft but the Three-Eleven never saw production. It was a missed opportunity for British aerospace, as it was a decade ahead of the Airbus A300.

## Deja Vu - Second Force Ambitions (1969-72)

It was ten years later but like a flash back to when he was made Managing Director of BUA. Once in his new Laker office, Freddie purchased two Boeing 707s, invested a 50% share in a ground handling company, took a 49% share in a Barbados airline, set up a base in Berlin... and then tried to buy BUA.

**Above:** Freddie with fellow aviation pioneer, Harold Bamberg. Laker's 707-138B aircraft, originally flown by Qantas were purchased from the Receivers of Bamberg's defunct British Eagle Airways.

**Above:** Freddie in his new office on the third floor of Laker's International Jet Centre at Gatwick where he started building Laker Airways into a powerhouse. He brought his 'lucky' oak desk from BUA and surrounded himself with aircraft models.

**Right:** Alan Snudden (L) - Managing Director of Dan Air, David Livingston - British Airports Authority Director of Gatwick and Freddie at the signing of the agreement for the Laker / Dan Air joint venture, Gatwick Handling Ltd.

**Below:** Laker's Boeing 707-138B G-AVZZ was re-painted 'International Caribbean' for the flights from Gatwick to (low fare friendly) Luxembourg and Barbados.

**Left:** A 707 crew about to head off to Barbados. Cabin crew and ground staff now wore a vibrant red uniform topped off with a bowler hat.

**Right:** A postcard from Berlin's Tegel Airport with a Laker One-Eleven at the gate. Berlin was an important Laker base and flew package holidays to the Mediterranean for tour operator 'Flug Union' and flights to Turkey for the workers employed in Berlin, via the strictly controlled air corridors.

## The 'Left-Handed Canary Club' and ABCs (early 1970s)

In the early 1970s, the only way to affordably cross the Atlantic was to take an Affinity Group Charter. Passengers were required to be members of an association of no more than 20,000 members for a period of at least one year and the association had to exist for reasons other than cheap air travel. The Affinity Group Charters spawned thousands of bogus groups with bizarre names where membership was back dated. Freddie was incensed by the lunacy of people having to 'lie to fly' and vowed to change things.

Laker Airways' 707s flew tens of thousands of charter passengers a year across the Atlantic during the early 1970s to over a dozen destinations in North America.

**Below:** The Boeing 707 cockpit with the Captain (L), First Officer and the Flight Engineer behind. For long-haul flights, a Navigator sat on the port (left) side of the cockpit.

**Left:** Robert M. Beckman, a respected Washington DC aviation lawyer was hired by Freddie to obtain the early route licenses for Laker's North Atlantic affinity group charter flights.

**Left:** Freddie speaking to distraught Affinity Group members who were denied boarding due to irregularities. The controversial Affinity Group charters led to the Advanced Booking Charters (ABC) Laker pioneered, that gave Freddie the idea for his revolutionary Skytrain 'walk-on, no frills' air travel concept. He immediately had Bob Beckman get to work in the USA for the licensing.

**Right:** Freddie with two of his first employees in the USA - Ricki Walsh (L) and Linda Earls at the tour operator Jetsave's travel agent seminar in Los Angeles. These young women almost single handedly managed the Affinity Group and ABC flights at Los Angeles and New York in the early 70s. In the spirit of Freddie's 'promote from within' philosophy, they went on to become Laker Airways' Station Managers of LAX (Ricki) and JFK (Linda) for the Skytrain service.

## Laker Goes Widebody (1972)

Freddie seized the opportunity to buy his first McDonnell Douglas DC-10s with financing by Japan's giant Mitsui corporation when All Nippon Airways suddenly cancelled their order.

**Right:** Sanford McDonnell urged Freddie to take advantage of the 'once in a lifetime' chance to buy the ANA DC-10s.

Laker's first DC-10-10 being built at MDC's Long Beach factory.

**Above:** L-R Charles Forsythe, John Brizendine - President of McDonnell Douglas, Freddie, and Bill Townsend. MDC knew the Laker deal would help sell the DC-10 to other independent airlines.

**Below:** Freddie signs the contract for his first DC-10s with Charles 'Widebody' Forsythe - VP of Sales for MDC.

**Above:** Freddie takes delivery of the first DC-10 seen through the empty nacelle of a GE CF6 engine.

Laker's DC-10s outside the McDonnell Douglas Corp. production hangar at Long Beach, California in 1972.

## The DC-10 Changes Everything (1972)

Freddie was ecstatic at taking delivery of the first DC-10s in Europe. Laker beat Swissair and KLM to the honour by a matter of a few weeks. G-AZZC (Eastern Belle) was flown to Gatwick from Long Beach by Manager of Flight Operations, Captain Alan Hellary (below L) on 26th October 1972.

**Left:** Ten cabin crew were needed for the DC-10 and an intense training schedule for the in-flight service and emergencies was rapidly initiated.

**Above:** A widely-used publicity photo - often copied by other airlines to promote the DC-10.

**Below:** All three aircraft types outside the Laker hangar at Gatwick. The DC-10-10 (G-AZZD) had just been delivered and is seen with the Boeing 707-138B (G-AVZZ) & BAC One-Eleven 320 (G-AVBW). Laker now had a versatile fleet of jet aircraft to serve a variety of international destinations.

**Right:** Laker's hangar had to be modified to accommodate the DC-10s; One-Elevens could be tucked in on each side.

## Showing Off (1972-73)

The DC-10s gave Freddie a unique opportunity to show off. He was never shy about creating publicity and Freddie embarked on a whirlwind tour to promote the new aircraft. He enrolled his attractive air hostesses to entertain the hundreds of guests and civic & travel industry luminaries on the new planes.

**Above:** An important first stop of the DC-10 promotional tour of Britain was at Liverpool - home of Arrowsmith Holidays. One of Freddie's favourites, Anne Clark (right) was a Manchester based In-Flight Director and flew Arrowsmith passengers to the Mediterranean and North America. Thousands of 'Im a Laker Liker' and DC-10 stickers were given out during the demonstration tours.

**Left:** Freddie in full voice as he entertains guests during a flight. A masterful showman, Freddie paved the way for other business leaders to follow his example.

**Inset Left**: Freddie and his mother, Hannah. She boarded a flight at RAF Manston in Kent near her Ramsgate home.

**Above**: Freddie on the DC-10's PA system extolling the virtues of his new aircraft and thanking his guests for flying on Laker Airways.

**Left**: George Carroll (L) and Gordon Nichols of Lord Bros. with In-Flight Directors Julie Poole & Beverley Blum (R).

## More DC-10s (1974-77)

Freddie had made an initial commitment for three DC-10-10s. The third (G-BBSZ) was named 'Canterbury Belle' after Freddie's birthplace in Kent, England. He was then given a terrific deal on a fourth, the MDC demonstration aircraft and the second DC-10 built, (G-BELO 'Southern Belle').

**Above:** Laker's third DC-10-10 (G-BBSZ), being built in the McDonnell Douglas production hangar at Long Beach, California. 'Canterbury Belle' was delivered to Laker's Gatwick HQ on May 20, 1974.

**Above:** An early publicity photo of Freddie showing the size of the GE CF6 engine.

**Below:** McDonnell Douglas President, John Brizendine holding a press conference with G-BBSZ at Long Beach.

**Above:** Freddie and Technical Director Bill Townsend (R) in the DC-10 cockpit.

**Below:** Freddie checking out the Flight Engineer's panel of a DC-10.

**Above:** G-BELO (Southern Belle) was delivered on June 3, 1977. Laker's unique 'Skytrain' logo was on all the DC-10s in anticipation of approval.

## Those Magnificent Men

Whenever he flew on one of his aircraft, if he wasn't in the cabin chatting to passengers, Freddie was in the cockpit with his flight crew. He enjoyed considerable mutual respect with his crew members, many of whom had been with him for their entire post Royal Air Force careers. Freddie's pilots couldn't imagine working for anyone else and flight crew turnover at Laker Airways was almost non-existent.

**Above:** DC-10 Fleet Captain, Steve James was one of Freddie's most long-serving, experienced and respected pilots.

**Right:** Captain Alan Hellary and First Officer Ray Hazzard flying a Laker Airways' DC-10.

**Above:** Freddie toasts Captain Nick Bevan on the successful delivery of one of the new DC-10s.

**Above:** Freddie in the jump seat flying with Capt. Jock Manson.

**Above:** DC-10 Flight Engineer, the popular Ted Burns. Laker's F/Es had typically come from the hangar and were trusted and capable cockpit crew members. They also added a useful third pair of eyes to the job which was appreciated by the pilots.

**Above:** Freddie observing Capt. Steve James and a DC-10 crew in action. Laker's DC-10s were equipped with Litton Inertial Navigation Systems that facilitated long haul flights without a Navigator on the crew.

## The Unsung Heroes

Laker Airways, despite its reputation as the pioneer of the 'low-cost transatlantic airline' model, was essentially an engineering-driven company. Freddie kept his engineer's licence current and he was as adept in the hangar as in the boardroom. Laker's engineering division was respected worldwide.

**Above:** DC-10 G-AZZD (Western Belle) is pushed out of the Laker hangar after routine maintenance.

**Left & Above:** A DC-10 centre engine change in progress at Laker's Gatwick hangar. The Engineering Department was headed by Engineering Director, Bill Townsend. Often the unsung heroes, Chief Engineer Peter Yeoman and his staff of highly skilled airframe, engine and avionics technicians performed all the line maintenance and the routine checks for the Laker fleet.

## The Battle for Skytrain (1971-77)

Freddie Laker's six-year battle with the authorities on both sides of the Atlantic for a licence to operate between the UK and USA made headline news. It was finally concluded in June 1977 but even then, Laker was at first approved to fly from the unfavourable Stansted and had massive restrictions imposed, including not being able to take reservations or sell tickets at the airports. Never before in the history of civil aviation had a major national airline been so unfairly discriminated against.

**Above:** Freddie looking exasperated after another frustrating session at the Dept. of Trade & Industry with his Publicity officer, Robin Flood and Deputy Managing Director, Cliff Nunn. Freddie promptly left for Majorca after the ordeal to relax on his yacht.

**Above:** 'Ever heard of the consumer, Mr. Shore?' read the banners. A Laker staff group travelled by bus to London and the House of Commons where they lobbied the UK's Trade Secretary, Peter Shore to licence Skytrain.

**Above:** Freddie and Laker executives outside the C.A.A. offices in London on 22nd January 1975 holding a petition of thousands of names in support of Laker Airways' Skytrain application. From left, Robbie Robinson - Finance Director, Geoffrey Street - Skytrain Service Manager, Christopher Brown - Group Solicitor, Cliff Nunn, Freddie, George Carroll - Managing Director of Laker Air Travel, and Lesley Chilton - Freddie's PA.

**Below:** In anticipation of being granted the Skytrain licence, in early 1977, Freddie moved into a spacious and somewhat out of character new office suite. He reluctantly gave up his 'lucky' English oak desk he'd brought from BUA for one in rose-wood. Freddie typically blamed the new desk whenever things went awry.

## "I'm Freddie - Fly Me" (1972-77)

While he battled governments on both sides of the Atlantic for the Skytrain licence, the four DC-10s Freddie had bought specifically for Skytrain were deployed on the Advanced Booking Charter (ABC) flights to North America, package holiday flights to popular Mediterranean sun spots, special group charters, and for the annual Hajj pilgrimage flights to Jeddah (for Mecca). Meanwhile, Freddie tried to take over the Concorde SST programme from British Airways... and then got married for the third time.

**Above:** Freddie with Bill Townsend (L) and Cliff Nunn. He was deadly serious about operating the Concorde and had petitioned the British government. His colleagues were justifiably skeptical.

**Above:** In Flight Director Sandy Doherty (R) with two of her crew and passengers at Corfu. Laker's Mediterranean package holidays had a competitive edge with the 345-seat DC-10s.

**Below:** Meg Vesty (L) and Irene McAdam before setting off on a Boeing 707 with The Rolling Stones for their 1975 Tour of the Americas.

© M Vesty

**Above:** After a chance meeting in Palma followed by a brief courtship, Freddie hastily married Patricia Gates in 1975.

**Above:** The memorable advertising line that prompted a book of (almost) the same name.

**Left:** Laker Airways was the largest operator of Advanced Booking Charters between Britain and North America.

**Below:** Hunt vs Lauda for the 1976 F1 championship. Laker Airways carried the Grand Prix teams' personnel to the European races and to LAX for the USGP at Long Beach.

**Above:** A Laker DC-10-10 was chartered to Air Algerie for the Hajj. Between 1972 and 1977, Laker operated the annual pilgrimage flights to Jeddah (for Mecca) on behalf of Saudi Arabian Airlines, Nigeria Airways, Royal Air Maroc, Iran Air, and Air Algerie. The Hajj fell in the off-season and generated significant incremental revenue.

## Victory at Last (1977)

Finally, the licencing authorities on both sides of the Atlantic granted a licence for the Skytrain service.

© Rex Features

**Above:** Freddie reads about the approval of Skytrain that made front page news in all the daily papers.

© Rex Features

**Above:** Freddie and his wife, Patricia celebrate the news of Skytrain's approval while relaxing in Palma on the 'M/V Tutinela' - at anchor behind.

**Above:** Freddie celebrating with some of his closest family and associates. L-R: Ian Wallace - Freddie's Merchant Banker, Lesley Chilton, wife Patricia, Freddie, daughter Elaine Seear, Cliff Nunn, and Harry Freeman - Freddie's chauffeur.

**Below:** Freddie sharing his jubiliation with some of Laker Airways' senior executives who had all done their part for Skytrain. L-R: George Carroll, John Jones - Commercial Manager, Charles Maxwell - Manager USA, Freddie, and Cliff Nunn.

LAKER
Skytrain
Trade mark
SCHEDULED AIR SERVICE

**Left:** Freddie celebrates finally winning the Skytrain service licence outside the offices at Gatwick with his elated staff, many of whom had sacrificed their time and energy for the cause. The monumental efforts of Freddie and his legal teams on both sides of the Atlantic had finally paid off. In 1977, Freddie Laker's Skytrain service would unknowingly pioneer the 'no-frills, low-cost' airline model.

Initially the Airbus A300s were planned to take over the flying from the aging BAC One-Elevens, which would be coming to the end of their economic lives in a few years. Inclusive tour (IT) holidays were still growing and there was a high demand from tour operators; the IT sector accounted for 50 per cent of Laker's charter operations.

The A300s would be the quietest and most efficient airliners in the world. They would be fitted with the latest avionics, including inertial navigation, colour radar, and autoland. An A300 would be able to carry three times the number of passengers of an 89-seat One-Eleven; it would have considerably more capacity than Laker Airways needed, except for a few high-density IT routes to summer Mediterranean destinations such as Palma and Alicante. However, the Airbus A300 was far from the perfect aircraft for Laker Airways at the time. The A310 and Boeing's 767 wide-body twin and 757 narrow-body twin were still a few years away, while McDonnell Douglas had short-sightedly all but shelved its DC-10 twin. For some unfathomable reason, Freddie had never seriously considered the Boeing 737 as a replacement for the One-Eleven, despite it being clearly the most logical platform for Laker's existing and future intra-European operations. Freddie had a long history of purchasing and operating American aircraft, including the DC-10 and Boeing 707, yet he was still predisposed to buying British, even if the aircraft in question was only partly British.

The British Government had been considering rejoining the Airbus consortium from which it had withdrawn in April 1969, citing concern about rising costs and an ability to recoup its investment. The Airbus was a highly political aircraft, and that in itself should have given Freddie warning signs. The British Government's participation had consisted of funding a stake on behalf of Hawker Siddeley (by then part of British Aerospace), which had designed and then built the wing structure for the A300 at its Chester factory.

Airbus explored moving the construction of the wings to Germany. Both VFW Fokker and the French Aerospatiale produced designs of their own for the A310, but they were no match for the British technology and expertise that was so far ahead in the area. They conceded that no one could build wings like the British. Nowhere else in the world, except the USA, had the automated machinery or capacity to fulfil this crucial production role.

Murmurings about British Aerospace (BAe) rejoining the Airbus consortium started in 1976 and Boeing made moves to block it. By 1978 there was a potential partnership with the Boeing Corporation on the table for BAe. The Boeing proposal was a cheaper, risk-sharing arrangement on the Boeing 757 aircraft. BAe was offered a 50 per cent share for an investment of $400 million. Instead, Boeing changed its mind and substituted an offer of a fixed-price contract to build the wings as a subcontractor with an allowance for profits and expenses. BAe didn't view it as a good deal, especially as Boeing wanted a 30 per cent haircut on the price it would normally have charged for making a pair of wings. BAe had surplus capacity and could have done with the work, but there were strong suspicions that this was little else but spoiler tactics by the Americans, leading the British away with promises that they wouldn't keep.

The Americans were keen to get European sales and feared that the success of the Airbus project in Europe would lead to European governments demanding that the numerous state-owned airlines buy from Airbus. The proposed arrangement would deal a serious blow to the Europeans by taking away their wing manufacturer. Fears were that a Boeing deal would reduce BAe to being merely a components manufacturer.

On 24 June 1978 British Prime Minister James Callaghan travelled to Washington to receive the first Hubert H. Humphrey International Award. There he had lunch with Frank Borman, the famous former astronaut and now Chairman of Eastern Airlines, which had orders on the books with both Airbus and Boeing. That evening he dined with Thornton 'T' Wilson, Boeing's Chairman, and Ernest 'Tex' Boullioun, head of the commercial group and known as 'the world's greatest plane salesman'. Callaghan was uneasy after the dinner, as he recalled: "Wilson dangled larger future projects, but the more he said, the less interested I became. I felt Boeing wanted to swallow us in." BAe's management remained intransigent; it had never wanted to deal with anyone other than Airbus. Before leaving Washington, Callaghan had one final meeting with Sandy McDonnell and John Brizendine of MDC. McDonnell slipped in his own proposal, which was a partnership between BAe, Airbus and MDC. It seemed attractive, but there was nothing really serious behind it.

Rolls-Royce was also a very interested party in all these negotiations. It wanted to supply its RB211-535/235 engine to British Airways for the new Boeing 757. The package was by far the preferred choice for British Airways over the Airbus A300. An earlier incarnation of the RB211 was already being used on BA's Lockheed TriStar aircraft. Rolls needed a $500 million investment from the British Government to develop the engine. It was hugely important for Rolls-Royce as it would be the first time that it would be a launch engine on a Boeing aircraft. Both British Airways and Eastern were ready to order the 757, equipped with Rolls-Royce engines. Rolls-Royce was only just recovering from its period in receivership in the early 1970s, which had been caused by the enormous cost of development of the engines' first incarnation. The company's chairman, Kenneth Keith, saw it as the only way to save Rolls-Royce from drifting towards another bankruptcy. He believed that any deal between BAe and Airbus would ruin his chances with Boeing. Among MPs in the British Parliament there was support for both sides, with many pro-Europeans taking BAe's side and the British Ambassador in Paris suggesting that a deal with Boeing 'would not help with industrialised cooperation generally in Europe'. It was a difficult situation in light of Britain having joined the European Common Market. Others thought the case for British Airways buying Boeing aircraft made more commercial sense, and there were some officials in the Treasury who thought that Airbus was just another public sector investment with the potential to go horribly wrong.

14,000 British jobs were at stake with the engine manufacturer, and at the height of the summer of 1978 Rolls-Royce's lobbying actually succeeded. A cabinet committee that had been set up to investigate had decided to allow British Airways to order 19 757s with Rolls-Royce RB211-535 engines. BA took an option for a further 18 of the narrow-bodied Boeing 757s, a far smaller aircraft than an A300 and far more suited to BA's routes in Europe. The choice left no room in its fleet for the Airbus, and called into question Britain's future collaboration with the Europeans. BA's decision, backed by the Government, was unquestionably a defining moment for British Aerospace.

For Britain to buy back into Airbus it would depend on a 20 per cent contribution towards the billion-dollar cost of the new version of the aircraft, the A310. The huge development costs of the Airbus had been mostly borne by the West German and French Governments. Additionally, the French were insistent that Britain's Airbus entry was conditional on an order from the national carrier, British Airways. But the more commercially minded Germans were far more sympathetic to BA's position and felt that its decision to purchase the Boeing 757 rather than the Airbus was sound. Predictably, the French were livid with Prime Minister Callaghan's decision to allow Britain's national carrier to buy aircraft from Boeing. The French President, Valery Giscard d'Estaing, called the decision 'bizarre' and his Transport Minister, Joel Le Theule, stated, "We do not wish for the British to work with the European industry at the same time as buying American aircraft." A suitable alternative major British airline needed to be found as a matter of urgency. Relations between the two nations became very tricky. The French firmly believed that the British Government should have forced British Airways to buy European. The British Government cabinet committee took three months to eventually abdicate itself from the decision and finally allow BA to make up its own mind. Not that British Airways ever had any intention of buying anything other than the Boeing 757. The French were told that they could not and would not force it to do so. Airbus now had to decide whether BAe could still be a partner, or if it was, in fact, an enemy.

The hunt was on for a suitable British candidate to buy the A300. Laker Airways, tiny in comparison to BA and BCal, was the next best thing. Freddie Laker's career had been built upon trading in aircraft and their spares, so when presented with such an opportunity he was hardly expected to refuse. The terms on offer by the manufacturer and the British Government, desperate to save face, were far too tempting for Freddie. Airbus was providing a standard 25 per cent first loss guarantee, which meant if the planes were sold on they would take the hit on the first 25 per cent of any loss in value before the purchaser or their lenders absorbed any loss.

Under pressure from the Germans, who were fed up with the high costs of the project, of which they were bearing the brunt, the French capitulated and grudgingly agreed that Laker Airways would 'just about do'. The French and German executives from the consortium had set a deadline for the end of the month, beyond which they were unwilling to wait. Freddie was quick to make sure that the world knew he was doing them all a massive favour. Conveniently overlooking the BAe involvement or the fact that most of his fleet was now American-built, he snapped at government officials with classic Laker hyperbole: "It's a terrible indictment that I am having to buy a new aircraft built abroad ... rather than in Britain."

Rolls-Royce had been hoping that the Laker Airways A300s might be an outlet for its engines. It was a slim possibility, as Rolls-Royce was not on good terms with the French, who had always ignored Rolls; in turn, the French had therefore always been ignored by Rolls. Kenneth Keith, Chairman of Rolls-Royce, called the French 'too difficult, too tricky'. It was also unrealistic to put the company's engines on Laker's Airbus A300s, as it would have cost Rolls an extra $25 million in certification costs. General Electric's CF6-50L engines would power the Airbus aircraft, and from a practical point of view they would be interchangeable with the engines on Laker's DC-10-30s. Freddie had been only too happy to play GE off, telling the company that he had a very attractive financing offer from another manufacturer.

Publicly, the sheer volume of the Laker Airways Airbus order took the industry by surprise, given that at the time of the announcement the Laker balance sheet could not support such huge aircraft purchases. It showed assets of £44 million of which £39 million was attributable to aircraft. However, the accounts might also have shown that the airline was growing at a phenomenal rate. Revenue for the financial year 1977 had increased to £76 million – up by 46 per cent. Pre-tax profit at the financial year-end of April 1978 was £1.5 million. In 1977, Laker Airways carried 1.1 million one-way passengers, with 360,000 on the Atlantic. Laker hardly needed any more debt on its books. However, because it was Freddie, no one questioned it beyond suggesting that the aircraft could perhaps be leased rather then bought. One London airline expert told *Newsweek* magazine: "Any other airline executive making a similar announcement would probably have been accused of harbouring delusions of grandeur. But no one doubts that Laker being Laker is doing the right thing." Freddie was an expansionist who incredibly had grown his airline with virtually no balance sheet capital. Freddie loved using other people's money and he was quite proud of it. "It was pretty amazing what he was able to accomplish with a balance sheet that had virtually no equity," recalled top Washington lawyer Bill Barrett. Over-borrowed and under-capitalised, Freddie needed a deal that required no up-front cash. The deal that emerged seemed at the time like a gift, and Freddie took full advantage of the ongoing political upheaval between the British, French and German governments. Laker Airways Airbus order naturally aroused the question from reporters as to how he was financing the purchases. Freddie answered all the media queries with, "There is no way I am telling you how I am raising the money," which naturally triggered speculation of government subsidies.

Freddie believed that, because of his proven expertise, there was actually no risk in buying the A300s because he had always been able to sell at a profit any aircraft he had ever owned. He had a well-deserved reputation for taking excellent care of his equipment, and said, "Regardless of whatever happens, I can always put these aeroplanes to work; they can be flown anywhere in the world where there is flying to be done." Freddie had an abiding confidence that he knew how to make them pay even when a recession hit. His self-belief was well-founded on past experiences and it had always worked for him. Regardless of the many obvious downsides, Freddie's order for the A300s was in fact placed with good intent. He needed them for his European quest and naively assumed that he would be given a nod for the routes as a quid pro quo. However, to any reasonable-thinking person, Freddie's 1978 vision for the expansion of the Skytrain concept bordered on the megalomaniacal.

CHAPTER 32

# The Years that Rocked

## Enjoying the spoils

1978 - 1979

After the hugely successful New York Skytrain service's performance from its inception, the Los Angeles inaugural flight seemed like a disaster, although Freddie was quick to say that the terrible performance was actually 'on target.' Despite the hoards of Skytrain passengers at Victoria, and camped out in central London waiting for the New York flights, anyone wanting to go to Los Angeles could be accommodated immediately. On 26th September Freddie was at Gatwick for the LA inaugural and had to face some tough questioning from reporters, especially as the initial flight was only half full. One television reporter asked Freddie if he wanted to be sold out.

"No, I hope not," he replied. "I don't want to be sold out because ... well I want to have some empty seats because that is what really happens every day." Freddie was clearly struggling for an excuse as to why the much-anticipated first flight to LA wasn't sold out. "We have empty seats and I expect to go out with 100 empty seats. The public and passengers will say this isn't a big queuing operation. Other than a few peak days of the year we can do what Freddie Laker promised. We can go when we like and come back when we like."

His response was bizarre and it's perhaps as well that none of his managers heard this classic Freddie Laker hyperbole, skewed to fit the situation at hand. At any other time, if there were empty seats on a flight, someone would get an earful.

When the reporter asked, "How do you manage to do it so cheaply?" his response was equally trite: "It's specialisation. It's horses for courses."

The television interview made it clear that Freddie Laker's self-belief was so strong that he would say almost anything to demonstrate that whatever he did was right. Even when it wasn't. Even saying that going out with 100 empty seats was OK.

Laker Airways' Los Angeles Skytrain service began just as Freddie had insisted, using the 345-seat DC-10-10 with a planned en route stop in Bangor, Maine, in both directions. Laker had been using Maine's premier airport for years as its transit point to Los Angeles, Oakland, Calgary and Vancouver. In the days before longer-range aircraft, Bangor was a very busy airport, handling most of the European and American airlines serving North America's West Coast cities. Laker crews enjoyed the layovers there at the Stable Inn, which was the scene of many a good party, as there wasn't a lot to do, especially in winter. Occasionally a crew had to be repositioned from Bangor to New York or Toronto for another flight schedule, and Laker had typically used the local commuter airline, Bar Harbor Airlines, which operated 15-passenger Beech 99s. However, in May 1978 the airline suffered a fatal crash that killed the company's founder. From that point on, Laker's captains refused to fly on small commuter planes, with good reason.

One of the operational problems of the Bangor transit was immediately highlighted when the LA Skytrain service commenced. Due to the low initial eastbound passenger loads from Los Angeles, the DC10-10 would often be able to make it to Gatwick non-stop. Sometimes this wasn't known until they were en route, so occasionally a crew in full uniform would be waiting at Bangor to take over the flight, only to be told that it had overflown and they had to go back to the Stable Inn. The overflights created all manner of problems for Laker's crew rostering department, but the crew members were often able to use the extended layover to enjoy the stunningly picturesque area of Maine, nearby Bar Harbor, Acadia National Park and Cadillac Mountain. Had anyone thought about it, Bangor could have been a popular destination in itself, especially for fly-drive vacations to explore New England. Sadly, as more and more airlines, including Laker, bought long-range aircraft, the magnificent Bangor Airport was only used for weather diversions and an occasional splash of fuel en route to New York.

After gaining the LA rights, Laker Airways only suffered one serious knock-back in 1978. In October the Australian Transport Minister advised the Australian Government against allowing ABC flights to Sydney and Melbourne. This effectively blocked Laker Airways from flying the 'Kangaroo Route' between the UK and Australia even on a modest charter basis. The ruling was a serious blow to Freddie's 'down under' objectives, but he vowed that Laker would fly there one day regardless, and ordered Beckman to appeal immediately.

Emboldened by the success of Skytrain, Freddie kept up his attacks on the protectionism of the global airline industry, with the CAB in Washington giving him an open forum to do so. Opening on 22nd October 1978, the CAB held public anti-IATA hearings to allow opponents and supporters of its plans to give evidence as to whether the CAB should remove antitrust immunity from IATA's member airlines. The opening session was a confrontation between the Director General of IATA, Knut Hammarskjold, and of course Freddie Laker. It was a little ironic, as Freddie and John Jones had just engaged in an illegal, clandestine meeting with representatives from British

Airways to discuss fares. Coming off the back of 'Lakerville' and the chaos it had created, it was decided among the carriers that a solution had to be reached to somehow stop it happening again.

Freddie's opponents saw the CAB's action as an attempt to impose US free market ideals on the world, which would have detrimental effects on their flag carriers – ideals that Freddie epitomised as much as he did the American dream, a man from humble beginnings who through his own hard work and determination had achieved success, fame and fortune. Freddie Laker had beaten the cartels that had tried so hard to stop him. He had faced down two governments, one in the highest court in the land. Now he was the glowing public example of the virtues of cheap airfares that the CAB was only too happy to present. Freddie was happy to oblige the CAB and join in its offensive against IATA. Before he left for Washington, Freddie said, "IATA has no useful part to play in any sphere." Influential US voices railed against the CAB, including Secor Browne, its former chairman, who warned that "the appearance, as witnesses, of officials of airlines which are government entities in other sovereign nations before a quasi-judicial body of the US government is, at best, creating resentment abroad and, at worst, risking serious retaliatory action by the offended governments against US carriers." The end result of the hearings was that the CAB was happy to accept IATA as nothing more than a trade association with a second level of membership that could include US carriers. This forced the likes of Pan Am out of the organisation. Before long, IATA would be rallying its member airlines and their governments to lobby the Americans to change their stance.

On 24th October 1978, President Jimmy Carter signed into law the Airline Deregulation Act. This historic piece of legislation removed governmental control of previously regulated domestic airfares, routes, new airline licensing and a number of other constraints. The Act essentially stripped the 40-year-old Civil Aeronautics Board of its powers over US domestic civil aviation. The CAB's bureaucratic complacency had often hindered licensing, as Laker Airways had experienced in the years before Skytrain had been finally approved by President Carter. The Deregulation Act was met with mixed reviews from industry analysts, some of whom felt that it would bring about the demise of many major US carriers. Laker Airways' Washington-based licensing attorney, Bob Beckman, surprisingly didn't agree wholeheartedly with the Deregulation Act when Freddie called him to enthuse about it. However, Beckman was careful not to be too negative about the Act to Freddie, who was the supreme 'de-regulator' – instead he simply cautioned that there would inevitably be some fall-out. It was an accurate assessment.

Just as Freddie had predicted in the years leading up to Skytrain's approval, the overall North Atlantic market appeared to have been stimulated, and the fear of diversion from the IATA carriers was, as he had said time and time again, unfounded. The total passengers carried by IATA airlines on the North Atlantic was up by 11.4 per cent in 1978 based on the same period in 1977. Freddie had also predicted correctly that Skytrain would not divert traffic from Laker Airways main IATA competitors. Worldwide scheduled air traffic had risen by

19 per cent. Bob Beckman highlighted this in Laker's future route application documents, with pages of statistics to prove the point. However, charter traffic, as also predicted, dramatically fell by nine per cent on the North Atlantic, as passengers slid across to Laker's Skytrain and the legacy carriers' Budget and Standby fares. It spelled the end for many of the independent charter operators. With the advent of Laker's Skytrain and the competitive low fares offered by Laker's main competitors, the charter operators' passenger numbers collapsed.

Freddie and Beckman had overlooked the diversionary effect on the main charter airlines of Britain and the USA. Skytrain had inadvertently been the cause of the ultimate downfall of some iconic names in civil aviation. Skytrain and its competitors' low fares on scheduled services also negatively affected the various consolidators (bucket shops) who specialised in selling transatlantic charter tickets. Notwithstanding, Laker Airways' North Atlantic ABC traffic to prime eastern cities in North America such as Toronto, Montreal and Halifax, as well as New York, due to the secure advance booking and fixed dates of travel, had somehow bucked the overall downward trend and was still increasing. Laker's Advance Booking Charter business was highly profitable and operationally efficient. The DC-10-10 aircraft was perfect for the job.

The diversion from the supplemental airlines may well have dispelled the concept of the mythical 'forgotten man' not being catered for by either the scheduled airlines or the charter carriers. What Laker's Skytrain service unquestionably did was to allow almost anyone to travel when they wanted at a price they could afford. They could get on a flight at the last minute without financial penalty, even if there was some inconvenience and they had to wait for the next flight or the one after that... or sometimes even the one after that as well. Freddie himself said, "I think the average person is sick and tired of being coddled out of their mind. They want to be left to make their own decisions and to some extent look after themselves." Another thing he was right about was that when the fares were slashed, the passengers followed.

Sir Freddie was now having the time of his life. During 1978 he was named that year's Man of the Year by numerous organisations. He had many honours bestowed upon him, including an honorary Doctorate from the University of Manchester Institute of Science & Technology (UMIST). He was also made a member of the prestigious Wings Club, the 'premier global society of aviation professionals' with its headquarters in New York. Sir Freddie was then elected for membership of the exclusive Jockey Club, an accolade of which he was incredibly proud. "There's no doubt it is harder to become a member of the Jockey Club than get a knighthood," he quipped. He was also made an honorary steward of the Lingfield racecourse in Surrey.

Freddie was no stranger to being financially in Britain's upper echelon and living very comfortably, and by his own admission he moved in both high and low circles. In addition to his primary residence of Furzegrove Farm in Chailey, Sussex, he owned Woolgars, a large working farm bought in 1964 where he grew wheat and barley. He raised Hereford cattle, sheep and poultry, including a few turkeys that he would send as gifts to his closest associates at Christmas. He also owned the 72-acre Woodcote Stud adjacent to Epsom Downs and bounded by Epsom Common. The whitewashed building, with red doors and black frames, comprised stabling for more than 40 racehorses. Woodcote was home to Freddie's thoroughbreds, and his yearlings would regularly be consigned to the Newmarket sales. Freddie named his horses after the Laker group's businesses, including 'Go Skytrain', 'Go Arrowsmith', 'Manchester Skytrain' and 'Skytrain Hostess'. Freddie now owned more than 1,000 acres of British countryside and often said that, "Basically I'm just a country boy."

Freddie's tycoon-level lifestyle was remarkable considering that he didn't take any dividends or salary from Laker Airways. Instead, he used his previously earned and smartly invested profits from the Berlin Airlift, and the sale of Air Charter and Aviation Traders. His other assets were paid for by the airline, including the 20-metre Italian-designed motor yacht called 'Tutinela', which was berthed in Majorca. Freddie loved boats and owned one for most of his adult life. "Aeroplanes are just an aluminium tube that you can use to make money. You can't love them the way you do a boat," he would say, usually followed by, "I'm in the airline business because sailors don't earn enough money to buy boats."

'Tutinela' was taken care of by Pablo Palmerini, an Italian sailor who also doubled as the ship's cook. Pablo was a bit of a playboy and Freddie was influenced by some of his first mate's more adventurous exploits with the opposite sex. Fortunately this hadn't landed Freddie in any hot water or made headlines in the taboids. 'Tutinela' had been named for Freddie's second wife, Rosemary, whom he had always called 'Tutin' – she had a striking resemblance to famed actress Dorothy Tutin – combined with the name of his daughter Elaine. This was a Freddie Laker tradition, except for his first boat, which he had called 'King', more than likely named for himself. His second vessel, 'Kevella', was a combination of his children's names, Kevin and Elaine. With the success of the Skytrain service he had ordered a new larger yacht, a 27-metre Italian-built steel-hulled Benetti motor yacht that he named 'Patrina' after his wife Patricia and her teenage daughter Bettina. Freddie's naming of his yachts reflected the fickleness of his affections for the women in his life. He had grown especially close to his 15-year-old stepdaughter and was by now seriously considering adopting her.

Freddie loved his luxury cars and almost from the beginning of his time as an entrepreneur he'd had the latest model of Rolls-Royce. In the late 1970s a white Silver Shadow with the personalised number plate FAL 1 was his company car. It was the latest of more than two dozen Rolls-Royces he had owned. Freddie always said he made money on each one when he traded it in each year, but no one believed him. It was more likely Freddie Laker hyperbole to perhaps justify the extravagance. He rarely drove the Rolls himself and typically sat in the front passenger seat unless he was working or had given a lift to one of his cabin crew. He'd then switch to the back seat so he could flirt with the young woman, who would likely be star-struck from being given a lift by the boss, then tell everyone on the flight about the experience.

Freddie's Rolls-Royces were also regularly used to ferry crews to the Gatwick ramp from the offices, usually with an engineer or an Ops guy driving. Greg

Dix recalls: "One time we stuffed almost an entire 707 crew with their bags into the old man's Rolls to get them to the aircraft and avoid a delay. When we arrived at the gate, the passengers had already assembled and watched in disbelief from the concourse windows as the crew about to take them to Canada literally fell out of the Rolls in a dishevelled state, laughing hysterically." Freddie often disparagingly said of the company Rolls-Royce, "It's just a four-wheeled fornicatorium," even in interviews, as a way of down-playing his wealth and status and perpetuating his 'working class hero' public persona.

Since his time as Managing Director of BUA, Freddie had always had a chauffeur, the latest of whom was the hugely popular Harry Freeman. Harry's wife Rita was the Laker family's housekeeper. His former chauffeur, Stan Abnett, who had driven Freddie for two decades, was switched to a less demanding role after a serious illness, managing the Laker uniforms department. Abnett was always treated as one of the family, as was Freeman afterwards. When Abnett retired in September 1968, Freddie bought him a small house in Guildford.

In the early years of Laker Airways, Freddie treated his staff like his family. When Robbie Robinson came down with meningitis and his wife came down with glandular fever he sent the Rolls-Royce to ferry them around and collect the children from school. Robinson only half jokes when he remembers, "He didn't bring any files to my hospital bed."

As an employer, Freddie was as equitable with his employment policy as he was with the passengers his airline attracted, except for perhaps one area he was hung up on, and that was mostly a generational issue. Despite his loyalty to many of his old guard from BUA and even before that, Freddie was a believer that you employed the best people for the job, irrespective of anything else. During a visit to New York, while meeting with Greg Dix and Linda Earls at the JFK offices, he was clearly stunned when a well-dressed handsome black man was shown in and introduced himself as the JFK Airport Affirmative Action Committee representative. "What the hell is affirmative action?" he asked. The man explained that it was his job to ensure that airlines operating at JFK, especially foreign carriers, employed a certain quota of minorities. And if they didn't, they would have a short amount of time to make up the numbers to an acceptable level. Freddie looked at Dix and Earls for clarity as he had never heard of such a thing and was about to give the visitor a piece of his mind.

Earls tactfully ushered the man out of her office and into the general area where she pointed at the employee roster board and went down the list of names while calling out their nationality or ethnic affiliation. Freddie and Dix followed her to see what it was all about. "So in summary," Earls concluded to the man from the Affirmative Action committee, "we have 34 staff of which 22 are women. We have six black Americans, four Puerto Ricans, three Cubans, six Jews, eight gay men, one of whom is perhaps undecided, and our most dominant minority of all – two English men," looking over at Dix with a smirk to make the point.

After Earls had finished her discourse for the man from JFK's Affirmative Action Committee, Freddie picked up the baton, turned to the young man and said, "See, we have more bloody minorities than any quota. Now bugger off and don't come here again."

Freddie had winced when he heard how many gay men they had at JFK. He had fought like mad to fend off hiring male cabin staff as long as he could. The group's solicitor, Christopher Brown, recalls that the initial interviews for male cabin staff were a sham, as there was really no intention of hiring any men on the boss's strict instructions. However, after Freddie had been told he may be breaking the law, he reluctantly allowed Joy Poirrier's cabin services department to employ a small quota of males. He instructed the crew rostering department to "try and keep it at just one per flight". He still smarted from the BUA days where he disapproved of the male cabin staff; he thought they were responsible for stealing from the bar and other misdeeds. Freddie was of a generation and an upbringing that encouraged 'men to be men'.

On one occasion he was incensed that his passengers had been exposed to what he obviously considered a serious internal problem. Greg Dix received a memo from Freddie on company letterhead, which his secretary Diane tentatively put on his desk with a suitably strong warning. Stapled to the internal memo was a two-page typewritten letter. The subject line simply said 'See attached', and hand-written in scrawling black ink rather than typed by his secretary, it simply said, 'Dix, the fucking queers are out of control. Get it sorted. Freddie.' The attached letter was from a passenger who had apparently arrived at JFK only to witness what she described as an 'outlandish display of homosexual behaviour by Laker employees', followed by how she had to endure a delay disembarking from the aircraft while 'your staff chatted to each other like giggling schoolgirls about Gucci handbags, paying no attention to the passengers.' It was no secret that a sizeable portion of Laker's JFK and LAX male passenger service agents were gay. It was similarly no secret that some of Laker Airways' new stewards who flew on the aircraft were of a similar orientation. Almost without exception they were exemplary at their jobs, giving Laker's customers extraordinary levels of service and attention. However, in the 1970s, gays of both genders were discriminated against in many fields of employment; fortunately the airline industry wasn't one of them. Despite its conservative, homophobic Managing Director's disapproval, Laker Airways was inadvertently a moderniser with its liberal attitude towards employees of different sexual orientations.

The knighthood and all the accolades Freddie had received in 1978 gave him a spring in his step like never before. Flushed with the overall success of Skytrain, Freddie was perfectly poised for a dizzying expansion of Laker Airways. The British public felt as if they knew him personally – he was their champion. He was often on a Laker Airways plane travelling back and forth across the Atlantic, typically at the back of the aircraft chatting with the passengers, or 'chatting up' someone who had caught his eye. It made them feel special and helped any who perhaps had a fear of flying. If he made an announcement over the plane's PA system, the entire plane full would always clap and cheer. Like an actor or a rock star, Freddie needed to be applauded, acknowledged and adored. Despite all his outgoingness and supreme self-confidence, deep down

Freddie Laker was actually quite insecure.

As 1978 came to a close, Laker Airways added two new routes to its network, flying from Boston and Baltimore to Barbados on behalf of International Caribbean Airways. The routes had become available and, without anyone conducting a thorough feasibility study on whether they were commercially viable, Freddie insisted that the services be added. He saw it as a way to penetrate the lucrative Caribbean market from the USA that Laker Airways would never be permitted to operate, and with a Barbados-registered airline it was an opportunity not to be missed. Unfortunately, the marketing and promotion needed for the services lagged way behind the operational capability, and the initial load factors were extremely light. No one at Laker Airways had the time or the inclination to get behind the routes so, despite the enormous potential, they weren't expected to have much long-term viability.

Laker Airways was now the 'go to' airline in the UK for many of the Asian and African carriers who had committed to operate the Hajj pilgrimage flights each year. For the 1978 Hajj, Laker's commercial executive Gerry Sharp had calmly and patiently negotiated a deal with the Malaysian Airlines System (MAS) for a wet-lease of two Laker DC-10-10s to operate the Hajj from Kuala Lumpur to Jeddah. The operation went without a hitch and the Malaysians were thrilled with Laker's aircraft, ground support, crews and in-flight service. Upon returning from Malaysia, Sharp, who had managed the two phases of the Hajj, immediately had MAS sign up for the following year.

The much-vaunted Los Angeles Skytrain service had a disappointing start, carrying 21,948 passengers between 26th September and 31st December at a load factor of only 34.3 per cent. As a result, the company swallowed a £2.5 million loss in its year-end accounts for the LA route. Some of the reason was in the way the service had been rapidly inaugurated following licensing. No one had had any time to catch their breath after the start of the New York service and what followed afterwards. Also, during the spring and summer of 1978 'Lakerville', on both sides of the Atlantic, had been a double-edged sword for the airline and had created negative repercussions for the new Los Angeles service. However, Laker's ABC flights to Los Angeles flown non-stop by the Boeing 707s had continued on a twice-weekly basis with high load factors. This proved that California was a destination requiring a longer booking term, and it was going to take time to develop the route for the more instant-booking/walk-on Skytrain concept.

The London-Los Angeles route was so seriously uneconomical initially as a Skytrain service that some of the flights had been combined with a New York flight. This again highlighted the problem of initiating a service prematurely before it had been properly evaluated and marketed, a point that more than one of Freddie's managers had warned of during the initial planning stages.

Overall, despite the poor performance of the LA Skytrain operation in the last quarter, 1978 was a successful year for the Laker group, and record revenues and profits were assured. But the financial success came at a price. 'Lakerville' and the queues of prospective Skytrain passengers in London and New York, with the resultant high load factors and with little or no advertising, was something every airline dreamed of. However, one of the downsides of 'Lakerville' was what it had done to Laker Airways' standing with airport management and other airlines. This was especially apparent in the USA where Laker was subjected to prejudicial treatment unheard of in the industry. On the one hand, the airports, tenant airlines and handling companies had the prerogative to refuse access based upon the (legitimate) fear of their facilities being overrun by prospective Laker passengers camping out for days. On the other, Laker had been duly licensed by the respective governments and had rights of access to the designated airports for its scheduled Skytrain service: London Gatwick (LGW) in the UK, New York's JFK, and Los Angeles International Airport (LAX). Laker's Washington lawyer, Bob Beckman, was asked to resolve the problem.

It was now clear that the original Skytrain business model was unsustainable in its original form and some drastic changes to its 'terms and conditions' were needed on both sides of the Atlantic. Following the secret meetings earlier with British Airways, Freddie had formally applied to the CAA for a rollover system so that no one would have to wait in line for more than a day. More significantly, as Laker Airways was still using a 1977-based fare schedule, Freddie asked for an increase in that too. "We could do with some extra money as well, and so could they," he chirped in an aside to the competition that was haemorrhaging money trying to compete with him.

By 1979 Laker Airways was making moves towards becoming an almost conventional fully scheduled service. It was flying the latest wide-body jets on the most competitive air routes in the world. Laker had stepped up its game considerably and now a host of entirely new functions, systems and procedures were needed. Many of the growth pains and problems that had faced them before Skytrain started were now highlighted and had become an even greater strain on resources and personnel. The management of what had been a modest charter airline only a year before now had to somehow deal with the enormous operational and administrative challenges that had been created by the indefatigable Freddie's developmental initiatives.

Beginning on 1st January 1979, United Airlines finally gave permission for Laker Airways to handle its own passengers at Kennedy Airport. It had taken a lot of negotiation and assurances to United that there would be no congestion or passengers sleeping in its terminal overnight. United was fully aware that throughout the previous year Laker's passengers had been camping out for days in nearby Queens, often with resultant lapses in personal hygiene, and this had been a matter of considerable unease to United since the start of Laker's Skytrain service. United was America's largest airline in 1979 and was extremely conservative. In its eyes it was like the Queen Mary while Laker was akin to a tramp steamer; Laker's operation was the antithesis of UA's business model.

On 19th January the CAA gave permission for Laker's 'rollover' system. Skytrain service seats for the next available flight could now be sold if all the seats on that day's flight were gone. This alleviated prospective passengers having to wait in line overnight, although an efficient precursor to the official roll-over system had already been implemented in New York. Within 48 hours of approval, Laker Airways put the system in place. The CAA didn't want a repeat of the summer of 1978 when thousands of Laker passengers were camping out in London and New York as the demand for available Skytrain seats dramatically outstripped supply. Freddie hoped that he might even tempt a few business travellers now that Skytrain had turned into what was being labelled a 'guaranteed standby'.

Although not quite an IATA-type carrier, Laker was now a far cry from Freddie's revolutionary 'walk-on, no-frills' experiment. It had been necessary to ask for the variation to counteract the predatory actions of the airlines attempting to drive Laker off the Atlantic. The competing carriers, in particular Pan Am and TWA, had been concentrating their low-fare quotas on New York and Los Angeles. Freddie said, "We need to be able to offer advance seat reservations so that we can attack our competitors' soft underbelly when they come at us with knives."

Despite his antagonistic public rhetoric, in February 1979 another meeting between Laker Airways and British Airways was held at BA's Victoria station offices to discuss fares. Freddie didn't participate as he recognised that any colluding could end very badly for him if word ever got out about it. So he dispatched John Jones to meet with Bernard Monks, BA's Product Planning Manager. While there, Jones was more or less threatened that if Laker didn't raise its fares and 'close the gap' to its competitors, BA as well as Pan Am and TWA would all match the Skytrain fares and drive Laker out of business.

It highlighted that by getting into the cut-throat transatlantic scheduled service game, Laker was now butting heads with some of the most experienced commercial executives in the world. By comparison, Jones, Laker's home-grown Commercial Manager, had little more than a year's experience in the scheduled service business and was somewhat at their mercy.

Jones's dilemma was that, while he could return to Gatwick and tell Freddie what had been threatened, the person he really needed to inform was Bob Beckman. However, he couldn't discuss it with Beckman as he knew the lawyer would strongly disapprove. Beckman would warn Jones of the consequences, which could include being indicted and possible incarceration under the USA's stringent antitrust laws. Instead, Jones kept the colluding and fare fixing with Laker's competitors between himself and Freddie, unwittingly jeopardising the entire future of Laker Airways.

CHAPTER 33

# On the Up

## More planes, more routes... more debt!

1979

In late February 1979 Freddie flew to Los Angeles on GK1. He was on his way to sign the purchase agreement for the five DC-10-30 aircraft he'd ordered and also to take delivery of the fifth DC-10-10 that bore his initials G-GFAL and was to be named 'Northern Belle'. No one was quite sure why he had chosen that name, but it was probably in deference to Laker's North of England operations. Arrowsmith Holidays, based in Liverpool, and Laker's Manchester base had been a great asset to the group for the past decade.

Freddie called Greg Dix to meet him at LAX. "Do you want to stay at the crew hotel in Santa Monica, the airport Marriott or down in Long Beach?" asked Dix, thinking his boss would probably like some female company and opt for Santa Monica. Freddie was still lamenting the closure of the Los Angeles Plato's Retreat a year earlier, which had engendered a quasi-obsession with the infamous sex and swingers' club. Fortunately for Freddie, Plato's in New York was still going strong and whenever he was in the Big Apple he cajoled whomever was around to join him for a couple of hours of voyeurism. Freddie always liked a good time whenever he was out on the West Coast, but as they had to be at McDonnell Douglas the next morning they opted for the airport Marriott and dinner with LAX Station Manager Ricki Walsh, who had worked for Freddie since the early charter days. Walsh didn't know that Dix had briefed Freddie that he may soon have to replace her, as her staff were on the verge of mutiny. Aware of Freddie's affinity, Dix wanted his take on it before making a difficult decision.

By the time the dinner with Ricki Walsh was concluded, it was already past 5.00am on Freddie's body clock. Nevertheless, he realised that the Carolina West strip club was just a stone's throw away up Century Boulevard. When the Los Angeles Skytrain had started four months earlier, a billboard located right before the 405 Freeway blared 'Welcome Sir Freddie Laker to Los Angeles'. Just behind the billboard, in flashing red and orange neon, was a huge sign that had 'Nude, Nude, Nudes' blinking rapidly and advertising the Carolina. The positioning of the Laker billboard adjacent to the Carolina couldn't have been more appropriate, and Freddie loved it. So despite the time and what he had to do the next day at McDonnell Douglas, he insisted they go and have a nightcap and some titillating entertainment to conclude his only evening in LA.

The next day they sped down to McDonnell Douglas at Long Beach in Dix's blue Pontiac Trans Am Avis rental, the powerful 'muscle car' provoking Freddie's obvious annoyance and trepidation. After lunch, he formally accepted G-GFAL. Standing at the top of the steps by the aircraft, Freddie could view the awe-inspiring sight of the DC-10 flight line and a dozen MDC tri-jets awaiting delivery to some of the world's most famous airlines. Laker Airways was now one of those airlines. MDC President John Brizendine asked if they'd like a tour that included seeing the sixth and final DC-10-10 destined for Laker, G-GSKY ('Californian Belle'), which was in its final stages of preparation before being delivered in a month's time. Freddie had already seen the main DC-10 production line in 1972 when he had purchased the ANA-cancelled aircraft that had put Laker Airways on the map, but MDC was now spitting out DC-10s at an incredible rate. Freddie was suitably impressed. When he saw a large scale model of the DC-10 twin-engined variant that MDC had proposed a few years earlier, he felt obliged to say, "We would have bought that instead of the Airbus A300, Briz," as he was still incredulous at MDC's missed opportunity at not building a competitor to the European wide-body. Brizendene didn't have a response; he knew it was a massive error. MDC made no secret that it had been disappointed at Freddie's decision to purchase ten Airbus A300s, but as he'd committed for five brand-new DC-10-30s he remained one of MDC's favourite airline bosses.

Before Laker's two new DC-10-10s could be delivered, a problem surfaced with respect to the Japanese financing. The 'Samurai money' racket had been exposed and the Japanese Ministry of Finance (Mifi) and the all-powerful Japanese Ministry of Trade & Industry (Miti) were at loggerheads over it. Their dispute threatened the anticipated delivery dates of the aircraft, so Freddie duly dispatched his English counsel, John Roney, to Tokyo. This type of negotiation was a far cry from what Roney typically did each day, but he was a gentlemanly lawyer whom the Japanese would probably embrace. Bob Beckman's name was kicked around on Laker's third floor, but the consensus was that he would irritate the Japanese with his combative approach. Everyone had believed that the finalising of the Japanese financing was a mere formality, only to find out when Roney arrived in Tokyo that Mifi and Miti had some disagreements. Miti had set aside the 'Samurai money' for Laker, but had not cleared it with Mifi, which actually held the money.

After some wrangling, the diplomatic and genial Roney won over the Japanese and managed to get the cash released for the two DC-10s. One of the bizarre stipulations of the 'Samurai' financing was that on the long-way-round delivery flight to Gatwick from Long Beach the two new aircraft were to make a rudimentary fuel stop at Tokyo's Narita Airport, thus technically conforming to the 'export' stipulations.

Before leaving Los Angeles, Freddie told Dix that he wanted him to go out to Hong Kong and Tokyo in a few weeks to begin setting things up for the London to Hong Kong and round-the-world 'Globetrain' routes for which they were applying. Noting Dix's questioning look at this directive, he followed up, "Beckman thinks these routes are ours for the taking and he's confident we'll get licensed." Dix already knew about Hong Kong as he and Bob Beckman communicated regularly. "And while you're out there go and see Singapore Airlines and get them on board to handle us for our Australia routes, and you may as well start things rolling in Bangkok too."

"Bangkok?" queried Dix. "What the hell are we going to do there?"

Freddie laughed, as he knew what he was referring to. "It's one of the dozen points in Asia we'll be flying ABCs to from Hong Kong." Laker already had the licence application ready to present to the Hong Kong Licensing Board (ATLA). "Call Beckman and he'll give you the low down."

And with that typically sparse brief on what Dix was expected to do during his first trip to Asia, Freddie boarded GK2 at LAX International Terminal Two and flew back to England.

Within weeks, Laker Airways had applied for a low-fare operation to Hong Kong via Sharjah in the United Arab Emirates. The application was designed to end BA's monopoly service, which carried only about 150,000 passengers a year. The Government of Hong Kong had long complained that the service provided by BA was inadequate and that competition from another carrier was needed. Freddie's objective was to serve the people who were denied the opportunity to travel between London and the colony for a reasonable price. This new potential market didn't fit into the discriminatory classifications of individuals that BA had singled out for special fares. Freddie estimated that up to half a million new passengers could be generated with his low fares, starting at £133 for a one-way Skytrain ticket, including a large ethnic Chinese market. However, Laker Airways faced stiff competition for the Hong Kong route from two other airlines, British Caledonian and Cathay Pacific, the national airline of Hong Kong. BCal applied for a three-class service to Hong Kong as a counter-measure to Laker's application, while Cathay was a powerful competitor and would likely object to Laker's application as a protectionist measure. Cathay was 60 per cent owned by Swire Pacific, 25 per cent by the Hong Kong & Shanghai Bank and 15 per cent by British Airways; it was well established to serve every prime destination in the Pacific Rim and made a significant contribution to the entire economy of Hong Kong.

In early 1979, the two Japanese-funded DC-10s arrived at Gatwick within a month of one another. G-GFAL, 'Northern Belle', arrived on 27th February and G-GSKY, 'Californian Belle', followed on 21st March. It was yet another interesting choice of name, as 'Californian Belle' would likely never fly to the Golden State once the DC-10-30s arrived. Laker Airways now had a full complement of six DC-10-10s and Freddie sold the 19½-year-old 707-138Bs, each with about 65,000 flying hours. He had much to be grateful for as these venerable old Boeings had launched Laker Airways on the North Atlantic, first with the Affinity Group Charters, then with the ABCs.

When the results came in for the 1978 financial year on 31st March 1979, Freddie was thrilled. Fuel prices had been stable and jet fuel could be bought for as little as 45 cents a gallon. This enabled Laker Airways to almost double its pre-tax profits for its financial year-end of 31st March 1979 to £2.5 million.

With the financial package still to be confirmed, and after six months of hard-fought negotiations, in April 1979 Freddie signed contracts to buy the ten Airbus A300B aircraft. In the latter half of 1978 Arthur Howes, the Airbus European Sales Manager, had installed himself in a hotel at Gatwick to work out the terms of the purchase. He later told author Stephen Aris about the tactics Freddie had used: "Freddie was adept at misapplying the rules of arithmetic to develop a price that was a long way from the truth. There was the aircraft price, the engine price, and the price of the equipment. He used to do his little sums. He would cover sheets and sheets of paper with these false calculations. He had a stack of them about that high by the end of the negotiations. It was wonderful. After several days of these rather difficult negotiations, I began to feel like I was being hit over the head with a heavy stick because it was the same argument all the time."

Howes responded by producing 20 identical sheets with his own calculations to hand to Freddie in answer to the ones that he was being given. It was stalemate. Reinforcements were called for and the remainder of the negotiations were conducted between Freddie and the head of Airbus Industrie, Bernard Lathiere, who flew in from Paris to take charge.

At their first meeting Freddie noticed that Lathiere liked to drink. So at the next rendezvous, which took place over breakfast, a strategically placed full bottle of the best whisky sat on the boardroom table. Sir Freddie was relentless in pursuit of a good deal that benefitted him the most. The weak position of BAe and the Government had not been lost on him. Freddie was an unsurpassed negotiator and his experience was unequalled in making a good deal. The two got on like a house on fire and Laker Airways' solicitor, Christopher Brown, remembers Freddie sitting on Lathiere's knee being bounced up and down having a great time while working out the finer points of the contract.

Freddie was given a very keen price and it was now just a question of he and Lathiere signing the memorandum of understanding. Freddie wanted it done on home turf at Gatwick, but Lathiere protested that he was far too busy and his calendar was full. Freddie suggested a date, Lathiere said he was expected elsewhere. Knowing that Lathiere would be under extreme time pressure, he suggested, "You will be in the company jet, fly into Gatwick, sign up and fly off." Lathiere reluctantly agreed.

As the documents were being copied, Freddie adjusted them – by as much as 10 per cent on some elements – just before Lathiere signed. Freddie was determined to at least get what he called his 'presidential 5 per cent'. Lathiere immediately noticed it but did not have time to argue about it. He wagged his finger. "Naughty boy, Freddie," he said with a laugh and a wink. Lathiere signed and flew off, thoroughly beaten.

Despite all his gamesmanship, Freddie didn't receive any discount on the purchase price of $42 million each for the A300s. He was paying the list price, but would receive a one-time credit of £8.468 million in March 1982, which was the difference between operating the A300 in lieu of the A310, the aircraft he would have preferred, although he did negotiate an option to convert the order for the last four A300s into A310s. He also always accomplished one thing that was completely unheard of, and that was not paying progress payments on his new aircraft; in general, these were paid prior to delivery and staged over the construction period, and might comprise a hefty 33 per cent of the delivery price. Invariably these stage payments would either be financed, or paid in cash. The Airbus deal was different, and meant that he would not have to lay out any cash or have a financing deal that would go on the balance sheet, or weigh the company down, before delivery of the aircraft. On delivery, when the finance was drawn down, it would cover the deposit as well as everything else. As the first British customer, Freddie received extra training for three crews for each aircraft; Airbus would normally include training for one and a half. He was also given letters of credit from Airbus for spares and ancillaries.

Alongside the Airbus order came a stunning announcement as Freddie made his biggest and possibly riskiest move yet. He had long set his sights on the European air transport market, and at the signing of his £250 million order for ten Airbuses, which had left the aviation world stunned, he fired off his opening shot. "The present European system of air transport is illegal and I will campaign for unrestricted air travel throughout Europe," he said. The Airbus order gained him a great deal of kudos and press coverage as well as early delivery positions for Europe's sought-after aircraft. However, behind the order was an astonishing announcement. Freddie was about to apply for multiple Skytrain services into Europe. He had been told by the Prime Minister's office that if he bought the Airbus he would be granted the European routes he so desperately wanted. That was the trade-off, and Freddie took the Government at its word.

His solicitor, John Roney, recalls that Freddie had a clear understanding that this was the case. "It was a stretch for him to buy them without a doubt, but in his mind it was a certainty that he would get the routes. He felt that the Government would support him at the other end of the bargain." Freddie was no fool; at the time much of the business he did was undertaken very casually, what he called 'the old pals act'. If he wanted to borrow money from his merchant banker, the Clydesdale, he would just go in and have a chat. When he could walk in and get a promise of $100 or $200 million on a handshake, it was perhaps not surprising that when someone from the Cabinet Office made him assurances, he naturally read them as a certainty. This admirable and unusual 'old school' quality was what made Freddie Laker so great. Unfortunately, not everyone did business Freddie's way, whereby a handshake over a pint could seal a multi-million-pound deal with no questions asked and no paperwork or lawyers involved.

At the time, aviation in Europe was the bastion of restrictive high-fare services.

The steep fares, capacity limitations and prioritisation of national flag carriers had long held back growth. Passengers had no alternative but to fly with their respective nation's airline. Every air fare for travel within Europe was disgracefully high; European passengers could up to pay three times per mile more than their counterparts in the US to travel the same distance. The European system was supported by the governments that owned and operated the major European airlines, many of which were linked even more closely financially to their governments than British Airways. They all vehemently opposed liberalised fare structures. Competition was excluded by their agreeing high fares at IATA meetings, which their governments automatically rubber-stamped. The fare levels were dictated by the costs of the weakest and most inefficient carriers that were protected by the system, and they used the intra-European fares to subsidise their entire worldwide networks. Even where there was the illusion of competition, carriers pooled their resources and shared the revenues.

Many believed the time was right for an airline with impertinence, a good lawyer and strong popular support to take them on. Step forward Sir Freddie Laker, for whom the bear-baiting of governments was all part of the fun. Guided by Bob Beckman, Freddie believed that the Treaty of Rome, by which European nations had created the European Economic Community (EEC), enabled him to operate Skytrain services at low fares throughout Europe.

Articles 85 to 90 of the treaty made specific provision for free competition. Freddie's view was that Laker Airways should be as free to sell an air service from Britain to Luxembourg as a British shirt manufacturer was able to sell his shirts in Luxembourg. Freddie threatened to take the British Government to the European Court in Luxembourg to prove it. Unfortunately for Freddie, the EEC nations had been known to disregard the court's rulings. A decision of the European Court of Justice in 1974 held that the general rules of the Treaty of Rome did in fact apply to transport. However, that decision had never been given practical effect and no legal action had ever been taken. Freddie had high hopes that he would be better supported if the Conservative Party was victorious in the upcoming May 1979 General Election, believing that the pro-competition Tories would be sympathetic to the opening up of European routes to lower fares.

Separately, Laker Airways made a third major route application. This was for the trans-Pacific route from Hong Kong to the US West Coast, including Los Angeles, San Francisco, Seattle and on to Vancouver, via Tokyo, Guam if necessary, and Honolulu. Route 6, as it was known, was a dormant route available to a British airline under the US/UK bilateral agreement.

London to Hong Kong and Route 6 together would enable a Skytrain ring around the world. Freddie called it 'Globetrain' and, as with the original Skytrain service, it was something that he had carried around in his head for years. It had long been an obsession; Freddie wanted to emulate Pan Am's famous simultaneous eastbound and westbound around-the-world flights, PA001 and 002. There was nothing else like it.

When advised of Freddie's latest whim, Finance Director Robbie Robinson felt that it was going to be difficult logistically. Undaunted, Freddie would not be put off. He told him: "Bob, I know the price – its $999 – but I haven't got a clue how we put it together." He convinced Robinson to make it work: "You just go out there and pull all the numbers for me. By the way, I want them for 11 o'clock tomorrow morning." Robinson got on with it despite his severe reservations. He felt that Laker Airways should instead be consolidating what it already had on its plate, and he wasn't alone.

Globetrain comprised operational and logistical challenges that went far beyond anything Laker Airways had addressed for the original Skytrain. Unlike the point-to-point Skytrain that emanated from London to New York and now Los Angeles, Globetrain comprised no fewer than six points around the world, each of which, if the licences were granted, would contain full traffic rights. In other words, Laker Airways would be able to transport passengers between London, Los Angeles, Honolulu, Tokyo, Hong Kong and Sharjah in both directions, and passengers could be picked up and dropped off at any point except between Hong Kong and Tokyo. The plan was to use the DC-10-30 aircraft Freddie had ordered, which would be arriving from December onwards. The overall elapsed times would be more than 51 hours eastbound and more than 59 hours westbound, due to the stronger headwinds. To achieve the objective of a daily round-the-world service in both directions, Laker would need six dedicated aircraft and crew bases at four downline points.

When the Conservatives under Margaret Thatcher convincingly won over Labour's Jim Callaghan with a 43-seat margin on 3rd May 1979, Freddie was absolutely thrilled. He expected to get more favourable treatment from the CAA and the Government for all the new routes he had proposed. The win made Thatcher the first elected woman leader in the history of the UK and Europe. Freddie's contributions to the Conservative Party's General Election campaign had finally paid off, and now he hoped to reap the rewards. For Sir Freddie and Laker Airways, things now appeared to be on the up and up.

## CHAPTER 34

# Tragedy in Chicago
## Applications for everything

1979

On 23rd May, Freddie's 80-year-old mother Hannah – better known as 'Gran' or 'Grandma' to senior members of Laker's staff – passed away. She had brought Freddie up single-handedly after his feckless father had abandoned them, so the two were understandably very close. He had cherished his mother all her life; when the third Laker DC-10 (G-BBSZ) had come into service in May 1974, Freddie had named it 'Canterbury Belle' in his mother's honour. When Hannah Laker travelled with the airline, schedules were juggled so that she could fly on this plane if operationally possible. When his stepfather died, Freddie bought his mother a comfortable three-bedroom apartment by the sea in Ramsgate. "He won't have me lack for anything," she was quoted as saying, while happily showing off cupboards full of hats and shoes, most of them unworn, all of which her son had bought for her. She had already suffered from two massive heart attacks and was ailing. "When she died, she had four shillings and threepence of old English coinage in her pocket and a betting slip. The horse was a loser," recollects a Laker wag. As an only child, losing his mum was a great personal blow, although Freddie's wife Patricia and friends rallied round as much as they could. Freddie found solace in his 16-month-old son, whom he described to friends as "growing into a strapping lad possessive of his daddy."

Just two days after the loss of his mother, while Freddie was at her funeral, another immense tragedy occurred, a disaster that had serious consequences for Laker Airways. At 3:04pm local time on 25th May 1979, immediately after take-off from Chicago's O'Hare International Airport, American Airlines Flight AA 191, en route to Los Angeles, fell from the sky and burst into flames. The plane plunged into an open field beside a mobile home park, destroying five homes, several cars and a nearby hangar. All 258 passengers and the 13 crew on board were lost, together with two employees at a nearby repair garage. Two other bystanders were severely burned. It remains to this day the worst air accident on US soil.

The transcontinental McDonnell Douglas DC-10-10 (N110AA) that had crashed was virtually identical to the DC-10-10 aircraft operated by Laker Airways. The repercussions of the accident affected Laker Airways immediately. The US air safety authority, the National Transportation Safety Board (NTSB), investigated the cause of the crash and found that at the point of the aircraft's rotation engine number one, suspended below the left wing of the aircraft, had separated from and flipped over the top of the wing, and had then fallen back onto the runway. Unbeknownst to the crew, the engine had ripped away a 3-foot portion of the leading edge of the wing and in the process had severed the hydraulic lines that controlled the aircraft. As a result, the outboard leading edge slats retracted due to the force of the air moving over the wings, increasing the maximum stall speed of the left wing. Meanwhile, the right wing, fully intact, continued to produce lift. The crew were unaware that the slats of the left wing had retracted and they had carried out a standard American Airlines one engine failure after take-off procedure that called for a reduced airspeed to V2, the minimum speed that must be maintained with one engine inoperative. A serious and unrecoverable asymmetric imbalance was created and, with one engine gone and a stalled left wing, the aircraft rolled to the left until it was partially inverted at 112 degrees, then fell from the sky. Barely 300 feet above the ground, the pilots had no time to recover; in any event, the electrical wiring in the wing was torn apart and vital cockpit instruments had failed.

Some senior and experienced pilots quickly commented that American's standard procedures for an engine failure after V2 may have been flawed. They suggested that if the flight crew had continued to build speed rather than reduce it, there might have been an outside chance they could have kept the DC-10 in the air. However, considering the damage the aircraft had sustained and that it all happened in less than a minute, any suggestion of pilot error was immediately negated. American's flight crews were renowned and AA's crew training facility at Dallas-Fort Worth International Airport was one of the finest in the world. Many airlines, including Laker Airways, used American Airlines for their routine simulator training.

Only eight weeks before the accident, during routine maintenance at American Airlines, the engine and the pylon that held it in place had been removed from the aircraft in one piece using a large variant of a forklift. The engine's shipping stand was used to support the engine on the forks. This saved the servicing costs of more than 200 man-hours per aircraft, as well as perpetuating the belief that fewer disconnections of wiring, hydraulics and fuel lines would add to safety. The aircraft's manufacturer, McDonnell Douglas, did not recommend this procedure, although the company stated that it 'does not have the authority to either approve or disapprove the maintenance procedures of its customers'. The removal of the engine and pylon on 29th and 30th March 1979 had not gone well. Mechanics had partially disconnected the engine and pylon, but for a period of time the forklift was not powered because it had run out of fuel, the pylon was found to be jammed on the wing, and the forklift had to be repositioned. The pylon's attachment fitting had struck the pylon-mounting bracket, and a fatigue crack had developed; over the eight weeks prior to the crash this had worsened to the point of failure on 25th May.

The FAA issued an emergency airworthiness directive to every DC-10 operator, to inspect the aft pylon attachment and immediately report back the results. Laker's DC-10s were inspected and proved to be undamaged. Two Continental Airlines aircraft were reported to have been flying with similar cracks, which had been repaired; the company's engineering personnel had been using a similar procedure to American and in the two instances had been alerted by the sound of the flange fracturing, which was 'as loud as a cannon'.

Despite the clean bill of health, of concern to Laker's engineers was that all the heavy maintenance of the Laker Airways' DC-10s had been sub-contracted to American Airlines at its facility in Tulsa, Oklahoma. AA, as with all the other DC-10 operators, was required to inspect its entire fleet of DC-10s for any damage after the Chicago crash, and the reports showed that only aircraft that had their wing engines changed with the pylon attached using the forklift operation showed signs of cracks. None of Laker's DC-10s had been subjected to the irregular maintenance procedure.

American Airlines reported to the FAA which of its aircraft had cracks and which did not. When the inspection reports came back, there were cracks in five or six American Airlines' DC-10s. American admitted that it had discovered a crack in the pylon of an aircraft that had been inspected not once but twice, and was found not to have any cracks. The FAA had little choice but to mandate that every DC-10 undergo a thorough top-to-bottom inspection until the type could get a clean bill of health. Then on 6th June, Langhorne Bond, the Administrator for the Federal Aviation Administration, withdrew the type certificate of the aircraft; grounding all 138 DC-10s operated by US-based airlines. He then banned every DC-10 aircraft operated by international carriers from flying in US airspace. In Britain the Civil Aviation Authority followed suit. Shortly thereafter, every European aviation authority as well as all others around the world followed the FAA's mandate.

Ironically, Freddie heard the news of the DC-10 grounding in the middle of a licence application hearing at the CAA in London. It had been filed in January for Laker to operate as a full-service scheduled airline without any ticketing restrictions. At the hearing, Freddie said that his airline had earned the right to offer a full reservation service on all its scheduled transatlantic Skytrain flights. Laker needed to be able to compete effectively against Pan Am and TWA, both of which were offering low fares on their New York and Los Angeles routes. Laker would keep the existing walk-on Skytrain fare and add an Apex fare with a 21-day booking restriction as well as a normal economy advance booking fare with no restrictions. Laker Airways also wanted to sell Skytrain tickets through travel agents and had asked for clearance to carry cargo and mail on all its transatlantic scheduled service flights. It was a massive departure from the original Skytrain walk-on/no-frills concept that had made history – and created chaos – just a year earlier.

The CAA officials quizzed Freddie for hours on how he would continue to serve his existing market while expanding his service. He had originally been awarded licences on the basis that he was creating a new market by offering cheap flights to sections of the public who could never have dreamed of flying across the Atlantic. But the fox was now in the henhouse, as Freddie would now be taking on his larger rivals directly as a competitor full-service scheduled carrier.

The final confirmation of the DC-10 groundings came just as the CAA official chairing the hearing, Raymond Colegate, was in the middle of cross-examining Freddie. Elgin and Ritchie, Sir Freddie's first biographers, described the tense meeting: "A CAA secretary slipped quietly in and gave Freddie a plain brown envelope. He opened it and glanced swiftly at the contents. Colegate asked, 'Do you want to read it out loud?' Firmly, Freddie read: 'The CAA has decided to suspend for the time being the UK certification of the McDonnell Douglas DC-10...' He paused, then added wryly: 'You have to do everything in these hearings.' Even under this enormous pressure he could still try to raise a laugh. The room fell silent as the memo was passed from person to person before Colegate suggested, 'Now might be a good time for a short adjournment for tea.'

It was coming into the summer and high season on the North Atlantic and, with no alternative aircraft except for its two 707s, the effect on Laker Airways was devastating. There was a huge penalty for not running six transatlantic flights a day, 83 per cent of the total lift of passengers was grounded and the airline was losing money at the rate of £350,000 a day. Laker was sub-chartering aircraft from wherever they could get them and cramming thousands of passengers as best they could onto much smaller planes. John Jones, who as Laker's Commercial Manager was responsible for scheduling the flying programme on a day-to-day basis without the DC-10s, recalls the chaos: "I had aircraft coming in from all over the world to carry our passengers, chartering substitute airplanes on a flight-by-flight basis to fulfil the programme. We were running an airline without any planes."

The grounding could not have happened at a worse time because Laker Airways' three major competitors were all flying 747s out of the preferred London Heathrow to the US. It was disproportionately damaging to Laker Airways as the DC-10 was the workhorse of its fleet. As a result of the crash of Flight AA 191 and the subsequent grounding of the entire worldwide fleet, the reputation of the DC-10 with the flying public lay in tatters. Moreover, it was the third serious incident involving a DC-10. An earlier near crash of another American Airlines DC-10 in 1972 was soon followed in 1974 by the Turkish Airlines Flight 981 disaster, when all 346 people on board were killed. There had been 747 crashes, too, but somehow the original 'jumbo jet' had managed to maintain its impeccable reputation. The flying public wanted to fly on a 747 and were naturally skittish, especially after another fatal crash, about flying on the DC-10, an aircraft that was assumed to have potentially fatal problems.

During the DC-10 grounding, Laker's LA Skytrain operation was forced to moved back to the West Imperial Terminal as Laker's Boeing 707s used on the route in place of the DC-10s could fly non-stop and therefore would need Federal Inspection Services upon arrival at LAX. Freddie told Greg Dix that he was to take whatever measures he deemed necessary to keep the LAX operation on track, which had now turned a corner. Aside from the terminal facilities problems, Dix also had to deal with a challenging personnel issue.

To avert a staff mutiny, he made the difficult decision to terminate the employment of the somewhat tyrannical LAX station manager, Ricki Walsh. It was a delicate issue as her father was the owner of Mercury Air Services, her husband its General Manager, and Mercury was Laker's ground handling and refuelling supplier at LAX. Mercury's base was on West Imperial Highway just down from the West Imperial Terminal where Laker's charter flights arrived and departed, and Laker's LA airport offices were located in Mercury's building. Fortunately, the turnover of station managers didn't affect the relationship with Mercury. When Dix told Freddie, he was typically pragmatic despite being saddened at losing one of his old-timers as Ricki had been Laker's representative at LAX since the Affinity Group era. Dix immediately replaced her with Patrick Holness who came from PSA and seemed to have the right background and temperament for the challenging position. The fickle LA staff took to Holness, one in particular. He earned their respect when the phone rang and instead of yelling for someone to answer as was his predecessor's way, he picked up the phone himself. He was also a Brit, so that was also useful.

The DC-10 grounding made headlines across the globe, and the bloodthirsty press speculated whether it was the end of Laker Airways. "No, of course not," responded Freddie, emphatically.

In the midst of the chaos, the formal application for Skytrain services in Europe was presented to the CAA in late June 1979, part of Freddie's assault on virtually the whole worldwide system of commercial aviation. His vision was that in 20 or 30 years time most of the world's high-density routes would be covered by similar Skytrain-type services. Freddie was oblivious to what the term 'Skytrain' meant outside Laker Airways, and it was a brave person who would dare to suggest that he and Bob Beckman should stop using 'Skytrain' for every route application. Freddie applied for permission to serve 36 different European points in 14 countries with his new A300 aircraft, at fares roughly half the existing economy fares. This included extremely contentious rights that, if granted, would allow Laker to offer services between non-British points, effectively sweeping away the bilateral regulations that governed Europe's air transport.

The points applied for ranged as far north as Stockholm and as far south as Las Palmas. Someone pulled out their calculator and worked out the possible combinations. Theoretically Laker Airways potentially had 666 new routes at its disposal, 36 from London and 630 other permutations. It was headline-grabbing but it was unlikely that Laker would ever be flying a route such as Corfu to Heraklion as a scheduled service. Even so, it was the most sweeping and revolutionary application submitted to the CAA in terms of both its extent and in the legal issues it raised. Freddie called it his 'massive interruption', by which he meant that the revolutionising of European air transportation was being achieved by a massive interruption to the status quo.

Thankfully, by the end of June the DC-10s were finally flying again within Europe, although in America it was a different story and the ban continued. Freddie described the difficulties: "The Americans were being bloody-minded, a bureaucratic machine took over and we had no idea when we would be permitted to take off and land in the USA again." As Laker Airways' two Boeing 707s were being used around the clock for Skytrain to New York and Los Angeles, DC-10-10 G-BBSZ ('Canterbury Belle') was repainted in International Caribbean livery and started operating between Gatwick, Luxembourg and Barbados with a fuel stop at Santa Maria in the Azores. It was a costly alternative but at that point the airline had no alternative.

Laker Airways was struggling from the consequences of the DC-10 grounding and having its fares targeted by its competitors, so in their battle to survive Freddie and John Jones participated in a third clandestine meeting with four representatives of British Airways. The meeting took place on 2nd July 1979 and they discussed their respective fares for the upcoming Autumn/Winter season. Freddie was seeking a higher fare differential, even if it meant increasing Laker's fares. They reached an agreement in principle but, as BA was also acting on behalf of Pan Am and TWA, it had to confer with them or risk the American carriers filing their own fares independently. Freddie pointed out to BA's executives that at that particular time Laker Airways didn't know when the DC-10 grounding would be completely lifted. Given the extreme circumstances in which Laker was operating due to the DC-10 situation, Freddie could have conferred with Bob Beckman to see if he could obtain anti-trust immunity. This would have allowed Freddie and Jones to then legally confer with their competitors, instead of continuing the risk-filled practice of participating in the unlawful fare-fixing meetings in secret.

On 13th July, following the investigations that indicated that the cause of the crash had not been a substantial design fault with the DC-10 but improper maintenance procedures, the FAA reinstated the type's certificate with the added clause '...removal of the engine and pylon as one unit will immediately render the aircraft un-airworthy'. The DC-10s were cleared to fly the very next day. To prove what had actually happened, Freddie had gone to the trouble of having his engineering department make a scale model of the pylon and another complete aircraft model made with the engine and the pylon, together with a model forklift to demonstrate what had happened. The government agencies involved were dependent on getting this type of detailed information from the airlines in order to write their final report.

Once the DC-10s were back in the air, the LA Skytrain service was set to expand with a second daily rotation, and more check-in counters were needed. The LA Airport Authority had erected an inflatable building on spare land next to Terminal One at LAX and insisted that Laker move in there to conduct its passenger check-in; the stigma of Skytrain and the potential for long lines of backpackers was still fresh in the mind. After some initial resistance, Greg Dix, who was responsible for the LAX terminal facilities and ground handling, reluctantly agreed. The LA staff nicknamed it the 'Bubble' and Laker had it pretty much to themselves initially. Operationally it worked quite well; after they had checked in, the passengers walked around to the gate at International Terminal Two for departure. The 'Bubble', while not optimum for Laker's long-term image at LAX, was light years better than operating from the West Imperial Terminal, which was two miles away on the other side of the airport. There were still a few months before the DC-10-30 would take over the LA route and fly it non-stop, necessitating Federal Inspection upon arrival. Laker's Los Angeles operation was finally starting to show some promise.

By July, Laker Airways had been granted all its licence revisions, allowing advance bookings to be made on its existing Skytrain services. From then on, 40 per cent of the aircraft was reserved for Skytrain walk-on passengers, 30 per cent for Apex, and 30 per cent for a 'Reservaseat' advanced booking, with a round-trip fare of £162 to New York and £249 to Los Angeles. This compared to British Airways' unrestricted economy fares of £207 and £307 respectively to the same destinations. Laker's Apex fares were priced at £204 to New York and £262 to Los Angeles. The Apex mandatory advance booking had been reduced to 21 days with a minimum stay of seven days. Laker was now looking more and more like a conventional scheduled airline, although it had a considerable problem with its reservations systems. Unlike its competitors, Laker Airways was suffering from growing pains; it didn't have the necessary scheduled service systems in place or, just as important, the management expertise to operate a network of full-service scheduled flights. Despite the term 'low-cost airline' being continually used to describe Laker Airways, the reality was that the company's actual costs were increasing at an alarming rate. However, Laker's new scheduled fare structure, despite there still being a modest differential compared with those of its competitors, was dependent on high load factors for sustained profitability. The long-term effects of the DC-10 grounding were still unknown; it was something that gave Freddie much food for thought.

By the autumn there were some encouraging signs that Laker Airways' application for routes into Europe was not a complete folly. The European Commission – the part of the European Economic Community charged with upholding its treaties – had been investigating airfares. In July 1979, it had issued a memorandum that articles 85-90 did indeed apply to air transport and intended to ensure that the principle was respected. Unfortunately there was a suggestion that, without further regulation, they had no rights to police and enforce the application of the Treaty of Rome. Several legal actions would emerge from the memorandum in belated attempts to clarify the rules. The laws appeared straightforward enough, and there was plenty of support for Freddie's view among some members of the European Parliament and in Britain, while the other nine EEC member governments enthusiastically backed the existing price-fixing arrangements. Contrary to the ethos of the European Community, they were determined to maintain their monopolies. Eventually, however, Freddie would have to take them all on in order to make his dream a reality.

In October, Australia's Transport Minister, Peter Nixon, was still resisting Freddie's charms. After much deliberation, he finally advised the Australian Parliament that he was not going to allow Laker Airways to operate its proposed ABC flights and that the UK-Australia market was to be reserved exclusively for Qantas and BA. One of the reasons he gave was that Laker Airways, by proposing to serve only two points in Australia, was being discriminatory in denying low fares to other parts of Australia.

Nixon recommended new low fares to and from Australia on existing services. A sudden spate of activity had arisen from Laker's applications, with both Qantas and BA having high-level talks in Sydney and the UK's Department of Trade meeting the Australian Government in London and Canberra. The result was a fares pact, one that agreed to a low-season round-trip fare of about £345, almost identical to Laker's proposals. To access the fares, which then turned out to be very limited in number, a lengthy advanced booking period of many months applied. The low fares were limited to Qantas and British Airways, flying their passengers on a third and fourth freedom basis, so as to shut out all competition. South East Asian carriers that had been operating under 'sixth freedom' rights, i.e. picking up passengers at each end and stopping off in their own country along the way, were deeply aggrieved. Nixon was rightfully given a hard time by the Australian press, the public and Parliament.

Freddie hit back in typical style when he realised his Australian dream was in danger: "The Australian minister thinks that the world is flat and has not yet heard that Australia has a number of regional carriers who now cover the whole of the country. The real reason that Australia wants to block our proposals is that the national carrier is treated as a sacred cow and just can't hold its own in the world of free competition." Freddie refused to withdraw, stating that he had no intention of taking back his proposals until negotiations between the UK and Australian governments on a new bilateral air services agreement, still under discussion, had been completed. Freddie added a further application for Australian ABCs to Melbourne and Perth, with a provision for full traffic rights to Singapore and Colombo in Sri Lanka. This application was carefully constructed to prevent British Airways from squeezing Laker Airways off the route by using up all the capacity in the bilateral agreement between the two nations.

Financially, 1979 should have been an exceptional year for Laker Airways. However, the DC-10 grounding put a huge dent in potential profits. The 5½-week grounding was calculated to have cost Laker Airways more than £5 million in lost revenue. There was also no way of knowing what the long-term effect would be with the decline of public confidence in the DC-10 aircraft. In the Washington offices of his law firm, Beckman & Farmer, on Connecticut Avenue, Bob Beckman, Laker's US attorney, was developing a legal action that could potentially recover some of Laker Airways' losses. He'd formed the opinion that it was American Airlines that was ultimately responsible for the FAA's decision to ground the world's fleet of DC-10s from 6th June to 14th July. Beckman took a special interest in Flight 191, the evidence surrounding the crash and the subsequent aircraft safety inspections. Beckman then consulted Don Madole, the USA's top air accident lawyer, former Chief of the Air Accident Investigation Section at the NTSB and a member of the Civil Aeronautics Board. American Airlines had been sued by all the families and

Madole was involved. All the new information on the crash was strictly confidential, and Madole was the one that had it. He agreed with Beckman; it was too far-fetched that the new cracks were simply unexplained, and it had to have been a case of negligent inspection. Their view was compounded by American Airlines' further failure to report to the FAA that it had been untrained staff who had performed its first two inspections incompetently.

Subsequently, Freddie went down to his hangar at Gatwick, climbed up a ladder and inspected the engine and pylon himself as Beckman stood by. Freddie had learned his trade from the ground up; it wasn't that he didn't trust his people, just that he knew exactly what to look for. They were seeking to determine whether an inspector could have failed to see the damage and the short answer was 'no', they absolutely could not have. Beckman believed he might have a legal claim for damages. It was not unfamiliar territory for Freddie; he had already made one successful claim over an earlier crash. In March 1974, Turkish Airlines flight TK981 from Istanbul to London had 346 people on board, mostly English rugby supporters returning from the Five Nations Championship. The DC-10's outward-opening left-side cargo door had been improperly secured and upon reaching altitude it blew out, the plane depressurised and went down outside Paris. There was a fundamental design problem, and critically there was a paper trail that showed the plane had been rushed into production. McDonnell Douglas was desperate to get ahead of Lockheed's competitor aircraft, the L-1011 TriStar, which it did by a few months. Freddie threatened an action against McDonnell Douglas over an 'undisclosed design flaw', and loudly alleged that he had been 'sold a pup'. No suit was ever filed, but Laker Airways did receive a nominal amount of compensation from MDC.

Through Madole, Beckman learned the real truth about what had gone on with the AA inspections. Madole knew that in Tulsa there was an A line and a B line for maintenance of DC-10s. On one of these lines the manager had decided that he could save seven hours on the maintenance time of an engine change by using the reverse engineering sequence to detach the engine. It wasn't that the cracks had suddenly started showing up – they had been there all the time. The engineers on the affected line knew what they had been doing and had misled the FAA. They had bought themselves a week to decide how they could control it, but quickly realised that 'there was no way to control this'. The fact that it had been only on one maintenance line and not the other was the slam-dunk. American Airlines had known what was going on. When everything came to light, the manager of that line, realising what he had inadvertently done, committed suicide.

Beckman rang Freddie saying, "Remember what we did a few years ago? We may have something again," knowing that he had a good claim against American for causing the grounding of Laker's DC-10 fleet. Beckman had done a brilliant job of sleuthing the situation and Freddie asked him to present his views to the company's board of directors. The Laker board voted unanimously to bring a suit against American for the multi-million-dollar losses, although Freddie insisted that they give American notice of their intention to do so. This

Beckman duly did on 27th October 1979. The industry was baffled when it was widely reported that Freddie was going to sue, but would not name the defendant, only that it would not be the aircraft's manufacturer.

"We have just posted our letter and don't want the people involved to find out about our claim from the newspapers; it's a matter of common courtesy," Freddie told *Flight International* magazine. Speculation was that it must be the US Government itself or the FAA under a 'right to fly' clause in the Bermuda II agreement, which had 'opened up the skies' between the UK and USA in 1977.

More than ever, Laker Airways now needed a successful Hajj, which could bring in many millions in incremental revenue at a critical time of the year. As a result of the DC-10 grounding, Laker's profits for 1979 would be less than £250,000, so the incremental Hajj revenue was never more essential. Gerry Sharp was once again in Kuala Lumpur supervising the operation. Laker sent two DC-10-10s to Malaysia with a support staff of engineers and operations personnel. Sharp told the Malaysians that Laker would have DC-10-30s for the following year; however, he didn't anticipate a huge increase in the wet lease rate. Nevertheless, it was obvious to Sharp that the Malaysians were being lured by more than one US carrier. The Hajj was also gradually moving forward due to the shorter lunar calendar, which meant that the following year's pilgrimage would now fall during the late summer. Each year the Hajj was becoming less and less viable as its dates started to compete with the Laker group's late summer holiday season. The 1979 Hajj made a significant contribution to Laker's year-end results, coming on the back of the DC-10 grounding and the resultant losses.

Ultimately in 1979, despite incurring huge losses due to the grounding, Laker Airways had been saved by OPEC. The oil-producing nations decided on a major escalation in the price of oil – the lifeblood of an airline – and the rocketing increase diverted the competition's attention away from Laker to their own survival. Instead of lowering their fares as they had threatened, they increased their prices to cover the rising cost of fuel, as their mostly Boeing 747-200s were notorious gas-guzzlers. The fare differentials to those of Laker were getting larger because the legacy carriers were filing for higher and more frequent fare increases to cover their rising costs, driven by the fuel price increases. By contrast, Laker filed to reduce its economy fares on the New York and Los Angeles routes in order to fill its planes. In the latter half of 1979 Laker Airways had acceptable differentials on its Walk-On and Super Apex fares, together with a very high differential on its Economy fare to New York. Freddie and John Jones knew that this advantage was temporary and would last only as long as oil prices remained high – then the gloves would come off again and Laker would be fighting for every dollar of fare differential.

Laker Airways' overall expansion in 1979 was quite modest. Laker had already overcome strong objections from British Airways to operate charter flights to Colombo, Sri Lanka. Many sceptics asked 'why Colombo?' Freddie was quick to point out that having a toehold there might help Laker's global aspirations, as Colombo was strategically placed to not only be a destination in its own right but also a viable transit point between the UK and Australia and the UK and the Far East.

From 6th November 1979, Laker entered the package holiday business to Israel when a contract was signed for a once-a-week DC-10 charter operation with Modernline Travel, Travel the World, Venus Travel, and Jaffa Holidays to offer package holidays to Tel Aviv for only £95. The contract was worth $3 million. Unbeknownst to Freddie at the time, it was his trip to Israel to close the deal that put some of his future plans in jeopardy.

On 21st December 1979, the NTSB finally published its full report on the Chicago DC-10 crash and confirmed that the improper engine change procedure by American Airlines had been the cause. There would have been no grounding of Laker's fleet, or the fleets of the other DC-10 operators that had followed the proper maintenance procedures if American Airlines had not been negligent in the engine change procedures of its own aircraft. While the NTSB report was somewhat reassuring, it did nothing to alleviate the public's fear of flying on the DC-10. MDC had hired retired astronaut Pete Conrad, the famed third man on the moon, to appear in DC-10 advertisements, where he lauded the aircraft in an attempt to restore public confidence. Freddie was quick to join in the 'Save the DC-10' crusade, but the damage was already done. The general public and the travel trade were naturally wary of the aircraft and no amount of cheerleading by Captain Conrad or Freddie would change that mindset.

Freddie had hinged the entire future of Laker Airways on the McDonnell Douglas DC-10. Restoring the confidence in the aircraft would be an enduring challenge. Regrettably, the tragedy in Chicago signalled a premature finale to one of the finest civilian aircraft ever built.

CHAPTER 35

# Global Domination
## The world according to Freddie

1979 - 1980

You could almost hear Freddie humming the Seekers' hit song from the 1960s, 'I'll Never Find Another You' – its opening lyrics, 'There's a new world somewhere, they call the promised land', were never more appropriate. If someone had thought about it at the time, a licensing deal could have been arranged to use the song in Laker's advertising. The song's third line, '...and I'll be there someday', could have been Freddie and Bob Beckman's mantra as they continued their ambitious quest for many of the most sought-after and protected air routes in the world.

Freddie's greatest obsession at that time was a route licence for a London to Hong Kong Skytrain service. The application proceedings had taken seven months to be heard and came before the Air Transport Licensing Authority (ATLA) on Monday 12th November 1979. It was being heard separately from the Hong Kong-Japan-US/Canada (Route 6) application for administrative convenience.

Freddie was, as usual, to be the star witness, and arrived in Hong Kong with his wife Patricia determined to enjoy himself. To that end, Bob Beckman had also brought along his wife, Angela. Freddie was in full flight mode: "This place is going to take off!" he said confidently as they arrived.

There was no permanent panel to adjudicate and its members were drawn from local business people, many of whom were affiliated with the Government. One member was the Managing Director of Shell, supplier of fuel to Cathay Pacific, BCal and BA. Freddie was immediately worried that these people had strong links to others who were against the awarding of Laker's licence. The Hong Kong Attorney General, John Griffiths QC, had already announced that it provisionally supported Cathay Pacific's bid to be the second carrier on the lucrative London-Hong Kong route. Citing these conflicts of interest, the Laker team successfully forced two panel members to stand down.

Freddie fancied himself as being a major player in the Hong Kong scene, but he was actually somewhat naive about it. He underestimated the clout of the Swire Group, which owned Cathay Pacific. Hong Kong was like being in Britain back in colonial times – in other words, more British than England ever was. Following a recommendation from Laker's Australian representative Athol Guy, Dr Freddie Watson, a well-respected Hong Kong gynaecologist, became Laker Airways' point person for the colony. Dr Watson was the senior partner in Hong Kong's premier medical firm of Anderson & Partners and one of the hard-partying 'ex-pat mafia', as they were known. He and his petite, attractive wife Jacqui were well-established in Hong Kong's elite society and moved in circles beneficial to Laker Airways' long-term objectives there.

During the hearing, British Caledonian's application was heard first. Lawyers acting for Cathay Pacific and British Airways accused BCal of presenting false forecasts, alleging that they were wildly inflated and exaggerated. Leonard Bebchick, BCal's lawyer, lashed out at Cathay Pacific for overstating its break-even passenger capacity. The second day of the public enquiry was as tense as the first, with the main protagonists lined up against each other. British Airways' lawyers claimed it would lose about HK$100 million a year with another carrier on the route. Christopher Brown, Laker Airways' in-house solicitor, who had accompanied Freddie to the hearings, recalled: "Nothing but lies were told at the hearing. British Airways, Caledonian and Cathay said that this market had reached its maximum of 100,000 passengers a year and there was no room for anyone else." Freddie believed passionately that there was a vast, untapped market and pointed out that all previous market projections were based on old, established figures and that no statistics existed showing the number of people who had not flown to Hong Kong due to the high fares. The Laker team dismissed the market research and statistical analysis undertaken by BCal, BA and Cathay as 'pure unadulterated rubbish'.

Bebchick focused the final BCal position on the political compromise that it had worked out, a three-carrier regime comprising BA, BCal and Cathay... but no Laker. Bebchick promised the Hong Kong authorities that if they licensed BCal they would in turn support Cathay's application to the British CAA. There was some doubt as to Cathay Pacific's position since it was not classified as a British airline, and the CAA could only license a carrier that was wholly or substantially owned in the UK.

The Hong Kong hearing closed on 18th November. Many weeks later Ross Penlington, the judge heading the panel, announced the decision. British Caledonian was licensed for four services a week and Cathay for three, while British Airways kept its seven flights a week. The ATLA rejected Laker Airways on the grounds that 'the Skytrain service was outside the terms of its reference', whatever that meant. So it was Round One in favour of the Hong Kong triumvirate, which perhaps naively thought that would be the end of Laker Airways' bid to serve the colony. However, the competition had underestimated the resolve and tenacity of Freddie Laker, who merely saw this first rejection as a way of strengthening his case next time.

And next time wouldn't be too long down the road. Before any rerun, however, Freddie and Beckman had business before the CAA in London. Just days later the CAA began what became known as the 'Great European Hearing', which now included three other airlines, BCal, Air UK and Dan Air, all proposing low fares to Europe. Adam Thomson, BCal's Chairman, called Laker's application an 'unrealistic proposal for a free-for-all network of 600 routes based on 34 European cities'. One BCal executive accused Freddie of trying to 'bomb his way' into Europe. The two airlines' opinions of what to do about gaining entry into Europe with lower fares differed vastly. BCal was taking an evolutionary approach that won plaudits with the CAA; it applied for unrestricted low fares to 22 destinations, and called it 'Mini Prix', but the fares would only be available on its lightly populated off-peak flights. Freddie's plan was to operate services to major hubs like Paris, Frankfurt and Munich at the most convenient times for business travellers. The gaps in the Laker schedule would be filled with holiday destinations such as Tenerife, Palma and Rhodes. Over the previous two years Laker Airways had carried more than 300,000 charter passengers to the destinations they were applying for and already flew to. The independent operation out of Berlin carried 100,000 more. If the application proved to be successful, this would lead to a massive increase. Laker's Airbus fleet would be in action for up to 15 hours a day on a 24-hour, seven-days-a-week basis. The lengthy hearings would run into the New Year, but the delivery schedule of the new Airbus A300 aircraft continued as planned.

By December the first of Laker Airways' five new long-range DC-10-30 aircraft, specially ordered to serve the proposed new routes to Australia and for 'Globetrain', in addition to the West Coast of the USA and Florida, was ready for delivery. Freddie called Greg Dix to see if he would represent him at the delivery ceremony. "Steve James is going to accept the plane and then fly it back, but ... er ... Robin has insisted on being there," Freddie told Dix.

"Well, you don't need me then," replied Dix abruptly. "Let her represent you – it's what she bloody lives for."

Dix did, however, fly to LA as Freddie had insisted, but stood at the back with Larry Raymond and others from MDC to watch the festivities over a glass of champagne.

The pre-Christmas 15th December handover was an elaborately staged ceremony at McDonnell Douglas's Long Beach factory. MDC's President had kept his promise, and the gleaming new plane was adorned with a giant red ribbon tied around its enormous fuselage – even Santa was in attendance. The plane was handed over to DC-10 Fleet Manager Captain Steve James by John Brizendine. As was the custom, 'Briz' ritualistically snipped off Captain James's tie as he gave him the keys to G-BGXE. The DC-10-30 heralded a new era for Laker Airways. If Freddie and Beckman's plans succeeded, Skytrain flights would now be flown to the farthest reaches of the globe.

After a couple of proving flights to JFK, G-BGXE took over the Los Angeles Skytrain service from the DC-10-10s on 1st January 1980. The second -30, G-BGXF, arrived on 5th January, with the third, G-BGXG, slated for February, The fourth, G-BGXH (named 'Florida Belle'), would arrive in April and the fifth and final -30 aircraft, G-BGXI, would be in service by June.

With imminent delivery of so many new aircraft, Laker Airways decided to rationalise its fleet and put all five BAC One-Elevens and the two 707-351s, which were relatively new to Laker, up for sale. Once all the new aircraft were in place, Freddie and Bob Beckman were anticipating a flurry of favourable licensing decisions for Laker Airways' global ambitions.

By the beginning of 1980, Laker Airways had increased its Gatwick to New York Skytrain flights to three a day. To accommodate the growing business an expansion of the Gatwick hangar began, effectively doubling its size, at a cost of £900,000. John Seear was once again tasked with the project management.

With the potential broadening of the US/UK Bermuda II bilateral agreement, Freddie made an application to Britain's CAA for Skytrain scheduled services from Manchester to New York, Los Angeles, Miami and Tampa; Prestwick to Los Angeles, Miami and Tampa; and Gatwick to Tampa. A service to Orlando was also sought.

The CAA proceedings on Europe concluded on 24th January 1980 and Freddie vigorously defended his plans. Laker Airways' statement in support said: "People fly three times less in Europe than in the USA since deregulation. This is not because they drive or take the train instead, or because incomes are lower; it is because the fares they have to pay are too high or so wrapped up in restrictions they are only useful to a limited segment of the market."

Within days of the completion of the 'Great European Hearing', the hearing concerning the London to Hong Kong route at the British CAA also came to a close. It had replayed the arguments that had been made in Hong Kong. As always, the hearings were a rollercoaster ride, as the parties presented their cases as to why they should be licensed for the prestigious route, often with undisguised hostilities. The CAA never really liked to see the aggressive and combative Bob Beckman before them; tensions usually flared when it was the turn of Leonard Bebchick of British Caledonian or Beckman, representing Laker Airways. Their performances were described by one of their colleagues as being like two rucking wildebeests. Their hostility to each other was a direct extension of the hostilities shared by their respective clients, as Adam Thomson and Sir Freddie Laker made no secret of their mutual loathing. But the difference between the Laker vs Thomson animosity and that of their respective counsels was that the lawyers invariably allowed their mutual dislike to play out in an important licensing hearing or a courtroom. More than once Freddie had cautioned Beckman that his aggression was counter-productive.

1980 looked to be a fantastic year. Laker Airways had already announced that it would be operating charters for one of its long-standing clients, Intasun. Harry Goodman, Intasun's principal, said at the time: "I have a good idea with these Laker DC-10-30s coming onto the market – they make new destinations available to us, the Caribbean, Florida and the West Coast of America, and I want to launch services to them."

Goodman was sick to death of the Spanish hoteliers that he was dealing with continually increasing their prices, and told them he would take his people elsewhere. He had realised that hotels in South Florida ran low occupancies in the summer months because it was so hot and humid in Miami. Typically the 'snowbird' North Americans only go to the southernmost part of the continent in winter. The Atlantic hurricane season starts in summer and runs to November, and that too is a deterrent for Americans.

The Brits on the other hand, anxious to have a sun holiday in the summer no matter what, would flock to Miami if Goodman could get the price right. He went to Miami only to find that most of the hoteliers there were not willing to drop their rates to the level he needed. However, he happened on one that would, The Shelbourne. They thought that he was mad, but agreed to give him rooms for $10 a night. Goodman knew that Laker Airways would have a spare DC-10-30, maybe two, so he called John Jones to do a deal.

"I want to launch services to Miami, John."

Jones said, "Fine, Harry – shall we put three flights a week on?"

The seat rate that Jones gave him was cheaper than the one he had been getting to Tenerife on a One-Eleven. It was to be a good business for Laker and a great start to 1980, but then came an unexpected blow.

On 13th March 1980, the CAA completely rejected Freddie's vision for Europe. Laker Airways, said the CAA, had failed to show that what it was proposing was economically viable. 'Laker Airways was, in effect, offering a map of uncharted territory in support of an application for carte blanche.' The panel ruled that Laker's case was 'a little thin'. Freddie thought they were wrong and that there had been more than enough evidence for him to be licenced for at least some of the routes. After all, hadn't he been told that he would get the routes if he bought the Airbus? Plucking a number out of the air, Freddie said he might have been happy with a dozen, or ... anything at all. He called it a tactical error by the CAA in 'not attacking the Europeans'. Bcal, on the other hand, was granted six routes; the CAA found that it had a better chance of being accepted by the European governments involved, and commended BCal's sensible approach. Freddie was told that he could return and apply for each route individually.

First came Freddie's inevitable appeal to the new Conservative Secretary of State for Trade, John Nott. It was a little surprising when Nott, who was openly in favour of more competition, turned down both Laker and BCal, who wanted more routes, and sided with the CAA. This went against his own previous comments and the mood within the British Government, which was beginning to lose patience with its European neighbours. Speaking in the aftermath of the French Government's out-of-hand rejection of a £20 'Channelhopper' fare to Paris, and on the eve of the CAA decision, Nott said, "I find it increasingly unreasonable that in all those areas where the British economy is highly competitive – banking, insurance, services, aviation and of course agriculture – we are frequently frustrated by the protectionism of our European partners. Yet in areas where we have temporary problems such as the motor industry, we maintain open markets for their manufacturing of goods." The trade imbalance with 14 of the countries to which Laker Airways had applied to fly, stood at a staggering $5,648 million.

Nott concluded that there was no point in approving licences, bilateral agreements notwithstanding, as they would simply be blocked by the European governments, thus making the exercise a waste of time. Nott added, "Freddie Laker is free to take the case to the European Court. Good luck to him." His own departmental lawyers had advised him that in the case of civil aviation, the Treaty of Rome did not apply and the rulings of individual countries prevailed. Freddie was scathing about the British Government's soft approach of letting the policy evolve naturally. "Trying to do it politically means they won't do anything and it'll come to nothing, like everything else done politically."

In 1980, there were in fact a number of political initiatives for change under way. The European Commission was sending out letters to governments and airlines seeking answers to questions on the relationship between them, on matters such as fare fixing. This was in response to legal action brought by Lord Bethell, who was a member of the European Parliament. Bethell had set up the 'Freedom of the Skies' campaign to force airlines into reducing their prices, which he believed were artificially inflated. The European Commission's earlier memorandum was under discussion, and in the summer the House of Lords Select Committee on the European Communities produced a report on European Air Fares.

In an echo of his legendary 'Skytrain' case, Freddie geared up to take the Department of Trade and the CAA to the High Court. He hired expensive counsel and began to devise a suit to test once and for all whether the articles of the Treaty of Rome compelled free competition in air transport.

Just days after the CAA's decision on Europe, Freddie had another fight on his hands when it announced its decision on Hong Kong. While it concurred with the Hong Kong authorities that the existing capacity and frequency did not meet demand, it gave the sole rights to compete with British Airways on the London to Hong Kong route to British Caledonian, refusing to license Laker Airways. In a decision that shocked all involved, the CAA also controversially ruled against Cathay Pacific. BCal's Chairman, Adam Thomson, was naturally elated at getting one over on Freddie, especially after Freddie had 'stolen' the valuable North Atlantic routes from under him.

The Hong Kong Government was appalled at the CAA's ruling, although British legislation at the time required the CAA to favour British airlines. The ruling had effectively ruled out Cathay, despite it being based in a British colony and majority owned by the Swire Group, one of the most respected British entities. As far as the CAA was concerned, Cathay Pacific was a 'foreign air carrier' no different from, say, Air France or Pan Am. Moreover, in anticipation of being a 'shoo-in' for the route Cathay had gone and purchased Boeing 747s, which were powered by British-built Rolls-Royce engines to give them compatibility with the company's fleet of Rolls-Royce powered L-1011 TriStars, the main competitor aircraft to the DC-10. Ironically, Cathay's proposed use of a high-capacity 747 was another key issue in the CAA's ruling, which concluded that the 747 would be inappropriate for a route demanding a rapid build-up of frequency more than capacity. The CAA considered that BCal's DC-10 aircraft, with less capacity and operating more frequently, were much better suited to a 'long, thin route' like London to Hong Kong.

Freddie and Bob Beckman had failed to convince the CAA that there was a market niche for Laker Airways despite the fact that, like BCal, Laker had DC-10s for the route. Ironically, no one brought up the issue of potential resistance to flying on the DC-10 in the wake of the American Airlines disaster and the resultant grounding of the world's DC-10s the year before. 'Lower fares will not increase traffic to the levels that Laker is suggesting,' the CAA stated in its ruling. Freddie had said that he would fly half a million passengers between London and Hong Kong in the first year of operation, but the CAA didn't believe it possible. 'Just because Laker has demonstrated it can fly a lot of people across the Atlantic doesn't necessarily correlate to London-Hong Kong, at four times the distance and a completely different market altogether,' stated one of the CAA's board members afterwards. The use of the term 'Skytrain' in the application had probably not helped Laker's case either. Despite the original 'no-frills, walk-on' Skytrain service being long gone, the name still had negative connotations and was a reminder of the chaos it had caused in 1978.

The two negative rulings on Europe and Hong Kong, however, did nothing to dampen Freddie's appetite for expansion, pushed along by Bob Beckman. Freddie had proved time and time again that he did not give up easily and would not be put off. He often joked, "I had to win that case nine times," before he could operate the Skytrain service between London and New York. He was not going to take no for an answer from the Australians either. He still had his heart set on operating to Australia. By 1980 three Australian State Governments, Victoria, New South Wales and Western Australia, were all strongly behind Freddie and they supported a new application to operate cheap fares between London and Australia. In April, all the different state tourism ministers met in Melbourne. Dick Hamer, Victoria's Premier, successfully urged all the other ministers to confront Ralph Hunt, the new transport minister, to allow a two-year trial period for a Laker-type service. Hamer intended to appear before the CAA in early June to make the case in London.

In the interim, Athol Guy, in conjunction with John Moore, Managing Director of Tour World International, had set up Laker-badged sales offices in Melbourne and Sydney. Ian MacIntosh was hired to manage the Sydney operation, and they sold Laker product to London via Singapore Airlines and bulk seats through Singapore's largest wholesaler. Some of the flights connected with Laker's Mediterranean packages. They also sold trips on Pan Am via the Pacific to Los Angeles, connecting with Laker's LA Skytrain service. At 14,000 miles, it was a long way to get to England, but the cost saving was worth the effort. Of greater importance than the revenue from ticket sales, which was not insignificant at AUS$1 million a year, was getting the Laker name in the Australian public's mind, long before Laker commenced flying there.

In the spring of 1980 the Intasun holidays to Miami were selling out quickly and Harry Goodman was filling all the capacity he'd been allocated. He excitedly called Jones: "We took 3,000 bookings today, John – I want to put another flight on." Three went to four and four soon became five. A holiday to Miami Beach became de rigueur, years before Don Johnson (as Sonny Crockett) and Philip Michael Thomas (as Rico Tubbs) put South Florida in the minds of millions with the hit TV show Miami Vice.

From 14th April, Harry Goodman's Intasun started to make serious money flying Laker's under-utilised DC-10-30 aircraft and filling up otherwise empty South Florida hotel rooms. Unsurprisingly, the Intasun/Laker London to Miami ABC programme was a smash at an unprecedented starting price of £139 per person for a flight and a seven-night hotel stay. It was the start of the Miami 'gold rush'. Sensing another opportunity, Freddie applied to convert the charter licence to a scheduled Skytrain service between Gatwick and Miami. This was easily won with no opposition, once BCal withdrew its own application, and Laker Airways' inaugural Skytrain service flight from Gatwick to Miami was slated for 22nd May. The CAA's Ray Colegate called the Miami switch to a scheduled service 'one of the more blatant pieces of transformation ever seen in air licensing'.

Unlike Skytrain set-ups at JFK and LAX, Miami was mostly trouble-free. Operations Manager North America, Greg Dix, had a much easier time setting up Miami. "We were given excellent terminal facilities without having to fight for them, the ground handling was being done by one of MIA's very best service providers, and the in-flight catering was by Marriott, who had a first class flight kitchen there." Laker was actually welcomed at Miami; it was a pleasant change from being vilified, considered a nuisance and prevented from performing the most rudimentary airline functions and services as at the other Skytrain locations in the USA. "The airport management couldn't have been more cooperative," Dix continued. "It was an entirely different situation to what we were still experiencing at JFK and LAX," Laker's first two USA Skytrain gateways, where they were still experiencing considerable resistance.

The flights to Miami took nine hours, so the in-flight service, food and beverages were an important feature of the flights. By the time the new Skytrain service began, most of the original bugs had been worked out. "We could now take reservations, we had a three-tier fare structure, a fantastic in-flight service, and we would soon have containerised baggage," Dix said. "The main problems we faced with Miami was that it was more seasonally sensitive than any other transatlantic route and we were relying 100 per cent on low-income British tourists. It was a bit like the Costa Brava in the sixties."

Laker's new Miami service clearly didn't tick all the boxes for a sustainable year-round operation. Realising this, Freddie asked David Tait to relocate from Toronto where he had headed up the sales effort for Laker Air Travel, Canada. Freddie needed someone experienced in developing North American originating traffic to balance the Miami operation and more especially to drive traffic in the winter time, when the Brits typically don't travel. Miami, as the de facto capital of Latin America, was almost exclusively bi-lingual and every Central and South American airline, as well as those from the Caribbean, flew to Miami. The potential for connecting to these Latin American carriers was limitless. Freddie told Manager USA Charles Maxwell that the mission of the new Laker Miami sales office was to stimulate traffic from Latin America as soon as possible. Freddie knew that by the time it got to October the typical

British holidaymaker wouldn't be flying anywhere and there would be lots of empty seats.

Once again, Freddie had initiated a challenging situation by impetuously and perhaps prematurely converting the Miami flights from a flexible, low-overhead charter operation to a considerably less flexible scheduled service. Once scheduled, Laker Airways was committed to operating the service come what may. With less than six months to generate interline arrangements with Latin American carriers, most of whom were already committed to Laker's competitors, Freddie had potentially set the airline up for a bleak winter. Whereas the New York route could be sustained with load factors in the 60s and even 50s using the economical DC-10-10, the Los Angeles and Miami services needed considerably higher load factors and yields in order to be profitable, as the DC-10-30's operating costs per hour were significantly greater.

The inaugural London to Miami Skytrain service, flight GK11, went to plan. All the passengers were excited and those who were seated by the windows gasped in awe when they had their first view of the clear turquoise waters off Miami Beach. As the wheels touched the tarmac at MIA, loud cheers and clapping erupted in the cabin and the atmosphere on board was festive. The Laker Airways DC-10-30, G-BGXH, the aptly named 'Florida Belle', had been delivered from MDC's Long Beach factory only a few weeks earlier.

One drawback of arriving at MIA in the evening was the simultaneous arrival of several flights from Central and South America, which meant that Immigration and Customs would get backed up. The 'Visitor to the USA' lines were long and the passengers had to wait behind those from several other countries. Moreover, visitors from Latin countries were given considerably longer scrutiny than their European counterparts – an unfortunate and possibly unfair side effect of the considerable drug-trafficking problem that existed at the time. Flights from Colombia could sometimes take several hours to clear, such was the magnitude of drug-trafficking via Florida in 1980. Finally, an hour after the plane had landed, the passengers started to appear from Customs into the arrivals area where Laker's Greg Dix and Linda Earls were standing to welcome them. Alongside was newly appointed Station Manager Joseph Strein, who had recently relocated from the New York operation, where he'd been the senior passenger services supervisor. The anxious tour operator reps were holding the Intasun and Laker 'Welcome to Miami' signs, while Laker passenger service staff checked in the small group of US originators, mostly travel agents who would head to London on the return flight. Miami was never expected to initially produce a large quota of US originating passengers. Nearly all available capacity had been blocked by Intasun, Laker Air Travel and a handful of other UK tour operators, so there weren't many (if any) seats for US originators on the eastbound flights for the anticipated summer season.

The passengers filing out of Customs into the landside arrivals area were easy to identify by their appearance, typically pale Britons with their unmistakable English accents. Then just as one group of elderly ladies was walking out, the distinctive sound of a high-powered motorcycle was heard screeching to a halt outside. The Terminal's glass doors then burst open and a man dressed head to toe in black leather, helmet still on and a mirrored visor obscuring any possibility of identifying him, ran into the arrivals area and drew a silencer-equipped pistol. The Laker passengers froze as the shooter took aim and released two sets of fast double rounds at a man coming out from baggage claim with the Laker passengers. Screams erupted and blood spattered everywhere, including on Laker's passengers as well as on Dix, who had been standing fairly close to the man who was shot. The shooter turned and quickly exited, hopped on his bike and rode off. Everyone stood frozen in shock at what had just happened. The tour operator reps and Laker staff quickly assured the shaking and terrified passengers that this was not a normal occurrence, there was nothing to be concerned about, and it was obviously another targeted, drug-related homicide. Surely this only happened in movies.

Welcome to the 'Sunshine State'.

Needless to say, the only person unhappy about the Miami Skytrain flights that had begun as ABCs exclusively for Intasun was Harry Goodman. He saw Laker's new Skytrain service as a threat to his Florida holiday goldmine. He had been credited with making Miami and South Florida the new Costa Brava, and he reacted by promptly cancelling what he could of Intasun's Laker contract and switched his tour programme to Air Florida, claiming that he would have better reliability, even though the cost was higher. It didn't create a problem for Laker Airways, as it immediately offered inexpensive package holidays through its integrated travel companies, Laker Air Travel and Arrowsmith, and attracted other UK tour operators. Goodman's decision proved to be short-sighted; he had simply handed the Laker capacity to his principal competitors eager to offer package holidays to Florida.

A few weeks after the harrowing Miami inaugural experience, Dix and Earls got married. It was all top secret and only a few key insiders knew, although it probably wasn't a surprise to most of Laker's New York staff. After a short, non-religious ceremony in the garden overlooking Long Island Sound, accompanied by the music of Led Zeppelin played in a classical style, the pair jumped on a United 747 and flew to Los Angeles. Dix had business meetings lined up and he had to accept the last DC-10-30 at Long Beach the next Monday. Freddie called him while they were in LA to see how things had gone at MDC. After giving him a detailed update, Dix informed him what had just happened. Thinking Freddie would be happy at hearing about yet another Laker union, as he was especially fond of Linda who had been one of his stalwarts for more than a decade, Dix was shocked at Freddie's reaction. "The old man just went ballistic," he said. "He swore at me using every awful name imaginable." Freddie had concluded his outpouring of vitriol by shouting, "One day I may forgive you, Dix, but Cliff never will" then slammed down the phone. When Dix told Earls what had happened, she piped up, "Maybe he's jealous." Seeing Dix's quizzical reaction to that tidbit, she concluded, "He once asked me to marry him and no, he wasn't drunk at the time either." As Freddie had predicted, things smoothed out quickly – everyone was far too busy to hold grudges and even Cliff Nunn came around after Dix had apologised.

In mid-1980, Laker Airways signed a contract with Pandair, the freight forwarding division of the renowned P&O shipping line, to act as Laker Airways' exclusive cargo agent. As Laker only had three scheduled service routes, having its own cargo division would have been commercially unviable, so Pandair agreed to contract for the entire cargo capacity on Laker's DC-10s. This necessitated LD3 and LD6 containers being positioned at Pandair's off-airport facilities at Gatwick, JFK, LAX and MIA. Freight shippers brought their cargo to the Pandair facility and Pandair did the rest. The cargo containers were sealed and loaded on to the aircraft about an hour before departure and before the baggage containers. Laker had begun its Skytrain service with bulk loaded baggage; now with containers positioned at all points, ground handling was faster, more efficient and baggage was less likely to be lost or damaged by rain or by being dropped.

With the CAA having rejected applications from both Laker Airways and Cathay Pacific to fly between London and Hong Kong, both carriers appealed against the CAA's decision to John Nott. Meanwhile, Hong Kong interests in Britain put strong pressure on the British Government to change the decision. Hong Kong's Governor exerted an unprecedented level of political blackmail by threatening to reduce the Crown colony's imports from the UK in retaliation for the CAA not granting its de facto 'national carrier' Cathay a licence. To his credit, and unlike many who held positions like his, Nott gave the submissions of the two air carriers due consideration, and on 17th June 1980 he became the first British politician to overturn a CAA ruling. He issued a mandate that would give both Laker and Cathay Pacific licences to operate the route together with BA and BCal. Nott announced this at a dinner given in London by the Hong Kong Trade Association. Both he and his junior minister, Norman Tebbitt, strongly favoured competition, so the minister decided to licence all three. "I will take a more dynamic view," he said, thus allowing all the carriers to make their own commercial decisions. He rejected the CAA's assessment that there was insufficient traffic on the route to support all four carriers, as well as the CAA's view that there was no such thing as Laker's 'forgotten man' on the Hong Kong route. It was controversial, as it was the first time that a CAA decision had ever been overturned by a government. Nott had effectively declared an open skies policy on the route. The CAA was particularly upset at the inferred criticism that it had taken a short-term view. As expected, BCal's Adam Thomson was livid and thought the ministerial reversal, which benefitted Laker, was only done because Laker was 'a poster child for the Tory Administration'. Laker's licensing lawyer, Bob Beckman, relished the prospect of having another round or two with his arch nemesis, BCal's Leonard Bebchick, who was probably thinking along the same lines.

BCal and Cathay Pacific started their operations to Hong Kong in the summer of 1980. By now, Laker Airways had taken delivery of all five of its brand-new long-range DC-10-30 aircraft, and Freddie was desperate to deploy them on additional long routes. He submitted a new licensing application to the Hong Kong authorities, as Minister Nott's game-changing decision had forced the Hong Kong ATLA into reconsidering Laker's application, and had effectively kept Freddie's dreams alive. He desperately wanted to operate the prestigious London - Hong Kong route as well as circling the world with 'Globetrain', despite the numerous logistical challenges.

Happily for Freddie, in June 1980 the CAA made the decision to license Laker for Route 6, Los Angeles/San Francisco/Seattle to Hong Kong via Honolulu and Tokyo, the first step to operating across the Pacific Ocean. It was relatively simple, since Laker was the only British airline with an interest in flying the route. It was no secret that the carrier would need deep pockets, the right equipment and a well-established wholesaler/general sales agent before tackling the trans-Pacific routes. Laker still needed to win rights from a number of other licensing authorities, including the USA's CAB, although it would likely rubber-stamp it, once everyone else concurred. The CAB was sworn to an open skies policy, so wasn't anticipated to be a problem; Route 6 was currently vacant and listed in the Bermuda II schedule. However, the Hong Kong ATLA was viewed as a major stumbling block. Cathay Pacific had a strong position with respect to its Hong Kong-Tokyo route, which could be threatened by Laker operating Route 6 in its entirety; it was one of the main arteries of its network.

However, it was the Japanese licensing authority that everyone knew would be the most difficult. The Japanese were notoriously ill-disposed towards opening up any routes to British carriers. Freddie felt that Laker needed to be able to pick up traffic in Tokyo for the trans-Pacific routes to be economically viable. Neither Freddie or Beckman had heeded Greg Dix's caution about the Japanese factor of Route 6 following Dix's March 1979 initial reconnaissance trip to the Far East. Dix had met with Mitsui on the subject of assisting with Japanese traffic rights, but had experienced nothing much more than a bit of head-nodding and a splendid sushi lunch.

Dix had also evaluated the logistics and discussed the flight operations' considerations with Dick Bradley and Captain Alan Hellary. "Freddie, this is not like flying across the North Atlantic" Dix had cautioned and he had been ably supported in this view by Bradley. They had sat in the Navigation office at Gatwick and plotted numerous trans-Pacific route permutations while evaluating the DC-10-30's payload/range performance. Hellary thought they needed a 747SP to do the job. Their rudimentary analysis was all fed back to Freddie. Nevertheless, the Pacific became another obsession, similar to the original Skytrain, and he wasn't going to let anything stand in his way.

Freddie was hoping that the Department of Trade would negotiate the Japanese rights on his behalf after the CAA had designated Laker under the UK-Japan air services agreement. Japanese approval was vitally important; by bringing up the trade imbalance, the British side hoped to claw something back by way of increased air services through Japan. The two favourable decisions from the CAA included provisional rights to Sharjah, the third largest emirate of the UAE and only 15 kilometres from Dubai. Sharjah had a new ultra-modern airport, but there was reluctance on the part of the existing airlines to use it as a transit point instead of Dubai or Bahrain. Laker's service via Sharjah was inspired and would create new traffic to the Gulf area. It would also provide a feed for connecting flights to the USA over Gatwick.

While Freddie's focus was on potential new routes on the other side of the world, his competitors were turning up the heat on the North Atlantic. By June 1980, TWA in particular had become both aware of and concerned about the increased traffic that Laker was carrying. Pan Am, TWA and BA, which had increased fares between the US and the UK by more than 50 per cent since 1978, now delayed the implementation of a planned 13 per cent increase.

In July, Freddie and John Jones increased Laker Airways' basic London to New York Apex fare by 15 per cent, but they left the walk-on fares where they were. The 'Big 3' feared that Laker's Apex fares had remained lower than their own while Laker also benefitted from significant across the board fare differentials; as much as £90 on the New York Apex and £60 on the New York and LA full economy fares. The Miami route had less differential to the point of Miami being a loss-making route, unless it achieved exceptionally high load factors.

All this was intolerable to the competition and on Monday 28th July 1980 TWA was the first to announce new Super Apex and Standby fares for the US-UK 'to counteract the inroads of Laker'. When and if Laker Airways lowered its fares, TWA would 'take whatever action was necessary to keep Laker out of the US'. It was cat and mouse, but Laker Airways nevertheless had a great summer, carrying record load factors on its three scheduled routes and supplementing them with ABCs to Toronto, Halifax, Winnipeg, Montreal, Vancouver, Windsor (Ontario) for Detroit, and Oakland. The inclusive tour programmes to the Mediterranean and North Africa, Canary Islands and Eastern Europe were also going well, with Laker Air Travel and Arrowsmith having their best year to date.

When Sir Lenox Hewitt, Chairman of Qantas and a powerful opponent of low fares, retired in July 1980, Freddie believed that with his departure from the scene he stood a better chance at securing a licence to serve Australia. So in another impulsive move, he withdrew his existing ABC application for a modest programme of charter flights to Sydney, Melbourne and Perth, and arrogantly replaced it with one for a scheduled Skytrain-type service.

Freddie was still completely hung up on the Skytrain concept, even though by now no one really knew what 'Skytrain' actually stood for. Due to the relative success Laker Airways had achieved on the London to New York Skytrain service, then more recently on the London to Los Angeles route, Freddie thought that Skytrain could be applied anywhere, even on 'long, thin routes' such as London to Sydney, a 23-hour ordeal of more than 9,500 nautical miles with two transit stops. Australia could of course never be a 'walk-on'-type service and it was perhaps an error of judgement on Freddie's part to think he could muscle his way into Australia with a service called Skytrain. The Australians hadn't even been receptive to a modest programme of relatively non-competitive ABC flights. So it was naïve to think they would simply hand over part of their prized and protected 'Kangaroo Route' for Laker to go head-to-head with Qantas on a scheduled basis. Nevertheless, Freddie continued to pull out all the stops with the help of his influential main 'guy' there.

By this time, Laker's man 'down under', Athol Guy, had left Parliament and joined the board of Clemenger Harvie, Australia's largest advertising and public relations agency. One of the agency's projects was a major promotional campaign for Laker Airways. Guy organised a TV interview via satellite with Freddie Laker and Ralph Hunt, the Australian Minister for Transport, with journalists present at both ends. The satellite hook-up was a big deal in those days and was often used for global media events. Freddie wanted Guy at his side at the UK end and bellowed down the phone, "Young man, can you come to London next week?" Guy can still hear Freddie's voice inside his head imploring him to make a 24-hour journey for one TV slot. But he did as he was asked and arrived at the studios in Camden, north London, straight off the plane with just an hour to go. On arrival he found chaos, with Hunt nowhere to be found in Canberra and Freddie nowhere to be found in the studio. Athol Guy panicked as the satellite time was very expensive and had taken hours to set up, and his credibility was on the line if the participants failed to show up at each end. He finally found Freddie in a dressing room with his feet up talking on the phone. When Guy appeared he quickly ended his call and said, "Hello, young man. Glad you made it. I was just chatting up a bird."

Guy quickly told him that Hunt hadn't showed up at the other end, and said: "We'll have to show just the empty chair in Australia" as he led Freddie into the studio. Freddie did a brilliant job of politely lecturing the chair and thanking the minister for his civility in not interrupting. The skit resulted in massive publicity for Freddie and embarrassed the Australian minister. But there was still no licence to fly to Australia forthcoming any time soon, despite a large number of provisional bookings being taken.

Attention swiftly turned back to Hong Kong. In July 1980, Sir Murray MacLehose, the 25th Governor of Hong Kong, said that his Government would support any application by Laker Airways for landing rights there. The hugely respected Governor was publicly taking a softer stance with respect to Laker Airways, and in the light of the UK Government's decision to allow Cathay Pacific onto the route in defiance of the CAA, he said that 'it would be inappropriate for his government to disapprove of the new 'open skies' policy that the decision implied.' However, few really believed that the Governor was actually as disinterested as he claimed. Despite his posture, BCal and Cathay Pacific, joined by British Airways, made it clear that they would vehemently oppose Laker's application for traffic rights when the London to Hong Kong application came to be re-heard. There was plenty of condemnation against Freddie because they all knew that he represented the future. So the incumbents continued to play down the potential growth of the Hong Kong route, despite all the predictions otherwise. Hong Kong was the only realistic outlet for Laker's DC-10-30s. The date was set for October 1980, and it would be the last chance. The Hong Kong ATLA's decision to allow Laker on the prestigious London to Hong Route depended largely on the attitude, or rather the 'approval', of Cathay as Hong Kong's carrier. It may have still been a British colony, but ATLA had unilateral rights when it came to licensing, and it didn't have to follow British Government directives.

If Cathay didn't object to Laker being licensed, it might possibly be approved by the ATLA, but that was a massive long shot. However, Bob Beckman was filled with confidence that they could persuade the Hong Kong licensing board to give them a chance. Freddie's attitude was 'the more the merrier – we've never been afraid of the competition', and based on Laker's North Atlantic record so far he had a point. Intuitively however, Freddie was somewhat more pragmatic than Beckman about Hong Kong. He knew that it wouldn't be as effortless as his typically over-confident lawyer would have him believe.

If the existing applications weren't enough to be dealing with, Freddie had also set his sights on more routes to the United States and applied for London-Baltimore/Washington and London-Detroit. Laker Airways had just received a licence to serve Tampa on Florida's Gulf Coast, close to Disney World and the numerous attractions that were springing up in the central Florida area. By giving Laker Tampa in October 1980, the CAA was accused by British Airways of failing abysmally. Minister Nott also overturned the CAA on its refusal to license Laker's Manchester and Prestwick to Miami applications. This now cleared the way for Laker to commence services from these strategic UK gateways to Florida's most popular tourism centres.

Laker's Hajj operation in the second half of 1980 was once again on behalf of the Malaysian Airline System (MAS) with two DC-10-30s. The contract for the 2½ weeks of flying the pilgrims to Mecca from Kuala Lumpur, then flying them all home again after the Hajj finished would be worth in excess of £8 million (£38.5 million at 2018 values). Unlike the Hajj operations Laker had undertaken from Nigeria, the Malaysian Hajj was considered the most desirable. The typical Malaysian pilgrims were of a high social and economic status, so the aircraft came back clean and ready to operate on the North Atlantic immediately. It was a major revenue producer for the contract carriers and Laker in particular needed the annual Hajj to bolster its revenue in the latter part of the year.

That year, Gerry Sharp, who usually handled the lucrative Hajj contracts from within the Commercial department, wouldn't be heading to Kuala Lumpur to assist with operations. Freddie had asked him to take over the management of International Caribbean Airways in Barbados, starting in November. Freddie wanted to bring Ian Allan back to the UK, from what he sarcastically called a 'paid vacation in the sun', and make him Scheduled Services Manager, replacing Geoffrey Street.

Allan, despite being close to retirement age, was also one of the old guard to whom Freddie was naturally loyal, yet Allan's experience of international scheduled service operations was extremely limited. Managing ICA didn't necessarily prepare anyone to take over the airline's main transatlantic business segment. But Freddie refused to go outside for expertise, preferring to promote from within; an admirable quality for sure, although it didn't always place the right people in some of the most critical roles in the organisation. Freddie should have known by now that if Laker was to ever have a chance against the Big 3 on the Atlantic, he needed more expertise in his commercial management team. While John Jones was unquestionably one of the most astute managers in the fold and had done an impeccable job with the ABCs in the seventies, he was now out-gunned by the commercial executives of Laker's competitors.

Other than expansion with the new North Atlantic routes, Laker had achieved little success so far with its licensing applications to other continents. Yet during the autumn of 1980, the details of the financing agreement for the Airbus A300s were being worked out and incredibly the purchase was still going ahead regardless. The Midland Bank claimed that it was being pressured by the Government and BAe, albeit discreetly, to lend the money to Laker for the Airbus purchase. The Laker order was the entry ticket the state-owned BAe required as part of the price for its 20 per cent stake in the Airbus consortium.

Allegedly, the Midland had turned down the first financing proposal. Now it would benefit from the Laker deal, gaining virtual exclusivity on the profitable financing of 20 per cent of Airbus sales, in proportion to Britain's share in the consortium. Without Laker, the Midland potentially faced exclusion and a substantial loss of future business, and it most certainly wanted the business. A full investigation had already been carried out by the Midland into Laker's finances. Laker Airways was highly geared and under-capitalised, but the Midland did not lend to the company blindly. Its Corporate Director of Finance, Robert Wyatt, speaking to a conference in August 1980, said of Freddie Laker, "The amount of money involved there is vast. His capital resources are not vast." Despite this, Freddie found that there were no barriers to raising the money for the A300s: "The bankers in those days thought so much of me that they were literally wheeling it in, in wheelbarrows. There were unlimited funds available." Christopher Brown, Laker Airways' solicitor, explains that "After having Sir Freddie speak at you for an hour about how successful aviation and Skytrain in particular was going to be, any lender would be 'gift-of-the-gobsmacked' into saying 'take what you need'. Sir Freddie was an absolute tour de force – just to listen was a privilege." There was plenty of enthusiasm among bankers for the loan, which was not limited to the Midland; as the lead agent it syndicated the loan among 13 banks in France, West Germany, Austria, America and Canada. Rather like a bookmaker laying off its bets, the Midland spread its eggs around the basket. Indeed, it had to turn down eager lenders.

Aviation and travel were booming and there were a few added attractions in providing the financing that swept any hesitation aside. Airbus was providing its standard 25 per cent first loss guarantee, which meant that if the planes were sold on, they would take the hit on the first 25 per cent of any loss in value before Freddie or his lenders absorbed any loss. There was a denial by the Government that there had been anything by way of inducements to either Freddie or the banks. But the Department of Industry agreed to pick up part of the interest rate tab, in effect subsidising the loan. The interest that Laker Airways would pay on the $131 million price of the first three A300s was fixed at a constant 10.2 per cent for the 10-year duration of the loan. For the times, it was quite generous.

The Government played a further critical role by insisting that all Export Credit Guarantee finance raised in Britain for Airbus sales was denominated in dollars. The weaker dollar attracted a lower interest rate, lessening the amount that thge Government would pay out by way of its subsidy. It meant that

Freddie's $131 million loan was based in US dollars, not UK pounds. His existing loans were already all in US dollars ... $228 million from EXIM and $58 million from Mitsui. It was a terrible mistake and one that could have been easily avoided. At a time before many of Britain's nationalised industries had been privatised, Britain had a large public sector, and Government borrowing was high to cover the wage bill. Borrowing in the Eurodollar market reduced the strain on Britain's balance of payments by lessening the amount of money perceived to have been borrowed by the public sector.

Currency fluctuation was something that Freddie's bankers could have and should have protected him against. It was even discussed by the bankers and the ministers behind the financing, but brushed aside. Freddie was left exposed to risk in the belief that the pound would remain strong beyond 1981, when the aircraft were delivered and the loan repayments would begin, and everything would be all right. There was no mechanism in place to secure Laker Airways against a change in the value of the pound against the dollar, such as a forward currency contract locking in the exchange rate, albeit at a further cost to Laker. The banks had taken steps to protect themselves through Government backing and the Airbus guarantee, ultimately covered by the taxpayers in Britain, France and Germany.

Freddie, however, was still without the European routes that he had been discreetly promised and for which the Airbus purchase was intended. In a matter of weeks, the aircraft would begin to arrive and Laker's Commercial department and the group's in-house tour operators would be tasked with finding work for these expensive planes. Similarly, the five new DC-10-30s, together with the six DC-10-10s, were also in danger of under-utilisation heading into the last part of 1980.

Freddie called Greg Dix to say he was coming over to New York for urgent discussions about Laker's Pacific Rim aspirations. He arrived on GK 30 at 2:30pm on Sunday 5th October. The USA team were just concluding a battle with the International Brotherhood of Teamsters; the IBT had launched a serious campaign to unionise all Laker's non-management employees in the USA and a top labour law firm had been hired to help Laker's USA management defeat it. It had gone well, as Laker Airways enjoyed a very high level of employee relations. Everyone was adequately paid, there were opportunities for promotion and an excellent esprit de corps existed at the airports and to an extent at the Rego Park headquarters. Freddie and Cliff Nunn had asked Dix to assume the management of the central reservations department shortly after Laker was given approval to take reservations, but Manager USA Charles Maxwell and his reservations manager, Ann Marsh, had failed to organise the critical department. John Jones complained regularly about the inefficiencies. It was challenging, as Maxwell had done everything he could to usurp Dix's influence on the department. Dix had written to Nunn saying that he was unable to do what was necessary without being able to turn over the department's top management. He'd already placed Tom Walter, one of his own trusted managers, in the Reservations department with a view to him taking it over as soon as Dix could 'redistribute' or terminate Mrs

Marsh, who enjoyed a protected position as one of Maxwell's devotees. Nunn had readily agreed as he had no time for Maxwell or any of his inner circle. However, before Dix was able to do this, it looked as if his responsibilities were about to change yet again and he would have another new title and business card; it would be his third in as many years since transferring to the USA.

Dix met Freddie off the plane at JFK's International Arrivals Building. On the drive into Manhattan, Freddie was anxious to brief him on his next assignment, but first he had to endure one or two not unexpected 'observations' on matters of great concern. The first agenda item was Freddie's plan to have Ian Allan take over the entire scheduled services operation the following month. "Sending Gerry to manage International Caribbean is robbing the Commercial department of someone who knows the ropes" Dix said. But more importantly, he challenged Freddie if Ian Allan was the right guy to head up the entire scheduled services division? It was typical of Freddie to give an important and massively challenging role to one of his loyalists. Allan had been with him at BUA and had worked for numerous airlines under the BUA umbrella. He'd also done a stint in the Middle East. But none of it prepared the 58-year-old for what he was about to take over – a veritable shambles. Dix urged Freddie to consider going outside and posting the job, in the hope of finding someone with significant scheduled service experiencc. Freddie acknowledged Dix's concerns were valid and that the company had no-one with the level of expertise Laker Airways needed to oversee its scheduled service operation. But he had already confirmed Allan's appointment, and that was that. Freddie started grinding his teeth and looking out of the car window which was a sign the subject was closed.

He then had to listen to Dix's observations on the August fare filings with the CAB that Bob Beckman had sent him. Throughout the summer of 1980, Laker had enjoyed reasonable differentials on its Apex fares, which were the most important summer fare category. However, from October onwards Laker's differential to the 'Big Three' had been slashed to just £5 ($10) on all flights. Of greater concern to Dix was that Laker's full economy fare that summer had been less than the Apex, and for the late summer shoulder season to the end of September, the economy fare was only £10 more. "Freddie, why would anyone buy an Apex?" Dix asked reasonably. It wasn't the first time he'd queried the logic of Laker's fare structure. "Look, I know we've had a good summer, the best yet, but if the Y fare had been higher, it would have been even better. The difference is less than trip insurance and it's impacting our Apex and the cash flow it represents." He paused, as it was clear he was being ignored.

Freddie was grinding his teeth harder and saying nothing in response, which would be the signal to anyone else that the subject should be changed. But Dix hadn't finished. "Bob sent me what's been filed for December and our Apex is higher than everyone else's on New York and LA. What the hell's that about, Freddie?" His voice was now a few decibels louder. The August 1980 fare filing with the CAB showed that for December, Laker's USA Apex fares were a clear $30 more from New York ($459 against $429) and an unprecedented $50 more from Los Angeles ($609 against $559). Miami retained its $10 differential in Laker's favour, for now. "How on earth can we be higher than the others?" Dix shouted.

Freddie was by now noticeably irritated and obviously wanted to change the subject. He hadn't even suggested a visit to Régine's or Plato's Retreat that evening, which usually would be the second thing out of his mouth after "Hello." 'Maybe Pat's having an influence on more than just his suits and hair after all' mused Dix, sensibly keeping the thought to himself.

Freddie was anxious to brief his man on his next assignment. "We must get these licences to fly to Hong Kong and across the Pacific, Greg," he said emphatically, signalling that any further discussion on fares was over. It was obvious by Freddie's demeanour that he was feeling some pressure; his usual humour and light-heartedness weren't apparent.

He continued, "I want you to get out to Sharjah, Hong Kong, Japan, Hawaii and maybe a few other places as soon as you can."

Dix quickly thought how he would continue to manage all of the North American airport operations as well as the now 50-plus-strong central reservations office while he was trekking around Asia. "Er, OK, but are we sure we'll get licensed? Do you want me to actually go ahead and set things up or merely see what's available" he asked cautiously.

"Beckman says these routes are ours – he's supremely confident we'll get Hong Kong and we need to have everything in place so BA and Cathay can't say we don't know what the fuck we're doing." Dix let this sink in before responding, as he knew they were already stretched to the maximum just operating point to point on the North Atlantic. Before he could make a sarcastic response that BA and Cathay may be right, Freddie continued, "They all think we don't have the wherewithal to operate the routes, so we have to prove that we do." Freddie had conveniently forgotten the briefing Dix and Dick Bradley had given him earlier about operating the trans-Pacific routes and that Captain Hellary had suggested they buy 747SPs. Freddie had laughed at Hellary's recommendation saying "he just wants to fly the 747 as it may be the only plane he isn't type-rated for."

Dix hadn't been in Asia since March 1979 when he had done some cursory evaluations in Tokyo, Hong Kong, Bangkok and Singapore, the latter for the much-anticipated Australian route licence. Now Freddie wanted commitments. Dix said he would have to relinquish his responsibility for the reservations department back to Charles Maxwell for now and hoped that was OK with him and Nunn. Freddie said, "You must – this is a much more critical job than what you've been doing in the USA for the past couple of years." Dix wasn't so sure about that, but sensibly didn't argue the point. It was clear that Freddie's tunnel vision was in overdrive again and all he had on his mind right now was global expansion, no matter what it took. Dix wasn't the only senior manager at Laker Airways who thought that they should be putting more of their efforts into North America, instead of running all over the world chasing rainbows.

Cliff Nunn flew over to JFK the next day and Monday was spent going through everything they needed to do so Dix could spend extended time in Asia. This included Maxwell re-assuming responsibility for the Reservations department that had seen some major improvements during the year under Dix's guidance.

Nunn was concerned that it would fall back into disarray; he was no fan of Maxwell and had already made noises to Freddie that he didn't think Maxwell was up to the task as Laker expanded its North American operations. There were still no Latin American interline arrangements in place in Miami, and the US originators out of Los Angeles were less than 30 per cent of the available capacity. This was insufficient for the two long-haul transatlantic markets to be sustainable unless the USA sales team under Maxwell stepped up its game.

Freddie, Nunn and Dix flew to Gatwick on Tuesday 7th October. Wednesday was mostly spent with John Jones, then Dix left the next day on BA 111, arriving late evening in Dubai. He was met by Sharjah Airport's deputy general manager, who drove him to the impressive beachfront Meridien Hotel. The next three days were jam-packed with meetings and tours of facilities together with an afternoon in Dubai and a drive across to Fujairah on the Gulf of Oman side of the UAE. Sharjah's new and expansive international airport, managed by German Jorg Riis, was immaculate, yet vastly under-utilised. Considering that Dubai was only 15km up the road, it was easy to see why. Dinner with Director of Civil Aviation Mohammed Al-Hajri on Dix's last evening in Sharjah confirmed that Laker would be most welcomed there, and Al-Hajri attested to the support of the Emir himself. The Emir had extended a dinner invitation to Sir Freddie when and if he was able to visit the Emirate soon.

As he climbed aboard a Cathay Pacific L-1011 bound for Hong Kong at 1:40am, Dix was sorry to be leaving the UAE. There didn't seem to be the same level of tension there that he'd experienced in Saudi Arabia; in fact, Sharjah seemed more like Bahrain with excellent hotels, great beaches and friendly staff. The hotel even had a proper bar. Overall, it had been a very productive visit, and he was looking forward to returning and briefing Freddie on the considerable potential of Sharjah and the UAE in general.

Laker's ability to transit Sharjah was pivotal to the London to Hong Kong and London to Australia routes. Freddie and Bob Beckman both thought that the Hong Kong hearing, slated for Monday 20th October, might finally offer some redemption. Otherwise Laker would have many more aircraft than it knew what to do with, and their quest for 'global domination' would be in jeopardy.

CHAPTER 36

# Tunnel Vision

## Freddie blows it in Hong Kong

1980

Greg Dix had been drawn into the Hong Kong route preparations, almost as if it was a foregone conclusion that Laker would be approved for the London to Hong Kong route. His main role was to make certain that all the logistics were in place for Laker to successfully operate the route if and or when the licence was granted. From city ticket offices to in-flight catering, terminal facilities to crew hotel rooms, each point of the route had to be properly set up and ready to go at a moment's notice. Once licensed, Freddie would insist on flying as soon as possible, just as he had with the Skytrain destinations in North America. Dix arrived in Hong Kong on Monday 13th October 1980 after a few days in Sharjah. There, he'd set up everything Laker would need to transit the Emirate on the anticipated routes to Hong Kong and to Australia via Singapore. It had been the first time anyone from Laker Airways had set foot in Sharjah and Dix had been mightily impressed with everything.

His first stop upon arrival at Hong Kong's Kai Tak Airport was to see his old friend Jerry Penwarden, who he had known since their Luton days. Penwarden had moved to Gatwick to manage the newly formed Gatwick Handling where he'd given Dix a job in 1972. Despite his understated Cathay Pacific business card showing a title of 'Traffic Manager', Penwarden's job was managing Cathay's entire airport operations and outstations, worldwide. When Dix contacted him to say he was heading out to the colony from Sharjah, Penwarden authorised a first class pass on Cathay from Dubai to Hong Kong.

As he entered, a familiar voice boomed from the inner office: "Granny, show Mr. Dix in." Granny turned out to be Penwarden's very attractive secretary, Llanu who showed Dix into her boss's office. It wasn't clear to Dix how she got to be called 'granny' as she certainly didn't look like one. The two hadn't seen each other since their Gatwick Handling days but there was no opportunity for small talk or reminiscing. Penwarden had a senior Swire Group executive in his office who had apparently insisted on meeting Freddie Laker's representative for Asia. After the cordial introductions, Dix explained why he was there and that the Hong Kong licensing board were giving Laker another chance to submit their application to serve the colony from London.

Penwarden, grinning like a Cheshire cat said nothing while the Swire man appeared to be fully aware of what Laker Airways was up to in Hong Kong. "Mr Dix, you need to know something," the Swire executive said, pausing for effect. "Laker will not be allowed to fly into Hong Kong." Seeing Dix's quizzical look and before he could respond, "Cathay Pacific will never permit it" he concluded. It was as clear as that. 'Never mind BA and BCal objecting,' thought Dix, remembering what Bob Beckman had told him. 'Never mind the ATLA not permitting it, it's Cathay who won't permit it.' Unsurprisingly, Hong Kong's 'national airline' was the main obstacle. Beckman was barking up the wrong tree.

Dix thanked his old colleague for the free pass and said his goodbyes. They arranged to have dinner soon and Dix left the Cathay offices at Kai Tak, hopped into the Regent Hotel's courtesy car, a Rolls Royce for the ten minute drive to the hotel. He had to speak to Bob Beckman as a priority and hoped he wasn't out shopping in Tsim Sha Tsui with Angela.

The brand new and contemporary Regent Hotel was located right on the harbour front on the Kowloon side of Hong Kong, across the road from the world renowned Peninsula Hotel. The staff were eager to treat their guests to an unbelievable experience. After checking in and eventually getting to his room after what seemed like a hundred bows to the Regent's staff, Dix rang Beckman. Dix wondered why the Beckmans had been at the Regent all week when the hearing didn't start until the following Monday. When he entered their huge suite he soon found out. Dix guessed it was 1,000 square feet with a dining room, sitting room, two bathrooms and a magnificent view overlooking Victoria harbour and Hong Kong Island. Beckman and his wife Angela were clearly living a life of luxury at the expense of Laker Airways.

Dix ignored Bob Beckman's excesses and relayed the conversation he'd had over at Kai Tak less than an hour before. He related to Beckman exactly what one of Swire's top government relations' executives had said, word for word and the firm manner in which he'd delivered the statement. Far from being concerned, Beckman shrugged it off almost as if it were hearsay. He was supremely confident that Laker would be licenced to serve Hong Kong despite the ATLA having to make its own decision. He went on about what a strong case they had. Beckman told Dix that Hong Kong's Governor, Sir Murray MacLehose supported Laker's application. He said, "remember Greg, Freddie will be our star witness, look how he blew their doors off in London, and he'll be even more on form here, you see." Beckman paid no heed to Dix's warning about the influence Cathay Pacific had on the outcome.

There was a note on Dix's door asking him to join the General Manager at the bar later. The Regent's PR Director, Monique Hochstrasser made the introduction to Rudi Greiner, who was fascinated by the entire Laker Airways' story and the prospect of Laker Airways serving Hong Kong from London. Dix complimented Greiner on his magnificent hotel and the incredible service. He had been particularly impressed at how they had unpacked his suitcase, ironed his clothes and polished his shoes before Dix had even made it up to his room upon arrival. Greiner explained they were late opening as they had to tear down a huge wall, pointing at the immense marble stairs that swept down to the bar area with its floor to ceiling wall of glass overlooking the bustling harbour. He explained that right before they were due to open they had hired the services of a local feng shui consultant who told them they must tear down the wall and open up the stairs to where they were standing. Dix asked why on earth they had to do that. With a dead-pan face, Greiner told Dix that the feng shui man had said the hotel would have very bad luck if they didn't allow for the dragon to come down the stairs and have easy access to the harbour so he could take a swim. He went on to say that before Laker published any fares to London, they had to be approved by the feng shui man or risk not attracting any Chinese passengers. 'Use lots of eights' he said, as that's the most auspicious number in Chinese numerology. Seeing that he was deadly serious, Dix made a mental note to ask Laker's local wholesaler Tommy Chen about this when he met with him later. Clearly, there was much more to doing business in the Far East than everyone perhaps realised.

Sir Freddie arrived in Hong Kong on Friday 17th October. Dix went in the Regent's courtesy Rolls Royce to meet him off his BCal flight. Freddie was high as a kite as he got into the back of the Rolls. The hair-raising approach into Kai Tak, one of the most challenging airports in the world was to be believed. "How was it" Dix asked, as he greeted his boss. "Well it was one of my old BUA guys driving so I sat in the jump seat for landing. Have you done it?" "Incredible isn't it" replied Dix, "I sat up front on our 707 with George Newby once, you can almost touch the washing on the lines.

Freddie was full of praise for BCal's in-flight service. "It was much better than I thought it would be Greg," he said with a grin that made Dix think he'd chatted up some of BCal's hostesses. "Some of Thomson's 'Tartan Tarts' are real lookers and they do a bloody good job." After they'd discussed the merits of BCal's tartan clad and typically very attractive cabin crew for a few minutes, Freddie asked how he'd got on in Sharjah. Dix told him about Sharjah's magnificent new airport, their beachfront hotels and the tourism potential of the UAE, but Dix was anxious to let Freddie know about what he'd been told in Jerry Penwarden's office a few days prior by the Swire executive.

Freddie replied "well Dix, I've been telling Beckman all along that Cathay are our main worry not BCal. But he's got this hard on about Len Bebchick, he just can't let it go and it's a personal vendetta for him." BCal's Bebchick and Bob Beckman weren't just professional adversaries; they didn't play the typical two-faced lawyer game, ripping each other's throats out in court one minute and having a friendly martini together the next. They really did hate each other. It wasn't clear why, but rumour had it that Bebchick had once made an insulting remark about Angela. The hostility was now clouding Beckman's judgment and perhaps affecting Laker's future.

It was a national holiday in the colony and the streets of Kowloon were untypically quiet, so in just minutes, the Rolls Royce limo had them whipping down the Salisbury Road and pulling under the Regent's opulent marble clad entrance canopy. At least a half dozen staff immediately gathered around the Rolls to welcome Sir Freddie Laker to Hong Kong.

After changing from his travel clothes and leaving his butler to unpack for him, Freddie marched down and found Beckman with his wife, Angela in one of the hotel's best suites, larger and with a better view of the harbour than his own. 'It's all naturally being charged to Laker Airways of course' Freddie thought 'which will make Robbie apoplectic when he gets the bill'. Freddie's half-kidding taunts about Beckman's extravagances were not unexpected and as always Beckman responded with "it's been business, business, business all the way Freddie" as he took another drag on his cigarette. Freddie glared back at him through the cloud of noxious smoke. He was partial to the odd cigar but absolutely hated cigarettes.

Already exasperated, Freddie rang Dix's room wanting to know what was on the agenda. A tight schedule of meetings, PR functions, lunches and dinners had been arranged for the next couple of days. Beckman needed Freddie for some concentrated time to go over his delivery at the licencing hearing, due to commence at 9:30am the following Monday. It would be a demanding ordeal and Beckman said Freddie's performance was critical.

From 11:00am on Sunday, Freddie and Dix were subjected to a somewhat hellish afternoon in Bob Beckman's suite. Papers were strewn all over the floor with Bob and Angela talking a mile a minute as they sipped endless cups of black coffee and chain smoked. Freddie was quite uncomfortable in these surroundings, but he dutifully went through what Beckman wanted him to say at the hearing the next day.

For once, Freddie didn't share Beckman's confidence he kept thinking about Cathay Pacific. "Bob, Cathay is the lifeline of Hong Kong's economy. Swire Group own more buildings here and have more influence than anyone, perhaps even as much as Jardines" he urged. Beckman shrugged off Freddie's concerns and came up with more and more reasons why ATLA would licence Laker. Dix chimed in as he had before with his perspective on their using the term 'Skytrain' for the London to Hong Kong route. Lakerville and the chaos that ensued in London and New York was still on everyone's mind and 'how on earth can this route be marketed as a walk-on service' he had said. It fell on deaf ears. The Beckmans would have gone on all night, such was the intensity Bob and Angela imbued, however by 6:00pm, Freddie called it a day with, "let's go Dix, see you tomorrow Bob, night Angela." And with that, the pair were free at last.

When Freddie and Dix left the suite, Beckman presumed they would have dinner and an early night. Far from it. As they were having a drink in Freddie's suite and admiring the view of Victoria harbour there was a knock on the door. Dix went to open it and there stood two beautiful young Chinese girls. He had arranged this with one of their local collaborators thinking Freddie might like a bit of fun after the intense Beckman briefing session. "Hallo hallloww" Freddie said as the girls were ushered in and offered champagne. "God Dix are they legal? which one do you like, I quite fancy the taller one." "No they're both for you Freddie, I have to go and meet Mary and talk about the press stuff." "What the hell am I going to do with two, you can't leave me now" he replied with genuine panic in his voice. "Oh you'll be fine, give them another glass of fizz and pop 'em in your jacuzzi or something, you know what to do Freddie. Anyway there's only two this time. Remember when we were in... oh nevermind, set your alarm for 7:30, the car leaves at 8:30 sharp. Bye."

Dix was laughing as he went off to meet Laker's new PR representative in Hong Kong, Mary Chiang. It wasn't the first time he'd fixed Freddie up when he was away from home and likely wouldn't be the last. He was quite certain that Freddie would have a well deserved fun evening with the girls, even though their English was somewhat limited to just a half dozen essentials.

Predictably, at 8:25am on Monday the 20th of October, the Beckmans were waiting under the ornate portico of the hotel. A nervous Bob, pacing up and down yelled "Greg, where the hell's Freddie," as the car was due to leave in five minutes. Beckman knew the traffic in the tunnel to Hong Kong Island would be horrendous and he couldn't risk being late. He was furious at Dix, blaming him for Freddie's tardiness and demanded that he find Freddie. Dix had a key for Freddie's suite and went off as requested.

He unlocked the door of Freddie's suite, viewed the chaotic state of the living room and then walked over to the bedroom. He was stopped dead in his tracks wondering if he was looking at a scene from Bob Guccione's *Caligula*, uttering 'what the...' out loud. A naked Freddie lay fast asleep with the two equally naked Chinese girls who were also fast asleep, one on each side of him. There was a mutilated fruit bowl, the bed and floor were covered in rose petals, and several empty champagne bottles were lying on the floor. A pair of bright red panties hung from the ceiling fan. It was a surreal scene and would have been hilarious if they didn't have to be at one of their most critical licencing hearings in a half hour. Dix quickly woke everyone from their comatose state, dispatched the confused girls and urged a drowsy Freddie to hurry up and get shaved and dressed. He ran down and told Bob and Angela to go on ahead and that he and Freddie would follow in another car. Beckman was furious with Dix and demanded to know why Freddie had overslept. "It's probably delayed jet lag Bob" replied Dix sheepishly, knowing the reaction he'd get if he'd told Beckman what had really happened.

Four cups of strong black coffee, an equal amount of paracetamol and an hour and a half later, Freddie rose to give evidence. He could hardly keep his eyes open, slurred many of his words and delivered an inglorious monologue that made little sense. It was a terrible performance and people in the room looked at each other wondering what was going on or if Freddie was ill. His delivery that day was so bad that Beckman was sure it was the only reason Laker didn't get the licence. While Freddie's lack lustre presentation and cross-examination responses probably didn't help Laker's case, it was fairly apparent by Cathay Pacific's submission to the panel that whatever Cathay directed was how it was going to be. Cathay and BCal, newcomers flying Hong Kong to

London both turned on Freddie and were joined by BA in hotly opposing Laker Airways' renewed application. It was a fait accompli.

The ATLA reaffirmed BCal and of course Cathay. Supposedly the presence of a Skytrain type service to and from Hong Kong would have put an intolerable strain on the other three airlines that had been licenced. Leonard Bebchick was smug as he'd once again prevailed over his nemesis, Bob Beckman while BCal's chairman, Adam Thomson thanked the panel for 'letting common sense prevail'.

Bizarrely, less than two weeks before Christmas, almost as though the rejection in Hong Kong hadn't happened, Freddie flew to Sharjah via Dubai together with John Jones. The third most prominent emirate of the UAE was essential to Laker Airways' global ambitions. Sharjah was to be a transit point for all the Pacific Rim initiatives as it was about seven hours east of London Gatwick and another seven and a half hours on to Singapore (for Australia) or Hong Kong (for Tokyo and Globetrain).

Freddie was scheduled to meet the Emir of Sharjah at a reception and dinner being held in his honour. He and Jones had flown out to the UAE especially for this reception with the Emir, while Dix was already there. Unlike Jones and Dix, who had packed appropriate light-coloured desert climate suits, Freddie only had an ensemble more appropriate for a meeting with his bankers on a cold February morning. Thoughtfully, he had brought an appropriate watch to wear; a £5,000 gold Rolex Datejust with a £1,000 stainless steel Rolex for back up, just in case. As he completed knotting his tie, he fished the two watches out of his jacket pocket. "These guys all have fantastic kit on their wrists. What do you think, stainless or gold? John, Greg, help me out, which of these should I wear tonight?" Jones and Dix looked at each other wondering how he ever managed to dress himself at home. Dix came to the rescue, "Freddie, wear the gold Rolex tonight." Jones nodded in agreement. "We'll both be in our working class stainless but you know our hosts will all be in pure gold, platinum or even palladium, plus emeralds, diamonds and god knows what else." "Maybe iridium" Jones interjected with a laugh. "Thing is, just be humble and appreciative" Dix briefed Freddie on protocol. "Don't over talk the Emir, stick to water or tea, remember where you are and for god's sake Freddie, absolutely no lewd jokes or remarks about Israel OK?" Dix had spent a fair amount of time in the Middle-East and understood the culture. He had overseen numerous Hajj pilgrimage operations where he'd diligently briefed the young Laker flight attendants on covering their shoulders and knees at all times and being respectful of their host country's rules and regulations.

"Won't we get a proper drink" asked Freddie as he wasn't sure if Sharjah was a dry state or not. In 1980, Sharjah, the third largest by population and economy of the seven United Arab Emirates allowed their hotels to have liquor licenses. This went against Islamic principles but Sharjah thought it important if they were to have any chance of developing tourism. They had excellent beach front hotel properties run by reputable companies, so a relaxed liquor law was considered essential if they wanted to attract the Europeans. John Jones, as a first time visitor to the Emirate, quickly saw the tourism potential there and was already formulating the package holidays that he could offer to Laker's tour operators in the UK, thinking Sharjah could be a new chic destination.

"I'm not going to eat the bloody sheep's eyes" Freddie's raised voice brought his colleagues' attention back. "Freddie, if it's offered you more or less have to or we risk insulting our hosts" Dix said firmly, but all it got was a stern face and raised eyebrows from the man in the dark suit. "Look, I've been here a while now Freddie and these guys are so keen to have us, let's not fuck it up over something as daft as a sheep's eye. Anyway, they may offer you the heart instead as you're the guest of honour." Dix laughed but he was determined to get his boss's attention before they headed off to what was a critical event for them in the Middle East.

It was Dix's second visit to Sharjah, arranging the ground handling, logistics and other operational necessities. He knew the lie of the land and felt it was his responsibility to guide Freddie to the extent possible so the Laker brand remained untarnished in the UAE. "The car will be here in ten minutes, so are you ready?" Freddie was resolute on the matter of the sheep's eyes but he donned the gold Rolex as his men suggested. "I hate this watch you know," he said laughing, much to the surprise of his colleagues. "Myles Wyatt gave it to me as a birthday present and I hardly ever wear it, you can imagine why" he chuckled, but nevertheless strapped the old Rolex onto his left wrist, not realising it may be the last time he would wear it. He buttoned his jacket and by that gesture gave the signal he was ready to go for whatever lay ahead.

Freddie was going to meet the 31 year old Sheikh Sultan bin Muhammad Al-Qasimi who had ruled since 1972. His palace was typically impressive and ornate. The Laker group was ushered into a lavishly appointed room set off the main parlor and were offered tea, coffee and dates. Freddie would have preferred a scotch and milk but he kept his cool and was unusually quiet as they waited for someone to show them to the dining room. Introductions were made to at least a dozen of Sharjah's hierarchy who were presented by their full titles and their numerous names, many of which contained His Royal Highness or Sheikh, which was followed by the Laker men being seated. The Emir was a gracious host and spoke in English to his guests; like many Middle-Eastern leaders, he had been to university in England. He appeared to be particularly honoured that Laker Airways had selected Sharjah instead of next door Dubai or Bahrain as their transit point for Hong Kong and Australia. Freddie sensibly didn't tell the Emir and his senior ministers that the Hong Kong license was still not a sure thing and Australia looked as if it may be a long struggle too. He did however, as Dix had urged, compliment the Emir on Sharjah's superb airport that he'd been able to quickly view that morning upon arrival. The evening went well, even though Freddie was clearly outside his comfort zone. For once, he didn't tell any racy jokes or insult anyone from the government and he didn't have to eat a sheep's eye after all; in fact he commented afterwards how great the food was.

Back at the hotel bar that evening over a night cap, Freddie told Jones and Dix that he felt positive about Sharjah and that once licensed, Laker would help make it into a de rigueur vacation destination just as they had done with the Black Sea resorts years earlier. "By the way Dix" he said before leaving the next day for London, "I need you to go to Australia first thing in January. We need to keep the heat on there. Athol will arrange your schedule."

Away from the madness of the blind pursuit of global domination, Laker Airways ended the year by more than doubling its Skytrain numbers. The transatlantic business was doing well. It was undoubtedly bolstering Freddie's conviction that the Skytrain concept was what the rest of the world needed and the licensing authorities and protectionists had simply got it wrong.

In 1980, Laker carried 727,952 Skytrain passengers at an overall load factor of 78.3 per cent. Laker's DC-10s also carried 4,696 tonnes of cargo. The New York route continued to increase its traffic with 346,457 one-way passengers, nearly double the prior year at a load factor of 77.6 per cent. Los Angeles more than doubled its traffic with 239,359 one-way passengers at a load factor of 69.0 per cent. The introduction of Miami in May as a scheduled Skytrain service added another 142,136 one-way passengers and boasted an 86.6 per cent load factor. Laker's market share also increased. In the height of summer, Laker had 25 per cent of the New York market, 39 per cent of Los Angeles and 33 per cent of Miami.

Laker Airways had jumped from being the eighth largest airline on the North Atlantic to sixth behind TWA, BA, Pan Am, Lufthansa, and KLM and was poised to eclipse KLM in 1981. Laker was now interlining with United Airlines' domestic network in the USA. The arrangement was somewhat one-sided as United were able to sell Laker's flights but due to the UK's reservations system, 'Brian' still being in development, reciprocity was not yet possible.

Laker's brand new DC-10-30s were already setting industry records for utilisation, with a minimum of 4,500 hours a year being the goal. Freddie knew only too well that high usage meant more profits and as important, less maintenance as aircraft that sat on the ground invariably went 'tech' more frequently than planes that were flying all the time. While the Los Angeles and Miami Skytrain flights were perfect operationally for the DC-10-30s, the aircraft were already showing performance shortfalls that Freddie had been cautioned about by MDC when he ordered them. It had taken a while to gather sufficient data, but after a full year of operation it had become clear Laker's DC-10-30s with the GE CF6-50C2B engines and upgraded 580,000lb maximum take-off weight, were burning more fuel than MDC had forecast. DC-10 Fleet Manager, Captain Steve James said, "I recall there being a problem with specific fuel consumption (SFC) being up on the book figure. Two Douglas performance engineers did a flight with me back from Los Angeles and set the power up very precisely and checked the readings every hour." Senior DC-10 Training Captain, Geoff Brookes followed up with, "We always did our best to conserve fuel at all times and for instance made it clear to the pilots that the use of auto-throttles in the cruise was not recommended because they were over sensitive and 'chased' the speed setting, drastically increasing fuel conumption. On critical sectors we would obviously use the Long Range Cruise settings and speeds. I well remember doing this on a flight from Colombo to Gatwick with 300+ pax and despite the computer flight plan's pessimism, we made it non-stop in 11 hours 30mins." Brookes confirmed that Laker's pilots also typically flew the DC-10 between 2 and 2.5 degrees nose up once at cruising altitude, for optimum fuel flow. Capt Brookes continues, "When we were off the NAT tracks in the cruise at say FL310 and the AUW suggested a climb to FL350 in order to bracket the optimum FL330, I found that we lost out on fuel consumption for some time at the new FL. Whenever possible after discovering this, I would delay the climb until the optimum was FL340, in other words climbing to 1000ft above and not 2000ft above optimum. In my opinion this seemed to work, so this was my method ever after."

The DC-10-30s had been purchased to operate Laker's anticipated London to Hong Kong, trans-Pacific Globetrain and London to Australia routes, for which governmental approvals were still pending. The aircraft's performance and its specific fuel consumption would be critical for these operations. And nowhere would this be more critical than trans-Pacific flights from the Far East, especially Hong Kong to Hawaii and then to the west coast of the USA. There were literally no diversion points within 1500 miles of the Hawaiian islands so a dog leg south to Guam for a fuel uplift would be necessary on almost every occasion. The eastbound leg to Honolulu would test Laker's flight crews like nothing before, as the margin for error flying to Hawaii was infinitesimal.

Laker's pilots weren't just masters of stretching the range of everything they flew; on occasion they could break speed records too, if only unofficially. Captain Jock Manson along with F/O Terry Fensome and F/E Phil Kelly checked in at LAX for their flight home on the 19th of December, only to find the computer flight plan was showing an almost unbelievable elapsed time to Gatwick. By the time they'd overflown Las Vegas en route they were experiencing tail winds of up to 200kts. They were going so fast they thought they may even have to dump fuel in order to get down to the maximum permissable landing weight. Air Traffic Control all down the line gave them direct routings and despite having to extend the approach into Gatwick and land to the west on runway 26, they were on the blocks in a record 8 hours and 49 minutes. Unfortunately, observers from the Fédération Aéronautique Internationale (FAI) weren't on hand to officially record the flight, so it never made the record books. Nevertheless, it was a fitting achievement to top off Laker Airways' best ever year.

Despite the DC-10-30's performance issues that cut into any potential profits on the Los Angeles and Miami scheduled services, and the fare matching on the North Atlantic at the end of the year, 1980 was a record-breaking year for the Laker group. Laker Air Travel and Arrowsmith had set records, Toronto and the other North American ABCs continued to make a significant contribution and the Malaysian Hajj had been hugely profitable. Laker had survived the dirty tricks on the North Atlantic and was for now, still thriving.

Heading into 1981, Freddie's renowned tunnel vision and Bob Beckman's relentless battering ram approach were not yet paying off with governmental decision-makers anywhere outside North America. Global domination wasn't going to be quite as straightforward as they had initially envisaged.

# CHAPTER 37

# The Doors Slam Shut
## Global ambitions fade

January - August 1981

1981 was set to open on a high, with the announcement of the finalisation of the purchase of the Airbus A300s, and their arrival at Gatwick. The press conference on the 7th January that took place at the Minema cinema in London, and arranged by Robin Flood, Laker Airways' publicity officer was almost an embarrassing disaster. When the conference started, the financing contract was still not fully agreed. Laker's Finance Director Robbie Robinson and Company Solicitor Christopher Brown were literally in the theatre's back row frantically negotiating the final bits and pieces with Airbus Industrie. Finally, from where they sat, they gave Freddie the thumbs up and the deal was signed. Rubbing his hands together he gleefully declared: "This is the best deal I have made in 31 years. We could sell these planes at a profit at the time of delivery when their value will have increased by 20 per cent. What you boys always forget is that the planes are there as collateral" he lectured the press corps.

Less than impressed was John Jones, Laker's Commercial Manager who describes the aircraft as 'the last thing we needed, they were a total disaster'. He knew the aircraft would turn up as up as 'three more lines on my blank sheet of paper.' Freddie was never one for producing advanced costings but would claim that he knew everything from every perspective and that he had done his sums working late into the night. The reality was a seat of the pants operation with Jones and Robinson sitting down after the event saying 'ok, how do we make this work.' Before they arrived, Freddie had offered them out on lease, to the Australian airline, Ansett. They were interested but found the charges were too high. So Laker Airways was stuck with more large planes to fill.

It was only thanks to Jones and the commercial teams' hard work that the A300s proved to be neither a problem to fill or to contract out. Laker's versions were configured for 284 passengers, far less than the maximum of 345, with a comfortable 32-inch pitch between seats. Jones made sure he had signatures on aircraft charter agreements from tour operators long before their arrival; companies like Harry Goodman's Intasun, never one to miss an opportunity to be on board a new and attractive aeroplane.

On the 8th January 1981, the first A300B4, G-BIMA named 'Metro' arrived at Gatwick with much fanfare and a really big show from Freddie for the benefit of the cameras. It was delivered from Toulouse by Laker's Airbus Fleet Manager, Captain Tim Davies - another of Freddie's remarkable captains who had been the One-Eleven Fleet Manager and once owned a famous WW2 Spitfire. Davies had a hand-picked crew of Laker and Airbus Industrie pilots and flight engineers for the first flight. Laker's A300s had traditional analogue cockpits with a flight engineer station, whereas later A300s and A310s would come with forward facing crew cockpits, thus eliminating the flight engineer position.

A Mini Metro car, resplendent with Freddie's personal registration plate FLY 1 had been loaded into the baggage hold and it was presented to him upon the plane's arrival. Airbus and GE hosted a celebratory lunch for Laker Airways at the Café Royal in London the following day. In a gesture of support for the struggling British automobile manufacturing industry, the chairman of British Leyland, Sir Michael Edwardes officially named the plane on 25th of February. The naming ceremony of Metro coincided with the announcement of the engagement of Prince Charles and Lady Diana Spencer and a coup in Spain just the day before, so for once Sir Freddie didn't steal all the headlines. Metro was sent straight to West Berlin for Flug Union, the tour operator that had been using Laker's aircraft since April 1969. The two A300s that followed were G-BIMB 'Orient Express' and G-BIMC 'Intercity Express.'

Just as he had done with the first DC-10s a decade earlier, Freddie wanted to show his new A300s off. First was a travel agent promotion in Palma, Majorca, Laker's most dominant European destination. Robin Flood organised the almost pantomime-like show which saw uniformed cabin staff acting like the Tiller Girls while Freddie dressed as an onion salesman, rode a bike wearing a beret. It was a very camp show and perhaps would have been more appropriate ten years earlier. Shortly after, he took the A300 over to Berlin where they did a slightly more subdued show which saw Freddie on his knees writing on the 'Free Berlin' sign. The Airbus A300 was well-received everywhere it went, rightfully. It was after all, a magnificient example of multinational engineering and was the undisputed forerunner of the wide-body twin engined concept. It was a shame that like many things 'Laker', the Airbus A300s were just a little premature.

Freddie's signature on the loan agreement for the Airbus A300s was either going to be his greatest folly to date or another masterful stroke of genius. Freddie was so self-assured that he told Brown and Robinson, in an echo of what he told reporters: "If we ever do go bust, we'll be on the beaches of the South of France. There's so much equity in the aircraft." Neither of his young executives were shareholders and were left slightly baffled as to how this would dramatically enable them to lead hedonistic lifestyles if it all went wrong. One thing Freddie was right about however, was that by aligning with Airbus Industrie early on, it ensured Laker would be at the cutting edge of civil aviation technology for years to come. Airbus had a clear vision of what was to follow the A300 and its smaller variant the A310, that Freddie already had options for. While he never admitted he may have been wrong about his earlier criticism of the joint European project, Freddie was nevertheless mightily impressed with the final product that Airbus Industrie delivered. The first twin-engined, wide body commercial airliner was about to revolutionise the entire air transport industry and was yet another example of Freddie's acute insight into the future.

Following the euphoria of the Airbus delivery, in the early months of 1981, Laker Airways pressed ahead with the introduction of a myriad of new services. From the early days of having a single BAC One-Eleven based at Manchester, there was now a brand new Airbus, a DC-10-10 for the four times a week Manchester to New York Skytrain and a DC-10-30 for the Tuesday and Friday Manchester to Los Angeles flights and the four times weekly Manchester to Miami service, with the Wednesday flight operating via Prestwick to facilitate Florida bound holidaymakers from Scotland's Glasgow area. Manchester was playing a significant role in Laker Airways' future.

After the failed Hong Kong application, Laker Airways was left with spare capacity in its DC-10-30 fleet. To alleviate this problem, John Jones had negotiated a very lucrative and timely contract with Lan Chile Airlines to wet lease a DC-10-30 from January to March. Lan Chile wanted to try the aircraft out on their three prime routes to the USA before committing to purchasing their own. Laker's engineering division repainted the DC-10 in Lan Chile livery and with Jones aboard, the aircraft set off for Santiago. The Chileans had laid on a big reception for the aircraft with the country's President in attendance. Upon arrival, the Laker team didn't quite understand why the hundreds of people welcoming the plane to Chile weren't as enthusiastic as they'd expected them to be. However, when they saw the outside of the plane they understood. Jones, who had organised the Lan Chile lease was particularly embarrassed. Much of the Lan Chile livery which had been hastily applied in the days prior to delivery had peeled off, making the aircraft appear as if it had been sitting out in one of California's desert airparks for ten years. Jones promptly got on the phone to Laker's Chief Engineer, Peter Yeoman and delivered one of his celebrated 110 decibel tongue-lashings before apologising to the Chileans. In a couple of days, all was well, the aircraft was freshly repainted and commenced service for Lan Chile. The wet lease went extremely smoothly and over 33,300 passengers were flown. Lan Chile was pleased with the DC-10-30 and confirmed their order with McDonnell Douglas for five planes which they deployed on routes between Santiago and New York, Miami and Los Angeles. Once again, Laker had assisted MDC's sales of the DC-10.

Aside from the extra transatlantic services from Manchester, very little had been achieved in the quest to take the Skytrain brand beyond the USA. A number of routes were applied for and a tight schedule of licencing hearings was now planned for the first six months of the year. Freddie needed more routes to make his expanded fleet pay and he was brimming with confidence that 1981 would be the year he would leave past route licencing failures behind him. At the very least, he hoped to finally crack open the Australian market.

Laker Airways officially applied to Britain's CAA for a scheduled 'Skytrain' service to Sydney and/or Melbourne and/or Perth in Western Australia via Sharjah and Singapore. The Laker fares would be £232 in the economy section and £490 for a new envisaged business class. The BA and Qantas economy fares started at £604. Freddie pledged he would dramatically reduce fares and confidently predicted that the Australian government would grant him a licence to fly by the 1st November that year.

In January, Freddie sent Greg Dix down under to pave the way. Since mid 1980, Dix's title had been changed to Manager, International Operations; it was his third new role since being transferred to New York in March 1978. He was met at Melbourne's airport by Athol Guy and his Range Rover which was equipped with a massive set of bumpers that went all the way to the top of the bonnet. Guy explained they were 'Roo bars' designed to deflect an errant kangaroo that might come hopping across the road. He insisted they swing by one of his local drinking spots on the way to Dix's hotel, where Guy proceeded to demonstrate to his jet-lagged British guest how 'proper Australian blokes' picked up girls. The pitch started reasonably politely with 'ello Shiela, wanna drink' and became rapidly more explicit from there. Dix asked how often he got slapped using that approach but Guy said "Aussie girls have a good sensayuma" and the hit rate was generally over fifty per cent. The massively popular Seekers' bass player, Member of Parliament and marketing guru had set Dix up for a hectic 19-day, five-city schedule. It included introductions to Dick Hamer, Premier of Victoria and other senior officials in Canberra, the capital and also in New South Wales, South Australia and Western Australia. Together they went to Sydney and then Adelaide to meet with South Australia's premier. In Canberra they saw Brian Ward, Australia's industry and commerce minister. Dix told Ward Laker Airways would bring 200,000 new visitors to Australia every year. His comment and a detailed report of Laker Airways' proposed services saw Dix's face in all the Australian daily papers. Out west in Perth, he had a positive meeting with Frank Gallagher of the Department of Trade who mentioned that '1978 Australian Businessman of the Year' Alan Bond was keen to meet Freddie if he ever came to Perth. Dix also met with executives from Qantas who on the surface appeared more than happy to offer ticket counter space and do the ground handling for Laker's DC-10s at the principal cities.

Overall, the Laker representative was enthusiastically received everywhere he went in Australia. Most of the logistics were in place thanks to Athol who had set up sales and ticketing facilities in Melbourne and in Sydney. The two offices were already selling tickets to London via Singapore Airlines and also to Los Angeles to connect with Laker's Skytrain. Dix reluctantly returned to London as he had enjoyed his first time in Australia. He now realised why Freddie was obsessed with flying there. After such a positive visit, surely the permits were now only a formality, providing of course Canberra rubber stamped what the individual states clearly wanted. Freddie and Beckman said they needed him in London for the start of the Australia hearings at the CAA on 2nd of February. So Dix flew back via Singapore and spent a few days there arranging Laker's logistical requirements for the Australia route before heading to the UK.

On arrival in London, after checking into the Waldorf Hotel with its creaky wooden floors and paper thin walls, he took a cab ride to the Carlton Tower Hotel where Bob Beckman had a luxury apartment. Freddie joined them for dinner. Dix gave Freddie and Beckman a thorough briefing on his Australia trip along with verbatim comments made by senior government officials in all the states he had visited. Without exception, every state premier and official wanted Laker Airways to serve Australia. Dix cautioned that despite the individual states and cities being extremely pro-Laker, it was likely they would meet serious opposition from Australia's federal government, based upon what he had gleaned while visiting Canberra. As always, Beckman was supremely confident they would be licenced, despite his track record so far proving otherwise, to Freddie's obvious annoyance.

The Australia hearings kicked off on Monday the 2nd of February with the usual back and forths between the various lawyers. It was clear that BA and Qantas had colluded prior, thus ensuring their respective objections to Laker's presence on the 'kangaroo route' were synchronised. Beckman objected time and again, pushing Laker's case, which once more was all based upon the trademark low fare 'Skytrain' approach. Dix had cautioned about highlighting 'Skytrain' on numerous occasions. He had advised Beckman and Freddie following his Australia trip that they should drop the use of the term 'Skytrain' as it was inappropriate for the route being sought. As usual, it fell on deaf ears.

Wednesday the 4th was a day off from hearings. Freddie said he had things to do and as Dix was going down to Gatwick for meetings anyway asked him to meet Athol Guy who was coming in from Los Angeles. With him was David Jull who chaired the tourism committee in Australia, They were making the trip over to vouch for Laker and would be key witnesses at the continuation of the Australia hearing the next day. Dix had to meet with Captain Alan Hellary and Laker's Chief Pilot, Captain Barry Rawlins. They had a full agenda, part of which had been submitted by Captain Gordon Steer who headed up the Laker Airways Flight Crew Association. LAFCA was a very low key, quasi-union set up to represent Laker's pilots and flight engineers. Captain Steer was highly respected and Dix met with him whenever he came over to New York, so he was fairly up to date on any potential grievances or suggestions for improvement the flight crews may have. Usually LAFCA's concerns were fairly minor and easily remedied issues such as crew positioning on regional airlines and hotel accommodation, but on this occasion Dix was taken a little of-guard.

Over lunch with Laker's top pilots, Hellary produced a letter Steer had written after he had returned from a trip to Miami. It contained an extremely well-detailed breakdown of the direct operating costs of the flight and a similarly thorough account of the passengers on both outbound and return legs. Laker's captains knew how much it cost to operate the planes, but few had taken the trouble to do such a comprehensive analysis. Steer's conclusion was that both flights to and from Miami had both been loss-makers despite high load factors in both directions. Apparently he had taken his conclusions to Freddie and had been immediately fobbed off and referred to John Jones. Hellary was concerned that Laker's management pilots weren't getting a fair hearing any more when they invariably had good suggestions on how to improve Laker's operations. Dix took all this in as well as listening to their observations and concerns about the forthcoming Australia and trans-Pacific routes. He gave them the benefit of everything he knew and said he thought Australia was a long shot based on what he'd experienced while in Canberra. Dix also said he thought it highly unlikely Japan would grant traffic rights but that he would be going there again in March to see Mitsui and seek their support with the government. He urged Hellary to get with Dick Bradley and look again at the Hong Kong to Honolulu leg as it would be a critical component of Route 6 and the one with the least margin for error. Dix promised to speak with Freddie when he saw him the next day at the resumption of the Australia hearings. On the train back up to London that evening, he wondered why Laker's top pilots weren't being listened to. Hellary had been with Freddie for decades, Gordon Steer was one of the most respected captains in the company, almost like a father-figure to the younger pilots. Anyone who flew wide-body jet aircraft for a living wasn't just an average guy and it would be a fool who didn't respect their observations. After all, they had lots of time to think about how to do things better on a nine hour flight to Miami or an eleven hour flight to LA.

At 10:00am on Thursday 5th of February, the Australia hearing resumed, with Leonard Bebchick of BCal making a typically powerful representation as to why BCal and not Laker should be granted the Australia licence. Guy recalls the hearing in London as being "unforgettable." He said: "Fred and his attorney Bob Beckman, performed for the committee like two old vaudevillians. The chairman would ask one a question, and the other would answer it. They would then discuss the merits of each other's answer." It was all done with much humour and laughter amongst old friends. British Airways' barristers relished the fun. Guy told them afterwards: "I thought you went a bit light on me, and I am grateful. It's pretty intimidating but fun." One barrister replied: "We all like Fred and if my parents ever found out I had given you a hard time, they would never forgive me. My family are the Seekers biggest fans."

Freddie told Ray Colegate, who was chairing the panel, that since his last application to fly to Australia in 1978, the attitude of Australia's airlines had changed. He thought that it was highly unlikely the Australian government would block his plans. His hyperbole even included him saying that Qantas was now more in favour but the application for a licence to fly to Australia was bitterly opposed by British Airways. Its lawyer claimed the Laker application was "a farrago of nonsense." Notwithstanding the anticipated opposition from BA, there should have been no doubt about the outcome, given that the benefits were obvious and tourism to Australia was so underserviced. Beckman hammered home that it was 'an expansion of the market and no threat whatsoever to existing cartels and IATA members currently servicing the route'.

At the end of the hearing, Athol announced everyone was to be his guest at a Petula Clark concert that Friday night so Freddie and Pat Laker, Greg Dix and his wife Linda accompanied Athol. They all got to meet Petula backstage after the show; it was fairly obvious that Athol and Pet were old 'mates'. The hearing resumed on Tuesday 10th of February in order to wrap everything up.

The CAA said a decision would be made quickly, although it was clear that even if the CAA gave a favourable ruling, the Australian government may not.

Freddie sent Dix off again, this time his brief was to ensure Australia and Japan were on side. After an encouraging two days in Seattle, Dix again went to Honolulu and over three days there set everything up for Laker to transit Hawaii on Route Six, that he'd been assured was Laker's for the asking. 12th-14th of March was spent in Melbourne and Sydney but then it was off to Japan for what would for sure be a challenging round of meetings. After three days of sitting patiently in Mitsui's boardroom with their top executives, it was still unclear whether Laker could expect their support with the government. Freddie felt they owed him a favour for buying the first three DC-10s, but it was clear it was just a drop in the bucket to Mitsui and in fact was never even mentioned. Dix called Freddie from the Grand Palace hotel while in Tokyo and urged him to speak to anyone who would listen in the Foreign Office and to have Beckman speak to someone in the US State Department. It was clearly going to need the strongest governmental lobbying if Laker was to have any chance at all of operating in and out of Japan.

After a week in Hong Kong and a further few days in Sharjah, Dix arrived back in the UK to brief Freddie and Beckman. He said before meeting any more high level civil servants in Australia or Japan, Laker needed someone who understood their language and related to how the bureaucracy worked. Freddie said he had just the man for that, Geoffrey Lowe who had worked in the Foreign Office. He pledged to send him along with Dix next time.

On the 1st and the 2nd April 1981, a hearing for Laker's application to operate to Sharjah, both as a transit point and as a destination was held at the CAA in London, during which Freddie was subjected to a devious and concerted smear campaign by British Caledonian and British Airways. A photograph of Freddie taken eighteen months earlier in Jerusalem at the Wailing Wall wearing a kippah was circulated to the leaders of the UAE, including Sheikh Sultan of Sharjah. The aim was to have Laker Airways put on the Arab boycott list and forever block Laker Airways from Sharjah and any other Arab nation. The Sheikh had to send the pictures to the Arab boycott office that organised the blacklisting of any companies sympathetic to Israel. Freddie made light of what happened, joking that he wanted to put in a prayer for his worldwide 'Skytrain' ambitions. The man who first circulated the photo was Abdullah Nasser, chairman of Nasser Air Travel and Shipping Agency, who just happened to be British Caledonian's agent in Dubai, Sharjah's next door neighbour. Mr Nair, of the Dubai National Travel Agency sent the copies to the Dubai newspapers. Nair denied there had been a conspiracy but claimed he did it 'because we are Arabs'. However, the smear campaign backfired as the Emir of Sharjah had sent Mohammed Al-Hajri, his Director General of Civil Aviation to London to speak up for Sir Freddie Laker personally.

In the meantime, Laker Airways inaugurated Gatwick to Tampa service on the 2nd April. Tampa's close proximity to Disney World and the beautiful beaches of Florida's Gulf Coast made it a superb holiday destination. Laker averaged healthy load factors of over 74 per cent on the Tampa route from its inception, but was facing tough competition from Air Florida on the Miami route, who undercut Laker with a one-way bookable fare of only £199 - £41 cheaper. Miami was a successful Skytrain route if judged purely on load factor, however as nearly all the traffic were UK originators heading to Florida on vacation, its year-round, long term sustainability was in doubt. Without a strong feed from Latin America, Laker's Miami route would inevitably be a low-yield, high cost, loss making operation. The uncertain commercial viability was compounded by the DC-10-30's performance degradation, that was being carefully monitored.

As with the DC-10 purchases and the six-year battle for Skytrain, Freddie had made an enormous financial commitment in the Airbus A300s for Europe. Freddie and Beckman had vowed to keep fighting for the European licences and on April 19th 1981 they continued the licencing quest on 'friendly' terms. The CAA and the Department of Trade, now headed up by John Biffen MP who had succeeded John Nott, were anxious to see some sort of definitive answer. They were openly encouraging Freddie in his efforts. Politicians were always happy to make use of Sir Freddie Laker when it suited them to do so and he was similarly happy to play his part. The statement of claim for the formative litigation was disclosed to the Ministry on a private basis. The UK High court action was a short cut to the European Court to which it had a referral procedure. It meant Freddie could expect a decision within a year. Freddie's persistence had paid off in the past, it had taken six years of lobbying and litigation to force his way onto the North Atlantic. Now, he was no less motivated and said "I'm determined to get a 'can opener on Europe."

Laker Airways continued preparing in Australia and in the UK as if the route licenses were going to be granted any day. Based on the struggle they'd had with the protectionist Australian government, just to be sure Freddie had Greg Dix return to Australia on 20th April 1981. This time, he was ably accompanied by Geoffrey Lowe, the former high level British diplomat who had experience dealing with the tricky elements of bureaucracy. They flew to Sydney and then drove to Canberra. The annual National Tourism Outlook Conference was being held there on 22nd and 23rd of April at which time Dix and Lowe had a meeting with the top Qantas executives. It was fairly obvious Qantas had played their hand with the Ministry of Transport. Undeterred, they met with the Minister and despite Lowe's considerable diplomatic skills, it was at that meeting where it became clear Laker would not be granted permission to fly to Australia, irrespective of the individual wishes of the states. The opposition from Qantas, aided of course by British Airways with whom they had a pooling agreement, was simply too strong... and perhaps the Minister too weak.

However, what the Australians decided didn't matter in the end, as on Friday 1st May 1981, the Laker application to fly to Australia was rejected by Britain's CAA. They also rejected an application from British Caledonian. The CAA concluded that the route could not support more than two carriers. Freddie's ten-year quest for an Australian licence was appealed to the British Secretary of State on the 22nd of May. The CAA, BA and BCal put in their typical responses and Laker's Bob Beckman drafted responses to theirs, as the tedious, time-consuming and money-draining Australian licencing process began again.

To compound the disappointment, all hopes of operating to Sharjah were dashed a few days later when the British CAA rejected Laker's bid to operate to Sharjah as a terminal point. Freddie and Beckman immediately began planning an appeal against this decision as well, as it was completely illogical.

The UK government was actively investigating European airfares throughout 1981. The Trade and Industry Committee sought their own information from a number of airlines and organisations by way of a select committee, frustrated that the draft regulation by the European Commission for enforcement was still pending. They believed that the European Community already had the legal powers and the duty to outlaw anti-competitive practices by its member states. As far as air transport was concerned the Commission had failed resulting in conspiracy against the consumer and frustration on the principles of the treaty.

The time was right to assess what progress had been made to enable the people of Europe to travel between the cities of Europe at prices they could afford. Many of the witnesses that came before them, including Laker Airways' in-house group solicitor, Christopher Brown repeated that the fares were over regulated; but no-one besides Laker supported substantial deregulation in Europe.

Nineteen airlines stood in Freddie's way, including BA and BCal. The CAA had the tricky task of balancing the protection of airline finances and the exploitation of travellers by way of high airfares. If new carriers like Laker Airways, who had just experienced their best year ever on the North Atlantic, introduced lower fares, it would force the European governments who owned their national airlines into paying higher subsidies. None of the EEC governments wanted more competition especially with a recession looming. There had been a lot of talk about the experience of the United States and their deregulation, most of it to the effect that it was bad for business. In other words, deregulation was a failure and would not work in Europe. While deregulation was sharpening competition and efficiency in the USA, it was said to be worsening service, especially to smaller communities. The effect on the top twenty US domestic markets had resulted in a rise in carriers serving the routes and an increase in round trip non-stop flights. The phrase being bandied about was "the jury is out on deregulation." Fearing contagion, the European airlines and their governments were terrified of the consequences should Laker be successful. In May 1981, Lord Bethell asked the European court for a ruling on the argument that the Commission of the EEC had failed to stop fare fixing and other restrictive practices. The EEC's new competition commissioner, Dutch politician Frans Andriessen started taking legal action against the governments and airlines over the anti-competitive practices and introduced some rule changes. Before the year was out, bureaucracy would have defeated him. Like Freddie's, his ideas were too revolutionary and too dangerous.

At the beginning of July, the Trade and Industry committee paid a visit to the European Commission in Brussels where they discussed the liberalisation of air transport with a number of senior officials. Finding general agreement that airfares in Europe were too high, reinforced the enquiry. Existing price fixing arrangements were hampering another principle of the EEC, freedom of movement of people.

The report that emerged in July 1981 strongly supported the view, persuasively argued by Laker's Christopher Brown that more competition to flag carriers throughout Europe was desirable. Liberalisation of route entry was the key to effective competition and he recommended that the government lost no opportunity in pressing the initiative.

Freddie himself came before the House of Lords sub committee investigating the European air fares and gave another bravura performance, demanding the de-regularisation, liberalising of air transport in Europe and the taking on of the wicked cartels.

Despite all the rhetoric, by August 1981 out of the revised applications, Laker Airways had only gained a tiny toehold in Europe with permission to fly to Zurich from the 1st April 1982. The day the decision was announced, Freddie's immediate reaction was 'this is a dirty trick by the CAA'. Zurich was his third choice, he would have preferred Frankfurt or Dusseldorf that were both in the European Economic Community, whereas Zurich was not. The bilateral air service agreement between the UK and Switzerland allowed only one carrier and BA was already designated. It would have required a renegotiation of the agreement with a country not exactly known for having liberal policies with respect to civil aviation.

The Swiss situation demonstrated the problem Laker faced no matter what the CAA were prepared to licence Laker for. It was perhaps the folly of the entire 'Airbus for Europe' quid pro quo initiative. Behind the apparent dual ambitiousness of the Airbus acquisition and the European route applications, there had been in Freddie's mind a clear understanding from the government that if he bought the Airbus A300 aircraft he would be given the routes within Europe to fly them. That was the trade off. However, the inferred 'promise' by the British was only the tip of the iceberg. Every single city pair the British CAA licenced Laker for would still need reciprocity granted by the dozen or more European governments, irrespective of The Treaty of Rome.

Freddie had committed the cardinal sin of naively believing politicians. He felt certain the British government would go into bat for him with their European counterparts. He was duped and another door was slammed shut.

CHAPTER 38

# Route Six

## Major misjudgements

June 1981

At just after 9:30am on Saturday 6th June 1981, a dark brown Rolls Royce Phantom limousine belonging to the Regent Hotel was standing outside the arrivals area of Hong Kong's Kai Tak airport. Greg Dix was there to meet Sir Freddie and Laker Airways' in house counsel, Christopher Brown who had flown into Hong Kong on Cathay Pacific's flight CX 200. It was the start of a two-week long trip, during which Freddie hoped to secure a valuable route across the Pacific Ocean for Laker Airways that would turn it into a true global enterprise. During the 12-hour flight from London, the pair had been pampered by Cathay's legendary first class service and managed to get some sleep. Eastbound jet lag could be quite disorientating, so Dix who was coordinating the itinerary had committed Freddie for some media work almost immediately so his body clock could adjust to Hong Kong Standard Time, which was seven hours ahead of the UK's Daylight Savings.

Dix had been in Hong Kong since the previous Wednesday working with PR powerhouse Mary Chiang drumming up interest in the new services that Laker Airways planned to launch in the east. He'd had productive discussions about ticket sales with Tommy and George Chen of CL Thomson Express who were one of the largest trans-Pacific travel wholesalers. The Chen's operation would be crucial to selling a large portion of Laker's trans-Pacific product between Hong Kong and the USA. As in his previous trips to the colony, Dix had been entertained in fine style by Laker's Hong Kong Director, Dr. Freddie Watson and his popular wife, Jacqui. They had introduced him to some key people in Hong Kong who were all excited about the prospect of Laker Airways' imminent arrival. Laker's American lawyer, Bob Beckman had flown in the day before from Washington with his wife, Angela. He was comfortably ensconced at the Regent in his usual palatial suite overlooking Victoria harbour.

"I thought Pat and Bettina were coming on this trip," Dix said to Freddie once they were in the limo heading to the hotel. "They're coming in tomorrow," Freddie responded with a look on his face that Brown and Dix took to mean he almost wished they weren't. There was a surprise for Dix, "we have to go to Tokyo" he continued, "the Japanese are being difficult and I've arranged for us to see Hattori at Mitsui. I need them to pull some strings for us with the Japanese licensing board." "Er, OK but when are we going to fit that in" Dix asked knowing they had a full schedule of hearings and PR activity in Hong Kong ahead of them. "Right after the hearings are done, can you get us a ride on Cathay?" Dix said he would ask Jerry Penwarden for a couple of tickets for Sunday the 14th, the earliest they could make it out, followed by "I'll have some business cards printed for you if we're going to Japan," knowing Freddie never carried business cards. Freddie replied "don't bother they all know who I am." He was booked for a photo session followed by a meeting with George Tan of the Carrian Group that would likely take up all of Saturday afternoon. Brown asked why they were still in discussion with Carrian as they all knew that Tan had a dubious reputation and they had been warned to steer clear of Carrian. "Because he wants to buy into Laker Airways" Freddie replied almost nonchalantly as Brown and Dix looked at each other with one of those 'what the ...' expressions. Laker Airways' precarious financial position meant Freddie was talking to anyone and everyone if they had money to invest in the airline. Despite a fairly strong start to the year, 1981 was now on track to be the first time in Freddie's life that one of his companies would make an operating loss.

After he had said a brief 'hallo' to the Beckmans and derided Bob about his luxurious accommodations, Freddie had a short rest and then was back in the Rolls for his first press engagement. He was spreading the word to all who would listen that Laker Airways would soon be granted a permit to fly across the Pacific. The PR offensive went well and the next day the story was splashed in the *South China Morning Post* as well as on all the local television channels.

On Sunday morning, Freddie took the Regent's Rolls Royce to meet his wife Patricia and eighteen year-old stepdaughter Bettina at Kai Tak. It was fairly obvious to Freddie's inner circle there was some tension in the Laker household. Sensibly, no-one said anything.

After he had dropped them off at the hotel, Freddie and Dix were back in the Regent's limo to visit with the renowned and reclusive Sally Aw Sian at her home. The meeting had been arranged by Tommy Chen who was a friend of Miss Aw and would also be there. The head of the international Sing Tao Publishing Group empire, Sally Aw was known as the 'Tiger Balm Lady' after inheriting her father's fortune that had mainly come from the Tiger Balm natural medicinal products empire he and her brother had built. It was important politically for Freddie to be introduced to everyone of prominence in Hong Kong and Miss Aw was hugely influential in the Far East and beyond. As they were leaving, Tommy Chen pointed to the number plate on Sally Aw's Rolls Royce parked outside. It was 8888. Freddie didn't get it at first until Dix reminded him on the drive back about the necessity for Laker's published fares from Hong Kong to be approved by the Feng Shui consultant.

Route Six was a critical component of Freddie Laker's global aspirations. It was a dormant route available to a British airline under the Bermuda Two bilateral agreement between the USA and Britain. At the time, Hong Kong was a British colony and therefore enjoyed some of the privileges of the mother country. Two US airlines, Pan Am and Northwest Orient were already operating a series of trans-Pacific flights. Hong Kong's Cathay Pacific was also planning its own trans-Pacific operations starting with Hong Kong to Seattle.

Slated for Monday 6th June 1981, the Hong Kong ATLA would hear Laker Airways' case for Route 6, the eastbound leg from Hong Kong to the North American gateways of Los Angeles, San Francisco and Seattle and on to Vancouver if desired. Freddie had already stated in an interview with *Flight International* he would introduce a fare of under £200 one way; it was based on nothing more than the need to say something to get ink in Britain's leading aviation publication and was an absurb statement, even by Freddie's standards of hyperbole. Tokyo was part of Route 6 but without considerable political support in Japan, traffic rights would be a long shot. Nevertheless, if licensed by Hong Kong it would be possible to operate the route via Honolulu and if necessary Guam. Not that there would be much traffic to Guam, but Honolulu was significant as Hawaii was a favourite vacation destination for most Asians.

Laker Airways' bid to serve Hong Kong from London had been turned down and the thinking now was to operate Route Six, if successfully licensed to do so to Hong Kong via the Pacific first, with the hope of perhaps being granted the Hong Kong – London portion later. The permit to fly Route Six in its entirety depended on approval from Britain, Hong Kong and Japan. Under the bilateral agreement between the USA and UK, the Americans were expected to rubber stamp it once all other approvals had been granted.

It wasn't clear in the bilateral agreement whether Tokyo was mandatory or an option. Notwithstanding, Laker's team was proceeding as if Tokyo was to be a component of the route, despite everyone being aware the Japanese would be extremely protectionist and not likely to grant Laker traffic rights without considerable governmental pressure. Hence, the forthcoming meeting in Tokyo with Mitsui, whose keiretsu was one of the leading conglomerates in Japan.

The London to Hong Kong route and Route Six together would enable Laker Airways to have a 'ring around the world.' The plan was christened 'Globetrain.' Like the original Skytrain, it was something that Freddie had become fixated on. However, after years of tireless work and considerable expense, Freddie and Bob Beckman had little to show for their efforts. This was Freddie's last shot to rescue something from his rapidly crumbling plan for global domination.

Hong Kong had been an obsession of Freddie's for years and he didn't hide his disappointment of not being granted the licence to operate between London and Hong Kong. He now realised the full extent of Swire Pacific's power base in the colony and he was clearly in awe of what Duncan Bluck had achieved in his decade as Cathay Pacific's Managing Director. After successfully guiding Cathay's global development, Bluck was now Chairman of the entire Swire group in Hong Kong and one of the most powerful men in the region.

Freddie and Bluck had crossed paths in the late 60s when Bluck was Chairman of Bahamas Airways that at the time was co-owned by Swire.

It was no secret to those close to him that it was more than air routes to Hong Kong Freddie coveted. He was too late to be one of the great white colonists of British East Africa, dictatorial regimes that were in alignment with Freddie's philosophies and autocratic business style. Now, with Hong Kong, he envisaged himself as being one of its modern day tai-pans, similar to the main characters in the fictional '*Noble House*' that had just been released. Author James Clavell's best-selling novel was actually based on the Jardine-Matheson organisation, with whom Laker Airways was affiliated through their subsidiaries, Jardine Airways, Hong Kong Land Co. and Dairy Farm. The fact that Hong Kong would inevitably revert back to China fairly soon didn't temper Freddie's pursuit for prominence in the British colony.

Freddie, Brown and Dix spent Sunday afternoon being briefed by Bob Beckman on what was to be presented to the Hong Licensing authority, ATLA starting the next morning. Beckman handed out copies of the Route Six licence application. It was an inch thick and filled with page upon page of statistical data. Beckman's competent statistics expert, Lynn Gramley had compiled the data and Angela Beckman had coordinated the production of the document. Much of the statistical analyses was actually irrelevant to Laker's bid for the route but it helped pad out the application, as was typical of the Beckman strategy for these type of route applications. Unsurprisingly, it was the first time anyone other than the Beckmans had seen the completed document, although Dix had been feeding pertinent technical and operational information to Beckman for several months.

Included in the application was a roughly drawn map showing the various permutations of trans-Pacific routes Laker Airways was applying for. Beckman felt that demonstrating every route they sought was vital to the success of their application. Freddie however was immediately sceptical; he believed it should have been confined only to the routes being applied for, "Bob, why are we clouding up this application by talking about Europe and the North Atlantic? I think this is why the ATLA got scared last time when we were applying for the Hong Kong – London permits. We muddied the water by showing them our plan for the trans-Pacific and Japan. There's no wonder Cathay used all their political muscle to have our application chucked out."

Laker Airways' failure to secure the London to Hong Kong licence was like an open wound and he was clearly still angry with Beckman, as Dix chimed in with, "bringing up the charter flight programme to Japan, Thailand, Taiwan, and all those other points in Asia at the same time probably didn't help our case either." They were all Cathay Pacific's prime destinations and Dix's observation prompted sour looks on both Freddie and Beckman's faces. Bob Beckman had been supremely confident Laker Airways would be granted the Hong Kong - London route. He had seriously under-estimated the power of Cathay Pacific and had focused his taunts at the hearings on his long time nemesis, Leonard Bebchick who represented BCal. At the time, Beckman had thought the failure to be licensed for Hong Kong - London was because Freddie had given a dreadful performance on the stand. Freddie and Dix had agreed to keep mum about Freddie's decadent night before with the Chinese girls and let Bob think it was just fatigue from jet lag. In reality, Laker's fate had been decided much earlier by the Swire Group and Cathay Pacific.

Cathay Pacific had colluded with BCal on the earlier London to Hong Kong application and succeeded in getting Laker shut out. Cathay was part-owned by the Swire Pacific Group, who along with a handful of other British-owned entities dominated the colony. They would do anything to protect their patch. Cathay wasn't as yet operating trans-Pacific between Hong Kong and the USA, but they were in the process of buying more 747s. They had made it clear that they wanted to start service to Vancouver and then Seattle once they had the equipment, pitting them head to head with Northwest. Cathay was therefore expected to object to Laker's Route Six application. Their case would perhaps not be as strong as it was with respect to the Hong Kong – London route which they had served with a 747 since July 1980. Nevertheless, the influence of Cathay Pacific in the colony was powerful and never to be underestimated.

Beckman was adamant that demonstrating all the European and North American connecting traffic potential for Route Six was just as important as the point to point traffic forecasts, but Freddie didn't agree. Dix, who had the strongest operational experience quickly pointed out another flaw in the plan. Laker Airways didn't own any aircraft that could actually fly most of the routes shown on the map. This remark drew surprised looks on everyone's faces. "Bob, I wrote to you in May advising that the DC-10-30 wouldn't do many of the routes you're showing here... unless it was flying almost empty" Dix said emphatically. The route map showed Hong Kong direct to Los Angeles, San Francisco, Seattle and Vancouver. Even the Boeing 747SP, that at the time was the civilian aircraft with the longest range, would be on limits to do 6,000 plus nautical miles. Laker's Dick Bradley had concurred with this point.

The payload-range limitations of Laker's DC-10-30s hadn't been considered when preparing the document. Dix added: "Hong Kong or Tokyo direct to Vancouver isn't part of the bilateral." Agitated, he went on, "and Vancouver's an add-on from a USA west coast city, didn't anyone read the bloody air services agreement?" Hong Kong non-stop to Honolulu was over 4,800 nautical miles and Laker's DC-10s could only just make it to Los Angeles which from Gatwick was a bit less, "and if necessary we can drop into Salt Lake or Vegas for a splash of fuel" Dix reinforced his point. "If you set off from Hong Kong for Hawaii and something changes en route, you either end up on a remote bit of coral or you get your feet wet." The room was silent. Laker's two-engine drift down minimums wouldn't be in compliance and the only en route diversion points were Wake or one of the Marshall Islands. Jet fuel in remote locations such as Wake would be extremely expensive, if it was even available.

Freddie looked over at Beckman who had stopped smoking and his eyes were now glowing. Freddie wondered if Bob would rebut Dix's analysis verbally or just walk over and punch him in the mouth to shut him up. But the room was silent. Seizing the opportunity, Dix continued his lecture pointing out that Laker Airways currently didn't have a reservations system that could handle multiple pick up and drop off points. So even if Laker was given traffic rights to operate Hong Kong, Tokyo, Honolulu, Los Angeles it would be almost impossible to avoid having empty seats on some or all of the sectors. Dix reminded Beckman that he had written to him earlier asking why he was planning for three flights a week from Honolulu to Tokyo but six flights a week in reverse. Laker couldn't even guarantee full flights point to point between New York and Gatwick, even with fifty standby's at the gate, because their respective reservations systems didn't communicate with each other." Seeing the quizzical looks from Beckman, he explained that in the USA they were using Braniff's Cowboy system, but in the UK they'd been developing custom software they'd named 'Brian' for over two years that still wasn't working." "Dix is right" Freddie shouted as he was now annoyed, "John Jones is tearing his hair out, he sends me memos every week about it. Without a really good reservations system you know what will happen don't you?" Dix didn't wait for Beckman's response to Freddie, "Bob, even if the Japanese give us an OK which we all know is highly unlikely, we'll have a mass of Japanese tourists on the Tokyo to Honolulu leg that we'll have to bring back at some point as they'll nearly all book an Apex. But we can't guarantee to uplift as many passengers in Honolulu as we drop off for the leg to LA and vice versa."

Freddie nodded in agreement as Laker Airways was challenged controlling its capacity on point to point sectors such as Gatwick to New York, so to do it on four or five live sectors would be impossible. Beckman sat silent for a moment then he chided them for being so luddite in their thinking. He felt that by the time Laker was ready to fly the route in 1982, they'd have sorted out the reservations system issue, but neither of them shared Beckman's confidence. Dix wasn't finished "look, let's say by some miracle, the Japanese give us a permit and we do manage to have a reservations system that can work for multiple points, why the hell are we then planning this massive dog-leg south to serve Honolulu en route to LA." He was making the argument that Laker's objective was to fly people from Tokyo to LAX and then possibly on to London on the LA service. Laker wasn't in the business of flying Japanese tourists to Hawaii or California. The Japanese knew that and were massively protectionist about that route. Also, an airline flying Japanese tourists needed to have Japanese speaking flight attendants and translators on board. Clearly, no-one would fly from Hong Kong over the Pacific to get to London when they could fly westbound faster over the Middle East. Yet the licence application showed potential traffic statistics from Hong Kong to London via LA. Dix suggested it was futile and Freddie nodded in agreement as Beckman accused Dix of always being able to find the cloud under the silver lining.

"So what do you suggest Greg" Freddie asked. "Why don't we change the application and show we intend to fly to the USA over the top. Tokyo to LA is about the same as Gatwick to LA – around 4,730 nautical, so we should make it eastbound non-stop with the tail winds. If it's marginal, we can drop into Anchorage, Vancouver or Seattle for fuel. Westbound is another matter and in almost all cases we'd have to stop at Anchorage for an en route uplift. Seattle to Tokyo is just over 4,100 nautical and over ten and a half hours flying, so if the headwinds aren't too strong, we should make it OK. We obviously have to skirt around Russia unless we want to be shot down." Freddie thought about what Dix had suggested but replied that they hadn't ever considered flying the great circle to the US west coast and that Honolulu had always been part of the plan. "Right, I understand," Dix responded, "but Honolulu is what will scare the Japanese, they told me as much when I was there. The bilateral is pretty clear to me, so why is Honolulu so critical? I've been there three times already gearing them up but I haven't been to Anchorage once."

The room was silent again for a few moments as Dix's words sank in. "As for the DC-10-30s," he went on, "quite honestly I wouldn't use them on the Pacific. They're long thin routes and to start with I doubt we'll get loads to fill a DC-10 and like I said, they don't have the range. We'll be diving into Guam for fuel on almost every flight to Hawaii." Freddie chimed in that he couldn't afford the fuel at Guam, confirming the point.

Dix then suggested they buy more 707-320s and start off with equipment more suitable for the expected passenger loads and with the range to do any of the legs non-stop. He recommended they develop the routes first and then buy 747s when the traffic warranted it. Laker's DC-10-30s weren't optimum for the job, especially with the performance degradation issues they were dealing with. Cathay Pacific were re-equipping and it was discussed they may have more 707-320s and that an aircraft purchase could help with relations in Hong Kong. Freddie quickly acknowledged the 707s they had bought from Cathay in 1978 had been fantastic work-horses. He also recalled both Dix and John Jones encouraging him to use the 707s to start with on the Los Angeles Skytrain back in 1978. He was adamantly against it only to experience half empty DC-10s and over £2 million pounds in operating losses for the first few months of the LA operation. Dix reiterated that the Boeings were Northwest's originally and they used them exclusively on the Pacific until they bought their 747s. "No airline, including Pan Am knows how to operate across the Pacific Ocean more efficiently than Northwest" he concluded.

Christopher Brown sat silently, clearly fascinated with the many operational considerations of the trans-Pacific route application and the challenges Laker would face if granted the permits to operate the routes. But he wondered why this hadn't all been discussed before they wrote the application. Brown muttered that it seemed to him they had shot first and aimed later. "Exactly Chris, just like we usually do, LA was a classic example," Dix said loudly enough for Beckman and Freddie to hear. Risking coming across like a know-all he finished off with "finally, even if we get Route Six approved we won't have enough DC-10-30 capacity to fly it in the summer of 1982, as all the dash thirties will be needed for the LA and Florida Skytrain. Remember we'll have one based in Manchester plus two flights a day each from Gatwick. Do the maths. And that's without any ad hoc charters, the Hajj, Barbados and all the other commitments." Dix reminded them he had outlined the round the world flight times in a memo, showing the elapsed time to be 59+ hours westbound and about 52 hours eastbound with ground time. "We'll need six planes to do the schedules, the weather is unpredictable and where will we get an engine in the Marianas" he finished off, while a speechless Freddie ground his teeth.

Despite the many arguments to the contrary, Beckman was extremely agitated at having his trans-Pacific plan torn to shreds and insisted on staying with the current application. He was adamant that it was too late now to change it for the next day and copies of the document had already gone to the ATLA.

As Freddie, Brown and Dix filed out of the Beckman's suite, Dix gave Freddie a polite earful about the lunacy of waiting until the day before a hearing before evaluating the contents of the application, that was already in a binder and couldn't be changed. Not for the first time, he wondered if Freddie was in over his head. He was doubting Freddie's decision-making abilities and wondering why he wasn't more involved in the business, especially with critical route planning. Something was distracting him from the job at hand and it was starting to affect the progress of the entire organisation. Risking a backlash, he told Freddie firmly, "I think you rely too much on the Beckmans Freddie. They may be great at the legal aspect of the licensing process, although that's sometimes debatable when Bob gets the red mist about Len Bebchick, but they know fuck-all about operating aircraft and the constraints we face." He again stressed that crossing the Pacific was perhaps more challenging operationally than flying in Africa or South America. "Going over the top, if you stray off course even slightly, you could be shot down by a Mig, and then if you get your calculations just a tiny bit wrong or something happens en route to Hawaii, you end up in the drink or on a tiny island where the locals wear grass skirts and probably think Jet A is cooking oil." Freddie looked shocked but acknowledged he had a point, even if Dix was deliberately overstating in an attempt to get his boss's attention back on track.

As the three men walked back to the Laker's suite, Freddie considered what Dix had said and realised that Laker Airways didn't have the best team in place to thoroughly oversee new, complex route applications from top to bottom. He was becoming increasingly frustrated with Bob Beckman with whom he had a love/hate relationship that he couldn't extricate himself from. His fees were outrageous and in the last four years, Laker Airways hadn't had one successful new route license outside North America that could be operated with any degree of commercial viability, including the loss-making Miami service. Freddie said he would have a meeting with his top managers in July where they would map out a new strategy, as it was becoming clear with so many license applications turned down, Beckman's approach may be misguided. To conclude his thoughts he burst out "and he pisses everybody off" as Brown and Dix hoped Freddie wasn't talking about them, "and then sends me a fucking great bill."

The hearing went more or less as expected with the usual posturing from the lawyers and hours spent debating seemingly irrelevant points. It was clear that unlike the London to Hong Kong hearings, the ATLA members who were a different group to previous hearings, seemed considerably more accommodating to Laker's Route Six bid, despite the numerous flaws in the route application document. Perhaps it was because Hong's Kong's Governor, Sir Murray MacLehose had always stated publicly that he supported Laker Airways serving the colony. More likely it was because no-one thought Laker had the wherewithal to actually operate the routes. It was a fair assessment given Laker Airways' financial situation and its operational capabilities at the time. Freddie was scheduled to meet the 64 year-old Governor the following Thursday but first he had to endure a dinner with George Tan of the Carrian Group on the Tuesday evening. Tan seemed determined to buy a stake in Laker Airways. Patricia and Bettina, Dix and Brown went along with Freddie and sat through Tan ranting about how a partnership would revolutionise travel in the region. Freddie agreed to give Tan a proper audience in his suite the following Saturday where specifics of the offer to buy into Laker Airways would be discussed. Brown cautioned it may not be approved by the CAA.

By the end of the week, Freddie had been in the hearings for five days, had done countless TV and press interviews, met with the Governor, and had breakfast, lunch or dinner with all the key Laker associates in Hong Kong. Mary Chiang, Laker's PR representative had done an impressive job with the press, radio and television schedule, prompting Freddie to comment, "where did you find her, Dix. She's terrific, maybe we could have her come over to London and give the chihuahua a few pointers," he said roaring with laughter at how that would go down with his effusive publicity officer, Robin Flood, with whom he had a similarly bizarre and costly relationship to the one he had with Robert Beckman. Unbeknownst to everyone at Laker Airways except perhaps Financial Director Robinson, Mrs Flood wasn't on the payroll but she and her husband had a lucrative consulting arrangement. Flood incredibly may well have been paid more than Captain Hellary or Deputy Managing Director Cliff Nunn; she enjoyed the many benefits of a 'special relationship'.

Laker Airways hosted a lavish reception at the Regent for Hong Kong's 'finest' on the Thursday evening. Dr Freddie Watson and his wife Jacqui had organised the exquisite event. They'd made sure the guest list included anyone who could be strategic to Laker Airways' ambitious Pacific Rim objectives.

A photographer from the high-society 'Tatler' magazine captured all the guests for a full page spread in their society pages that was tagged 'Laker Cocktails'. A wonderful photo of Freddie with Patricia and Bettina on either side of him was the feature photo at the top of the page. An ebullient Freddie was right back on his game at the party, doing the rounds and getting Hong Kong's upper echelon firmly on side, while a tanned Lady Patricia Laker looked stunning; many of the guests commented on what a lucky man Freddie was.

Bettina had chosen to wear a black silk Chinese dress that no-one had dared to suggest may be a cultural faux pas, even if it was being worn by a teenager. She spent the evening being wheeled around by Freddie while Dr Watson made sure everyone was bedazzled by Lady Laker. It had been a good week overall and approval for Laker to operate Route Six, despite the sketchy application the Beckmans had compiled, looked for now at least, quite positive.

Freddie realised that the voluminous licensing documents and the protracted hearings were mostly a charade and an opportunity for the lawyers to strut their stuff. The decisions on whether or not to licence Laker Airways had likely already been made, behind closed doors and many weeks earlier. Freddie had missed the fact that Hong Kong still had a strong class system, decades after social status was perhaps not as prevalent in the UK. It took more than wealth and fame to be accepted in one of Britain's colonies. Freddie's often overbearing demeanour was tolerated and perhaps even lauded in the UK and the USA. However, it didn't necessarily endear him to the right people in such a class-driven, closed society such as the predominantly ex-patriot community of Hong Kong. If Freddie had aspirations of being a tai-pan there, he would need to soften his approach and play the colonial game better. But it was highly unlikely that he would... or could.

On Friday 12th June, Freddie and Dix had a productive meeting with Trevor Bedford, managing Director of the Hong Kong Land Co. a division of the mighty Jardine-Matheson organization. Afterwards, they had to rush off to a studio for a Television engagement where Freddie made an appearance on Hong Kong's popular '*Here and Now*' show. Apart from his obvious annoyance with Beckman, everything seemed to be going well in Hong Kong until suddenly Freddie dropped a bombshell. "Pat's going back tonight," he announced irritably as he sat having his make-up removed. Seeing Dix's obvious surprise, he went on "she needs to get back for Charlie" and before Dix could ask if Freddie wanted him to line up some suitable 'entertainment' for that evening he quickly followed up with "but Tina's staying on with me and she's coming with us to Tokyo on Sunday. Can you get her a ticket on Cathay and would you change my room at the Imperial so I have a suite."

It wasn't obvious if this was a sudden change in the schedule or if Patricia had always planned to fly back to London that evening. Nevertheless, Freddie's demeanour was noteworthy. "That's a shame Freddie," Dix replied, "we have a few more important functions including Bedford's party and Pat's a terrific asset for us." He received an irritated response that Freddie would have Bettina there and not to worry, so he knew not to pursue it further.

Freddie and Jacqui Watson took Pat out to Kai Tak airport for her flight home. It was obvious to the Watsons that Patricia wasn't happy even though she had seemed fine the previous evening. Nothing was said as to what had brought about her departure, or more significantly why Bettina was remaining behind with Freddie for the next week. After a photo session on Saturday morning, where Freddie looked slightly worse for wear, they had the lunch meeting with George Tan of Carrian. Tan again ranted on about their forth-coming partnership as if it were already a done deal. "Fifty-fifty, fifty-fifty" Tan shouted over and over again waving his hands in the air, "together we can rule the world. I'll even paint Laker on the side of my building" as he pointed across the harbour to Hong Kong island where the Carrian group had its headquarters. Dix and Brown stood on the sidelines witnessing the spectacle and wondered how Freddie could possibly have been drawn into this, despite Carrian's assets and apparent influence in Hong Kong. Brown leaned over to Freddie and whispered "careful, you've got a tiger by the tail here." "Don't I know it" Freddie whispered back. Dix had earlier cautioned that an alliance of any sort with Tan would likely strain relations with Tommy Chen and C.L. Thomson. The Chens and their wholesale operation were vital to Laker's success in the region and they had been highly supportive of Laker for several years. Tan had been introduced to Freddie by John Wimbush, a senior partner at the esteemed law firm, Deacons who represented Tan and his Carrian group. Laker Airways' Hong Kong lawyer, the young and energetic Tony Fox also worked for Deacons and he'd cautioned against any involvement with Carrian. But Freddie was desperate to woo an investor in Laker Airways. Even if Tan and his Carrian Group didn't tick all the boxes, it was perhaps as good as Freddie could hope for given the company's precarious financial situation in mid-1981. The over commitment on new aircraft and declining north Atlantic traffic was now taking its toll. He turned down an invitation to Tan's Sunday 'morning prayers' ritual but committed Brown and Dix to attend on his behalf. It was met by frowns from his junior men who knew what they'd be in for at Tan's cult-like ritualistic event.

There were a few free hours before the Hong Kong Land Co's party so Dix asked Bettina if she wanted to accompany himself and Brown to the Regent's pool for a swim. Before she could reply, a clearly agitated Freddie said "absolutely not" and hustled the girl back into the suite. Dix was taken aback by Freddie's hostile reaction as he went off to meet Brown at the pool, wondering to himself if Freddie didn't trust him with his stepdaughter. It wouldn't be the first time that Freddie had concerns about the exploits of his young executives; one of the downsides of his being an influential role model.

That evening, Trevor Bedford and the Hong Kong Land Co. hosted a cocktail party for the Laker group. Freddie proudly showed off his step-daughter Bettina for the entire evening. His open and obvious affection for the attractive teenager drew quizzical glances from some of the party's guests who, perhaps naturally, wondered where his wife was. After recovering from the Carrian Sunday 'morning prayers', Brown flew back to London. Meanwhile Freddie, Bettina and Dix boarded Cathay Pacific's flight CX500 bound for Tokyo and what would be a game-changer for Laker Airways.

After lunch on Monday 15th of June, Dix knocked on the door of Freddie's suite at Tokyo's five star Imperial Hotel. Freddie was ready to go to the Mitsui offices and it was evident Bettina was coming too. Dix was quite certain it wasn't appropriate for her to come to Mitsui, as it was a decidedly male-dominated work environment but he said nothing for fear of raising Freddie's ire. They were duly met at the Mitsui head office reception area and taken up to the Aerospace Services Division. Upon entering the vast office that housed several hundred employees sitting at rows of perfectly aligned metal desks, the entire roomful of identically dressed Mitsui staff stood up from their desks, turned to the Laker party at the door and bowed in unison. It was a moving experience. They were shown to the 'office' of Mr Hattori, the head of Mitsui's aerospace department. It comprised of nothing more than an eight-foot square corner of the room, his desk was wood instead of metal, there was a small rug and two guest chairs. Considering his position in the organisation, this was about as understated as it could be. It was something Freddie in his former years would have embraced. However, by 1981 his earlier frugality and minimalist business practices had given way to arrogance and grandiosity, as if he felt the need to exhibit his wealth and success at every opportunity.

"Konnichiwa Hattori-san" Freddie greeted the younger man whom he had not met before, in his best Kentish-accented Japanese that he'd practiced an hour earlier, together with a quick bow of his head and an embarrassed grin. The Mitsui executive acknowledged Freddie's greeting with an appropriate bow followed by a presentation of his business card held in both hands. Freddie of course never had a business card as he assumed everyone knew who he was. Dix stepped in with a quick bow and presented his own card to the Mitsui top man with both hands, followed by a presentation of gifts he'd quickly cobbled together in Hong Kong. The small model Laker planes shaped like an egg and Skytrain bumper stickers were graciously accepted.

This was a very different Mitsui Corporation to the one Freddie had dealt with ten years prior when he bought the first DC-10-10s financed by the giant Japanese conglomerate. In 1971, Mitsui were massively grateful for Freddie's purchase of the cancelled ANA DC-10s and were more forgiving of his gregariousness and the occasional social and cultural faux pas. For the next hour, Freddie 'talked at' the Mitsui senior executive about everything Laker had achieved since the initial DC-10 acquisition. He lobbied for support with the Japanese government with respect to Laker's Route Six application and the traffic rights to serve Tokyo. Throughout, Hattori remained expressionless and said little. Freddie, as usual did nearly all the talking while Bettina sat patiently and Dix excused himself for a few minutes to say hello to some of Hattori's young management team with whom he'd met previously. The meeting concluded with Hattori confirming Freddie and Dix would have dinner with him and his executives later.

The Mitsui dinner had been arranged the week before and at that time, it was just for Freddie and Dix and had naturally not included Bettina. It soon became clear that Freddie was bringing Bettina anyway, whether she wanted to attend or not. That evening when Dix arrived at the door of Freddie's suite he was truly shocked. The teenager was once again wearing the same gaudy black silk Chinese dress, resplendent with embroidered dragons she had worn at the Regent party a few nights before. It was inappropriate attire in Hong Kong, but she had got away with it due to her age and who she was with. "You can't wear that, Bettina" Dix said firmly as he stepped into the suite. Freddie came rushing up "She looks fine Dix." But Dix was insistent, "Freddie, we're in Japan, the dress is Chinese and totally inappropriate and unacceptable; she should wear western clothes. They'll be insulted." But it wasn't Bettina's Chinese dress that was of concern to Dix, it was the fact she was coming at all. "You know it will be just Hattori and all his guys there don't you" Dix urged, hoping Freddie would comprehend. But he quickly realised his concerns no matter how valid, were falling on deaf ears. Freddie's insistence that his stepdaughter attend was ridiculous. He was about to compromise a carefully cultivated business relationship with Mitsui and perhaps even higher up the chain in Japan.

The dinner was to be a typical men only affair, followed by the customary gentlemen's entertainment the Japanese were known for; nothing salacious but traditionally not for women, especially a teenager. Dix's anxiousness was born out as the Laker party arrived for the Mitsui dinner. The exclusively male Japanese hosts all looked embarrassingly at their esteemed guest, the 58 year old English knight with his arm tightly around a young girl wearing a Chinese dress. In characteristic Japanese style, they quickly recovered their composure and politely ushered the Laker party to the table. The dinner proceeded more or less as expected although the conversation was untypically polite and muted. Freddie seemed to be in a world of his own at the dinner, chatting more to Bettina than to his hosts and unaware of the puzzled faces around the table. He was completely oblivious to what he'd done by this enormous social faux-pas and how it may affect future relations with Mitsui and the Japanese. For once, Dix bit his tongue and didn't get into it with Freddie afterwards. It was clear there was simply no listening to any reason; the obsession with his 18 year-old stepdaughter was clearly beyond logic and any counsel offered on the matter was likely to fall on deaf ears.

Upon returning to Hong Kong on Tuesday, Freddie and Dix had a meeting with Brian Keep, Hong Kong's Director of Civil Aviation. Keep gave them some assurance that he thought the Route Six application would go through and asked what Freddie thought the chances were of the Japanese giving them traffic rights. Freddie naively thought the meeting with Mitsui had gone well and that he would have their support. Dix remained silent but it was obvious Freddie wasn't thinking with a clear head. If he'd bothered to read the body language and facial expressions of the Mitsui executives while in Tokyo, he might have picked up on their reactions. Realistically, there now wasn't a hope in hell of Laker being granted any traffic rights by Japan.

They met Freddie and Jacqui Watson at the Mandarin Hotel for a drink before heading over to the bustling Aberdeen harbour. The Watsons had thoughtfully arranged a junk cruise to Lamma Island thinking Freddie may enjoy being out on the water. The trip down the Lamma Channel went without incident with Freddie closely chaperoning Bettina and hoping the junk wouldn't capsize. The incisive Watsons were by now wondering what was going on with Freddie, especially after Patricia's sudden departure from Hong Kong earlier.

Dinner ashore was at one of the numerous restaurants lined up on the esplanade. The strip was known as the Lamma Hilton and the food there was renowned. They were on their first drink having just ordered the food when the boat boy from the junk came running up yelling 'master, master, boat sinking'. The men all jumped up and ran down to the junk. Their suit jackets and Freddie's briefcase containing all the confidential documents for the Route Six licence were still aboard. The junk was a hive of activity as the boat boys from other junks helped bail out the water. Friends of the Watsons who were also on Lamma Island for dinner offered to give them a ride back to Aberdeen on their junk after they'd eaten. "Never again Dix, never again" admonished a noticeably rattled Freddie after the somewhat harrowing experience, as he and Bettina disappeared into their suite at the Regent.

Two more days were spent in Hong Kong doing an endless round of PR, lunches, dinners, and meetings. Freddie's schedule concluded with a meeting at the Civil Aviation Department followed by a last dinner with the local team who had all been supportive over the past few years. Freddie and Bettina were inseparable throughout and the pair were arm in arm with each other as they stepped into the Regent's Rolls Royce for the ride to the airport. They departed for London on Thursday evening the 18th of June on BCal's flight BR 381. Dix left the next day for Tokyo, then caught flight PA16 on Pan Am's 747SP, non stop to JFK. As he reclined his over-sized first class seat, he thought to himself 'this is the aircraft we really need if we are serious about operating across the Pacific. 5,860 nautical miles non-stop to New York, just touching the Arctic circle'. Followed by the worst jet lag imaginable.

During the exhausting flight home across the International Date Line, Dix wondered what on earth was going on with Freddie and his fanatical behaviour with Bettina. It was now indiscreet and being gossiped about. Considering all that was happening at Laker Airways, everyone needed to be fully engaged; the survival of the company was at hand and Freddie couldn't afford any domestic upheaval. It had been clear in Hong Kong and Japan that the infatuation with his teenage stepdaughter and his strange behaviour had perhaps compromised Laker Airways' future standing in the Far East.

One thing was certain; based upon what had happened in Tokyo, any chance of support from Mitsui whether it was for traffic rights or refinancing, was a lost cause. Freddie had blown it with the Japanese by bringing Bettina to a men-only business dinner and acting as he did. Dr Freddie Watson had taken Dix aside when they were together and asked what was going on. Watson had been put in a compromising position, given his reputable standing in the colony and after witnessing Freddie's imprudence at the Hong Kong social gatherings the Watsons had organised. Dix explained that Freddie was always demonstrative with his affections and he was protective of his stepdaughter, tactfully stopping short of likening him to Svengali. The astute Dr. Watson, who after decades of experience as a top gynaecologist had heard every tale of domestic turmoil and relationship issues imaginable, clearly wasn't buying it. But he diplomatically said no more.

Dix felt sympathy for Bettina; she seemed like an innocuous young girl who was clearly beguiled by her influential 58 year-old stepfather. She was the latest moth to be drawn to the Laker flame and he hoped she wouldn't get burnt, like so many others. Dix decided to discuss the sensitive issue with his wife when he got home. She usually had a good perspective on this sort of thing and Linda knew Freddie better than most. Perhaps she could knock some sense into him.

While they were together, Freddie had told Dix he had instructed Cliff Nunn to reorganise the USA. He didn't elaborate but hinted that it may mean Dix would now be spending more time in the USA than running around Asia, Australia and beyond. This was disappointing news as he loved it in Asia, especially Hong Kong. Dix and his wife Linda Earls had been getting ready to move to Hong Kong to manage Laker's Pacific Rim operations. The Hong Kong Land Company had already assigned a stunning apartment for them next to the funicular railway on Hong Kong Island, as well as prime office space in the Central district. Laker had a good team in Hong Kong and everyone knew they could make a real go of it in Far East Asia, once they had a foot in the door. Dix thought Route Six seemed like the best way to achieve that, with or without the Japanese factor. 'In fact,' he thought to himself, 'it could even be better without Japan and a 100 per cent concentration on Hong Kong to the west coast USA cities via Honolulu, even if it did mean a stop for fuel at Guam'. Freddie had always made it clear that without Tokyo, Route Six would probably not happen. There was, as always, a chance he would change his mind if the Japanese didn't play ball with traffic rights. After the Mitsui debacle, that now looked quite certain.

Shortly after, the Hong Kong ATLA agreed to grant Laker a licence for Route Six on the condition that if it proved to interfere with Cathay's existing traffic, Laker would lose their permit. Despite being unable to operate the route immediately, the Route Six approval raised Freddie's hopes for the reciprocal London-Hong Kong designation from the ATLA, that would connect the chain of destinations to make up his dream of the around the world service, Globetrain. However, Route Six, Hong Kong, Japan and beyond would all have to wait, as the USA had now become an urgent priority.

Following what Freddie had said in Hong Kong about reorganising the USA and formulating a new strategy for licensing applications, Dix was summoned to Gatwick to meet with Freddie, Cliff Nunn, John Jones and others. He arrived on 7th July at which time Freddie told him that Charles Maxwell was being fired and that Dix was to take over most of his responsibilities including the seventy-person strong central reservations operation. He said that he'd put Cliff Nunn in charge of the USA as he was too busy with trying to keep the airline afloat and "the thousand other things I have going on." Nunn had unilaterally decided to decentralise the USA as it was so large. He'd split the country into three sales regions, simplistically divided geographically. His plan called for David Tait to be promoted from Sales Manager, Florida to Regional Manager, South-Eastern USA & Latin America and Charles 'Skip' Clemens from Sales Manager, California to Regional Manager, Western USA.

Dix appealed to Freddie and Nunn that decentralising the USA in this way was fundamentally flawed. He suggested Tait, who had no airline operations experience, manage the sales and marketing functions while he would oversee the airports, operations, cargo, reservations and logistics, just as he had before all the globetrotting began. Clemens was new to Laker and despite his solid credentials would need some time to be effective. Dix suggested he come under Tait who could guide his sales initiatives. To strengthen his argument, Dix made the point that no-one in Georgia or the Carolinas, that would now fall under the Miami sales office would fly to the UK via Miami, similarly no-one in Colorado, that under Nunn's new map would be part of the LA sales office's responsibilities, was going to back-track to Los Angeles to get to London. He pulled out CAB statistical data to prove his point, showing that except for residents local to Los Angeles and Miami and those connecting by air from another point, everyone else in the USA flew to the UK via New York.

Frustrated, Dix then had a long session with Freddie and John Jones going over all the latest traffic figures for the UK-USA Skytrain routes. The forecasts for the 4th quarter of 1981 were hardly encouraging. Jones brought out the fare grid he had formulated for the winter of 1981-82, ostensibly the recovery plan for the company. There were four fare categories including a new 8-day walk-on, the original same-day walk on, full economy and Apex.

"What the hell is that?" shouted Dix, pointing at a line item on Jones's matrix. Freddie quickly jumped in and mumbled something about it being his 'secret weapon'. The three of them went over the fares Jones was proposing. Dix pointed out the full Economy fare was still way too close to the Apex to be viable. He had protested about this for the summer 1981 fares but it had fallen on deaf ears. "And why have you got Miami fares less than New York?" Clearly, Jones and Freddie were up to something as none of the proposed fares made very much commercial sense, especially given the high operating costs of the DC-10-30s on the Los Angeles and Florida routes.

After Jones had left, Dix got into it with Freddie. He rarely raised his voice at Freddie if anyone else was there, even Jones. But his frustration with everything that was happening, especially after the last trip to Asia and now the sudden re-organisation of the USA, was now stretched to the limit. First he told his boss that Cliff's absurd reorganisation plan clearly demonstrated just how little Nunn knew about North American travel. Then he lambasted the fares Jones had proposed for the winter. Finally he put Freddie on the spot by demanding "just what the hell is going on Freddie, I think you need to come clean," hoping he would explain his recent conduct. Freddie was shocked at Dix's affront but meekly responded that he had everything in hand and that he would be informed soon enough. It was obvious Freddie had no intention of coming clean. He was clearly under a great deal of pressure and it wasn't all work related, as Dix had witnesed first hand three weeks earlier.

Realising he was getting nowhere, Dix said an abrupt goodbye to Freddie, gave Lesley a pat on the shoulder of encouragement and empathy on the way out and went off to meet with Ian Allan, thinking maybe he would have a perspective on what was going on. Dix liked Allan and felt badly Freddie had put him in the unenviable position of Scheduled Services Manager; a thankless role in which he would be unlikely to make any serious headway.

Allan confirmed that an 'all hands on deck' directive had been given for the USA and that Freddie had told him any new route developments were on hold for now. Dix relayed to Allan what had gone down in Freddie's office. He knew Allan and Freddie went back decades, so perhaps Allan had some influence. It was clear Allan didn't think much of John Jones and the feeling was likely mutual. It was another dysfunctional aspect of Laker Airways' top commercial management team. Dix thought to himself how great the company would be if every department operated as well as Flight Ops and Engineering, or the USA for that matter. It looked as if Freddie's head was somewhere else now. He wasn't focusing on what was going on right under his nose at Gatwick or the USA... or in fact very much at all to do with Laker Airways.

Freddie's current state of mind was born out further, as on Friday 10th July, he and Dix along with a small group of Laker executives met with the Carrian Group's Chief Financial Officer, Rod Bell in Freddie's office at Gatwick. George Tan had sent Bell over to negotiate a better deal with Freddie for all or part of Laker Airways. No-one except Dix and Christopher Brown were aware of the discussions with Carrian or that the talks of a total buy-out of the Laker group had now reached this level. There were a couple of surprised faces in the room.

Freddie, in typical fashion had kept all of this very close to his chest. Cliff Nunn likely wondered why Brown and Dix, who both reported to him, knew more about the future of Laker Airways than he did. Nevertheless, Freddie was still keen to sell out if it meant the survival of the company, despite the enormous risks of an involvement with Tan and his Carrian Group and the tricky aspect of transferring the airline's routes to a foreign entity.

Laker's financial position in July 1981 was dire but it had not yet been made public. At the meeting with Bell, Freddie made a serious and desperate attempt to sell the entire group of Laker companies to Carrian Holdings. While in Hong Kong, Freddie had told Tan the value of the group including the two tour operations was \$200 million; this figure included \$33 million of goodwill. It was perhaps a reasonable valuation of the group less than a year earlier. A sale or major investment (for at least 50 per cent of the equity) by Carrian had been discussed with Tan at the June meeting. However, only a few weeks later, with his back to the wall, the company in serious difficulties and his head focused more on matters at home, Freddie told Bell that he would let George Tan and Carrian take it all off his hands for \$120m. However, once he saw the latest Laker Airways' accounts and declining load factor projections for the remainder of 1981, Bell on behalf of the Carrian Group, declined.

After the Carrian executive had left, Brown mentioned again, as he had in Hong Kong when the prospect of a Carrian investment first emerged, that significant foreign ownership may not be approved by the CAA. Brown and Dix had conferred on this point after sitting through the meetings with Tan and felt neither the CAA or the American CAB would approve of Laker Airways being even partially foreign owned and that it would put Laker's route licences and operating permits in jeopardy. Freddie was typically bullish and didn't think it would be an issue. Nevertheless, Dix said he thought Bell's decision was a good thing; Brown nodded in agreement as he and Dix had seen first hand what Tan's crazy operation was like. They had lobbied Freddie hard in Hong Kong, saying that a partnership with Carrian would definitely end in tears. Freddie however, wasn't listening to reason, he was desperate and his priorities at the time were clearly elsewhere.

POSTSCRIPT

*John Wimbush, the classy British lawyer and senior partner at Deacon's in Hong Kong who had first introduced George Tan and Carrian to Sir Freddie, was found dead in his swimming pool on 13th April, 1984. A rope tied around his neck had been attached to a concrete manhole cover. The official report gave the cause of death as suicide, however Wimbush had been about to testify in connection with the collapse of the Carrian Group.*

CHAPTER 39

# Enter the Bankers

## Thatcher's recession strikes

1981

Laker Airways' financial problems started in the second half of 1981 with oil prices looking to remain high for the second year and running at over $35 dollars a barrel. The timing of this significant increase in the airline's principal operating expense collided with the rapidly declining value of the UK pound against the US dollar.

Three years earlier, crude oil was $25 dollars a barrel, but that was about to change. On the 11th of February 1979, Shah Mohammed Reza Pahlavi of Iran was overthrown by a revolution. His family dynasty had ruled Iran (formerly Persia) since 1925. The Shah had been toppled because of an effective withdrawal of support by the United States ordered by president Jimmy Carter. By pushing too hard for constitutional reforms and the imposition of human rights policies in Iran, the ramifications of that decision would be felt by the United States for many decades on. In fact, Carter's participation in easing out the Shah was probably the most catastrophic foreign policy decision ever taken by a US president in recent times, or perhaps even at any time. By withdrawing funding and threatening to withdraw support of social and military aid, the US completely misjudged the fragility of the Shah's position. The resulting chaos led directly to the hostage crisis later that year and then to the loss of hundreds of thousands of lives under the new regime in the Iran - Iraq war. The fallout brought about the rise of the murderous dictatorial regime of Sadam Hussein of neighbouring Iraq, with whom ironically the Americans initially sided. Following the demise of the Shah, the westernised living standards of the Iranian population collapsed and the freedoms they had enjoyed evaporated. So misguided was America's thinking on Iran that *Time* magazine named the Shah's successor, Ayatollah Khomeini as its Man of The Year in 1979. The magazine and President Carter would come to regret that. As a direct result of the USA's mis-guided foreign policy, the whole world was plunged into a huge recession, arguably the worst in modern times directly because of what happened in Iran and the subsequent effect on the price of oil.

Driven by hatred of anything connected to the Shah, the Khomeini government sought to systematically destroy any vestiges of the old regime, including murdering anyone connected with it. Khomeini's lust for revenge was thought to be driven by the death of Mustafa, his eldest son who died in 1977 while he was in Iraq. Khomeini believed that Mustafa was killed by the Iranian secret police, Savak. Within 12 months, Iran was at war with Iraq and the price of oil went through the ceiling inevitably throwing the world into a recession.

The ramifications of the Shah's fall was manifest in Britain in the form of rising inflation and huge wage demands by unions to compensate. The inexperienced Labour prime minister, James Callaghan over reacted, frightened by world events of which he had little understanding. Britain was already in economic disarray fighting a war against inflation and the winter of 1978 - 1979 became known as the 'winter of discontent'. Callaghan's well-intentioned attack on rising inflation had directly caused the debacle. His answer was to limit pay increases across Britain to five per cent. Predictably it had little effect, except to ensure that British workers were five per cent worse off every year. By 1978 it was biting hard and by October, everyone wanted to strike. The main damage was caused by gravediggers and refuse collectors, as the rubbish piled up in the streets and bodies were literally stacked up in morgues one of on top of another waiting for burial. Inevitably side deals were done to get vital workers back to work well above the five per cent level. The situation destroyed any chance of Callaghan's Labour government winning the 1979 general election against a resurgent Conservative party, led by Britain's first and only woman prime minister, Margaret Thatcher. When Thatcher came to power she inherited a recession that had already started. It was made worse by the austerity measures that she imposed on a Britain already down on its luck. The recession was not her fault and had been effectively caused by economic misrule from a well meaning but ultimately clueless socialist government. Aside from out-of-control raging inflation, unemployment was the other big problem. This had risen in Britain alongside interest rates and inflation as the three-pronged enemies of real prosperity ever since Harold Wilson was Prime Minister in the early sixties.

As with most of the developed world, recession hit the United Kingdom at the turn of 1980s, although the economy had been plagued by a string of crises for most of the 1970s. Unemployment had gradually been increasing and some 1.5 million people were unemployed while inflation was running at ten per cent.

In 1979, passenger traffic on the North Atlantic began to slow. It still grew by 5.7 per cent and a total of 18.4 million passengers were carried between Europe and the USA. Laker Airways' Skytrain passenger numbers were 301,734 at a 71.7 per cent load factor, albeit severely dented by the DC-10 grounding. Laker's North Atlantic charters mainly to Canada were a credible 531,853 passengers – slightly down on the prior year due to an increase in Skytrain capacity. However, by 1979, aviation fuel averaged $1 a gallon, as the cost skyrocketed. Despite the fuel price increase, 1980 was business as usual for Laker Airways who had sold 14,000 one-way transatlantic seats a week on its 42 Skytrain flights during the summer season. By the end of July 1980, the airline had already carried as many Skytrain passengers as it had in the entire year prior. In August 1980, Laker introduced more aggressive ticket prices. The walk-on Skytrain fare to New York was £78, and a 'Super Economy' fully bookable ticket was introduced. It was half the cost of a normal scheduled economy fare and significantly lower than all the other airlines' Super Apex fare. Laker was no longer the 'no-frills' carrier that made headlines in 1978 with Lakerville. It was now competing for every segment of transatlantic passenger except for the legacy carriers' first class and Laker now offered every level of service including advance reservations.

By the end of 1980, a total of 727,952 Skytrain passengers were carried and 1.35 million people had now travelled using the revolutionary service since its inception in September 1977. Laker's aircraft were flying over 16 hours a day; the fleet was fully utilised. The capital reserves of the Laker group of companies had now risen to £23 million. These were happy days for Sir Freddie and Laker Airways; 1980 was the pinnacle of the airline's existence. However, the glory days as wonderful as they were, were already in jeopardy as the problem over the price of aviation fuel lingered. There was no tax on bonded jet fuel used for international flights, every increase to the price of oil went straight on the price per gallon paid by the airlines. Airlines were hit first as the price inexorably rose. Before the collapse of the Shah's Iranian regime most people believed that the oil price was about to plummet as the west gained the upper hand in world affairs. The fall of the Shah changed everything.

Margaret Thatcher's austerity measures since taking office had kept inflation from creeping above ten per cent, but that was all. Thatcher and her chancellor Geoffrey Howe confronted the recession in a brutal way. Rather than cutting taxes, they raised them, and rather than increasing government spending, they cut it and rather than cutting interest rates they raised them. The tightening of fiscal policy in this way almost immediately reduced the budget deficit.

The restrictions in money supply sharply reduced consumer spending, business investment and curtailed exports. The increase in interest rates caused a rapid appreciation of the pound sterling, further harming exports. The only good thing was that the strengthening of the pound reduced the cost of expensive imported oil and other goods. In doing so it destroyed the balance of payments, creating another fiscal headache, especially as British North Sea oil was starting to come on stream. The early benefits of that were subsumed by the strengthening of the currency. The side-effects of the recession saw the closure of factories, shipyards and coal mines deemed inefficient. All in all, the 1981 recession quickly became the perfect economic storm, which only time and ironically high inflation could cure.

Britain was well behind what was already happening elsewhere. The recession had started in the United States and Canada whose economies had been effectively destroyed by the sharp oil price rises. America had the same problem as the aviation industry in that its gasoline price was untaxed or low-taxed; every cent of oil price increase went on the price of petrol at the pump. As it doubled, doubled again and then doubled again so did the price at America's 'gas' stations. In Britain, as 75 per cent of the cost of petrol was tax, the price increases on the price of a gallon of petrol were somewhat mooted.

The main enemy, as viewed through Margaret Thatcher's eyes was always inflation. Things became a lot worse before they became better and the inflation rate that she inherited of ten per cent became 22 per cent within a year. Rising fuel prices made the battle against inflation almost unwinnable, although it was a battle Thatcher felt she had to fight nonetheless. She handled the problem with monetarist policies. Her policies created a huge backlash from trade union leaders seeking to protect their members' standards of living. To combat that, Thatcher sought to change trade union laws to reduce strikes in the public sector. She also embarked on a prolonged period of privatising state owned industries to get the problem off the government's hands. Gradually it all began to work.

All this had been at the expense of employment and the unemployment rate doubled to three million, an unprecedented rise which accounted for 12.5 per cent of the workforce in England. It was even worse in the other regions; Northern Ireland hit 20 per cent and Scotland 15 per cent. Industrial areas such as Tyneside, parts of Yorkshire and the West Midlands, Merseyside, South Wales and Scotland became almost unrecognizable. Only the southeast of England escaped with unemployment levels of less than ten per cent.

With all the bad news, perhaps unsurprisingly, in 1981, civil disobedience in the shape of mass rioting broke out for the first time since the war years. For several weeks, unprecedented violence and protests, exacerbated by a hot summer raged in Liverpool and London. The riots under control of militants had one aim, to bring down the Conservative government. In the end it was stopped and contained from spreading only by an outbreak of heavy rain and firm action by the police.

The US and Canada weathered the recession far better. The US was far better off because Ronald Reagan's newly elected Republican administration did not impose direct austerity measures but instead severely tightened money supply and sharply raised interest rates to as high as 21.5 per cent. This measure effectively squeezed inflation, which topped out at 13.5 per cent, out of the system. The US unemployment rate peaked at 7.7 per cent. The US was also far better off because it had its own domestic oil supply. When the effects of the global oil price rise were absorbed, it quickly recovered.

But not so in Britain. It endured four years of terrible recessionary pressures that forced many otherwise sound businesses into bankruptcy. The people who lost their jobs in that period never forgave Margaret Thatcher for the misery that was caused. Before the worst was over, Thatcher's approval rating amongst the British public fell to as low as 25 per cent. The Prime Minister was further hindered by the rise of the Social Democrat party in Britain. Split off from the Labour Party and led by David Owen, Roy Jenkins, Shirley Williams and William Rodgers, it was a serious threat to Labour, especially after it merged with the Liberals.

Despite a stellar 1980, from February 1981 passenger numbers on Laker's flagship transatlantic New York route declined significantly. Not only were the overall numbers falling, Laker's market share of the New York – London route declined to 12 per cent whereas the average just a year earlier had been a healthy 19 per cent. The expansion of the Skytrain service with six new transatlantic city pairs was increasing the overall passenger numbers in 1981. However, it was misleading and gave Laker's management a false sense of security. By June, both the Los Angeles and Miami routes from London had started to decline at an alarming rate. All three prime Skytrain routes continued to weaken throughout the second half of 1981. The rising oil prices and devaluation of the UK pound notwithstanding, the timing was unfortunate with Laker expanding its overall capacity just as its existing passenger traffic was falling. The ebbing away of passenger numbers was compounded by the fall in the value of the pound. It had started the year trading at US$2.40 = £1 and by June it was down to $1.97 = £1, with the movement in a steady downward trend.

Laker's US originating traffic was insufficient to compensate for the decline in UK originators, deterred by the unfavourable exchange rate. Had Laker's passenger mix been equal, it wouldn't have mattered if the pound devalued against the US dollar, or vice versa. In theory, a weaker pound should have meant more Americans flocking to the UK. And they may well have been... but not on Laker Airways.

There was no getting away from the permanent loss of income. Something had gone very wrong and it appeared to be not just the weakening of the pound and loss of competitiveness on fares or increasing oil prices. Freddie and his management had banked on the UK to provide the bulk of Laker's revenue, as it had done in the prior years since the beginning of the Skytrain service. Yet it was the USA that could have provided the bulk of the transatlantic scheduled service revenue, especially with an increasingly strong dollar, had it perhaps been given more priority sooner.

The weakening pound was not only affecting traffic on Laker's prime US routes. Freddie had negotiated all his aircraft loans in US dollars. The exchange rates applicable to Laker's loans averaged at $2.16 for the DC-10s and $2.19 for the A300s. With the majority of Laker Airways' revenue in the devaluing pound, Laker's dollar revenue for 1981/2 was predicted to be only $100 million. Ninety per cent of the airline's fixed costs were paid for in US dollars while 80 per cent of the airline's revenues were in UK pounds. Fuel, which accounted for almost thirty percent of the company's direct operating costs, was also paid for in US dollars. It was a double financial whammy of the worst kind.

Freddie had periodically made major gains or losses at the hand of the exchange rate. Canny businessman that he was, Freddie normally forward bought currency where appropriate, to balance things out. The banks' foreign exchange experts had advised that it had not been in Laker's best interests to hedge the pound against the dollar. The advice was that the UK pound would harden and that there should be no forward buying because of the instability of the rate. Notwithstanding, in the following year, if things returned to normal, a profit looked possible. This was just as well, as Freddie would likely need all the profits he could get.

During a period when he needed to be a hundred per cent focused on his business, Freddie was instead engaged in legal combat with his second wife Rosemary. Although six years had passed since Freddie's divorce from wife number two, in mid-1981 the relationship with Rosemary had come back to haunt him. At the time of their hasty divorce in 1975 to enable him to marry the already pregnant Patricia Gates, Freddie had misled Rosemary over the state of his finances. He had told her in a letter: "I'm not a millionaire, as my net assets do not exceed a million pounds, or even a million dollars." He gave her the impression that he could be made bankrupt at any moment. The reality was that he was extremely well off and in fact he was a millionaire many times over both in cash and non-business assets. Perhaps the only truth was regarding the wobbly finances of his main business asset, Laker Airways. The future of the company had looked uncertain when Freddie made the statement, six years prior. Aside from constant cash flow concerns, he was battling governments on both sides of the Atlantic for the licences to fly the Skytrain service that had become an obsession. He'd also purchased three expensive widebody Douglas DC-10 aircraft for routes he didn't have licences for. Nevertheless, when he told his soon to be ex-wife that he was actually a minus millionaire and by his own calculation £115,000 in debt, Freddie had risked perjury charges. He said his annual income was £5,500 less than his expenditure and pointed out a personal £500,000 guarantee he had given to his bankers over loans to Laker Airways. Nevertheless, in 1978, the Laker group posted a profit of over half a million pounds, an increase of 61 per cent over the prior year and the best result so far.

By early 1981, Freddie was driving a Rolls Royce Silver Wraith II with a Jaguar XJ12 as a back up, both owned and paid for by Laker Airways. In addition to the Chailey estates, he also personally owned Woodcote Stud and Woolgars Farm. He had hidden significant assets offshore in Bermuda plus an enviable stock portfolio worth millions. The Laker group of companies of which he was a 90 per cent shareholder and had total control, remained his largest asset and may have been worth as much as £200 million; its balance sheet didn't accurately reflect the company's true market value.

Meanwhile, his second wife Rosemary enjoyed a reasonably affluent lifestyle in London. But she felt it wasn't enough. Her timing in 1981 couldn't have been worse to make her claim on Freddie. Rosemary felt she had been cheated and she hired new lawyers to go back and demand more money. They were astonished when they saw what Freddie had managed to pull off. So they hired Coopers & Lybrand, a top accounting firm, to undertake a thorough appraisal of her ex-husband's financial status. The report was enlightening and Coopers assessed his net worth at £11.5 million. It showed that he derived an income of as much as £180,000 a year (£740K - 2018). Although Freddie drew no salary from Laker Airways he received huge benefits in kind, including the luxury cars, yacht and unlimited entertainment on his company credit cards.

Following the audit it looked like Freddie was going to get his pockets picked by wife number two. As always however, he managed to stall proceedings while he dealt with considerably more pressing matters that would significantly change his financial position.

Ironically, Freddie was first alerted to what was happening at Laker Airways by his first wife Joan who had met with Laker Airways' finance director Robbie Robinson. Joan had seen the danger signs and had written to her ex-husband, warning him. Unfortunately he did not take her seriously. Robinson, who understood every minute detail of the day-to-day position of Laker Airways' finances, finally convinced Freddie that his airline was about to fall into serious financial difficulty. Freddie had been distracted from the day-to-day business in early 1981 chasing his global ambitions that included Australia, the Far East, the Middle East and beyond. He had also been embroiled in domestic distractions that had caused him to take his eye off the ball.

Left with no choice, Freddie went directly to his bankers and told them the hard truth about the swirling economic winds. As he recalled: "I went to the bankers and said, look, there is a lot of competition and jugular marketing out there and there's a possibility I may need to do some restructuring on my loans. Let's talk about it now so that if there's anything to be done, it isn't a panic measure." He went on to remember those early meetings with the bankers: "We were talking about cash, and on the basis of the falling dollar, and competition across the board, there was a chance that our load factors would drop, and we did a sensitivity graph of what would happen. There was a distinct possibility we would default on our loan repayments."

And that is exactly what happened. On the 13th July, Laker Airways failed to make the first payment for the Airbus A300s. The interest alone was $6.9 million. Laker should have been issued with a notice of default, but it never happened as it would have automatically lost the export interest rate subsidy on the Airbus loans. The Bank of England stepped in, the payment was quietly put back and the interest rate subsidy remained. The UK's membership of the Airbus project had hung on Laker Airways' significant order, it was a sensitive time and a default so soon after delivery would have been very embarrassing for the British government.

Unfortunately, instead of Freddie's candour and caution being seen as virtues, the bankers were panicked. In the second half of 1981, the bulk of Laker's payments on the annual loan commitments were fast approaching. The vast majority were due on the 15th September and payable to the Japanese and Americans banks. On the 31st July 1981, Laker Airways owed over $415 million, borrowed from no less than twenty-four different international banks and lenders who had financed his aircraft. The annual capital repayments, excluding interest, amounted to over $55 million dollars. The interest on the huge aircraft loans was approximately another $40 million dollars a year. Aside from the aircraft loans, the overheads at the airline had risen to about $168 million a year. In a good year, the payment schedules were perhaps manageable providing the company's revenues remained steady, but in the latter half of 1981, revenues from all Laker's business segments were in decline.

1981 was different from the year before when Laker Airways' cash position was reasonably healthy. The cash on hand had now entirely eroded and Laker was regularly dipping into its overdraft facility to get through each month. It became abundantly clear there was no chance of Laker Airways making the bulk of its payments for the DC-10-30s due on the 15th September. The only hope was to reschedule the loans until a date when revenues had recovered and the pound had risen enough so a repayment of the capital could resume.

Freddie realised he would have to reschedule the entire debt in order to ride out the financial crisis. During the first week of August he and his legal advisor John Roney, drafted a schedule of proposed visits to the lenders. Roney would travel to the USA and meet with EXIM Bank. Freddie would do the rounds with the other lenders, presenting his proposals and financial information. Although Freddie and Roney did not see it that way at the time, the survival of Laker Airways would come down to what short-term concessions each lender was prepared to offer.

The EXIM Bank as the biggest lender was approached first, and Freddie met with them on the 4th of August. They played hardball and said the most they would consider was putting back one payment for 30 days. It was lost on no one that the negotiations were going to be tough, especially with the EXIM Bank and there was to be some hard bargaining ahead. EXIM, in underwriting aircraft sales to foreign competitors who directly competed with American companies, had long been of deep concern to the U.S. government. In truth, the last thing the EXIM Bank wanted was an embarrassing default, and it would eventually have to soften its stance.

The Clydesdale, Laker's long time merchant bankers, were at this stage extremely supportive. On the 14th August, a crucial emergency meeting of all Freddie's lenders was hastily convened to take place four days later.

However, on 16th August the story of Laker Airways' financial difficulties broke and the headline in the city pages of *The Sunday Telegraph* read: 'Laker in crucial £130 million debt talks'. The entire world had been alerted; it then spread to every newspaper, television and radio station in the UK and beyond. The timing of this was compounded by a devastating upheaval at home; Freddie was getting it from all sides as he dodged back and forth between his respective domestic and business crises.

The damage of the story in *The Sunday Telegraph* was potentially catastrophic. Freddie knew how much public confidence mattered with the thoughts flashing through his mind of thousands of holidaymakers cancelling their bookings. The Telegraph's reporter had rung Freddie out of courtesy the night before they ran the story? Freddie didn't deny the story but in words that may have come across far too glibly for his bankers' liking, he was quoted as saying: "I said to myself, Laker you are an innovator. You have innovated the airline business. Now you must innovate the banking business." It was classsic Freddie Laker hyperbole and a quote that he was never allowed to forget.

He dismissed further rumours that his three Airbus A300s were for sale as "totally untrue. It's pure unadulterated rubbish. You don't sell wide bodies, you buy wide bodies. You sell junk."

Everyone now knew that the airline that bore Freddie's name was in grave financial difficulty. He would have to find a way of refinancing his airline in the glare of the public eye. It could not be done by conventional means. Everything was already either mortgaged or charged to the banks.

Back in July 1979, Freddie had borrowed £700,000 against each of his three BAC One-Elevens and their spare engines from the Clydesdale to fund further purchases. The situation in regard to Laker's six DC-10-10s was complex. Mitsui held multiple liens on the aircraft. Laker Airways' supply of aircraft spares was also secured against these aircraft. EXIM Bank and Pefco, (Private Equity Finance) a financing house, also held various liens on DC-10-10s.

When he next spoke to the press a few days later, Freddie mentioned a new term with a 'release and recapture' clause inserted into the existing agreements. It meant a postponement of repayments for what was expected to be as short a period as six months. There would be no exchange rate penalty and Laker Airways could resume its payments at a later date on exactly the same terms, thus reducing the losses on dollar sums. Freddie bullishly told *The Times* newspaper that it was just a hiccup: "There is no question of us not making our repayments. We are attempting to get the banks to be more flexible when dealing with an industry like ours, which is highly cyclical."

Behind closed doors, the Civil Aviation Authority began warning other government departments about what they perceived to be the dire financial state of Laker Airways. The passenger numbers were falling and its market share spoke for itself, the CAA continued to monitor the numbers on a weekly basis throughout the crisis. The CAA was all-powerful and it had a responsibility to protect the public. If they perceived the airline's cash flow to be insufficient for it to continue, Laker Airways could have its air operating certificate (AOC) revoked.

The CAA and the British government were both keenly aware of the important role Laker Airways had played in democratising air travel and market expansion. They decided to tread carefully. Freddie's popularity, high profile and his association with the British public's demand for cheap air travel had to be carefully considered. The CAA therefore left it to the Bank of England and Laker's creditors to decide whether or not they would continue to support Laker Airways. They had only one condition; lenders could not call in their loans during the months between March and September, which was the height of the flying season.

The disruption to the passengers and the other airlines who would inevitably have to pick up the pieces would have been too great. It could also mean the maximum draw on the Air Travel Reserve Fund. The Bank of England had its own stipulation; Laker Airways needed to put $50 million on its balance sheet as soon as possible. They had decided to assist, but there would not be any direct bail out for Laker.

While Freddie may well have innovated the airline business, he was about to find that innovating the banking business, as he quite arrogantly stated, would be considerably more challenging.

CHAPTER 40

# The Final Straw

## Freddie pushes them all too far

August 1981

On Wednesday the 19th of August, 1981, after a full day at the Laker USA headquarters at Rego Park, New York, Greg Dix headed out to JFK to catch the last flight of the day to London. GK60 left at 10:15pm and arrived at Gatwick at 10:00am the next morning. Dix was scheduled to meet with Cliff Nunn in the afternoon to go over the plans for the USA operations. Freddie had put his deputy in charge of the USA and Canada after firing the USA Manager, Charles Maxwell a few weeks earlier. Nunn was keen to demonstrate that he had North America firmly in his grasp despite the reality being anything but. Dix thought it was an aberration. Nunn's geographically based division of respective USA sales areas was already showing its flaws. As Dix had predicted to Freddie, Nunn and John Jones in July when the reorganisation plan was broached, no-one from Denver had flown to London from LA and similarly no-one from Atlanta had flown via Miami; not that there were any seats for US originators out of Miami as the route was still almost 100 percent occupied by low yield British holidaymakers.

Dix was hoping to see Freddie alone while there as Freddie had called him earlier to let him know that Patricia had abruptly left for Florida, taking the three-year old Freddie Allen with her. While Dix perhaps wasn't all that surprised to hear this, given what he'd experienced in Hong Kong and Tokyo in June, he was nevertheless concerned for Freddie's well-being, which now seemed close to breaking point. He was distraught and angry. One minute Freddie was raging mad, swearing and using words like 'abducted' while calling Patricia every insulting name imaginable and the next minute in tears and sounding as if he was on the verge of topping himself. It was quite disconcerting.

Freddie already had a lot on his plate in mid-August 1981. His bankers were huddling to evaluate whether Laker Airways was worth saving and the press were milking it by splashing the airline's woes in all the dailies with headlines like 'Laker heads for bankruptcy'. Now, when matters perhaps couldn't get any worse, Patricia had left for Florida, wrenching Freddie's beloved son from him. The now nineteen year-old Bettina remained behind in England for the time being. Upon arrival in Miami, Patricia and Freddie Allen had moved into the Key Biscayne hotel just outside downtown Miami. Despite the considerable stress Patricia's actions created, Freddie most certainly wanted to keep his family unit together if possible. He was especially distraught about the loss of his son, who was unquestionably the most important aspect of his life. His devotion for Freddie Allen was made all the more intense by the fact he had already lost two sons; seventeen-year old Kevin in July 1965 and four-hour old Freddie Robert in December 1975.

Freddie's latest domestic crisis coincided with everything that was happening at Laker Airways. With his airline in serious financial difficulty and after suffering such a devastating personal crisis, Freddie started making out of character, irrational decisions that would affect the future of the business. Freddie had always prided himself at being able to leave his domestic worries at home when he came to work, but this time he couldn't. He had difficulty even functioning, let alone leading his airline through its most troubled period. Most staff members at Laker Airways were unaware of what he was dealing with, as Freddie had a remarkable ability to put on a brave face and appear as if nothing was wrong. Only a few insiders and those really close to him, fully realised the extent of what he was enduring at the time.

He pleaded with Patricia to return and bring his son home. She point blank refused and told him it was her intention to remain in Florida. Then Patricia called Bettina and insisted she leave England immediately, or else. To Freddie's dismay, Bettina acquiesced and flew to Florida and her mother. Almost overnight Freddie had lost his entire family. But it was the agonising loss of his son that was the most damaging and what risked de-railing him altogether.

Freddie and Patricia were together during the zenith of Freddie's success. At no other time in his life had he achieved so much and been acclaimed by so many across the globe. Patricia, with her glamorous looks, great fashion sense and engaging personality, topped off with an endearing Oklahomian accent had given him enormous credibility and enhanced Freddie's image. She was kind-hearted, well liked by everyone at the company and had been an asset with the promotions for Skytrain in the late 70's and for the launch of the new Airbus. She looked perfectly at home in the owner' circle at the races, typically dressed in one of her full-length fur coats and dripping with diamonds that Freddie had lavished on her. Patricia had insisted that Freddie smarten himself up too, from his clothes to his hair. He even had his crooked teeth fixed at her behest. New York Station Manager and Freddie's first employee in the USA, Linda Earls said, "we all really liked Pat and thought she made Freddie a better person in every way. We were really saddened when we heard about them splitting up."

There's no question that being married to Freddie meant Patricia enjoyed an enviable standard of living. She had a title by virtue of being married to an English knight, a country estate in a sought after part of Sussex, the yacht in

Majorca, a chauffeur- driven Rolls Royce and staff for the house, memberships to exclusive clubs, and a long list of VIP friends. Her daughter benefitted from the best English education possible and was given as many horses as she could ride. It was a privileged lifestyle of the rich and famous. For Patricia to leave so suddenly and so terminally, her rationale had to be considerably greater than mere 'irreconcilable differences' or that Freddie was too busy with his work. Needless to say, the rumour mill at Laker Airways which had previously only been a whisper, was now quite loud. Freddie merely went through the motions day after day, reeling from the shock of what had happened. Fortunately, since his loyal staff never took any gossip outside, Freddie averted what might have been intense and embarrassing press scrutiny. The merciless British tabloids would have paid handsomely for a scandalous story about the 58 year-old 'champion of the forgotten man'.

Following Patricia's departure, relations between Freddie and his wife were as acrimonious as they could be. The press reported that Patricia stated her husband had sent her to Florida to buy a home and set up there. He maintained that it was a 'temporary sojourn.' However, behind the scenes it was very different. Money was an acute issue, so Freddie arranged for Patricia to have a job with Laker Airways at its Coral Gables sales office. Shortly after, he claimed she had walked out of her job while she said she had been sacked from her new, highly-paid position. She stated that her bank accounts were empty, while he maintained she had plenty of money. Even with all the wrangling going on, Freddie wrote to Patricia that he had no intention of instituting divorce proceedings. He was still hopeful she might return to England with Freddie Allen and unrealistically proposed she allow him full custody of the boy.

It was clear that Patricia had other ideas and a scorned, unforgiving and emotionally distressed woman emerged. She clearly felt justified in her actions and was determined to wreak havoc on her husband's life. She had in her control the most potent weapon of all, their son, Freddie Allen. His father adored Charlie beyond all reason. This was another watershed moment in Freddie's life, arguably as painful as when he lost his first son Kevin; perhaps even more so, as the high expectations for this boy were at another level.

In a flash back to 1965, Freddie's domestic crisis was once again in lock-step with his business challenges. The negative publicity when the financial problems of Laker Airways finally became known, soon became self-fulfilling as the public perception of the airline took a down-turn. This was serious in a customer-based industry where the confidence of travel agents as well as the consumer were arguably more valuable than cash. Journalists, who just a few months before had been praising him to the heavens, now piled in with their attacks. All through the summer of 1981, the public was eager to read about Sir Freddie Laker's business misfortunes. Fortunately this was all they were able to read about, as Freddie's PR and legal representatives kept the dogs at bay and he avoided any muckraking. As if he didn't have enough going on with Laker Airways, losing Charlie was going to test Freddie's resolve and resiliance like at no other time in his life.

After Freddie had vented about his latest domestic crisis, he told Dix he was looking forward to seeing him as he considered him one of his closest friends. He also asked him to 'be discreet' in case he was contacted by anyone. Dix knew immediately what Freddie was asking and responded 'of course, you don't even have to mention it'. Freddie wanted to hear his suggestions at the untypically large gathering of senior management to go over the plans for his latest initiative, the 'Regency Service.' Dix, had already spoken at length to Ian Allan and Cliff Nunn as well as his colleagues in the USA about it. He knew he wasn't the only one at Laker Airways who thought competing with the legacy airlines for their highly prized business-class passengers was foolhardy. But he refrained from saying anything to Freddie on the phone; the timing was clearly inappropriate for anything that smacked of criticism.

When he'd been initially called by Cliff Nunn about the Regency Service, Dix deliberately didn't mention what he'd been privy to back in July when he'd flown over to meet with Freddie and John Jones to discuss fares and strategy for the USA. Jones had revealed the Fall/Winter Economy and Apex fares that had prompted a justifiably irate Dix to give Freddie an earful. Freddie had as much as given his Regency intitiative away when he called it his 'secret weapon'. Dix had good reason to be angry. Freddie had told him the main objective in his new role was to increase traffic from the USA, as the company urgently needed US dollar revenue. Without a reasonable fare advantage, the USA management team had an almost impossible job on their hands. At the time, Freddie couldn't divulge to Dix, or in fact to anyone what he and Jones had been doing that had driven them to formulate the latest fares, and introduce the controversial and perhaps ill-advised Regency Service.

The other transatlantic operators had been attacking Laker Airways' at the low-fare end of the market, which aside from a few transatlantic charter flights had been completely dominated by Laker's Skytrain since September 1977. From the outset, Laker had enjoyed substantial fare differentials that had gradually been whittled down to being almost non-existent. Freddie's original plan for retaliation to the fare-matching was to modify one of Laker's DC-10-10s with a business class cabin. The intention being to attack the Big Three's lucrative business class services – BA's 'Club Class', Pan Am's 'Clipper Class' and TWA's 'Ambassador Class' – for a trial period on the New York route. His thinking was to divert some of his competitors' revenue from their business class and perhaps some of their first class with Laker's aggressively priced Regency product. This, Freddie felt would have the effect of disabling the competitors' ability to subsidise their 'economy class' and thereby offer lower fares to attack Laker. He had the Regency concept in his back pocket thinking that if the others didn't play ball, he would use it as leverage.

Earlier, on 2nd June 1981, TWA had matched Laker's new 21 day Super Apex in both directions by reducing its fares by $31. Even British Airways and British Caledonian complained that the fares could not possibly be economic because they were lower than the year before. However, the CAA approved TWA's fares and on the 5th June, British Airways changed their tune and matched them. By the end of June, the airlines knew that Laker Airways' traffic was depressed because Freddie was seeking permission from the CAA to offer selective 25 per cent discounts across Laker's fare structure on all their UK-USA Skytrain routes. Freddie had explained to the CAA that the passenger numbers on Laker's flagship route between London and New York were down almost 20 per cent in the first half of 1981 compared to the same period in 1980. The Los Angeles service was slightly up and Miami was at the time stable, as Miami was still almost all UK originating holidaymakers. But it was the New York route that was the real problem. Recognising this, albeit perhaps too late, Freddie had abruptly re-organised his USA management in an attempt to increase the USA originating traffic and the essential dollar revenue. He complained to the CAA that the major carriers had all matched Laker's fares and therefore he needed to take this extreme action.

Then, on the 6th July, Freddie had inexplicably backed out of the fare filing. BA had called for a clandestine meeting ten days later to discuss and agree across the board transatlantic fare increases. After ten years, since the start of the north Atlantic high growth period, passenger traffic was dropping considerably and the revenue and yields were getting worse each month. The principal North Atlantic airlines were all being hurt by the greatly reduced fares mainly due to the ascendancy of Laker Airways. Freddie of all people knew an overall increase in economy class fares would be beneficial to everyone. There was only one way to ensure all parties cooperated and that was once again to do the unthinkable. That meant he had to again collude with his main competitor.

At the covert gathering on 16th July, BA was to act as a conduit for Pan Am and TWA. Freddie was naturally anxious about this particular meeting; Bob Beckman had already cautioned both Freddie and John Jones that they would be in serious breach of US antitrust laws if they were ever in cahoots with their competitors, especially in regards to fare fixing. Beckman's voice once again rang loudly in his ear... 'Freddie, you can go to jail here if you're caught colluding.' Beckman had obviously never been given a hint about the fare-fixing meetings Freddie and Jones had been involved in with their principal competitors since 1978. In fact, since the Route 6 hearings in June, Freddie had barely spoken to Bob Beckman. But Freddie knew he had no choice than to take the risk if he was to have any chance at all of averting a fare war; one that he would for sure lose and one that could put Laker Airways out of business.

Freddie and John Jones had to clamber over the rooftop of BA's Victoria terminal to reach the designated secret meeting spot British Airways had chosen. Charles Stuart, BA's commercial manager had a maintenance man assist them as they navigated their way around air conditioners and other rooftop hazards before finally arriving at BA's Victoria boardroom. Top BA executives Ossie Cochrane – Western Routes Manager, John Meredith – BA's US General Manager and Bernard Monks – Product Planning Manager for the Western division, were all there. They were tough, experienced adversaries. At the meeting they amended the tariffs and then worked on the question of fare differentials for the across the board increased Y class fares. Freddie, knowing the implications of his presence at the meeting, sensibly remained silent and allowed John Jones to do the negotiating. Jones was firm and did a good job, provisionally agreeing all the fares except one or two full economy fares.

But Freddie wanted more. He wanted bigger differentials for Laker Airways. He needed to play his trump card and decided that this was the time to tell BA that Laker Airways was going to introduce a business class in November that would be called 'Regency'. The £253 one way Regency Service fare from London to New York deliberately matched Laker's competitors' unrestricted full economy fare. He hoped that the threat of Laker Airways targeting their most coveted business-class customers would bring them into line. The hostile reaction to Freddie's revelation from the British Airways' executives was exactly as Jones and he had anticipated; they had played into his hands perfectly.

Seizing the opportunity he had hoped for, Freddie almost immediately offered to withdraw Regency in exchange for higher differentials. In his mind, he hadn't decided to really operate Regency; it was still conceptual and he was using it mostly as a negotiating ploy. And it worked. After considerable further discussion, Laker Airways actually won all its differentials back for the proposed increased autumn fares that would now come into effect at the beginning of August. On July 31st 1981, Laker Airways filed the agreed upon package of higher fares. They gave Laker differentials of £15 and £10 below the competition on the peak, shoulder and low season Apex fares. It was a far cry from the much greater fare differentials Laker had been able to negotiate with their competitors during the heyday of Skytrain in 1979 and 1980, but now, Freddie and Jones would have to take what they could get.

Then, BA, Pan Am and TWA blind-sided them and reneged. They didn't introduce the higher fares they'd all agreed at the secret meeting, while Laker conformed to the agreement and published theirs. The net result was that for about ten days in August, Laker Airways, the perceived lowest cost operator on the North Atlantic, incredibly had the highest fares. Freddie was apoplectic, although he perhaps shouldn't have been surprised. He received a telephone call from BA in which he was told that the agreed fare differential was more than BA and the others carriers could accept.

Freddie went mad, they had done this to him before. He thought John Jones had misread what had been agreed and proceeded to give him hell. As Freddie admitted later 'I led John a dog's life about the whole thing.' A bruised and humiliated Jones got on the phone and shouted at the executives of Laker's competitors for not introducing the fares when they were supposed to. Those who hadn't before experienced a 110 decibel, full on John Jones tongue-lashing were now trembling in shock. Pan Am apologised for not introducing the fare on the correct day because the typist was on jury service and they couldn't get anyone to type up the document. TWA, through British Airways were tinkering with the fares thus delaying the filing. The lamest excuses imaginable were offered for not conforming to the agreement. They were guilty as hell and they all knew it. But the damage had been done and Laker Airways' phone lines simply stopped ringing.

Eventually, BA filed fares with £10 - £20 differentials above Laker Airways' Super Apex fare to New York and Los Angeles. TWA decided to file only £10 above Laker. Pan Am targeted Los Angeles to London with special economy fares very close to Laker's pre-increase levels. TWA and BA implemented their new special economy fares LAX-LON exactly as Pan Am had done. TWA waited for Laker's reaction, hoping that the contagion would be limited to the Los Angeles route and not spread to New York. The Big 3 matched Laker's all-important standby fares exactly. They thought their actions would force Freddie into withdrawing his increases.

Freddie was incensed at the betrayal. He retaliated by immediately filing the fares for Laker's Regency Service at £253 on London to New York, as he had threatened. He hoped that by taking this action his phone would ring, his competitors would all try and talk him out of starting a business-class service and then give him the fare differentials Laker needed to survive. The call never came. With his hubris quotient red-lining, in a retaliatory public statement, Freddie lashed out, "I have constantly warned the others if they attack my end of the market I will attack theirs." So instead of just converting one or two aircraft to operate Regency on the New York route on a trial basis, an angry and clearly irrational Freddie Laker completely disregarded his top managers' counsel. He immediately issued an instruction to convert most of Laker's fleet of DC-10-10 aircraft used for New York and the DC-10-30s used on the Los Angeles and Florida routes, into a two-class configuration.

Laker Airways was already dealing with acute fare matching by their main competitors as well as being 'out-commissioned' at the retailer level. Now, launching a business-class service going into the winter and pitting Laker against established transatlantic operators on all the principal Skytrain itineraries seemed on the surface to be about as reckless a scheme as Freddie had yet come up with. The London - New York route was clearly the only one that could possibly produce anything close to a reasonable quota of business-class passengers in both directions during the winter months. London – Los Angeles was still developing and if it wasn't for an interline agreement with Air New Zealand, the US originators from LAX would have been nominal. In fact, there were more passengers originating in Aukland than in all the neighbouring states around California put together.

Miami was still hampered by being primarily a destination for British tourists and there were few Floridians who would travel to London. The vital Central and South American markets hadn't yet come to fruition. Regional Manager for Florida and Latin America, David Tait had only been in his new role a little over a month and Laker still had no secure interline agreements with any of the Latin American carriers. It highlighted another flaw in Nunn's regionalised management. Newly appointed Skip Clemens whose responsibility was only for the western states, spoke Spanish fluently and had proven experience in the Latin American market. Yet he hadn't been enrolled to assist. Miami needed all the help it could get, it was a loss-making route despite the high summer load factors. It could never be sustainable year round without a significant increase in US originating passengers. Regency could never be the Miami route's salvation.

When Freddie had first conceptualised a business-class he wanted to call it 'Pullman'. Christopher Brown, Laker's in-house lawyer, tried his best but he was unable to secure the rights to the Pullman name. It was owned by the estate of the American industrialist, George Pullman who had famously devised the renowned Pullman Sleeper car that became standard on all the world's railways. Freddie instead settled for 'Regency' even though most of his senior staff felt it had a pretentious tone to it. The drab maroon branding and ornate gold typeface of the name and logo were the antithesis of the young, vibrant airline with its stylish black, red and white livery. It reflected Freddie's mood of the moment.

The Regency Service created an enormous amount of additional work and staff training just at a time when everyone needed to be 100 per cent focused on what they had on their plates already. The strain on Laker's infrastructure was immense and virtually every department was affected in some way. The DC-10s' 80 standard economy class seats in the front cabin had to be replaced with 46 sumptuous, deep red 'business class' style seats. Senior cabin staff were trained for the higher standard of service, while the catering and bonded store units started ordering the upgraded food, wines and amenities. Freddie insisted the Regency passengers would be served premium champagne, fine wines and a choice of high quality menus served on Wedgewood china. At the initial strategy talks for Regency, Freddie apparently had balked at using 'Laker' monogrammed Wedgewood saying "I'm not buying my crews and half the passengers a Wedgwood dinner service." He knew from his BUA days that china and cutlery with the airline's name on it would be taken as souvenirs. The Cabin Services management assured him that strict inventory controls would be in place to ensure nothing would ever be pilfered, so he reluctantly gave in. But deep down, he knew exactly what would happen and instructed the accounting department to allow for a significant replacement of Regency Service china and cutlery in the flight costs. He also knew that a lack of strict controls on the liquor and wines was going to be another area of concern. Notwithstanding, the high quality food and beverage service, combined with complimentary in-flight entertainment, priority check-in and expedited baggage at the destination made Laker's Regency Service a first-rate product for a drop-dead price. In fact, Freddie insisted that Regency had to be as good or better than any business class of any airline, not just those on the North Atlantic. "If we're going to get into this game, let's do it right" he had said once he'd decided to go down this road. Most of his top management thought Freddie was being absurdly unrealistic when he told them to use Singapore Airlines, with whom he'd flown to Australia as the benchmark.

What Freddie hadn't fully considered when he made his reactive decision to launch a two-class Skytrain service was how the re-configured planes would work on the company's other operations such as the U.S. and Canadian ABC flights and ad hoc charters should a 345-seater be unavailable. Or conversely, how they would compensate up to 46 Regency passengers if a two-class plane wasn't available and an all-economy class 345-seater had to be used. Laker's already stretched to the limit engineering division would more than likely be re-configuring DC-10s and then back again on a regular basis. Needless to say, if Freddie had wanted to turn his company on its head, at perhaps the worst time imaginable, he couldn't have chosen a better way. More than one senior manager thought Freddie was losing the plot and that his judgment had been seriously compromised by all his domestic problems.

Nevertheless, Freddie had signalled to his competitors he was going after the business traveller, their most coveted customer on every one of the main transatlantic routes that Laker Airways flew. Regency Service was to take no more than two and a half months to come to fruition. It was an ambitious and expensive departure from Laker's core business, just when the airline could perhaps least afford it. The Regency Service required a massive capital outlay. Aside from the logistics and operational upgrades, the marketing, advertising and travel agent incentives needed to attract the entirely new demographic of traveller would be more challenging than Laker had ever experienced. The margins would be higher per passenger, but Freddie had always been about the mass market; he was a 'bums in seats' advocate, preferring as an example 200 passengers at £100 each as opposed to 50 people at £400.

The Regency Service was a total contradiction of the original Laker ideology and Freddie risked not only bad press but also potentially turning off the so-called 'forgotten man' to whom he had appealed since the birth of Skytrain. Some of the rationale he used to justify Regency was to try and shake off the image as an airline that only carried students, back-packers, or those on a tight budget who were prepared to compromise for the lowest fare. The chaos of 'Lakerville' and the negativity Laker Airways suffered in 1978 was still on Freddie's mind, despite his reluctance to modify the use of the term 'Skytrain' that perpetuated the stereotyping. Being able to take reservations had helped the company's image and most importantly, travel agent acceptance. But the high-volume, low fare market was what Laker Airways was best known for and it had successfully built its brand around this targeted business model. Regency created an 'identity crisis' for Laker that would take time and great marketing before Laker became a viable alternative for the business traveller.

At 11:00am on the 21st of August 1981, perhaps the largest group of senior managers ever assembled in the history of the company, squeezed themselves into the most spacious open office at Laker's Gatwick headquarters. Some of them were meeting each other for the first time; anyone with a vested interest in the Regency Service was there. Freddie seemed distracted as if he was somewhere else for the first couple of hours that was taken up discussing the in-flight service. There were some yawns and bored expressions evident, as protracted discussion on which white wine to offer was debated.

During the meeting, Freddie clearly had other things on his mind. This was understandable given what he had going on at home. Everyone in the room knew what had happened the week before and that Freddie was still reeling from his latest domestic upheaval. At one point in the Regency meeting he mistakenly called Nina Griffin, the company's popular catering manager whom Freddie had at one time during the BUA years tried to lure into an affair, 'Bettina'. Freddie's gaff raised a few eyebrows and confused exchanges by a few of the senior managers in the room. To be fair, Freddie often made errors with names, but on this particular day, it was obvious his monumental family matters were dominating his mind. The distractions couldn't have been happening at a worse time, as Freddie needed all his faculties for what was arguably Laker Airways' most challenging period in its fifteen-year history.

He wouldn't be the first man to be pre-occupied by domestic problems so serious that they came to work with him. For most of the time, Freddie handled it admirably and was able to delineate home from office as best he could, but on this particular day, the Regency Service meeting was unquestionably not at the top of his agenda.

The meeting dragged on well into the afternoon without Freddie. While sympathetic to the enormous challenges Laker's superb cabin services and catering units had to deal with, after hours of discussing food, wine and in-flight service for the Regency product, Dix quietly left the meeting. He was surprised nothing had been discussed as to how they were going to promote the new product due to start in just a few months. Equally surprising was that some of his colleagues such as John Jones, who was not known to be the most patient of men, had sat through it all. He had enthusiastically offered his suggestions for the Regency in-flight service, prompting Dix to wonder if Regency was in fact Jones's brainchild and not Freddie's, as Cliff Nunn had suggested earlier.

He felt some anger building up at the lunacy of starting the Regency service on every North Atlantic route in November, before it had been given a trial on the London to New York Skytrain service first, obviously the only feasible winter business-class market. Dix thought about the level of competitive marketing that was now being done by the Big Three in the USA for the back of the plane, Laker's passengers in other words. 'What will they do once Regency gets going?' he muttered to himself.

He'd considered flying back to New York on GK 50, scheduled out at 1630 and he could still make it, but Dix decided to stay another night and visit with old friends nearby. England in August was a welcome respite after what had been a crazy year of endless travel to Asia and Australia in pursuit of Freddie's Globetrain. He knew the months ahead would be just as frantic as they were about to do battle with the Teamsters union again, which was a draining, time-consuming exercise. Now they had the Regency Service to try and sell to a sceptical travel trade.

Before leaving the building, Dix stopped by Freddie's office in case he was still there and to say hello to Lesley Chilton, with whom he was on quite familiar terms. Freddie had left, so he told her about the Regency meeting. He expressed his concern about Freddie's current state of mind which prompted a raised eyebrow. Lesley was the most discreet person in the company and she was doggedly loyal to Freddie. She said she would keep Dix informed if Freddie needed him for anything.

He went down to the Operations department and did the usual ribbings with his old colleagues, including asking the day shift Duty Officer Brian Koering "do you want to swap jobs?" Seeing Koering's quizzical expression he followed up with "I'm honestly not kidding Brian" before ambling down to the hangar. A DC-10 was undergoing maintenance, the huge doors were open and sitting outside were the two dormant 707-351Bs and two of the four remaining BAC One-Elevens. But also sitting out on the ramp was a DC-10-30 and an A300. It was an afternoon in August, the peak month of the summer season, when every serviceable plane should have been operating.

As he was pondering this, Dix heard the familar voice of Peter Yeoman, Laker's Chief engineer. Yeoman was a 'Laker Lifer' who had come over from BUA right after Freddie had started Laker Airways. Before that, he'd worked for Aviation Traders for sixteen years. He was hugely respected and did an impeccable job, that at times must have been challenging. Already 60 but didn't show it, Yeoman was probably considering retirement. He asked his younger colleague what was going on, perhaps thinking Dix had an inside track to those who were making the decisions that directed the company. Yeoman had been at the Regency meeting briefly before he too had ducked out, as selecting white wines wasn't exactly his speciality. He intuitively knew something was amiss. His department had the unenviable task of reconfiguring the bulk of Laker's DC-10s for the new two-class service.

It was obvious Yeoman was concerned, not just about Freddie whom he had known for over thirty years but why Laker's business was so down. Internal communications had never been the company's strong point and that emanated from Freddie himself. Even someone in Peter Yeoman's position with 600 staff in his department, often found himself to be amongst the last to know.

The Laker offices were clearly lacking their usual vibrant energy. Dix made a mental note to call Bob Beckman when he was back in the States. Bob would surely have some perspectives, even though Freddie wasn't speaking with him. In the past, who else did Freddie turn to whenever he needed encouragement, advice and support? Perhaps if Bob refrained from sending in a massive invoice after every phone conversation, Freddie might contact him more, he thought.

As he walked over to his company-owned loaner car, Dix felt troubled by what was happening at Laker Airways and of course with Freddie. It didn't feel like the same upbeat, trend-setting airline any more. Desperation had replaced innovation and knee-jerk reactions had displaced intelligently considered strategy. The grave financial status of Laker Airways had made the newspapers and Freddie was obviously distracted dealing with his monumental domestic issues. Hopefully, Freddie could keep his personal life out of the press, as any adverse publicity about his affairs would likely sound the death-knell for Laker Airways.

Freddie was being pulled in so many different directions; the latest turmoil at home couldn't be happening at a worse time and had all the signs of perhaps turning nasty. He was now making irresponsible business decisions driven by emotion; the ill-advised Regency Service was the latest example. Based upon the reaction of Laker's competitors, it was fairly clear that this was the final straw.

CHAPTER 41

# High Noon on the North Atlantic

## War is declared

October - November, 1981

From its inception, the IATA members and legacy carriers had viewed Laker's Skytrain service as a threat to the entire IATA system of maintaining high prices by airline agreement. The first meetings to discuss a joint response to Laker's competition had been held in the summer of 1977. The airlines agreed to a predatory pricing scheme designed to destroy transatlantic charters and Laker's scheduled Skytrain service by offering among other things, high cost service at fares that were allegedly below the costs of those services. In August 1977, Laker's competitors had agreed the fares, service and products to systematically attack Laker's US-UK scheduled and charter services.

The IATA members agreed which of them would offer below cost services on the New York - London route. The airlines expected to experience short-term financial losses in carrying out this scheme, but intended to recoup these losses by raising prices after they had eliminated the competition of charter services and Laker's scheduled Skytrain service.

Despite the joint efforts by the key competitors to hinder Laker's progress, Laker increased its number of scheduled service routes between the United States and the United Kingdom. Even as Laker was applying for government permission to provide scheduled service between Los Angeles and London, Pan Am, TWA and BA instituted below cost fares on that route, seeking to prevent Laker's entry. After Laker began providing Los Angeles-London Skytrain service in 1978, Pan Am, TWA, and BA acted in concert to offer below cost services on that same route.

The carefully formulated predatory pricing the Big 3 had published was successful and prevented Laker from offering the public a significant price differential. As early as May 1978, TWA openly admitted that their super Apex budget and standby fares were not economic. Having virtually eliminated charter competition, in August 1980, BA, Pan Am and TWA had attacked Laker's nascent super Apex (Advanced Purchase Excursion) service, the last vestige of the old Advanced Booking Charters (ABC) Laker had pioneered in the seventies. Laker's success in attracting traffic in 1980 with a lower priced, perceived inferior service resulted in conferences in the summer of 1980 to adopt a common strategy to deal with Laker's success. The strategy they agreed was to threaten Laker with a lowering of BA, Pan Am and TWA fares to Laker's level, so that Laker would abandon competitive pricing altogether.

For the winter season 1980/81, they allowed Laker Airways to have a mere $10 differential. It was insufficient to reflect Laker's perceived lower value service. The three legacy carriers conferred again in early 1981 to agree their fares and a common strategy vis-a-vis Laker, for the summer of 1981.

So how had Laker Airways survived all the attacks? Unbeknownst to everyone other than Freddie and Commercial Manager John Jones, Laker Airways had negotiated a relationship with their competitor airlines. Freddie told no one and thought he could do this on his own. He had become involved with price fixing, a criminal act in the United States. He was always looking for that little niche, he called the 'differential' and they gave it to him. The airlines would accommodate Laker at a £30 margin. "We could live with that. We could earn a good living trading £30 below. The cheap fares were not the ones that British Airways had been filling their planes with," explains John Jones.

It was all cloak and dagger. In addition to his 'day job' where he was busy working 16 hours a day filling planes, Jones was also Freddie's emissary in the pricing discussions with Laker Airways' main competitors. The meetings were all highly irregular as well as illegal, but Freddie knew they had guns to their heads and he was prepared to take the risk. Sending Jones to collude with the competition and doing it in the USA was truly irrational. You could perhaps get away with it in the UK but not in America. Jones had a good job, a wife and children and what he did at Freddie's behest could have landed him behind bars. Sir Freddie had enough past experience and knowledge of the US antitrust laws from the earlier potential suit his DC attorney, Bob Beckman had pursued, to be seriously afraid of them. He studiously avoided the meetings with the other airlines when he could. He was afraid he may say something potentially incriminating. Beckman had been vociferous in his warnings about any sort of collusion with Laker's competitors.

Pan Am and TWA were also aware of the prohibitions in the U.S. antitrust laws against discussions between competitors on prices. The communications between BA, Pan Am and or TWA were held on the telephone, referred to as the 'secret telephone' and were typically held after normal business hours at equally 'secret' locations. Negotiations were also conducted in person by BA officials going to New York and meeting with their opposite numbers at Pan Am and TWA in bars or in private homes. There were even secret over the roof top meetings, the last of which was held in July 1981.

When their concerted predatory action failed to destroy or deter Laker, the other airlines expanded the scope of their predatory scheme. Laker nevertheless survived, rapidly and systematically expanding its scheduled operations, and with its extraordinarily high load factors, generated a profit each year.

By April 1981, Laker Airways was operating nine scheduled non-stop UK-US routes: London - New York, Manchester - New York, London - Los Angeles, Manchester - Los-Angeles, Prestwick - Los-Angeles, London - Miami, Manchester - Miami, Prestwick - Miami, and London - Tampa. New York and Los Angeles were served with multiple daily frequencies that adjusted by season. Up to sixteen Skytrain service flights a day were crossing the Atlantic using Laker's DC-10-10s and DC-10-30s. In addition, Laker was still the predominant airline offering Advance Booking Charter flights to numerous other North American destinations, with Toronto having at least five flights a week in the high season.

Passengers going to or from continental European countries such as Germany and Switzerland travelled via London in order to use Laker's Skytrain service across the Atlantic. European IATA members, including the state owned Lufthansa and Swissair, found that Laker was attracting thousands of passengers flying between continental Europe and the United States, thereby directly competing with them and putting downward pressure on all fares.

The North Atlantic market after years of significant annual growth had by now turned. Scheduled air traffic had only grown 2.9 per cent between 1980 and 1981. There were 96 weekly scheduled flights available from the UK to the USA utilising 747s, DC-10s, and L-1011 wide bodied jets as well as the Concorde. There was massive daily capacity, yet everyone's planes were flying with very low load factors. Except Laker, who had consolidated flights and reduced capacity to maintain reasonable load factors on the flights being operated. For example, in June 1981 the London to New York load factor was 72.5 per cent. At the time, the IATA carriers would have been thrilled with that. Except that Laker's June 1981 total traffic to the Big Apple was over 40 per cent down on the previous year; 24,084 passengers vs 40,367 in June 1980.

Despite the downturn in Laker's traffic numbers, Sir Freddie's incredible achievement of guiding Laker Airways into becoming the world's largest privately owned airline, one that was no longer just a small independent, could be tolerated no longer. It was now a major carrier stealing market share from the legacy airlines, many of whom were state owned icons.

None of them was perhaps more iconic than Pan American World Airways. However, despite its legendary status, in June 1981, Pan Am announced its disastrous financial results. It was an airline in serious decline with an operating loss of $80 million per year and America's most famous international carrier was flirting with insolvency. They had been forced to sell their profitable hotel chains, The Intercontinental and The Grand Metropolitan Group in Britain after being refused a credit line of $475 million by Chase Manhattan, their bankers. The sale bolstered their books by $348 million dollars. Pan Am raised approximately $800 million from the sale of assets; without it, the company would have been in default of its own loan agreements. Although these extraordinary sales of assets temporarily provided Pan Am with a large amount of cash, the company continued to suffer massive losses with its airline operations and something had to be done about it.

Pan Am's financial woes occurred at approximately the same time during mid-1981 as Laker Airways' financial problems also became publicly known. On the 1st October 1981, Pan Am's recently appointed Chairman and CEO, Edward Acker was only in the first month of his new job. Acker had been parachuted in from Air Florida, fortuitously right before Air Florida experienced a well publicised crash of one of their 737s into the Potomac River in Washington DC, killing 78 people including four bystanders on the bridge. Air Florida had its own transatlantic service using a DC-10-30 between London and Miami. Acker had been instrumental in undercutting Laker on this prime route by £41 a seat. When he joined Pan Am, Acker had declined a salary until he was able to get the airline back into profit. He described his new job as akin to being 'the Captain of the Titanic'.

Unabashed and brazen, Acker held a press conference saying that Laker could not offer a service on any route served by Pan American at a fare that Pan Am did not like. "We will no longer allow a competitor to undercut us, no matter how loud that competitor screams," he said. Pan Am had just applied to the CAA to reduce their one-way economy fare from London to New York to just £124. The proposed fare matched Laker's. Acker predicted that in 90 days or less, Laker would come to heel and the fares would rise. In response, British Airways' Director of Commercial Operations, Gerry Draper publicly called the Pan Am fares 'economic suicide'. "We have not matched some of the crazy fares being introduced by some airlines. There is no joy in flying empty seats across the Atlantic," Draper called it 'lunacy'.

Sir Freddie was no less aggrieved, "If there are no passengers around, are we going to get any more business because we put the fares down? No, the fares were right. Our planes are full and our fare increase in September had no impact on the number of passengers travelling" he railed. While this was classic Freddie Laker hyperbole to suit the occasion, Laker's planes, while not exactly full were definitely somewhat more full than their competitors' planes.

Shocked by Pan Am's announcement, Laker Airways, BA and British Caledonian convened a meeting on the 16th October with the CAA and the Department of Trade and asked the government to exercise its right under the Bermuda agreement to postpone the implementation of the Pan Am fares. Freddie provided the convincing arguments for the filings to be refused. "I believe that Bermuda II is the bible which lays down the way that air transport should be run on the North Atlantic. It says there, in words of one syllable, article 12, under tariffs, that every fare should be tested to see that the cost relates to the fare. The British and American governments are not adhering to this treaty." Article 12 of Bermuda II gave the CAA power to seek cost data from Pan Am. At the very least, the CAA could force Pan Am to observe a 75-day notice period delaying implementation until mid December. At first the CAA agreed, despite the obvious challenge of accurately testing the fare vs its actual cost, something they had never actually done before.

A phone call from Pan Am's president, William Waltrip to BA's Draper soon changed Draper's tune. An hour later Draper telephoned the CAA and told them that the position expressed at the meeting by BA's US general manager,

John Meredith was 'incorrect.' BA wished for the Pan Am and matching filings of its own to be approved "so that BA would be able to match Laker's fares and in particular their recently filed, new Regency Service fares."

Like Pan Am, British Airways had experienced massive losses in 1980 and 1981. Money was draining away at £200 a minute. BA's auditors said later, in October 1982, that the company could only be considered a going concern because the British government guaranteed $1.7 billion of its debt. British Airways also sold significant assets to raise cash in 1980 and 1981. Prime Minister Margaret Thatcher was keen to privatise the national carrier. The depth of their pockets to trade 'below cost', regain their monopoly and put Laker out of business in time for their proposed stock market flotation was something Freddie was going to find difficult to combat.

Despite what had been said about economic suicide, BA went along with the targeting of Laker. Gerry Draper called it jugular marketing. It was not a fair fight as BA's financial position was guaranteed by the government and therefore enabled them to lose money. They made it clear they would be sitting on Freddie's head. Most of it emanated from Draper. When they saw that they could actually kill off Laker Airways they decided that they would. Laker was bleeding and in trouble. They just had to keep this up for a few more months and the dastardly Freddie Laker and his airline would be gone. It was personal.

Notwithstanding, the deep fare cuts on British Airways' economy seats across the Atlantic would come into effect on 1st November 1981. By obtaining the CAA's support, BA was effectively gaining government backing, and therefore government approval for their initiative, with the sole objective of driving Laker Airways out of business. TWA and BCal were in no better position than Pan Am and BA. They too were losing large sums of money on their UK-US operations in 1981. All the airlines had stated in public that they needed to increase their fares, particularly their lowest fares. Despite this, BA followed along and their prices fell by as much as 66 per cent.

John Jones claimed "Our arithmetic was wrong to the tune of £8-10 million, but we could have come through that. We could have traded satisfactorily if our main competitors had not been matching our fares penny for penny." What Jones omitted to say at the time was why Laker's fares had been matched.

It was left to Iain Sproat, the young Scottish MP, newly arrived that September to the post of Parliamentary Under Secretary for Trade responsible for aviation, shipping and tourism, to give Sir Freddie Laker the bad news. He telephoned Freddie personally to let him know that he would be approving the Pan Am fares. Freddie was naturally livid and raged down the phone at Sproat "Minister I will be out of business in three months, we are dead." Sproat had no reply. He would later say Pan Am had told him categorically that the fares they were charging were economic. Freddie's appeals reached the ear of Sproat's boss, Trade Secretary, John Biffen. He offered to overrule the CAA's decision on the condition that Laker increased his base line price above Pan Am's. Biffen could then justify the rejection of the fares because Laker Airways was known to be highly efficient and had the lowest operating costs on the North Atlantic. Freddie rebuffed the very suggestion, conspiring to raise prices went against everything that Laker had ever stood for. The revolutionary Skytrain Service was very much a personal triumph. His victory was for the concept, one that was consumer orientated. It set Laker apart from the high cost cartels that had controlled international air transport for decades. Freddie responded "There is no way Pan American can knock 50 per cent off the fare; there is no way BA can lower their fares by 80 per cent. At the end of the day, we are the low cost operator, and if we say it can't be done, there is simply no chance for them to do it." Freddie was right in principle and Biffen should have listened, even though Freddie had no idea what BA and Pan Am's costs were.

It was impossible not to see who the absurdly low fares were aimed at, but if there was any doubt, Pan Am's Waltrip confirmed as much. On a trip to the UK on the 4th November he admitted that the October 1981 fares were uneconomical but were introduced 'to make sure that the competition understands that there is not going to be a niche for them anymore'. He added that he expected Laker to understand this. In a blatant and naked power game, the airlines had set themselves a target of 90 days to kill off Laker. The fares, Waltrip said, would go up by 15 per cent in the next three months and a further 20 per cent in the spring.

Freddie was furious: "This precipitous action by Pan Am is nothing less than suicidal marketing and could endanger the fabric of the airline industry as a whole. "Pan Am's tactics are like the death throes of a giant whale and are totally irresponsible." In trying to match Laker's fares "the other major transatlantic carriers are behaving like a lot of lemmings following each other over a cliff." He went on: "I wasn't against lower prices but this was an obvious 'get Laker' ploy." The prices were predatory because it was impossible for the major airlines to make a profit on such low fares – their prices were below cost. They were running their flights on the same routes as me at a loss, solely to put us out of business." Freddie was an instinctive competitor and believed that he could out compete anybody, but not when the rules were so skewed that his competitors were prepared to lose £50 on every passenger they stole from Laker's flights. That was Freddie's assumption despite his not knowing what the Big 3's actual 'below cost' was or their percentage of discounted seats.

None of this had passed unnoticed by two preeminent Washington D.C. law firms who specialized in civil aviation; Metzger, Shaydyac and Schwartz, and Beckman, Kirstein and Farmer. An article in the *Wall Street Journal* caught the eye of former U.S. Department of Justice counsel, Bill Barrett, of MSS. The report alleged that the North American commercial carriers were meeting in the context of IATA and were trying to deal with skinny traffic, tiny demand, low pricing by Laker and exacerbated by Pan Am. "At some point that day I walked into Carl Schwartz's office and said something like the antitrust division is soon going to have some interesting anti-competitive activity to deal with, in respect to the disruption caused by Laker Airways and world demand."

An identical scene had just played out in the Beckman law firm when the Pan Am fare struck. Pierre Murphy, by then a very capable new recruit remembers the panic vividly as his colleague Don Farmer rushed into his office shouting, "have you read today's *Wall Street Journal*, Pan Am have gone and done it, their Apex is about 50 per cent below cost; we have to do something." Bob Beckman could have and would have filed an antitrust suit on the Thanksgiving holiday in late November 1981 if only Freddie had confided in him about the predatory pricing going on. Inexplicably, Freddie wasn't speaking to Beckman around that time so no antitrust suit was filed and an opportunity for counter-measures against the attack was missed.

The October 1981 fare reductions to match Laker across the board by BA, Pan Am and TWA were unlike anything the industry had every seen before. Whatever Laker's fare was, they'd match it. But only on the routes where Laker was operating. They were not lowering the fares on any of their other routes.

Freddie, not just Laker Airways had been targeted by individual people, not just competitor airlines, intent on putting him personally as well as his airline, out of business, no matter the cost. It was something new in the industry where an arline owner was so vilified that it had become a personal vendetta against him. Simultaneously, the secret fare fixing meetings were suddenly broken off. There would now be no more back door negotiations or discussions about fares between Freddie, John Jones and British Airways. It was war!

Laker Airways had lost its price advantage. It was now trapped in the jaws of a much bigger problem than an exchange rate here or a fuel price there. Hell bent on putting Laker out of business, the competition drained off passengers simply by offering the same fare for their higher cost services. They were all prepared to lose substantial sums of money to achieve their objective. Furthermore, the attacks were not only on fares. As part of their predatory schemes, Pan Am, TWA and BA agreed an initiative for travel agents, by way of an offer the agents simply couldn't refuse.

By 1981, 75-80 per cent of Laker Airways' capacity on the North Atlantic was being sold through travel agents. It had been a struggle to get the travel agency community to accept Skytrain. Initially no-one in the travel trade would, as Skytrain's early walk-on service sold directly to the public had bypassed the travel trade. It had drawn off a big chunk of the travel agents' business and in general they were seriously put off Laker. Once Laker was allowed to take advance reservations, Freddie's sales teams on both sides of the Atlantic had worked hard to gain acceptance from the travel agencies. They joined the Association of British Travel Agents (ABTA) and the American Society of Travel Agents (ASTA). The sales teams attended travel agent conventions and Laker's off-duty cabin staff and pilots were scheduled for travel agency visits and activities. At that time, no other airline optimised their flight crews in this way. The travel agent community, especially in the USA responded favourably to Laker's attractive, red-uniformed air hostesses and handsome British pilots visiting their offices. Freddie himself had also been pro-active with the agents, often dressing up and making fun at his expense at travel agent gatherings. He re-introduced the 'I'm Freddie, Fly Me' phrase that had caught on earlier and became one of the airline's most successful marketing campaigns and it had worked. Laker was now well thought of by the travel trade on both sides of the Atlantic, especially as Freddie Laker's popularity with the public made a Laker booking an easy sell.

However, despite all these prior efforts to get Laker back in favour with the travel agents in both countries, Freddie's sales teams and reservationists had no response for what the competition did in late 1981. They all came out with massive overrides. Standard commission was ten per cent, after which the override went into effect. The overrides offered by Laker competitors, most notably Pan Am, took the overall commission up to as high as 28 per cent. It was unprecedented. It was commercial lunacy and possibly illegal but they didn't care. They would stop at nothing to see the back of Laker Airways.

"They were overriding to the travel agents to the point where they would simply call and cancel the Laker economy fare booking and then rebook them on Pan Am. How could they possibly refuse a commission schedule like that?" said Greg Dix. "And because our full unrestricted Economy fare was only $25 more than the Apex from New York, most people bought the full Y fare. Why wouldn't they, as they could then cancel without penalty." Laker's Low Season Economy fares were perhaps one of the many pitfalls of the fare fixing Laker had agreed with their competitors. The differential to their Apex out of Los Angeles was only $24 and out of Miami just $10. It was cheaper than the Apex cancellation / change or trip insurance. Had the Economy fare been priced with a much higher differential to the Apex, unquestionably fewer people would have cancelled and Laker would have benefitted from the APEX cash flow.

Dix continues, "Also, Pan Am and the others were offering full service to the favoured London Heathrow with 747s, the most popular wide-bodied aircraft of the day. We of course also had full service and reservations, but we operated DC-10s. The public and the travel agents still had serious misgivings about the aircraft ever since the crash in Chicago. The Americans didn't understand Gatwick either, no matter how much we promoted its benefits, the better rail transportation system to London and the fact that other US carriers were now flying to Gatwick." Laker may have been able to overcome some of the resistance to the DC-10 and Gatwick, but they had no response for the excessive commissions that were more than double anything Laker could offer.

The major airlines also pressured the travel agents to switch their business from Laker Airways by spreading false rumours that Laker was going bankrupt. The effects of all these measures, the fare cuts, excessive commissions and the negative rumours about Laker Airways were immediate and extremely damaging. John Jones said: "It happened very quickly, from October on it was just like watching the tide go out, the load factors dropped off the edge."

That October, it wasn't just load factors that were dropping off the edge, Freddie's emotional state was compromised too; the fall-out from the traumatic loss of his family two months earlier was by now at breaking point. He was desperate to put it all back together. Freddie had only seen his son three times since Patricia had left for Florida, taking his son away. It was not enough and Freddie felt he was losing him forever. He would never consider counselling, so his only emotional outlet was to put his thoughts down on paper, which he did frequently. Freddie's letters covered intensely personal subjects and revealed a man under considerable emotional and mental stress and perhaps someone who, given the extreme circumstances wasn't thinking with a great deal of logic.

In a heartfelt three-page letter to Patricia dated 9th October 1981, Freddie affirmed his concerns. He started by stating that he had hoped to have face-to-face discussions when he was last in Miami but as Patricia was unwilling to talk to him he had no alternative than to write. He continued, "My first and major concern is Charlie. You know my love for him is total, he is very close to my heart and I would not wish anything we do to affect him and therefore it is essential we both act in a sensible way." Freddie went on to say that he felt it was important their son grew up knowing both parents and it was his intention to see him as often as possible. He then pleaded, "I ask you, therefore, to return to this country with Charlie so that I can see him regularly and that he can be brought up in England as an Englishman, eventually to inherit whatever I may have." Accepting that the marriage may be unrecoverable, Freddie pledged to provide them with a 'reasonable home,' but if Patricia did not wish to return, he begged for her to let him have his son, for whom he would hire a nanny/governess as well as a full-time housekeeper to care for him.

Astonishingly, in the same letter he then turned on Patricia and castigated her for leading an expensive lifestyle whilst he faced potential ruin in his business. He told her his view on her renting an expensive apartment, driving a Cadillac and her use of his credit cards, all being paid for out of the Laker Airways' accounts. He asked her to return the credit cards, vacate her expensive Key Biscayne apartment and trade in the Cadillac for a smaller vehicle. Freddie had obviously not consulted with anyone before writing this letter to Patricia. He would have been advised that pleading for her to return or give him full custody of his son followed immediately by threats over finances, would hardly generate a satisfactory result. It showed the irrationality embedded in his emotional state and the fact that by the later part of 1981, he was fighting for his very survival.

Freddie then addressed what may possibly have been the trigger point for Patricia's sudden departure from England seven weeks prior. He wrote, "I must now mention the very painful subject of Bettina. The hideous lie has made it impossible for our very natural father/daughter relationship to continue. I cannot understand how you could believe such a wicked rumour and I must ask you very strongly not to spread it further. The person who will be most hurt will be Bettina, your own daughter. The rumour is categorically and absolutely untrue." The 'wicked rumour' Freddie was referring to was the nature of his relationship with Bettina. Numerous people had been in the company of Freddie and Bettina when they were together and had observed his preoccupation with the attractive teenager. Freddie was hardly discreet.

His letter to Patricia continued: "As to whether or not Bettina accompanies you to England, should you come, is a matter entirely for her." Clearly, he held on to the slim hope Patricia may return with Charlie and perhaps with Bettina. Despite his earlier comments, Freddie was firm on discontinuing his financial support for Bettina and wrote, "She is now an adult and must support herself. Much as I love and adore her, I can no longer accept responsibility for her and she must make her own way."

Not once in his pleading letter to Patricia had he spared a thought for Bettina's feelings or what she may have gone through. He perhaps felt she betrayed him by leaving England when Patricia told her to. It was not untypical of Freddie to take this stand. He had a history of turning off from anyone he considered to be 'disloyal', including those close to him.

He concluded, "This is not of my choosing, but I must protect her and my interests." Cutting his stepdaughter off financially was perhaps an act of cruelty or even retribution for her leaving, but he obviously felt he had no choice. Given the circumstances, it was an odd position for Freddie to take and again pointed to the intense emotional stress affecting his judgment.

Just a few months earlier, Freddie had committed £5,750 (£23,500 - 2018) to buy a three-day eventing horse for Bettina to ride in competition. His stud farm manager, George Plowes, wrote to Laker Airways' Finance Director Robbie Robinson rationalising the purchase and the supplemental expenditure, saying that the events would be watched by thousands on television, royalty would be there and so on. Laker Airways' finances were precarious in 1981, there was a freeze on advertising, pay cuts and staff layoffs were looming, yet an expensive horse for his stepdaughter was considered a necessary expenditure. It demonstrated how Freddie's personal priorities were influencing his decisions.

Freddie had tried to adopt Bettina in late 1979 when she was 17 and he was aware of the intense scrutiny this entailed. But now that Patricia had laid down the gauntlet to him, despite pledging his 'love and adoration' of Bettina, he had immediately distanced himself from his stepdaughter.

Freddie's letters were clearly the writings of a confused and desperate man as they kept flowing from his secretary's typewriter. In his 9th October letter, he confessed to Patricia that he had a permanent shake due to 'sheer pressure, both domestic and financial'. His closing paragraph was: "Finally, I want you to know that I have no intention whatsoever to institute divorce proceedings." He was presumably still clinging to the hope that Patricia may be forgiving and return to England, so they could all resume life just as it was before.

Whatever the principal cause of Patricia leaving him so abruptly, it was fortunately never leaked or even widely spoken about. Insiders were aware that the loss of his family and the life they had enjoyed for six years had devastated Freddie. The scene was set for a potentially messy divorce battle just at the worst possible moment for him. As well as losing his wife, his beloved son and his stepdaughter, whom up to then had been his focus, he was also losing the battle against his larger and more powerful competitors. Freddie had few cards left to play. However, the personal situation that compounded his business difficulties was entirely of his own making. A quirk of his personality was that he would forever be in denial and would consider himself entirely blameless about the part he himself played. Freddie was now teetering on the brink of losing everything... and his reputation along with it.

On the 1st November, a Laker DC-10 had departed from Gatwick for New York with Laker's new 46 seat Regency cabin. It was about as far from the original Skytrain concept as it could be. The question many people asked was why had Freddie become obsessed with the Regency Service initiative. Few, if any of his management team were 100 per cent on board with it, they were all stretched to the max with what they already had on their plates. Most of them wondered what Freddie's motivation was, beyond perhaps thumbing his nose at Laker's competitors? The timing for such an aggressive initiative was felt to be potentially suicidal. To launch Regency, let alone trying to then sell it at the same time as Laker's North Atlantic scheduled routes were already under considerable attack was more than a bit ambitious, even by Laker's standards. Laker Airways was in dire need of a period of stability in tough trading conditions, where they could focus on developing all the new routes and maximise their commercial position, especially in the USA. Now, Laker's Regency Service, aimed at the coveted business traveller had gone too far for the competitor airlines' tolerance. And they had reacted accordingly.

It was Laker's Regency Service that instigated the transatlantic fare war of late 1981. After quietly getting on with the job for nearly four years and stimulating overall traffic growth without stealing too much market share from the Big 3, "we then went head to head for their prime business and VIP passengers. The product itself was fantastic, but it was perhaps the stupidest thing we could have ever done at the time," admits Dix. John Jones concurs, "If people were going to jump off BA First Class and jump on to Freddie's front cabin, it was always going to be one antagonism too far." All bets were now off. The Big 3 airlines on the North Atlantic couldn't afford to have their vital front of plane revenue under threat, especially by Laker Airways, a carrier they considered to be nothing more than an upstart renegade.

Business travellers accounted for half of British Airways' passengers. Four in ten in the US market were Business Class passengers and made up two thirds of BA's revenues. The introduction of Laker's Regency Service brought about a swift response from Laker's competitors; Pan Am and BA offered an identical fare to Laker. The introduction of Laker's Regency Service had now put everything beyond any kind of negotiation.

There was no coincidence in the timing of the concerted measures by Laker's main competitors to drive Laker out of business. They were initiated the minute Freddie laid down the gauntlet during the summer by filing Laker's Regency Service fares. Not only did the Regency fares match to the dollar the Big 3's full unrestricted economy class fare, but Laker's 'first-class' type product was geared towards their most coveted segment of passenger, the business traveller.

The gloves were well and truly off and the major competitor airlines serving the North Atlantic were unanimous in their goal to drive Laker Airways out of business as soon as possible. Pan Am's Chairman, Ed Acker, who probably saw this more as a personal vendetta than anyone and clearly detested Freddie Laker and all he stood for, smugly said, "they all went along in the end."

POSTSCRIPT

*On consecutive evenings in November, Angus Kinnear the General Manager of Gatwick Handling - arguably one of the most detail-oriented and eagle-eyed executives in civil aviation and Alastair Pugh, a Director of BCal flew Regency to Gatwick. They both telexed Greg Dix who authorised their passes to compliment Laker and the 'outstanding Regency Service'.*

# CHAPTER 42

# Are You Ready... For Sir Freddie?

## The 1982 lifesaver

November 1981

On Monday the 23rd November, Laker Airways' New York based General Manager, Greg Dix and his wife, Linda Earls who was Laker's JFK Airport Station Manager, walked two blocks from a midtown Manhattan parking garage to the offices of Lord, Geller, Federico, and Einstein (LGFE) on Madison Avenue. They had been called there to view the storyboards for the 1982 TV commercials that had been assigned to the agency earlier and were scheduled to be filmed with Sir Freddie after the New Year's holiday.

They were coming off a busy weekend that included being with Cliff Nunn, who at the last minute the previous Friday had decided to spend the weekend in New York. He said that he wanted to check on how things had gone with David Tait and Skip Clemens who had been with Dix earlier in the week, strategising how they would combat the latest unionisation attempt by the Teamsters. In a reprise of the previous year's IBT campaign, the management team were again being challenged. But this year, given the dire financial state of the company, looming cost cuts and redundancies, their job would be considerably more arduous. "Do you think Cliff's got a girlfriend" Earls had asked, "this is his third time in New York in a month, maybe he's knocking... er I mean having a relationship with one of the crew, he always insists on staying at the Doral." Of all the people at Laker Airways, the least likely to have a girlfriend on the side, especially one of Laker's staff, would perhaps be Nunn. However, after decades with Freddie Laker, anything was indeed possible.

Nunn had accompanied Earls and Dix to the Kennedy Airport Airlines Management Council dinner, then they'd all gone to the British Consular Ball at the Plaza Hotel, where he had displayed some deft-footedness on the dance floor. He was surprisingly good company and had by now forgiven them for not inviting him to their wedding in June. After seeing Cliff off on

Sunday night from JFK, the pair had rushed back into the city for a reception hosted by Manhattan socialite and philanthropist, Gloria Starr-Kins. For some reason Starr-Kins had taken to 'Mr and Mrs Laker Airways' as she called them. Whenever she had one of her 'get togethers' of the world's rich, famous and influential, she invited Dix and Earls along. Taking one on each side, arm in arm, Starr-Kins would wheel the pair around, introducing them to a variety of sheikhs, ambassadors and Saudi royalty, including H.H. Prince Abdullah A. bin Jalawi for whom Kins was his U.S. representative. She had numerous Middle Eastern associates, one or two of whom were most intrigued by Laker Airways and had hinted they had money to invest. Dix had commented "we must bring Freddie next time he's in town, Gloria would love him and there may be some investor opportunity. It's too bad we didn't know these people when Freddie was hitting on George Tan." Tan's Carrian group in Hong Kong were courted by Freddie for a partnership deal or perhaps to buy out the entire Laker group. Dix acknowledged that Carrian's investment wouldn't have been legal, due to the foreign ownership stipulations governing British airlines, but at the time it was of no matter, as Freddie was desperate.

It was public knowledge that Laker Airways was not in good shape, so Dix and Earls had some trepidation about the meeting with the LGFE creative team. Their account executive, Victor Emmanuelle had been living almost full time at the Laker offices in Queens and had done his best to assure the agency's principals that they should continue with the advertising campaign for 1982, as planned. This LGFE advertising campaign was arguably the most important in Laker Airways' history. It was hopefully going to turn around the airline's dire financial situation by stimulating essential U.S. originating passengers and the respective dollar revenue. Even though the USA teams were putting out numerous immediate fires created by the fare war and the introduction of Regency Service, Freddie had instructed Dix to plan ahead for 1982. He was confident Laker would get through the winter and the refinancing plan he'd been working on for most of the year would soon be in place. A new television advertising campaign was therefore key to the company's future.

The agency had been well briefed and had assigned their brightest and best to the task. Even the agency's principals, Dick Lord and Norman Geller had added some creative input; they were both renowned advertising industry copywriters. Creative Director Arthur Einstein was there along with senior Art Director Larry Aarons and an assembly of writers and graphics experts. 'They all look very positive' Dix thought, as he and Earls walked into the spacious conference room meaning 'they have something really great to show us.' Victor Emmanuelle, the agency's point person responsible for the Laker Airways' account had virtually lived at the Laker offices in the months prior. Dix had encouraged him to bring one of the creative department's writers with him to the Laker management meetings at their Rego Park offices, which often went past most people's bedtimes. 'Sometimes the best ad campaigns and creative ideas come from the company's management meetings' Dix had told him. Emmanuelle knew the ins and outs of Laker Airways as well as anyone and he was pivotal to LGFE coming up with a great campaign for what was Laker Airways' turnaround year. Everyone knew about Laker's financial difficulties, the fare war and what had transpired since October. They had done some quick print ads, but now there was no greater incentive for the agency than to present a new campaign that would knock the socks off America.

When everyone was assembled in the conference room, LGFE's Creative Director, Arthur Einstein started things off with a brief rundown on what the campaign was based upon. As he proceeded with his preamble before revealing the storyboards that were lined up on a long shelf facing inwards, Dix felt Linda tapping his leg under the table and glancing sideways as if to say 'what the hell is he going on about.' Not long after, the first story board was turned around, then another and another with an appropriate explanation from one of Einstein's team until about a dozen brightly illustrated boards were now facing everyone in the conference room. The creative department all looked eagerly at Dix and Earls hoping for a positive reaction. Instead all they got was quizzical looks. Dix finally broke the silence as he looked at another pile of storyboards sitting on the floor, with "hmm what else have you got there." By his facial expression, he was clearly not excited about what he saw lined up along the wall. Fortunately, LGFE had a back up, just in case their clients weren't overly impressed with the first campaign they'd presented. Advertising agencies often did this as a ploy to enhance the impact of the ad campaign they really wanted approval for. So the first batch of story boards were removed and another dozen large cards were placed facing inwards on the long conference room wall shelf. As each of the second batch of storyboards were turned around with an explanation given by a member of the creative team, it became obvious the agency was massively wide of the mark. Dix looked over at Victor Emmanuelle as if to say 'what have you guys learnt from being in my office for the last month as they had clearly not captured the essence of Laker Airways, or of Sir Freddie. But it wasn't really the fault of Emmanuelle or the agency. They were still new to the Laker account and had unfortunately become involved when the airline and its staff were not at their optimum. They hadn't known Laker in some of its glory years of 1978 to 1980.

"Guys, I think what you have done is wonderfully creative... but it's just not us. Actually it's probably perfect for British Caledonian and Adam Thomson" he said, laughing. By their expressions it was obvious the LGFE team didn't know what or who he was talking about. "It's not Laker Airways and it's certainly not Sir Freddie. He would never say much of the script you have on either of these two campaigns." The LGFE creative team looked forlorn.

They'd obviously worked hard on the two ad campaigns, only for Laker's senior man telling them they weren't appropriate. Seeing their downtrodden faces, Dix took control and commenced by giving them a brief history of the company, it's monumental achievements with Skytrain and what Freddie Laker was all about. After nearly a decade of working for Freddie and especially after travelling extensively with him for the past couple of years, he was in a unique position to inform the assembled creative team what he would be at ease saying and just how he'd say it. "Sir Freddie won't be comfortable with 'you'll enjoy my new Regency service with unlimited champagne, hors d'oeuvres and a complimentary headset. And he will definitely balk at saying 'and you won't have to queue for days' as that's what destroyed the entire concept of Skytrain." Dix was hedging his words in case LGFE's team were sensitive to criticism.

"We're hell bent on shaking off the image of being the airline that created 'Lakerville' and all the chaos back in 1978" he went on, trying to buy some time and think of a suggestion. "You probably don't remember our earlier campaigns, they were quite simplistic but really punchy, 'I'm Freddie Fly Me' and "I've Got My Name on Every Plane' were absolute winners. We need something like that again. Something catchy, even a bit corny because that's more Freddie than what you have up there right now guys… sorry." Dix and Earls sat staring at LGFE's creative team of art directors, copywriters and producers who all looked as if someone had stolen their lunch. No-one responded, so Dix was on the spot for a solution. "I think you're being a bit too cerebral, too sophisticated" he continued. "That's not us, we're pretty simple down to earth types; remember who Freddie is and what he represents. He may be worth millions, own thoroughbred race-horses and a large yacht, but horse breeders and sailors aren't our customers and he's not pretentious. Remember, Freddie's put himself out there as the 'champion of the forgotten man'. I realise you don't know him like we do" looking over at Earls next to him. She had been Freddie's first employee in the USA, had worked for Laker Airways even longer than Dix and knew Freddie on a personal level far better than most. "And he never takes himself too seriously" Earls concluded.

The LGFE creative team were all stone-faced and silent which meant they had to come up with a suggestion. If there was one thing that irked Dix more than anything it was one of his staff complaining about something and then not being able to offer a few solutions or alternatives; he didn't want to now be guilty of this himself, so he thought quickly and went on.

"Any of you remember Freddie and the Dreamers, the British Invasion band from the sixties? They had this song called 'Do the Freddie'. It was a huge hit and created an entire dance movement. You could perhaps contact the publishers and do a licensing deal to use the hook line, maybe even the rights to use the song as a jingle." Suddenly, faces that a few minutes earlier had been solemn started to light up around the table. "You have to remember that the company and the man whose name is on the planes are inseparable. "Do the Freddie, do the Freddie" Dix sang the lines to make the point but thought twice about doing the absurd dance that went with it, "think about it." Everyone laughed and then Linda piped up, "yes and how about the Flintstones." The pair now had the full attention of the LGFE creative team. Everyone around the table clearly loved the Flintstones and were probably thinking she was going to suggest they use 'yabba dabba doo.' "Do you remember how Wilma used to be annoyed at Fred because he was always late" she continued. And she'd call out 'Ready Fred' to him." That prompted a few nods around the table and some brief exchanges between the creative team but then Dix chimed in as he'd now thought of another example along the same lines, "and last year Queen had a massive hit with 'Crazy Little Thing Called Love' you've probably heard it" as everyone appeared to get more animated in anticipation.

We used the song in Asia to introduce Freddie at a function. "In the last verse, Freddie Mercury sings 'and take a long ride on a motorbike, 'til I'm ready' and then the band all chorus back 'ready Freddie.'We'd cue it so everyone in the room, maybe two or three hundred people, would all yell 'ready Freddie' and he'd walk out in his tuxedo looking like he was about to get an Oscar. Anyway..."

Dix stopped talking as the room had gone quiet. Sensing they may have overstepped the mark and were trivialising the work this vibrant young ad agency were doing, he looked over at Linda sitting next to him for a bit of guidance as to what to say next. Earls often had to save Dix from himself and explain what he really meant, usually after staff members were in tears. "Look guys, I'm sorry, you're the experts here, we just know the man and our airline. We're really not trying to be facetious or insulting about the work you've done for this campaign. We just know Freddie won't be comfortable with most of what you've shown us and..."

"Greg." It was Creative Director, Arthur Einstein loudly interrupting whom Dix assumed was about to give him a piece of his mind based on the level of his voice. "Why don't you guys and Victor go and have lunch and come back in about an hour." So the meeting broke up and Emmanuelle, Earls and Dix left to go and have lunch nearby. In the elevator, Dix turned to Victor who looked glum and probably thought his days at the agency were numbered "I think we may have fucked up Victor. Arthur, Larry and all their guys probably feel insulted with what we said in there." Emmanuelle didn't have an answer, as he was surprised at what had gone down in the meeting. He thought the campaigns LGFE had produced were appropriate and tasteful. But knowing his colleagues at the agency were a pretty thick-skinned group and used to rejection from clients, he'd also sensed that some of what the Laker pair had said to the creative team may have hit home.

As Emmanuelle, Earls and Dix filed back into the LGFE conference room after lunch they had no idea what had been happening in the agency's creative department during the last hour. Arthur Einstein kicked things off by thanking Dix and Earls for being so honest with their views on the campaigns they'd presented earlier. He acknowledged that even after his staff had spent considerable time at the Laker offices, been embedded into the management meetings and shown over one of the aircraft during a routine three-hour turnaround at JFK, the agency hadn't quite grasped the essence of the airline they now represented. Einstein was keen to stress that after just one very brief meeting with Freddie earlier in 1981 after they had won the account, where he was distracted, ill-tempered and clearly not himself, they didn't really know him. Or how vital his role as the company spokesperson was and what he may be comfortable saying.

"So we have cobbled together, very fast I should add, a revised campaign for your consideration." Einstein turned to Larry Aarons, his senior art director and nodded for him to turn around the first story-board. No explanation was necessary, as written in simple white block letters on a blue background was 'ARE YOU READY... FOR SIR FREDDIE?'

# CHAPTER 43

# Saving Laker

## Freddie's early Christmas gift

Late 1981

Back on the 26th August, 1981, at the behest of Lord Benson, advisor to the Bank of England, Dennis Kitching, the Assistant Chief General Manager of the Midland Bank, was called to a meeting. Benson and his assistant, David Walker had told Kitching that Laker Airways appeared to be in severe financial difficulties and asked the Midland to lead an attempt to arrange a refinancing package.

The Midland Bank, as the lead bank in the Airbus consortium and the largest creditor of Laker Airways was itself far from blameless in the crisis. It could not have been that much of a shock, when the payment for the A300s failed to materialise. The bank had gambled that any future Airbus lending would offset any potential losses should the Laker Airways' loan go wrong. They had encouraged Freddie in the acquisition of the A300 aircraft that Freddie openly admitted he could not afford. Supposedly they had done their due diligence before approving the loan. Of the $131 million dollars owed to the Airbus lending syndicate, $26 million was being carried by the Midland.

Kitching was told that the position was critical because Laker was about to default on a large payment due to EXIM Bank. Kitching soon discovered just how rapidly Laker's problems had escalated during the summer of 1981. The Midland Bank's own position via its subsidiary the Clydesdale Bank was covered, it held floating charges over all the principal Laker companies; International, Services, Airways, Arrowsmith, and Laker Air Travel.

Midland's security comprised four BAC One-Elevens, two Boeing 707s, the hangar and the freehold office complex at Gatwick. The book value of the 707s was £3 million and three of the One-Elevens were worth about £1 million. However they had been on the market since March 1980 with no takers. From its Marine Midland division, Freddie had borrowed $10 million towards the purchase of DC-10-10 (G-BELO) jointly with the Royal Bank of Canada. There was $10.8 million left on the loan but the aircraft was worth substantially more. The banks had a lien on G-BELO plus a spare engine. It was this loan that was actually hurting the airline the most, as Robbie Robinson, Laker Airways' Finance Director explained: "We knew what all the loan repayments were going to be except the one for G-BELO – that was Libor (a variable rate of interest) related. It was a killer."

It was Kitching's initial view that he didn't think Laker Airways was worth saving and the bank ought to have called it a day on the over extended airline. If Laker was to go into 1982, there was an additional cost of renewing the TOSG bond that was about to expire. The TOSG bond required ABTA members to obtain a bond equivalent to five per cent of their annual revenues. It existed to provide the funds to rescue stranded holidaymakers and to refund people who had paid for future holidays in the event of a failure of an airline or tour operator. In the case of Freddie's package holiday businesses the bond was about £4.8 million. The money was held in a deposit account and required the bank to release it.

There was not much love lost between Freddie and Kitching. Freddie would later say, "I think Dennis Kitching is an ass. He really made a cock up of it. I think that says it all." John Roney thought that the Midland Bank had its fingers in too many Laker pies. The Clydesdale Bank, a Midland subsidiary were also Laker Airways' commercial bankers.

At the request of Lord Benson, the Midland drafted in its merchant bank, Samuel Montagu and one of its managing directors Ian McIntosh to head up the rescue. Unfortunately, McIntosh was described as 'very nice' but not the heavy hitter Laker Airways required; he was 'a city banker of the lunchtime variety'. The Montagu appointed accountants, Thomson McLintock were tasked to write a review of the Laker group and its prospects.

For much of the of the time in the early stages, Freddie was not involved in any of the meetings nor was he kept informed of what was going on. Samuel Montagu was always felt to be a creature of the Midland. Information that was given to Freddie and the finance department of Laker Airways was heavily edited. "Eventually Freddie had to force his way into the negotiations" recalled John Roney. Roney had grave concerns about Samuel Montagu and Thomson McLintock's involvement. He was sufficiently alarmed to ask them straight out who they were advising. McIntosh said he did not know, but 'probably Laker'.

Thomson McLintock had prepared an initial report on the financial state of Laker Airways. One of its partners, Bill Morrison was drafted in full time as financial advisor to Laker's young financial director, Robbie Robinson. Freddie and others invariably referred to Robinson as 'smart as paint'. Despite his undoubted talents in a pivotal role, he was clearly overloaded in this particular crisis. In terms of willingness to put in effort, Robbie reminded his colleagues of 'Boxer' in George Orwell's, Animal Farm – "The solution, as I see it, is to work harder. From now onwards I shall get up a full hour earlier in the mornings." And so he did, Robbie worked truly punishing hours for Laker and it is said nobody worked harder. Even John Jones.

Refinancing talks were now fully underway and agreement from all the lenders was the prerequisite to their success. It was almost certain the EXIM Bank would make it a condition of their assistance that Laker Airways not take delivery of the next three Airbuses that were on order. Fears were that if word of this was reported back to Toulouse, the negotiating position with Airbus would be catastrophically weakened.

By the 25th August, Freddie had heard nothing from EXIM but a proposed tide-over letter was still circulated by Laker Airways' financial advisors. On the 28th August, Mitsui said they were unable to deal with the draft tide-over letter and the proposals until they had cleared a few things up, but would get back to them the following week. No one seemed to be in any kind of a hurry.

An increasingly desperate Freddie, who was still reeling from his wife Patricia leaving with his son less than two weeks earlier was thinking up new ways to raise cash. During August, he came up with an idea for an issue of what he called Travel Bonds and actively explored the legality of the idea. The bonds would be available to the public for £100 each and that would allow them to buy any Laker product in perpetuity with a ten percent discount. They were effectively giant sized gift coupons and no one took the idea very seriously.

Two days later, on Sunday 30th August, John Roney had flown first to the U.S. and then to Canada for urgent face-to-face talks. From his hotel room at the Plaza Hotel on 5th Avenue in New York, he'd spoken to Claudette Cristian, the general counsel of the EXIM Bank. Roney was told there would be a final decision by the following Wednesday. Just three days later whilst in Ottawa meeting with the EDC, (Canadian EXIM Bank) to whom Laker Airways owed $6.5 million, Roney was given a very rough ride. Their attitude was not the least bit sympathetic. Laker had been their first ever application for a deferral and Roney left the meeting empty handed. Two weeks later they would relent, but only agreed another month's extension while negotiations continued. So Roney spoke again with Claudette Cristian. She told him that EXIM expected payment as usual on the 15th September. Apparently she had spoken to Freddie who had told her the payment would be made. Roney quickly disabused her of this position. What made it all the more difficult was that EXIM had found gaps in the numbers that Laker Airways had presented and it still had questions about the airline's operations as a whole; they wanted clarification.

A meeting with Robbie Robinson and Freddie had been hastily scheduled for the following week to include General Electric and McDonnell Douglas, the two American corporations who had co-funded the purchase the DC-10-30s. When Sandy and John McDonnell heard about Freddie's problems they had instructed Jim McMillan, the President of McDonnell Douglas Finance Corp oration to 'keep Laker flying'.

John Roney was tasked with preparing a skeleton report outlining what had been considered to reduce costs or for introducing additional equity. The clock was ticking and Roney had been given only ten days to complete it. Nonetheless, somehow and with great difficulty, an interim deferral of Laker's repayments was given, but only for a limited period of thirty days, this had allowed further talks to continue.

Completely out of the blue, on 15th September, Midland Bank had struck the first critical and damaging blow. They informed Freddie that they would be exercising their rights by way of a notice of default and they refused to release any money out of the Laker group's deposit accounts. Robbie Robinson was stunned when he received the letter and asked Roney for advice on how to respond. It was a sneaky move by the bank as it had no real entitlement to withhold cash from accounts with money in them. But it made little difference as the sums of money involved were quite small. However, its significance as a 'tightening of the noose' by Laker's financial institutions was all too real.

Throughout the remainder of September it was apparent that all the talking, let alone the necessary deeds of variation to the loans could not be completed before the next financing instalments were due. The earlier meetings had gone reasonably well and Freddie and Roney were certain there would eventually be some kind of offer to assist from the lenders.

Meanwhile Bob Beckman, Freddie's tenacious Washington lawyer, had been chomping at the bit ever since the news of Laker's financial problems broke. He believed that he and not John Roney should have been leading the refinancing talks. Greg Dix recalled: "Bob was tearing his hair out trying to get through the door and he was so hurt by being excluded." In his own opinion, Beckman genuinely felt he was far better qualified to deal with the international issues at hand than John Roney. Freddie however, had put his complete faith in Roney, who was acquainted with all the participants by virtue of his involvement with the aircraft purchases. If ever there was a time when Freddie perhaps needed more specialised counsel it was now. By this time, partly skewed by his current state of mind and emotions, Freddie had turned off to Beckman and was leaning on Roney more than ever. After all, Roney was going to have to deal with Freddie's messy personal situation at some point, so keeping him close was Freddie's proven standard operating procedure.

Beckman did in fact have an interesting take on the situation with the EXIM bank in particular. His opinion was the US government's action in creating and maintaining high interest rates by intentionally constricting the money supply in the US, had depressed the value of the pound. This of course substantially increased the cost of Laker's repayment of EXIM's financing. As the EXIM was an agency of the United States government, Beckman believed that the law was clear; the US government could be held liable for its actions that hindered a private party's (Laker Airways) performance of a contract with the government (EXIM). Freddie was therefore entitled to postpone his repayments. Beckman would have happily sued the Federal Reserve, United States Government and the EXIM Bank in the blink of an eye. However EXIM was only one lender and acting quite reasonably, so Beckman's view didn't have legs.

Undeterred, late in September, Beckman made another pitch in an attempt to get himself involved. He had produced his own figures to show Freddie just how badly the American carriers had fared on the Atlantic so as to present a useful comparison. Beckman urged Freddie to stress the significance of the DC-10 grounding as the prime reason for the current problems and that he had considerable research showing there was still public resistance to flying the DC-10s. Dix and Laker's other managers in the U.S. concurred with this; after all, they were the ones trying to sell the American public on flying Laker's DC-10s instead of the competitors' considerably more popular, and in the eyes of the public, safer 747s. But it was a route that Roney refused to go down; his view was that if the DC-10, the primary long haul aircraft Laker Airways flew at the time was the problem, it was a problem there would be no way out of, or at least not for a very long time. Roney wanted to show that Laker Airways' future was bright, arguing it would be highly damaging to their position with the public if there was anything that might suggest otherwise. "Laker Airways", he bluntly told his American legal counterpart "has already pinned its colours to the mast by blaming the entire airline's troubles on the poor exchange rate. To shift from that position now, would be irresponsible."

Beckman didn't give up. The telexes went back and forth to no avail and the phone calls were brief and often tense. "You don't understand Bob, you do not understand what is going on," Freddie would say to him without explanation. In one of their final conversations Freddie growled at him, "Why do I need you, when I have the Bank of England helping me?" Freddie's reticence to hire Beckman to assist at this critical time was partly due to Beckman's high fees and Freddie's deference for Roney, who would doubtless charge a fraction of what Beckman would bill the company. This was always a powerful argument with Freddie and eventually, Freddie stopped answering the phone calls from Washington. It had caused Beckman to become quite despondent as a result. Despite his outer toughness, Beckman was a sensitive man and more than anything wanted to be loved and needed. He would have done anything for Freddie and being ostracised hurt him deeply. After all, Beckman and Freddie had almost single-handedly revolutionised the airline industry. Now his 'friend' had turned his back on him. Beckman knew Freddie had been through the ringer emotionally, although he wasn't in the loop on the details or reasons. He just knew Freddie was distraught and perhaps not thinking clearly. After all, why would Freddie, after all they had been through together be ignoring him, just when he perhaps needed him the most.

Laker Airways had stumbled into October, its passengers numbers were running at below half of their August high point. Even though the re-organisation of the USA management had made some immediate improvements in US originating traffic and revenue, it may have all been too little, too late. The efforts simply weren't enough to generate the dollar cash flow the company required. Moreover, the passenger numbers and load factors were about to plummet further as Laker's competitors took their gloves off. Laker Airways was by now regularly drawing on the overdraft at the Clydesdale to make ends meet.

EXIM Bank granted another one-month deferment after Freddie had presented them with a study prepared by McDonnell Douglas. The MDC analysis had given everyone cause to be optimistic. If Laker Airways could hang on until the following summer, the traffic forecasts showed there was a sufficient cushion for the airline to weather the storm. But the CAA and the Midland Bank hadn't believed a word of the report, suggesting it was 'unnecessarily rosy'. Despite the report being generated by highly qualified

MDC analysts, the traffic and revenue projections had been submitted by Laker's commercial and financial executives, ratified by Freddie himself. Airbus Industrie claimed that there were disturbing errors in the report, which clearly favoured the DC-10s. They thought the operating revenues had been exaggerated while the costs, especially those of the DC-10-30s were underestimated, this despite the MDC report clearly stating the DC-10-30s were loss-makers. They also concluded that the DC-10-10s were 30 per cent more expensive than their own aircraft on the European routes being operated.

The EXIM Bank's extension had not been long enough, it was anticipated that the negotiation period would fall beyond November. Then EXIM relented and extended for another 30 days. Diplomatic efforts by the UK government in Washington were said to be behind the decision, or maybe the fact that EXIM stood to lose $30-40 million in the event of a Laker collapse. Another leading lender, the Bank of Tokyo deferred its payment until the 16th November. But this was the final deadline for a workable proposal all the lenders – including the Airbus syndicate – could adhere. Representatives of both syndicates would convene in London on the 4th November for more urgent talks.

For as long as possible, Laker Airways had resisted selling any of its aircraft, always rebuffing the suggestion as being 'in the realms of speculation'. At the time of the purchases, when asked what he would do if he got into trouble, Freddie's worst-case scenario was always that he would sell the aircraft, or just hand them back.

That time had arrived and Dennis Kitching told Freddie he must reduce the capital debt of the aircraft, that stood at $422 million, by half. But the world had changed and what looked like the obvious answer to his problems was no longer so simple. The DC-10s were practically unsalable due to the public perception of them as being unsafe, following two fatal crashes. There was zero market for the wide bodies, more than forty DC-10 aircraft languished unsold around the world. Prices were severely depressed in late 1981. A used DC-10-10 could be bought for $15 million and the 10-30s were selling for an average of $20 million.

McDonnell Douglas and Airbus jockeyed for position and each insisted that their competitors' aircraft were sold. The brand new Airbus aircraft were easily the most saleable assets, being pristine and efficient and with no history of incidents. It made sense to off-load them first. The underutilised DC-10-10s could operate the European flying the A300s were slated for without having to lease back or charter extra aircraft to fulfil the package holiday contracts for the summer of 1982. Although an A300 had the range to cross the Atlantic, legislation governing twin-engined aircraft at the time precluded them from doing so. ETOPS was still a few years away.

Since the arrival of the A300s, in the 1981/82 financial year, the DC-10-10s were forecast to fly approximately only sixty per cent of their available block hours. The 707s were not flying at all and the One-Elevens were also effectively redundant. However as the recession began to bite and affect the travel industry, when the crisis hit hardest, the Airbus aircraft had lost their value.

Freddie would happily have parted with just one Airbus; but in that event the favourable interest rate subsidy would be lost on all three. At interest rates running in excess of 15 per cent, Laker Airways would not be able to afford the repayments on the other two. Freddie proposed leasing one of the A300s to Pan Am for the coming winter, but Pan Am just weren't interested.

John Jones, Laker Airways' astute commercial manager, to no-one's surprise had devised another aggressive and innovative commercial strategy for the European sun destination vacations for 1982, in order to achieve maximum utilisation of the new widebody aircraft. Unfortunately, the A300 initiatives had taken Jones's focus away from Laker's extensive North Atlantic programme at the worst possible moment when the load factors were down, the competition was eating away at Laker's market share on every route and when Laker Airways needed life-saving US dollar revenue. In September for instance, the differential between Laker's New York unrestricted, refundable full Economy fare and the advanced purchase (APEX) with 21 day booking restrictions and a minimum stay of 7 days, was just £10.

"Why would anyone buy an Apex with such a minimal differential" Dix continually asked Laker and Jones. His view was born out once the September figures came in and were analysed. It showed what was happening. A savvy passenger would book a full Economy ticket then call on the day of departure, check if there were seats, turn up at the airport and buy a Walk-on. They would then cash in their full Economy ticket for a full refund. Laker would lose £53 each way on every full Y fare transaction cancelled, plus the administrative headache of refunds and the goodwill lost with travel agents, who would also lose their commission on every cancelled ticket.

Dix had earlier urged Freddie to get rid of the same day Walk-On fare as it was uncommercial and bypassed the travel agents they were desperate to get on side. But Freddie wouldn't hear of it, "that's how Skytrain was bloody well started" he'd scream. In September, the 8-day bookable Walk-On fare and the full Economy were Laker's best sellers on the New York route. Apex was basically a non-event, only 17 per cent bought it, even less from Manchester. Going into the last quarter of 1981, Laker had more than a fare war with its competitors to deal with. They had an internal fare war. The frustrated managers in the USA and the equally vexed Skytrain Services Manager in the UK continued to battle with Freddie and Jones that the fares they had been given to sell were unworkable. By this time however, perhaps the last thing on Freddie's mind was the transatlantic fare schedule.

The A300s were still only expected to break even for the first three years before they would be profitable. By contrast, the DC-10-10s had made Laker Airways a lot of money; they were especially profitable on the London to New York and Toronto routes where they were at their payload-range limitations. The DC-10-30 fleet however had incurred significant losses on the Skytrain services to Miami and Los Angeles, but were needed for their range in order to operate the routes non-stop. Laker couldn't afford to abandon or reduce service on any US dollar earning route. The McDonnell Douglas report that had been specially compiled to assist with Laker's refinancing and used data supplied by Laker's own management, was quite specific. It forecast that for 1981-82, the

11 DC-10s would lose £10.2 million and the three Airbus A300s would lose £7.3million. It was an eye-opening conclusion that got everyone's attention.

Keeping the DC-10-10s that carried approximately $40 million less debt than the A300s made perfect sense. Selling all the A300s was clearly the most practical solution and would reduce Laker's debt down to $291 million. The Midland Bank's Dennis Kitching however, was insistent that at some point some of the DC-10s would have to go as well.

The situation between the two rival manufacturers created a great deal of tension, Airbus and its British partner, BAe were not going to readily agree to a solution that would only benefit McDonnell Douglas at a cost to themselves. Both demanded to be treated equitably. Airbus was already smarting from the cancellation of the seven aircraft Laker Airways had on order, one of which was approaching completion at Toulouse. They justifiably felt hard done by, especially since they had done more than anyone else to help, and they told Freddie so.

Airbus had underwritten a first loss guarantee of 25 per cent on the aircraft if and when they ever came to be sold, this loss would be passed onto the stakeholders in Airbus, the governments of West Germany, France and Britain. In theory, it made Airbus Industrie the biggest losers in the affair, but fully protected the banks in the consortium.

Airbus did have a right of subrogation; in other words they could still pursue Laker Airways through legal channels for causing the loss. With increasing worries that the loan rescheduling would leave them with greater exposure, Airbus Industrie would do no more than strictly abide by its contract.

Sitting pretty and massively hostile were two German banks, the Dresdner Bank and Bayerische Vereinsbank and the single Austrian bank, Creditanstalt Bankverein. All three deemed Laker unsalvageable. They decided they were not going to go along with the proposed 12-month rescheduling. They thought the aircraft should be sold so as to get most if not all of their money back as soon as possible. The West German government had invested heavily in the Airbus programme, whereas the British and their national carrier BA had chosen Boeing, causing residual bitterness. The German banks couldn't care less what happened to Laker Airways; in fact due to their close links with West German national airline, Lufthansa they would happily see Laker disappear. Lufthansa was well connected within the German banking system and could use their connections to lobby the German banks to shut Laker down. The chairman of Lufthansa's supervisory board, Dr Hermann Abs held the identical post in Deutsche Bank. Lufthansa was a deeply entrenched member of Laker's archenemy, the International Air Transport Association (IATA). Laker wasn't directly competing with Lufthansa on any routes, but Laker's European route applications and the threat to go to the European Court had set Laker on a collision course with the mighty German national carrier.

On the 4th November, all of Laker's lenders gathered in the boardroom of the Midland Bank's city headquarters for a summit that would decide Laker Airways' future. There were representatives from each of the banks plus executives from McDonnell Douglas, EXIM Bank, General Electric, Airbus

Industrie, and British Aerospace. Observing were government representatives from the Bank of England and the CAA. Freddie was not invited and instead he was represented by his two bank designated financial advisors, Ian McIntosh of the Midland's subsidiary, Samuel Montagu and financial advisor Bill Morrison.

Before them, was a newly completed report from Thomson McLintock and the 82 page report from McDonnell Douglas that since the 1st October had been circulating for everyone to digest. It highlighted Laker Airways' efficiency in terms of usage of its aircraft, it read, 'Laker easily leads the field'. The report contained long-term traffic and financial forecasts, but also showed increased losses of £11.6 million. However, even though things would go from bad to worse in 1982, the MDC report forecast that by mid 1983 Laker would once again be healthy and highly profitable.

Samuel Montagu thought Laker Airways needed a cash injection of £40 million. Their figures were bleak and they projected that by the 31st March 1982, Laker Airways was going to be overdrawn by £19 million. However, internally produced figures by Laker Airways told a somewhat different story. By Laker's reckoning, in December the overdraft would stand at £6.8 million, rising to £6.9 million in January. As revenue came in from deposits on holidays in February, the overdraft would reduce to £2.9 million. In March the overdraft would peak at £9.2 million. There was some quick number crunching by the bankers. The rescheduling, savings in interest payments and an increase in package holiday deposits would add £22.6 million to the Laker group's balance sheet. Ironically, the bankers somehow came up with the exact same number of minus £9.2 million as the end of March balance. This had been accurately predicted by Laker's top accountants. It left Laker still needing £10 million to be solvent again. The time had come to either shut the company down there and then, or agree to support Laker Airways by way of its overdraft and the rescheduling of the long term aircraft debt. The bankers chose the latter.

McDonnell Douglas were the keenest to assist. Freddie had genuine close personal relationships with the McDonnell Douglas executives and they liked him. Freddie's decision to rely on its DC-10s for Laker Airways major services and the relatively successful operations of its DC-10 fleet contributed to MDC's ability to export DC-10s to other non-US airlines and supplementals.

Freddie had been quick to tell the world the DC-10 was the safest aircraft flying and the crash in Chicago was nothing to do with the aircraft but caused by American Airlines' improper maintenance. MDC were eternally grateful for Freddie's support and confidence yet they too faced deep recession, not knowing where the next DC-10 sale was going to come from. They most definitely didn't want any aircraft returned to them. Freddie thought MDC's mistake was in not pointing the finger firmly at American. So the DC-10's reputation continued to languish. Clearly MDC were concerned about any disruption to their long-standing relationship with AA. Logically, it should have been obvious that American really had nowhere else to go for planes at the time. Boeing had more orders for the 737 and 727 it knew what to do with, AA already flew the 747 and DC-9 and they'd ordered the only wide bodied twin engined plane available, the Airbus A300. Lockheed wasn't in the frame at all. Freddie urged the MDC executives to back him more in trying to rescue the reputation of the maligned DC-10, but he got nowhere.

EXIM Bank pressed for the capital repayments to be deferred by only six months just to the 15th March 1982. This date fell into the high point of Laker's projected borrowing. Acknowledging that this would do nothing more than draw out the whole painful saga, they acquiesced and agreed to a year. The Japanese preferred to schedule an additional loan to cover the existing loans.

There remained one last difficulty and it was the trickiest; the Airbus loan and how the first loss guarantee was to be dealt with. The two German and Austrian Banks would have to be forced into line by the Midland and/or the Bank of England. The Airbus Syndicate planned to meet in early December and only then would its true position on Laker Airways be clear.

In desperation, John Jones had committed a DC-10-30 to Nigeria Airways for a Hajj programme from Llorin in central Nigeria to Jeddah (for Mecca) in Saudi Arabia. While the revenue was adequate, the risks were considerable. Nigeria was by now not under a military government, nevertheless operating out of such a remote location with no back-up whatsoever, could have compromised the aircraft, crews and ground support staff. Laker was prepared to take those risks in late 1981 and had to capitalise on every available revenue opportunity.

Freddie and Cliff Nunn flew on GK10 to New York on Wednesday 4th of November. On the drive into Manhattan with Greg Dix who had met them, Freddie rubbed it in how brilliant and visionary he was in launching Regency; both he and Nunn said it was a terrific service despite only a handful of people being in the front cabin. Freddie was in high spirits, which considering everything going on was surprising. Dix assumed he'd chatted up some of the cabin staff for later. They then huddled with Dix in his office on how to stimulate more US dollar revenue. The November forecasts were appalling and David Tait was brought up for the day to explain what was happening in the Miami office. The interline agreements with the Latin American carriers, without whom Laker Airways' future in Florida was inevitable, were not forthcoming, much to Freddie's consternation. The USA management was in the midst of another battle with the Teamsters' union which was taking up a lot of their time and energy, yet they had nevertheless made significant improvements since the July re-organisation.

True to form, no matter how challenging his life was at the time, Freddie had insisted on breaking away that evening. Strategically leaving his deputy Managing Director to fend for himself in the Doral bar, surrounded by attractive Laker cabin staff, Freddie cajoled Dix to accompany him to Régine's. He knew his man would gripe about the extravagance and the 'over-priced food' as they drove up Park Avenue to the Delmonico Hotel where Régine had her empire. Expensive champagne was consumed while the petite, smoky-voiced, red-headed Régine flirted with Freddie, as she did with perhaps two hundred of her flock every night. She then introduced the pair to two of her 'VIP' members who would accompany the Laker men to Plato's. It was a perfect night in the Big Apple for Freddie - a couple of hours fun at Plato's before returning the girls to Régine's and a nightcap. Unusually, Freddie didn't

**Above:** Freddie Laker stands in a reflective mood in front of his flagship DC-10 just before boarding the aircraft for the inaugural Skytrain service flight to New York, JFK on 26th September, 1977. The history making flight concluded a six-year battle with governments on both sides of the Atlantic. They had done everything they could to obstruct Laker's entry on one of the most valuable and sought after air routes in the world. Freddie had finally achieved his quest to offer affordable air travel to millions who could never have dreamt of having the experience. It was a defining moment in aviation history.

## Making History (September 26, 1977)

After six years, Freddie finally realises his dream with the inaugural Skytrain service to New York.

**Above:** Freddie at Gatwick airport and being greeted by grateful passengers before the inaugural flight of the Skytrain service took off from London Gatwick to New York JFK on 26th September 1977. With all the publicity Skytrain had generated, Freddie was already a folk hero in Britain and the United States.

Freddie in his signature flying pose before the flight.

**Below:** Freddie is besieged in a media scrum of British press before the flight left for New York.

**Below:** Celebrations at Gatwick. Freddie was happy to share the special day with his mother Hannah next to him and PR officer Robin Flood (L).

**Below:** Freddie was in a jubilant mood on the day of the first flight of his Skytrain transatlantic service from Gatwick airport, London to JFK, New York. He proudly waved the flag of England before the DC-10 took off across the Atlantic.

## ‘GK10 Clear for Take-Off’ (September 26, 1977)

Laker Airways’ flagship DC-10, G-AZZC (Eastern Belle) flew the inaugural Skytrain service to JFK. Crew: Capt. Basil Bradshaw, F/O Mike Willett, F/E ‘Spud’ Murphy and Chief Stewardess Joy Poirrier.

**Above:** Freddie straps himself into the jump seat behind Captain Bradshaw for the historic take-off.

**Right:** Inaugural flight passengers - with their complimentary flight bags - board the aircraft as Laker’s Skytrain Service Manager, Geoffrey Street (L) welcomes everyone.

This is to Certify that
Gregory Dix
was a passenger
on the first Laker Skytrain
Air Passenger Service
from Gatwick Airport – London
to Kennedy Airport – New York
on Monday September 26th
1977

**Above:** McDonnell Douglas DC-10-10, G-AZZC ‘Eastern Belle’ takes off from Gatwick Airport bound for New York on 26th September 1977. The historic event was heavily televised. It was fifty years since Charles Lindbergh crossed the Atlantic in May 1927.

**Inset:** An inaugural flight certificate signed by Captain Bradshaw and his crew and by Freddie himself.

**Above:** Freddie chatting with the passengers during the flight to New York.

**Right:** Freddie celebrates with his inaugural flight’s cabin crew on arrival in New York. He enjoyed an almost messianic loyalty from his flight crew members; many of Freddie’s pilots and cabin staff had been with him for decades. From left: Joy Poirrier, Sue Barnes, Sandy Doherty, Siobhan Hunter, and Kym Turner.

## A Movement is Born (1977-78)

Prospective Skytrain passengers formed at Gatwick and then at London's Victoria terminal and outside Laker's terminal in Queens, New York. Under the strict terms of the Skytrain licence, Laker was unable to take reservations and passengers queued up to fly on a first come, first served basis. Skytrain created fervour similar to a grass roots movement; all in support of affordable air travel.

©Getty Images

**Above:** The queues of Skytrain passengers at Gatwick Airport caused the British Airports Authority to insist Laker find an alternative ticketing facility. Victoria Station was chosen.

**Above:** Freddie opening the Skytrain ticket office at London's Victoria Station. The direct rail link to Gatwick made it a convenient ticket sales point.

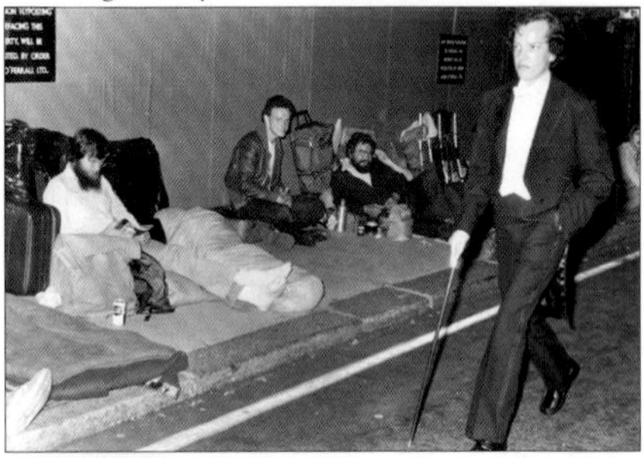

©Rex Features

**Above:** A London 'dandy' creates an amusing contradiction to the weary Skytrain passengers camped out on the pavement at Victoria.

©Getty Images

**Left:** Prospective passengers organised themselves and created a self-managed 'reservations' system. When Skytrain was first approved, the prospect of thousands of Laker's passengers camping outside for several days terrified airport authorities and other airlines. In New York, airport access was blocked and Laker's passengers were processed 10 miles from JFK.

## 'Lakerville' (Summer 1978)

Thousands camped out for days enduring the weather and lack of food and sanitation facilities. The residents of affluent Eccleston Square near Victoria endured the squatters for the entire summer. No-one could have known how the frenzy would impact the Skytrain concept and Laker Airways' future.

**Above:** Freddie signs autographs while he visits the queues of people camping outside Laker's Victoria Station ticket office in London. **Inset:** The elusive Skytrain service ticket was akin to the Holy Grail for Laker passengers. People had never gone to such extremes to fly between Britain and the United States.

**Below:** Desperate for a cheap flight to America, enterprising Skytrain passengers created a shanty town while they camped out on London's Millbank, a mile from Victoria, as they waited to buy a ticket.

**Insets:** Skytrain passengers created signs some of which warned queue jumpers what they could expect for an infraction.

**Above:** Freddie checking on the rain-soaked passengers.

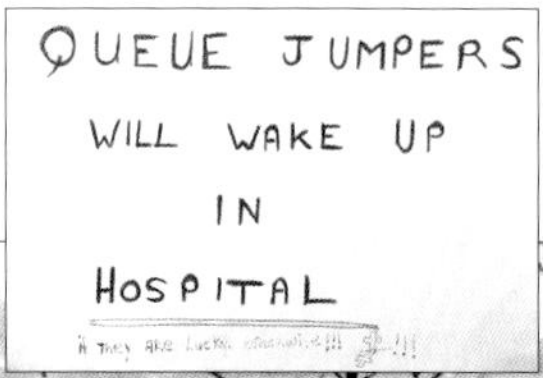

## "Arise Sir Freddie" (1978)

The greatest honour for any Englishman is to be knighted by Her Majesty, Queen Elizabeth II. Following his knighthood, Sir Freddie was voted 'Man of the Year' and received numerous awards. A long- awaited membership of the prestigious 'Jockey Club' came later and was another highlight.

**Left:** Acknowledged for the success of Skytrain, the newly honoured Sir Freddie with his wife, Patricia (R) now 'Lady Laker' and his mother Hannah (L). He was knighted by H.M. the Queen in her birthday honours list for services to civil aviation. The investiture was held on 19th July 1978.

**Below Left:** Sir Freddie outside Buckingham Palace.

©Alamy

**Right:** Freddie with his wife Patricia (L), 16 year-old step-daughter Bettina (R) and long awaited son, Freddie Allen (b Jan 4, 1978) at Furzegrove Farm in Chailey, Sussex.

**Above:** The UK distributors for Apple Computer turned up at the Laker offices with Steve Jobs' latest innovation and asked Freddie to be the spokesman in their advertising campaign. They left the Apple 2 behind. Sir Freddie never used it and John Jones eventually procured the computer.

**Below:** Freddie holds his Mac cartoon (by the popular Daily Mail cartoonist) after receiving honorary lifetime membership in the prestigious Cartoonist's Club at their St. George's Tavern, London HQ.

## Enjoying the Spoils (1978-80)

With the initial perceived success of the Skytrain service, his new title, an idyllic domestic situation, and honorary Doctorates embellishing his reputation, Freddie enjoyed the fruits of his efforts.

**Above:** Freddie often said the only reason he was in the airline business was so he could own boats. His new yacht, the 'M/V Patrina' named for his third wife Patricia and stepdaughter Bettina was a 27m Italian built Benetti that he berthed in Palma, Majorca.

**Left:** A Rolls Royce Silver Shadow, Freddie's latest company car.

**Left:** Freddie felt he'd finally completed his education when the renowned University of Manchester gave him an Honorary Doctorate.

**Left:** Sir Freddie studying the form book before bidding on thoroughbreds. He is with Epsom trainers Vic and Tony Smythe, the brothers of Freddie's great friend and trainer Ron.

**Below:** Freddie with the celebrated Welsh jockey, Geoff Lewis after Freddie's thoroughbred 'Go Skytrain' won the Anniversary Stakes at Lingfield.

**Right:** Harry Freeman (L), Freddie's loyal chauffeur opens the front passenger door as Freddie typically sat in the front. "It's a four-wheeled fornicatorium" Freddie laughingly described his numerous Rolls Royces.

**Left:** With the success of Skytrain, a knighthood, and other accolades, Sir Freddie assumed the persona of 'SuperFred'. There was nothing he couldn't do. Fueled by hubris, he now set forth on his most ambitions ventures.

## Developmental Initiatives (1978-81)

Flushed with the success of Skytrain and finally with a stable domestic life, Sir Freddie embarked on a host of new initiatives. Lenders were throwing money at him and he couldn't resist the opportunity to apply for new routes to the USA, buy many new aircraft and expand the company's infrastructure.

**Above:** Freddie and Pat's son Freddie Allen had turned one in January 1979.

**Above:** Two Boeing 707-351B aircraft were purchased in 1978 for Caribbean Airways and North American ABCs.

**Above:** Freddie at Disneyland.

**Left:** A promotion at the Queen Mary.

**Below:** A billboard positioned on Century Blvd Los Angeles, by the infamous Carolina strip club.

**Above:** In anticipation of ten new wide body jets arriving imminently, Director John Seear oversaw a massive expansion of Laker's hangar and offices, effectively doubling its size.

**Above:** Legal department secretary, Joan Vaughan surrounded by the already antiquated terminals and rotary-dial phones of 'Brian' the Laker UK's reservations system. After two years of custom programming, 'Brian' never operated efficiently.
**Inset Above:** The affable Ian Allan came back from Barbados to be Scheduled Services Manager.

**Above:** Laker's cabin services training team worked hard and efficiently to graduate new groups of cabin staff for the rapidly expanding fleet of wide body aircraft. Freddie was extremely proud of Laker's industry leading in-flight service.

**Above:** Operations Manager for NA, Greg Dix finally secured terminal space at JFK & LAX after considerable obstruction by competitor airlines and airport authorities. Laker co-hosted with Braniff's 'Cowboy' for reservations and airport functions.

## Committed to the DC-10 (1979-82)

In early 1979, two brand new DC-10-10s were delivered, one of which bore Freddie's initials (G-GFAL). In May 1979, flight AA191 crashed on take-off from Chicago and as a result the worldwide fleet of DC-10s was grounded for five weeks. Between December 1979 and June 1980, Laker took delivery of five new McDonnell Douglas DC-10-30 aircraft, financed by the Ex-Im Bank.

**Above:** The pre-Christmas 1979 delivery ceremony of the first Laker DC-10-30 (G-BGXE) at Long Beach, before its flight to Gatwick. The bow and card acknowledge the new non-stop service from Los Angeles.

**Right:** Laker's DC-10 Fleet Manager, Captain Steve James has his tie ritualistically snipped by John Brizendine, President of McDonnell Douglas as he officially receives G-BGXE on behalf of Sir Freddie.

**Above:** As the USA took longer to lift the DC-10 grounding ban, Laker Airways used one of its DC-10-10s (G-BBSZ) for the Caribbean Airways' Gatwick, Luxembourg to Barbados flights in July 1979.

**Left:** After Laker's DC-10s were grounded for five weeks, Freddie was pleased to announce that Skytrain was finally back in the air again.

**Right:** Pete Conrad, renowned astronaut and third man to walk on the moon was a Vice President of the McDonnell Douglas Corp.

**Below:** Laker's DC-10-30 (G-BGXF) was leased to Lan Chile in early 1981 as many of Laker's new long-haul route licenses hadn't yet been granted.

**Above:** Sir Freddie with astronaut, Pete Conrad. They were proactive spokesmen to restore the much needed consumer confidence in the maligned DC-10 after the five week grounding of the worldwide DC-10 fleet on 6th June 1979.

## Global Domination (1979-81)

'There's a new world somewhere, they call the promised land'. Inspired by the opening line of the Seekers' hit song, Freddie's ambitious 'Globetrain' was to operate around the world daily: London - Sharjah (UAE) - Hong Kong - Tokyo - Honolulu - Los Angeles - London and vice versa. He also sought London to Australia (via Singapore), new cities in North America and 666 European routes.

**Left:** Freddie with Greg Dix (L) and John Jones in Sharjah, UAE, December 1980. They were being honoured at a banquet held by the Emir of Sharjah.
**Right:** Freddie wanted Skytrain to connect every point on the globe.

©J Watson

**Above:** Sir Freddie saw himself as a tai-pan in Hong Kong. He hosted a lavish party for Hong Kong's upper echelon at the new Regent Hotel in June 1981 during the trans-Pacific licence hearings. L-R: Bettina Laker, Sir Freddie, Jacqui Watson, Dr. Freddie Watson - Laker's HK Director, and Lady Patricia Laker. Shortly after, Patricia abruptly left Freddie and moved to Florida.

**Right:** The widely circulated, controversial photograph of Freddie at Jerusalem's Wailing Wall during his trip to Israel, that almost cratered his global ambitions.

**Above:** Cathay Pacific's 747, purchased for the Hong Kong to London route they started in July 1980. Cathay successfully objected to Laker's bid to serve HK from London.

**Left:** Athol Guy, the popular bass player singer of 'The Seekers' and a former M.P. for the state of Victoria was the Managing Director of Laker's Australian company in Melbourne.

## 'Quid pro quo' - Europe for the Airbus (1979-81)

Sir Freddie's impulsive order for ten new Airbus A300Bs in 1979, immediately after the purchase of seven new DC-10s, committed the financially stretched airline to an unprecedented aircraft purchase debt. In exchange, Freddie was promised 666 European Skytrain routes. He was duped.

**Above:** Freddie with Bernard Lathiere, Chairman of Airbus Industrie signing the contract that made him a hero in France.

**Above:** Laker's first Airbus A300B being assembled at the Airbus Industrie factory in Toulouse, France.

**Below:** Sir Freddie was thrilled with the new Mini Metro sporting his personal number plate 'FLY 1'. The Metro was a gift from Airbus Industrie courtesy of British Leyland, in gratitude for his unprecedented order for ten A300s.

Airbus A300-B 'F-WZEL' flying over the Alps on a test flight. For Laker, it was re-registered 'G-BIMA' and named 'Metro' after the revolutionary Mini Metro vehicle made by British Leyland.

**Above:** Sir Michael Edwardes, Chairman of British Leyland (L) Freddie and Bernard Lathiere, at a 'liquid luncheon' to celebrate the arrival of 'Metro' the first Laker A300.

**Below:** Freddie painting an appropriate message during an A300 promotion in the West German capital where he had a long history and Laker had an operational base.

**Below:** Sir Freddie with his A300 Fleet Manager, Captain Tim Davies (second from right) and flight crew members of Laker and Airbus after the delivery flight of the first A300B (G-BIMA) 'Metro' from the Toulouse factory.

**Below:** Sir Freddie and a group of Laker Airways' hostesses promoting the Airbus in Palma - Majorca in 1981.

## The Final Straw (September 1981)

Ignoring the advice of nearly all his top managers, Sir Freddie launched the 'Regency Service'. It was a purely antagonistic gesture against BA, Pan-Am & TWA; he was enraged they had matched his Skytrain fares so 'Regency' targeted the Big 3's most lucrative customers. In desperation, he then turned the USA operation upside down in an attempt to increase life-saving US dollar revenue.

**Above:** The Regency Service brochure promoted the oversized seats, flowing champagne, lavish china service, and upgraded in-flight entertainment.

**Above:** Charles Maxwell, Manager USA, held a pivotal position until mid 1981, when Freddie, frustrated with a perceived lack of progress in America had him fired. The reorganisation that followed was instigated to increase the percentage of US originating passengers taking advantage of the strong dollar.

**Right:** After two years pursuing Laker's global aspirations in Asia and Australia, Greg Dix was 'grounded' in New York and tasked with improving all areas of Laker's business.

**Left:** Freddie sent Stuart Alderman over to New York to head up Laker Vacations. Alderman had been with Wings prior where he'd been mentored by Ernest Welsman.

**Above:** "I have constantly warned the others if they attack my end of the market I will attack theirs" was Sir Freddie's brash challenge. For his competitors, it was the final straw.

**Above:** An early Regency Service print advertisement that ran in Los Angeles.

**Left:** Freddie and David Tait, the Regional Manager for Florida & Latin America. Tait's job was to generate US originating traffic from Miami and Central & South America.

## The Perfect Storm (late 1981)

An economic recession, a massive financial over commitment for aircraft, aggressive competitor fare matching, the mis-timed Regency service, and half his fleet of aircraft sitting idle created a 'Perfect Storm' at the end of 1981. Meanwhile, McDonnell Douglas, GE and the banks were all desperately trying to save Laker Airways and over 2500 jobs, while Freddie was distracted by a monumental domestic crisis.

**Right:** Freddie and his son Freddie Allen and stepdaughter Bettina. Freddie had a lot on his plate and Laker Airways was in deep financial trouble. In August, consumed by business challenges, he was blind-sided when his wife Patricia abruptly left him, taking his beloved boy away. The heart-wrenching domestic upheaval caused him to take his eye off the ball, just when he needed to concentrate on survival.

© Pablo Palmerini

**Right:** John Roney, Freddie's lawyer, worked hard on the Laker re-financing, yet vital clues were missed that might have eventually changed the outcome.

**Left:** In a last minute attempt for revenue in late 1981, a DC-10 operated from Llorin in Nigeria to Jeddah (for Mecca).

**Below:** Nearly half of Laker Airways' entire fleet of aircraft sat idle outside the Laker hangar towards the end of 1981. Numerous factors had struck a devastating blow to travel between Britain and the US.

**Left:** Laker's Victoria ticket office, that just a few months earlier had queues around the block, had more staff than customers in late 1981.

## 'Action' (February 2-3, 1982)

Sir Freddie had experienced a tough winter. At the end of 1981, the future of Laker Airways looked bleak and his personal life was in disarray. After months of exhaustive negotiations with his principal lenders, they gave Freddie a green light and he flew to New York to shoot TV commercials for 1982.

**Left:** Sir Freddie flew on the Concorde to New York's JFK on 2nd February, 1982. He had missed his Laker flight the day before due to an overly long call with the Midland Bank. Freddie was relaxed and looking forward to being in the TV commercials for the 1982 summer season. He felt he had finally turned the corner and could now get back to what he loved doing the most.

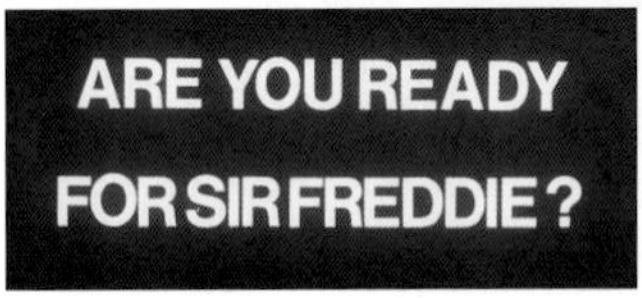


**Above:** The first story board of the ad campaign Laker Airways' New York advertising agency presented for the 1982 Skytrain Service.

**Right:** Sir Freddie in a reflective moment before shooting the spots for his controversial Regency Service.

**Below:** Amanda Cooper (L), Steve Wren and Meg Vesty were specially selected for the ad campaign.

**Below:** George Steinbrenner (C), renowned owner of the New York Yankees baseball team appeared in the TV commercial. His line "I'm Ready for Sir Freddie - I thought I was Ready for the Dodgers" played on the humiliating defeat to their LA rivals.

**Above:** Freddie delivering his opening line "Are you Ready... for Freddie" for the television ads that would air in all Laker Airways' USA markets.

## 'Ready for Freddie' (February 3, 1982)

Sir Freddie loved the new ad campaign and was confident it would drive essential US dollar business in 1982. The 'Regency' commercials would transform Laker's image from 'no-frills' to a 'full service' airline. After Director Fred Levinson called for a wrap, Freddie hit the champagne and had some fun.

**Left & Right:** Sir Freddie was relaxed during the shoot in New York and excited for the future. Just the night before he had been forced to give up his bid for the 666 European routes to appease his lenders. They then assured him the refinancing for Laker Airways was approved; Freddie was ecstatic.

**Left:** Laker Airways' In-Flight Directors, Amanda Cooper and Meg Vesty were good sports and unruffled by Freddie's boisterous behaviour at the wrap party. Fueled by Moet & Chandon, Freddie was right back on his game, after months of stress and personal traumas.

**Above & Left:** Freddie and Amanda... who hadn't experienced her boss's good-natured lasciviousness prior to the shoot.

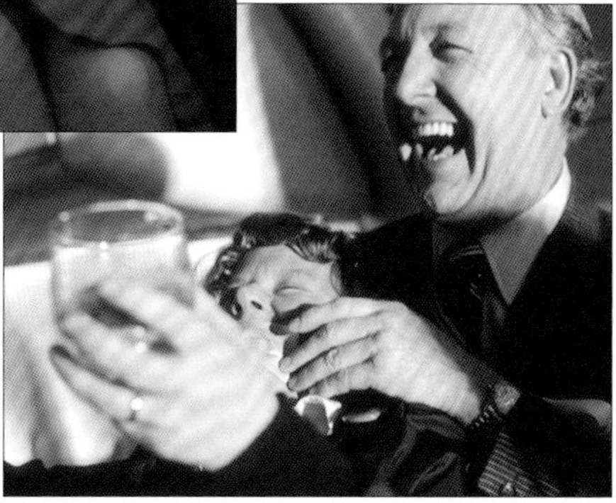

**Above Centre:** 'I'm Ready for... Sir Freddie' buttons were made up for the 1982 ad campaign.

**Right:** Freddie and Meg, who after ten years of flying for Laker had 'got all the tee shirts' and could handle anything... including Freddie.

**Above:** Freddie used gaffer tape to silence Robin Flood, his exasperating publicity representative. He was oblivious to the news he was about to make.

## 'Grounded' (February 5, 1982)

**Above:** The grounded Laker Airways' aircraft outside the hangar at Gatwick. Within hours of the receivers being called in, all flights had been returned, the offices locked and Laker's assets seized.

**Above:** John Roney (L) with Sir Freddie. On arrival from New York, Freddie had been summoned by the Midland Bank and ordered to call in the Receivers. He and his lawyer had both missed an earlier hint of the Midland's intentions.

**Left:** Shocked, exhausted and alone, Sir Freddie had endured a grueling two days. After being told to call in the Receivers he then had to meet with a divorce lawyer handling the acrimonious proceeding with his wife, Patricia. Following an all-night vigil with his directors trying in vain to raise the cash to float the company, on the 5th of February 1982, Laker Airways was grounded and Freddie's life (and those of 2,500 staff) was in tatters.

**Above:** A Laker Airbus A300 (L) and a DC-10-30 at Manchester Airport after the Receivers had grounded the entire Laker fleet.

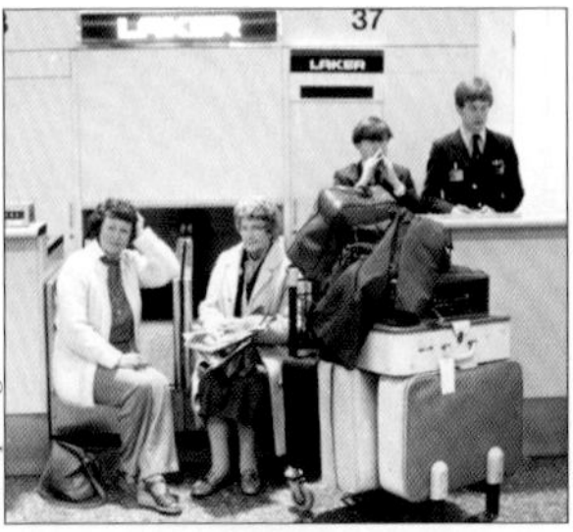

©Getty Images

**Above:** Stranded passengers wait for news if they'll ever fly home.

**Above:** Distraught ground staff taken off-guard by the collapse.

**Left:** Laker's exhausted New York team trying to lighten up the worst day of their careers.

**Below:** Bravo Whiskey sits idle at Gatwick after 16 years service, with a seizure notice attached to the door.

©Rex Features

care for either of them, probably from fatigue, stress and jet lag, It was gone 2:00am by the time they stumbled into the Doral and by 9:00am the next morning they were back in Dix's Rego Park office, with Nunn none the wiser.

A select group of New York area Travel Agents escorted by one of Dix's sales managers were all surprised to have Sir Freddie on GK20 with them that Friday evening as they headed to London. As soon as he had heard Freddie was coming over, Dix had hastily put the fam trip together. He knew they would be wowed by Freddie during the flight and from then on, even if Pan Am were paying them more commission, they would likely favour Laker; he really was that effective. Dix said to Nunn if Freddie could do more of that instead of having to spend day after day with bankers, accountants and lawyers, the company may well be in a different place.

On the 19th November, an emergency board meeting of Laker Airways was held at Gatwick. Finance Director Robbie Robinson presented the problems to the board. The overdraft that was offered was not going to be sufficient. Of greatest concern was that the two German and one Austrian bank had still not agreed to the refinancing even though they were being assured by Samuel Montagu that they would. A discussion was held about the selling of the subsidiaries, but the Laker group did not work without the inter-relationships of its various components. The holiday companies provided 40 per cent of the airline's passengers and £37 million in value for flying. In fact, the two holiday companies with their low overheads and impeccable reputations with the travel trade, would easily survive as independent entities. However, the financial situation was now too tight and there was not enough margin for error. "If the company ceases trading, so be it" said Freddie almost resigned to his fate.

At this point its fair to say that Freddie had more than just his airline's woes weighing on his mind. He had flown back and forth to Florida to try and smooth things out with his wife Patricia but had got nowhere. On the 25th November 1981, Patricia applied to the courts for alimony, child support and an order preventing her husband from abducting their son. Freddie meanwhile had made his own custody application in the British courts for the boy. There was more than a fare war happening on the North Atlantic and in much the same way as with the airline war, there was no sign of an imminent resolution.

The Midland's Dennis Kitching, when he had reviewed Laker's traffic forecasts had thought the end was nigh. The aggressive price cuts brought in by Pan Am had succeeded. Laker Airways' passenger numbers had halved, whereas those of Pan Am and BA had risen. Laker had averaged 15 per cent market share of the London - New York market in 1981, but now it was down to eight per cent and still losing ground. Not only had the prices been cut, but the legacy airlines were also paying over-the-top commissions to travel agents to drive Laker out. With no rescue plan formally announced, travel agents sat on the cash owed to Laker until the very last moment. Laker's customers were booking one way, just in case. Compounding matters, the railway strikes affecting the entire country had effectively cut off Gatwick. The fast, direct rail link from Victoria was one of Laker's much touted selling points and one of Gatwick's few advantages it had over London's Heathrow.

November turned out to be a disaster as Laker Airways carried only 26,848 passengers on its three principal transatlantic scheduled routes. It was 47 per cent down on 1980 when 50,596 were carried in the same month. 9,360 passengers at a 58.5 per cent load factor were flown between London and New York compared to 16,116 at 75.3 per cent load factor during the same month of 1980. The Big 3 also coordinated their London – Los Angeles services and provided a nonstop service every day of the week, having only operated the route five days a week prior. The increase in capacity in the low season hurt Laker's previous high market share on the LA route and in November 1981, Laker carried 9,625 passengers at a load factor of 51.4 per cent compared to 14,312 passengers at 69.1 per cent load factor in the same month of 1980. London - Miami, a loss-making route even with high load factors, was even harder hit and a mere 7,863 passengers flew at a load factor of just 47.4 per cent, compared to 20,168 passengers at 80.1 per cent load factor in November 1980. The 'Miami gold rush' was well and truly over. Heading into Low season with a weak pound and almost no US originating passengers, it looked ominous for the prime Florida route to survive the winter.

The advanced bookings for December and early 1982 for all the main Skytrain routes between Britain and the USA painted a bleak picture. The volume of traffic had declined against Laker's own forecasts that earlier had estimated traffic would improve. The Midland's Kitching said he was no longer prepared to talk to German and Austrian banks once he had seen the November results. It was left to the Bank of England to encourage the three obstinate banks into line, but they still remained discontented.

Lesley Chilton called Greg Dix in the afternoon of the 8th of December to say Freddie and Cliff Nunn were flying in the next day on GK10. Dix had just survived a bruising interview with *Travel Trade Magazine*, where he had been grilled on Laker's financial position and why they weren't paying agents more commission. So he wasn't in the best of moods. "What the hell are they coming here again for Lesley" was perhaps not the response Chilton was expecting. She explained that as well as needing to meet with Dix on Thursday they also had an important meeting in New York on Friday 11th. "I can't see them on Thursday as I'll be with American Airlines through lunch." After a few seconds of silence except for the sound of a page being turned Chilton said, "Oh, hmm well I have the meeting with American down for Friday at 10:00am." Dix thought about what Freddie's secretary had said and wondered if with all the stress everyone was perhaps going mad. "Lesley" he said his voice somewhat firmer, "I'm having lunch with two guys called Baldwin and Lloyd-Jones to discuss check-in counter and office space at American's terminal. Don't tell me somehow Freddie got wind of it and is flying all the way over to participate. Or is it another excuse to go down to Miami?" Chilton stifled a laugh and then explained that Freddie and Cliff Nunn along with Bob Beckman had a top secret meeting planned with American Airlines' CEO, Robert Crandall. That's why they were coming over and she then gave Dix the address of their meeting asking if he thought a limo should be booked for them. "No Lesley, they don't need a bloody limo, they can walk the few blocks over to 6th Avenue from the Doral. I thought everyone was on strict austerity measures, I've just laid off thirty staff." Dix heard a frustrated sigh at the other end and assumed that Chilton must be under a fair bit of pressure also; likely more than anyone.

Once it had been established that their respective meetings with American Airlines were for entirely different purposes, Dix confirmed he would meet Freddie at JFK and drive them into town. He then had Karen, his secretary book Freddie, Nunn and himself into the Doral for the nights they were in town. He assumed Beckman would book a suite in the Waldorf Astoria across the road; no austerity measures would apply to Bob's accommodations. 'Now what the hell's all that about', Dix mused to himself before calling Washington. Beckman filled him in on the reason for the meeting with Crandall and then complained that Freddie never spoke to him or asked him to do anything any more. He was particularly aggrieved Freddie hadn't called him personally to summon him to New York, when the entire case against American was his idea.

The short notice and imminent arrival of Freddie and Nunn was hardly convenient. Adding Bob Beckman to the visitor list inevitably meant more 'baby-sitting' as all of them would need the usual 'welcome to New York' amenities, which meant Dix's tight schedule would be massively disrupted. He had a management meeting with the labour lawyers for the Teamster battle and planned to now bring Nunn into it so he could see first hand what they had to deal with. He would also get Freddie to give a talk to the staff, as he was always motivational. The New York staff Christmas party had been arranged for that Friday evening. It was deliberately early to help employee relations in light of the unionisation campaign. Dix had asked Laker Air Travel's Managing Director George Carroll to fly over for the party. Carroll was a renowned party animal and never missed a chance to hang out with the staff socially. But now, Dix would also try and keep Freddie or Nunn in New York for an extra night, as that would show his over two hundred Rego Park and JFK Airport employees that Laker's top management really cared about them. Once he had mobilised his team to shift gears, something they were extremely familiar with doing, he felt more positive about the head office visitors arriving the next day.

It had been some six weeks since the start of the fare war proper and on the 11th December, while Freddie and Cliff Nunn were in New York, John Roney found himself summoned to meet with The Bank of England's Lord Benson at 5pm. South African Henry Benson had enjoyed a long and glittering career as a director of the renowned accountants, Coopers & Lybrand. He had impeccable credentials. During the meeting, Benson told Roney straight out that his client should close down. The Bank of England had lost faith that Laker Airways could be saved beyond only the very short term. Laker needed to consider its position that very day, and immediately cease trading. It was reiterated more than once to Roney that in the bank's view it would be very difficult for the Board of Directors to decide anything else. Roney was speechless at Benson's opinionated audacity. He came out of the meeting furious. "I thought, what the hell is going on? As an independent solicitor I would not be told by somebody not directly involved in the case what my advice should be to my client. It was very much a matter for me to decide."

The situation was so serious that Benson offered some other advice; Laker should consider placing all holiday deposit money received from Monday in a protected designated account.

Immediately after the meeting with Roney, Benson picked up the phone and called Ray Colegate at the CAA. Benson had Colegate's ear and his opinion carried a lot of weight. His devastating analysis was that Laker Airways would not survive without an injection of £50 million.

"I can't stay over Dix" Freddie said after Nunn, Beckman and Pierre Murphy, Beckman's young barrister who had done most of the leg work for the DC-10 grounding case, had left. "I need to get back by tomorrow morning, sorry. Roney was at the Bank of England today." Dix knew to not ask about what had gone down at the meeting with Crandall, but Beckman's demeanour hinted there was a great deal of tension in the air. Freddie too, seemed stressed and distracted, unlike the night before when once again he and Dix had started the evening at Régine's. As usual, Freddie had been wheeled around by the hostess who knew everyone's name and with one look could have them quaking, while Freddie shook hands with people who had familiar faces but whom he obviously didn't know. It was always an eye-opener to see megastars of stage, screen, sports and music drop anyone or everything they were doing and go gaga when they met Freddie. Obviously, being a titled Englishman in New York was advantageous, but it was the same in London at Johnny Gold's Tramp that in many respects was very similar to Régine's. At both, Freddie was a magnet.

With two of Régine's 'regulars' in tow, Freddie decided they would have a light dinner at her bistro in the same building aptly called Réginette's. They would then be heading to Plato's at Freddie's insistence, for a last hurrah there of 1981. Over dinner, when the ladies had excused themselves and someone wasn't trying to shake Freddie's hand or try and sell him something, Dix told him that he had an important interview with *Travel Agent* magazine on Monday afternoon. He wanted to know what he should tell the travel and tourism industry's premier publication about Laker's re-financing plan. Freddie said he honestly didn't know until he got home and had spoken to Roney about it. Dix knew by the response not to push it further. He also didn't tell him that David Tait and Skip Clemens were both coming in for a meeting with the labour lawyers that same morning. He realised it was pointless for Freddie to be told things weren't looking good with the unionisation campaign and that laying off staff right before the Christmas holidays had naturally created a lot of uncertainty. Uncharacteristically, Dix bit his tongue and didn't bring up the fact they had probably blown the equivalent of a week's wages of a passenger service agent on champagne and nouvelle cuisine that evening. All so Freddie could indulge in the New York celebrity scene and have his ego stroked by phoney, sycophantic celebrity-seekers, even if most were celebrities themselves.

On Tuesday the 15th of December, with the next deadline for the temporary deferment with the EXIM about to expire, officials gathered from government departments to voice their concerns – including representatives from the CAA, the Bank of England and the Trade and Industry departments. The CAA was now saying that the required overdraft to get the airline through the winter would be nearer £14 million and not £10 million.

It called for a new plan devised by Bill Morrison. If the BAe took back the A300s at no loss to Laker with perhaps Airbus Industrie taking preference shares on the shortfall and... if McDonnell Douglas were asked to take shares in lieu of their monies due, a deal could be done. In addition, if MDC and GE agreed to inject £5 million in new capital and if Airbus, MDC and GE agreed, the Midland would continue to support the overdraft the CAA sought.

They had until 6pm on the 16th December to come up with a workable solution on this basis. Failure would mean the revocation of Laker Airways' licences. The CAA would force a shutdown of the company. At the end of the memo from Morrison to Roney there was a stinging condition. Freddie was ordered not to contact anyone directly. He was to curtail his public pronouncements like the one he had made earlier in December at the opening of a new sales office in Glasgow where he told the press that he was heading for a '£15 million profit in the next financial year'. After the worst slump for years 'we are turning a corner' proclaimed Freddie. It was a ridiculous thing to say, and to his exasperated helpers a most unwelcome statement. Laker Airways may never have failed to make a profit, but those profits had always been minimal. In 1979 they had been £1.52 million, in 1980 £2.53 million, but in fiscal 1981 after the final reckoning they were predicted to be anyone's guess. Despite his earlier prediction that 1981 would be his first loss in sixteen years, Freddie was now unrealistically forecasting a modest profit of £0.18 million. His bravado performances behind the scenes with the bankers were equally as infuriating as the ones he made in public.

"We understand that Laker Airways is going bankrupt tomorrow," the *Daily Mirror* was on the phone to Laker's press officer, Robin Flood. Even though the newspapers were generally too frightened to print stories in exactly those terms, any sort of reporting of this kind scared travel agents, many of whom were holding on to passengers' deposits. The 16th of December 1981 was the worst moment so far of the crisis at Laker Airways. That same day, Freddie's lawyer, John Roney had been forced to send a letter to the BBC's news editor, Peter Woom, threatening him with a libel writ over 'irresponsible reporting'. Roney warned Woom specifically about an article on Laker Airways' troubles that was scheduled to appear on the Nine O'clock News that evening.

On the 17th December, Ian Wallace, Laker Airways' account manager at the Clydesdale wrote giving mixed and disappointing news. He called the 'confirmation of willingness to defer' the Airbus loan and its loan on the DC-10-10 G-BELO, for a period of twelve months as 'premature'. The Clydesdale was prepared to continue to provide an overdraft, but only £4.5 million. It was much less that had been hoped for or had been verbally agreed in August. The Clydesdale did suspend their right to demand immediate re-payment of the overdraft until after the 14th September 1982 and with some further pressure increased the overdraft from £7 million to £9 million. The terms of this increase were suffocating as it was on the understanding that another pre-existing $5 plus million US dollar loan used to purchase the two 707s was repaid immediately and that any aircraft sales would reduce their overdraft before anything else. Word got back to the EXIM Bank about the reduction of Laker's overdraft facility. They were deeply upset with the Clydesdale letter, as their grapple for security threatened to destabilise the tentative agreement.

The Canadian EXIM agreed to reschedule on the 17th December. On the 21st December, a letter was sent from the Bank of England to BAe with agreed terms. Roney was unhappy that he and Freddie had not been able to preview its contents and it was delivered as a fait accompli. Kitching was to approach the German and Austrian banks that afternoon to settle things despite saying he wouldn't. A later telex that day to all lenders from the Midland confirmed that McDonnell Douglas and GE had agreed to inject £5 million in new capital. They would receive preference shares in lieu of a proportion of the DC-10-30 debt. Representatives of MDC would come to London on the 4th January 1982 to finalise the deal. The three Airbus A300s would be sold. Airbus agreed to defer their payment until July 1982 and if necessary until September 1982 if the A300s weren't sold. They were still waiting on Mitsui although confirmation that the approval of the board was just a formality. Nevertheless, the loose ends were strung together, even if the schedule overran.

The telex from the Midland that Roney and Freddie had been waiting for had finally come through. It read, 'We now have approval in principal of all other lenders including the Airbus syndicate'. Ian McIntosh and his fellow director Gervaise Boote ended the telex with the words, 'We are very anxious to make an outline announcement on Wednesday 23rd December. An urgent reply is therefore requested'. Freddie responded that he had a better idea and suggested that the press release was put out by Samuel Montagu and that the Bank of England had given it their support. Freddie felt coming from the bank instead of Laker Airways gave the news better credibility. Public confidence was key.

On Christmas Eve, 1981 a short press release was issued by the bank, confirming the deal had been done. It simply said, "Samuel Montagu announces on behalf of Laker Airways that agreement has been reached in principle on the restructuring of Laker's financial affairs with a view to securing its long-term viability. The Bank of England has participated in the discussions."

The normally verbose Freddie had not spoken to any journalists on the record since mid December. He thought that when Samuel Montagu & Co, the merchant bank owned by the Midland Bank, announced that a refinancing agreement had been reached in principle, in a Christmas Eve press release, it would be the end of it. But it wasn't. The refinancing was intended to ensure the airline's long-term future. It had said that the deal had the Bank of England's approval. As Montagu's chief executive, Ian McIntosh told the *Financial Times* a few days later: "It is a real package. The Bank of England doesn't attach its name unless they are happy about it." Freddie had gone on the BBC News that evening and said: "This is the best Christmas present of all time. We have secured our long-term future. We are not going to lurch from one crisis to another."

The wording of the statement had not been easy, nor had the memo about the deal been initialed by all the parties. General Electric (GE), the American conglomerate and airplane engine-maker, had supported the refinancing in secret. Joe Gallina, the company's lawyer, insisted that all mention of his company be removed. It was an extremely sensitive issue both for GE and for McDonnell Douglas (MDC). They didn't want to be seen helping Laker. Both companies knew the dangers of such a deal, directly supporting a customer, becoming a stakeholder while also supplying competitors, many of whom blamed Laker Airways for low fares and their own losses. Neither the final press release nor the memo about the deal made any reference to either GE or McDonnell Douglas as being the sources of the extra cash, only mentioning them as 'the lenders'. Both companies were big contributors, rescheduling their combined debt of $56.4 million and converting it into preferential shares. GE and MDC were in an invidious position. Laker was one of their best customers and had supported both manufacturers when no other airline would. The direct conflict of interest made it essential that no one should find out that MDC and GE were involved in the refinancing. But it proved an impossible secret to keep, as the *Financial Times* leaked full details of the deal a few days later.

While the Montagu press release wasn't quite what Freddie would have written and the typical wishy-washy 'bankspeak' should have been anticipated, it nevertheless gave him the assurance that he needed. It was the best early Christmas gift Freddie could ever have hoped for... well almost.

Supposedly, back on the 10th December he and Patricia had 'kissed and made up' on a Florida beach, or that is what he told a journalist who sensed that there was more to the story. All was far from well between them, however Freddie would get what he so desperately wanted. His son Freddie Allen would be returning to England over the holidays and he would be able to spend some time with him. To facilitate the reunion, Freddie had to make a legal agreement with Patricia to put her up in a hotel in Piccadilly, loan her a car and pay her a per diem of £50 in expenses for each day of the planned visit.

On the 26th December (Boxing Day), Patricia flew in with Freddie Allen and Bettina. Freddie was naturally thrilled to see his boy on home ground. But Patricia had wrong footed him, he discovered by accident that she was staying on until the 5th January. Freddie didn't question this at first and figured it was a good thing. Freddie Allen's birthday was on the 4th January and it would be an opportunity to have his son for the day. However, Patricia made every excuse possible why this could not happen. After numerous phone calls, heated exchanges and even a telex sent to the hotel she finally agreed that he could have Freddie Allen until midday. Unbeknownst to Freddie was the main reason for Patricia coming to London in the first place. Her US attorney Melvin Frumkes had accompanied her and before the year was out, she blind-sided Freddie for a second time on Thursday the 31st of December by petitioning for divorce. Her timing was less than ideal.

That wasn't Freddie's only immediate problem. The challenge for Laker Airways was keeping the cash flowing at a difficult time of the year for the airline industry. Christmas had come and gone and Easter, when bookings traditionally picked up was still in the distant future. Positive cash flow was everything in the airline business. Despite the weak pound, the British holidaymakers who were known for never giving up their traditional summer holiday in the sun no matter what, were booking their 1982 holidays through Laker Air Travel and Arrowsmith at a fairly positive rate. The tour operations were highly profitable in their own right and over £200,000 in advance deposits by passengers booking for the summer had been taken. It was vital to cash flow. The bookings taken during the 1981 Christmas/New Year holiday had surprised everybody, including Freddie and a reasonable European tour operating picture for summer 1982 was emerging, even though the summer season and the holidaymakers' final payments were still a long way off.

However, Laker's advance bookings for its Skytrain service on the North Atlantic were decidedly lack lustre. The weak pound and the aggressively competitive onslaught by the Big 3 was continuing to take its toll. Unless there was a massive swing in US originating traffic with the associated dollar revenue it generated, saving Laker was going to take something akin to a miracle.

# CHAPTER 44

# The Perfect Storm

## A critical state of affairs

Late 1981

As with most catastrophes, there is usually more than one component contributing to the outcome. Typically, an untimely collision of several events and circumstances all happening simultaneously creates a phenomenon that is often referred to as a 'Perfect Storm'.

In the case of Laker Airways, during 1981, no-one realised the company was heading for a clash of so many of these major elements, almost all of which in isolation may not have presented an insurmountable challenge. Yet happening within the same time frame and coinciding with the on-again, off-again refinancing plan, these same issues had a multiplying effect of devastating proportions. Heading towards 1982, they put the continuation of Laker Airways in jeopardy. The economic recession, air traffic control strikes, the rail strike in Britain, soaring oil prices, and the weak pound were all serious challenges during 1981, but none of these issues were isolated to Laker Airways. Conversely, resistance of passengers and travel agents to booking the DC-10, the flawed purchase of the Airbus A300, the mistimed Regency service, and the transatlantic fare war were all issues exclusive to Laker. Compounded by numerous other events and circumstances, not least of which was a monumental personal crisis, Sir Freddie was dealing with unprecedented challenges, all happening concurrently.

### AIRPORT RESTRICTIONS

From the inception of Skytrain in September 1977, the Port Authority of New York and New Jersey had tried to force Laker Airways over to Newark. Laker's licence under the Bermuda II air service agreement was for a London to New York route and as Newark was in New Jersey, it therefore fell into a different set of licencing parameters. Nevertheless, the various airlines at JFK did everything they could to prevent Laker from having satisfactory terminal facilities. Negotiations for space with several major carriers located in JFK's International Building were on-going. Meanwhile, Laker was stuck with the two terminal operation it had endured since 1977; its flights from London arrived at the International Building and the aircraft was then towed (or taxied) over to the United Airlines terminal for the eastbound departure. It extended the ground time, created a double ground handling expense, it was inconvenient for passengers and needed additional staff. By 1981, United allowed Laker to have two check-in desks at JFK that were equipped with Braniff's 'Cowboy' terminals for Laker's passenger and baggage check in. With up to four flights a day departing New York within a three and a half hour window, a potential 1,380 passengers had to be processed. Over In Los Angeles, a similar situation was in effect with Laker Airways relegated to a temporary inflatable building for passenger check in. Incredibly, airlines with far less prominence or number of flights per week were given preferential facilities at Laker's principal North American gateways. The respective airport authorities did little to assist even as Laker was poised to be the fifth largest carrier on the North Atlantic in 1982.

## AIR TRAFFIC STRIKES

Air traffic control disputes, just like the weather, are out of the hands of the world's airlines. In May 1981, Laker Airways endured an air traffic controllers' strike in the UK. One in every three of its flights had to be rerouted; it created a costly operational challenge and a great deal of inconvenience to passengers, e.g. one fully loaded DC-10 bound for Los Angeles sat on the ground for four hours at Manchester before it was given permission to proceed, by which time the crew was technically 'out of hours' to do the eleven and a half hour flight. Any other airline's crew would have gone off duty, but this was a Laker crew and the Captain, as they typically did, used his discretion to operate the flight and mitigate further inconvenience to the passengers.

Then another Air Traffic Controllers' strike arose in August, this time in the USA and considerably more serious. In response, President Ronald Reagan fired 11,345 out of 13,000 air traffic controllers who had participated in the illegal strike. He then banned them from Federal service for life in a sweeping move that shook the entire civil aviation industry. Naturally, everyone feared the worst with air traffic control across the USA so compromised. However, the FAA did an incredible job training new air traffic controllers in record time and despite some delays and re-routings, the strike wasn't nearly as disruptive as everyone originally feared. Laker Airways didn't cancel a single flight, even though many other airlines cancelled flights, day after day. Occasionally, Laker consolidated some of its flights such as a Manchester flight with one from London, a process that extended the overall flight time but eventually got the passengers to their destinations. President Reagan set a precedent with his bold initiative, sending a clear message that industrial action by Federal employees would never be tolerated.

## BATTLING THE TEAMSTERS

In late 1981, Laker Airways had its own union battles to contend with. Almost exactly a year on from their first unionisation campaign, the International Brotherhood of Teamsters (IBT) once again lobbied hard for Laker's USA employees to sign up for membership. The IBT was one of the most powerful trades unions in the world, thanks in part to the notorious Jimmy Hoffa's leadership in the 50's through the mid 70's, before he mysteriously disappeared. The IBT's two million members were devotees, to the point where even when they were on the payroll of a company, they referred to themselves as a 'Teamster' first and foremost and proudly wore apparel and badges with the IBT logo. When Freddie, one of the most staunch anti-labour union executives on the planet, heard the Teamsters were trying again, he instructed the USA management to 'spare no expense or resource to defeat them'. The first IBT organisation attempt a year earlier was defeated convincingly. A major contributing factor in beating the Teamsters the first time was that Laker Airways had been incredibly successful during 1979 and 1980. The company had created new job openings and promotions, salary increases and fringe benefits. "We had a promote from within policy that emanated from Freddie himself," Laker senior executive Greg Dix says. "There wasn't an airline out there where you could go from being a passenger service agent to a Station Manager in just a couple of years." In late 1981 however, it was a different story. Everyone knew Laker was in difficulties, a pay freeze was in effect and staff layoffs were imminent. It was a perfect time for a unionisation campaign. Dix remembered what they all went through. "It was brutal, the IBT stopped at nothing, as organising Laker would have been such a feather in their cap" Dix says. "It would have given them leverage with so many privately-owned companies that didn't have anything like the same level of employee-relations and staff loyalty that Laker enjoyed." IBT representatives had swarmed into the Laker ticket offices and airports, bribing the Laker staff with gifts and being quite convincing they would be better off joining the Teamsters. The specialist labour lawyers Laker hired to combat the IBT campaign were equally as vicious as their adversaries. Dix continued "sitting in meetings with our legal team was actually quite scary. They came up with such aggressive counter measures I felt the safety of our managers may be compromised." Having to spend considerable time dealing with the IBT campaign was diversionary just when the entire US management was trying to stimulate life-saving dollar revenue. It couldn't have happened at a worse time. Nevertheless the Teamsters were beaten again and Laker USA remained non-union, much to Sir Freddie's considerable relief.

## WHERE ARE THE DOLLARS?

By mid-year 1981, Freddie realised the company's dollar revenue was not forthcoming. The UK pound had de-valued further by September to $1.81. It closed out the year well under $2 and all the economists predicted a significant further drop in the pound's valuation throughout 1982. By now, Laker Airways should have been able to rely on Americans coming to Britain in droves, taking advantage of the strong dollar. However, throughout 1981, the percentage of US originating passengers on all Laker's scheduled Skytrain routes gradually declined, when it should have increased. In 1980, US originators on the New

York and Los Angeles routes made up almost 50 per cent of Laker's passengers. In mid-1981 it had dropped to 38 per cent and looked to be heading even further south. Given the population of the United States, and New York being the principal gateway for travel to Europe, Laker's US originators should have comprised at least half of the available capacity. By the time the imbalance had been identified, Laker was being attacked on all its prime routes. The London - Miami route that had started in May 1980 was still almost 100 per cent UK originating passengers and therefore produced little or no US dollar revenue.

## THE ESSENTIAL USA

Since the commencement of the Affinity Group Charters of the early seventies, followed by the Advanced Booking Charters and finally the Skytrain service, North America and in particular the USA had played a vital role in the success of Laker Airways. Shortly after the start of the Los Angeles Skytrain operation in September 1978, for some inexplicable reason - beyond perhaps everyone being too busy putting out fires and distracted, chasing new routes across the globe, the USA never received the top management attention from Laker's head office that it warranted. Subsequently, under Manager USA Charles Maxwell, the American side of the business was left to its own devices, with little or no oversight. The net result was an inadequate and invariably misguided sales and marketing effort to stimulate US originating traffic and the corresponding, vital US dollar revenue. This, together with a lack of 'intelligence' with respect to what Laker's competitors were doing, prompted an unprecedented reaction from an abnormally intolerant and clearly frustrated Freddie.

Shortly after returning from Hong Kong in June 1981, he instructed his deputy, Cliff Nunn to fire Maxwell and re-organise the USA. The dismissal of a senior manager was certainly not something Freddie did every day; in fact it was a first in the company's 16-year history. While the re-organisation did in fact slightly improve US originating traffic and the respective dollar revenue almost immediately, it was too little too late. The North Atlantic fare war that had been prompted by Laker's controversial Regency service meant that all bets were now off. Had the USA been given a greater priority, essential US originating passengers and US Dollar revenue would have been stimulated much earlier and Laker Airways' financial position at the end of 1981 would have almost certainly looked quite different.

## GROWING PAINS

When Laker Airways was granted its Skytrain service licence and commenced transatlantic scheduled service in 1977, the operation was clear cut. Laker's licence initially didn't permit advance reservations, so prospective passengers queued up at London's Victoria Station where Laker had a ticket office, or at the company's expansive New York travel centre in Queens. It was obvious after the chaos of Lakerville in 1978 that the original 'Skytrain' concept was not sustainable. So over the next two years, with continual pressure being brought to bear on licensing authorities and airport management, Laker's scheduled service operations became much the same as everyone else. This included being able to take advance reservations either directly or via travel agents, selling tickets and checking in passengers and baggage at airports, carrying cargo and mail, providing a full in-flight service and so on. In order to facilitate the move into the big league, Laker had to invest in costly telephone and computerised reservations systems along with the necessary hundreds of new staff on both sides of the Atlantic. Going 'scheduled' was nothing like what the airline had done before and the transition from being a charter carrier incurred monumental growing pains and increasingly immense costs.

In 1981, Laker Airways was still plagued by chronic problems with its phone system in the USA. From the initiation in 1979 of being able to take reservations for its Skytrain service, there were huge demands on the phone lines from both passengers and travel agents. A system tracking how many incoming calls or uncompleted calls were made, showed that Laker had a call volume that was beyond any airline's wildest dreams, and no equipment available could have handled it. Not that this was known at the time. At the peak of its booking seasons, Laker Airways was receiving over 16,000 calls a day at its central New York reservations centre. But there wasn't the infrastructure in place to handle it all and essential bookings for later in the year were lost to Laker's competitors. The damage to Laker's reputation was unquantifiable.

When it first started taking reservations, Laker only had eighteen phone lines in New York. A shortage of suitably experienced staff meant at best, ten were being used at the busiest times of the day. Half of the calls were lost. More lines were installed and staff numbers in the central reservations office in Queens swelled to 50 and then eventually to over 70 on a 24-7-365 basis. But staffing didn't solve everything and on many days the phones were still permanently 'busy' and playing background music to the frustrated callers. There were structural problems with the telephone system itself and Laker had to sue Telesources, the company from which the phone system was purchased, for its failings in rectifying the problems and the equipment. It still didn't solve all the problems and it took until the mid summer's re-organisation and the dismissal of the Manager USA and the Reservations department manager, before this critical issue was finally addressed.

Furthermore, Laker didn't have a network-wide computerised reservations' system that allowed travel agents to view availability for Laker's flights on their computers and book seats for their clients. Unlike other airlines, every reservation for a Laker flight had to be made directly with Laker's reservations office by phone. In the USA, Laker had been using Braniff's state of the art 'Cowboy' system for airport check in from September 1978 in Los Angeles and January 1979 at JFK. As soon as Laker was given the go ahead to take advance reservations, 'Cowboy' terminals were then installed everywhere in the USA and Laker's sales and reservations staff were trained on the system. By 1981, travel agents could access Laker's flight inventory directly and providing space was showing available, they could book their clients without having to call the Laker Reservations department in New York. However, it had been a long and painful process and the lost business as a result of an inadequate reservations system was incalculable.

## THE FOLLY OF 'BRIAN'

Over in the UK, it was a different story altogether. In mid-1981, the software development of the new custom system, that was named 'Brian', had been struggling along since 1979. It showed no sign of being completed any time soon. Nonetheless, Laker UK continued to persevere with 'Brian' and it required staff at both ends to continually manage the capacity on every flight. Laker's Commercial Manager John Jones was apoplectic and wrote to Freddie with a typically understated 'we are drifting into 1982 without a satisfactory computer system'. Jones had several permanent staff in his office working in unison with reservations controllers in New York, juggling space and seats in order to try and maintain full flights. Communications Software of North London, the developers of 'Brian' were unable to write a programme specially tailored for Laker's reservations and ticketing that was capable of interfacing with any other system. Laker Airways was trying to reinvent the wheel with a custom system when co-hosting with a third party for an existing tried and true platform would have been a much better option.

'Brian' was operated out of Laker's UK reservations centre at Norfolk House in Horley under the Scheduled Services Manager Ian Allan, who had assumed the role from Geoffrey Street. The affable Allan, who was already close to retirement age was thrown in the deep end by Freddie. He had previously been the Managing Director of International Caribbean Airways based in Barbados, so he went from being on more or less a 'paid Caribbean holiday' to the considerably high-pressure job managing Laker's scheduled service operation. An operation that was essentially a shambles. Allan's appointment was typical of Freddie's penchant for giving pivotal, challenging jobs to one of his old stalwarts. Through no fault of his own, Allan had little idea of what he was doing and like everyone else in the organisation, he had minimal previous scheduled service experience. The failure to launch the 'Brian' reservations system was a significant contributory factor to the airline's woes and throughout 1981, Freddie often alluded to 'Brian' as being to blame... for everything.

After nearly three years in development, the UK's reservations' platform was still a long way from being ready and was only being used in the UK offices by way of a test bed. The hardware was already antiquated, even to the point of it still using rotary dial telephones. At the airports, passengers were often turned away because Brian showed that the plane was full. Aggravated, prospective passengers stood at the gate, while planes left with empty seats. The situation was absurd and had to be rectified. As soon as the reorganisation of the USA management took place mid year, Greg Dix who was once again overseeing the USA's central reservations operation, recommended, or rather insisted that Allan install Braniff 'Cowboy' screens at all UK sales and ticketing outlets, including the airport. It was a reasonable quick fix as 'Brian' was clearly a long way from being ready, if ever.

It was impossible to assess what the lost business amounted to or how Laker's reputation may have been damaged due to the reservation system debacle. It had all come at a price in both the UK and the USA. The travel trade was still apprehensive about Laker since the original Skytrain walk-on concept had excluded them. Compounded by the inadequate reservations systems and by Laker's 1981 summer fare structure, as the airline headed towards the winter and 1982, Laker's forward bookings would be the make or break if the company was to survive.

## LACKLUSTRE ADVANCE BOOKINGS

On the 17th of November 1981, Scheduled Services Manager Ian Allan dropped a bombshell by way of a sales forecast for the transatlantic Skytrain service. It was sent to all Laker's senior managers and the numbers were nothing short of catastrophic. For the period of 20th November, 1981 through March 1982, all Laker Airways had on its books for its principal scheduled service routes were:

| | | |
|---|---|---|
| New York: Capacity 99,046 | Seats Sold 15,030 | Load Factor 15.17% |
| Los Angeles: Capacity 95,007 | Seats Sold 20,045 | Load Factor 21.10% |
| Florida: Capacity 109,282 | Seats Sold 32,949 | Load Factor 30.16% |

It was of little consolation that New York was typically a later booking market than California or Florida with a higher percentage of business travellers.

The early 1982 forecast was merely a continuation of the decline in North Atlantic passengers Laker had experienced in 1981 on their principal Skytrain routes. London - New York, Laker's flagship route was down by 32 per cent with 237,014 one-way passengers carried compared to 346,457 in 1980. The decline had started as early as February. London - Los Angeles fared slightly better and its traffic decline hadn't started until June. Nevertheless LA was 13 per cent down on the prior year with 209,089 one-way passengers carried vs 239,359 in 1980. London-Miami from May on the month-to-month variance was minus 25 per cent overall with 107,296 one-way passengers compared to 142,136 in the same period of 1980. The overall traffic numbers for the year were skewed by six new routes from Manchester and Prestwick (Glasgow) to Miami, New York, LA and Tampa. The additional passengers carried on these services helped the 1981 Skytrain passenger total to increase by nearly 15 per cent to 834,526 vs 727,952 in 1980.

The overall result was illusionary however, as Laker should have carried well in excess of a million passengers in 1981. It was almost incomprehensible that an airline that had returned profits for every year of its existence and had grown exponentially in terms of size and stature, could now be facing closure because of the sudden downturn in traffic on its prime scheduled routes.

Unquestionably, a principal factor influencing the decline was Laker's scheduled airfares. The low fares that had once been the bedrock of the airline's earlier success, had now pigeonholed Laker Airways... and become its biggest liability.

## THE SKYTRAIN FARES DEBACLE

Nothing was perhaps more challenging and crucial to Laker Airways' long term viability as a North Atlantic scheduled carrier, than its fare structure. The initial Skytrain service fares were simpler than reciting the alphabet. £52 London to New York and $125 New York to London. Every seat on every flight. Turn up on the day of departure, buy a ticket and go flying. Nothing could have been simpler. With this formula, Freddie Laker had hung the future of Laker Airways as being a 'low cost' or rather a 'low fare / no frills' airline; the actual 'costs' by going 'scheduled' were clearly escalating. However, it soon became clear that for Skytrain to succeed long term, it would need much more than merely having a single low fare. Especially a fare that Laker's principal competitors were prepared to match.

Once it became clear that British Airways, Pan Am and TWA, aka the 'Big 3' were going to take Laker Airways on no matter what, Freddie and his Commercial Manager John Jones had commenced a collaboration with them. Freddie had initiated a doctrine of 'if you can't beat 'em, join 'em' and Jones was his unwitting emissary. What they did was highly illegal and all done in total secrecy. It could have ended badly if they had been caught, as it was a clear breach of the USA's stringent antitrust laws. These laws were designed purely to regulate and promote fair competition to benefit the American consumer.

As a result of the chaos of Lakerville and thousands of stranded passengers queuing for days, a 'rollover system' was introduced in February 1979. Then, Laker applied for and received approval to have a full reservations service, starting 19th July that same year. A three tier tariff was published for New York and Los Angeles: 'Reservaseat' was an unrestricted one-way or round trip Economy class fare that could be changed / cancelled without penalty; Excursion was bookable 21 days in advance, required a minimum stay of 7 days and incurred change and cancellation penalties; finally the Walk-on fare was a continuation of the original day of departure, non-refundable concept. The 'Reservaseat' was £162 one way (£324 round trip) to JFK while the 'Excursion' was £204 round trip. The 'Walk-on' fare was £70 each way. Travel agents were finally able to book a Laker flight and only the Walk-on was a direct sell by the airline.

The differentials between the fare categories encouraged the purchase of the 21-day Excursion fare by the typical vacationer / tourist and those visiting friends and relatives, just as they did with the hugely popular Advance Booking Charters. The Economy fare was low enough to attract the potential business market and those needing flexibility of travel dates. Students, budget travellers, and anyone with time on their hands and needing flexible travel dates were accommodated with the one-way Walk-On fare. Significantly, due to the IATA carriers' fare increases in October, Laker's differential to their competitors was advantageous; Walk-on £34 less than their Standby, Apex was £58 less and Economy a whopping £234 less. The Laker tariff was well-formulated and equally well received. Despite the losses sustained during the five-week DC-10 grounding, 1979 was a solid year overall and Laker carried 301,734 passengers at a 71.7 per cent load factor on its two scheduled transatlantic routes.

Ditto 1980, again with similar differentials and an attractive 'Excursion' fare, Laker seemed headed for another stellar year. The IATA carriers had met in Geneva on 24th of January and agreed to increase their fares by between 8 and 12 percent from 1st April thus continuing Laker's fare advantage. Going into the summer of 1980, Laker's differentials to its main competitors were:

| | | | |
|---|---|---|---|
| London - New York | - Economy £57, | Apex £89, | Walk-on £13.50 |
| London - Los Angeles | - Economy £57, | Apex £58, | Walk-on £12 |
| London - Miami | - Economy £5.50, | Apex £25, | Walk-on £5 |

However, from August on, BA's Product Planning Manager continually urged Laker to 'close the gap'. It was a polite 'threat' that if Laker didn't get its fare schedule closer to the Big 3's, then they would take drastic action. Laker ignored the directive, so in unison BA, Pan Am and TWA all filed exactly the same Apex fares and essentially decimated Laker's advantage. BA matched Laker's Economy fare from 1st September. They also introduced their 'Pond-hopper' fare which was priced at Super Apex fare levels but also offered one-way at half the round trip fare. By October, BA had matched Laker's Economy fare and Laker's Apex advantage had been reduced to just £5 on the New York and the new Miami route and a £10 differential on Los Angeles. In December, Laker had the highest Apex fare on the New York and Los Angeles routes.

While this closing of the gap affected Laker's end of year load factors, it wasn't catastrophic. Laker still carried great momentum and 1980 nevertheless ended well, with record passengers carried of 727,952 at a 78.3 per cent load factor. New York and LA almost doubled their previous year's numbers while Miami, that commenced in May contributed 142,136 new British tourists to the mix. Cautious high-fives were in order. However, the commercial decision-makers at Laker Airways were in no doubt that their position as the lowest cost airline on the North Atlantic was now being seriously challenged.

For 1981, Laker again published a three-tier fare structure comprising the same Economy, Excursion and Walk-On categories. However, unlike previous years, Laker's Excursion fare to New York for June was set extremely close to the unrestricted Economy fare; Excursion was £259 round trip while the unrestricted Economy was £128 one-way (£256 round trip). July-September Excursion was £286 and Economy £148 one-way (£296 round trip). Little wonder the advance purchase Excursion fare, the one that produced the best cash flow and the least risk to the airline, was clearly outsold. There was almost no financial advantage in buying the Excursion fare and as a result many passengers, even those who typically would have accepted the Apex fare's restrictions, sensibly opted for the unrestricted Full Economy instead. It was an easy sell for a Travel Agent and a third of Laker's bookings in late 1981 was at the full Economy level.

The benefit of purchasing the full Economy fare was no minimum stay, no advance booking (deposit) requirement and no change or cancellation penalty. But the real danger for Laker in a growing hostile environment was that a travel agent, given an incentive to do so, could cancel their client's Laker Economy reservation and re-book the passenger on British Airways, Pan Am or TWA to London's Heathrow and on the preferred Boeing 747 or TWA's L-1011 that all offered more legroom. And that's exactly what they did. In the thousands.

The situation was exacerbated when the Big 3 gave travel agents much higher commission incentives than Laker could ever offer. By the end of September, the prime New York route was down by no less than 81,724 passengers (-29%) from the same period in 1980. The Los Angeles decline didn't start until June but then quickly accelerated downward for the remainder of the high season. The Miami route decline also started in June, then had a short blip in August before plummeting dramatically, as it was the end of the British tourist season.

It was the worst possible timing. It hadn't been helped that Freddie had spent a large part of 1981 distracted from the day to day business. He was flying all over the world trying to persuade various governments to grant Laker licences to serve Australia, the Middle East, Far East and to revolutionise Europe. Then the upheaval in his personal life during the summer deeply affected his focus.

Laker's published high season fares were a significant factor in the declining passenger numbers of 1981, long before the fare war of later that same year. For a few weeks in August, due to a deliberately bungled fare launch by the competition, Laker once again incredibly had the highest APEX fares on its prime routes: £15 more on New York and £25 more on Los Angeles. The net financial impact was devastating. It perhaps proved the folly of colluding with the competition, who by now had clearly got the upper hand and were essentially dictating Laker's fares. Their sole objective of driving Laker off the North Atlantic was now being realised. Unfortunately, by that time, Laker was too entrenched in the collaboration activities to break away and risk going it alone or perhaps more importantly, risk the penalties for their participation.

Freddie was no fool and knew the risks of collaboration. He strategically left it to Jones, putting his main man in an extremely compromising position. Jones was pitted against a half dozen top British Airways' commercial executives who between them had over 100 years combined experience in scheduled service operations. Jones had four. Freddie's bombastic approach and Jones's high energy and often abrasive personality perhaps didn't help negotiations with men who operated more like civil servants. Behaving diplomatically was never the Laker way and while the brashness may have been applauded by the man in the street, it wasn't optimum when dealing with powerful adversaries, especially if their jobs and decisions were backed by the British government.

By late 1981, Laker's lower cost advantage had gradually declined to the point where it was so insignificant there was no longer a genuine price advantage. Hinging the company's entire future on always needing to be the lowest cost airline had inevitably characterised Laker. Every time a Laker DC-10 took off for New York, Los Angeles or Miami it effectively had a target on its back.

The main downside of Laker collaborating with its competitors was a pricing structure formulated primarily upon the negotiated differentials. Despite the risks, Freddie and Jones continued to collude with the Big 3 competitor airlines throughout 1981. Even as late in the game as the 19th of January 1982, Jones was in Miami 'agreeing' (or otherwise) fares with Laker's competitors. He was by now between a rock and the proverbial hard place. If Laker had not colluded or fixed the fares with their competitors, there was for sure the risk of the Big 3 matching Laker's fares, no matter what they were. BA's Commercial Manager, Gerry Draper had left Freddie in no doubt at the Waldorf meeting in February that BA were prepared to reduce their rates to have the lowest fare. "Even to zero?" Freddie had asked. He shouldn't have been surprised as from the time Skytrain was made public, BA were hell-bent on seeing Laker off and were prepared to do whatever it took to make it happen.

However, had the Laker men not colluded with Laker's competitors, it would have allowed Freddie the opportunity to have Bob Beckman file an antitrust suit against the Big 3. It was a suit that might have had legs, given that Laker's competitors were colluding and operating below cost to drive Laker off the North Atlantic. Predatory pricing was illegal, both the British CAA and the US CAB knew that, so their respective approvals of the tariffs filed by the legacy carriers, especially when the Big 3 all filed fares that matched to the penny, would also have come under scrutiny. Unfortunately, using the USA's stringent antitrust laws was never an option while ever Jones and Freddie were willingly collaborating, thereby putting themselves in violation too. In the circumstances following Lakerville and the chaos of 1978, it may have been the only way they felt that they could survive and was perhaps naively done in self defence.

What had become clear by 1981 or perhaps even earlier, was that they now couldn't extricate themselves from the fare-fixing. The flawed 1981 summer fare schedule and the resultant decline in passenger numbers on all three primary Skytrain routes would have given Freddie and Jones sleepless nights. Laker's public posture of blaming the recession and devaluing pound, fuel prices and other external factors, could only go so far. It was by now apparent that the hugely flawed fare schedule, over which they now only had very limited control, was the principal cause of the company's dire financial position. It created a situation where an inordinate amount of time and energy was spent in late 1981 developing re-financing / loan re-scheduling strategies.

Nevertheless, for the pivotal winter of 1981/82, with Laker struggling to stay alive, Jones published no less than five different fare categories; Regency (business class) plus four economy class fares. It was the most complex fare grid the company had ever formulated. To start with, many of the fares weren't particularly marketable, whether in UK pounds or US dollars, for example £113, £141, $204, $261 etc. They wouldn't have passed muster with Hong Kong's feng shui consultant, who had insisted Laker must use lots of 'eights'. Added to the complexity of the fare matrix was the cold hard fact that Laker Airways no longer had a fare differential that gave it a reasonably competitive advantage over its main competitors.

For winter 1981/82, arguably the most critical period of Laker Airways' entire 16-year lifecycle as the airline was by now literally fighting for its life, the following fares were published: For November - March excluding the Christmas/New Year holiday travel period, London to New York fares were: Unrestricted Full Economy (cancel or change without penalty) £124 one-way or £248 round trip; Super Apex (bookable 21 days in advance, a 7-day minimum stay and £25pp cancellation fee) £223 round trip; 8-day advance purchase £109 one-way or £218 round trip; Same Day Walk-On £90 one-way or £180 round trip. With only a £25 differential, the Apex fare that would contribute the best cash flow and held the least risk for the airline, was once again severely compromised. The cancellation fee or the cost of trip insurance, that everyone who purchased an Apex was urged to buy was the same as the fare differential. Every travel agent knew that and would therefore encourage a customer to buy a full Economy ticket instead of an Apex.

After Laker announced its intention to launch the controversial Regency Business class, the gloves came well and truly off and the price war of late 1981 coupled with an unprecedented travel agent commission schedule, decimated passenger figures and load factors. During November and December 1981, Laker carried only 53,344 passengers on its three prime transatlantic routes compared to 101,215 the prior year; an over 47 per cent decline.

It couldn't have happened at a worse time as Laker urgently tried to formulate its re-financing and debt re-structuring package. The British CAA were monitoring the forward bookings and passenger figures on a daily basis and they had made it clear that Laker's air operator's certificate may be pulled if revenue and load factors didn't rapidly improve.

Despite the November and December results and the dire traffic forecast for January and beyond, similar fare categories and respective differentials were formulated for all three principal Skytrain routes for the 1982 mid and high seasons. The fare schedules were distributed as a fait accompli to those responsible for selling the Skytrain product in the UK and USA. Only Jones and Freddie knew how the fares had been formulated and they were frequently a source of heated discussion, especially in the USA. Everyone knew if they got through the winter, a return to profitability in 1982 was primarily in the hands of the USA generating a significant increase in passengers and the respective dollar revenue. The transatlantic fare structure was therefore the most essential component of this initiative.

A meeting in New York with the USA management was slated for as soon as possible in January once Freddie's availability had been determined, so that the crucial 1982 fares could be discussed. It was perhaps a meeting neither Freddie or Jones were particularly looking forward to; the reaction from their managers responsible for selling the Skytrain product in the USA was already a foregone conclusion. As Laker looked towards a financial recovery heading into 1982 and a boost in life-saving US dollar revenue, the unwieldy and uncommercial fare structure was clearly not about to offer redemption any time soon.

## LAKER'S OPERATING COSTS

In late 1981, Laker Airways was taking a triple hit on its transatlantic long haul routes. It was firstly compromised by low-yielding fares as described in The Skytrain Fares Debacle above. Driven by load factors in serious decline, the revenues of the Los Angeles and Miami routes were spiralling downwards. The third component that significantly affected the financial return of the routes being operated by the DC-10-30 aircraft was the direct operating costs (DOC).

The McDonnell Douglas report of October 1981 showed the DC-10-30's DOC per block hour to be £2,638. However, this hourly rate was based upon each of the five DC-10-30 aircraft achieving 4,865 block hours per year. With the reduction in service due to the fare war and other factors, Laker's DC-10-30s were flying 70 percent of budgeted hours in 1981. Some operating costs such as maintenance, passenger expenses and positioning costs had been amortised over the forecast number of block hours. With the reduction in block hours actually flown, the pro-rata increase in the DOCs may have been as much as £350 per block hour, ie an additional £6,125 on a round trip Miami flight, or approximately 30 extra passengers needed to offset the extra cost.

This point is significant for another reason beyond the additional DOCs affecting Laker's financial performance on its long-haul routes. Predatory pricing was one of Freddie's principle issues with BA and Pan Am, especially after the fare war commenced in late summer. However, it is quite probable that BA and Pan Am, who operated 450-seat Boeing 747s on the North Atlantic's longer routes to Miami and Los Angeles, had a better cost per available seat mile (CASM) than Laker, who operated the DC-10-30. The perception by both the general public as well as Laker's competitors was that Laker was 'the low-cost airline'. After all, Laker's entire business model had been based on that principle and Freddie continually made the point that no-one's 'costs' were lower than his. However, had Laker's fares and direct operating costs been challenged and evaluated, a case could potentially have been made that in 1981, Laker themselves might have been operating at 'below cost'and therefore would have been in contravention of the Bermuda 2 Air Services Agreement stipulations.

A 707 FOR LA AND MIAMI?

Freddie had insisted on using the medium range DC-10-10 on the Los Angeles Skytrain service when it commenced in late 1978. It involved stopping in both directions for fuel and a crew change in Bangor. The route lost several million dollars in its first few months. Laker Airways had two perfectly capable long-range Boeing 707s that could have done the job adequately non-stop until the passenger loads improved and the DC-10-30s had been delivered to fly the route non-stop. Freddie had good reason to want to use the flagship DC-10 on such a prestigious route and was prepared to take the hit. Laker was having a good year, revenue was flowing and everything was generally on the up and up. The LA route would turn around soon enough. And it did.

However, in November 1981 it was a very different picture. The airline had its back to the wall and was suffering massive losses. The LA load factors plummeted to around 50 per cent and the forecast for the winter was bleak. The same two 707s were mostly sitting idle at that point outside Laker's hangar at Gatwick. They could have operated the LA route more economically than the DC-10-30; the Boeing's direct operating costs were some £800 per hour less. Five days a week, the passenger loads were less than 189, the 707's capacity. Landing / handling fees, crew overheads and numerous other cost savings could have been realised. The number of Regency passengers midweek on the LA route was minimal and could have been refunded, re-booked or even given an incentive such as a future discount. Switching aircraft types on the LA route in the lowest of low seasons ever experienced could have saved over £18,000 per round trip or up to £100,000 a week; ie. a potential £1.3 million cost saving between November and January 1982.

Similarly, as with the LA route, a Boeing 707 could perhaps have taken over the London - Miami service for the winter, with a resultant saving in operating costs of approximately £80,000 per week. For the three months between November and January 1982, in excess of £1 million could potentially have been recovered with a simple switch to a more cost-effective aircraft.

Even if one or both aircraft were in need of a 'C' check before they could resume passenger service, it may have been worth the expense given the cost savings that could have been realised throughout the winter of 1981/82.

However, in light of Freddie's single-mindedness about the DC-10 always having to operate the Skytrain services, it is unlikely that using the Boeing 707s on the Los Angeles and Miami routes was ever seriously considered.

## THE END OF THE MIAMI GOLD RUSH

Since the commencement of the Miami Skytrain scheduled operations, Laker, had quickly achieved a reasonable market share of the London - Miami route of 26 per cent, not far off BA at 33 per cent, with Pan Am and Air Florida having 41 per cent between them. However, market share alone was never going to make the Miami route viable long term. It had been started as an extremely low risk operation, with all capacity contracted to Intasun and 100 per cent of the aircraft for UK holidaymakers. From 22nd May 1980, when it was converted to a scheduled service, Laker Airways and its two in-house tour operators assumed the entire risk. There was no sharing of capacity with a US based tour operator as Laker had done with great success on the New York, Los Angeles and Toronto routes. Laker had put all its eggs in one basket on the route.

By the end of 1981, the London to Miami route had never achieved its full potential or any level of profitability, mainly because the Latin American and Caribbean feeder market had not been developed. By the time Laker started to get serious about Miami as more than a summer holiday destination for Britons, Braniff and Pan Am were already major players in the Latin American markets. They both operated 747s on a regular basis to every major city in South America. Penetration of Latin America was considerably more challenging than anyone imagined due to the political and economic volatility of almost every country, where hyperinflation was a regular occurrence. There was no easy short-term solution to make London-Miami a viable high-yield, year round route without a balanced mix of UK and USA originating traffic.

Due to the competitive nature of the Miami route and because it was populated almost 100 per cent by UK originating vacationers, the London to Miami APEX fare for November 1981 through March 1982 (except for the holiday period) was set at £228 round trip. Miami was a thousand miles further flying than New York, an additional hour and a half flight time each way and Laker used its considerably less cost-effective DC-10-30 aircraft on the route. Yet to fly round trip to Miami cost only £5 more than flying to New York. Similarly, the low season Same Day Walk-On was only £5 more than New York while the 8-day Walk On fare to Miami was a mere £3 more than to New York. However, the unrestricted Economy fare to Miami was not only £5 less than the New York Economy fare but at £119 one way (£238 round trip) it was only £10 more than the Miami APEX. The differentials were set higher for the Mid and High Summer seasons but it was winter 81-82 Laker had to get through, otherwise there would be no summer. Once again, Laker's essential APEX fare had been compromised partly because fare differentials had been determined through agreement with Laker's main competitors and also because Air Florida was competing on the route with aggressive loss-leader fares.

By late 1981, the Miami 'gold rush' from Britain was rapidly declining and the British tourists reverted back to booking Spain or other Mediterranean and North African destinations for 1982. The increased hotel costs for the winter season put South Florida out of reach of most Britons, who typically didn't flock to sun destinations in the winter anyway. Laker's over-reliance on the British holidaymaker and their seasonal preferences, compounded by a rapidly devaluing UK pound, resulted in a downturn that appeared to be unrecoverable in the short term. By November 1981, Laker's Miami Skytrain service suffered a catastrophic decline in passengers with the resultant load factors in the 40s and no immediate recovery in sight.

## REGENCY SERVICE

Following the successful commencement of the Skytrain service, many of Freddie's developmental initiatives raised eyebrows, from impulsive purchases of aircraft to the relentless pursuit of routes around the world. No decision was considered more precipitous and provocative than the Regency Service. However, some of these same initiatives, given just the slightest shift in circumstances, could also have been heralded as 'pure genius' and Regency was no exception. It started as an antagonistic measure against British Airways, Pan Am and TWA. They then matched Laker's fares in retaliation, creating a serious downturn in Laker's passenger numbers in the second half of 1981.

Regency Service turned Laker Airways on its head. Every department was affected, none more than Engineering, Catering and Cabin Services who all pulled off a near miracle to launch the first-class type service in just a couple of months. As many expected, by the end of 1981, the statistics showed that Regency was essentially a non-event, with the possible exception of the London - New York - London route where seven per cent of the passengers had chosen Laker's new business class. With the November and December load factors on the New York route between 50 and 60 per cent, this equated to an average of between 11 and 15 passengers per flight being served in the 46-seat Regency cabin. The Los Angeles route averaged five to eight Regency passengers per flight while Miami languished below five, as the Florida route was populated by budget-conscious UK holidaymakers heading to America's vacation capital. Furthermore, during the initial months of Regency, many of the occupants of the forward cabin were non-revenue such as family members of staff, positioning crew, other airline personnel, travel agents and so on.

On the surface, Regency was a commercial disaster, when the company could least afford it. The 'genius' factor however could have been by shifting from a single class aircraft, Freddie was changing the perception of Laker Airways. The reasonable start on the key New York route where it had the best chance to work long term and year-round, showed some promising signs. It was about as far from the original 'Skytrain' concept as it could be, but heading into 1982, Regency wasn't quite the lost cause that everyone had initially projected. Unfortunately, Freddie's timing for the introduction of Regency service was premature as well as misadvised. It was singularly responsible for the fare war that devastated Laker's load factors and revenue in the latter part of 1981.

## INTERNATIONAL CARIBBEAN

ICA was a loss-making enterprise. The twice-weekly flights from Gatwick to Barbados via Luxembourg were beneficial perhaps only to the flight crews who enjoyed long layovers and the stunning beaches of Barbados. However, ICA was another missed opportunity. The 49 percent share holding of ICA presented Laker with potential routes the airline could never have realised as a British carrier; ie a penetration of the lucrative Caribbean market from the USA and Canada. Two routes, Baltimore to Barbados and Boston to Barbados were launched in November 1978, but quickly faded out due to zero marketing effort. Nevertheless, ICA might have become a major operator to Barbados from North America and via a tie-in with LIAT it could have served multiple Caribbean destinations. Furthermore, ICA's considerable debt of £2 million should have been a positive contributor to Laker's precarious finances in late 1981, had stronger measures been applied to recovering what was owed.

## THE 'SKYTRAIN' CONUNDRUM

There is no question when the term 'Skytrain' was conceived it was one of the most attention-getting brand initiatives of the civil aviation industry; perhaps even any industry. Its unique logo with the distinctive Stars and Stripes juxtaposed with the British Union flag, painted on the side of Laker's DC-10s was a civil aviation phenomenon. The media coverage of 'Skytrain' was unprecedented. The name itself, while synonymous with an affordable, trans atlantic scheduled air service, when no such thing had existed before, had considerably broader ramifications. Single handedly, Freddie Laker created a revolution, a quasi grass roots movement supporting a long overdue and much needed cause. In the late seventies, it's unlikely anyone in Britain and to a large extent in the USA hadn't heard of Freddie Laker's Skytrain.

Just as Freddie himself and the airline that bore his name were inseparable in the minds of the travelling public, similarly Laker and Skytrain also became as one. For instance, holidaymakers flying down to Majorca from Manchester on a Laker DC-10 after buying an Arrowsmith holiday, may have thought they were flying on 'Skytrain'. Similarly, travellers who had purchased a flight on a Laker Air Travel, Suntours or Jetsave Advanced Booking Charter flight to visit relatives across the Atlantic may have assumed they were flying on 'Skytrain'. Every Laker Airways' widebody aircraft, eleven DC-10s and then the three Airbus A300s, had 'Skytrain' emblazoned on their hull in six foot high letters. Airport check-in desks had the 'Skytrain' signs hanging over the counters. Skytrain bumper stickers, tee shirts and bags were everywhere. Laker Airways was by then, albeit incorrectly, referred to as 'Laker Skytrain'. And no-one perpetuated or championed the 'Skytrain' brand more than Freddie himself.

Ironically, while 'Skytrain' was known as a trail-blazer, it had also garnered a reputation in the industry as a conveyance of the 'great unwashed' and being singularly responsible for long lines of prospective passengers camping out in the streets, dirtying up airport terminals and wreaking havoc on civilised neighbourhoods. The spectre of 'Lakerville' still loomed, long after the 1978 chaos it had caused. 'Skytrain' was now a double-edged sword. In fact, by 1981 what was once Laker Airways' greatest asset, had actually become a liability.

Laker's 'Skytrain' brand and name scared governments, airport authorities, handling agents and airlines in the far reaches of the globe where Freddie had set his sights. Well into 1981, Freddie continued to be obsessed with operating a Skytrain service to Hong Kong, Skytrain to Australia and the Skytrain derivative, 'Globetrain' around the world service. The 666 routes in Europe for which he ordered no less than ten Airbus A300 aircraft were also badged as Skytrain. Every new route application document had Skytrain highlighted throughout. Even after Freddie and Bob Beckman had been advised the term was seriously unpalatable to decision-makers, they continued to use it at every opportunity. Naturally, those in authority in Hong Kong, Japan, Australia and beyond only knew about Laker's Skytrain from reports that highlighted the turmoil it had created. Skytrain's real message, which was simply a lower fare alternative to what was currently available, was invariably lost in translation.

## DIVERSIONARY GLOBAL ASPIRATIONS

An inordinate amount of time, management effort, legal fees, and travel costs had been incurred in pursuit of Laker Airways' new international route licences. However, no new long-haul route licences had come to fruition except for Britain and Hong Kong's approval of the trans-Pacific Route 6. It was a route that would have been logistically and operationally challenging, if not impossible and it also needed approval from Japan and the United States before it could be flown. Meanwhile, only two scheduled routes in Europe had been approved, Gatwick to Berlin and Gatwick to Zurich. Being refused the majority of the applied for routes was a severe blow, especially as a fleet of expensive brand new, wide body jet aircraft had been purchased specially to operate them.

A side effect of Freddie's global aspirations was the diversionary effect it had on the running of the existing business, together with the considerable drain on overheads. Laker's global initiatives had all been started well before the transatlantic Skytrain service had anywhere near stabilised. Ever since the September 1977 Skytrain service inaugural, Laker's management had been dealing with the enormous challenges that Skytrain had created on both sides of the Atlantic. So the prospect of successfully operating further afield to Asia, Australia and beyond, was at the time not merely challenging, but implausible.

## TOP DOWN MANAGEMENT

Freddie's management style was an extension of the post WW2 private company dynamics where the owner was referred to as 'Sir' and employees were often addressed by their last names. Freddie's style had worked well for him in the early years of Air Charter and even during BUA. As Laker Airways grew and Freddie became more and more out of touch with the day-to-day business, his autocratic style of management was showing its flaws.

From 1978 on, the 'Icarus factor' was unrestrained as Freddie embarked on a host of new initiatives that took him away from managing his company. Freddie would have done well to perhaps hire a General Manager / COO type executive who could direct the day to day business. Instead, a few executive directors and several department heads, some of whom didn't see eye to eye or even communicate with each other, kept the company going. It had all worked well in the formative years and even going into the 80s. But as 1982 approached, many of the management were in over their heads and close to burning out. They all had unprecedented levels of responsibility.

Quite often, decisions made by Freddie took time to filter down to those who had to put it all into play. Key departmental managers were on a 'need to know' basis. His top down style had worked well in the fifties and sixties and somewhat well in the early seventies, but by 1981, it wasn't working well at all. The company had grown too large for Freddie's type of management where everything emanated from him. Despite their unquestioned competence and dedication, almost all the principal departments were managed by home grown managers who had only ever worked for Freddie. Most of them only knew his way and they had 100 percent faith in their leader and his decisions. Laker Airways was akin to a business version of the Stockholm Syndrome.

In one of the most challenging periods of his eventful career, Freddie must at times have felt like he was all alone. Laker Airways' board of directors was comprised of only executive directors who (at least in Freddie's eyes) were little more than senior managers. His first wife Joan was the only non-executive director and she played no part in the decision-making process at Laker Airways. She had distanced herself from Freddie since his marriage to Patricia, for whom she had considerable disdain. It was perhaps fortunate that Joan, a 10 per cent shareholder of the entire Laker group of companies, was unaware of Freddie's earlier estate plan. Incredibly, he had left everything to Patricia and providing she survived him by 28 days, she would inherit Laker Airways.

By the end of 1981, the Laker group had over 2,500 employees and the small team of four executive directors was perhaps inadequate for the size and diversity of the company. The organisation clearly needed a more balanced board especially given Freddie's global ambitions and everything it entailed. One or two outside 'non-executive directors' could have brought objectivity, fresh perspectives, experience in other industries, and perhaps a degree of dissent to some of Freddie's more outlandish initiatives. It may have shifted the dynamics of the company and influenced more considered decision-making at a critical time. Whether the resolute Freddie Laker would have listened to anyone else's opinion or taken their advice is another matter altogether.

## AN UNWIELDY, UNDERUTILISED FLEET

At the end of 1981, Laker Airways' fleet of 20 aircraft comprised:
Four BAC One-Eleven 320 (89Y seats) Used sparingly and up for sale;
Two Boeing 707-351B (189Y seats) Used infrequently and up for sale;
Six McDonnell Douglas DC-10-10 (345Y or 46F/268Y seats);
Five McDonnell Douglas DC-10-30 (345Y or 46F/268Y seats);
Three Airbus Industrie A300B4 (284Y seats).

Laker's small fleets were proving to be inefficient with five different types of aircraft from four different manufacturers and four different engine types. While the plan was to sell the 707s and BAC One Elevens, an all wide-body fleet of DC-10 and A300 aircraft could not have efficiently served Laker's short-thin routes in Europe nor its long-thin routes planned for Asia and Australia. Furthermore, the DC-10-30 was unsuited for the envisaged trans-Pacific operations between Hong Kong and the west coast of North America. It was also a loss-maker on its North Atlantic deployments, through only partial fault of the aircraft. As if Laker's fleet wasn't unwieldy enough, by November 1981, over half the DC-10s had been re-configured to a 46F/268Y configuration from 345Y, to accommodate the Regency Service.

The number of available seats at the close of 1981 was 5,381; it was a massive 151 per cent increase on the seats available in 1977 and a 16.5 per cent increase from 1980 due to the Airbus A300s. The fare war that had commenced in the autumn of 1981 together with the global recession, compounded by being turned down for many new route licences, created a situation where a good portion of Laker's entire fleet was sitting on the ground, often for days at a time. The Manchester base had a DC-10-10 for the 4 X weekly Skytrain service to New York plus a DC-10-30 to operate the 2 X weekly Manchester to Los Angeles via Prestwick and the 4 X weekly Manchester to Miami services, one of which each week went via Prestwick. Manchester also had an Airbus A300B and a BAC One-Eleven for it's Mediterranean package holiday operations on behalf of Arrowsmith. Berlin had an Airbus and a BAC One-Eleven for the Flug Union package holidays to the Mediterranean and Canaries, and for the Turkish worker flights from Berlin to Istanbul, Ankara and Izmir.

The remainder of the fleet was based at Gatwick. The One-Elevens that had been used for package holiday flights to the Mediterranean, Canaries and Black Sea destinations had been superseded by the Airbus on the most popular routes. The Boeing 707s mostly sat idle except for ad hoc charters or ABC flights to Canada or western USA. One DC-10-10 operated the daily New York Skytrain service while another flew the twice-weekly ABCs to Toronto, twice weekly Luxembourg to Barbados for International Caribbean and any ad hoc charters. A DC-10-30 flew the daily Los Angeles while another operated to Miami daily and to Tampa twice a week. The DC-10-30 was unsuitable for short sectors due to maximum landing weight constraints. A late contract for one DC-10-30 for a Hajj pilgrimage operation from Llorin in Nigeria to Jeddah (for Mecca) provided some late 1981 revenue. Heading into the winter, Laker's fleet was about to be vastly under-utilised.

## MCDONNELL DOUGLAS REPORT

The McDonnell Douglas financial analysis of October 1981, formulated to support Laker's refinancing and debt re-structuring, was quite clear in its assessment of the DC-10 fleet's commercial viability. The DC-10-10 aircraft used for New York, Toronto and a few other eastern North American routes were excellent money-makers. Conversely, Laker's DC-10-30 aircraft, despite fairly high utilisation, lost the airline money on almost all applications. It was a stunning revelation from the manufacturer, proving that Laker's fare structure and yields compounded by declining load factors on its long-haul routes, were inadequate to offset the direct operating costs of the DC-10-30s.

## THE UNFAIRLY MALIGNED DC-10

There were many disparate factors influencing the decline in Laker's business during the second half of 1981. Perhaps nothing outside the airline's direct control was as detrimental as the unjustly compromised reputation of Laker's principal aircraft, the McDonnell Douglas DC-10.

To be fair, Laker Airways could perhaps have done a better job highlighting the merits of the DC-10 after the AA191 Chicago disaster of 1979 and the subsequent six-week grounding. No-one could have known the American Airlines' crash would have such a far-reaching effect on the type. Astronaut Pete Conrad and Freddie did everything they could to regain public confidence in the superb aircraft. However, Laker's PR machine that worked well for the build up of Skytrain was noticeably lacking in the aftermath of the DC-10 grounding. At a time when Laker needed an impactful publicity initiative in support of the DC-10, even if it had pointed a finger at American Airlines as Bob Beckman had urged, there was nothing forthcoming. Instead, Laker's publicly stated excuses for its financial woes of 1981 were pinned mainly on the devaluing UK pound, the recession and Laker's US dollar loans. Beckman had a strong case against American Airlines, but it was kept under wraps, even after American agreed to settle. Laker's PR machine never highlighted the irrational and unjustifiable resistance to the DC-10 and the aircraft continued to be denigrated. As a result, the much-maligned aircraft was an extremely hard sell both to travel agents and the general public alike, especially in the USA.

Meanwhile, Laker's competitors took every opportunity to highlight they flew the more popular and perceived 'safer' Boeing 747 and Lockheed L-1011 TriStar. A premature ending of passenger service by the McDonnell Douglas DC-10, one of the finest aircraft ever built, seemed inevitable.

## A MISSED OPPORTUNITY

Following the global grounding of all DC-10s for six weeks in 1979 after the American Airlines' tragedy in Chicago, most DC-10 operators tempered their promotion of the DC-10. Ironically, Laker was the only air carrier to challenge American Airlines that their improper maintenance caused the Chicago crash of AA191. MDC were apprehensive about publicly laying blame at the feet of one of their biggest customers, so they were happy to let Freddie Laker do it. However, this initiative subsequently became another missed opportunity that could have changed Laker's financial picture heading into 1982. After they had threatened American Airlines with a multi-million dollar law suit, Laker Airways then engaged in months of settlement negotiations with AA.

The culmination of these negotiations took place in New York on December 11th 1981 at 10:00am; a big dog and pony show organised by Bob Beckman at an American Airlines' safe house in midtown NYC with Freddie and Cliff Nunn in attendance. Pierre Murphy, Beckman's young barrister colleague was also there. The meeting was top secret and no-one knew what they were up to. Ironically, this was Beckman's first assignment on behalf of Laker Airways since the Route Six hearings in Hong Kong six months earlier. He had been out of touch with Freddie in the interim as Freddie had inexplicably stopped speaking to him. Freddie had also discontinued using Beckman for assignments he was perhaps better suited for than Laker's 'go-to' counsel, whom Freddie had leaned on more and more during the latter half of 1981.

There had been one condition to the meeting taking place with American; Freddie and Beckman were under no circumstances to show up with Don Madole – former Chief of the Air Accident Investigation Section at the NTSB and member of the Civil Aeronautics Board. In the eyes of Bob Crandall, AA's President and CEO, Madole's work with the relatives of the victims of AA191 made him persona non grata. "If Madole is there, Crandall is not coming in the room," was the message. After taking their seats around the table, Crandall came in through a side door, and sat down without introducing himself; he didn't need to, as everyone knew who he was. Undeniably a genius, Crandall was arguably the toughest executive in the air transport industry, he was feared and revered in equal parts. He put one leg up on the head of the table and casually put down two packets of cigarettes in front of him. He pushed his glasses on to the top of his head and finally spoke, 'let's proceed.' Beckman launched himself, 'Mr Crandall this and Mr Crandall that,' Beckman - always a great one for coming in really high and working down – was demanding big numbers in excess of $20 million dollars. Crandall just carried on smoking, he didn't say a word... not one word. He showed no emotion when Beckman brought up that AA had lied to the FAA over the AA191 crash. After an hour of Beckman's rhetoric, Crandall finally spoke "Mr Beckman thank you. Sir Freddie meet me in my room."

As Freddie stood to walk off with Crandall, Beckman cautioned, "Freddie I don't think you should be meeting..." "Don't worry Bob" said Freddie. Beckman immediately turned into paranoid mode; he could not believe what had just happened. Being locked out was the recurring theme of his professional existence. Once again he was not even the kid looking through the window. After an hour, Freddie came out without saying anything and the Laker team retreated to a suite at the Doral Hotel, the Laker Airways' crew hotel for a debrief. "Freddie what is going on?" demanded Beckman. "We are going to settle and I am going to meet with the man in Florida in January," replied Freddie. Beckman said "let's co-ordinate." "No, no Bob you don't understand? You're not going to be there," Freddie replied firmly, to Beckman's obvious dismay.

## SIR FREDDIE, THE PROVOCATEUR

Sir Freddie Laker was deliberately provocative towards competitors and government agencies. He'd called Peter Shore's Department of Trade 'bums and gangsters', then announced to the dismay of his lenders 'I now have to revolutionise the banking industry', and termed TWA 'Teeny Weeny Airlines' and 'Try Walking Across'. No attempt was ever made to shore up the rift with BCal's Adam Thomson, on the contrary, Freddie took every opportunity to exacerbate the hostility. Similarly, the antagonism levelled at British Airways and the legacy / IATA carriers went way further than simply offering a competitive air service with low fares. His brash David and Goliath spirit won Freddie enormous popularity with the masses, who embraced his cavalier attitude and arrogance. Freddie was now paying a heavy price for cocking a snook at the establishment and his competitors, as in 1981 they all ganged up against him.

SACRIFICES TO SURVIVE

As 1981 came to a close, it was clear that for the Laker group to survive the winter, some sacrifices had to be made. The company prided itself as being a conscientious employer and during the over fifteen years it had been in business the airline and associated tour operations had never had staff cuts, layoffs or furloughing. Some people had retired, a few had gone to positions elsewhere, usually with a promotion or an increase in salary, but aside from one or two who had been dismissed for pilfering and the senior managers in the USA who had been terminated, no one had been 'let go' for economic reasons. This was about to change. The first department to experience cut backs was Flight Operations. Twenty-one senior pilots were given early retirement or terminated and a further ten were demoted. The next two planned pay increases for Laker's pilots were cancelled. Cuts were also made in Cabin services. Less flying also meant less work on the ground so Laker's Customer Services department at Gatwick was also reduced. Cliff Nunn delegated the unenviable task of informing the department of the cuts to company solicitor Christopher Brown, who recalls "I remember standing on a table in an office in the terminal at Gatwick, telling our Customer Services department that their numbers were about to be decimated (or worse). Angrily, they wanted to know why Cliff Nunn, the deputy managing director wasn't telling them himself as Roy Boutell, head of customer services reported directly to him." They had a point.

The US division of Laker Airways employed many part-time and temporary staff. No-one aside from one or two key management who had been employed in the UK prior had employment contracts, or company supported pensions. As a result, lay-offs were relatively easy to achieve, despite being no less painful for those concerned. In addition to overall reductions of head count, some full-time staff were made to go part-time, paid lunch hours were eliminated, cost of living increases were frozen, and perquisites like travel allowances were cancelled. Cross-training many of the staff to slot into other jobs was also done, so that when one department was slow, such as reservations, staff would double up in the sales area or even at the airport. "It was easier for us in the USA" says Greg Dix, "as we had a lot more flexibility with staffing and job assignment."

In Britain there was still a 'job for life' mentality and it was doubly strong within the Laker group. The company cars assigned to the UK managers numbered in the dozens; it was a perquisite worth thousands of pounds a year over and above salary. Freddie didn't pay his staff at the same level as other airlines, however he ensured the British employees all had a good pension. This was his 'old-school' management style and Laker's pension scheme was something he was revered for. Unfortunately, with almost all employees in Britain being in full time, pensionable positions, it made staff cuts challenging, especially in a recession with double digit unemployment nationwide.

The company-owned yacht, 'Patrina' that was based in Palma had a book value of over £600k, yet it was never put on the market. In fact, if the Laker group was in financial difficulties, most of the time it wasn't apparent. Freddie still had his chauffeur-driven Rolls and there was a fleet of expensive company vehicles sitting in the management parking area every day. The construction and development of a new £975,000 office building continued unabated. Laker Airways had plenty of tangible assets. It was as if no-one believed it would ever come down to having to actually sell or re-mortgage anything to survive. There was a huge 'denial' factor present, even when everyone stared at half the Laker fleet of jet aircraft sitting idly outside the hangar at Gatwick, day after day.

## SLASHING THE LEGAL BILLS

One of the easier cuts in overheads Freddie had achieved in the latter part of 1981 was a reduction of Laker's legal bills. It had been reactionary rather than strategic and appeared to have been driven by personal undertones. In order to deal with the complex refinancing initiatives, Freddie had leaned more and more on his UK based personal lawyer, John Roney. For reasons known only to Freddie, he had stopped speaking to his long time trustee, Bob Beckman.

The rift with Beckman was partly due to Laker not obtaining the route licenses for Hong Kong and Australia that Beckman had been supremely confident were Laker's for the asking. Freddie blamed Beckman for the airline's over-capacity problems and related financial challenges that were partly caused by these failed route applications. It was compounded by Beckman's outrageously high fees and travel excesses. "After we got back from Hong Kong following the Route 6 hearings, Bob called me regularly to ask what was going on," says Greg Dix. "He had tried phoning Freddie as he always did, but Freddie never called him back. He clearly felt left out and was hurt by the snub." Bob would be at the hush-hush DC-10 grounding claim meeting with American Airlines on the 11th of December, but that was about all.

Having Beckman in Freddie's camp was a considerable asset as there was perhaps no-one more tenacious and fearlessly adversarial. Bob Beckman had made it his life's mission to be Freddie's de facto 'knight in shining armour' and when Freddie perhaps needed Bob the most, he had thoughtlessly ostracised him. It left Freddie with inadequate legal representation with respect to the US antitrust laws had he needed to use them. With the fare war and the Big 3 throwing everything they had at Laker, Freddie should have been seriously considering that option, irrespective of the potential downsides.

## FOR SALE BY OWNER

At the end of 1981, Freddie started to off-load some of his assets. However, this wasn't to save his company but in anticipation of having to make a sizeable payout in the pending divorce from his third wife, Patricia. It was yet one more stressful matter, based in desperation that he was dealing with on top of everything else at Laker Airways. Freddie's net worth had taken a dive during 1981, mostly because his day to day existence was directly linked to the airline's fortunes. He put his Furzegrove Farm estate in Chailey on the market, but the only offer Freddie received was £230,000, far less than he had hoped for. He had Woolgars Farm on the market along with its two cottages, as well as a parcel of land he owned in Clandon.

Freddie's former chauffeur, Harry Freeman and his wife Rita, the Laker's housekeeper lived in one of the Woolgars' cottages. Freddie had allowed them to occupy the cottage rent free as Harry had fallen sick after years of loyal service and being on call day and night. Despite this, Freddie, who always prided himself as a benevolent employer issued an eviction notice to the Freemans in order to liquidate his assets. He wrote to them "It hurts me more than I can say to two of my good friends, that it will be necessary for you to move from East Clandon." His actions were being influenced by fear and despair, but it would have made little difference to Freddie's publicly stated precarious financial position.

Liquidating his assets would have attracted a capital gains tax bill of £485,000, thus wiping out most of their value to him. As Freddie fought for the survival of his airline, Ian Wallace, his lifelong close friend at the Clydesdale Bank chose that moment to heap on more pressure. Freddie was overdrawn on his personal account by £880,000, and the bank called the overdraft. Clydesdale was determined to recover everything they could by whatever means they deemed necessary. It was perhaps one of the downsides of befriending your bank manager. Freddie had his back to the wall as the bank leaned on him, just as he was about to face a bitter divorce proceeding and custody battle for his three year-old son, Freddie Allen.

## DOMESTIC UPHEAVAL

After Patricia left him and moved to Florida in August 1981, Freddie's life had changed beyond all measure. It had been compounded by the loss of his stepdaughter Bettina and of course his beloved son, Freddie Allen. He was obsessed with maintaining contact with his son at all costs. His visitation trips to Florida became like pilgrimages. The timing of them compromised the Laker Airways' re-financing talks and caused several delays to an important marketing initiative for the USA. At the most critical time of his life, he gave more priority to visiting his son than to potentially saving his airline. He was paranoid about losing the boy, no matter over 2,500 employees' jobs were on the line at the time. Freddie's personal affairs and distractions played a significant role in the fortunes (or misfortunes) of Laker Airways throughout most of 1981, although Freddie was masterful at putting on a brave face and shielding almost everyone from his domestic woes.

The heart-wrenching loss of those most dear still haunted him and caused Freddie to take his eye off the ball, just when he needed to be fully engaged on survival. The domestic upheaval was the epicentre of the perfect storm of events he was dealing with at the time. Now, the world was asking, could Sir Freddie pull off another Laker miracle?

# Part 4

## The End Game

LAKER

CHAPTER 45

# New Year's Resolutions
## Implementing a done deal

January1982

Despite confirmation that the restructuring deal had been done, Freddie had little else to celebrate that New Year. From a personal standpoint it had been a turbulent festive season, topped off by Patricia's unwelcome New Year's Eve surprise by filing for divorce. Any peace making resolutions were now void.

He had initially been absolutely thrilled to be spending at least part of the Christmas period with his son. He was less pleased when he found out that he had been completely played and that the visit only happened at all because Patricia had flown to London and extended the stay to coordinate her legal representation on the 4th and 5th of January. It was a pre-planned first strike. Determined to prove this, Freddie went as far as recovering attorney Melvin Frumkes' ticket coupon. Incensed, he had called upon his industry contacts to find out when his flight reservation had been made; Frumkes' ticket was issued on 26th December, a full four days before Patricia filed for divorce. Freddie was livid that Patricia had taken both Bettina and Freddie Allen with Frumkes to a meeting with a London barrister and in an angry letter to his Florida lawyer Dan Paul, urged 'nail this shyster for something'.

To add even more fuel to the fire, throughout their stay in England, Patricia and Bettina had run up considerable expenses at the Piccadilly Hotel and instead of using the £350 in cash that Freddie had supplied them with, Bettina had informed the hotel's cashier to send the entire bill to Freddie.

However, there was no time to dwell on what had happened as it was straight back to work in the New Year. On the 5th January, a status meeting with Freddie, John Roney, Bill Morrison, another Midland Bank director Gervaise Boote and Ian MacIntosh was held. Freddie reported that he had received some tentative interest for the three A300s from Cyprus Airways who he and Morrison were planning to meet under the strictest secrecy. Airbus Industrie was not to know, as Freddie didn't want the consortium spooked. Offloading the A300s was complicated by the fact that the British Government had dictated that they did not want them sold to a British airline, but hadn't actually said why. Freddie explained that his allegiance was now wholly with McDonnell Douglas and he did not want anything further to do with Airbus or the syndicate.

Laker Airways had also just received a much-needed payment of $800,000 from Air France for sub chartering one of the A300s. Even so, revenues from the transatlantic scheduled services were deteriorating further and Laker's overdraft was now predicted to be as much as £13.7 million by the 12th January which was in line with the CAA's earlier estimate. Laker Airways was by this point walking a tightrope, despite having a record prior year.

During 1981, Laker had flown 834,526 revenue passengers on its Skytrain transatlantic services at an average load factor of 72.5 per cent. Traffic on Laker's three principal transatlantic route from London took a hit from mid-year, mostly due to aggressive fare-matching by Laker's competitors. Had Laker been able to equal its 1980 passenger counts during the second half of 1981, it would have carried well in excess of a million passengers. At its peak, Laker was flying 42 weekly scheduled round trips between the UK and USA. The Skytrain service operated from London Gatwick, Manchester and Glasgow Prestwick to New York, Los Angeles, Miami and Tampa. Although still a relatively small carrier in terms of aircraft and employees and taking into acount the traffic downturn from mid-year, Laker nevertheless had vaulted itself into 6th place of all 43 transatlantic airlines. In 1982, it was predicted to eclipse KLM and there would only be the giant legacy airlines, British Airways, Pan Am, TWA, and Lufthansa ahead of Laker in terms of transatlantic passengers carried. Considering that Laker had only commenced its scheduled services a mere four years earlier, this towering achievement wasn't lost on anyone, especially Laker's main competitors. Since the 26th September 1977, 2,180,825 people had flown on Laker's Skytrain service across the Atlantic.

Notwithstanding the 1981 results, the challenge for Laker Airways was keeping the cash flowing through the challenging winter period. Christmas had come and gone and Easter, when bookings traditionally picked up was still in the distant future. Positive cash flow was everything in the airline business. Despite the weak pound, the British holidaymakers, who are known for never giving up their traditional summer holiday in the sun no matter what, were booking their 1982 summer holidays to the Mediterranean destinations through Laker Air Travel and Arrowsmith, at a positive rate. The tour operations were highly profitable in their own right and the advance payments by passengers booking for the summer were vital to cash flow. The bookings taken throughout the 1981 Christmas / New Year holiday had surprised everyone, especially Freddie. A satisfactory tour-operating picture for summer 1982 was emerging. This was just as well, because Laker's advance bookings for its Skytrain service on the North Atlantic were decidedly lack lustre. The weak pound and the competitive onslaught by the Big Three compounded by Laker's compromised fares, were all taking their toll as the last few months of 1981 demonstrated.

Laker's refinancing agreement was almost a work of art and a tribute to

Bill Morrison's skills and his desire to save Laker Airways. It was necessarily complex with thirteen lenders, comprising mostly European banks in the Airbus Consortium alone. Morrison had persuaded the three reluctant banks in the consortium that Laker Airways was not doomed and with the backing of the Midand he had brought them into line. The deal terms were cleverly constructed in Laker's favour. It called for seven undelivered Airbus A300 aircraft to be cancelled without penalty. The three existing Airbus A300s in the fleet were to be sold to clear the outstanding loans. Mitsui, who had supported the DC-10-10 purchases agreed to defer all capital repayments for 12 months and reschedule interest payments by providing Laker Airways with an additional loan to cover the existing debt. The six other main lenders, EXIM, PEFCO, Morgan Guaranty, Bank of Tokyo, Marine Midland, and the Royal Bank of Canada, had struck similar deals, and deferred payment to September the following year. McDonnell Douglas agreed to convert $46.3 million of debt into preference shares. General Electric agreed to convert a $10.1 million loan into equity. Additionally MDC would lend a further $8 million (£4m) and GE a further $2 million (£1m).

On the 6th January, Jim McMillan the President of McDonnell Douglas Finance Corporation had a teleconference with Samuel Montagu's Ian McIntosh. He reconfirmed MDC's commitment that they would insert their £4 million and the injection of the capital would be completed as soon as possible. The Midland's Dennis Kitching flowed this information back up the line to BAe and Airbus Industrie the next day, "was this adequate for their purposes?" he asked.

Aside from the rescheduling of Laker's loans and the cash injection from MDC, the figures produced by Laker's own finance department estimated the amount of extra cash they needed to see them through the winter was £9 million. This was viewed to be a sufficient cushion for Laker to trade for the foreseeable future. Mainly because of Freddie's renowned 'old pals act' and his long term alliance with Ian Wallace, the Clydesdale Bank agreed to increase Laker's overdraft facility by £2 million to £9 million. The cash infusion from MDC and GE would then bring it up to a comfortable £14 million. Freddie also agreed with the Civil Aviation Authority (CAA) to raise his Tour Operators Bond to £4.6 million. Laker Airways had to keep the money in its bank account to cover holidaymakers' deposits in case it went out of business. It had been difficult, but somehow it had all come together.

The entire, complex re-financing deal was scheduled to be completed and the paperwork signed by 31st March 1982. A draft heads of agreement and new articles of association were drawn up, and on 6th January, John Roney sent them off to the Midland Bank's chief executive, Dennis Kitching. The proposed injection of funds and conversion of debt by McDonnell Douglas and GE were to be dealt with separately. Everyone indicated they were happy with a 31st March deadline for signing contracts, it would give them time to kick it around for a bit. Mitsui's solicitors, Linklaters & Paines, who would be coordinating the paperwork for all lenders sent John Roney a draft for a new mortgage covering the Mitsui debt. However, Mitsui probably had the least to lose, the early DC-10s were virtually paid for. In the cold light of day following the December announcement, other lenders proved more difficult to round up.

EXIM Bank asked for more clarity on the complex cross-guarantees that were a central part of the deal. EXIM was concerned about the sale of the three Airbus A300s. If they were not sold by 15th September the bank wanted alternative contingency arrangements in place, since EXIM would have been disadvantaged in the overall deal. Treating all lenders equally had always been a key factor in getting consensus. Substantial repayments were due to EXIM on the same date and EXIM wanted an extra provision for these to be rescheduled into the remaining maturities for January 1983.

Behind closed doors at the Midland, it was apparent all was not as well as it seemed. The Airbus syndicate was being described internally as now being 'too hostile'. The German and Austrian banks were being heavily leant on by Lufthansa and SwissAir, with whom they were deeply connected. They had now decided not to agree to the rescheduling after all.

It also seemed that nobody had properly informed Airbus of the plan, or so they claimed. Pierre Pailleret, Airbus's Senior VP of Sales and Marketing, responded to a telex from John Roney during the early evening of 7th January: 'Airbus is not in a position to react as you so positively suggest'. He had not received an earlier telex. "Nor do we know the substance of what the lenders are contemplating, have agreed to or are expecting from either party," wrote Pailleret. Throughout the saga, Airbus had been described by the Midland syndicate as 'intransigent, not lifting a finger to go beyond their contractual obligations'. An overview of the building situation was given by John Gentling, a Senior VP with McDonnell Douglas Finance Corporation: "Midland were acting tough and AI were very unsupportive and wanted out. The burden of the problem was being carried by MDC." Laker Airways was the unfortunate piggy in the middle of a complete falling out between the Midland Bank and Airbus Industrie. AI had been making rude comments about the Midland even to the point of wanting to switch to another UK lead bank.

From this point onwards, the Midland Bank began reading from an entirely different script and came up with a nickname for Freddie. They called him the 'Tudor King' or 'Sir TK' in all their correspondence; it stuck and was picked up by the other lenders. Despite the Christmas agreement, Dennis Kitching inflicted yet more pain on Freddie and the stricken airline, possibly as some kind of retribution. A year before, on 7th January 1981, when the financing of the Airbus purchase had gone through, as part of the package, £6.5million was placed in a deposit account as an A300 spares reserve. This money was to be released to Laker Airways upon the presentation of certified invoices in respect of spares purchased for the Airbus fleet. The Midland was contractually obliged to refund Laker under this unusual arrangement.

Laker Airways had bought £2.35 million of spares and a request for £1.35 million had been lodged with the Midland Bank. Laker had indicated they required the other £1 million within the next thirty days. However, the Midland and the Airbus consortium simply didn't want to reimburse Laker Airways; the Midland certainly didn't after releasing £4.6 million for the TOSG bond.

Halting this expected cash flow at such a critical time placed Laker Airways in even greater financial hardship. Freddie tried to contact Kitching personally after all efforts by Robbie Robinson to be reimbursed had failed. The Midland was only willing to release the money on the 12th January if Laker Airways agreed to leave £1 million in the spares account as additional security for the consortium and make no further requests for the cash until the rescue deal had been fully documented. Furthermore they would only agree to this compromise on the condition that the next interest payment was made on the Airbus loan.

Jim McMillan, President of MDC Finance Corporation had planned to fly to Gatwick on Monday 11th January 1982 for a crucial strategy meeting with Freddie to help save Laker Airways. However, to the considerable dismay of his bankers and his top management, Freddie told McMillan the meeting wouldn't be possible as he would be in Miami visiting his son. Freddie's timing couldn't have been worse. Many of McDonnell Douglas's top executives had dedicated months to the refinancing initiative and Freddie desperately needed the backing of MDC for the plan to be consummated. It wasn't the first time since his domestic upheaval of August 1981 that Freddie had put his domestic affairs ahead of the potential survival of his airline.

On 12th January 1982, the principal capital payment due to the Airbus syndicate by Laker Airways wasn't paid, although they had managed so scrape together the interest payment. Given the financial position of Laker Airways, this was not unforeseen or unexpected. Despite Laker meeting the Midland's conditions, the bank reneged on the deal over the spares money. Finally, in order to have the spares money released, Freddie and Roney had little choice but to agree to a supplementary mortgage with the Midland over the A300 spares reimbursement.

Of even greater concern was that the failure to make the capital payment was not seen as an official default as it would have created a number of problems with the other lenders. The arguments bubbled away for two weeks until the airline was finally served with a formal notice of default, with one small caveat that the bank 'did not plan to call the loan given the ongoing negotiations'.

The hardening stance of the Midland could only have been a cynical ploy, an attempt to gain preference over as many of Laker's assets as possible. Nevertheless, it was felt, maybe somewhat optimistically, that everything seemed to be moving in the right direction. By mid-January the lawyers for the Airbus syndicate, Mitsui and EXIM had met and there was overall agreement between the three big creditors that the rescheduling would go ahead as per the terms of Samuel Montagu & Co's Christmas proposal. There was a bit of jockeying for position over security amongst the myriad of lenders, all on different terms and looking for a bit of clarity.

However, day after day in January, the £5 million that MDC and GE had agreed to put in failed to arrive; Freddie continually urged the MDC people: "Put up the money, the Midland will be furious." Nobody had explained to Freddie why they hadn't sent the £5m and he had no idea why. He had continuously been reassured that the money was on its way, but McDonnell Douglas were getting cold feet. Their finance executives and lawyers had by now realised they would lose their security and that their competitor, Airbus Industrie could directly benefit from money paid into Laker Airways by MDC. MDC had grave concerns about increasing their exposure and losing their security position.

Then, Freddie's principal backers, the Clydesdale Bank, despite increasing the overdraft for Laker Airways, had taken a closer look at Freddie's personal financial situation. They concluded it was now beyond what they were comfortable with. Despite Freddie's renowned 'old pals act', his friend Ian Wallace had to act responsibly on behalf of his employer. On 13th January he wrote to Freddie's lawyer, John Roney advising him that Freddie's overdraft now stood at a whopping £880,753 (£3.2 million - 2018). It was secured by his principal residence Furzegove Farm, Woodcote Stud, Woolgars Farm, some land and a couple of buildings at New Manor Farm, and a stock portfolio. The value of everything plus his personal guarantee of £250,000 still wasn't enough collateral to support the overdraft. Wallace wrote that Freddie's remuneration from Laker Airways, which was basically zero, was insufficient to meet the interest payments for the overdraft. He concluded by asking for an increase in Freddie's personal guarantee to £500,000 and stated ' the Bank is now insisting that he takes steps in early course to rectify what is considered to be too onerous a burden on his resources'. Despite his long and successful history with Freddie, Wallace's divided loyalties were now being tested to the fullest.

By 22nd January, Laker's schism with the Midland over the Airbus aircraft spare parts money that still hadn't been paid, was widening. In fact, it was now doubtful that the £1.35 million – due in three separate payments on the 27th, 28th and 29th January – would ever be paid.

But Freddie wasn't around to deal with it, as he was yet again spending a few precious days in Miami visiting his son that week. He was also meeting with the President and CEO of American Airlines, Bob Crandall to finalise the DC-10 grounding claim Laker had against American. On 23rd January 1982, Bob Crandall and Freddie met for the final time at Sir Freddie's rented condo in Key Biscayne, Florida where an agreement in principle was reached. American would pay Laker $2.5 million, in exchange for mutual releases. The settlement terms and discussions were to be kept extremely confidential. Freddie agreed to defer AA's payment of the $2.5m until 1st September 1982. By then, the statute of limitations for anyone else to sue American would have expired. Freddie assumed the Laker Airways' debt restructuring and refinancing package was coming to a satisfactory conclusion in the last week of January 1982. He had no contingency plans in case the re-financing fell through; he was supremely confident of the bail-out by the banks. Incredibly, perhaps not thinking clearly at the time, Freddie believed he didn't need American Airlines' $2.5 million.

The trip to Florida had also resulted in the third postponement of the filming schedule in New York for the Laker Airways' 1982 advertising campaign that was then re-scheduled for 28th January. However, Lesley Chilton telexed Greg Dix on Tuesday the 26th of January to advise him Freddie had again changed his plans suddenly and was now going to Miami instead of New York the next day. Dix went mad and called Freddie immediately. Upon being told

Freddie was out, Lesley had to endure an angry two minute monologue on what this all meant and how many people would be disrupted, not to mention essential advertising to drive business was once again being compromised. "Lesley have you any idea how many people are involved with this shoot? We've already cancelled two flights to free up a plane and we'll now have to call the passengers back and tell them their flight's going after all. They'll think we're idiots." Dix asked her to have Freddie phone him immediately but she counselled him that Freddie wasn't listening to any reason at that point, especially if it was anything to do with his visits to Florida to see Freddie Allen. She cautioned Dix that anything he said to Freddie would not only fall on deaf ears but make him angry too.

While Freddie's paternal devotion would in any other circumstances be perhaps admirable, his skewed priorities were now compromising the future of Laker Airways and over 2,500 jobs. Not being available to deal with critical issues of the complex re-financing package was serious enough. But another delay to the new advertising programme, that he himself had urged was a priority, caused chaos in the USA. It made Laker's advertising agency skittish with good reason and risked their walking away from the Laker account.

Robbie Robinson, Laker's Finance Director was then told by Ian Wallace at Clydesdale that there would be a delay in the repayment of the Airbus spares money; the orders not to pay had come from much higher up. In desperation, Robinson telexed John Roney seeking his intervention with the Midland's senior management. The longer this dispute went on, the greater the pressure on cash flow and the overdraft. So the typically diplomatic Roney wrote 'denial of drawdown at this stage, despite the valiant efforts made by the Laker staff, Thomson McLintock staff and invaluable assistance of the Airbus themselves is intolerable', in a rapidly fired off letter to the Midland. As should have been anticipated, Roney's appeals received a negative response.

Bob Wyatt, an Assistant General Manager at another branch of the bank was standing in for Dennis Kitching who was on holiday. He wrote back to say that as much of the original $13 million had been drawn, an agreement from the Airbus syndicate was sought for the payment of the $4.7 million. These were weasel words, the agreement on the spares money was supposed to have been decided upon by the syndicate by the 8th January and Wyatt had personally assured Freddie, only the week before that they would release the money. However, By the 28th January, the monies owed to Laker for the Airbus spares had increased to £1.8 million, knocking sideways all cash flow forecasts for the airline and reducing the available overdraft facility by 20 per cent.

A concerned Freddie upon hearing about this, immediately rang Kitching from Florida. During their conversation, Kitching dropped a bombshell and informed Freddie that Bill Morrison, Laker's bank appointed financial advisor was being fired. Freddie should have been highly suspicious, but inexplicably responded: "You hired him, you can fire him." He never thought to ask why they were replacing Morrison, or more importantly with whom. The relationship between Freddie and Morrison could have been a hostile one, but instead they had got along pretty well. At the start, a naturally wary Freddie had looked

Morrison in the eye and asked him his intentions. Morrison had told him firmly that he was 'his man'. Despite Freddie's distrust, which never really went away, Morrison had nevertheless pretty much lived up to his commitment.

Morrison had recruited another Thomson McLintock colleague, Andrew Jones, to join him on the Laker Airways rescue package. Jones was stationed full time at the Laker HQ at Gatwick Airport, and they both worked with Robbie Robinson and Chief Accountant Martin Ballard to keep the airline afloat. Significantly, Morrison had always thought the top job was beyond Robinson's capabilities, with the current situation putting an enormous strain on Laker's Accounting department staff. It remained a bone of contention between himself and Freddie. Freddie's opinion of Robinson was well known; he thought his Financial Director had no equal at Laker Airways and while he recognised the stress he was under, he wouldn't allow him to be maligned.

Freddie was nevertheless naively reassured by Morrison's departure. In his mind it signaled that his work was over and that the refinancing was complete. With Morrison being let go, he firmly believed that the deal was now a 'go'.

Then without any warning, GE pulled out, terrified of the impact the Laker refinancing deal would have on its business relationships with their other customers. The head of GE's Engine Division, Brian Rowe who did not care much for Sir Freddie Laker, pulled rank and declared that "there is no way we are putting equity in Laker." A revised plan suggested by Freddie and John Gentling of MDC was that a £1 million cash infusion would suffice in lieu of the debt-to-equity conversion. But the engine supplier had lost its patience and its nerve. GE was deeply mistrustful of the Midland and had felt that the burden of saving Laker Airways should be placed on the bank and not on GE.

On the 1st of February, Freddie telephoned GE's lawyer, Joe Gallina in one last push for the much needed cash. He told him he needed to pay fuel bills. Laker Airways was now up to its overdraft limit. An exchange between two of GE's executives close to the deal read: 'Frankly we don't know who to believe anymore and I think we should seriously consider rejecting the latest proposals and force the hand of the UK banks. It is conceivable that they are playing the game of 'milking' the manufacturers for all they can to keep their risk exposure within more reasonable limits. In addition, if our actions cause the plug to be pulled, I suspect that we will get one more crack at changing our minds'.

That same morning, MDC's David Sedgwick was at the Midland Bank enduring a bruising ordeal with Dennis Kitching. Kitching told him that he had issued instructions to the Clydesdale to pay no cheques on Laker Airways account. It was made clear to Sedgwick that the Midland would not increase its exposure beyond the £9 million with or without the MDC cash. He expressed intense dissatisfaction that the overdraft had already been extended and their exposure was already increased having relied on the £5 million, which with GE's withdrawal was now only £4 million. Sedgwick tried to reach another General Electric official, Ed Hood to see if they would change their minds. The answer, many hours later when it did eventually come, was negative.

During his meeting with Kitching, Sedgwick was informed that a man named Bill Mackey had been hired as an advisor replacing Bill Morrison and that he was an expert Receiver. After Sedgwick had revised the numbers, he concluded that an immediate £4 million from MDC, would be the last chance to save Laker Airways. He never considered what the appointment of a receiver to replace Morrison perhaps indicated.

Despite such a bleak outlook, Sedgwick formulated a plan and spoke with Jim McMillan about how they could still go ahead. Their £4 million would be put in a new facility, allowing the Clydesdale a line of credit, out of which the Midland could draw funds to immediately reduce the £9 million overdraft to £7.75 million. This would buy a little breathing space; an extra £1.25 million over and above the £4 million could be added later so that it matched Laker Airways' estimated requirement of £13 million. McMillan approved the plan and the pair headed to the Bank of England for a 5:00pm appointment to see David Walker with their proposals. Walker's reaction was positive and he called Kitching at the Midland. After much discussion, Kitching finally, albeit reluctantly agreed. It theoretically gave a green light to the resolution.

CHAPTER 46

# Plan B

## An early warning goes unheeded

Monday 1st February 1982

With so much at stake due to Freddie's chaotic and unpredictable schedule, the risk-management of Laker's General Manager in New York was in overdrive. Greg Dix had phoned Lesley Chilton every day since the last postponement of the shoot caused by Freddie suddenly going to Florida to visit his son. They had re-re-scheduled him to fly to New York on Monday the 1st of February and Lesley had been told, 'there can be no more postponements'.

Freddie would fly out on GK10 to New York at 1:00pm that afternoon with Cliff Nunn, John Jones and Scheduled Services Manager Ian Allan. They were all going in anticipation of the refinancing deal being done. An important USA strategy meeting had been scheduled with Dix, David Tait – Laker's Regional Manager for Florida & Latin America, and Skip Clemens, who was responsible for the Western States. The meeting was to give Commercial Manager Jones a chance to discuss and also justify the Spring / Summer 1982 fares that he had allegedly 'agreed' at a top secret conference in Hollywood, Florida with Laker's competitors on the 18th and 19th January. These fares, and the marketing and sales strategies supporting them were crucial to turning around Laker Airways' fortunes and stimulate much needed US dollar revenue. The initiatives they agreed could 'make or break' the financially distressed airline. The next day, Freddie was scheduled for a morning of photography followed by the filming of new TV commercials for the 1982 Spring/Summer season. The shoot had been rescheduled three times already due to Freddie's commitments elsewhere, including the last postponement due to a last minute '"I absolutely must go" trip to Miami to see Freddie Allen. Freddie was completely oblivious to the chaos that he had created. This time however, he simply had to appear in New York, no matter what. He had been firmly told that he couldn't postpone again.

Deputy Managing Director Nunn was flying over as he had been put in charge of the USA, despite having less than a thorough grasp on what was happening on the other side of the pond. Laker's publicity representative, Robin Flood had invited herself even after being told by Nunn her portfolio didn't now include the USA after the firing of Manager USA, Charles Maxwell the previous July. Nevertheless, Flood felt obliged to be in attendance if there was anything going on with advertising or with Freddie, whom she fussed over like a clingy, jealous girlfriend. She also wanted to make a final plea to Dix before he fired her long time associate, New York PR representative Evelyn Heywood. Flood wasn't aware Dix had already obtained both Freddie and Cliff Nunn's blessing to terminate Heywood, for whom Freddie had considerable disdain. She was the final remnant of the Maxwell era in the USA and everyone thought some new energy was long overdue.

With the exception of Freddie, everyone would return home on the evening of the 2nd February after the 1982 strategy meeting. The UK executives were to fly back on Pan Am because the evening Laker flight was to be cancelled so the aircraft could be used for the shoot on Wednesday 3rd February. The plan was to have the DC-10 towed over to United's hangar at JFK after flight GK10 had landed at 3:45pm on Tuesday. Wednesday's GK10 from Gatwick would also be cancelled to get the flight rotations back on track. Laker Airways was operating only one flight a day to New York in February with low load factors on all but the weekend flights. It was the company's worst winter ever and half of Laker's entire fleet stood idle outside the Laker hangar at Gatwick. After the filming had wrapped on 3rd February, the plane would be cleaned and prepped to fly GK20 back to Gatwick at 7:30pm. A lucky Laker aircrew would get an extra night in Manhattan and some equally fortunate New York businessmen may meet an attractive English air hostess in the Doral Hotel's bar that evening. Everyone thought it was a good plan.

The previous Friday, when Karen – pronounced 'Kaahrun' on account of her German heritage – Dix's petite, blonde-haired secretary had said who was on the line for him, he had feared the worst. But Lesley Chilton was just calling to give him a reassurance that everything was still 'go' for Monday. Dix was breathing a sigh of relief when she nervously said "But I have a Plan B… just in case." "Plan B" queried Dix, already getting the jitters. Resuming her firm and reassuring voice, Chilton advised him in case Freddie's schedule on the 1st February was compromised in any way and he missed the Laker flight at 1:00pm, that to ensure he would be in New York by lunchtime at the latest on the 2nd February, she had secured a seat for him on the 10:30am British Airways' Concorde flight out of Heathrow. It didn't make for the most relaxing weekend as Dix made numerous contingency plans in case Freddie didn't make it out to New York… again.

Around 9:00am on Monday 1st February, Karen knocked and entered Dix's office. He had just started reviewing the passenger counts that Tom Walter, his Reservations Manager had dropped off earlier. The unusually serious look on Walter's face meant the January results for the entire USA were worse than they had forecast. Karen was an attractive, effervescent 23 year-old who typically brought a ray of sunshine to Monday mornings with her all-smiling, upbeat demeanor. She had the usual cheques to be signed, Dix's daily reading under her arm and a fresh mug of coffee for him. Untypically, she too had a grave air about her as she announced "Lesley Chilton's on hold for you on the hot line." Dix reacted predictably: "Oh fuck, this can't be good news," as Karen made a quick exit and he grabbed the red phone. "Morning Lesley" was followed only by an emotionless voice at the other end informing him that Freddie had missed GK10 and would not be arriving with the others. Dix paused for a second and then asked if Plan B was now in motion. "Yes" said Chilton and asked him to pick Freddie up off the Concorde at 9:30am. After responding in the affirmative and with as polite a voice as he could muster given the circumstances, Dix said that should Freddie inexplicably miss the Concorde, Plan C was that he must stay put at Heathrow and catch the first flight, anyone's flight, that would get him to JFK by early afternoon on Tuesday. He didn't want Freddie returning to Gatwick for the only Laker flight at 1:00pm, only to miss that as well and put the entire schedule in jeopardy. He advised Lesley that a full programme was planned for Freddie on arrival and losing another entire day would compromise everything. In addition to the TV commercials they had planned to shoot, the still photo session called for Freddie to be craned up to the top of the DC-10, over thirty feet off the ground where he would stand above the cockpit of the plane with his arms outstretched and... Dix shouted "there will be no bloody safety net" laughing at the absurdity of what he'd just said. Chilton laughed at the other end which prompted a slightly calmer Dix to ask if Freddie had packed his trainers so he wouldn't slip. The call concluded on a lighter note and they had a laugh recalling the last time Freddie stood on top of a plane, albeit a much smaller one. On that occasion, he'd complained of experiencing vertigo, a disorder he had often suffered from but fortunately few people knew about. The inner ear condition that caused Freddie's vertigo had plagued him for decades; it was a legacy of his near death experience during pilot training in the ATA. Chilton wished Dix good luck as they clicked off. He didn't dare inform the advertising agency about yet another re-scheduling of Freddie's arrival in New York; they might have walked away from the Laker Airways' account in disgust, and no-one could blame them. So the plans for Wednesday's shoot went ahead, assuming Freddie would somehow make it there on Tuesday 2nd February and hopefully be in good shape for everything he had to do.

Dix then opened the traffic statistics folder; he had the day to day numbers for the New York route but hadn't seen Los Angeles' and Miami's final counts until then. It was the worst month in the entire history of Laker Airways. London - New York ended up with 8,519 one-way passengers at a 37.2 per cent load factor, 51 per cent down on January 1981. The London - Los Angeles route produced 7,202 one-way passengers at a 32.6 per cent load factor, 47 per cent down on January 1981. London - Miami dropped right off with 7,882 one-way passengers at a 35.7 per cent load factor, 54 per cent down on January 1981. February's forecast looked to be no better. He resisted the temptation to fire off another telex to John Jones recommending they cancel some of the mid-week rotations, knowing it would likely be met with resistance. He'd already suggested to Freddie they dust off the 707s and use them for LA and Miami mid-week to save millions in direct operating costs. That too, fell on deaf ears.

Unsurprisingly, none of what was happening at his airline was at the forefront of Freddie's mind. For months, the majority of his waking hours had been spent dealing with bankers, accountants and lawyers and when he wasn't, he was flying off to Florida to visit his son. Earlier that Monday morning, despite knowing he had to go to New York, he became lost in a telephone conversation with George Gilhespy, the Midland Bank's general manager. Gilhespy was a man he had not met before and whom he knew very little about. They spoke broadly about Laker's overdraft and Freddie told him he was off to New York that day. Gilhepsy urged him not to go, telling him that he would be better off dealing with his financial problems and his business than leaving the country to make a commercial at such a critical time. Freddie told him that he had to go, otherwise people would realise his business was in trouble and that he'd already had to re-schedule several times already. The telephone conversation dragged on past the 1:00pm departure time of GK10 that was Laker Airways' only flight to New York that day. An agitated John Jones had called up to Lesley Chilton from the gate, five minutes before departure wanting to know 'where the hell's the old man'. Chilton said Freddie was tied up, that she had made other arrangements and for them all to go on to JFK as planned and Freddie would catch up with them the next day.

Freddie had anticipated that he may miss GK10, and with his Concorde ticket already arranged he had made plans to meet Ian Wallace of the Clydesdale and the McDonnell Douglas Finance Corporation team who were all staying at the Intercontinental Hotel in London. Freddie had Lesley book him a room there for the night. When he told Gilhespy he was coming up to the City that afternoon, Gilhespy suggested he come by his office before his evening commitments and that he would welcome the opportunity to meet him at around 5:00pm. Freddie agreed and met with Gilhespy at the Midland Bank that evening. They had a general discussion about the Laker companies and where things currently stood with the refinancing plans. Gilhespy claimed that the Midland, after months and months of work, still did not have enough information from Laker Airways to complete the refinancing. Gilhespy then confirmed what Freddie had been told by Dennis Kitching, Gilhespy's boss just a few days earlier that they were replacing Bill Morrison of McClintocks. He went on to say that the replacement would be a man named Bill Mackey of Ernst & Whinney. Freddie, who hadn't heard of Bill Mackey despite his reputation in the City, responded "that's fine by me, I have no problem with it."

Freddie was in a hurry to make his important rendezvous with Ian Wallace and the MDC people. They had been at the Bank of England concluding the finer points of the Laker Airways' rescue deal and working out the last remaining issues that would allow the complex refinancing to go ahead. That evening, a rather tense Freddie was hoping for the best news possible as he headed over to the Intercontinental Hotel on Park Lane. He never spared a thought about the man Gilhespy had mentioned and had probably forgotten his name already... Bill Mackey, renowned in London's financial circles as 'Mack the Knife'.

CHAPTER 47

# Sausages at Tramp

## A false sense of security

Monday 1st February 1982

It was an unusually mild February evening as Sir Freddie Laker marched along Jermyn Street in London at his usual brisk pace. Trailing along behind were four companions, David Sedgwick, the Vice President of Finance for McDonnell Douglas, Ian and Jane Wallace and Robbie Robinson, the young Laker Airways Finance Director. Freddie had insisted the cab bringing them from the Intercontinental dropped them at the corner as he didn't want to pay the additional pound to go around the one-way system in order to drop them off at their destination. Robbie Robinson was perhaps the only one who understood Freddie's inconsistent frugality.

It was an intriguing group and three of them had been instrumental in the recent history of Laker Airways. Wallace was the manager of the Piccadilly Branch of the Clydesdale Bank a subsidiary of the Midland Bank. He was a tall thin Scot with twinkling eyes and he had known Freddie for over 30 years. Their relationship had grown close and there was both mutual respect and admiration. As a member of Freddie's inner circle, he was often a guest on Freddie's yacht in Palma. Wallace had arranged the finance for Freddie's first aviation enterprise after the Second World War. Freddie's business ventures had always been profitable for the Clydesdale Bank; he had always borrowed big but he had proved to be an excellent customer with a very high profile. In turn, Wallace's financial support had helped make Freddie the equivalent of a millionaire before he was 30 and a multi-millionaire by the age of 40. When Laker Airways had hit trouble in the oil crisis of the mid-seventies, Wallace had been right there at Freddie's side, helping him through it, just as he was assisting him in the current crisis. Wallace had always been in a tricky position, his enduring friendship with Freddie occasionally conflicted with the allegiance to his employer, the Clydesdale Bank. Less than two weeks earlier he'd had to write to John Roney, Freddie's lawyer and call in Freddie's personal overdraft.

They had all been invited to join Freddie that evening for supper as they had something to celebrate. The group stopped at No 40 and the brass plate on the wall indicated they had arrived at Tramp. The orange Lamborghini Muira parked outside with a registration comprising just two letters followed by the number one meant that either a football superstar or a rock god was inside. Freddie was quite at home rubbing shoulders with celebrities although he didn't have a clue who many of them were, especially if they fronted a band or kicked a ball for a living. But they all knew who he was. Tramp was Freddie's favourite place in London. He had been a member since it was opened by Johnny Gold and Oscar Lerman (husband of the novelist Jackie Collins) in 1969. They had named the club after Charlie Chaplin's most famous character. In the succeeding years, Tramp had become a famous destination and was frequented by the more louche members of international society. It was here that the likes of Frank Sinatra, Paul McCartney and Mick Jagger partied until dawn alongside royalty such as Monaco's Princess Caroline and Britain's Princess Margaret. Freddie paid £10.50 a year to be a member and came as often as he could. He'd never failed to have a good time.

They all walked down the metal steps to the basement and into the wood-panelled foyer. Lorraine and Julie, the two receptionists on duty that night, smiled broadly and mouthed in unison as they always did: "Good evening, Sir Freddie." Freddie answered back as he always did: "Good evening Julie, good evening Lorraine." He signed in his four guests and they went straight to the restaurant. Freddie glanced to the right to see if Johnny Gold was sitting at his usual table. If he'd been on his own, or in happier times with his wife Patricia, Freddie would join Gold at his table, but tonight he needed a table for five.

As they sat down Freddie immediately announced to the waiter: "Bangers and mash for five." He looked round and no one demurred. Sausages and mashed potatoes was a popular Tramp speciality. Gold remembers that night as though it was yesterday. Freddie was one of his dearest friends and there was no one he liked to see in the club more. "He was an amazing man, larger than life. It was a Monday night. I was sitting having something to eat at my table with a friend of mine, and suddenly there was a tap on my shoulder and it was Freddie. He said, 'Johnny, stand up and give me a huge hug,' and he gave me, well, we gave one another, a big hug and with a flourish he turned round to these people who were standing behind me and said, I was forty-five minutes away from bankruptcy and these are the people who saved your old mate; these are the ones who have kept us flying."

The evening had started earlier at the bar of the Intercontinental Hotel on Park Lane. Robinson and Wallace had spent the entire day at the Midland and were met by Freddie later who had joined them there for his 5:00pm meeting with George Gilhespy. Afterwards, they shared a taxi to Clydesdale's office at Piccadilly, where they had collected Wallace's wife Jane and Alex McMillan, the managing director of the Clydesdale Bank who also sat on the board of the Midland. Freddie had mentioned he would invite McMillan onto the board of Laker Airways to restore some confidence in his airline with the financial world once the refinancing deal was put to bed. From there they had hurried on to Park Lane to meet McDonnell Douglas executives David Sedgwick, Jim McMillan, John Gentling, and Tony Carbonair at the Intercontinental. They were all staying at the hotel for the night.

Sedgwick, a Yale-educated lawyer, had previously been in house counsel to Exim. Jim McMillan a former Patent Engineer with Douglas was president of the airline's financial offshoot and Sedgwick's superior. The two men had spent the latter part of the afternoon at the Bank of England in Threadneedle Street with David Walker and it was there that they had agreed to see the Laker Airways' rescue operation through. They had all been working on the refinancing for months, and as soon as they saw Freddie they broke into huge grins. McMillan, a tall hearty man with a slick of thick black hair pushed across his head in a wave, moved ahead of the even taller Sedgwick and boomed out: "It's done, Freddie! We've just been to the Bank of England. The deal is done."

Freddie looked at Sedgwick, who had been worrying about the details. Despite being given this good news, Freddie was still sceptical. After he'd left Gilhespy's office an uneasy feeling had come over him, it was more about the man himself than anything Gilhespy had said. In fact Freddie had already forgotten what Gilhespy had told him about Bill Morrison's replacement. He asked Sedgwick if Gilhespy agreed. Sedgwick made the point that it didn't matter as Kitching was Sedgwick's boss and he had agreed. Despite Kitching being Gilhespy's boss, Freddie sensed that Gilhespy could still make or break the deal. He wanted more assurance and asked Sedgwick to call Gilhespy at home, 'just to make sure'. Freddie waited anxiously on his own by the bar, the clock showed it was just past 8:00pm. As he was taking another sip of his usual scotch and milk, Sedgwick returned with a smile on his face and to Freddie's relief said, "Gilhespy agrees."

With those words, Freddie finally believed that the refinancing deal was really done after months of ups and downs, broken promises and endless previous agreements had fallen apart. Now everyone was agreed and everything would be all right. The deal memo, which had been initialled, stated simply that repayment of Laker Airways' debts had been postponed until the following September. This ensured that the company had more than enough funds to meet its day-to-day cash flow needs for 1982. Cash was king in the airline business. Freddie now knew that he had the funds to see his airline through what was clearly going to be a very tough winter and into the summer when he was confident Laker's business would pick up again.

Everyone had a drink to celebrate. And then another. By about 11:00pm it was too late to get a meal at the hotel's restaurant, so Freddie invited everybody to Tramp. Jim McMillan begged off. "Early night for me. I'm off to Germany and Switzerland tomorrow to talk to bankers. We're selling US$50 million in Eurobonds and I'm doing the rounds of the German and Swiss banks. You go and enjoy yourselves." With that, McMillan squeezed Freddie's hand, slapped him on the shoulder and went off to order room service and get some rest. McMillan had always liked Freddie and he was happy that Laker Airways' finances were now taken care of. He was also pleased that he could go off and do other things and didn't have to think about Laker Airways any more.

There was plenty for Freddie to reflect upon as he and his guests sat down at Tramp to sip champagne and anticipate a hearty meal. Johnny Gold watched as Freddie ordered the first bottle of Krug, on the menu at £62.50 (£255 in 2018). They toasted the fact that Laker Airways had been saved, as talk of airline business reverted to normal social chat with Freddie regaling everyone with his old war stories and off-colour humour.

"Freddie loved the bangers and mash that we used to serve," recalls Gold. "Our chef, I think he had quite a pornographic mind, would shape the sausage with two tomatoes, one on each side, and he had the mash going down the sausage so it looked like a penis. And he used to write rude notes in cheese on the bangers; for Freddie he might write 'Fly Laker' or something more racy." Johnny Gold remembers how he had first met Freddie in the seventies around the clubs of London. He says that Freddie always had his airline's prettiest stewardesses in tow and as a result he was a very popular member of the elite London club scene.

Eventually, Gold wandered off leaving the Laker table to celebrate well into the morning hours. Everyone was just relieved to have got through the day. Freddie ordered five more bottles of Krug before everyone had had enough. Just after 2:00am the party broke up and Freddie went off to say goodbye to Gold. "Johnny, I'm going to New York in the morning to do a commercial. I'll be back on Thursday and we'll have dinner." "It'll be great to see you then."

With that, Freddie and his guests staggered out into the gloom of London, bleary-eyed and quite intoxicated, looking to hail a cab and wishing they'd perhaps called it a night a bit earlier.

CHAPTER 48

# Welcome to New York

## Debating the 1982 revitalisation plan

Tuesday 2nd February 1982

Sir Freddie strode towards the special Concorde check-in area at London's Heathrow Airport feeling both tired and hung over. His bankers and lenders had given him their blessings the previous night and despite only having verbal confirmation, he was absolutely certain in his mind that the agreement to refinance his airline was in place. The financial problems of the last six months were behind him, he would sign the contracts on his return and he was now off to New York. He would have preferred flying on one of his own planes but he'd been told that he must be in New York by lunchtime... or else. Flying on the Concorde, however wasn't as thrilling for him as it was for many of its passengers; he thought it was cramped but acknowledged that being able to get to New York an hour earlier than you left London was quite something. Freddie had only flown back from Miami just a few days earlier after visiting his son. He had been dismayed that his plane was two-thirds empty and it was one of the main reasons why he was going to New York.

The British Airways check in agent at the special Concorde desk immediately recognised Freddie as he walked up. She greeted him with an easy familiarity, "Good Morning Sir Freddie, I have your ticket for you, may I just see your passport." Freddie set down his briefcase and his small travel bag and handed her his passport. The agent barely glanced at the passport, it wasn't necessary as everyone knew who Sir Freddie Laker was, especially since he had hardly been out of the newspapers or off the TV screens in recent weeks. She passed him his ticket and boarding pass and Freddie had just turned towards the stairs that took Concorde passengers to immigration, when a photographer confronted him. 'That's all I need, the bloody press' he thought. He had no desire to speak to a journalist as they had made the last six months of his life hell. The media had almost single-handedly killed Skytrain. Day after day, newspapers had printed progress reports on the refinancing and stories that the airline was going bust. Every time a new article appeared it had chipped away at public confidence and cost Laker Airways hundreds of thousands of pounds worth of advance bookings, seriously affecting cash flow. Despite his hangover, Freddie beamed broadly for the camera, even though he was actually seething inside.

There was still one thing bothering him. He wondered why the Midland Bank were so keen to replace the architect of the refinancing agreement, Bill Morrison. In the cold light of day it seemed a bit suspicious. Gilhespy had urged Freddie not to go to New York the evening prior. Freddie had asked Gilhespy for his assurance that the Midland Bank would do nothing to Laker Airways while he was out of the country. Later that evening Gilhespy had confirmed to David Sedgwick the rescue plan was going to be carried through as agreed, even though the promised MDC money was still pending. Freddie knew nothing of Bill Mackey of Ernst & Whinney, Morrison's replacement, and so he was oblivious to Mackey's reputation as a 'hatchet man'. Surprisingly, he hadn't mentioned Mackey to Ian Wallace, McMillan or Morrison. Nor had he called John Roney to have him do a routine check on Mackey.

On his way to the Concorde lounge, Freddie stopped by a pay phone. He fished out a 10p piece and dialed the Intercontinental Hotel's number as he needed to check in with David Sedgwick, in case there was anything he needed to know before leaving. "Good morning, David, it's Freddie. I hope you don't have a hangover." "Hello, Freddie. I thought you were off to New York this morning." "I am. I'm in the Concorde lounge at Heathrow and the press are here, what do you think I should say David? Sedgwick chuckled before saying "tell them you're going to New York to make a commercial that's going to put Laker Airways back on the map." "Thanks David. That's good to hear. "I just wanted to clear it with you. I don't want to say anything wrong." He had another 10p piece so he called Ian Wallace at the Clydesdale Bank.

"Hello, Ian. It's Freddie here. How's your head?" "Morning Freddie, well we probably should have stopped on the fourth bottle, I'm fine but Jane's a bit worse for wear. Is your flight on time?" "Yes everything's fine, I'm in the departure lounge. The press are here, Ian. I'm not sure how they got wind of me going to New York this morning. Anyway, should I speak to them?" "Yes yes, of course Freddie, it will be a change to get some good publicity." He thanked Wallace, replaced the receiver, and stepped outside the safety of the lounge into the corridor between the Concorde room and its departure gate just as a scruffy-looking man with a notepad came towards him.

"Good morning, Sir Freddie. Can I ask you some questions?" "Yes," he said. Inevitably all the questions were about the health of Laker Airways, so Freddie gave him a great sound bite. "Altogether I have raised £60 million and for the first time in weeks you can say I am buoyant and talking to the press. I am flying high today and couldn't be more confident about the future." By the evening editions, his words were on every front page. A beaming Sir Freddie peered out of the newspapers beneath headlines such as 'Happy days are back again for Sir Freddie Laker' and 'Cash boost for Laker'. Unfortunately they were qualified with unattributed quotes that his claims 'surprise banks' and that 'Sir Freddie's optimistic statements were understood to be premature'. The 'flying high' interview, as it came to be known, would come back to haunt him. His flight to New York was being called, so Freddie hurried to the Concorde departure gate.

Concorde was a technological marvel but its small cabin was both narrow and utilitarian. Freddie made his way down to the less popular rear of the aircraft. He squeezed himself into the just large enough but luxurious grey Connolly leather seat to prepare for take-off. He declined the vintage champagne and Beluga caviar Concorde passengers were offered before take off. The SST hurtled down Heathrow's runway 28R at over 200 knots much like a top fuel dragster. As it lifted into the air at a steep incline, Freddie's eyes started to water and his ears began to ache as the aircraft climbed and headed towards the Irish coast. In about three hours, Freddie would be landing in New York. He was looking forward to being in the Big Apple again and doing the television commercials. Although he was desperate to sleep, there was no chance to nod off. Twenty minutes into the flight, as Concorde reached the Atlantic coast of Ireland, the afterburners kicked in to take the plane supersonic. The speed increase was barely noticeable, only a slight nudge in the small of his back that often gave him trouble.

Once the Concorde had levelled off at its cruising altitude for crossing the Atlantic, Freddie retrieved his briefcase from underneath the seat in front. He took out an old letter from Jim McMillan and in blue ball-point on the back of it, in his distinctive handwriting he began to draft a press release:

*Laker Airways Financial Restructuring*
Laker Airways announced that agreement had been reached today regarding the restructuring of its loans, Sir Freddie Laker said in New York today after making a flying visit to the United States to make his television commercial. "Like most airlines, Laker Airways is in financial trouble due to the general recession in Europe and the United States and the weakness of the pound against the dollar. Since early last year we have been working to fix it to assure the long term future of the airline. Today we put it to bed. The final financial package includes an injection of cash, increased bank facilities, guarantees, and conversion of debt to equity. To understand the complexity of the negotiations one must appreciate that the capital employed in Laker exceeds 500 million dollars and the total money involved in the current negotiations exceeds 100 million dollars. The main negotiations regarding the restructuring have been with McDonnell Douglas Finance Corporation, the Clydesdale Bank, the Midland Bank and the Bank of England. They all have been involved in the discussions."

Sir Freddie went on to say that the company was now in better shape than ever before and financial terms have taken a more traditional form, he hastened to add that Laker would continue as the market leader in low fares on the Atlantic and intended to continue the fight for low fares in Europe.

He also said that he intended to eventually sell the A300s (Airbus) and if necessary expand the fleet of 11 DC-10s.

When asked the question was he going public? He said, "yes that is now my ambition, to make Laker Airways what it really is, a truly people's airline, now we have got the equity base right I can concentrate on a flotation. During the last few months literally thousands of the general public from all walks of life have offered to buy shares in the company + what it represents to the people is too big for one man to control. It should go to the people for the people." Talking about fares, he said fares are going up so buy now, he said no other airline is lower than Laker now and they wouldn't be in the future.

About Regency he said Laker was already about Budget and Regency was now accepted as a genuine First Class Service but at a much-discounted fare.

On the subject of senior management & control, Sir Freddie said "I will continue as the Chairman and Managing Director and have not disposed of any of my shares. I still control the company as in the past, however I have offered seats on the board to two people that have not yet accepted. The present management team will continue as before. Unfortunately to reduce costs generally and to increase productivity even more it has been necessary to reduce staff and to have a wage freeze." Sir Freddie referred to his staff as "Hard working, loyal, helpful remarkable people." When asked who was to blame for his recent problems he said bluntly "me. I got it wrong" and went back to star in his own television commercial. *Ends.*

A little more than three hours later in what seemed like no time at all, Concorde's passengers were treated to a low-level view of Jamaica Bay as they sped over the Rockaways before the aircraft crossed the Canarsie VOR, the final navigational waypoint before its destination. Then the Concorde made a steep right hand turn and lined up for the approach to JFK's runway 13R. It was one of the longest commercial runways in North America and with more than 14,500 feet of asphalt, the Bay Runway as it was known was also a Space Shuttle emergency landing point. The unique, hinged droop-nose was extended downwards so the pilots had a visual of the runway and the SST commenced its descent into JFK. As the aircraft taxied to the British Airways terminal, the purser did the standard "Welcome to New York the local time is 9:25am. You have just flown across the Atlantic in three hours and twenty-two minutes at a speed of over 1,340 miles per hour and an altitude of 56,000 feet." Concorde was a time machine; for once they hadn't endured any Air Traffic delays and it wasn't even 9:30am in New York as Freddie adjusted his Rolex back to Eastern Standard Time.

As soon as the plane came to a standstill and the seatbelt sign extinguished, Freddie stood up, grabbed his leather coat from the overhead bin and put it on over his double-breasted suit jacket. He still didn't feel 100 per cent and was hoping for a quiet ride into Manhattan with Greg Dix, who would likely harangue him about the postponement, the appalling load factors and of course the never-ending subject of the air fares. He picked up his briefcase and travel bag then followed all the other passengers disembarking the aircraft into BA's arrivals area. One or two of his fellow passengers had given Freddie a nod of acknowledgement, but as Concorde was always full of celebrities, star-struck autograph seeking fans were a rarity. For some of the passengers, it had been the trip of a lifetime, but it was just another flight for many of the regulars, some of whom had recognisable faces or were carrying guitar cases. U.S. Customs and Immigration agents rarely bothered to detain a Concorde passenger, including rock stars with dubious vices; their bags were hardly ever searched.

As Freddie finished clearing, he spotted Dix walking at his usual high speed into the customs area, who upon seeing his boss broke into a grin. "Morning, Freddie, welcome to New York. Nice of you to finally make it, we were all beginning to think you didn't love us anymore." When they were together, only the two of them, Dix took liberties and it was always just 'Freddie', typically followed by something sarcastic, but when in company the 'Sir' was always added. Freddie was anticipating being immediately lambasted for the latest re-scheduling, but the admonishment thankfully was not forthcoming.

"Good flight" Dix asked cheerfully as they shook hands and he grabbed Freddie's black Samsonite briefcase as he always did. Freddie wondered where the 34 year-old got all his energy as he knew he hardly ever slept. "Glad you made it as we have a lot to get through today and tomorrow." He hurried Freddie to his gleaming black Chevrolet Blazer wagon, with a 'GK1' New York registration, all-access NY Port Authority plates and huge tyres, parked in the tow away zone outside the BA terminal. "I hope you got some rest as you need to be fully present for the meeting this afternoon," Dix said, thinking back to the Regency meeting of August when Freddie's mind had been somewhere else the entire time. Freddie was silent as he hoisted himself into the high vehicle, but for once didn't complain about the car. Ever since the 1978 winter, when the newly appointed JFK Station Manager's controversial purchase of several four wheel drive vehicles had saved the day during one of New York's famous snow storms, he and Robbie Robinson who had complained about the cost, now accepted JFK's big Chevy wagons were perhaps a good choice.

Freddie didn't own up to being at Tramp until the wee hours as he knew he would likely be chastised. Dix wasn't shy at telling him what he thought about the 'absurd extravagance of private celebrity nightclubs' like Tramp and Freddie's second favourite haunt in New York after Plato's Retreat, the equally renowned Régine's. The last time he and Dix were at Tramp, Johnny Gold told them he'd just had to evict Ringo and Barbara for being disorderly. Freddie had seized the opportunity for a wind-up and had asked Gold with a dead-pan face "who the hell's Ringo." It had the desired effect.

Coming back to the present, Freddie finally answered the question, "No I didn't sleep, the Concorde is pretty uncomfortable and I'm fighting a bit of a headache. But I did draft a press release as they told me all the financing was in place and we're in the clear, finally." "OK, that sounds positive" Dix replied, knowing what Freddie had been going through, "but I assumed you wouldn't have come if you didn't have a green light from the wankers - er bankers. I can get one of my girls to type it up for you and we can publish it this afternoon if you want." Freddie laughed "well you can read it at the hotel and we'll do some final tweaks on it. I've said that we're going public."

"What" Dix was astonished at what his boss had just announced. "You can't do that Freddie. The whole world knows our financial predicament so how the hell can we do an IPO when we're about to publish the company's first ever loss. Best not to put it out there. Who said you could say that?" Freddie was staring at a Pan Am 747 that was parked by their hangar; he ground his teeth but didn't respond, which meant Dix shouldn't ask any more questions.

Freddie knew better than to try and pull the wool over his man's eyes. He knew Dix made it his mission to always be fully informed and that he, sometimes annoyingly, wrote everything down; dates, names, phone numbers and often entire conversations. It came from his five years in the Ops department where the Duty Officer kept a meticulous log of every event, no matter how trivial.

As they drove out of JFK on the Van Wyck Expressway, Freddie asked Dix if he'd met with everyone after they'd got to the hotel the evening before. "No, I was in pre-production for the ads till late" Dix responded. "Oh, hmm... so you haven't seen the summer fares John's prepared then?" Freddie cautiously enquired. "Well we haven't had chance to discuss them, but he telexed them over to me. I imagine they're what he, er 'agreed' in Florida a couple of weeks ago" emphasising 'agreed' to Freddie's surprise, as he naively didn't think Dix knew about Jones's supposedly top secret trip to Miami. "They're erm..." the younger man paused trying to find the right words "obviously not optimum Freddie, but..." He would have normally taken this opportunity to get into it about the fares but Dix sensibly stopped talking. He didn't want to risk getting angry and having a row with his boss, minutes after he'd just flown in. Freddie was silent, except for the sound of his teeth grinding as he considered the untypically tactful response.

His thoughts drifted back to another occasion when Dix had met him off a United flight and had been less than polite about the fares he'd been given to work with. Freddie remembered the encounter had not been pleasant. On that occasion, he and his wife Patricia had flown in to New York from Los Angeles one Sunday evening. Dix, accompanied by his wife and JFK Station Manager, Linda Earls had met them at the United Airlines' gate. As soon as Freddie appeared on the jetway, Dix, who always favoured directness over diplomacy and without as much as a 'good evening', had launched into him with "Freddie, just what the fuck is going on?" Walking a few yards behind and witnessing her husband enduring a tongue lashing from one of his senior employees, Pat Laker in her Oklahomian drawl urged Linda to "shut Greg up before Freddie gets mad." "No Pat," responded Earls, "Greg's right, what on earth's going on with these idiotic fares, we've just lost the only advantage we had." Up ahead, Freddie who was annoyed at being attacked had yelled back that if Dix didn't like it, he was fired. But that simply created even more antagonism. Exasperated, tired and brow beaten, Freddie suggested they go to United's Red Carpet Room... for drinks and possible job reinstatement for Dix, providing he'd just "please shut up about the bloody fares."

As he sat in United's spacious lounge, sipping his scotch and milk, Freddie still didn't tell his man what was going on but it was fairly obvious. Dix had been advised by his Reservations Manager that travel agents had been calling to cancel their clients' bookings and were then re-booking them on Laker's competitors. At the time, they didn't know why travel agents were cancelling so many bookings and thought it was because of the bad press Laker was generating. It also turned out that all of Laker's other fare categories were being attacked mainly because their competitors, Pan Am especially had been offering travel agents massive additional incentives beyond the basic commission. It was a no-brainer for a New York area agent to cancel the Laker booking in favour of one of Laker's competitors. Even after Dix challenged him directly on the similarity of the competitor's fares as well as Laker's dramatically reduced diferential, Freddie continued to stall and be vague. He was shaken back to the present as the big Chevy wagon lurched upon hitting one of the Van Wyck's notorious potholes. So he quickly changed the subject.

"Sorry I had to reschedule Greg, but Charlie was sick and I had to go to Miami at the last minute." Dix knew Freddie had been in Florida but wasn't sure if he was telling the truth. Sensibly, he didn't pursue it bearing in mind Lesley Chilton's earlier counsel. Before he could reply, Freddie said the passenger load out of Miami on his flight was dreadful. That remark opened the door for Dix to bring up the worst month in Laker's history on the three main North Atlantic scheduled routes that between them had achieved an overall load factor of only 35 per cent. Freddie, I suggested to John last week we go down to four flights a week to Miami for now and he said he would discuss it with you." "No no, we can't do that, we must maintain a daily service no matter what" Freddie replied angrily; obviously this was a sensitive issue. Dix wondered if his personal need to be able to fly to Miami at a minute's notice was clouding his commercial judgment. The prime Florida route was seasonally precarious, the Brits had now fallen away for the winter and there were virtually no US originators. It was a massive loss-maker and more than one top manager had rued the day when the Miami flights had been converted from an ABC to a scheduled Skytrain service. Dix decided the timing perhaps wasn't right to bring up what he and Ian Allan had discussed about the disastrous Miami service.

"How's this ad campaign of yours then?" Freddie was anxious to change the subject. Dix brightened at the shift in the conversation. "Really good. We've tweaked the script for the TV spots that you're going to make tomorrow. You'll like it. It's a bit hokey, but I think it'll catch on. We've borrowed United's hangar and the plane will be towed there after it lands today. I'm glad you didn't go back to Gatwick for our flight and took Concorde. Did Lesley give you the schedule? You're planned for photos first thing and we're shooting your spots inside the plane after. You'll be a smash." Dix was talking at his usual fast pace then finally took a breath so Freddie could get a word in. "That's great Greg; I know all you chaps here are busting your arses to make things work and the US originating traffic has improved a bit. I'm looking forward to doing the commercials, it'll be a welcome break from dealing with all those bloody bankers and lawyers." "Well a couple of your favourite girls are coming in today for the shoot, so you better behave yourself" Dix admonished with a laugh. They were soon in the Midtown Tunnel that crossed under the East River and shortly after, they turned into Lexington Avenue and pulled up outside the Doral hotel. "We're here," he said. "Everyone's on for eleven in your suite, it's the smaller, one-bedroom again I'm afraid. We can get going whenever you're ready." "I'm ready," said Freddie, sliding down from his seat and taking in the car horns, police sirens and the general chaos of Manhattan, oblivious that what he'd just said was the theme of the TV commercial he was about to make the next day.

Freddie and Cliff Nunn were certain that the future of Laker Airways was now the responsibility of a small group of young men whose sole mission was to generate life-saving US dollar revenue. In just the few months since the re-organisation of the USA, even though the overall numbers were still in decline, they'd seen a modest improvement in the US originating passengers and cargo, despite not having a fare advantage and with everything against them. Something was working, now it was up to Freddie, Jones and others to get firmly behind the USA operation. With none of the global route licences coming to fruition and with Britons reluctant to fly to the USA due to the appalling exchange rate, the future of Laker Airways was now mainly in the hands of their North American operation.

After pouring a cup of tea, Freddie looked around the room at his assembled top management team. He obviously saw a lot of Cliff Nunn and John Jones, although that morning Jones's dark glasses appeared to be darker than usual. Perhaps, Freddie thought it was in anticipation of the roasting he was about to get because of the 1982 fares he'd published. The diminutive Ian Allan was typically quiet. Freddie didn't get down to Norfolk House much where Allan ran the Skytrain service from. He had been with Freddie since their BUA days and was the longest serving Laker man in the room. Skip Clemens, whom Freddie had only met once before was the new guy. While not exactly a surfer dude, Clemens gave off the air of a typical laid-back Californian. Scottish-Canadian David Tait had seen a fair bit of Freddie since Patricia had left. He had typically been there to do the necessary for Freddie during the numerous visits with his son in Florida. The red-haired, mustachioed Tait had already broken out in a sweat, probably on account of wondering if his days were numbered. Miami had fallen into disrepair quite fast on his watch and there were rumblings of the route being seasonal only. And that left just Dix, who Freddie hoped had vented enough in the car and may be untypically quiet at this meeting. But he knew there was no chance of that whatsoever.

Freddie apologised for missing Monday's flight, then gave the assembled team a brief rundown on what had transpired the day before. He confirmed that he had been given assurance the refinancing plan would go through. He also confessed about celebrating at Tramp with Robbie Robinson and some of the bankers and then admitted how many bottles of Krug they'd consumed. John Jones did a quick mental calculation and interrupted with "that's like spending the fuel cost for a One-Eleven to Zurich." No-one thought it was the least bit funny and wondered why Freddie was being so ostentatious, especially when they were all applying austerity measures and laying off staff.

The conversation became even more serious when the proposed 1982 fares were written up on the flip chart. The sore subject of Laker always having to maintain a fare advantage was the debate everyone in the room feared. Especially Freddie and John Jones. Freddie was reminded in no uncertain terms of the importance of the USA having a fare differential as well as a significant differential between their own unrestricted Economy fare and the Apex. It was hammered home, mostly by Dix and Tait that in the UK Freddie had his reputation, immense popularity and that he generated lots of great publicity. He was revered as the 'champion of the forgotten man' and all that. The Brits probably thought flying Laker was 'cool' and somewhat anti-establishment irrespective of anything else. But in the USA, it was only about who had the lowest fares, or at the very least was perceived to be the lowest fare carrier.

Sensing things were about to get hostile, Freddie quickly changed the subject, so they went over the never-ending problem of adequate terminal facilities at JFK and LAX. Dix had been trying for years to get Laker a single terminal operation at JFK but had been thwarted at every turn. But he was now able to report that just a week earlier he'd received a positive response from American Airlines at JFK. "American Dix, are you sure we want to get into bed with them" he'd asked thinking about the DC-10 grounding claim that only a few including Dix, knew about. Freddie was reminded that Laker already used AA for crew simulator training and for DC-10 major checks, so he said nothing more. At Los Angeles, Laker was still checking in passengers at an inflatable temporary structure set up outside the main terminal area they called the 'Bubble'. It wasn't the image Laker Airways wanted in California but it couldn't be changed in the immediate future due to all the construction at LAX.

While the terminal facilities at Miami weren't an issue, having adequate seat capacity to sell for US originators in the summer high season and the daunting task of stimulating feeder traffic from Latin America were the main agenda items. From the commencement of service to Florida's major city there had been an over-reliance on British holidaymakers, who until recently had flocked to Miami in droves. It had created a serious imbalance of revenue and the route, despite high load factors had appalling yields. It was an even bigger loss-maker than the International Caribbean operation to Barbados. Generating considerably more US originating traffic from Miami was the goal, especially since the instantaneous seasonal drop in UK passengers and the pound's devaluation.

Moreover, despite Florida's high season being the opposite to Europe's, the Brits simply didn't go to sun destinations in winter, regardless of how inexpensive the air fare may be. The Latin American market was still to be captured through interlining with Central and South American airlines. Until November, there hadn't been guaranteed capacity, so no interline agreements could be signed. As a result, traffic from Latin America and the Caribbean area was still almost non-existent. Everyone agreed that Spanish language advertising was needed and Spanish speaking cabin staff a necessity. Miami was a sensitive subject, so despite being tempted to bring up what he had suggested to Freddie in the car earlier, Dix kept quiet about reducing service to Miami for the winter. He looked over at Ian Allan hoping he was going to speak up about what he and Dix had discussed. The Scheduled Services Manager tactfully decided the timing wasn't perhaps right to propose that he and Dix both thought Miami should revert to being a summer only charter operation, as Tait likely breathed a sigh of relief.

Instead, risking Freddie calling him a smart-arse as he had done in Hong

Kong when he had suggested it to Beckman one evening during the trans-Pacific hearings, Dix put forward his recommendation to apply for Route 9. No-one in the room except Freddie knew what he was talking about, so Freddie piped up "Dix thinks we should apply to fly from Miami to a bunch of Caribbean islands... like St Kitts" which prompted a few sarcastic faces and laughter by the group, all except Tait who was in the hot seat to make Miami work at any cost. Dix chimed in, "look we have the perfect plane for the job with the A300 and Route 9 isn't about St. Kitts, it's about potentially viable routes from Miami that could be ours under Bermuda 2. Traffic rights to Barbados, The Bahamas, Jamaica... even Cuba" which drew raised eyebrows. "As a British carrier we could legally serve Havana from Miami if licenced." Beckman had never proposed licencing for the routes being discussed and Freddie hadn't been too keen while ever Australia, Hong Kong and Globetrain had been his focus. But now they were all on the back burner. Freddie was desperate to do any routes that kept the fleet employed, so he now had renewed interest. As Dix had exclusively been working on route development for the past two years, Freddie promised to review the suggestion carefully. He said he would get Beckman to look at the licencing, despite having severe reservations about giving him an assignment that was likely to cost the company a lot of money.

The controversial Regency service was then discussed and evaluated. Freddie said he was quite pleased with how the service was going, even though only the London - New York route was showing signs of producing anything close to a break-even load factor. Anticipating some of his managers may suggest they scrap it altogether, he quickly said they were past the point of no return. Freddie deliberately ignored the fact that Regency had created the latest fare war.

"It helps change our positioning" he reinforced, knowing he was about to make some new TV commercials specifically for Laker's business class. Everyone in the room was abundantly aware Regency had turned the entire airline upside down just a few months before. It was the principal reason behind the Big 3 matching Laker's fares dollar for dollar. No-one commented; they knew debating Regency at this point was futile. Ian Allan said he was impressed, 'it's better than BA' he had said, which was met by nods of agreement by everyone. There was no question Laker's Regency Service was a superb product and all it lacked was a full cabin of fare-paying passengers on every flight.

Cliff Nunn who appeared to have been dozing off, seized the pause in conversation to bring up the recent unionisation attempt by the Teamsters. During a recent visit to New York, Dix had coerced him into one of the meetings with the labour lawyers and Nunn had been visibly shaken by what went down. He congratulated the USA management team for defeating them and an untypical short round of applause was given by Freddie and the Gatwick based executives; they all knew how crucial this was to the well-being of the USA operation and how arduous the Teamster battle had been for everyone.

Despite all the other issues, the fare differential was the one they kept coming back to. Jones took the criticism on the chin and remained stoic despite the battering he received, whilst acknowledging the competition had many advantages such as their better airport facilities, 747s, Heathrow and the ability to cross-subsidise their transatlantic routes.

During the winter, Laker Airways' load factors were typically lower and there was more seat availability, especially mid-week. There was far less risk for a prospective passenger turning up at the airport to buy a cheap 'Walk-on' or standby ticket. The Walk-on was the fare that produced the least yield for the airline and bypassed travel agents, to their considerable annoyance. It was a different matter in the spring and summer where booking in advance was highly recommended. It was why the Apex fares were so popular and important for Laker. The original Skytrain concept's most serious flaw was that it had displaced many typical travellers. People with jobs and reduced flexibility, older passengers, those visiting friends and relatives, and business travellers. All of whom needed to be able to book in advance and know they had confirmed seats in both directions. The greater the distance to the destination, the more this applied, as the London to Los Angeles route painfully demonstrated in 1978. LA had proved that Laker's 'Walk-On' product was unfeasible between cities that were a full day's travelling time, 6,000 miles and eight time zones apart, except perhaps in the depths of winter when there were more seats available.

After a short break, the controversial Apex and the necessity for these popular fares to have a considerable price advantage over Laker's unrestricted Economy fare, was brought up again. No amount of reasoning by the USA management about the fares they had been given to work with would change Sir Freddie's or John Jones's rigid position. Ian Allan reminded everyone about the massive drop-off in load factors on all routes during the latter part of 1981 due to the fare war. A fare war that Laker itself had initiated.

The USA management all considered the high season differentials Jones had presented between the unrestricted Economy fare and the Apex – New York £24, Los Angeles £26, Miami £9 and their US dollar equivalents, were insufficient. Allan chimed in that he thought the unrestricted Economy fare should be almost double the Apex, which prompted nods from the USA team. Freddie was getting agitated and told them it was a fait accompli at this point and further dialogue on what they had been given to work with was futile. He and Jones both knew full well that Laker needed to have bigger fare differentials to effectively compete with BA, Pan Am and TWA, while at the same time have higher yields, especially on the longer routes to LA and Florida.

Freddie's position was as Laker Airways' costs were lower than those of the Big 3, they could still make money with the 1982 fares. "Our competitors have already lost hundreds of millions of dollars charging the same fares, just to put us out of business" he hammered home. There was no opening for further debate as Freddie explained how they would target the larger travel agents who produced high volumes and offer them higher commissions. He acknowledged Laker's traditional advantage over the competition was all but gone, then explained that he didn't see how the 'Big 3 cartel' could keep their fares low indefinitely. "I expect an across the board tariff increase as soon as the high season commences. And as their fares go up, Laker's fares will go up too," he concluded presumptuously, "but perhaps not as quickly."

Even though he hadn't yet seen the scripts or story boards, Freddie thought the new advertising campaign would drive the consumer to demand flying on a Laker flight and all the travel agents would have to do was process the booking and collect their commissions. "We'll do all their work for them" he concluded as Dix, Tait and Clemens looked at each other wondering who should pipe up first and rebut Freddie's apparent ignorance. The USA management team, who knew more about the fickle North American travel agents than anyone, made their strong counter arguments to Freddie's overly simplistic solution. Despite a prospective Laker passenger possibly demanding a Skytrain ticket as a result of Laker's fantastic marketing, the harsh reality was that a travel agent being paid 25 per cent or more commission by Pan Am would almost certainly be able to convert the Laker booking in favour of the competitor, they protested. There was clearly much more to the competitive situation in the USA than just fare matching and having adequate differentials.

The meeting thankfully wrapped up after about six hours. The marketing strategy was approved. The staffing and facilities problems reviewed and the touchy fare differential issue had been debated ad nauseam. In the end, Laker's USA management team had been forced to accept what they still felt was a ludicrous situation with respect to the published fares, especially the hugely compromised 21-day advance purchase Apex fare.

From the commencement of the Affinity Group charters, through the ABC era and then Skytrain after reservations had been approved, advance purchase fares had been the lifeblood of the airline. Freddie and Jones both knew the CAA were looking closely at Laker's forward bookings on an almost daily basis. However, the general public and the travel agent community were stalling; they weren't booking Laker's flights because of the bad publicity and the knowledge that they could wait until the very last minute before making a commitment. And then buy the lowest "Walk-On" fare at the airport. It was a dire situation for Laker Airways, with no immediate solution.

What neither Freddie or Jones admitted to was that by now, Laker's fares were more or less being set by British Airways in collusion with Pan Am and TWA. Jones's ability to negotiate a differential to the Big 3's published fares and even satisfactory differentials between Laker's own fares, was now almost non-existent. Freddie couldn't tell anyone what Jones had been doing. Dix, who had caught on earlier, tactfully kept it to himself during the meeting; it was obviously an extremely sensitive issue and Freddie had already got himself into an agitated state. More than anything, Dix wanted Freddie to be in the best possible frame of mind for the all-important TV commercials he had to shoot the next day.

He needn't have been concerned, as despite the anticipated heated dialogue on the fares, Freddie was actually buoyed by what had been discussed and was in better spirits than any of them had seen in months. David Tait and Skip Clemens tried to appear positive, John Jones was typically smug while Cliff Nunn, who had been silent for most of the time looked ever more confused.

The usually sanguine Ian Allan shook his head, clearly perplexed at what had transpired as he likely wondered why on earth he had agreed to come back from Barbados. He quietly announced "I need a drink" and made a swift beeline for Freddie's mini-bar.

CHAPTER 49

# Blackmail

## MDC caves in

Tuesday 2nd February 1982 (New York)

As the Laker executives were raiding Freddie's mini-bar, the phone in the room rang. It was MDC's David Sedgwick. "Hallo David" and before Sedgwick had a chance to speak, Freddie, who was excited after his meeting and feeling quite bullish told him that he wanted to announce the sale of the Airbus A300s and the possible purchase of more DC-10s. He was still confident of getting licences for Hong Kong, Japan and Australia and they'd already been given provisional approval for Route 6, meaning Laker Airways could operate from Los Angeles to Hong Kong via Honolulu and Guam. They would need more DC-10-30s and DC-10-10s for these and any new USA and Canadian routes. It wasn't just a ploy, Freddie still thought it was just a matter of time, some lobbying and exerting a bit more pressure on the governments involved before he was granted all the routes he'd applied for. After listening patiently to Freddie's blather for a minute, Sedgwick burst his bubble, "what did you say to the press because we've got aggravation from the bankers?" A more subdued Freddie told him what he had said and that Sedgwick himself as well as Ian Wallace of the Clydesdale had urged him earlier that morning to make a statement."Is everything alright, David?" "Yes Freddie" answered Sedgwick before abruptly ringing off. The call left Freddie visibly confused.

Late that morning, Robbie Robinson had reported that the cash requirement at the end of March would be £11.2 million. Therefore the adequacy of the £4 million was now in question and from thereon the problems had escalated. Both Sandy and John McDonnell had called Sedgwick earlier in the afternoon before he'd put in his call to Freddie. They had wanted to 'hold up' on the highly sensitive Laker deal for a few days. However, knowing how desperate things were, Sedgwick made it clear that they didn't have a few days and that once the telexes confirming the deal went to the Clydesdale Bank they 'should not back out'. The McDonnells therefore agreed to proceed but with considerable trepidation. By now, the Laker saga was becoming a very real problem.

Something that Sedgwick held back from telling Freddie was the reason why the McDonnells were getting cold feet. For the past couple of weeks McDonnell Douglas (MDC) and General Electric had been receiving threatening telexes and phone calls from their European customers. They had started at the end of January, even before Freddie had set off for the States and had spoken to the press confirming the re-financing was all in place. They were now reaching a crescendo. Senior VP of MDC Finance Corp. Jim McMillan, reporting back from his trip to Germany, said that he was also getting flak and the agreement with Laker was 'causing competition ire'.

Warren Kraemer, MDC's London-based public relations man, was taking the brunt of the abuse in the form of angry phone calls from their customer airlines' senior executives. Shaken by the vitriole, Kraemer sent a telex to Sandy McDonnell and John 'Briz' Brizendine, President of the Douglas Aircraft Division of McDonnell Douglas. The subject heading was simply 'Laker', and it read: "Today each of the following carriers has called me with their understanding of the soon to be consummated arrangement in support of Laker Airways." He proceeded to list some of Europe's major airlines, most of them state owned. Adam Thomson, Chairman of British Caledonian had phoned Kraemer and dictated the text of a cable he had dispatched to McDonnell and Brizendine, which he wanted to be certain was clearly understood. "I will absolutely forbid any further negotiations with McDonnell Douglas for DC-9 Super 80s or any other aircraft now and in the future," read Thomson. BCal had already deliberately and at the last minute cancelled a sales meeting to make its point. Thomson dictated a report from the company's group finance director, Trevor Boud that was based on information received in a phone call from MDC's John Gentling. Apparently Gentling had indicated that MDC 'had decided to rescue Freddie Laker from his own failure and to take the equivalent of an equity position in the most disruptive airline on the North Atlantic'.

Thomson apologised to Kraemer for being almost incoherent with anger at the thought that MDC would be so insensitive. Kraemer unsuccessfully attempted to placate Thomson, saying that MDC was not moving into the management of Laker and that the proposed short-term loan facility was very modest in comparison to the exposure they faced. But Thomson was a bitter and jealous man who hated Freddie and his airline, and he would not be calmed. He told Kraemer 'he did not regard Laker as being the same as any other carrier with whom they competed and the MDC rescue package would cause a storm in the entire air transport industry across Europe'. Thompson then rang GE, still frothing; he threatened to shift his business to another manufacturer. The GE executive who took the call ran through the maths of buying spare engines and an inventory of spares from another manufacturer as well as the retraining of all the mechanics. He concluded his mental arithmetic and got the number up to about $30 million. Recognising that Thomson was a Scotsman and did not throw money away, he disregarded Thomson's bile as an idle threat. MDC could have done the same but they didn't. Instead they cowered to Thomson's biased hostility. Joining in the concerted boycott frenzy was the Vice Chairman of Lufthansa, Reinhardt Abraham, he telephoned another GE executive, Ed Hood. Abraham demanded to know what GE was doing about Laker. Hood told him "we are not going to put any money into Laker or take an equity position." That immediately brought the conversation to an end but Abraham then made a more threatening telephone call later that day to Sandy McDonnell.

Adam Thomson had instructed his colleague Ian Ritchie to send the threatening telex to John Brizendine and copy it to all other operators in Europe who were MDC customer airlines, including Lufthansa, Swissair and Scandinavian Airlines System. It did the trick. Kraemer subsequently received telephone calls from Martin Junger, Senior VP of Swissair, Abraham of Lufthansa, and Bo Stahle, Senior VP of Administration and Legal Affairs at SAS. In the preceding weeks comments in a 'similar vein without specifics' referring to Laker as 'violently disruptive', 'knowingly generated the crisis' and having 'indulged in malpractices' were made by the Belgian national airline Sabena and the French carrier Union des Transports Aeriens (UTA).

And there had been others; Dan Air, Britannia and KLM among them. Umberto Nordio president of Alitalia had suggested that the Chairman of IATA, the trade association of the world's airlines, should "secure the support of as many members as possible and then register a formal complaint to MDC and GE impressing upon them the impropriety of their proposed action and the possible countermeasures they may expect of the airlines."

Finally, Kraemer wrote. 'It is now clear that the vehemence of the opposition to Laker, and directed against MDC for our perceived role in creating a potential solution to the Laker financial problem, has spread beyond the opposition from BCal to an orchestrated basis throughout Europe of most of the scheduled carriers. As was indicated in previous discussions, the Laker filing of 666 point-to-point fares intra Europe which he proposed to serve with the A300 Airbus fleet and the ultra low inclusive tour fares and packages also aimed at the European Market, has formed the basis of a violent reaction against MDC now that it has become clear that a potential for Laker's survival has been developed by the financial agreement'.

The telexes later came to be known as the 'nastygrams', and the unashamed ringleader and instigator was BCal's Adam Thomson, backed by French airline UTA and its boss, Rene Lapautre, who had sent his telex to six other airlines encouraging them to follow his example. They all made one thing crystal clear, none of them would consider any further purchases from McDonnell Douglas.

Commercially, it was understandable that a company might not wish to do business with a supplier that had become a shareholder in a competitor. Gentling's disclosure to Adam Thomson may not have created the uproar it did had he not mentioned that MDC may take an equity position in Laker Airways. A simple infusion of cash on a short-term loan basis or a re-scheduling of interest or loan payments, may have been reluctantly accepted or even understood, especially by DC-10 operators who had also suffered from the 1979 grounding. But a share-holding in an airline that was arguably the most vilified anywhere, was beyond the pale. Freddie Laker, with the low fares revolution through his Skytrain service had made enemies of the airlines, who now blamed him for all their own failings. It was a well-organised and vicious campaign, the vitriol spilling from the pages. Even by the standards of the cut-throat airline business, this was a bloodthirsty baying mob, with a clear message. If MDC and GE stepped in to help Laker Airways, they too would be destroyed, despite the questionable logic of the threats.

About 30 minutes went by as the Laker executives chatted amongst themselves over a well-earned drink, when the phone rang again. Freddie answered it. It was Sedgwick. It was now 5:30pm in New York meaning that it was 10:30pm in London. Sandy McDonnell had spoken to Sedgwick after taking Reinhardt Abraham's call. Sedgwick told Freddie that Lufthansa was demanding he withdraw his European route applications. In exchange, Lufthansa would withdraw its pressure on MDC and the German and Austrian banks, which were part of the Airbus consortium and whom Lufthansa was also haranguing. "That's a bit unfair David?" replied Freddie. He stiffened, his pulse racing "we could agree something now and try to do something at a later date?" Freddie figured he could fight this later. "No Freddie. If you agree to pull out, you've got to pull out properly," insisted Sedgwick. It was blackmail. Breaking the stranglehold of the IATA airlines in Europe was an obsession of Freddie's and crucial to Laker Airways' future viability. Europe was why he had bought the A300s, incurring a debt burden on Laker Airways like never before. It was the main reason why the refinancing package was so critical. "Will that be the end of everything, no more trouble? Does that mean the financing goes through?" "Yes," came the reply. "No more trouble. You will get all of your £4 million, as agreed." Freddie's eyes focused on the far wall. 'Should I give in to blackmail?' he thought. 'Should I give up Europe?' Seconds ticked by as Freddie deliberated his next move. "All right David. We will withdraw from Europe." "Good," said Sedgwick. "Now, is this it? No more problems?" "No more problems, Freddie. Good night." "Good night, David" as Freddie let out a sigh of defeat.

Laker's bid for scheduled service rights to fly low-fare Skytrain type services all over Europe, had so far won just one route, a twice-daily service from Gatwick to Zurich granted on the 23rd December. Even so, with Laker's brand new Airbus A300s, full scheduled service amenities and with advanced bookings available, it was a terrifying prospect for the European airlines. Freddie had seen the future; as always, he was way ahead of his time. But he had seriously underestimated the animosity he had created with the success of Skytrain and the relentless thumbing his nose at the establishment. He slowly replaced the receiver, reached for his drink and took a big gulp. The room was silent and his top managers' eyes were all on him. He told them what Sedgwick had said, word for word, concluding with "it's pure, unadulterated fucking blackmail."

The meeting broke up. Dix turned to Jones, Nunn and Allan "I'll drive you guys out to JFK for your Pan Am flight as I have to check on our plane for tomorrow, see you down in the lobby." "Hope the shoot goes OK, cheers everybody" said Jones as everyone but Dix left the room, who then turned to Freddie, "Get an early night Freddie, you're knackered. No going down to the bar or grabbing a couple of girls for Plato's, you have a big day tomorrow."

CHAPTER 50

# Touch and Go

## The lenders play games

Wednesday 3rd February, 1982 (Morning, London)

David Sedgwick was up and already showered when he answered the ringing telephone in his high floor hotel room overlooking London's Park Lane. He knew it was his automated wake-up call and didn't need 'good morning, this is your wake-up call', shouted at him by the phone. Sedgwick replied as he always did with 'thank you and good morning' even though he knew it was just a machine.

He paced the room while awaiting his room service breakfast that he had ordered the night before. Before turning in, he'd telephoned Freddie in New York and had told him that his European dream was over. He hadn't liked doing it but he was trying to blunt the European airlines' opposition to Freddie's scheme. The European airlines were threatening to not buy any more McDonnell Douglas aircraft and even cancel existing orders if MDC continued to support Laker Airways' refinancing. These sales were vital to his company's continued existence. To Sedgwick it seemed like a good trade off. He would use McDonnell's leverage with Laker Airways to stop the airline's expansion into Europe in exchange for a continuing good relationship with MDC's European customers. After finishing his breakfast, Sedgwick made his way to the Midland Bank's main office with a spring in his step. He had put out the last fire and arrived still expecting the deal to be a go.

Meanwhile, the Midland's Chief Executive, Dennis Kitching, was putting into effect his plans to protect the Midland's interests. That meant Laker Airways would more than likely have to shut down unless it could find a significant amount of cash... fast. A week before on 25th January, when Kitching had returned from his three-week holiday in Egypt, he had been concerned that the £4 million promised by MDC had not arrived. He thought Laker Airways' trading position appeared to be worsening and the appalling cash flow and overdraft requirements were intensifying. He needed to protect his position. Kitching had called William Mackey of Ernst & Whinney, one of the largest accounting firms in the world who counted British Airways amongst their clients. As BA's auditors, the company was working on the due diligence required for its stock market flotation. Mackey was the company's liquidation partner and the leading receiver of bankrupt companies in England. However he wasn't involved with any of the British Airways' privatisation initiatives.

On the morning of the 28th January, Kitching had instructed the Midland's General Manager, George Gilhespy, to dismiss Laker's financial advisor Bill Morrison of McClintocks, as soon as possible. When Gilhespy tried to terminate Morrison he resisted, saying that only Freddie could conclude his services. Gilhespy told him that his replacement would be William Mackey. Morrison was shocked as he knew exactly what that meant. It was not the doctor the Midland had sent for. It was the undertaker.

Mackey would effectively replace Morrison and he would be positioned at the heart of Laker Airways. Freddie had already been forewarned in advance by Kitching that Morrison's role would be terminated and he'd flippantly said to the Midland's top man 'you hired him, you can fire him'. When Freddie had met with Gilhespy on the evening of the 1st February, he had again been told who Morrison's replacement would be. At the time, Freddie had been anxious to keep his evening engagement so he had been quite nonchalant about it. Bill Mackey meant nothing to Freddie and it was likely that by the time he met up with his associates that evening, he may have already forgotten the name. If Freddie had given it more thought, he could have bounced Bill Mackey's name off Ian Wallace, his merchant banker with the Clydesdale and a friend for thirty years. The financial district of the City of London was like a village. Wallace would have for sure known of Mackey, what he did for a living and exactly what it might have signaled for Laker Airways.

Similarly, Freddie could have phoned John Roney and instructed him to do a thorough background check and find out who Bill Mackey was. He did neither. This non-action wasn't indicative of the super smart, second-guessing Freddie Laker of earlier times. The enormous challenges of 1981 that should have made him paranoid and distrusting, instead appeared to be having the opposite effect. Freddie had seemingly become complacent and it was about to bite him.

Immediately after hearing from Gilhespy what the Midland's intentions were, Morrison went straight over to John Roney's office located nearby. He arrived upset. When Morrison asked Roney if he knew who Bill Mackey was, Roney replied that he hadn't a clue and as far as he was aware, one accountant was simply being replaced with another. At that time, there had only been two famous insolvency experts in the history of the City of London. The first was Sir Kenneth Cork who went on to become the Lord Mayor of London and the other was Bill Mackey of Ernst & Whinney. Roney's office at London Wall was in the heart of the City so it was surprising he had never heard of Mackey. Morrison informed Roney that Mackey was one of the leading liquidators in the city. Roney was shocked at this disclosure. He simply could not comprehend that despite the obvious clue of their replacing Morrison with Mackey, it was the Midland's intention to close Laker Airways down altogether. However, whether it was disbelief, complacency or some other reason, Roney didn't think this was serious enough to immediately strategise a counter plan or phone Freddie in New York and give him a heads up. Clearly, Kitching and Gilhespy wanted the Laker men to know the Midland's intentions; why else would they have given them the name of a renowned receiver and liquidator. They could have just said 'we're replacing McLintocks with Ernst and Whinney' and left it at that. They had given both Freddie and Roney due notice that the Midland Bank was about to pull the plug on Laker Airways. Incredibly, the Laker men hadn't read the tea leaves.

Freddie called Roney from New York on the morning of 3rd of February and at his behest, Roney finally telephoned Gilhespy. He expressed his concerns about the withdrawal of Thomson McLintock, the Midland's accounting firm who were Morrison's employer and the impact this would have at such a delicate stage of negotiations. He said it would be damaging to change horses at that stage. The other consideration was the burden that would be laid upon the company and in particular Robbie Robinson if a new firm without any knowledge of Laker's accounts was put in. Roney seemed more concerned about the potential handover challenges between the two accounting firms and he never questioned Gilhespy as to Midland's intentions or why they had replaced an accountant with a liquidator. Gilhespy fobbed him off. Roney was told that the bank had the problem very much in mind and in particular the problems that such a replacement would create for Laker's Robinson. The proposal was for a gradual takeover and they expected Thomson McLintock to fully brief the new Ernst & Whinney accountants. During the call with Roney, Gilhespy had become agitated saying that the bank needed a vast amount of information quickly as they were 'hidebound without an atom of information'. It was an odd comment given how deeply entrenched the Midland was in the refinancing and that Morrison had been working with the Laker accounting team for months. This should have rung some alarm bells.

After the phone call with Gilhespy, Roney put his concerns in a letter to be sent the next day, the 4th of February to Freddie. However, he and Freddie were scheduled to be together in the afternoon of the 4th of February as they had an important meeting with Freddie's divorce lawyer in London. It was why Freddie was returning from New York after the shoot and not heading down to Miami as he would have preferred. Roney didn't contact Freddie by telephone or telex to advise him what he had learnt from his conversation with Gilhespy. Instead he wrote a single page outlining his concerns. He thought the bank's proposals were impractical and commented on 'the general effect on confidence that the withdrawal of Thomas McLintock would have at this delicate stage of negotiations'. He highlighted 'the impossible burden that would be laid upon the company and in particular Robbie Robinson, if a new firm without any knowledge of Laker's accounts were put in'. In the next paragraph, Roney wrote that Gilhespy had agreed his point was valid and that they (the Midland) were proposing a gradual takeover. They expected McLintocks to fully brief the new accountants and that they needed a vast amount of information quickly. Roney reiterated Gilhespy's statement that the bank was 'hidebound without an atom of information', this despite the fact that Bill Morrison had been reporting regularly on the status of Laker Airways and the bank was receiving almost daily traffic and revenue updates. Roney's final paragraph included a comment that if McLintock pulled out altogether it may raise a few eyebrows and he concluded 'if I am wrong on this however, I do strongly believe that it would be quite impossible to have a new firm come in and it is unrealistic to expect Thomas McLintock to spend the time teaching this new firm the ropes'. Roney never mentioned Bill Mackey in his letter to Freddie. He appeared to have missed the point entirely that the Midland's intention was not simply replacing one accounting firm with another. It was actually replacing an accountant tasked with saving Laker Airways with a renowned receiver and liquidator who's only job would be to shut the company down and sell off its assets.

The day before, Robbie Robinson had reported that the cash requirement at the end of March would be £11.2 million even with the refinancing in place. Therefore the adequacy of the £4 million was now in question and from thereon the problems just escalated.

With Freddie out of the country, Kitching sent Samuel Montagu's Ian McIntosh to the CAA to see Raymond Colegate. The CAA was the regulatory body with ultimate direct control over every aspect of civil aviation in the UK. Colegate was an unabashed Freddie Laker supporter and held an all-powerful role as the Economics Director. He had legitimate concerns as to whether Laker Airways had sufficient financial resources to get through the slack winter period until revenue picked up with the traditional spring / summer surge in traffic. McIntosh asked Colegate whether MDC's back-up credit of £4 million, after the withdrawal of GE's million, and over and above the Clydesdale's £9 million overdraft was enough. Colegate repeated that there should be a back-up commitment nearer £5 million, and that the CAA needed to be assured that Laker Airways had sufficient financial backing to see the company through the winter. And if not, the company should cease trading immediately. Indeed, Colegate was adamant that Laker probably needed more, much more, regardless. McIntosh now had what he had been sent for and quickly returned to the Midland and reported back. Now Kitching had not only a statement that the £4 million cushion was insufficient, but he could dress up Colegate's 'sufficient financial backing to see the company through the winter' as an official demand from the CAA for unlimited finance. The CAA's position, combined with the dreadful cash flow figures sent over to the Midland from Laker's Financial Director Robbie Robinson were compounded by a worsening situation on the North Atlantic generally. For Kitching and the Midland, this was the last straw and exactly what they needed in order to shut down Laker Airways.

Dennis Kitching took all this to his superior, Stuart Graham who was the Midland Group's Chief Executive. He wanted Graham's approval to pull the plug. Kitching, who had perhaps never been properly committed to rescuing Laker Airways now had his chance to kill the company off. While Laker's summer revenue from 1981 was rolling in, the overdraft had hardly been used. Indeed, the previous August, the Clydesdale had even agreed at one stage to extend Laker's overdraft to £20 million.

But now, it was the depth of the winter season and with the original £9 million overdraft all used up it was the perfect opportunity for Kitching to call time on Laker Airways. He had not done it earlier because he was keen to avoid a backlash aimed at the bank for taking action prematurely.

Kitching rang the Assistant Director at the Bank of England, David Walker and a private meeting was hastily convened. Walker still needed to be fully convinced and the Midland needed to overcome the Bank of England's support for Laker. In 1979, Margaret Thatcher had run for Prime Minister on a platform of supporting free enterprise. She had campaigned publicly with a speech that proclaimed, "It wasn't British Airways that gave you low fares, it was Freddie Laker and free enterprise. Competition works." Margaret Thatcher genuinely liked Freddie. They had known each other for years, mainly through her husband. Thatcher wanted Laker Airways to survive and it was on her explicit instructions that the Bank of England was assisting with the refinancing package. Thatcher had asked Ray Colegate of the CAA what he thought about a £5m cash injection to save Laker. Colegate, who she knew was a fan of Freddie's said he didn't think it was enough. In fact, Colegate advised the Prime Minister that possibly within weeks, another £5 million may be needed. Thatcher's response was predictable. She couldn't in good faith use government funds for a bail out that may be open-ended.

Meanwhile Kitching had told Walker that the CAA was demanding more financial support than McDonnell Douglas and the Midland Bank, the two principal providers of Laker's finance, were willing to give. As a result the Midland concluded that it could no longer continue to support Laker. Kitching then told the Bank of England that the CAA believed it was better for everyone, especially Laker's passengers, if Laker went out of business now rather than during the height of the summer holiday season.

Meanwhile, Ray Colegate had already phoned Walker himself when he'd seen the latest traffic figures from Laker Airways. He told him that it was entirely unacceptable that the '£5 million headroom' would be reduced but rather it could turn out that Laker Airways might well need more. The money on offer was inadequate to cover contingencies. Colegate pointed to Laker's (over optimistic) traffic forecasts as proof that there was need for more headroom, rather than less. Walker told him he might be able to coax the bank to increase its commitment. Colegate later discussed the matter with Sir Nigel Foulkes the CAA's chairman who told Colegate that he thought the margin should be £10 million. Colegate then rang Kitching and repeated what Foulkes had said. Kitching now had exactly what he wanted.

Freddie's lawyer, John Roney believed that there were good arguments to take a more lenient view of Laker's traffic figures and that they were not insurmountable. This could all be overcome with a little time and funding. He stated: "Probably the major cause for the load factors being below forecasts was the reluctance of passengers, and particularly travel agents, to book forward in view of the adverse publicity, which had created a lack of confidence. This depression was artificial, and traffic would have revived once confidence had been restored." Under different circumstances, Roney's view may have had some validity but now it was quite naive. The economic climate was dire, the pound was forecast to drop even further against the dollar and Laker's main competitors were matching Laker's fares dollar for dollar and offering travel agents massive commissions. Ray Colegate was one of Britain's top economists and had always been supportive of Sir Freddie Laker. Yet even Colegate had severe reservations as to the future viability of Laker Airways without a significant cash infusion to guarantee the company's survival through what was to be a very tough winter season.

Dennis Kitching was now armed with many good reasons for not extending any further credit. He could actually force Freddie to call in the receivers himself. Freddie, the CAA or someone else other than the Midland would take the blame. Kitching would inform Freddie at the earliest opportunity that the bank could no longer support Laker Airways. Everyone involved in the refinancing would need to be told of the decision. Kitching knew that at this point, the Midland Bank and in particular the Airbus consortium that it led, would almost certainly not be out of pocket in the final result. There was a 25 per cent manufacturer's first loss guarantee on the A300s, the virtually brand-new planes had a good resale value, and there was money in the deposit account as a result of the bank's retention of the A300 spares money. There were also the spares themselves plus two brand new engines. The Midland's subsidiary, the Clydesdale Bank was also sitting pretty; it held a joint charge with the Royal Bank of Canada over a DC-10-10, G-BELO (Southern Belle), and a spare engine. The plane was valued at between $12 and $15 million, with $10.8 million outstanding. They had charges over the two Boeing 707s, four BAC One-Elevens and the hangar and office complex at Gatwick. It was more than enough to pay off any indebtedness. The overdraft facility was fully secured by floating charges and cross guarantees between profitable member companies of the Laker group such as Laker Air Travel and Arrowsmith, that had significant credit balances. The assets available to the Midland group as security stood at £26.8 million against lending of £11.5 million. The earlier missed payment on the Airbus loan meant it could be called at any time, despite the earlier assurance in writing that it would not be. The overdraft that should only have been called in September 1982 was used up, artificially helped along by the Midland's refusal to reimburse the £1.8 million of Airbus spares money due to Laker. The bottom line was that the Midland Bank would not be out of pocket because of its demise. Dennis Kitching was satisfied.

David Sedgwick arrived at the Midland and went up to Kitching's office located on the third floor. Kitching wasn't there. Gilhespy wasn't around either, so Sedgwick sat down in the conference room and finished the paperwork on the agreements they had made at the Bank of England on Monday afternoon while he waited. This was supposed to be a busy day; he couldn't understand why there was no-one around and he decided to make some phone calls. He then received some troubling news; the crucial telexes from MDC's head office for the deal to go forward had not been sent. He knew how much this mattered. Eventually the Midland's Gervais Boote turned up and took him to lunch. To Sedgwick's further dismay, Boote let it slip that the bank was still holding onto the A300 spares reimbursement cash. Sedgwick had not known about this and couldn't believe it, as freeing up this money was an essential component of the refinancing package. Earlier, John Roney had sent a tersely worded letter on behalf of his client to the Midland about the reimbursement of the spares reserve monies owed Laker Airways. It had no effect and was simply ignored. Sedgwick next went to Samuel Montagu's office thinking that Ian McIntosh would know what was going on, but he was out. His secretary told Sedgwick that he and Bill Morrison were at the Civil Aviation Authority going over the figures. Fearing the worst, Sedgwick decided to wait, and sat with Bill Chase, one of McIntosh's colleagues, working out the possible mechanics of an emergency loan facility.

Finally McIntosh returned, and announced that all Laker's advisors would be having a dinner meeting at the Waldorf Hotel that evening with the CAA's Ray Colegate. 'OK', thought Sedgwick, 'I'll find out what is going then'.

By now, it was late afternoon in London. Kitching told Gilhespy to get a message to Freddie that he was to come up to the Midland's offices upon his return from New York the next morning. Gilhespy called Freddie's direct line at the Laker headquarters at Gatwick Airport and spoke to Lesley Chilton, Freddie's private secretary. He didn't say why Freddie was to come and she didn't ask. Chilton confirmed she would get the message to him in New York. Freddie was busy shooting his commercials at JFK Airport but he was given the message as soon as they wrapped. Freddie assumed he had been summoned to the Midland to sign routine paperwork related to the re-financing. The message from the Midland didn't ring any alarm bells with him, even though it perhaps should have done had he considered what Morrison's replacement meant. It was the only message he received while in New York. Freddie was scheduled to come back anyway since he and Roney had to meet the divorce lawyer handling the undoing of his third marriage.

It had obviously not yet dawned on anyone involved that Freddie could be heading into a trap, one that he could never reverse out of once he was back in the UK. However, there was always a chance John Roney would realise, given the appointment of Bill Mackey, what the Midland's intentions really were. There was still time for him to call Freddie in New York and warn him.

CHAPTER 51

# I'm Ready

## Redefining the brand

Wednesday 3rd February, 1982

Freddie had slept well. He knew he had a long day ahead at JFK airport. Everyone had flown home after the strategy meeting the previous day except Robin Flood, who had remained in New York. She had insisted on being present for the shoot even though Cliff Nunn had emphatically said it wasn't necessary. Fearing a tantrum, Freddie stayed out of it. Greg Dix had driven Nunn, John Jones and Ian Allan out to JFK for their Pan Am flight. He'd then headed over to the United hangar to make sure the aircraft was properly cleaned and prepped and for the pre-light for the next day's shoot. Dix hadn't made it back to Manhattan in time to have dinner with Freddie, but before leaving had instructed his boss to get an early night so he'd be fresh the next day. A 9:00am photo session had been planned where Freddie would be craned on to the roof of the DC-10 followed by an all-day shoot in the aircraft. Dix needed Freddie to be 100 per cent as they had a lot on the line.

There was a knock on the door and a voice called out 'room service.' Freddie gratefully downed the orange juice and coffee. He was feeling human again. He felt relaxed, despite the troubling call the evening before with David Sedgwick of McDonnell Douglas Finance Corp. Being coerced to give up his European route applications was particularly disturbing. He figured that he'd fight that later, but if that was the compromise he had to make to keep Laker Airways alive, then so be it. He'd had a short phone call with John Roney to confirm he'd be back the next day for the meeting with his divorce lawyer and to have Roney check in with the Midland's George Gilhespy. Then he had switched gears as there was work to do, his favourite kind. Freddie loved being on camera, especially when surrounded by his attractive girls. He was feeling light again, for the first time in many months.

Freddie's domestic situation was far from OK, he hadn't yet resigned himself to Freddie Allen living in Miami with Patricia, but there was little he could do about it. He'd regularly flown over to see his son since she had abruptly left for Florida the previous August, taking Freddie Allen with her. The timing couldn't have been worse for Freddie as he was dealing with the fare war, re-financing, the drop off in traffic on the Atlantic, rejections from Hong Kong, Australia, Europe and Japan, the rapidly devaluing pound making his debts even greater, and a dozen other problems. It was more than one person should have had to deal with and a lesser man would have cracked under the pressure.

Freddie had clearly not been himself for months, his manic-depressive mood swings concerned everyone around him. He was masterful at convincing others, even those close to him that there was nothing wrong. Today however, the 3rd of February 1982, Freddie felt he was back in the groove once more. He knew Dix would be banging on the door in fifteen minutes to take him out to JFK for a full day of media work. He didn't know much about what lay ahead for him that day. Lesley had been sent a brief with the script and the revised schedule following the latest postponement so that he could once again fly to Miami to visit Freddie Allen. He'd then been too tied up with his bankers on the Monday, a bit worse for wear on Tuesday morning and then had to endure a six-hour management meeting. So he hadn't had time to look over the script. Normally for a new advertising campaign, Freddie would have been involved much earlier, but this time he had to trust that others knew what they were doing. "I better get ready" he muttered to himself as he headed to the shower.

Ten minutes later and another knock on the door meant it was Dix, typically a few minutes early. "Morning, sleep well?" he asked jovially, "ready for your big starring role?" Freddie confirmed he had slept well and as he knew what the next question would be quickly followed up with "and I didn't go to Plato's or even down to the bar" he gloated. "Well you look rested, it's been a while since you were in front of a camera for all the right reasons," Dix responded with a laugh. There was much truth in his comment as for past six months all Freddie's face to camera work had been answering awkward questions about Laker Airways' financial status and whether the airline would survive or not.

"I don't have any decent clobber with me Dix" Freddie said as he pulled on his socks. "No, all you need is your fine black Oxfords, I told Lesley we had suits, shirts and ties for you but that you must bring your own shoes. I know how fussy you are about them, even though they probably won't be in the frame." Freddie was known to be very particular about his footwear. He may have occasionally compromised on other things but never his shoes. "Anyway, we would never have got the right size for those dainty little plates of yours" laughed Dix staring down at his boss's slender feet he was slipping into a brand new pair of black Oxfords that he guessed were hand sewn and had probably cost at least three hundred pounds. "Oh, and I hope you brought some trainers for the top of the plane." "Even better my lad," answered Freddie smugly, holding up a blue Sperry Topsider yachting shoe he'd grabbed from his carry on bag. Anyway, never mind the bloody shoes Dix, which watch should I wear" Freddie took out his old gold Rolex and a cheap-looking Timex with a faux leather strap. "Oh no, not the watches again

Freddie, we had to do this in Sharjah so you'd be properly 'accessoried' to meet the Emir. Anyway, it doesn't matter for the shoot, the cuffs will cover it."

Still laughing at the absurdity of Freddie's wrist watch dilemmas, the pair went out to the elevator that served the top two garden suites of the Doral Hotel. "Who's in the big suite Dix, not Richard Harris again surely" Freddie asked with a smirk, as he was usually assigned the larger two-bedroom suite but this trip he'd had to settle for the slightly less spacious one-bedroom facility next door. Both top floor suites had enormous rooftop gardens with stunning views of the City. Freddie loved having the two bedrooms when he was in New York, "one to play in and one to sleep in" he'd say. Earlier in November, Dix had also been assigned the smaller suite. When he came out one morning he'd bumped into famed Irish actor Richard Harris. Dix had greeted Harris by saying "you're in my room" at which the Irishman had laughed and asked in his inimitable voice, "just who the hell are you?". When Dix told him he worked for Freddie Laker, Harris was appropriately impressed, as everyone was when you said that. After some banter in the elevator, Harris said he'd leave tickets under the door for Camelot in which he was again starring on Broadway. The next day, Laker's insurance manager, Tony McCarthy had called Dix and asked him to meet with Laker's underwriters who were flying in from Omaha, as he couldn't make it over. So Dix took them to a swank Manhattan restaurant he thought they'd like to go over the policies. During the lunch, one of the insurance men was fixated on a corner table where ironically, Richard Harris was dining with two stunning looking women. The Nebraskans were clearly in awe at being in the same restaurant as such a famous celebrity. As they were all walking out of the restaurant, Harris saw Dix and yelled out 'hey how's it going" in his distinctive smoky Irish voice to which Dix replied as if they were old pals, "hey Richard, are you still messing up my room." The Omaha men were completely dumbstruck at this exchange. Laker's insurance policy was naturally renewed without a hitch and thereafter Freddie, who loved the story told it to anyone who would listen.

GK1, the freshly washed Laker Airways' Chevy had been brought around to the front of the Doral by the hotel's valet as they went out into Lexington Avenue. "I guess it's too early to ask if you've heard anything more from the Midland or MDC" Dix was probably stating the obvious but was checking that Freddie's state of mind was clear for the day ahead. "No, I just called Roney that's all, as I wanted him to check in with the Midland bloke. We're good I think Greg, but you never know with these bastards, if they get more pressure from their European customers, who knows what they're capable of." "Yeah, that's for sure," agreed Dix, "we've seen it before. We think we're a pretty decent sized carrier with eleven DC-10s but when you add up those dash thirty operators in Europe, they have seventy aircraft between them, their tight little KSSU group and half a dozen governments behind them." "I know" Freddie replied as he thought back on the evening before when David Sedgwick of MDC Finance Corporation had passed on the message from Sandy McDonnell himself, telling him he had to let go of his 666 European route applications if Freddie wanted their money. "I hate being blackmailed like that, it's bad enough I have to go through it all the time with Patricia, just to get a day or two with Charlie. Dix bit his tongue about the postponements to the shoot due to Freddie's trips to Florida in January to see his son. But there was nothing he could say on the subject as he knew only too well the anguish his boss had been through over losing his son, wife and stepdaughter Bettina in August of the previous year. He hadn't been the same man since. Dix was hopeful the old Freddie would be fully revived for the shoot and all the signs looked good.

As they entered New York City's mid-town tunnel en route to JFK, Freddie changed the subject as he didn't want to risk being depressed or melancholy on what had the makings of being a really fun day. "Right, let's see the script then. This better be good Dix, I understand you've got one of the top directors in advertising." "Well the agency pulled out a few stops to get Fred Levinson; you'll love working with him Freddie, the bloke's brilliant, he's been NW Ayer's main guy for decades. He does his own camera and from what I gathered at the pre-production meetings, he tries to work fast." Freddie took the paper from the folder Dix had stuck by his seat and looked over what had been prepared for him, the script, rundown sheet and the scene schedule. He noted the 'talent' list, which included photos of the Laker personnel and all the extras including a personal favourite, the flirtatious blonde-haired Meg Vesty, a senior Laker In-Flight Director and one of his old guard. She had been doing the company's promotional events with Freddie for a decade and knew the ropes... and Freddie. He wasn't so familiar with Amanda Cooper but said he was looking forward to changing that after lustily staring at her photo. He was impressed they had picked the popular steward, Steve Wren, for the shoot. This was noteworthy considering Freddie's widely-known homophobia and earlier resistance to having any male cabin staff. There was also a dozen 'extras' the agency had selected, who would act the part of passengers. Freddie nodded his approval and was clearly getting back into the groove. This was what he loved more than anything, perhaps as much as hanging out with his engineers in the hangar; although it was all business there and none of his girls to flirt with down on the hangar floor.

"Are you ready for Freddie" he said aloud and then laughed. "You did warn me it was a little hokey Dix, but I must say I really do like it and think it'll catch on. By the way I hope you know what a hokey is, you know, the hokey-pokey" Freddie was laughing at his jibe but Dix didn't pick up on it and remained serious."Well there are a bunch of derivatives around the basic theme" he explained, "and the ten second tags we've shot already include celebrities or a celebrity look a like. They have one guy who's the spitting image of Ed Sullivan, another who's a dead ringer for Fred Astaire and this five year old kid who's on the verge of being a big star here, his name's Joey Lawrence." "What does he have to say?" asked Freddie. "Oh it's brilliant, they have him sitting on the stairs with his face pressed into the baluster rails and he puts on a big pout and says 'I'm ready for Sir Freddie... but my Mom won't let me go.' They both laughed as they got up to speed on the Grand Central Parkway. "And what about Steinbrenner, I'd like to meet him, he made all his money building ships before he bought the baseball team," Freddie said as he knew a bit about the New York

Yankees' owner. "Well his part is a throw back to last year when the Yankees lost to the L.A. Dodgers in the '81 World Series. He was pretty embarrassed about it at the time," Dix explained to a clearly fascinated Freddie. "Anyway his piece goes 'I'm ready for Sir Freddie… I thought I was ready for the Dodgers.' Freddie laughed and it was obvious he was getting caught up in the theme of the campaign and becoming excited at doing his part, "oh, and the agency also got his permission for you to use his name in our print ads where you'll be standing on top of the plane with your arms outstretched and the caption goes "I want George Steinbrenner on my plane." Freddie hmm'd at that one, "I'm thinking it may be better for the caption to say 'I want George Steinbrenner in my Regency service cabin' or something like that. We don't want to put anyone off." Dix nodded in agreement as he too had some misgivings about anything that could be viewed as pretentious, which he'd conveyed to LGFE's copywriters.

As they drove along the busy freeway, Freddie thought how critical to the company's future the USA was. His global expansion plans to Asia and Australia had for now fizzled out and just the previous night his dream of revolutionising travel in Europe looked like it was also on indefinite hold, or perhaps even gone for ever. They'd spent an inordinate amount of time, energy and funds chasing their Pacific Rim aspirations but he was now convinced North America was where the company should be putting all its efforts. Perhaps where the company should have been putting all its efforts for the past few years in fact.

As if he was reading his mind, Dix broke into his thoughts, "you know I've been thinking about yesterday's meeting Freddie," he started off and immediately noticed Freddie's face turn to a grimace almost as if he was expecting another diatribe about the fares. "Maybe I've been wrong about the fare differential issue and our always having to have the lowest fare no matter what." "What on earth do you mean," Freddie seemed surprised at the remark. "I thought you were the one who gave John and me the hardest time about our always having to have a fare advantage," as he remembered the heated discussions they'd had about the fare schedules, the latest not sixteen hours earlier. "Right, and I am," Freddie looked puzzled but said nothing as Dix went on, "but I think it's really dangerous if that's our only unique selling point, our only advantage over the others. We've hinged the company's entire future on having the lowest fare being our sole criteria... and it was probably a mistake. Look at the fucking aggro it's caused us." Freddie allowed what Dix was saying to sink in for a few moments before replying, "Greg, you of all people know that John and I have had a hell of a time maintaining a fare differential. We had to make compromises… massive, almost unacceptable compromises. But I think I hear what you're saying. We're big enough and well established now that we can promote other reasons to fly with Laker apart from the fare, right." "Yes exactly," Dix replied quickly, "and I think that's why this new ad campaign may be a turning point in the States, Freddie. We've only ever promoted Laker as the lowest fare to Britain and the very day we weren't the lowest, the bloody phones just stopped ringing." Freddie nodded in acknowledgement as he knew he was right. They desperately needed to re-brand Laker Airways as something more, much more than simply the lowest fare. "You were vehemently opposed to Regency Dix, if I remember you were one of its biggest detractors." "Right, I was when you came up with it and decided to launch it last Fall as an antagonistic initiative. But not so much now Freddie. At the time, I thought it was idiotic and I know you just did it to cock a snook at the Big Three. You did it at the wrong time and for the wrong reasons and let's be honest, it was stupidly expensive and unnecessary to convert so many planes." Freddie ground his teeth and then nodded. He would never fully admit he was wrong about something, even though the timing of Regency had proven to be a serious error of judgment. It was perhaps his biggest mistake since the Accountant, although the misguided Airbus deal had now eclipsed them all.

"As we discussed yesterday, Regency's still not producing much out of LA or Miami, but it's doing much better out of New York and it's a really fantastic product… probably the best value for money out there." Dix was giving a nod to the hard work by Laker's engineering, cabin services and catering units who had made Regency a reality at short notice.

He went on, "John Cleese flew from JFK with his young daughter and he told me at check-in how great it is. We have rock bands like Elvis Costello and The Attractions; they flew over when my Mum and Dad visited, my mother was appalled as all Elvis did was swear the entire flight." "Elvis... I thought he was dead" Freddie exclaimed. "Actually his real name is Declan" the explanation was clearly only confusing Freddie more, but Dix hadn't quite finished name dropping. "Yes and we get movie stars too, Lynn Redgrave's another Regency regular…" "Oh she was in Georgy Girl" Freddie interrupted "I saw it, remember Athol and the Seekers had a huge hit with the song, it was right after we'd started, I hadn't met Athol yet" Freddie paused for a moment thinking, "So there are people actually paying full price to fly Regency now," he said sarcastically, as he knew only too well that his controversial Business Class had largely been a flop since November when it was launched. Most of the initial occupants of the re-vamped front cabin were either non-revenue Laker staff, relatives of staff, travel agents, or "bloody free-loading airline executives, like Alastair Pugh" Freddie laughingly concluded as he knew his old BUA route planning manager and BCal Director had checked out Regency already.

Everyone was helping themselves to the 'Laker' logo'd cutlery, Wedgewood china, and bottles of champagne, including his crew members, as Freddie had predicted. "I bet the crew parties are something else now with all the wine and champagne leftovers," Freddie said with a smirk as Laker Airways' rowdy crew shindigs were legendary throughout the industry. Dix knew this only too well having signed numerous apology letters and compensation cheques for wrecked hotel rooms, stained carpets and terrified room service waiters.

"I think we're on the right track, we've hopefully got our re-financing so we can forget about Europe, the Far East and Australia for now and just focus on the States. We need the dollars Greg, so let's get these ads done and start rebranding Laker Airways as not just the cheapest way to Britain… but the best way." "Well much as I hate being 'grounded' in New York, I agree Freddie" Dix responded. "We're almost at the hangar so are you ready?" Freddie laughed, he sensed it was going to be a great day and shouted back "I'm Ready."

# CHAPTER 52

# Collusion at The Waldorf

## The noose tightens

### Wednesday Evening 3rd February, 1982 (London)

On the evening of the 3rd of February, 1982, around a circular table in a secluded alcove off the grand colonnaded dining room of the Waldorf, sat the people who for months had been working to make the refinancing of Laker Airways a reality.

The Waldorf was much more than a hotel. There was literally nothing quite like it and the Waldorf perhaps represented civilised England at its finest.

Established in 1908 by William Waldorf Astor or 'Viscount' Astor, the uniquely curved building followed the line of the semi-circular, tree-lined avenue in the Covent Garden district of central London called Aldwych. The Waldorf was close to all the capital's main attractions. It was equidistant to the financial district of London to the east, commonly referred to as The City and the bustling tourist havens of Mayfair and Soho in the opposite direction. It was also in the heart of London's theatre district. Being an old hotel, it had creaky oak floors, paper thin walls and the doormen had been in jobs passed down through generations. Every afternoon, a traditional English tea was served with buttered scones and a variety of mini sandwiches and delicacies, while guests participated in ballroom dancing, often to the bemusement of the hotel's American guests. Elegantly-dressed couples, sipping champagne and waltzing in the middle of the afternoon wasn't an everyday occurrence in Kansas.

Freddie and the Laker team, except for Bob Beckman who stayed at the Carlton Tower in Knightsbridge or the Savoy, always stayed at the Waldorf whenever they had meetings or licencing hearings at the CAA offices, that were located just up the road. Naturally, Freddie insisted on the airline discount whenever they stayed, although he was typically given a spacious suite, complimentary.

The group of anonymous looking middle-aged men at the table that evening were all people Freddie believed were helping his airline to survive. In fact they were perhaps the only people who could make it happen apart from two men who shared the same Scottish last name and were in St. Louis. The group comprised George Gilhespy of the Midland Bank, Ian McIntosh and Gervaise Boote of the Midland Bank's merchant bank division Samuel Montagu who were overseeing the re-financing, Laker's financial advisor Bill Morrison of Thomson McLintock's who had technically been replaced, and finally David Sedgwick representing the McDonnell Douglas Finance Corporation. Ray Colegate, the powerful and highly influential Economics Director of the CAA rounded out the group; he was the main figure at the dinner. Sedgwick was there to hear what had been decided by the Midland Bank along with the approval of the Bank of England, to save Laker Airways.

Colegate, holding court did most of the talking and laid out the situation as he saw it. Laker's trading advantage was gone except for their lower costs. The airline clearly needed higher load factors as he read out what they were that week on Laker's prime scheduled routes. The traffic was seriously down at the end of January with load factors in the mid-thirties and the forecasts he'd been given by Laker Airways were bleak. The CAA wanted assurance that Freddie could continue trading through the summer, otherwise 'he must stop right away'. The CAA wanted an 'unlimited guarantee' to September, and the amount, Colegate said appeared to not be measurable.

Colegate also stated that the CAA was 'very upset' that John Jones, the Commercial Manager of Laker Airways had told BA that Laker might not fall into line over the proposed IATA fare increases. The ongoing fare war was bound to have casualties and it was time to call it off. Noting the nodding of heads by the Midland representatives at these conclusive remarks, Sedgwick, who had been taking notes during Colegate's rhetoric wrote in his notebook 'there is no chance for Freddie'. Stunned, he realised this was not a meeting to confirm the survival of Laker Airways but instead, a plan to put it out of business. Everything that he had worked toward over the last few months had been a complete waste of time. He could not believe what he was hearing.

Sir Freddie had not been told what was being planned. Neither had John Roney, although both of them knew Morrison was off the Laker account and the Midland had now assigned Bill Mackey, the well known receiver to Laker. Sedgwick had known about the Morrison/Mackey switch since the 1st of February, but was finding out himself at this very dinner just what that meant. He suddenly realised Freddie was in fact being ambushed. Sedgwick knew the promised £4 million from his employers, McDonnell Douglas had not yet been sent to the Midland; this despite assurances just the evening before that if Freddie gave up his applications for the European routes, the funds would be forthcoming. He was seething inside and didn't know what he should do. He naturally felt betrayed by his own company and considered excusing himself from the table, finding a phone and calling Freddie or John Roney immediately to warn them what was being planned. Guilt and anger was coursing through his entire being. He now felt personally responsible for pressuring Freddie to give up his European dream. It was tantamount to blackmail and he hated doing it, but he had been given no choice.

As the dinner ended, Ray Colegate said goodnight and left. The rest sat at the table silently, considering everything that had been said. Ray Colegate, who had been one of Freddie's greatest cheer-leaders, appeared to have lost confidence Laker Airways could be saved without a disproportionate injection of funds that none of the lenders were prepared to pony up. Surely then, that meant the end. Morrison, who had been tasked with assisting Laker's Robbie Robinson didn't raise any objections. He had realised when Kitching had told him he was being replaced by Bill Mackey that it was Midland's intention to put Laker Airways into receivership. Freddie's earlier suspicions about Morrison were proving to be correct and it was now becoming clear where Morrison's loyalties lay. His employer, the esteemed accounting firm Thomson McLintock, not only represented the Midland but also worked with Airbus Industrie.

Sedgwick looked around at all of them sitting there, trying to assess their facial expressions and whether he would be supported if he said that he wanted to immediately call Freddie in New York to tip him off. Before he could say anything, Ian McIntosh, who had now assumed the authoritarian position after Colegate left, said "right that's it then. Tomorrow morning at the Midland. No-one must warn Freddie, OK" he said looking around the table for nods of concurrence. Gilhespy and Boote, both Midland group senior managers nodded, Gilhespy even gave off a wry smile as he knew his boss, Dennis Kitching had been relishing this moment for some time.

McIntosh then looked at Morrison who hesitated, perhaps having some last pangs of guilt at his involvement in the plan. He had got to like all the Laker people during his time there, especially Laker's Financial Director Robinson who he felt was unfairly under the gun. No-one spoke. They knew Morrison had mixed loyalties and while he hadn't exactly 'gone native' and become a Laker man, it was obvious he was conflicted about what to do. The silence of the others at the table was intimidating. Morrison realised his salary was paid by McLintocks and therefore his allegiance had to be with the Midland group even if they had removed him from the Laker assignment. Slowly and without making eye contact with anyone, he nodded his head. That left only David Sedgwick. He was the 'outsider' at the table. Everyone else worked for the Midland or an associated entity. Sedgwick worked for the McDonnells and his allegiances were to the McDonnell Douglas Corporation and to its customer airlines. His loyalties were not to banks or lending institutions of MDC's customers, although on occasion he had to do the bidding of bankers if MDC wanted to make a sale. Some of his work was clearly distasteful, but he felt no affinity to the Midland group and the others around the table knew it. In fact, at that moment he felt nothing but hostility towards everyone he was with. They were all undoubtedly wondering if Sedgwick would spoil their party.

Finally, instead of nodding his head like the others, Sedgwick spoke. He said that he felt duty bound to speak with his principals, Sandy and John McDonnell before committing. It went against everything he stood for and Sandy McDonnell would disapprove of an MDC executive participating in anything that wasn't strictly above board. Strangely, none of the others spoke up or tried to dissuade Sedgwick from acting on his conscience. The Midland men said their good-byes and left together. They were perhaps going to continue the discussion elsewhere. Morrison remained behind looking at Sedgwick. It was clear he was now feeling some guilt and perhaps wished he hadn't nodded his head in agreement. "I'm going to call Sandy then Freddie" Sedgwick said. Freddie's still in New York and his flight doesn't leave for another few hours. I can stop him from coming back." Morrison's face told Sedgwick he wasn't sure that was a good idea and he finally said, "I'm planning to go over and tell Roney in the morning that he should come to the Midland." Sedgwick told him by then it would be too late. The pair got up, collected their coats and quickly left the Waldorf. Morrison said "goodnight, see you tomorrow" leaving Sedgwick to wonder just where Morrison stood. He knew Morrison had been removed from the Laker account but he hadn't lost his job, merely his assignment. By Monday, he would be given something else to do and wouldn't even think about Laker Airways or his replacement, Bill Mackey, whose mission was now crystal clear.

Sedgwick walked towards the Strand trying to hail a cab but they all had their orange 'taxi' lights off as they sped by him. He continued to walk fast, thinking about nothing else other than what he was going to say to Freddie when he got him on the phone. Sedgwick knew he was in the middle of filming his TV commercials, but he had to warn Freddie that he was about to be ambushed.

# CHAPTER 53

# Take Two - Action

## High jinks in the hangar

### Wednesday 3rd February, 1982 (New York)

Fred Levinson was sitting in one of the Regency cabin's first class seats of the DC-10 parked inside United Airlines' hangar at JFK on the 3rd February, 1982. He had arrived at the site early and was sipping coffee while quietly observing the production crew readying the aircraft for the shoot. Levinson was renowned as one of the top advertising directors in the country and Laker Airways' U.S. advertising agency, Lord, Geller, Federico, & Einstein (LGFE) had called in a few favours to secure his services. He had been hired to direct the new Laker Airways' TV campaign for the spring/summer 1982 North Atlantic Skytrain service. Levinson's camera 'grip' was busy setting up the Panaflex 35mm motion picture film camera for him; he preferred to operate the main camera himself, as well as direct the shoot. This was the only 'location' shoot Levinson would direct for the campaign. They'd already done a few days in the studio filming the actors and celebrities for their cameo appearances slated for the end of the 60-second TV commercials. The New York Yankees' owner, George Steinbrenner had been the agency's big coup for Laker Airways' new and controversial 'Regency' first-class service, that had been introduced the prior November. The LGFE creative team had pulled out all the stops once the basic theme of the campaign had been formulated... almost by chance at a lunchtime session just a few months earlier at the agency's Madison Avenue offices.

A separate crew were preparing to do the still shots of Freddie on top of the aircraft. They didn't have long to accomplish this or it would compromise the filming schedule. By the time the stills were done, Levinson would have run through the script with Laker's Meg, Amanda and Steve and the dozen extras who would all be made up and stylised for their parts. Everyone was already there and being prepared by a small army of wardrobe assistants, stylists and make-up artists. A movie set type trailer, parked inside the hangar next to the DC-10 had been rented for this purpose. The director's thoughts were interrupted as one of the agency's production staff came up and suggested he may want to consider placing his Panaflex 35mm motion picture camera on the crane they had for the still shoot's Hasselblad and get a few seconds of footage of Freddie on top of the plane. This hadn't been scheduled or even thought about prior, and it was tempting, especially as it would create some continuity with the print ad campaign. But knowing they had a full day ahead and the plane was needed for the London flight early that evening, they decided to stick with the plan and not risk the schedule, or the expensive rented Panaflex. Another cherry picker, normally used for maintenance on United's DC-10 vertical stabilisers would take Freddie and a production assistant thirty feet above the hangar floor. The crew had hung an array of Fresnel lights from the girders of the hangar roof that lit the forward part of the aircraft. It had been freshly washed down on arrival the previous evening, making it look almost surreal, as well as immense. One of New York's best portrait photographers had been hired by the agency to shoot Freddie standing on top of the plane with his arms outstretched, smiling. There was an element of risk in scheduling the stills to precede the main shoot as typically a photography session of this sort would take a full day. But with Freddie's itinerary being so tight, they had no choice.

Dix had briefed all the production people that Freddie was really easy-going and he would do anything that was asked of him. It was a hard sell. All they'd ever seen of Freddie was interviews on TV with him answering tough questions and trying to convince journalists and viewers that his company was solvent. An earlier, very brief meeting with him at the agency after they had won the Laker Airways' account proved him to be anything but jovial and easy-going. To the LGFE creative team, Freddie Laker didn't seem like someone who would be comfortable on camera or do 'impromptu' naturally. Little did they know.

"Meg!" Freddie yelled as he leapt out of Dix's big Chevy wagon he had driven into the hangar. The vivacious blonde-haired senior In-Flight Director was standing in her bright red Laker Airways' uniform by the makeup trailer. Bucking the new almost midi-length Laker uniform dress code, Meg's hemline was a good 3-4 inches above the knee, just as Freddie liked it, and she had the legs to carry it off. Obviously thrilled to see a familiar face and one of his favourites, Freddie gave her a mighty hug with his trademark backside patting and a proper kiss on both cheeks. "I'll only kiss you on two cheeks not the usual all four today" was one of Freddie's favourite flirtatious greetings, no matter who was in his grasp. "It's a good job they haven't done my hair and make-up or you'd be in trouble" she admonished laughing; "you look well Sir Freddie, did you get some sleep or were you out on the raz last night," she jokingly quizzed her boss. Meg was on very familiar terms with Freddie after years of being on the road with him doing Laker Airways' promotions and PR activities. "Well Dix and I would have taken you and Amanda to Plato's but he made me get an early night. I think we're going to have a good day Meg, have you seen the script?" "Yes and we all think it's really great, the agency guys have given us these buttons they made up, look." Freddie took the two and half inch white button she handed him and read it aloud... "I'm Ready for Sir Freddie." He stared at the button silently and for a moment his eyes glistened, but he quickly broke out of it and grabbed Vesty again in another bear hug, "well you better be ready for Freddie my girl and where's Amanda, she better be ready too." Freddie was fired up now and feeling properly energised. "He's obviously ready for something," Meg said aloud to the crew, straightening her dress down and laughing as she disappeared into the trailer to be prepped. The agency personnel just stood there wide-eyed, incredulous at the scene they had just witnessed.

Dix walked up, "Freddie, I want you to meet Victor Emmanuelle, he's our account exec with the agency and he's been more or less living in our office for the last few months and this is Fred Levinson, your Director for the shoot." He shook hands with Victor and the two Fred's met eyes, shook hands warmly and before Levinson could even say hello, Freddie blurted out "Fred, Victor, I am so sorry you guys have been jerked around so much, it's all my fault and I apologise. I've had a hell of a time of it. I'm still not completely out of the woods but we're looking pretty good now and I'm really looking forward to working with you. So just tell me what to do, where to stand, what to say and when... and I'll do it." The renowned director looked quite surprised at this humility, he wasn't used to his 'star' being so easy-going. Usually he had to deal with egos, tantrums and even 'A' list celebrities walking off his sets in a huff. After a similarly respectful exchange back to Freddie and a "good luck up there, see you later" it was time for Freddie to be suited, coiffed and made up for his still photos on top of the DC-10.

Several weeks earlier, after the entire 'Ready for Sir Freddie' campaign had been mapped out, there was still some uncertainty that Freddie would be able to pull it off. The agency had been briefed Freddie was embroiled in re-financing discussions as well as his on-going domestic tug of war. They'd read the newspaper reports that Laker Airways was going out of business and they'd grilled Dix at their regular meetings as to whether the airline would make it. The numerous delays and rescheduling of the shoot had made them nervous and didn't help an already tense situation. They'd been paid for the interim print ads and for the media placement, but they were on the hook for today's shoot with Freddie. The bill for the studio time and the celebrities they'd hired for the ten second tags at the end of each sixty second TV spot was still pending. It was a massive financial undertaking for a relatively small agency and the principals were naturally skittish. So when Freddie arrived at the United hangar and immediately started hugging one of the girls, laughing and just being himself, the assembled agency team breathed a huge sigh of relief. They didn't know what to expect as they'd only ever met Freddie once before and at that initial meeting he was clearly preoccupied, dour and distant. Now, they were seeing the real Freddie Laker for the first time. And they realised why Dix and Linda Earls at that earlier November meeting had been disapproving of the first campaigns they'd presented. They had been right. In just a few minutes of his being on location for the shoot, they were seeing an entirely different Freddie Laker to what they'd expected, or seen on TV fending off awkward questions. 'If he can maintain this temperament' they said amongst themselves, 'he's going to knock it out of the park today'.

"Why don't you come up, the view's great from here" Freddie yelled down to no-one in particular and everyone in general. "Can you kill the lights for a sec while I get to my spot, I can't see a bloody thing," as he shaded his eyes from the glare. Once the lights had been doused he gingerly made his way to the front of the aircraft and stood on the roof above the number one door and the British flag, awaiting his directions. He didn't look at all scared. One of the production assistants stood nervously about ten feet back and out of the frame. He wasn't sure why he'd been told to accompany Freddie to the top of the aircraft as there wouldn't me much he could do if Freddie slipped. But Freddie wasn't about to slip. He'd owned and operated boats for decades, so he had superb balance and he was wearing his Sperry Topsiders with their patented non-skid soles. The crew had offered to tether him with a safety harness but he had declined saying it would wreck the look of his suit. The Fresnels came back on bathing the aircraft and Freddie in light. Everyone came out and stood watching, looking up nervously. Even United's maintenance crews took a break and came over to see one of the industry's most renowned personalities standing on top of one of the world's biggest planes. The camera platform rose up to get the best angle for the optimum impression of size and height of the plane. The idea was to shoot it so Freddie looked quite small standing atop the huge aircraft. They'd checked it before he'd arrived with a nervous stand-in placed on his spot, but with Freddie there, some minute adjustments were now necessary. "OK, we're going to do a couple of Polaroids first Freddie, arms outstretched please as if you're inviting someone on to your plane, here we go." The large Kodak Polaroid camera took its one shot and the camera was handed to the photographer's assistant. After a few seconds she pulled the film out of the camera, waving it in the air to dry and handed it to her boss who reviewed it with the agency's creative director and Dix. After a couple more Polaroids followed by minor adjustments and with everyone satisfied they had the right angle for the shot, Freddie was directed to assume his posture. The Hasselblad's shutter started clicking.

"That was fun, I'd never been up there before on the DC-10. I've stood on the wings and inside the engines but I'd never been on the top, did you get something usable," Freddie asked excitedly wishing he could see what he'd just done. "Here's the Polaroids, but they aren't really representative, you'll have to wait a few days for the real thing Sir Freddie" replied the photographer's assistant, just as the familiar squawk of a woman's voice was heard nearby. "Oh god Dix, didn't you send her home with the others" Freddie's mood suddenly shifted from jovial to annoyed as the all too familiar cackling of his publicity officer could be heard echoing across the vast United hangar. Mrs Flood's presence on the set quickly changed the atmosphere. The agency team knew her already as she and Charles Maxwell had been the ones to instigate LGFE's bid for the Laker account back in the Spring of 1981. For some reason, Maxwell and Flood thought Laker Airways had run its course with New York's esteemed advertising agency, D'Arcy, McManus and Masius and needed a new marketing direction. It probably wasn't the smartest time to switch advertising agencies given Laker's dire situation on the North Atlantic. It was either done out of desperation or because D'Arcy wanted out, which is more likely. However, LGFE's award-winning IBM personal computer campaign had impressed the Laker decision makers and so they had landed the account. It was their first airline or travel company. Freddie hadn't been involved in the ad agency selection decision for the first time ever; he typically always had the last say when it came to anything brand related and marketing but he'd been too tied up with everything else he had going on with the company's refinancing and his personal problems. Nevertheless, LGFE seemed like a good choice, Freddie thought when he had reviewed the latest campaign in the car. He didn't know what had transpired the previous November when Dix and Linda Earls had steered the LGFE team in a different direction, or how much time the LGFE team had spent learning everything there was to know about the company.

Strategically, and with Cliff Nunn's approval, Robin Flood had been excluded from the formulation of the new ad campaign and was as surprised as anyone when she read the scripts. She had been deliberately kept out of the loop but now was itching to inject herself into the day's proceedings. Whenever Freddie was scheduled for something to do with advertising, publicity or in fact just about anything at all, Mrs Flood felt duty bound to be at his side, annoyingly fussing over him. For some reason, perhaps known only to the two of them, Freddie tolerated her. They had a bizarre 'odd-couple' type relationship that he didn't exactly encourage and seemed mostly exasperated by, yet couldn't disengage from. Flood was obsessed with him, often to his embarrassment. Freddie's first wife Joan, hated her and the influence she had over him. Today however, none of the production team were going to stand for any unwanted interference. Dix had been told by the agency and the director that if Flood made a nuisance of herself he would have to literally fling her off the plane.

Freddie was already made up and his hair neat and tidy from the still shoot, so he only needed a quick powder down on his face and a final makeover. The charcoal double-breasted suit the agency had purchased fit perfectly and he clearly looked the part. "Hallo hallo ladies," he air-kissed the two smiling red-uniformed girls so as not to smudge their make-up. He gave Amanda an embarrassingly obvious full up and down check out as he entered the DC-10's cabin, now transformed into a movie set. Freddie got away with salaciousness and behaviour that would land anyone else in hot water. "Steve, I'd kiss you too but I'm told that you're actually quite a ladies man" as Freddie shook the young steward's hand with both of his, winking knowingly and laughing. The handsome young man looked clearly embarrassed that his boss may know something about him. Freddie excused himself from his three exquisitely turned out cabin staff who were scheduled to be in the next scene after his opener and turned to the director, who was waiting patiently. The lights were all on, technicians were manning tape machines, grips were standing by to do any lighting adjustments the director called for. "Where do you want me Fred?" One of the production assistants came over and guided Freddie to his spot marked with an X in gaffer's tape on the cabin floor. "OK Freddie, here's what we're going to do. We'll start off with you looking straight ahead, after you hear 'action' continue looking ahead for a few seconds so I can push in on your profile. Then you turn to the camera, smile and say your lines, or rather your line, as it's only five words. Think you can remember them or do you need a cue card," Levinson said laughing, which prompted a chuckle from the dozen production crew, agency personnel and Laker representatives. "He always likes to have a cue card," a shrill voice shouted from the back in an octave usually only dogs can hear, which brought a scowl from the Director. 'Oh god, here we go' thought Dix, standing next to Levinson, thinking he'd have the unenviable task of booting her off the set. "Let's just try one Freddie." "OK, I'm ready" Freddie replied, with a grin and flirtatious wink as he looked directly at Amanda.

With that, the director called for quiet on the set.' The air conditioning unit below was silenced, a couple more lights blazed on, the camera's record button was pressed as the production assistant said "Freddie scene one, take one." The director called 'action' to cue the talent to commence his part. The camera was rolling but Freddie stood frozen on his spot looking straight ahead with a deadly serious look on his face for an extraordinary long time. Standing next to the camera, Dix wondered if for once in his life Freddie had stage fright or if all the troubles that had plagued him for the past eight months had now come flooding back. The seconds ticked by and the crew and agency personnel looked anxious. They all thought the director would call for a cut at any moment for Freddie to regain his composure. They needn't have worried as he eventually turned to the camera as directed, smiled and delivered his lines, all five words… and without a cue card. "OK cut, relax for a minute Freddie, I need an adjustment as he ushered a grip to change the positioning of one of the soft lights. "Right, lets try another, this time a slightly longer pause after 'ready' OK." Freddie nodded in acknowledgment and now appeared to be fully present, "OK let's do it." "Quiet on the set. Freddie scene one, take two. Roll speed, stick please, and… action." Freddie, now fully composed and focused, paused, looked ahead for a few seconds as directed, then turned to the camera, cracked one of his signature contrived smiles and in his inimitable persuasive voice recited his opening line: "Are you Ready… for Freddie."

"Cut. Much better Freddie, take five everyone. After a short break during which Freddie seemed lost in his thoughts for a few minutes, he resumed his takes. He nailed it and after they'd shot the safety take, they went quickly to Scene 2 with Meg, Amanda and Steve and the Regency service scenes with the extras. The shoot lasted over five hours and they had enough footage to make several sixty-second TV commercials for Skytrain, including special Regency service ads. The agency personnel were overjoyed after being quite tense before the shoot about what may happen, or not happen. The heat in the aircraft cabin was excruciating. They had an air conditioning unit plugged in outside but it had to be turned off during the takes, as it was quite loud. The dozen extras who had been hired to simulate passengers in the cabin were patient and had taken their direction well. The Laker flight crew team were stars in their own right and seemed to relish their new acting roles. Meg and Steve were especially vibrant while the more demure Amanda gave the scenes a touch of elegance, especially in the Regency service takes. Dix as the company's de facto 'executive producer' for the campaign was thrilled with what they had accomplished. He couldn't wait to start the post-production and editing for the various ads with the LGFE creative team. The only interruption to the shoot had been when Robin Flood was called to take a phone call in one of United's hangar offices. It was Lesley Chilton with an urgent message for Freddie. Flood had rushed back on board the aircraft to deliver the message personally to Freddie, but Dix had stopped her and asked what it was all about. She relayed the message Lesley had given her and insisted on giving Sir Freddie the message immediately. Dix put his foot down and told her absolutely not, he didn't want Freddie distracted when he was on a roll, potentially wrecking his state of mind and compromising what they were doing. The urgent message was that Freddie had been summoned to a meeting at the Midland Bank in London the next morning, immediately upon arrival back in England. Apart from that narrowly averted hiccup, the entire day went better than anyone expected.

When director Levinson finally clicked off his Panaflex and announced "ok everyone, thanks for all your good work, that's a wrap" they all cheered and more bottles of Regency Service Moet & Chandon were expertly uncorked by Meg, Steve and Amanda. The crew immediately started breaking down the lights, as the plane had to operate GK20 to Gatwick in less than three hours.

Everyone toasted a good day's work amid lots of laughter and congratulations all round. Freddie downed several glasses of fizz in short order and then got boisterous with the girls, obviously making up for lost time. Meg and Amanda were typically good sports, as you had to be if you worked for Laker Airways. They went along with Freddie's high-handed, amorous behaviour and were happy to see him back to being his old self again. He was after all, known to be one of the most outrageously flirtatious and lascivious bosses in the world... and he had his reputation to uphold.

In the closing moments of the impromptu wrap party and after a few more glasses of Moet, Freddie who by now was on top form, partying hard and fairly inebriated, spotted a roll of gaffer's tape and peeled off a piece. He stalked Robin Flood from behind as she was chattering away to one of the production crew, who seeing what was about to happen, sensibly ducked out of the way. Freddie pounced on the unsuspecting Flood, slapped the sticky tape around her mouth and hauled her back into one of the Regency class seats and onto his lap. She was still clutching her glass of bubbly as Freddie, laughing his head off yelled, "maybe this will bloody well shut you up once and for all."

Everyone clapped and cheered. It was a fitting finale to what had been a very good day indeed.

# CHAPTER 54

# Ambush

## Why didn't you warn me?

3rd & 4th February, 1982

It was more than a mile and a half from the Waldorf back to the Intercontinental Hotel on Hyde Park Corner. By the time David Sedgwick had arrived at Trafalgar Square he'd given up trying to hail a cab. He picked his pace up as he started down the Mall. The lights of Buckingham Palace twinkled a half mile down the arrow straight, tree-lined boulevard that even late in the evening was still populated by tourists. He urgently needed to speak with John and Sandy McDonnell about what had gone down at the Waldorf earlier that evening. It was obvious that all the Midland executives were anxious to see the back of Laker Airways, as well as the man whose name was on the side of the planes.

It was only six o'clock in the evening in St Louis by the time he got back to his room around midnight. Sedgwick called John McDonnell at home and told him what had happened at the Waldorf earlier. He received a curt response, as if the younger McDonnell knew it would come to this when the £4 million MDC had promised wasn't sent. Sandy McDonnell listened to his report of the whole sorry business without offering any solution or in fact giving any opinion, beyond expressing sadness. He acknowledged Sedgwick for his diligence but assured him MDC couldn't do much more than they already had. In closing, McDonnell told him that nothing must be said to Freddie, which placed the MDC Finance Senior VP in a compromising position.

Sedgwick was feeling nervous, he couldn't reach Jim McMillan who'd cut his phone off. He poured himself a drink from the mini-bar, seconds later the phone rang. "Hallo, David, how're you doing? I'm at the airport and about to get on the plane." Sedgwick hesitated for a moment before acknowledging. His voice was shaky, then Freddie asked him just what he had hoped he wouldn't. "Is everything still OK David." Sedgwick, by now at his wits end, responded by saying that 'yes everything was OK except the CAA wasn't satisfied with the cash availability'. Freddie had been dealing with bankers, lawyers and accountants long enough to be able to read between the lines. "David, level with me," Freddie's tone was now not friendly, "is everything really OK." Sedgwick could feel the sweat beading on his forehead. He hated telling lies and recalled what Sandy McDonnell had instilled into all the executives of MDC about integrity above all else. He wondered why his CEO was now not following his own principles. After a few seconds of silence Sedgwick finally replied "Yes Freddie, everything's fine" his hand holding the phone was shaking nervously. He could still tip Freddie off. What should he do? Freddie didn't respond, it wasn't like Freddie not to say anything. The line was silent for a couple of seconds that felt like minutes. Finally he said, "See you tomorrow Freddie, have a good flight." Sedgwick wanted the call to end as soon as possible and prayed Freddie wouldn't dig deeper and ask him more questions. He heard someone beckoning Freddie to go to the gate as the doors were about to close and he breathed a sigh of relief as he said slowly "OK goodnight David, see you in the morning." And in that moment, David Sedgwick had made his decision. He knew he was culpable and it would be something he'd have to live with for the rest of his life.

Freddie was seen into the cabin of the Laker DC-10 by Greg Dix. He thanked Dix again for the hard work of the US teams in preparing the 1982 sales and advertising programmes and said he'd see him soon. He stuck his head into the cockpit and said hello to the flight crew and acknowledged Meg, Amanda and Steve who were already strapped into their seats, giving them a thumbs up for a job well done. There were over thirty revenue passengers in the front cabin for the GK20 flight to London and the main cabin was almost full due to the cancelled flight the night before. But it was still less than half of what they had been carrying at the same time the year before. Despite the grueling day and all the champagne he'd consumed at the wrap party, Freddie still had the energy to do a quick round of handshakes with the Regency passengers before finally tucking himself into seat 1A. He was exhausted and soon after take off began to fall asleep while wondering about the call with Sedgwick and why MDC hadn't sent the promised £4 million.

Six hours later he was woken by the In-Flight Director as the DC-10 was on its final approach to Gatwick. It was 7:00am local time when the aircraft came to a standstill, fifteen minutes ahead of schedule. As usual, Ops had arranged for Customs to clear Freddie on the plane.

As soon as the door opened and the stairs were positioned for disembarkation, a Laker Airways' staffer ran across the tarmac handing him a note from Lesley Chilton. 'Please go to the Midland Bank as early as you can this morning.' Freddie had already received the message the day before so this was merely a reminder. He wondered briefly what could be so important but assumed it must be routine paperwork he had to sign for the financing package. He then hopped into an engineering department van and was driven around the airport perimeter road to the Laker Airways' headquarters building. Climbing the stairs to the second floor he stopped by Operations as he always did. Once he'd seen the movement board showing everything was on time and had chatted briefly to the day shift operations staff, he went up to his third floor office to shower and shave in his private bathroom. Having changed into fresh clothes, Freddie walked back down to the car park, got into his Jaguar and drove to London up the M23 motorway listening to the Today programme on the radio. He was completely oblivious to what had taken place the night before at the Waldorf Hotel and he hadn't spoken to anyone; unlike the Rolls his Jaguar sedan didn't have a car phone. Assuming traffic wasn't too bad by the time he was near Southwark Bridge, he estimated that he would be at the Midland by around 9:30am.

Meanwhile, Freddie's lawyer, John Roney was heading to his office at London Wall in the City. Roney had no idea that it was the Midland's intention to close Laker Airways down. In his phone call to George Gilhespy just the day before, he hadn't brought up Mackey and had merely suggested that switching from McClintocks to Ernst & Whinney at this point may be problematic for Laker Airways' Financial Director Robbie Robinson. Roney, like Freddie had been hoodwinked into thinking that Ernst and Whinney's Bill Mackey was being installed to ostensibly 'assist' Laker Airways in place of Morrison.

As he was settling in for the day, Roney received an unexpected telephone call from Bill Morrison, who enquired if he was going to the meeting at the Midland that morning and if they should go together. Roney knew nothing about it, he had not been invited and said he was not intending to go. Morrison insisted that he had better go and shortly afterwards he appeared at Roney's office, which was not far from his own. He proceeded to tell Roney what had transpired the evening before at the Waldorf and what was about to happen. Roney hurriedly pulled on his coat and he and Morrison set off on the short walk to the Midland Bank's HQ together that was located on a City of London street named simply 'Poultry'.

Freddie parked his Jaguar behind the bank and the receptionist told him to go straight up. A large conference room had been prepared on the fourth floor for a meeting of 12 people but Freddie was shown into a small bare room next to the one that had been prepared. This was deliberate so Freddie could be advised of the position in private to avoid any humiliation in front of a large gathering. He sat down and waited. The door opened. It was John Roney and Bill Morrison, whom Freddie had been told was now replaced. They exchanged greetings and it was Morrison who broke the news: "The Midland has decided it can no longer support the growing financial requirements of Laker Airways." Freddie was stunned and looked at Roney, his eyes asking 'when did you know about all this?' George Gilhespy, the Midland's General Manager entered the room. He closed the door behind him, and leaned his back against it nervously. Gilhespy looked at Freddie and confirmed what he had just been told. Laker's overdraft provided by the Clydesdale Bank would be withdrawn within the hour. "Sir Freddie, I want you to call in the receivers," said Gilhespy moving away from the door. "When?" asked Freddie. "Now" answered Gilhespy. Before Freddie had time to respond, the door opened again and David Sedgwick appeared. Freddie looked directly at him and said, "Did you know about this when I rang you last night?" "Yes," admitted Sedgwick, his voice trembling. Freddie glared at him "I knew it, I could tell you were hiding something. Why did you lie?" Freddie bristled and by now was extremely angry. "I was instructed not to say anything," replied Sedgwick, visibly shaking and perhaps wondering if the burly six-footer standing a few feet away would walk over and deck him.

Freddie looked at Morrison; he too confirmed he had been sworn to secrecy and that they all had. Next, Ian McIntosh of Samuel Montagu walked in and he too confirmed the need for secrecy. McIntosh had nothing further to say and sat down to listen. Freddie also sat down, stunned. He turned his attention back to Gilhespy who had positioned himself back against the door: "Why must I call in the receivers?" Gilhespy explained that the CAA had requested the Midland Bank and McDonnell Douglas to provide an unlimited guarantee to see Laker Airways through to the end of summer 1982 and neither the Midland nor McDonnell Douglas were willing to do this. "That's impossible, they wouldn't, I want to call the CAA right now." Gilhespy pointed to the telephone situated at the end of the room, "you can use that one." Freddie pulled out his address book and found Ray Colegate's direct line number. He carefully dialed 379-7311 on the rotary phone, which was Colegate's private line at the CAA and waited. His secretary answered and put Colegate on the line.

"Hallo, Ray. It's Freddie Laker. I'm at the Midland. They want me to call in the receivers. They tell me that you demand an open ended guarantee." Colegate paused for a moment collecting his thoughts before responding. He wasn't going to be held personally responsible for the destruction of Laker Airways and replied: "That's not true, I merely posed the question, 'what if Freddie needs a little more...' that's all." Freddie had what he wanted, an admission from Colegate that the CAA had not requested an unlimited guarantee. They chatted some more and Colegate reiterated the CAA's position on the airline getting through the tricky March and April period and into the summer high season, when cash flow would help see the airline through. He said that a collapse had to be avoided between March and September, as it would cause the most disruption for passengers and a maximum call on the Air Travel Reserve Fund. To get through to September, Freddie's lenders would not only have to provide sufficient 'headroom' but also support the company even if it did require more funds later. Colegate said he understood that this may have been interpreted by the bank as an unlimited guarantee 'in the sense that the effect of any further adverse circumstances could not be quantified'. Given the present economic climate and the economic forecasts for 1982, this was a fair comment. Freddie knew the longer the call lasted the worse it would get and realised he wasn't getting any more out of Colegate. He hung up and dialed the number for Sir Nigel Foulkes, chairman of the CAA and Colegate's boss. Foulkes came on the line. Freddie told him that he was at the Midland Bank and they had told him to call in the receivers. He asked if it was true that the CAA had asked for an unlimited guarantee. Like Colegate, Foulkes denied it. This time Freddie kept it short, thanked Foulkes for his support and hung up the telephone.

Gilhespy was still in the room, leaning back against the door. His claim that the CAA had asked for an open-ended guarantee that underpinned the Midland's reasoning to call the overdraft had been demolished. But it made no difference, Gilhespy was adamant that Laker Airways was finished, there was nothing more that could be done. He said Freddie had no support and gave him until two o'clock to pull the plug. With that, Gilhespy opened the door and left. Freddie beckoned John Roney and they walked down the corridor out of earshot of Morrison and Sedgwick. "John, what's going on?" Roney replied: "Freddie, it's the end. They are absolutely determined to put you out of business. There is nothing you can do about it. If they don't get you today, it will be tomorrow, or Monday. The airline business is based on public confidence. Passengers and travel agents will not buy tickets in advance if they think the airline will stop operating." Freddie listened. He and Roney had known each other for more than eight years. While Freddie trusted Roney and knew there was practical sense to what Roney said, he didn't accept there was 'nothing he could do about it' as Roney had stated. That wasn't Freddie Laker and Roney should have known it. Of course, if the Midland made a public announcement that Laker Airways did not have sufficient finance it could well be the end, Freddie thought, 'but would they dare do that?' Any other man would have accepted the inevitable. But Freddie refused to give up. He thought of his over 2,500 employees. He thought of his four-year-old son, Freddie Allen who he wanted nothing more than to take over from him when he was old enough. He thought of how it all began after the untimely death of his first son Kevin. He thought of his mother Hannah and the sacrifices she'd made for him to get where he was. Freddie pulled himself together and walked back in.

He spent most of the next couple of hours on the phone. He talked to McIntosh and Sedgwick and Morrison and Kitching, refusing to accept that Laker Airways was finished. Around lunchtime, Freddie telephoned Iain Sproat, the British parliamentary Undersecretary for Trade. Sproat already knew what had happened. Prime Minister Margaret Thatcher had been briefed throughout the process and was also well informed. Nevertheless, Thatcher made a public display of going through the motions, calling a meeting of senior cabinet ministers and members of the Treasury including the chancellor, Sir Geoffrey Howe. She also spoke to Ray Colegate. Ironically, that very day, and in those same meetings, she had authorised £53 million to be paid to British Airways to cover redundancies. She had briefly considered a cash injection of £5 million for Laker Airways on the condition that it would be an end to the matter and said to Colegate: "I can't bear to think of all my passengers being stranded abroad, my passengers, my poor passengers. Couldn't we put in £5 million and put a ring fence about it so that is the end of the story?" But Colegate told her that it wouldn't be the end of the story and it would essentially be an open-ended situation. There would be the same decision to face again in two or three months' time. She said, "Oh dear, an open-ended situation. I couldn't wish that upon my poor taxpayers." But she knew it was wholly inconsistent of the British government to be funding British Airways' redundancies and refusing to help the 2,500 employees of Laker Airways. Colegate readily admitted that he found the dichotomy of the Prime Minister's situation all 'rather astonishing'.

The monumental losses being racked up on a yearly basis at the state owned British Airways were caused mostly by poor management. Laker's problems were partly caused by a recession that a large part of had been perpetuated by Thatcher's extreme austerity policies. In the Commons that afternoon Sir Michael Neubert, the Conservative MP for Romford, brought up the tricky facts and pointed out that British Airways was still flying the flag for Britain with a loss of £120 million. What had taken place within Laker Airways looked insignificant by comparison. Iain Sproat stood up and corrected Neubert. British Airways had in fact made an eye-watering pre-tax loss of £141 million, all from the British taxpayer's pocket. British Airways' external borrowings, the loans that it had taken out to purchase aircraft were £800 million, double its equity capital. BA's overall debt stood at £500 million, and rising. Sproat, who had lobbied hard for British Airways' privatisation, continued, "The Government has to look closely at the way in which taxpayers' money is being used to prop up nationalised industries." The next morning George Clark in *The Times* newspaper quoted a senior government source as saying: 'Everyone, a number of ministers and the Prime Minister were considering everything and anything that could reasonably be done to help Sir Freddie. However, the conclusion was that no government intervention was advisable... or possible'.

Prime Minister Margaret Thatcher was caught between a rock and a hard place. It was a dilemma she had never faced before and her decision could not be made lightly. Much as she personally wanted to save her friend Freddie Laker, in her role as head of state she had to take the advice of her ministers and economists on the matter, especially the CAA's Ray Colegate, arguably the most knowledgeable of all of them. Acting against her key advisers on the Laker Airways' issue would set a precedent for every private business in the country to ask for a government bail out when they were in trouble. After due consideration, regrettably, the PM was forced to take the harder line.

The two o'clock deadline was fast approaching. Freddie went to find David Sedgwick and brought him back to the conference room. John Gentling of MDC's Finance arm arrived after he had been summoned from his hotel room. Incredibly, Gentling had been oblivious to what was happening. Sedgwick, with whom he had been working closely on the refinancing, had not informed Gentling or his MDC colleague O.P. Curtis that Kitching had a receiver on short notice, or what had happened the previous night at the Waldorf dinner. Gentling and Curtis had been left behind in a room at the Intercontinental working on the numbers which they had received from Laker's John Jones and Robbie Robinson the night before. They were working on justifying the £4 million capital facility from MDC in exchange for non-voting shares; that was supposedly already agreed. For reasons unknown, they had been excluded from the latest situation. Needless to say, Gentling, a senior Vice President of MDC Finance, was disappointed and annoyed, with good reason.

Just before 2:00pm Freddie said: "So, what does the Midland want?" No one answered. "All right," he said, "let's get Kitching in here and find out what he wants." Sedgwick went to find Kitching in his office. "Freddie wants to talk to you," he said. Kitching got up from his desk and walked with Sedgwick to the conference room where everyone had gathered. Freddie stood up, looked straight at Kitching, and said, "Tell me what you want?"

"I want MDC's five million pounds right now and five million in thirty days," said Kitching. "Right," said Freddie. Kitching left. Everyone was shocked; MDC's Gentling thought the demands were unreasonable and unjustifiable. The demands made by Kitching weren't what any of them had been working towards. Kitching had effectively asked Freddie for a blank cheque.

The United States would soon be open for business and it was time to call the McDonnells. "Let's talk to Sandy," Said Freddie. Sanford 'Sandy' McDonnell was chairman of McDonnell Douglas. He had joined MDC in 1948 as a trainee stress engineer with a boat load of degrees from Princeton and the University of Colorado in both economics and engineering. He had turned down his uncle's starting offer of janitor. Eventually he had succeeded his uncle in 1980 when James S. McDonnell, known as 'Mac' died. Laker Airways had bought over $300 million worth of DC-10 aircraft and spares from MDC during the preceding ten years. Sandy McDonnell preached good corporate citizenship, and his concern with ethics reflected his personal code of conduct. Surely he of all people would not abandon Freddie Laker. Just three days earlier, on Monday night, Sedgwick and McMillan had told Freddie that everything was agreed. They had given him their blessing to go to New York and plan the 1982 programme with his key executives and make his commercials. Certainly, thought Freddie, MDC will honour the agreement they had made in principle already for £4 million and he thought he could convince them to find the extra £1 million Kitching was demanding that was originally coming from GE. After all, £5 million for MDC was a drop in the bucket for them.

Sedgwick took out his address book. It was only eight o'clock in St Louis. Sedgwick dialed the phone he knew rang in Sandy McDonnell's bedroom. "Good morning, Sandy. It's Freddie Laker here. "I've got a problem and I need your support." McDonnell interrupted him. "I don't handle the finance," he said bluntly. "You'll have to talk to John." Freddie apologised for disturbing him and told him he would do that. John McDonnell was Sandy's younger cousin and the son of the founder. He too had started near the bottom of the ladder as an engineer, but his career began on the highly prestigious NASA collaboration Project Gemini that preceded the Apollo moon landings. Freddie dialed his number and McDonnell's wife told him that John had already left for the office. Freddie hung up and said to Sedgwick, "He's left for the office." 20 minutes later, Sedgwick dialed John McDonnell's direct office line. He came on the line. Freddie explained that he needed £5 million, the four as promised and another £1 million. John McDonnell said they weren't prepared to put up the money and they would not be providing any financial assistance to Laker Airways. It was a conclusive telephone conversation. Inexplicably, Freddie reluctantly accepted what McDonnell had to say with no response. He didn't even remind McDonnell he'd given up Europe just two days earlier for MDC's funding. He looked at Sedgwick as if to say 'you double-crossed me'. Freddie was stunned at the rejection, especially as a half dozen of MDC's most senior executives had worked continually since the summer to save

Laker Airways. The report they had produced and circulated to Laker's lenders was perhaps the most comprehensive analysis of Laker Airways ever completed. Robbie Robinson, Martin Ballard and John Jones had all worked tirelessly to ensure the MDC report was a solid document. When Freddie put down the phone, he rued the day he had mistaken these people for his friends. At that moment he probably wished he had bought Boeing 747s instead of supporting the underdog. Didn't John McDonnell realise that without Freddie supporting the DC-10 when no one else did, McDonnell Douglas probably wouldn't have survived the backlash of the 1979 grounding of the worldwide fleet of DC-10s.

Desperate to save what was left of his credibility, Sedgwick plucked a few ideas out of the air, a possible investment from American Airlines or United. Or a partnership of some kind with one of the smaller US carriers, but it was all hopeless. McIntosh and Morrison had no suggestions. Gilhespy returned and asked Freddie if he had decided a course of action. "No" Freddie replied, he had not done so. The wily Freddie Laker kept an unsuspecting Gilhespy talking as another hour slipped by. At three o'clock it would be too late to put Laker Airways out of business that day. It was then that Dennis Kitching returned to the conference room and made his position crystal clear to Freddie. Unless Laker Airways obtained a cash injection of £5 million by 8:00am the following day, Friday 5th February, the Midland Bank would call the overdraft and stop Laker Airways' cash flow. Freddie and John Roney were left in no doubt that the Midland Bank was deadly serious.

By then, Freddie realised he had been ambushed. Had he known what the meeting was for he would never have come back to England. "Why didn't someone call and warn me" he lamented. "I would have gone straight to McDonnell Douglas in St Louis and then on to Tokyo." Freddie now had only seventeen hours to save his company.

The clock on the wall showed 3pm. After being cornered by the Midland Bank, Freddie had somehow fended them off for nearly six hours and bought himself a bit more time. A stillness came over him, he sat back down, he knew he had to think of something, anything, and fast. "What can I sell tonight to raise £5 million in cash by tomorrow morning?" he asked himself. Then it came to him. He would sell his Airbus A300s to Harry Goodman, the most successful tour operator in England. Failing that, he would offer Goodman his two profitable tour operations, Arrowsmith and Laker Air Travel. Goodman, the Chairman of International Leisure Group, would for sure be able to come up with £10 million. Freddie assumed he had helped Harry Goodman when no one else would. In 1980, Goodman's Intasun began offering package holidays to Miami for £139 and helped fill Laker's new DC-10-30 planes. But Goodman had been none too pleased when Freddie turned the Miami service into a Skytrain route, and then through Laker Air Travel and Arrowsmith, competed directly with Intasun. While they hadn't exchanged harsh words over this, Intasun nevertheless took a hit with the Miami experience and Goodman was no friend of Freddie's... and Freddie should have known it.

Nevertheless, Freddie called Goodman's office, but he was out. He explained that he needed to speak to him urgently. Goodman was in Madrid at a travel show, but his office tracked him down and he called Freddie, who explained the situation. Goodman said that he would fly to London that evening in his private jet, and they agreed to meet in the new Hilton Hotel at Gatwick Airport at 10:00pm. Freddie naively felt sure he could raise £10 million from Goodman that night.

Beleaguered, Freddie left the Midland Bank with John Roney for the 4:30pm appointment with his divorce lawyer. Earlier, on the 25th November 1981, his wife Patricia had applied to the courts for alimony, child support and an order preventing her husband from 'abducting' their son. Freddie had made his own custody application in the British courts for the boy and he'd travelled back and forth to Florida trying to smooth things out. He was optimistic that after he and Patricia had supposedly 'kissed and made up' on a Florida beach on the 10th December, he would get what he so desperately wanted. Over Christmas, she had returned to the UK for a week and Freddie was thrilled to be able to spend the holidays with his son. But Patricia had wrong footed him, blind-siding Freddie for a second time and she had filed for divorce on the 31st December. The inordinately painful proceedings were now getting underway, with Freddie naturally hoping there wouldn't be any muck-raking during the process.

Following the stressful appointment, Freddie and Roney drove back to Gatwick and collected Cliff Nunn for the meeting with Harry Goodman. They went up to the suite on the fourth floor of the Gatwick Hilton Hotel reserved by his staff, to wait for Intasun's top man. The news had somehow got out and reporters surrounded the hotel. Some disguised themselves as waiters, while others tried to get through on the phone, posing as relatives. Paradoxically, just a few floors below in the hotel ballroom, BCal's sales and marketing people were relaxing at dinner following their annual marketing conference. Finally, just after midnight Goodman and his entourage arrived, two hours late.

They got right down to business. Goodman flatly turned down an offer to purchase one of Laker's three Airbus A300s. He wanted to know all about Laker's tour companies. When he reviewed the booking projections and other data, he knew everything he needed to know. Goodman was as smart as they came and he also knew that Freddie would be out of business within hours. His response to Freddie's proposal was delivered in one line, "I don't see why I should pay you for what I can get for nothing in the morning." With that, he closed his briefcase, nodded to his entourage, left the suite, got into his jet and flew off to secure all the hotel rooms that he knew would be released when Laker Airways went bust the next day. Freddie was left stunned and could not believe Goodman. He looked sadly at his executives and they went back to the Laker offices. By now, it was past 1:00am on Friday 5th February.

Desperate, Freddie knew Japan was still open for business and he decided to call his 'friends' in Tokyo. It was a massive long shot and he knew it, even if he didn't comprehend why. The giant Mitsui Corporation had financed some of Laker's DC-10-10 aircraft. Freddie had dug them out of a multi-million dollar black hole by taking on three of the six DC-10s Mitsui had financed on behalf of ANA. He would therefore try Mitsui's Hattori, the Director and General Manager of their Aerospace Systems Division whom he had met in June of the previous year. £10 million was nothing to the Japanese he speculated and he thought that they owed him a favour. Freddie was oblivious to the social faux pas he had made in Tokyo earlier in June 1981, when he and Greg Dix had been invited to what was a 'men-only' dinner with the Mitsui executives. Hattori-san was insulted when Freddie turned up to the dinner with his step-daughter Bettina. Freddie had compounded the affront by allowing the teenager to wear a highly inappropriate Chinese dress and had then spent the evening engaged in chit-chat with the girl instead of being sociable with his hosts. It was perhaps one of Freddie's biggest ever blunders. As he should have expected, Freddie was politely told that Mitsui would need to consult with each member of its committee. Freddie hung up and looked at his executives. "They said they'd call back." He was aware how the Japanese did business and intuitively knew Mitsui would never call. He made an aside that dealing with them was like dealing with 'the committee of 400'. Freddie had run out of ideas and could think of no way to meet Kitching's demand for £5 million cash by 9:00am. He looked around the room at his directors and at John Roney who had stayed on and announced "It's over, we're done for."

Dawn had broken, there was only one thing left to do. The directors of the airline were gathered for an impromptu board meeting of Laker Airways International. The time was approaching 8:00am. John Jones, John Roney, Cliff Nunn, Robbie Robinson, John Seear, and Bill Townsend had been there with him all night. Freddie's first wife Joan was summoned; she was the only non-executive director. The board meeting was brief, the minutes show only five points. Freddie as Chairman first explained that both the Midland and McDonnell Douglas had withdrawn support and all the considerable efforts made overnight had proved fruitless. There was only one resolution of the meeting and it was unanimously agreed. The Clydesdale would appoint a receiver and manager for the group. Draft notices and press releases were produced and approved and with no other business, the final board meeting was adjourned.

Laker Airways was finished.

# CHAPTER 55

# Grounded

## Judgement day

5th February, 1982

At around 8:30am Freddie began calling the few people who should be told personally what the world would hear that morning. His first call was to Bob Beckman, whom he hadn't spoken to since the December meeting with American Airlines in New York. It was an emotional but short conversation. Meanwhile, John Roney had picked up another phone and dialed Dennis Kitching's number. He had been waiting for the call. Roney told him that Freddie would invite the Midland to call in the receivers. Kitching said, "Good" and that Freddie had "done the right thing."

A press release was hurriedly drawn up by Roney and it read as follows:

*It was announced on 24th December 1981 that agreement had been reached in principle on the restructuring of Laker's financial affairs with a view to securing its long-term viability.*

*On Monday night it was firmly believed that the most stringent of these conditions had been met and the way forward was clear. However, on Wednesday events took a sudden and dramatic turn.*

*Yesterday the facilities available to the company from its bank, Clydesdale, and the arrangements reached with McDonnell Douglas, are unhappily not considered adequate by others to meet the anticipated requirements of the company over the next few months, although Laker's (sic) strongly disagrees with this view.*

*However, as the holiday season approaches Laker's (sic) are vitally concerned that there is no risk whatsoever that passengers are stranded as a result of the airline's collapse in the summer months.*

*Laker's (sic) are mindful of the views of others and recognise that they must act in a totally responsible way. Accordingly, it is with the deepest regret that*

*Laker has requested Clydesdale Bank to appoint a receiver and manager.*

*Sir Freddie would like to thank the enormous support he has received from the public over the years and he hopes that with the demise of his airline any benefits gained for the ordinary traveller will not be lost.'*

As soon as the Clydesdale Bank received the call from Kitching, it sent for Bill Mackey, partner in the accounting firm of Ernst & Whinney . He had been waiting in the wings since the last week of January. Mackey was now appointed as the official Receiver of Laker Airways and he and his colleague, Nigel Hamilton, were called to action.

The news spread throughout Laker's headquarters. Operations had asked if they should dispatch the morning flights and Freddie naively told them 'yes'. He assumed the receivers would continue operating the airline normally until assets had been sold to pay off the creditors. Having never been in receivership before, Freddie had no idea of the procedures. In the sixteen years since Freddie had started the business in 1966, it had turned a profit, however modest every year, until 1981. This was something that could not be said of his competitors. He simply assumed Laker Airways and the associated tour operations would continue to operate, then be sold as going concerns. Surely that was the logical process Freddie thought to himself. He had no idea the intention was to shut down every Laker company and the entire organisation right then and there on Friday the 5th of February 1982.

At around 10:00am Bill Mackey arrived at the airline's headquarters and was shown into Freddie's third floor office. He introduced himself as the receiver appointed by the Clydesdale Bank. Freddie asked him what he wanted him to do. He received a short curt response "nothing." After sitting quietly for a few minutes, Freddie walked to the waiting car and was driven away by John Roney. They turned on the car radio just as the announcement was read out on the morning news. Roney broke down in tears.

As soon as Freddie was out of the building, Mackey had sprung into action and taken charge of Laker Airways. In the operations room at Gatwick it was John Jones who had been given the unenviable task by Mackey of calling back the planes. Now realising the airline was through and had to cease trading altogether, he went down to Operations to turn the planes around and tidy up; "I called back the plane that was halfway to Tenerife with 280 people on board and turned it around in mid-air." The fully loaded Airbus, which had just left packed with holidaymakers set to enjoy some winter sunshine in the Canary Islands was ordered to turn back. One of Laker's DC-10 pilots, Terry Fensome remembers: "We'd taken off for the Mediterranean from Manchester and I got a call, I think it was two hours out, to turn back to Manchester. Nothing was told to us at that time what the reason was."

Mackey's actions had immediate consequences as chaos ensued. Worst hit were the holidaymakers and passengers who suddenly found themselves stranded abroad. A New York bound DC-10 that had already departed Manchester before the order was given, was made to land back at Prestwick, Scotland, for fear that it would be impounded by the US authorities. The passengers were forced to disembark and initially left to fend for themselves. They wouldn't be going anywhere. The British Airports Authority impounded one of the other DC-10s to cover the company's unpaid landing and parking fees. A lucky plane load of passengers were returned to the UK from Malaga by Britannia Airways.

Deputy Managing Director Cliff Nunn had already called Greg Dix in New York who at the time was sound asleep, to break the news that it was all over and to shut down the USA offices. Unable to believe his ears, especially given what had taken place just two days earlier, Dix refused to be moved. "I want it in writing Cliff," he demanded and headed over to his Rego Park office to receive the telex confirming it was true. He then called all the US managers and urged them to get to their posts. There were no aircraft in the USA, but several thousand ticketed passengers as well as the entire US press corps would have to be dealt with. However Dix hadn't been in his office long before a nervous looking individual from Ernst & Whinney arrived. He told Dix he was there to take over Laker's operation in New York. "Take over eh?" asked Dix. "How many years of airline experience do you have then" "Well none, I'm an accountant" the supercilious young man responded. Sleep deprived and not feeling in a particularly tolerant frame of mind given the circumstances, Dix grabbed the E & W accountant and physically flung him out of the Laker offices. He yelled at him not to come back until they had finished dealing with the stranded passengers, the press and the dozens of creditors. Fuel suppliers, landlords, catering and ground handling companies would all be turning up and demanding payment as soon as they heard the news of Laker shutting its doors.

A traveller who was in Miami that day witnessed the scenes there. "I said to my wife, what are all these people doing? There were people in tears, people sitting on suitcases. Skytrain had gone bust. I did not realise it at the time until I had got off the plane back at Heathrow. I had a flight on BA, unlike all the stranded passengers. It was a zoo, there were hundreds in the part of Miami airport where Skytrain was supposed to go from and it was just besieged. The staff were harassed, there were people weeping, there were people shouting because they had no way home." The sudden shut down had all come as a complete shock to passengers and staff alike.

For the over 2,500 employees in the Laker group, their lives were shattered. Apart from a handful who would be needed to initially assist the receivers, everyone else was now technically unemployed. Nevertheless, many loyal Laker employees volunteered to man the desks at Gatwick and in the USA over the weekend, unpaid, to handle questions from still-stranded passengers.

It had been three months and three weeks since Freddie had told Iain Sproat, the Minister responsible for aviation, that he would be put out of business. He had been proved right.

On the morning of the Laker collapse, Sproat had made a statement to the House of Commons to that effect. He said, "Funds from the bonding arrangement and the Air Travel Reserve Fund will be adequate: the total amount available from those two sources is over £23 million and that will certainly cover all those on charter holiday packages."

Worryingly, Sproat estimated that up to 5,000 Skytrain scheduled service passengers could be stranded in the UK and the USA. He confirmed that there was no financial support available for them to be repatriated. Unlike those who had booked holidays through Laker's tour operators, any passengers who had not made their outward-bound journeys by Skytrain were not covered, and those already abroad had to pay for another flight to get themselves home, thus becoming unsecured creditors of the company. They numbered in the thousands and would be owed over £4 million.

People who had purchased Laker tickets found they were now unusable and invalid. With the doors of the Laker offices shut throughout the world at the behest of the receivers, there was little if any information available to the travelling public who were now caught up in the mess, despite the heroic efforts of Laker staff.

It was now up to Bill Mackey and his team to sort it out. The competition stepped in, as Mackey put it, 'to protect the name of the airline industry'. After a late-afternoon meeting, the airlines, among them BA and Pan Am, agreed to honour Laker Airways' return scheduled tickets until the end of February.

Adam Thomson, Chief Executive of British Caledonian, who was so envious of Freddie and his success, relished this opportunity for some free publicity. As he recounts in his autobiography: "The Laker story veered off into other highly publicised directions, but our job was to look at the immediate aftermath of the collapse. Our first task was to help Laker passengers stranded overseas, mainly in the USA. This we did at no charge whatsoever, bringing in our partners Eastern Airlines to carry the Laker people from places such as Florida to our gateways so that we could carry them to London."

As soon as Laker Airways closed down, the ATOL travel bond automatically came into action and was used to repatriate holidaymakers stranded abroad. All customers of Laker subsidiaries Laker Air Travel and Arrowsmith Holidays, and people booked on Laker charter flights, were covered by the various bonds, guaranteed by the leading banks. Having the bond was a condition of Laker's Air Travel Organisers' Licence, and the funds were immediately available to enable alternative arrangements to bring home people who were stranded abroad.

Additionally, Laker customers who had booked and paid for their holidays in advance would be compensated from the bond and if that proved insufficient to meet all legitimate claims, from another bond called the Air Travel Reserve Fund. The TOSG Trust Fund Ltd, the company that actually ran the bond, had already had meetings about the Laker situation, anticipating that a rescue might be necessary. For those that were left stranded or out of pocket, while the situation was distressing, they would eventually get home and many would be refunded despite plenty of recriminations in the press.

A week earlier, Mackey himself had been quoted in a newly published book, Managing for Profit: "Mr Mackey gives his own list of warning signs: Rolls Royces with personalised number plates; a fountain in the reception area; a flag pole; the Queen's Award for Industry; a chairman who is honoured for services to industry – every industry but his own; a salesman or engineer as chief executive; a recent move into modern offices." Intentionally or not, it read as a thinly veiled attack on Freddie, who was perhaps culpable on almost all of those counts.

By the end of the day, Mackey had done his work. All twenty aircraft in Laker's fleet were now on the ground at airports in Britain. He had all the airline's main assets under his control in the UK, including the DC-10 the BAA had impounded. All Laker's offices were now closed. Freddie's company owned Rolls Royce parked outside at Gatwick was seized. An order went down to Palma to seize Freddie's company-owned yacht 'Patrina', but the Spanish authorities had already impounded it against unpaid port charges and other accrued expenses.

As Thursday had already come and gone with Johnny Gold's promised dinner invitation unforthcoming, Gold thought. "He must have been caught up in the excitement of the rescue and forgotten; he'll show up at the club at some point." At noon on Friday, Gold was making the short trip into central London to the Tramp nightclub for an early meeting. Over the radio of his old Mercedes came the announcement that Laker Airways had been grounded. After the initial disbelief only one thing came into Gold's mind. "I honestly thought Freddie's gonna sue the life out of these people. I thought somebody had made a mistake, how could the airline be grounded. How mad, what a mistake they've made." Freddie had been in his nightclub just a few days earlier and Gold had heard Freddie's guests saying, "you're rescued" as they all celebrated before he went to New York.

As expected, the press were brutal and Laker's demise was headlines in all that evening's papers and the first breaking news story on television channels. Once the darling of the media, the newspaper editors now laid the blame squarely at Freddie's door. They had been given an official line from the receiver, the bankers and the Government that they all eagerly put to ink: "Freddie went bankrupt because he had bought too many planes that he did not need at too high a rate of interest. Laker's loans were in dollars, his income in sterling; the falling pound against the dollar left him short of cash." The public statement made it all sound very simple when the real reasons behind the demise of Laker Airways were anything but.

Exhausted after dealing with stranded passengers and press all day, at around 8:00pm on the U.S. east coast, Greg Dix's managers all gathered in his office on Queens Boulevard for one last time before they went their separate ways. No-one believed what had happened. Just two days earlier, Freddie had been there in New York making commercials and on top of the world. Victor Emmanuelle from the ad agency came over to help as soon as he heard the news. Stuart Alderman produced the Clydesdale Bank's cheque book and wrote million pound gag cheques from the now frozen bank account. Someone had thoughtfully grabbed a couple of cases of Regency champagne from the JFK bonded store before they too were impounded. The New York team made a serious dent in the Moet while trying to still have a laugh on perhaps the worst day of their careers.

John Jones lamented "16 years of my life were down the drain at a stroke; I had spent the last 16 years building a better mousetrap, solving problems and making the machine work better and better. The world was beating a path to your door and all of a sudden it was gone." It highlighted one of Freddie's famous Lakerisms, probably one he thought up after his first son Kevin was tragically killed. "Life has this way of changing so fast it takes your breath away." There was never a truer statement on the 5th of February 1982.

Late that afternoon, Freddie headed to Woodcote Stud. It was a place of sanctuary where he could find solace with those closest to him, including George Plowes, who was not just his stud and farm manager but for the last thirty years his best friend in the whole world. Woodcote provided Freddie with some privacy as his Sussex home 'Furzegrove' had by now been besieged by the press.

That evening, Freddie drank himself into oblivion; finally giving in to his emotions as he uncontrollably wept in the arms of his daughter Elaine and her family. The enormous strain of many months battling his business and domestic problems had finally swallowed him up.

It was the end of the glory years of Sir Freddie Laker.

Or was it?

# EPILOGUE

# Hindsight

## *"Bucketsful for nothing"*

Sir Freddie often said "you can get bucketsful of hindsight for nothing." After having read the story of Laker Airways, one might be confused as to what actually caused the demise of perhaps the greatest privately owned airline in the world. In writing The Glory Years of Sir Freddie Laker, every effort was made to not engage in finger pointing, but rather to present the facts based on many years of research, an unprecedented body of documents, exhaustive interviews, and the personal recollections of the main characters still living and those who were around when the project first started.

As described in The Perfect Storm chapter and Appendix X, the demise of Laker Airways was almost certainly not caused by a single individual or event. Initially, Sir Freddie appeared to be responsible, something he at first readily admitted. But over time, his perspective on it all changed. He subsequently proclaimed himself blameless and that Laker Airways was brought down solely by a conspiracy. Others, including Laker spokespersons echoed this convincingly in numerous interviews. The conspiracy theory was maintained over and over, until it became the 'official' party line. And it was never disputed.

There is no argument that Laker's competitors colluded and deliberately matched Laker's fares to drive Freddie off the North Atlantic, while in an unconnected and simultaneous assault, Laker's principal lenders caved under pressure and failed to reach an agreement for a refinancing package. However, there is also little doubt that Freddie left them an open goal and full advantage was taken. Nevertheless, the conspiracy theory became the widely proclaimed, accepted angle. It then became the cornerstone of a billion-dollar antitrust lawsuit that continued for three years and sustained Freddie's assertions.

Biographers, magazine editors, documentary film-makers and others also perpetuated the conspiracy theory, most of whom in the process have exonerated Sir Freddie of any responsibility. Typically, the liability for Laker Airways' cessation has been directed at the Midland Bank, British Airways and Laker's other North Atlantic competitor airlines, McDonnell Douglas, and Prime Minister Margaret Thatcher.

Curiously, no-one until now had ever revealed that Freddie's nemesis, British Caledonian's Adam Thomson was behind the blackmailing of McDonnell Douglas or that Ray Colegate of the British CAA played a significant part with his vote of no confidence. Furthermore, the Midland Bank gave the Laker men advance warning they had a renowned receiver / liquidator waiting in the wings; those few days may have made a difference. There is no short answer to the 'whodunnit' question, although perhaps by now it is fairly apparent that Sir Freddie was hardly as irreproachable as he always claimed.

Of the other reasons publicised as the cause of Laker's demise, perhaps none has been beaten to death more than the 'Laker expanded too fast' theory. Yet many companies, including airlines, expanded fast and took advantage of situations and opportunities presented to them. Maintaining the status quo is tantamount to going backwards, so pushing forward is essential in any business, especially in an industry as competitive as civil aviation. Despite some of Sir Freddie's expansion initiatives being mis-timed, overly ambitious or impetuous, they were quite conservative compared to some airlines today.

An over-reliance on sterling revenue and perhaps not hedging sufficiently for a rapidly devaluing pound against the dollar was another well-publicised reason for Laker's downfall. Exchange rates weren't exclusive to Laker and other independents in the UK such as Britannia, Monarch, BCal, and Dan Air all purchased American-made aircraft in dollars while their revenue was in UK pounds. None of the aforementioned went out of business due to the exchange rate. If Laker had developed its North American originating business sooner, a weak pound / strong dollar would have worked in its favour.

Had third party creditors, McDonnell Douglas and GE stepped up to the plate in 1982 as promised and not cowered to their customers threatening a boycott, the Midland Bank would have had no choice than to ratify Laker's refinancing plan. Once the promised collateral failed to appear, the Midland had few options, especially as Laker's Clydesdale overdraft was already overdrawn.

They say 'timing is everything' and at no time was this truer than in summer 1981. Laker's competitors declared war because Freddie angrily launched the Regency Service while he was embroiled in a massive domestic upheaval. Laker's load factors dropped like a stone. It was a classic 'Perfect Storm' of events.

None of the foregoing in isolation brought Laker Airways down. However, there is little doubt that the involvement in fare-fixing and colluding with competitors inhibited Laker's commercial independence. Bob Beckman was vociferous in warning Sir Freddie and Laker's managers about collusion or discussion with their opposite numbers at competitor airlines. By voluntarily participating in the fare fixing, Laker was impeded from taking action against the alleged predatory pricing tactics of their competitors (ie. the 'conspiracy').

Proving 'predatory pricing' however would have been challenging. On many occasions, Freddie made angry, unsupported claims that the Big 3 were offering fares at below 'cost'. The US-UK Air Services Agreement (Bermuda II as it is known) in Article 12 (2) states: 'Each tariff shall, to the extent feasible, be based on the costs of providing such service assuming reasonable load factors'. How operating 'costs' are assessed varies by air carrier. Whereas a 'reasonable load factor' for the legacy airlines may have been say 60 percent, Laker needed significantly higher load factors on some services just to break even on its direct operating costs. In 1981, Laker was hardly a 'low cost airline'.

Laker's competitors had a large percentage of high yield fares to off-set the loss-leader standby and heavily discounted fares they offered to attack Laker's fares. Laker on the other hand never had high-yielding fares in any great measure, even after their full Economy fares were introduced. In fact, Laker's highest yielding fares were so low in late 1981 that the long-haul scheduled routes lost money unless unrealistically high load factors were achieved.

Fortunately, Laker's competitors never challenged Laker's actual costs and the perception of their being a 'low cost operator' was sustained. Otherwise the tables may have been turned and upon scrutiny there is a distinct possibility that Laker was in fact operating 'below cost' - perhaps even from as early as the commencement of the LA Skytrain with the DC-10-30 in September 1978.

In retrospect, Laker's foray into North Atlantic scheduled services may well have been its downfall. After the spontaneous purchase of the first DC-10s, Laker Airways had become the unrivaled transatlantic charter operator. As Skytrain had yet to come to fruition, the new DC-10s had to be gainfully employed somehow and the Advanced Booking Charters between the UK and the east coast cities of North America were the perfect solution. Laker's ABC programme was unsurpassed and could likely have been a cash cow for many more years. However, once Freddie's Skytrain concept gathered momentum during the six years of the licencing campaign, there was no going back. Every time he was turned down, it only made Freddie more resolute in seeing Skytrain become a reality. The potential downsides of Skytrain were never considered, or perhaps never even envisaged. Freddie's Skytrain was singularly responsible for revolutionising air travel; there had been nothing like it before, so it would have been challenging to apply any legitimate risk management to the venture.

There are many things that should have been done differently after Skytrain commenced in September 1977. But nothing is as obvious as the ill-advised fare fixing and colluding with Laker's competitors. Not only was it illegal under American consumer protection laws, it was commercially irresponsible and Freddie should have known better, especially in the wake of the affinity group violations. There would likely have been no conspiracy, no fare war and no necessity for re-financing and deferral of loans, if Laker had focused on generating its revenue independently, earlier. And no perfect storm of 1981.

Nevertheless, there's no question that what Sir Freddie's small airline achieved in just a few years was breathtaking. Frustratingly and with just a slight shift in circumstances, some of his more outlandish and ambitious initiatives after Skytrain commenced, such as the purchase of five brand new DC-10-30s, the mis-timed Regency Service, the commitment for ten Airbus A300s based on nothing more than a verbal 'promise', and the international expansion projects like 'Globetrain' and Australia, could all have contributed to Laker's long term viability. Freddie would have been hailed as a 'visionary genius' had Laker been able to survive the winter of 1981-82 and see these initiatives come to fruition.

What makes the demise of Laker Airways even more confounding is that operationally the company was amongst the best of the best. Laker's pilots flew the planes to the absolute highest standards as McDonnell Douglas, BAC and Airbus Industrie all acknowledged. Similarly, the cabin crews gave outstanding in-flight service with pizzazz, efficiency and good humour. Laker's superlative engineering division was the envy of the industry while its airport passenger services in the USA won travel trade awards. Exceptional on-time performance and a 100 per cent safety record placed Laker Airways in the top echelon of all airlines, while the autocratic Sir Freddie engendered respect and staff allegiance like no other airline boss in the history of civil aviation.

Laker Airways, the largest privately-owned airline in the world at the time, by rights should never have been forced into receivership and wouldn't be today. The company was not 'bankrupt', in fact, it wasn't 'balance sheet insolvent' either. By the end of 1981, Laker's financial highlights were:

| | | |
|---|---|---|
| Fixed assets (book value) | £ | 234,570,498 |
| Investment in subsidiaries | £ | 1,005,187 |
| Current liabilities | £ | (33,052,678) |
| **Balance:** | **£** | **202,523,007** |
| Year end 1981 Profit (Loss) | £ | (560,530) |
| Long Term Debt (due 31st March 1982) | US$ | 53,164,000 |
| Interest (due 31st March 1982) | US$ | 41,598,000 |
| **Total 1982 debt payment** | **US$** | **94,762,000** |

*Aircraft loans calculated at $2.2445 = £1 Loans repaid at $1.84 = £1*

The long-term loans (10-year DC-10 & A300 & 3-year B707) for the aircraft amounted to £193 million. Laker had no progress payments due for any ordered aircraft. The downside of organising the group under one umbrella company (Appendix IX) became apparent on 5th February 1982. Laker Air Travel and Arrowsmith could have continued profitably using other airlines and Laker's engineering division may have survived as an independent entity.

However, the Laker Group as a whole was 'cash flow insolvent'. The final balances with the Clydesdale Bank on the 5th of February, 1982 were:

| | | |
|---|---|---|
| Laker Account re 707s | £ | (2,780,000) |
| Laker Airways Current Account | £ | (1,538,000) |
| Laker Airways Wages Account | £ | (930,000) |
| Eurodollar Loan Account ($5 million) | £ | (2,744,000) |
| Laker re: DC-10 G-BELO ($5.4 million) | £ | (2,951,000) |
| L.A. (International) Ltd Current Account | £ | (170,000) |
| L.A. (Services) Ltd Current Account | £ | (559,000) |
| Laker Air Travel Ltd Current Accounts | £ | (45,000) |
| Arrowsmith Holidays Ltd Current Account | £ | (130,000) |
| *Less Amounts in credit:* | | |
| Reservations Account (Deposits for '82 holidays) | £ | 243,000 |
| Currency Deposit Account | £ | 40,000 |
| **Total** | **£** | **(11,564,000)** |

Guarantees subsequently met by Clydesdale amounted to almost £7 million including money paid out under the TOSG bond. In total, the Laker Group's liabilities to the Clydesdale bank were £19.2 million (= £70 million - 2018).

Ironically, £5.6 million was owed to Laker on 5th February; £2 million from International Caribbean, £1.25 million from AA and £2.35 million from the Midland Bank for A300 spares reimbursement, yet none had been recovered.

Whether that, or the injection of the original £5 million promised by MDC and GE would have actually saved Laker and the over 2,500 jobs, is debatable. It might have bought some valuable time and that for sure could have been a game changer. It is anyone's guess what rabbits Freddie may have pulled from the hat if he'd had another thirty days to obtain the additional £5 million demanded by the Midland Bank. Sadly, he never got the chance.

Not long after his life was shattered and he had lost most everything he held dear, Freddie had a rare moment of introspection. "We had just returned to Freddie's apartment at Key Colony" Greg Dix recalls. "The antitrust case against Laker's competitors had been kicked off by Bob Beckman and Freddie was uplifted by the prospect of handily winning the case and the billion dollars Bob had confidently felt would be awarded." Key Colony was a deluxe residential complex on the ocean at Key Biscayne, Miami. Freddie and Dix stayed there while they were developing a new business venture in Florida and The Bahamas for Lonrho - at the time one of Britain's largest conglomerates.

"As usual, we had ended the evening at the English Pub. It was handily located across the road from Key Colony and meant we didn't have to drive, which was just as well given our condition." The pair had walked back from their favourite local tavern, unusually with no-one in tow. Dix continues "Freddie was enjoying bachelor life again to the full and he was masterful at the chat up. On any given night, he could have his pick of Florida's suntanned, tastefully dressed, single for the night women who would be mesmerised by his sense of humour, flirtatious charm and wit. And it probably didn't hurt if the barman whispered do you know who that is?"

Unwilling to call it a night, Freddie had grabbed a bottle of champagne and said "come on Dix, let's go down and have a walk along the beach." Influenced by a copious amount of alcohol along with some gentle prodding, Freddie opened up about Laker Airways for the first time since February 1982. "He started by conceding that the fare-fixing and colluding with BA had been an error of judgment. He was sorry he'd risked John Jones by forcing him to participate, with so much at stake. I was quite taken aback by Freddie's admission" Dix says despite his knowing what Freddie and Jones had been doing at the time. "Then even more incredibly, he confessed that his domestic situations had affected his common sense at a critical time and he'd taken his eye off the ball. He didn't go into detail or mention any names and I knew better than to push it further."

Nevertheless, it was perhaps one of only a very few times in his life where Sir Freddie had acknowledged his vulnerability; he wouldn't be the first man to have his entire world devastated because he hadn't exercised prudence in his personal affairs.

"Freddie was coming out of another business downfall in the UK and had more or less moved to the States full time" Dix continues. "He was probably the most unassuming and authentic in all the years I'd known him, in fact, he was a pleasure to be around at that point in his life. Our new business venture was coming together well and we were having a terrific time."

Ever the optimist and typically only looking forward to what's next, Freddie mentioned there were a couple of 727s he had his eye on. Then he became uncharacteristically retrospective and concurred that the sixteen years of Laker Airways were to be celebrated. Before finally calling it a night, he recalled some highlights and his favourite hostesses, then concluded by mumbling, with a tear or two rolling down his face "we broke down so many barriers and had great fun, didn't we?"

# APPENDIX I

# CAST OF CHARACTERS

| LAST NAME | FIRST NAME | ROLE IN THE LAKER STORY |
|---|---|---|
| Aarons | Larry | Lord, Geller, Federico & Einstein - Art Director for Laker Airways a/c |
| Abnett | Stan | Laker Airways - Freddie Laker's chauffeur |
| Abraham | Rheinhardt | Lufthansa - Chairman & Chief Executive |
| Acker | Edward | Pan Am - Chairman and CEO |
| Alderman | Stuart | Laker Airways - Manager, Laker Air Travel USA / ex Wings |
| Al-Hajri | Mohammed | Director of Civil Aviation - Sharjah, UAE |
| Allan | Ian. H | Laker Airways - Scheduled Services Manager / ex MD ICA |
| Allavie | Jack (Capt.) | McDonnell Douglas Corp. - Senior Training / Demonstration Pilot |
| Allin | William | Hannah Laker's partner / Freddie Laker's adopted father |
| Anderson | Donald (Sir) | Dept of Civil Aviation, Australia - Director / Quantas Board Member |
| Angermeir | Arno | Laker Airways - Station Manager, Berlin Tegel |
| Atkinson | Leonard (Atty) | Laker Airways - Operations Manager / ex BUA & Hunting Aviation |
| Aw Sian | Sally | CEO - Sing Tao Publishing Group, Hong Kong |
| Ayling | Robert | Department of Trade - Solicitor |
| Ballard | Martin | Laker Airways - Chief Accountant |
| Bamberg | Harold | British Eagle Airways / Eagle Aviation - Founder & Managing Director |
| Barrett | Bill | Law firm of Metzger, Shaydac and Schwartz - Senior Partner |
| Batt | Bob | Aviation Traders - Chief flight engineer |
| Bebchick | Leonard | British Caledonian Airways - US Legal counsel and director |
| Beckman | Angela | Wife of Robert Beckman / ex Statistical Analyst |
| Beckman | Robert M. (Bob) | Laker Airways - Aviation Licensing Lawyer, Washington DC |
| Bedford | Trevor | Hong Kong Land Co. - Managing Director |
| Benson | Henry | Bank of England- Advisor |
| Biffen | John | Secretary of State for Trade - UK |
| Black | Rosemary (Tutin) | Second wife of Freddie Laker |
| Boote | Gervaise | Samuel Montagu - Senior Partner |
| Booth | Beryl | Laker Airways - Chief Stewardess, Manchester |
| Bouttell | Roy | Laker Airways - Passenger Services Manager / ex Ops Duty Officer |
| Bowden Smith | Harry | Arrowsmith Holidays - Founder and Managing Director |
| Bradley | Richard (Dick) | Laker Airways - Chief Navigator / Performance specialist / ex BUA |
| Bradshaw | Basil (Capt.) | Laker Airways - Snr DC-10 Captain / Captain of first Skytrain flight |
| Bristow | Alan | Bristow Helicopters - Founder & Managing Director |
| Brizendene | John (Briz) | McDonnell Douglas Corp. - President, Douglas Aircraft division |
| Brookes | Geoffrey (Capt.) | Laker Airways - DC-10 Trng. Captain / ex Boeing 707 Fleet Captain |
| Brown | Secor D | U.S. Civil Aeronautics Board - Chairman |
| Brown | Christopher | Laker Airways - Group Solicitor |
| Callaghan | James (Rt Hon) | Prime Minister of the United Kingdom (1976-79) |
| Carpenter | John Boyd (Lord) | U.K. Civil Aviation Authority - Chairman |
| Carroll | George | Laker Air Travel - Managing Director / ex Deputy MD-BUA |
| Carter | Jimmy (Pres.) | President of the United States (1977-81) |
| Champion | John | Pan Am - senior executive, representative to IATA |
| Chen | George | C.L Thomson Express - USA (San Francisco) - CEO |
| Chen | Tommy | Thomson Express Travel (Hong Kong) - CEO / Hon. Consul - Tonga |
| Chiang | Mary | Laker Airways - PR representative, Hong Kong |
| Chilton | Lesley | Laker Airways - Private Secretary and PA to Sir Freddie Laker |
| Clemens | Charles (Skip) | Laker Airways - Manager, Western USA |

| LAST NAME | FIRST NAME | ROLE IN THE LAKER STORY |
|---|---|---|
| Clinton Davis | Stanley | U.K. Parliamentary Under Secretary of State |
| Cochrane | Ossie | British Airways - Western Routes Manager |
| Cohen | Marvin | U.S. Civil Aeronautics Board - Chairman |
| Colegate | Raymond | U.K. Civil Aviation Authority - Economics Director |
| Cooper | Amanda | Laker Airways - In-Flight Director |
| Crandall | Robert | American Airlines - President / CEO |
| Cremin | Tim | Laker Airways - Station Engineer |
| Crush | Harvey (Hon.) | Laker Airways - QC for Skytrain application |
| Davies | Tim (Capt) | Laker Airways - Fleet Captain, Airbus / ex One-Eleven Fleet Captain |
| Dell | Edmund | U.K. Secretary of State for Trade |
| Denning | Alfred (Lord) | U.K. Appeal Court Judge, Skytrain hearings |
| Dix | Gregory | Laker Airways - Manager, International Operations / ex Stn Mngr JFK |
| Docherty | Jean | Laker Airways - Station Manager, Toronto |
| Doherty | Sandy | Laker Airways - In-Flight Director |
| Doyon | Bob | General Electric Corp. - Senior executive |
| Draper | William | Export Import Bank of America (ExIm) - Chairman |
| Draper | Gerry | British Airways - Director of Commercial Operations |
| Earls | Linda | Laker Airways - Station Manager JFK |
| Edwardes | Michael (Sir) | British Leyland - Chairman |
| Edwards | Ronald (Sir) | Author of the Edwards report |
| Einstein | Arthur | Lord, Geller, Federico & Einstein - Creative Director |
| Emmanuelle | Victor | Lord, Geller, Federico & Einstein - Laker Airways' Account Executive |
| Estella | Tony | Laker Airways - Palma, Majorca representative |
| Evans | Don | Laker Air Travel - Sales Director |
| Farmer | Donald | Beckman, Kirstein and Farmer - Partner |
| Fensome | Terry (Capt.) | Laker Airways - DC-10 Captain |
| Flood | Robin | Laker Airways - Publicity Officer / ex BUA |
| Flood | Thomas | General Electric Corp. - executive |
| Forster | George | Laker Airways - Commercial Manager / ex Air Charter & BUA |
| Forsythe | Charles | McDonnell Douglas Corp. - VP Sales |
| Foulkes | Nigel (Sir) | U.K. Civil Aviation Authority - Chairman |
| Fox | Tony | Deacons - Hong Kong lawyer for Laker Airways |
| Freeman | Harry | Laker Airways - Chauffeur for Freddie Laker |
| Freeman | Gerald | Transair and Airwork - Director |
| Freeman | Rita | Housekeeper for Laker household |
| Frumkes | Melvin | US Divorce attorney for Patricia Laker |
| Gallina | Joe | General Electric Corp. - Lawyer |
| Gates | Patricia | Fiancee of Freddie Laker |
| Gates (Laker) | Bettina | Daughter of Patricia / Step-Daughter of Freddie Laker |
| Gentling | John | McDonnell Douglas Finance Corp. - Vice President Intl Services |
| George | Peter | Solicitor for Patricia Laker |
| Gilhespy | George | Midland Bank - General Manager |
| Goodman | Harry | Intasun - Managing Director |
| Greenhead | John | Laker Airways - Station Manager, Manchester / ex Stn Manager, JFK |
| Griffin | Nina | Laker Airways - Catering Manager / former Chief Stewardess / ex BUA |
| Guy | Athol | Laker Airways - Dir. Australia / Dir. Clemenger Harvie / MP, Victoria |
| Hamer | Rupert (Dick) | Premier of the State of Victoria, Australia |
| Hammarskjold | Knut | IATA - Director General |
| Harvey | Joy | Laker Airways - Chief Stewardess / ex BUA |
| Hattori | T | Mitsui & Co. Ltd. - Director & Gen. Manager Aerospace Systems |
| Hayley-Bell | Dennis (Capt.) | Laker Airways - BAC One Eleven Fleet Captain / ex BAC Test Pilot |
| Heal | Toby | Aviation Traders - Designer of the Accountant |
| Heath | Edward (Rt Hon) | Prime Minister of the United Kingdom (1970-74) |

| LAST NAME | FIRST NAME | ROLE IN THE LAKER STORY |
|---|---|---|
| Hellary | Alan (Capt.) | Laker Airways - Manager Flight Ops / formerly Chief Pilot / ex BUA |
| Hewitt | Lenox (Sir) | Qantas - Chairman |
| Heywood | Evelyn | Laker Airways - PR Consultant, New York |
| Higgs | Bernadette | Laker Airways - Deputy Cabin Staff Manager |
| Holness | Patrick | Laker Airways - Station Manager, LAX |
| Howes | Arthur | Airbus Industrie - Sales Director |
| Hunt | Ralph | Australian Minister for Transport |
| Hunter | Siobhan | Laker Airways - In-Flight Director / Laker Cabin Attendants' Assoc. |
| James | Steve (Capt.) | Laker Airways - DC-10 Fleet Manager |
| Jenkins | Roy | U.K. Minister of Aviation |
| Jennings | Norman | Aviation Traders - Senior Engineer |
| Johnson | Johnny | Aviation Traders - Manager of the Accountant project |
| Jones | John | Laker Airways - Commercial Manager / ex ABC Manager |
| Kaffenberger | Red (Capt.) | McDonnell Douglas Corp.- Senior Training & Demonstration Captain |
| Keep | Brian | Hong Kong D.O.T. - Director General |
| Kennedy | John F. (Pres.) | President of the United States (1961-63) |
| Kennedy | Edward (Sen.) | Senator of the United States |
| Kent | Felix | Laker Airways - corporate lawyer (USA) |
| Khan | Alfred E | U.S. Civil Aeronautics Board - Chairman |
| King | John (Lord) | British Airways - Chairman |
| Kinnear | Angus | Gatwick Handling Ltd. - General Manager |
| Kirstein | David | Beckman, Kirstein and Farmer - Partner |
| Kitching | Dennis | Midland Bank - Assistant Chief General Manager |
| Knight | Geoffrey | British Aircraft Corporation - Sales Director |
| Koering | Brian | Laker Airways - Operations Duty Officer |
| Kraemer | Warren | McDonnell Douglas Corp. - PR Director for UK |
| Kurkjain | Ara | Pan Am - Regional Managing Director, UK & Northern Europe |
| Laker | Bettina (Gates) | Step-Daughter of Freddie Laker and daughter of Patricia Laker |
| Laker | Elaine | Only Daughter of Freddie and Joan Laker |
| Laker | Freddie Allen | Son of Sir Freddie and Lady Patricia Laker |
| Laker | Freddie Robert | (decd.) First son of Freddie and Patricia Laker |
| Laker | Frederick Henry | Natural father of Freddie Laker |
| Laker | Hannah | Mother of Freddie Laker |
| Laker | Joan | nee Stallwood / First wife of Freddie Laker |
| Laker | Kevin | Only Son of Freddie and Joan Laker |
| Laker | Patricia (Lady) | nee Gates / Third wife of Sir Freddie Laker |
| Laker | Rosemary | nee Black / Second wife of Freddie Laker |
| Lapautre | Rene | UTA - Chairman and Chief Executive |
| Lathiere | Bernard | Airbus Industrie - Chairman |
| Levinson | Fred | Film Director - Laker 1982 advertising campaign |
| Lord | Christopher | Lord Brothers - Director |
| Lord | Stephen | Lord Brothers - Director |
| Manson | Jock (Capt) | Laker Airways - DC-10 Captain |
| Marsh | Ann | Laker Airways - Reservations Manager USA |
| Marshall | Colin | British Airways - Chief Executive |
| Marshall | Morgan | Lawyer to Joan Laker |
| Maxwell | Charles | Laker Airways - Manager USA / ex International Caribbean Airways |
| McCarthy | Tony | Laker Airways - Insurance Manager |
| McDonnell | Sandford (Sandy) | McDonnell Douglas Corp. - Chairman of the Board |
| McDonnell | John | McDonnell Douglas Corp. - President |
| McIntosh | Ian | Samuel Montagu and Co - Director |
| McMillan | Harold (Rt Hon.) | Prime Minister of the United Kingdom (1957-63) |
| McMillan | Jim | President of McDonnell Douglas Finance Corporation |

| LAST NAME | FIRST NAME | ROLE IN THE LAKER STORY |
|---|---|---|
| Meredith | John | British Airways - General Manager, USA |
| Miller | Sandy | UTA - USA legal counsel |
| Mocatta | Alan (Justice) | Appeal court judge, Skytrain hearings |
| Mollison | Jim | Husband of Amy Johnson |
| Monks | Bernard | British Airways - Product Planning Manager |
| Morrison | Bill | Thomson McLintock - Accountant |
| Murphy | Pierre | Beckman, Farmer and Kirstein - Lawyer |
| Newby | George (Capt) | Laker Airways - DC-10 Captain |
| Nicholls | Alan | BUA - Chief Accountant |
| Nichols | Gordon | Laker Air Travel - Commercial Manager |
| Nixon | Richard (Pres.) | President of the United States (1969-74) |
| Nott | John | U.K. Secretary of State for Trade |
| Nunn | Cliff | Laker Airways - Deputy Managing Director / ex BUA |
| O'Brien | Bruce | Trans World Airlines - Senior executive |
| O'Melia | Richard | Civil Aeronautics Board - Chief enforcer |
| Owens | Sid | Arrowsmith Holidays - General Manager |
| Page | John (Capt) | Laker Airways - DC-10 Chief Training Capt. / ex Boeing 707 Trng Capt. |
| Pailleret | Pierre | Airbus Industrie - Director of Sales |
| Palmerini | Pablo | Caretaker of Laker yachts in Palma, Majorca |
| Paul | Dan | Divorce attorney for Sir Freddie Laker (Miami-Florida) |
| Penlington | Ross | Hong Kong ATLA - Judge Presiding |
| Penwarden | Jerry | Gatwick Handling Ltd. - General Manager / to Traffic Manager, Cathay |
| Plowes | George | Stud farm manager for Freddie Laker |
| Poirrier | Joy | Laker Airways - Head of Cabin Services / nee Harvey / ex BUA |
| Powell | Taffy | Silver City Airways - Founder |
| Powell | Charles | British Caledonian Airways - Senior executive |
| Price | Charles | U.S. Ambassador to the U.K. |
| Pugh | Alastair | BCal - Route Planning Manager / BCal board member / ex BUA |
| Rawlins | Barry (Capt.) | Laker Airways - Chief Pilot |
| Reagan | Ronald (Pres.) | President of the United States (1981-89) |
| Robinson | Robert (Robbie) | Laker Airways - Finance Director |
| Rogers | George | U.K. Board of Trade - under secretary |
| Roney | John | Laker Airways - Solicitor / Freddie Laker's personal lawyer |
| Runnette | Charles | Pan-Am - Vice President Atlantic Division |
| Sanderson | Bobby | Freddie Laker's early benefactor |
| Schweitzer | Karen | Laker Airways - Secretary / PA to Gregory Dix |
| Sedgwick | David | McDonnell Douglas Finance Corporation - Vice President |
| Seear | Elaine | Only daughter of Freddie & Joan Laker / wife of John Trayton Seear |
| Selley | Peter | Laker Airways - Accounts Manager, New York |
| Sharp | Gerry | Laker Airways - Commercial executive / to ICA - General Manager |
| Shore | Peter | U.K. Minister for Trade. |
| Shovelton | Patrick | U.K. Diplomat |
| Smythe | Ron | Race horse trainer for Freddie Laker |
| Snudden | Alan | Dan Air Services, Ltd.- Managing Director |
| Starr-Kins | Gloria | Representative for HH Prince Abdullah bin Jalawi, Saudi Arabia |
| Sproat | Iain | U.K. Under Secretary of Trade |
| Steer | Gordon (Capt) | Laker Airways - Senior DC-10 Captain / Laker Pilots' Association |
| Stein | Jacob | Lawyer to Freddie Laker |
| Street | Geoffrey | Laker Airways - Tariffs Manager / ex Skytrain Service Manager |
| Strein | Joseph | Laker Airways - Station Manager, Miami |
| Stuart | Charles | British Airways - Commercial Manager |
| Sy | Mike | Laker Airways - Canary Islands representative |
| Tait | David | Laker Airways - Regional Manager, SE USA & Latin America |

| LAST NAME | FIRST NAME | ROLE IN THE LAKER STORY |
|---|---|---|
| Tan | George | Carrian Group - Chairman / potential investor in Laker Airways |
| Thatcher | Dennis | Husband of PM Margaret Thatcher / personal friend of FAL |
| Thatcher | Margaret (Rt Hon) | Prime Minister of the United Kingdom (1979-90) |
| Thomson | Adam | British Caledonian Airways - Chairman |
| Timm | Robert | U.S. Civil Aeronautics Board - Chairman |
| Townsend | Ron | Laker Airways - Deputy Chief Engineer |
| Townsend | William F. (Bill) | Laker Airways - Technical Director / ex BUA |
| Trayton Seear | John | Laker Airways - Director / Freddie Laker's Son in Law |
| Varley | John | Pan Am - Regional Director, Passenger Marketing UK & Europe |
| Vesty | Meg | Laker Airways - In-Flight Director |
| Walker | David | Bank of England - Advisor |
| Wallace | Ian | Clydesdale Bank - Senior executive / personal friend of Freddie Laker |
| Wallace | Jane | Wife of Ian Wallace, Solicitor for Freddie Laker |
| Walsh | Ricki | Laker Airways - Station Manager, Los Angeles |
| Walter | Thomas | Laker Airways - Reservations Manager, New York |
| Waltrip | William | Pan Am - Chairman and Chief Executive |
| Watson | Freddie (Dr.) | Laker Airways - Dir. Hong Kong / Sr. Partner - Anderson's Hong Kong |
| Watson | Jacqueline | Wife of Dr. Freddie Watson / ex Nursing Sister |
| Watson | Arnold | ATA - Chief Test Pilot / Castrol board member |
| Welburn | Hugh | British Airways - Tariffs Manager |
| Welsman | Ernest | Wings - Managing Director |
| Wenzel | Cliff | Laker Airways - Coordinator of Canadian tour operations |
| Wheelhouse | Brian | Laker Airways - Purchasing Manager / ex BUA |
| Whybrow | Douglas | Channel Air Bridge - Chief executive |
| Wilson | Harold (Rt Hon) | Prime Minister of the United Kingdom (1964-70 & 1974-76) |
| Wiseman | Jack | Aviation Traders - Chief Engineer |
| Wren | Steve | Laker Airways - Steward |
| Wyatt | Myles | BUA - Chairman / Director of Airwork |
| Wyatt | Robert | Midland Bank - senior executive |
| Yeoman | Peter | Laker Airways - Chief Engineer / ex BUA |

# APPENDIX II

# TIMELINE

# *1922 - 1982*

**PART ONE August 1922 - November 1965**

| | |
|---|---|
| 6th August 1922 | Frederick Alfred Laker born |
| 1929 | Starts at Simon Langton Grammar School |
| 1930 | FAL's mother, Hannah Laker meets William Allin |
| 1st July 1938 | Leaves school (not yet 16) |
| 6th August 1938 | Joins Short Brothers as an apprentice on his 16th birthday |
| 1941 | Enrolls in the Air Transport Auxiliary (ATA) |
| 10th May 1942 | FAL (age 19) marries Joan Stallwood (age 25) |
| 18th Jan 1944 | Elaine Laker born |
| March 1946 | Demobbed from the ATA |
| 1st April 1946 | Joins British European Airways for three months |
| October 1947 | Starts Aviation Traders buying and selling surplus aircraft parts |
| 1947 | FAL works for LAMS and buys a cherry orchard |
| March 1948 | Kevin Laker Born |
| 28th May 1948 | 10 Halifax aircraft bought from BOAC / loan from Bobby Sanderson |
| June 1948 | Start of the Berlin airlift |
| August 1948 | Reconditioned Halifaxes join the Berlin Airlift |
| 12th May 1949 | End of the Berlin Airlift |
| February 1951 | Surrey Aviation purchased as the first airline for Air Charter Ltd |
| November 1951 | Buys Fairflight Ltd - contract flying freight between Hamburg & Berlin |
| 1951 | Took part in the second Berlin airlift |
| 1951 | Rescues the Avro Tudor with a redesign, renamed the Super Trader |
| 1951 | Air Charter trooping flights for the government |
| 11th March 1952 | FAL is nearly killed in a Berlin air crash |
| 1953 | Starts work on the Accountant |
| 1953 | Establishes Channel Air Bridge |
| February 1954 | Avro Tudor now certified as the Supertrader |
| 1956 | Buys Percival Prentices, FAL's first big business blunder |
| March 1957 | Key staff in the Accountant project resign |
| 9th July 1957 | First flight of the Accountant |
| 1957 | Air Charter and Aviation Traders put up for sale |
| 10th Jan 1958 | Stops the Accountant project |
| January 1958 | FAL sells Aviation Traders to Airwork for £900,000 |
| 1958 | FAL builds new home 'Charters' in Epsom, Surrey |
| 1959 | Airwork companies merged to become BUA |
| 1960 | Civil Aviation Act is passed |
| 1960 | FAL buys Bristow helicopters for BUA |
| May 1961 | FAL orders BAC One-Elevens for BUA |
| 1st March 1962 | Appointed to the board of Air Holdings and becomes MD of BUA |
| 20th July 1962 | Launches the world's first passenger hovercraft service |
| 1962 | FAL carves up BUA between himself and Myles Wyatt |
| 1964 | FAL buys 'Woolgars Farm' as a hobby |

**1965**

| | |
|---|---|
| April | BUA's inaugural One-Eleven flight from Gatwick to Genoa |
| July | Kevin Laker dies from injuries sustained in car crash |
| July | FAL tenders his resignation from BUA |
| 1st August | Myles Wyatt starts circumventing FAL at BUA |
| 15th Nov | Fall out with Myles Wyatt |
| 16 Nov | FAL resigns all directorships of the BUA group & Air Holdings |
| 30 Nov | Official date of departure from BUA |

## PART TWO End 1965 - September 1977

**1965**

| | |
|---|---|
| 1965 | FAL starts planning Laker Airways with Joan & John Jones |
| 1965 | Elaine Laker marries John Trayton Seear |

**1966**

| | |
|---|---|
| 8th Feb | Launches Laker Airways at the St Ermins Hotel, Victoria |
| April | First Bristol Britannia arrives from BOAC |
| April | Offically registers the Laker companies in Jersey |
| May | First Britannia sent to Zambia with John Jones supervising |
| June | Capt. Alan Hellary joins Laker Airways as Chief Pilot |
| August | Second Bristol Britannia arrives from BOAC |
| 1966 | Both Laker Britannias seized in Africa |
| 1966 | William Allin, Freddie's step father dies |

**1967**

| | |
|---|---|
| 24th March | Signs contract with Wings (Ernest Welsman) |
| May | First commercial flight of a Laker Airways' One-Eleven for Wings |
| May | Britannias and Jones return from Zambia |
| 18th Nov | Value of the £ falls by 14.3% |

**1968**

| | |
|---|---|
| January | Buys Lord Brothers Holidays |
| April | FAL divorces Joan Laker |
| 10th July | FAL marries Rosemary Black |
| August | Laker Airways flies arms to Nigeria |
| 6th Nov | British Eagle goes into receivership |
| 6th Nov | Buys two ex-Eagle / Qantas Boeing 707-138Bs (158 seats) |

**1969**

| | |
|---|---|
| April | British government withdraws from the Airbus project |
| 5th May | Edwards report published, calls for a second force in British Aviation |
| December | Meets Athol Guy of The Seekers band / discusses Australian tourism |
| 1969 | Starts Affinity Group charters to the USA and Canada |
| 1969 | Pan Am lands the first 747 at Heathrow airport |

**1970**

| | |
|---|---|
| March | FAL's natural father dies, aged 72 |
| April | BUA put up for sale |
| October | Laker takes 49% interest in Intl. Caribbean Airways of Barbados |
| 30th Nov | BCal formed by purchase of BUA by Caledonian (Adam Thomson) |
| December | First flight on behalf on International Caribbean |
| 1970 | Ernest Welsman of Wings retires |
| 1970 | George Carroll joins Laker group to manage Lord Brothers Travel |

| | |
|---|---|
| **1971** | |
| 26th March | Affinity Group charters raided by the authorities |
| April | FAL travels to Australia with John Seear to prospect flights from UK |
| May | Second Affinity Group charter raid on Laker Airways |
| 15th June | First Skytrain Application |
| 30th June | FAL holds press conference to announce Skytrain |
| August | PM Ted Heath passes the aviation act that forms the CAA |
| October | Application for Australian ABC's |
| November | ANA cancels purchase of 6 McDonnell Douglas DC-10-10s |
| November | MDC approaches FAL to buy three DC-10-10 aircraft |
| November | Skytrain turned down by ATLB |
| 1971 | Athol Guy becomes an MP for the State of Victoria |
| **1972** | |
| 24th Feb | Announces purchase of 3 DC-10-10s from MDC financed by Mitsui |
| March | Appeal for Skytrain heard |
| 6th April | Revised application for Skytrain now using DC-10s |
| April | The ATLB becomes the Civil Aviation Authority (CAA) |
| 1st Oct | CAA grants Laker Airways its first Skytrain licence |
| 26th Oct | 1st DC-10-10 (G-AZZC) 'Eastern Belle' delivered (Capt. Hellary) |
| 16th Nov | 2nd DC-10-10 (G-AZZD) 'Western Belle' delivered from Long Beach |
| 21st Nov | First revenue paying flight of a DC-10 in Europe |
| November | Hajj for Saudia (707s) |
| 28th Dec | BCal's appeal against Laker's Skytrain licence dismissed |
| 1972 | CAA approves BCal for London to New York and Los Angeles |
| 1972 | Gordon Nicholls joins Laker from Air Holdings |
| 1972 | Gatwick Handling is formed with Dan Air in a 50:50 deal |
| **1973** | |
| January | Dick O'Melia asks the CAB to suspend Laker's Air Operators Permit |
| 26th Feb | Laker designated as a UK scheduled carrier under Bermuda Agreement |
| February | Suntours of Canada contract worth $15 million is signed |
| 10th April | First ABC flight between Manchester and Toronto |
| July | Laker pays a $101,000 fine for a breach of affinity group rules |
| 6-25th Oct | Yom Kippur war (Egypt & Syria vs Israel) |
| October | First oil price increases due to turmoil in Middle East |
| November | Hajj for Saudia (707's) and a DC-10-10 operates 2nd phase |
| 10th Dec | U.S. CAB hearings on Skytrain begin |
| **1974** | |
| 31st Jan | Horizon Holidays goes into receivership |
| February | Ted Heath loses the UK general election |
| 31st Mar | British Airways is formed by a merger of BOAC and BEA |
| March | CAB recommends a two year temporary permit for Skytrain |
| April | Applies to Min. Tony Benn to take over Concorde operation from BA |
| 20th May | 3rd DC-10-10 (G-BBSZ) 'Canterbury Belle' delivered from Long Beach |
| 15th Aug | Clarksons Holidays goes into receivership |
| August | Donaldson goes into receivership. Laker buys shed for its ABC office |
| 23rd Sept | US and UK North Atlantic carriers agree to limit capacity on routes |
| October | Beckman threatens to sue legacy airlines under antitrust laws |
| Oct-Nov | Hajj - Rabat & Fez Morocco (1 DC-10-10) for Furness Withy |
| 23rd Dec | BA applies to have Laker's Skytrain licence revoked |
| 1974 | Laker Airways expands its ABC programme to the USA and Canada |

**1975**

| | |
|---|---|
| February | BA's application to have Laker's Skytrain licence revoked is rejected |
| May | FAL tells 1st wife Joan about Patricia; generates hostile reaction |
| 7th July | Buys Furzegrove Farm, Chailey - Sussex |
| July | FAL divorces Rosemary Laker |
| 9th July | FAL marries Patricia Gates; Joan disrupts reception; has to be evicted |
| July | Peter Shore (Sec State for Trade) says he will never allow Skytrain |
| 29th Sept | FAL moves into Furzegrove with Patricia and step daughter Bettina |
| Oct-Nov | Hajj - Kano, Nigeria (2 DC-10-10) |
| October | Survey into the potential of Skytrain done by Mori |
| 10th Nov | Freddie Robert Laker is born; dies four hours later |
| 1975 | Lord Brothers Becomes Laker Air Travel |
| 1975 | Night Rider Holidays Introduced |

**1976**

| | |
|---|---|
| 23rd June | Edmund Dell gives notice UK exiting the Bermuda Agreement |
| July | Letter of intent for 4th DC-10-10 (an MDC demo aircraft) |
| October | Hajj - Tehran, Iran (2 DC-10-10) |
| 1976 | The Court of Appeal rules on Laker Vs Peter Shore in Laker's favour |

**1977**

| | |
|---|---|
| 18th Feb | British Embassy in Washington asks US to process Lake'rs permit |
| March | Starts funding Margaret Thatcher's election campaign |
| May | Laker proposes ABCs to Australia (FAL & John Seear go to Melbourne) |
| 3rd June | 4th DC-10-10 (G-BELO) 'Southern Belle' delivered from Long Beach |
| 6th June | CAB signs off for a Skytrain permit |
| 13th June | President Carter signs off Skytrain landing rights in the US |
| 22nd June | Bermuda II agreement is reached |
| 5th July | IATA traffic conference held in Geneva to discuss Skytrain threat |
| July | Stansted airport set up for Skytrain operation |
| 10th August | 2nd IATA traffic conference |
| 15th Sept | Capacity restriction of DC-10 removed / Skytrain moves to Gatwick |

## PART THREE 26th September 1977 - 31st December 1981

**1977**

| | |
|---|---|
| 26th Sept | Inaugural Skytrain service - GK10 LGW-JFK (Capt. Bradshaw) |
| October | Application to the CAA for Australian ABC's |
| October | Hajj - Algiers, Algeria (2 DC-10-10) |
| 12th Dec | First Boeing 707-351B ex Cathay / Northwest delivered (Capt. Brookes) |
| December | Application for Los Angeles Skytrain service (served by BCal prior) |
| 1977 | Two new DC-10-10s (G-GFAL & G-GSKY) are ordered |

**1978**

| | |
|---|---|
| 4th January | Freddie Allen Laker born |
| 21st Feb | Places order for 5 DC-10-30s with McDonnell Douglas Corp. |
| 28th March | FAL sends Dix to New York (Manager-JFK then Ops Manager - NA) |
| March | Skytrain sales office moves into a kiosk on Victoria station |
| March | Los Angeles Skytrain Application heard |
| 5th May | Los Angeles Skytrain licence approved / BCal's appeal fails |
| 10th May | Second daily round trip Skytrain service flights to JFK added |
| 13th May | FAL receives Hon. Doc. of Law degree from Manchester University |
| May | BCal launches appeal against Laker being approved for LA route |
| May | 2nd Boeing 707-351B ex Cathay / Northwest delivered |

**1978 (cont.)**

| | |
|---|---|
| 1st June | FAL has lunch with the Queen and Prince Philip at Buckingham Palace |
| 3rd June | FAL's knighthood is announced |
| 19th July | FAL knighted by the Queen at Buckingham Palace |
| July | Lakerville - the streets of London are swamped with Skytrain passengers |
| 1st August | JFK office safe robbed / staff polygraphed / no conclusions |
| 7-8th Sept | Dix sets up Boston and Baltimore for ICA flights to Barbados |
| 13-14th Sept | Braniff 'Cowboy' computer training at DFW for US staff |
| 14th Sept | Contract for five new DC-10-30s with financing by ExIm Bank |
| 26th Sept | Inaugural Skytrain service flight from Gatwick to Los Angeles |
| September | Provisional order for Airbus A300B4 at Farnborough Intl. Air Show |
| 24th Oct | President Carter signs the United States Airline Deregulation Act |
| October | Denied ABC rights to Australia by Australian Transport Minister |
| October | Hajj - Kuala Lumpur, Malaysia (2 DC10-10) |
| 16th Nov | Inaugural Intl. Caribbean flight Baltimore to Barbados |
| 19 Nov | Inaugural Intl. Caribbean flight Boston to Barbados |
| 20th Dec | Application for Hong Kong filed with UK CAA |
| December | The 'winter of discontent' in the UK begins |
| 1978 | Boeing 707-138Bs G-AWDG & G-AVZZ sold |
| 1978 | Apple's UK distributor use FAL in ads for the new Apple 2 computer |

**1979**

| | |
|---|---|
| 1st Jan | Laker commences own passenger handling at JFK Airport |
| 16th Jan | The Shah of Iran falls from power |
| 19th Jan | Permission granted for Skytrain rollover (next day) system |
| January | Application for Skytrain full reservations service, APEX fares & cargo |
| 11th Feb | Margaret Thatcher becomes Prime Minister of the UK |
| 27th Feb | 5th DC-10-10 (G-GFAL) 'Northern Belle' delivered to LGW from MDC |
| 20th Mar | Dix sent to Japan, Hong Kong etc for Globetrain route analysis |
| 21st Mar | 6th DC-10-10 (G-GSKY) 'Californian Belle' delivered to LGW from MDC |
| 1st April | F1 teams (LGW-LAX) for US Grand Prix at Long Beach |
| 5th April | First ABC Flight LGW-Oakland |
| April | FAL starts campaign for 666 European routes |
| April | Application for London to Hong Kong via Sharjah |
| April | Application for trans-Pacific Route 6 (Globetrain) |
| April | Formal order placed for ten Airbus A300B4 aircraft |
| 4th May | First ABC flights to Detroit and Chicago |
| 23rd May | Hannah Laker dies after suffering three heart attacks |
| 25th May | American Airlines AA191 DC-10 crashes after take off at Chicago |
| 6th June | Hearing in London at CAA for Skytrain reservations service and cargo |
| 6th June | DC-10 worldwide fleet grounded (FAL receives notice while at CAA) |
| June | Hannah Laker's funeral |
| June | Application filed for 666 routes in Europe |
| June | Application for ABC's to Australia via Singapore and Colombo |
| 2nd July | FAL & Jones meet with BA executives at Victoria to agree fares |
| 13th July | DC-10 fleet reinstated after 6-week grounding |
| July | Approval for Skytrain flights to carry cargo and take reservations |
| September | Signing of financing agreement for DC-10-30s with ExIm Bank |
| September | FAL applies to adopt Bettina Gates / Laker |
| 27th Oct | Beckman gives notice of suit against AA for DC-10 grounding |
| October | Australia makes public statement that it will never approve Laker |

| | |
|---|---|
| 12th Nov | Licencing hearings in Hong Kong for London-Hong Kong route |
| November | Great European Hearing of airlines applying for European routes |
| November | Holiday flights to Tel Aviv commence |
| November | Hajj - KL, Malaysia (2 DC-10-10) |
| 13th Dec | DC-10-30 (G-BGXE) officially handed over at Long Beach |
| 15th Dec | First DC-10-30 (G-BGXE) delivered to LGW (Capt. James) |
| 15-18th Dec | Hong Kong Hearing at the CAA, London |
| December | Application for Route 6 filed (Los Angeles - Honolulu - Tokyo - Hong Kong) |
| 1979 | Skytrain sales office moved into the old London Tourist Board office |
| 1979 | Transport and General Workers Union attempt to infiltrate Laker |
| 1979 | FAL Signs contract for the Airbus A300s |
| 1979 | M/V 'Patrina' - a 27m Benetti Motoryacht purchased for FAL |
| 1979 | FAL receives Hon. Doctorate of Engineering from the UMIST |
| 1979 | Oil Prices increase to $35 a barrel from $15-20 |
| 1979 | FAL becomes a member of the Jockey Club |
| **1980** | |
| 1st Jan | First DC-10-30 non-stop flight from LGW to Los Angeles |
| 5th Jan | 2nd DC-10-30 (G-BGXF) delivered to LGW from MDC, Long Beach |
| 24th Jan | Conclusion of the great European Hearing |
| 4-7th Mar | Skytrain strategy meeting at LGW with all senior managers |
| 12th Mar | Loan agreement for the DC-10-30s signed |
| 13th Mar | Denied European licences by CAA / BCal granted six European routes |
| 13-14th Mar | Demonstration of 'Brian' reservations system by Com Soft at LGW |
| 24th Mar | 3rd DC-10-30 (G-BGXG) delivered to LGW from MDC |
| March | Denied licence for London to Hong Kong by CAA |
| March | Two Boeing 351Bs and five BAC 1-11s put up for sale |
| 15th April | Move terminals at LAX from WIT / Term 2 to the 'Bubble' |
| 30th April | 4th DC-10-30 (G-BGXH) 'Florida Belle' delivered to LGW from MDC |
| 14th April | First LGW-Miami ABC flight for Intasun |
| April | Route 6 hearing at CAA, London for trans-Pacific flights |
| 22nd May | Inaugural LGW to Miami Skytrain service |
| May | Skytrain service now operating 3 flights to JFK, 2 to LAX and 2 to MIA |
| 17th June | Hong Kong licence - John Nott overturns CAA decision and licences Laker |
| 24th June | 5th DC-10-30 (G-BGXI) delivered to LGW from MDC |
| June | Australia hearing at CAA, London. |
| June | Laker granted trans-Pacific Route 6 by the CAA |
| 11th Aug | New reservation system in USA |
| August | Application filed for London-Baltimore and London-Detroit |
| 22nd Sept | Seear & Dix meet w/Bill Marriott Jr in DC re global catering contract |
| 9-12th Oct | Sharjah for Hong Kong and Australia route preparations |
| 13-31st Oct | Dix in Hong Kong setting up for LGW-HKG Skytrain & Globetrain |
| 17th Oct | FAL in Hong Kong for a replay of the London-Hong Kong hearing |
| 20th Oct | Hong Kong Hearing commences |
| October | LGW-Tampa Skytrain licence approved |
| 1-16th Nov | Dix in Hong Kong, Malaysia & Philippines for Skytrain & ABCs |
| 29th Nov | Ian Allan returns to UK from Barbados to be Skytrain Service Manager |
| November | Gerry Sharp replaces Allan as Gen Mngr ICA in Barbados |
| November | Hajj - KL Malaysia (2 X DC-10-30) |
| 13th Dec | FAL, Jones & Dix at formal reception/dinner with Emir of Sharjah |
| 1980 | Hangar Extension started at LGW |

| | |
|---|---|
| 1980 | Application for Miami & Tampa from LGW, Prestwick and Manchester |
| 1980 | Application for London-Baltimore/Washington and London-Detroit |
| 1980 | Hong Kong ATLA approves Route 6 / Denies London - Hong Kong |
| **1981** | |
| 7th Jan | FAL signs the final loan agreement for the Airbus A300B4s |
| 8th Jan | 1st Airbus A300 (G-BIMA) 'Metro' Arrives at LGW (Capt. T Davies) |
| 14th Jan | Applies to CAA for Skytrain to Sydney, Melbourne and Perth |
| 16th Jan | FAL, Dix & Nunn meet John Nott to discuss Sharjah & Hong Kong |
| 26th Jan | Frankfurt, Dusseldorf, Zurich Hearing starts in London |
| January | Inaugural Skytrain service Manchester to Miami |
| January | DC-10-30 wet lease to Lan Chile for three months |
| 1st-5th Feb | Australian hearings in London |
| 17th Feb | FAL & Jones meet BA executives at Waldorf Hotel to agree fares |
| 25th Feb | Airbus Industrie lunch to celebrate the naming of the Airbus |
| March | Inaugural Skytrain service Manchester to New York & Los Angeles |
| March | Inaugural Skytrain service Prestwick to Los Angeles |
| 1st April | Emir of Sharjah sends his envoy to London to speak on Laker's behalf |
| 1st-2nd April | Sharjah Hearing at CAA |
| 2nd April | Inaugural Skytrain service Gatwick to Tampa |
| 19th April | Start of legal action over Govt. interpretation of the Treaty of Rome |
| 20th April | Dix & diplomat G Lowe lobby Australian govt. for licence in Canberra |
| 27th April | Australia hearing commences at CAA - London |
| April | Inaugural Skytrain service Prestwick to Miami |
| 1st May | Denied Australia Route by CAA |
| 22nd May | Appeal lodged for Australian route application |
| May | FAL meets with principal lenders to warn them of Laker's financial difficulties |
| May | CAA rejects Laker's application to operate to Sharjah |
| May | Beckman / FAL present claim for DC-10 Gounding to AA |
| 5-13th June | FAL, Beckman, Brown, Dix + Patricia & Bettina Laker in Hong Kong |
| 8-12th June | Route 6 hearings & promotional events in Hong Kong |
| 12th June | Patricia Laker returns to UK |
| 13th June | FAL offers to sell entire Laker Group to Carrian for £100 million |
| 14-18th June | FAL, Dix & Bettina Laker in Tokyo (Mitsui) and back in Hong Kong |
| 4th July | FAL writes to Carrian and drops his asking price for group to £62.5m |
| 10th July | FAL, Dix & Brown meet w/Carrian's Rod Bell who turns down Laker |
| 10th July | Nunn reorganises the USA / changes management |
| 13th July | Fails to make the first payment for the Airbus |
| 16th July | FAL & Jones meet BA executives at Victoria to agree fares |
| 20th July | Dix, Tait & Clemens take over USA in reorganisation |
| 27th July | Charles Maxwell (Manager USA) terminated |
| 3rd-5th Aug | FAL, Nunn & Allan in NYC - meet w/Dix re US Res and Tels systems |
| mid-Aug | Patricia Laker leaves FAL / Flies to Miami with Freddie Allen |
| 16th Aug | Laker Airways' precarious financial position becomes public |
| 21st Aug | Regency Service Meeting at LGW with all Laker's senior Managers |
| 26th Aug | Bank of England meeting with Lord Benson and David Walker |
| 11-13th Sept | Beckman and Dix meet in DC re Laker's current status |
| 14th Sept | FAL, Robinson & Roney in DC for refinancing discussions with ExIm |
| 15th Sept | 1981 Payment due for the DC-10-30s |
| 15th Sept | Midland Bank gives Laker Airways notice of default |
| 15th Sept | FAL in NYC for urgent USA strategy meetings with Dix |

| | |
|---|---|
| 16th Sept | FAL flies to Barbados for ICA meeting |
| 22-23rd Sept | Beckman meets Dix in NYC for discussions on state of Laker Airways |
| 24th Sept | Dix, Tait & Clemens meet in NY re IBT unionisation campaign |
| 1st Oct | Ed Acker becomes Chairman and CEO of PanAm / leaves Air Florida |
| 9th Oct | FAL writes to Patricia imploring her to return with Freddie Allen |
| 15th Oct | Fare War on the North Atlantic / Laker's fares matched by BA, PA & TWA |
| 16th Oct | GK, BA, BCal all meet at the CAA to respond to Pan Am's price drop |
| 26th Oct | Regency Service demo flight to JFK (to test in-flight service) |
| October | MDC report on status of Laker is produced for re-financing |
| October | Hajj - Llorin, Nigeria (1 DC-10-30) |
| Oct-Nov | IBT (Teamsters union) capaign to organise Laker staff in USA |
| 1st Nov | Transatlantic Fare War continues with BA, Pan Am and TWA |
| 1st Nov | Regency Service Inaugural on GK10/20 (LGW-JFK-LGW) |
| 4th Nov | Laker's lenders meet in London to determine a strategy |
| 4-6th Nov | FAL & Nunn in NYC for survival strategy discussions with Dix |
| 23rd Nov | New ad campaign devised w/ LGFE in NY w/Dix & L Earls |
| November | Half of Laker's fleet sits idle at Gatwick |
| 4th Dec | Meeting of all Laker's lenders in London |
| 9-12th Dec | FAL, Nunn meet with Dix in NYC re desperate survival strategies |
| 11th Dec | FAL, Nunn, Beckman & Murphy w/AA's Crandall re DC-10 grounding |
| 11th Dec | Bank of England tells Roney that Laker Airways must cease trading |
| 23rd Dec | Staff meetings held at all USA offices to defeat Teamsters unionisation |
| 24th Dec | Official Press Release that Laker Airways has been saved |
| 26th Dec | Patricia Laker returns to England for a week with Freddie Allen |
| 31st Dec | Patricia Laker files for divorce |
| 1981 | Laker Airways granted LGW-Zurich route |
| 1981 | Legal action against the government over the Treaty of Rome |

## PART FOUR 1st January - 5th February 1982

**1982**

| | |
|---|---|
| 1st-3rd Jan | Beckman in NYC for urgent discussions with Dix on Laker's survival |
| 6-7th Jan | Dix, Tait, Clemens meet with NY lawyers re US employee situation |
| 7th Jan | Tudor King Letter confirming terms of Laker's refinancing plan |
| 22nd Jan | Midland Bank refuses to reimburse A300 spares reserve money |
| 23rd Jan | FAL & AA's Crandall in Florida to agree DC-10 grounding settlement |
| 26th Jan | Casting & pre-production for Laker's 1982 TV commercials |
| 30th Jan | Japan denies Laker fifth and seventh freedom rights |
| 1st Feb | Midland & MDC give FAL verbal assurance of refinancing |
| 1st Feb | FAL, Robinson & others at Tramp in London celebrating refinancing |
| 2nd Feb | FAL flies via Concorde to New York / met by Dix at JFK |
| 2nd Feb | Strategy meeting in NYC - FAL, Nunn, Jones, Allan, Dix, Tait, Clemens |
| 2nd Feb | FAL forced by MDC to forego Europe routes for refinancing package |
| 3rd Feb | FAL & Dix in all day ad shoot on DC-10 at JFK for 1982 programme |
| 4th Feb | FAL flies back to LGW / summoned to meet the Midland Bank |
| 4th Feb am | Midland Bank tells FAL to have £5m by am on 5th or call in Receivers |
| 4th Feb pm | FAL & Roney meet with FAL's divorce lawyer |
| 4th Feb pm | FAL fails to sell H Goodman an A300 and tour operations for £10m |
| 4th Feb pm | FAL calls Mitsui to borrow £5m / no response / acknowledges defeat |
| 5th Feb am | Final Board meeting / Laker Airways goes into Receivership |
| 5th Feb | Laker planes grounded / Laker offices worldwide closed |

# APPENDIX III
# LAKER AIRWAYS TOTAL PASSENGERS CARRIED
## *1966 - 1981*

| Year | North Atlantic Charter Passengers *(incl Affinity Group charters & ABCs)* | Total One-Way Passengers *(incl Europe, ABCs, Skytrain & charters)* |
|---|---|---|
| 1966 | | 9,800* |
| 1967 | | 131,050* |
| 1968 | | 233,739 |
| 1969 | | 334,514 |
| 1970 | 37,021 | 369,461 |
| 1971 | 52,227 | 424,870* |
| 1972 | 31,621 | 634,000* |
| 1973 | 102,102 | 668,773 |
| 1974 | 179,690 | 758,444 |
| 1975 | 228,726 | 960,800* |
| 1976 | 280,409 | 939,900* |
| 1977 | 305,013* | 1,150,732 |
| 1978 | 606,653 | 1,380,719 |
| 1979 | 531,853 | 1,306,040# |
| 1980 | N/A | 1,984,427 |
| 1981 | N/A | 1,941,175 |
| **Total:** | **2,355,315** | **13,239,884** |

Between 1970 and 1979, Laker Airways was the undisputed leader of North Atlantic charters, regularly carrying over 50% of the total traffic. Once Skytrain was launched, Laker's ABC traffic declined significantly and due to the aggressive response to Skytrain by Laker's competitors, it brought about the end of North Atlantic charters and the downfall of charter airlines.

* Unverified from company records and possibly approximate

\# Affected by the DC-10 grounding

Source: Laker Airways' company records

# APPENDIX IV

# LAKER AIRWAYS SKYTRAIN SERVICE ONE-WAY PASSENGERS

## *Comparison: 1981 vs 1980*

## *Total Passengers: 1977-1982*

| | Route | 1980 | % L/F | 1981 | % L/F | 1982 | % L/F | Variance 81 vs 80 | Variance% 81 vs 80 | Cumul. 81 vs 80 |
|---|---|---|---|---|---|---|---|---|---|---|
| Jan | LGW-JFK-LGW | 15,166 | 68.7% | 17,226 | 69.4% | 8,519 | 37.2% | 2,060 | 13.6% | |
| Feb | | 10,733 | 53.6% | 10,032 | 51.9% | | | -701 | -6.5% | 1,359 |
| Mar | | 16,852 | 69.8% | 14,130 | 68.3% | | | -2,722 | -16.2% | -1,363 |
| Apr | | 23,487 | 89.6% | 21,972 | 78.6% | | | -1,515 | -6.5% | -2,878 |
| May | | 29,680 | 82.7% | 22,566 | 77.0% | | | -7,114 | -24.0% | -9,992 |
| Jun | | 40,367 | 79.5% | 24,084 | 72.5% | | | -16,283 | -40.3% | -26,275 |
| Jul | | 51,334 | 85.5% | 29,651 | 83.2% | | | -21,683 | -42.2% | -47,958 |
| Aug | | 56,476 | 89.9% | 36,120 | 86.5% | | | -20,356 | -36.0% | -68,314 |
| Sep | | 37,929 | 88.0% | 24,519 | 89.2% | | | -13,410 | -35.4% | -81,724 |
| Oct | | 28,275 | 73.8% | 17,299 | 82.7% | | | -10,976 | -38.8% | -92,700 |
| Nov | | 16,116 | 75.3% | 9,360 | 58.5% | | | -6,756 | -41.9% | -99,456 |
| Dec | | 20,042 | 74.5% | 10,055 | 56.3% | | | -9,987 | -49.8% | -109,443 |
| **TOTAL JFK** | | **346,457** | **77.6%** | **237,014** | **72.8%** | **8,519** | **37.2%** | **-109,443** | **-31.6%** | |
| Jan | LGW-LAX-LGW | 9,784 | 45.7% | 13,628 | 61.7% | 7,202 | 32.6% | 3,844 | 39.3% | |
| Feb | | 7,430 | 37.8% | 9,236 | 47.8% | | | 1,806 | 24.3% | 5,560 |
| Mar | | 12,854 | 56.5% | 12,503 | 60.4% | | | -351 | -2.7% | 5,299 |
| Apr | | 15,144 | 73.2% | 16,717 | 80.8% | | | 1,573 | 10.4% | 6,872 |
| May | | 19,098 | 85.2% | 18,864 | 68.3% | | | -234 | -1.2% | 6,638 |
| Jun | | 24,520 | 78.9% | 19,483 | 67.6% | | | -5,037 | -20.5% | 1,601 |
| Jul | | 31,563 | 73.8% | 22,867 | 68.3% | | | -8,696 | -27.6% | -7,095 |
| Aug | | 37,905 | 88.6% | 32,659 | 78.9% | | | -5,246 | -13.8% | -12,341 |
| Sep | | 28,754 | 80.7% | 24,610 | 79.3% | | | -4,144 | -14.4% | -16,485 |
| Oct | | 24,664 | 76.0% | 20,222 | 77.1% | | | -4,442 | -18.0% | -20,927 |
| Nov | | 14,312 | 69.1% | 9,625 | 51.4% | | | -4,687 | -32.7% | -25,614 |
| Dec | | 13,331 | 62.3% | 8,675 | 46.8% | | | -4,656 | -34.9% | -30,270 |
| **TOTAL LAX** | | **239,359** | **69.0%** | **209,089** | **65.7%** | **7,202** | **32.6%** | **-30,270** | **-12.6%** | |
| Jan | LGW-MIA-LGW | | | 17,114 | 70.9% | 7,882 | 35.7% | 17,114 | | |
| Feb | | | | 12,834 | 66.4% | | | 12,834 | | 29,948 |
| Mar | | | | 16,136 | 75.4% | | | 16,136 | | 46,084 |
| Apr | | | | 19,400 | 80.4% | | | 19,400 | | 65,484 |
| May | | 5,901 | 81.4% | 15,262 | 62.1% | | | 9,361 | 158.6% | 74,485 |
| Jun | | 19,950 | 94.7% | 10,700 | 51.5% | | | -9,250 | -46.4% | 65,595 |
| Jul | | 17,569 | 82.1% | 15,760 | 68.9% | | | -1,809 | -10.3% | 63,786 |
| Aug | | 21,083 | 95.5% | 21,993 | 81.6% | | | 910 | 4.3% | 64,696 |
| Sep | | 19,056 | 93.5% | 14,131 | 75.3% | | | -4,925 | -25.8% | 59,771 |
| Oct | | 21,163 | 92.9% | 13,721 | 75.0% | | | -7,442 | -35.2% | 52,329 |
| Nov | | 20,168 | 80.1% | 7,863 | 47.4% | | | -12,305 | -61.0% | 40,024 |
| Dec | | 17,246 | 72.4% | 7,866 | 43.3% | | | -9,380 | -54.4% | 30,644 |
| **TOTAL MIA** | | **142,136** | **86.6%** | **172,780** | **66.5%** | **7,882** | **35.7%** | **30,644** | **21.6%** | |
| *Comparison (MIA from May 81)* | | | | *107,296* | *63.1%* | | | *-34,840* | *-24.5%* | |
| **TOTAL (x 3 Routes)** | | **727,952** | **77.7%** | **618,883** | **68.3%** | **23,603** | **35.2%** | **-109,069** | **-15.0%** | |
| *Total Comparison (MIA from May 81)* | | | | *511,587* | | | | *-174,553* | *-24.0%* | |
| **Supplemental Routes - 1981** | | | | | | | | | | |
| From Jan | **MAN-MIA-MAN** | | | 63,359 | 82.1% | | | | | |
| From Mar | **MAN-JFK-MAN** | | | 42,099 | 74.2% | | | | | |
| From Mar | **MAN-LAX-MAN** | | | 31,024 | 88.3% | | | | | |
| From Mar | **PIK-LAX-PIK** | | | 14,025 | 82.1% | | | | | |
| From Apr | **LGW-TPA-LGW** | | | 48,668 | 74.1% | | | | | |
| From Apr | **PIK-MIA-PIK** | | | 16,468 | 83.6% | | | | | |
| **TOTAL (Supplemental Routes)** | | | | **215,643** | | | | | | |
| **GRAND TOTAL (All Routes)** | | **727,952** | **78.3%** | **834,526** | **72.5%** | **23,603** | **35.2%** | **106,574** | **14.6%** | |

**1977-1982 Skytrain Passengers**

| | Pax | %LF |
|---|---|---|
| 1977 (Sep-) | 54,489 | 80.8% |
| 1978 | 262,124 | 72.3% |
| 1979 | 301,734 | 71.7% |
| 1980 | 727,952 | 78.3% |
| 1981 | 834,526 | 72.5% |
| 1982 (Jan) | 23,603 | 35.2% |
| TOTAL: | 2,204,428 | 73.5% |

Airport Codes UK: LGW - London (Gatwick) MAN - Manchester PIK - Glasgow (Prestwick)

Airport Codes USA: JFK - New York LAX - Los Angeles MIA - Miami TPA - Tampa

Source: Laker Airways' company records

## APPENDIX V

# THE FARE FIXING MEETINGS AND PARTICIPANTS

## *1978 - 1982*

Following the chaos of 'Lakerville', in the summer of 1978, Sir Freddie and Laker's Commercial Manager, John Jones had numerous secret (and illicit) meetings with executives of British Airways and Pan Am. They negotiated transatlantic fare levels and differentials in an attempt to give Laker a competitive advantage.

Main Protagonists:

| | |
|---|---|
| **Laker Airways:** | FAL - Sir Freddie Laker, Chairman |
| | JJ - John Jones, Commercial Manager |
| **British Airways:** | Draper - Gerry Draper, Director of Commercial Operations |
| | Welburn - Hugh Welburn, Tariffs Manager |
| | Monks - Bernard Monks, Product Planning Manager |
| | Cochrane - Ossie Cochrane, Western Routes Manager |
| | Stuart - Charles Stuart, Commercial Manager |
| | Meredith - John Meredith, US General Manager |
| **Pan Am** | John Varley, Regional Director, Passenger Marketing UK and Europe |
| | Ara Kurkjian, Regional MD UK and Northern Europe |
| | Charles Runnette, Vice President Atlantic Division |

| | |
|---|---|
| **November 1978** | Agreement with BA regarding Fare levels & Differentials. No objection to Laker removing tariff provisions from Skytrain licence. PA and TW confirm agreement with BA. |
| **3rd May 1979** | FAL had lunch meeting with Welburn. Discussed BA's desire to increase fares and Laker's intention to provide reservation products. |
| **2nd July 1979** | FAL and JJ met with Stuart, Cochrane & Welburn at Victoria. Discussed fares, fare levels and fare increases. FAL & JJ understood agreement re Fall/Winter 1979 Super Apex fares. |
| **Aug/Sept 1979** | Monks telephoned JJ to arrange a meeting to discuss fares |
| **On or About 19th September 1979** | JJ met Monks to discuss specific fares, levels and differentials. |
| **Sept 1979 - Feb 1980** | FAL & JJ telephoned frequently by Cochrane, Stuart & Monks concerning US-UK fares, differentials and pricing principles. |

| | |
|---|---|
| **14th February, 1980** | JJ met Monks at Victoria Air Terminal. Discussed fares, fare levels and differentials. |
| **Feb 1980 - Aug 1980** | Monks telephoned JJ frequently to say Laker 'must close the gap'. |
| **August 1980** | Monks advised JJ that BA, TW & PA reduced Standby & Super Apex differentials to $10, because Laker failed to 'close the gap'. |
| **5th Nov 1980** | FAL & JJ had lunch meeting at Intercontinental Hotel with CW Runette, Ara Kurkjian and John Varley of Pan Am |
| **Several days after 5th. November, 1980** | JJ met John Varley in Varley's office to discuss fares, fare levels, differentials, and fare increases. |
| **17th January, 1981** | JJ met Monks and John Elliott & Mike Paddy? (BA) at Victoria Air Terminal after Canadian Charter discussions. Discussed fare increases, differentials and fare increase timing. |
| **Jan & Feb, 1981** | JJ and Monks discussed on telephone specific fares & fare levels in preparation for Waldorf Agreement. |
| **17th February, 1981** | Waldorf Hotel meeting. FAL & JJ with Draper, Cochrane & Monks (BA). Specific fare agreement regarding entire Spring / Summer 1981 fare package. No differentials on Standby. Understood TW and PA agreed also. Draper threatened FAL that all three would reduce fares to zero if necessary. |
| **18th Feb 1981** | FAL had lunch meeting with Welburn |
| **On or immediately after 18th. March, 1981** | Laker repudiated 'Waldorf Agreement' resulting in phone calls between JJ and Monks and between FAL and Cochrane & Stuart |
| **July 1981** | Telephone calls from Monks to JJ regarding fares, fare levels, increases, and differentials for Fall 1981 Fares package. |
| **16th July, 1981** | FAL & JJ had 'over the rooftop' meeting in BA board room at Victoria Air Terminal with Cochrane, John Elliott, Monks, (& Welburn?). Discussed fares, levels, increases, and differentials. BA advised FAL & JJ the amount of differentials which BA, TW & PA would allow Laker. FAL advised them about Regency Service idea then FAL offered not to do Regency in exchange for higher differentials. Fare war followed. |
| **18-19th Jan 1982** | JJ met with Terry Cox, John Meredith and Derek Harwood (BA) in N. Hollywood, Florida. |

# APPENDIX V

# THE FARE WAR

## FARES FILED WITH THE US CAB

## *1981*

| ROUTE | AIRLINE | ECONOMY (One-Way) July 81 *Agreed with Laker* | ECONOMY (One-Way) Nov 81 *Agreed by British Airways Pan Am & TWA* | STANDBY (Walk-On) Nov 81 |
|---|---|---|---|---|
| London - New York | Laker | \$299 £148 | \$261 | \$204 |
| | British Airways | \$552 | \$261 | \$204 |
| | Pan American | \$552 | \$261 | \$204 |
| | TWA | \$552 | \$261 | \$204 |
| London - Los Angeles | Laker | \$399 £198 | \$346 | \$284 |
| | British Airways | \$1,016 | \$346 | \$284 |
| | Pan American | \$N/A | \$346 | \$284 |
| | TWA | \$N/A | \$346 | \$284 |
| London - Miami | Laker | \$282 £143 | \$249 | \$199 |
| | British Airways | \$368 | \$249 | \$199 |
| | Pan American | \$368 | \$249 | \$199 |
| | TWA | \$N/A | \$N/A | \$N/A |

Following the 16th July 1981 fare fixing meeting, Laker continued to have a reasonable differential to its competitors on its one-way unrestricted Economy fare. Laker could have actually filed a higher full economy fare for Summer 1981 but didn't, instead positioning its Economy fare close to its round-trip APEX that had been hotly contested, eg. LGW-JFK Economy round trip £296 & APEX £286. Laker's main competitors reneged on filing their new APEX fares that resulted in Laker having the highest APEX for about ten days in August 1981; Laker's phones stopped ringing.

The crucial Winter 1981 / 82 fares filed in November 1981 were matched by Laker's main competitors. Laker had by now, lost any price advantage it had enjoyed since the inception of Skytrain in 1977. Laker also positioned its unrestricted Economy fare on all three of its prime routes too close to the APEX. The net result was virtually no vital APEX tickets sold when Laker urgently needed advance bookings and positive cash flow. Then, when Laker's competitors offered considerably higher travel agent commissions, thousands of full Economy tickets were cancelled. By this time, Laker was not in control of determining its own fares and the folly of collaboration and fare-fixing was being realised.

Source: CAB Tariffs

# APPENDIX VI

# THE 1981-82 SKYTRAIN SERVICE

## REGENCY SERVICE

The controversial Regency Service one-way fare was positioned at the same level as the competitor scheduled carriers' unrestricted full Economy fare. Laker's introduction of Regency was singularly responsible for provoking the fare war of late 1981 when Laker's principal competitors matched Laker's Economy, Apex and Standby (Walk-On) fares across the board.

The Laker Airways DC-10 aircraft has been newly equipped to provide the utmost privacy for the frequent traveller, with the added comfort of wider, spacious seating.

The new

*Regency* **FRONT CABIN SERVICE**

will feature the following Laker luxuries:

- 46 first-class type seats with a 6 and 7 abreast configuration providing extra leg room for your comfort.
- Advance seat preference.
- Separate check-in facilities.
- Pre-boarding and priority baggage handling
- Champagne prior to take-off followed by complimentary drinks and liqueurs throughout the flight.
- Hors d'oeuvres and choice of entrees with complimentary selection of fine wines.
- Meals will be served on fine English wedgewood china on a linen setting.
- Newspapers and magazines for your reading pleasure.
- Complimentary full ear headsets for movie and stereo.

In addition, there will be other frills such as complimentary Elizabeth Arden toiletries, hot towel service, individual comfort packs and the sale of duty free items during flight.

### FLIGHT SCHEDULE

**FROM NEW YORK/JFK**

**To London/LGW**

| DEP | ARR | FLT# | FREQ |
|---|---|---|---|
| 7:30P | 7:15A | GK20 | Daily |

**To Manchester/MAN**

| DEP | ARR | FLT# | FREQ |
|---|---|---|---|
| 8:20P | 7:55A | GK22 | M/TH |

**TO NEW YORK/JFK**

**From London/LGW**

| DEP | ARR | FLT# | FREQ |
|---|---|---|---|
| 1:00P | 3:45P | GK10 | Daily |

**From Manchester/MAN**

| DEP | ARR | FLT# | FREQ |
|---|---|---|---|
| 3:00P | 5:20P | GK21 | M/TH |

SCHEDULES EFFECTIVE FROM NOVEMBER 1, 1981

### FARES

**TO/FROM NEW YORK**

The Regency Service airfare will be totally unrestricted without penalty for change or cancellation.

| One-Way | One-Way |
|---|---|
| $526 - Low Season | $622 - High Season |

### FARE SEASONS

| From New York | To New York |
|---|---|
| Low: Sep 15 to May 14 | Low: Oct 15 to Jun 14 |
| High: May 15 to Sep 14 | High: Jun 15 to Oct 14 |

Round trip fares are double the one-way fares for the appropriate season.

- All Flights are operated by DC-10 aircraft -
- Schedules are subject to change -
- All fares subject to change without notice -

APPENDIX VI

# THE 1981-82 SKYTRAIN SERVICE

## BROCHURE COVER

# APPENDIX VI

# THE 1981-82 SKYTRAIN SERVICE

## ECONOMY CLASS FARES

For the Winter of 1981-82, the most critical period of Laker Airways' lifecycle, an unprecedented five Skytrain products were offered on all nine of Laker's transatlantic scheduled service routes. All fares, except the same day Walk-On were bookable through travel agents. Laker's Apex fares were set too close to the unrestricted Economy fare, compromising vital advance reservations.

Round trip Winter 1981-82 fares for New York (JFK), Los Angeles (LAX) and Miami (MIA) shown under each fare category

**Skytrain** SCHEDULED AIR SERVICE

**ECONOMY**

Reserved seats on any flight, one way or round trip. Bookings may be made at any time prior to departure and there are no length of stay or other restrictions. The fare includes in-flight meals. Changes of reservation or cancellations may be made without penalty.
**Children's Fares:** Infants under 2 years of age travel at 10% of the adult fare, children under 12 at half the adult fare.

**JFK: £248 LAX: £338 MIA: £238**

**Skytrain** SCHEDULED AIR SERVICE

**SUPER APEX**

Reserved seats on any flights. Advance purchase round-trip fare. Bookings must be made 21 days or more prior to initial departure with minimum overseas stay of 7 days, including day of departure and arrival. The fare includes in-flight meals. Reservations may be changed or cancelled upon payment of £25 per person per cancelled or changed booking.
**Children's Fares:** Infants under 2 years of age travel at 10% of the adult fare, children under 12 at half the adult fare.

**JFK: £223 LAX: £314 MIA: £228**

**Skytrain** SCHEDULED AIR SERVICE

**8 DAY WALK-ON**

Outward seats may be reserved for travel within 8 days of booking, and firm return reservations also made, through your travel agent or at any Laker Skytrain Service ticket sales office. Tickets can be re-validated for another flight operating within 8 days of cancelled reservation at a charge of £10 per ticket sector amended, but are non-refundable. Fare includes in-flight meals.
**Children's Fares:** Infants under 2 years of age travel at 10% of the adult fare, children under 12 at two-thirds the adult fare.

**JFK: £218 LAX: £294 MIA: £224**

**Skytrain** SCHEDULED AIR SERVICE

**SAME DAY WALK-ON**

Reserved seats for travel the same day. The fare includes in-flight meals. Same Day Walk-On tickets are non-refundable and reservations may not be changed.
**Children's Fares:** Infants under 2 years of age travel at 10% of the adult fare. No reduction for children under 12 years.

**JFK: £180 LAX: £262 MIA: £190**

# APPENDIX VII

# LAKER AIRWAYS FLEET

## *1966 - 1982*

| Manufacturer | Type | Regn. | Origin | Name | In Service |
|---|---|---|---|---|---|
| Vickers | VC10 | G-ARTA | BUA | | |
| Leased to MEA | | | | | |
| Bristol | Britannia 175 | G-ANBM | BOAC | | 1966 - 69 |
| Bristol | Britannia 175 | G-ANBN | BOAC | | 1966 - 69 |
| BAC | One Eleven 320 | G-AVBW | New | | 1967 - 82 |
| BAC | One Eleven 320 | G-AVBX | New | | 1967 - 82 |
| BAC | One Eleven 320 | G-AVBY | New | | 1967 - 82 |
| BAC | One Eleven 320 | G-AVYZ | New | | 1967 - 82 |
| BAC | One Eleven 301 | G-ATPK | Bahamas | | 1971 - 81 |
| Boeing | 707-138B | G-AVZZ | Eagle | | 1969 - 78 |
| Boeing | 707-138B | G-AWDG | Eagle | | 1969 - 78 |
| MDC | DC-10-10 | G-AZZC | New | Eastern Belle | 1972 - 82 |
| MDC | DC-10-10 | G-AZZD | New | Western Belle | 1972 - 82 |
| MDC | DC-10-10 | G-BBSZ | New | Canterbury Belle | 1974 - 82 |
| MDC | DC-10-10 | G-BELO | Demo | Southern Belle | 1977 - 82 |
| Boeing | 707-351B | G-BFBS | Cathay | | 1977 - 82 |
| Boeing | 707-351B | G-BFBZ | Cathay | | 1978 - 82 |
| MDC | DC-10-10 | G-GFAL | New | Northern Belle | 1979 - 82 |
| MDC | DC-10-10 | G-GSKY | New | Californian Belle | 1979 - 82 |
| MDC | DC-10-30 | G-BGXE | New | | 1979 - 82 |
| MDC | DC-10-30 | G-BGXF | New | | 1980 - 82 |
| MDC | DC-10-30 | G-BGXG | New | | 1980 - 82 |
| MDC | DC-10-30 | G-BGXH | New | Florida Belle | 1980 - 82 |
| MDC | DC-10-30 | G-BGXI | New | | 1980 - 82 |
| Airbus | A300B4-200 | G-BIMA | New | Metro | 1981 - 82 |
| Airbus | A300B4-200 | G-BIMB | New | Orient Express | 1981 - 82 |
| Airbus | A300B4-200 | G-BIMC | New | Intercity Express | 1981 - 82 |

| | | |
|---|---|---|
| **Seating Configurations:** | DC-10 | 345Y |
| From Nov 1 1981 | DC-10 | 46F / 268Y |
| | A300 | 284Y |
| | B707 | 189Y |
| | One-Eleven | 89Y |

# APPENDIX VIII Flight Times & Distances

| Route | Time | Distance (NM) |
|---|---|---|
| **Skytrain Service Westbound** | | |
| LGW-JFK | 7:45 | 3,015 |
| LGW-LAX | 11:20 | 4,762 |
| LGW-MIA | 9:10 | 3,858 |
| LGW-TPA | 9:05 | 3,847 |

JFK = New York, LAX = Los Angeles, MIA = Miami, TPA = Tampa

Also: MAN-LAX, MAN-MIA MAN = Manchester

Also: PIK-JFK, PIK-LAX, PIK-MIA PIK = Prestwick / Glasgow

| Route | Time | Distance (NM) |
|---|---|---|
| **International Caribbean (Barbados) Westbound** | | |
| LGW-LUX | 1:20 | 262 |
| LUX-BGI | 9:15 | 3,869 |

LUX = Luxembourg, BGI = Barbados

| Route | Time | Distance (NM) |
|---|---|---|
| **Advance Booking Charters (Toronto) Westbound** | | |
| LGW-YYZ | 7:50 | 3,108 |

YYZ = Toronto Also: Montreal, Ottawa, Halifax, Windsor, St. John's, Winnipeg, Calgary, Vancouver, Oakland & others

| Route | Time | Distance (NM) |
|---|---|---|
| **Australia Westbound**** | | |
| SYD-SIN | 8:10 | 3,395 |
| MEL-SIN | 7:50 | 3,253 |
| PER-SIN | 5:15 | 2,104 |
| SIN-SHJ | 7:45 | 3,150 |
| SHJ-LGW | 7:50 | 2,960 |

SYD = Sydney, MEL = Melbourne, PER = Perth

SHJ = Sharjah - UAE, SIN = Singapore

| Route | Time | Distance (NM) |
|---|---|---|
| **Globetrain Westbound via Japan** (Incl. ground time) | | |
| LGW-LAX | 11:20 | 4,762 |
| LAX | 2:00 | |
| LAX-HNL* | 6:00 | 2,216 |
| HNL | 1:30 | |
| HNL-NRT** | 9:15 | 3,317 |
| NRT | 1:30 | |
| NRT-HKG** | 5:20 | 1,601 |
| HKG | 2:00 | |
| HKG-SHJ** | 9:05 | 3,207 |
| SHJ | 1:30 | |
| SHJ-LGW** | 7:50 | 2,960 |
| LGW | 2:00 | |
| **TOTAL:** | **59:20** | **18,063** |
| **Alternate 1** | | |
| HNL-GUM* | 7:45 | 3,302 |
| GUM-HKG* | 5:05 | 1,825 |
| **Alternate 2** | | |
| LAX-ANC | 5:50 | 2,038 |
| ANC-HKG# | 11:05 | 4,406 |

HKG = Hong Kong, NRT = Tokyo, HNL = Honolulu

SHJ = Sharjah - UAE, GUM = Guam, ANC = Anchorage

---

| Route | Time | Distance (NM) |
|---|---|---|
| **Skytrain Service Eastbound** | | |
| JFK-LGW | 6:45 | 3,015 |
| LAX-LGW | 10:25 | 4,762 |
| MIA-LGW | 8:20 | 3,858 |
| TPA-LGW | 8:10 | 3,847 |
| **International Caribbean (Barbados) Eastbound** | | |
| BGI-LUX | 8:30 | 3,869 |
| LUX-LGW | 1:15 | 262 |
| **Advance Booking Charters (Toronto) Eastbound** | | |
| LGW-YYZ | 6:50 | 3,108 |
| **Australia Eastbound**** | | |
| LGW-SHJ | 7:00 | 2,960 |
| SHJ-SIN | 7:15 | 3,150 |
| SIN-PER | 5:15 | 2,104 |
| SIN-MEL | 7:25 | 3,253 |
| SIN-SYD | 7:55 | 3,395 |

*Licenced / not operated ** Not licenced / under appeal

1 Nautical mile = 1.15 Statute miles (1,852km)

Flight times approx. for DC-10 at long range cruise (0.82M)

Distances based on great circle. Actual air distances may vary

| Route | Time | Distance (NM) |
|---|---|---|
| **Globetrain Eastbound via Japan** (Incl. ground time) | | |
| LGW-SHJ** | 7:00 | 2,960 |
| SHJ | 1:30 | |
| SHJ-HKG** | 7:05 | 3,207 |
| HKG | 2:00 | |
| HKG-NRT** | 4:10 | 1,601 |
| NRT | 1:30 | |
| NRT-HNL** | 6:55 | 3,317 |
| HNL | 1:30 | |
| HNL-LAX* | 5:30 | 2,216 |
| LAX | 2:00 | |
| LAX-LGW | 10:25 | 4,762 |
| LGW | 2:00 | |
| **TOTAL:** | **51:35** | **18,063** |
| **Alternate 1** | | |
| HKG-GUM* | 4:50 | 1,825 |
| GUM-HNL* | 7:10 | 3,302 |
| **Alternate 2** | | |
| HKG-ANC# | 10:30 | 4,406 |
| ANC-LAX | 5:20 | 2,038 |
| **Alternate 3** | | |
| HKG-HNL* | 11:30 | 4,824 |

Alternate routeings if Japanese traffic rights not granted

#Actual time & distance possibly longer to avoid Russia

# APPENDIX IX

# THE LAKER GROUP 1982

## *Ownership, Legal Status and Capital Structures*

**The Laker Group of Companies** evolved around a single theme: the production and sale of commercial civil aviation services. Each company existed as a part of the whole and each strengthened the business structure of the Group's undertaking.

**Laker Airways (International) Limited** was owned by Sir Freddie Laker (90%) and Mrs. J.M. Laker (10%). It was the holding company of the Laker group and all the subsidiary companies were wholly or partially owned by it. It also owned three DC-10-10 aircraft.

**Laker Airways Limited** was the airline operating company, registered in Jersey to enjoy certain legal freedoms. It held the Air Transport licences, employed the flight crews and administered the operational aspects of the airline. It owned all the other aircraft.

**Laker Airways (Services) Limited** undertook engineering and general administration, and carried out extensive engineering work on the Laker fleet at the International Jet Centre, Gatwick Airport. The company employed the non-flying personnel of the airline, owned support equipment and held property leases.

### THE LAKER GROUP

| | |
|---|---|
| ***Registered in England:*** | |
| Laker Airways (Services) Ltd. (Administration & Engineering services) | 100% |
| Laker Aircraft Consolidation Ltd. (Tour Operator) | 100% |
| Laker Air Travel Ltd. (Tour Operator) | 100% |
| Arrowsmith Holidays Ltd. (Tour Operator) | 100% |
| The Middleton Travel Agency (Lancs.) Ltd. (Travel Agency) | 100% |
| Gatwick Handling Ltd. (Aircraft passenger & cargo handling) | 50% |
| ***Registered in Jersey, Channel Islands:*** | |
| Laker Airways Ltd. (Aircraft Operator) | 100% |
| ***Registered in Canada:*** | |
| Laker Air Travel (Canada) Ltd. (Tour Operator) | 100% |
| ***Registered in Australia:*** | |
| Laker Airways (Australia) Pty. Ltd. (Airline Promoter) | 100% |
| ***Registered in Hong Kong:*** | |
| Laker Airways (Hong Kong) Ltd. (non-trading) | 100% |
| ***Registered in West Germany:*** | |
| Laker Holidays (GmbH) (Tour Operator) | 100% |
| ***Registered in Palma de Majorca:*** | |
| Viajes Trans-Espana S.A. (Travel Agency) | 50% |
| ***Registered in Belgium:*** | |
| Belgian Arrow Express (Travel Agency) | 80% |
| ***Registered in Scotland:*** | |
| Thistle Air Brokers Ltd. (Air Brokers) | 26% |
| ***Registered in Barbados, West Indies:*** | |
| Caribbean International Airways Ltd. (Aircraft Operator) | 49% |

# APPENDIX X

# THE PERFECT STORM

## *Summary of events, situations and components contributing to the perfect storm of late 1981*

**EXTERNAL ISSUES:**
- Rapidly devaluing UK pound
- Global recession
- Oil Price increase
- Air Traffic Control strikes
- Overall decline on North Atlantic

**INDIRECT CONTRIBUTORS:**
- Skytrain brand - Lakerville aftermath inhibited licences & operations
- Resistance to flying on the DC-10
- Resistance to Gatwick Airport and a strike cutting off LGW from London
- Perception as low-cost / no frills airline impossible to change quickly
- Resistance from Travel Agents due original Skytrain direct sell
- Press & Media reporting that Laker was going out of business

**EXCLUSIVE TO SIR FREDDIE:**
- Missed vital clue given by Midland Bank of their intentions
- Provocateur - thumbed his nose at competitors, banks & governments
- Hostility with BCal's Adam Thomson
- Untimely rift with Robert Beckman
- Separation and upcoming divorce
- Loss of son - relocated to Florida
- Potential tabloid scandal
- Personal stress affected judgment
- Resistance to outside counsel / advice
- No non-executive directors
- Top-down dictatorial management style not coducive to challenges
- Naively mis-judged government's verbal promises re Airbus for Europe
- Relied too much on the 'old pals act' and presumed 'friends'
- Hubristic, egocentric, undiplomatic

**EXCLUSIVE TO LAKER AIRWAYS:**
- Unpredictable re-financing initiative
- Unable to recover £2+m A300 reserve
- Regency service - costs, operation and split configuration of DC-10s
- Regency instigated 1981 fare war
- Devastating Fare matching by Big 3
- Inadequate fare differentials to Big 3
- Compromised APEX Fares
- Fare-fixing / colluding with competitors
- USA re-organisation too late
- Inadequate US dollar revenue
- Miami route - low margins / losses
- Miami - no US tour operator or Latin America market interline agreements
- Teamsters' unionisation in USA
- Airport terminal facilities at JFK & LAX
- DC-10-30's performance issues
- DC-10-30's high operating costs
- Airbus purchase (10 A300s) / repayments
- European Routes unforthcoming
- Loan repayments in US Dollars
- Most Direct Operating Costs in USD
- Majority of revenue in UK Pounds
- Hong Kong & Australia licencing
- American Airlines' debt of $2.5m
- High legal expenses
- Unwieldy, inefficient fleets of aircraft
- Management inexperienced in North Atlantic scheduled service operations.
- Computer reservations issues in UK
- Telephone systems issues in USA
- Miami 'gold rush' in steep decline
- Using 707s for LAX & MIA may have saved millions in operating costs
- Catastrophic winter 1981-2 bookings
- International Caribbean - loss maker and owed Laker over £2million
- Reluctance to take cost-saving measures
- Unable to sell assets quickly

# Index

## C

## D

## E



## F

# I



# J

## M

## N

## S

# T